Readings in ——————
SOCIAL PSYCHOLOGY
General, Classic, and Contemporary Selections

EIGHTH EDITION

WAYNE A. LESKO
Marymount University

Boston   Columbus   Indianapolis   New York   San Francisco   Upper   Saddle River
Amsterdam   Cape Town   Dubai   London   Madrid   Milan   Munich   Paris   Montreal   Toronto
Delhi   Mexico City   Sao Paulo   Sydney   Hong Kong   Seoul   Singapore   Taipei   Tokyo

With love to all of my children: Matt, Brennan, and Angelica

Publisher: Susan Hartman
Project Editor: Kerri Hart-Morris
Editorial Assistant: Alexandra Mitton
Marketing Manager: Nicole Kunzmann
Marketing Assistant: Craig Deming
Production Manager: Meghan DeMaio
Creative Director: Jayne Conte
Cover Designer: Suzanne Behnke
Cover Design: © James Thew / Fotolia
Editorial Production and Composition Service: Integra Software Services/George Jacob
Printer/Binder: Edwards Brothers
Cover Printer: Lehigh-Phoenix Color

Many of the designations by manufacturers and seller to distinguish their products are claimed as trademarks. Where those designations appear in this book, and the publisher was aware of a trademark claim, the designations have been printed in initial caps or all caps.

Library of Congress Cataloging-in-Publication Data
Readings in social psychology : general, classic, and contemporary selections/Wayne A. Lesko.—8th ed.
    p. cm.
  Includes bibliographical references and index.
  ISBN-13: 978-0-205-17967-1 (alk. paper)
  ISBN-10: 0-205-17967-3 (alk. paper)
  1. Social psychology.   I. Lesko, Wayne A.
  HM1033.R43 2011
  302—dc22

                  2011006243

10 9 8 7 6 5 4 3 2 1 15 14 13 12 11

ISBN-10:   0-205-17967-3
ISBN-13: 978-0-205-17967-1

Contents

v

Preface

THE TYPICAL SOCIAL psychology class ranges from sophomore through graduate levels, and the members may include majors who are required to take the course as well as nonmajors who have elected to do so. Regardless of the level or the audience, many instructors—myself included—feel that a collection of readings is a valuable means of promoting an understanding of the discipline.

Most collections of readings typically fall into two categories: professional articles from journals in the field or popular articles reprinted from such magazines as *Psychology Today*. The category of professional readings may include contemporary articles, classic articles, or a combination of the two. These articles provide excellent insight into the core of social psychology by describing not only the research outcomes but also the detailed methodology for how the results were obtained. Popular articles, on the other hand, lack the scientific rigor of journal articles but often present a broad overview of a number of findings pertaining to a particular topic. Clearly, both types of readings have advantages and disadvantages associated with them, depending on the particular level at which the course is taught.

In over three decades of teaching social psychology at both the undergraduate and graduate levels, I have found that students seem to respond best to a variety of reading formats. Popular articles are easy to understand and provide a good overview, while also generating critical thinking about an issue. Research articles provide insight into the methodological issues in social psychology and help the student develop a critical attitude in evaluating research contributions and conclusions. Classic research articles familiarize the student with early research that has had a lasting impact on social psychology, while contemporary works illustrate issues currently being studied and the methods used to investigate them.

Like the first seven editions, this eighth edition of *Readings in Social Psychology: General, Classic, and Contemporary Selections* is designed to provide exactly that breadth of exposure to the different sources of information available in the field. As in the previous editions, each chapter begins with an introduction to the topic, which is followed by three articles: one general (popular), one classic, and one contemporary. Each article begins with a short introduction that sets the stage, or provides a context for the article. Each article is followed by a set of Critical Thinking Questions, which ask the student to examine critically some part of the article presented, to speculate about generalizations and implications of the research, and, in some cases, to suggest new studies based on the information in the article. Each classic article is also followed by a list of Additional Related Readings for students who may wish to examine more contemporary articles on the same topic. At the end of each chapter is a section called Chapter Integration Questions. These questions are intended to link the three chapter articles, usually by identifying a theme or themes common to all of them. As with the Critical Thinking Questions, these questions can be used in their entirety or in part, as best meets the needs of the instructor.

The topical organization of *Readings in Social Psychology: General, Classic, and Contemporary Selections* (eighth edition) directly parallels that of many social psychology textbooks. As such, it can be adapted readily for use with any text or used in lieu of a text, depending on how the course is taught. Likewise, the book can be used with classes of varying levels, by structuring which articles will be emphasized and in how much detail they will be examined.

Finally, all articles are presented verbatim, in their entirety, since it is my firm belief that one valuable skill gained by students from reading research articles is the ability to abstract pertinent information from an original source. The only exception to this, necessitated by copyright ownership, is found in Table 1 of Article 14, which is an abbreviation of the Bem Sex Role Inventory.

Because the articles are presented in their original forms, some of them, especially the contemporary articles, may be difficult to understand. However, I selected these particular articles for a variety of reasons. First, the topic of each of these articles is one that not only represents the type of research being conducted on this topic today but that also usually has interest to the reader. Second, these contemporary articles were selected to give the reader a broad exposure to the different types of professional publications in the field. Most of the more difficult articles are from journals published by the American Psychological Association (APA) or the American Psychological Society (APS). In fact, if only less complex articles were included in this book, then APA and APS publications virtually would be excluded. This would be a disservice to the reader, from my view.

For even the most complex contemporary articles, I have found that users without much background in psychology (e.g., sophomores with little or no prior research exposure) can read them effectively with the proper guidance. In addition to the guidance provided by the instructor, students will benefit by reading A Note to the Reader, which follows this Preface. That section provides some useful suggestions for how to read a research article without getting lost in all of the statistics and technical details.

At this point, perhaps some notice is in order about several of the articles. Understandably, everything is representative of the time in which it was written, both in terms of the ideas presented and the language used. Some of the classic articles in this collection were written 40 or more years ago and are out of step with current language style. Moreover, some of the descriptions made and observations offered would be considered condescending and even offensive by today's standards. Please keep this in mind, and consider the context in which each of the articles was written.

ACKNOWLEDGMENTS

At Pearson, I would like to thank Susan Hartman, Executive Editor, and Kerri Hart-Morris, Editor, Assistant, for their guidance and help with the format of the book. I am especially indebted to my graduate and undergraduate students in social psychology at Marymount University, whose honest feedback on the contents of the first seven editions helped me create a new, improved book of readings.

I also want to thank the various friends, colleagues, and graduate assistants who helped me and provided encouragement and advice over the many editions of this collection of readings. Without their input, this work would not have been possible.

Last but not least, I thank all of the authors and publishers of the articles contained in this book for their permission to reprint these materials. Their fine work in advancing the field of social psychology is literally what made this book possible.

A Note to the Reader

As YOU EMBARK on your study of social psychology, you will soon discover that the field is broad indeed. You will encounter many different topics, but they all are related by the common thread that defines social psychology—namely, the study of individual behavior in social situations.

As a collection of readings, this book is designed to expose you to some of the most important areas of study within social psychology. Just as the topics found in the area of social psychology are diverse, so, too, are the ways in which social psychological knowledge is disseminated. If you are new to the field, most likely you have encountered one common source of information: articles in nonprofessional sources. For example, newspaper and magazine articles may present the information from some study in social psychology. Typically nontechnical pieces directed to the general public, these articles summarize a number of studies on a given topic and are fairly easy to comprehend. Each of the 15 chapters that comprise this book begins with such an article—what I have termed a *general* reading.

A second source of information is actually the backbone of social psychology: articles that appear in professional journals of the field. These articles are the primary means by which new ideas and the results of research are shared with the professional community. While they tend to be more technical and difficult to read compared to the general works, professional articles have the advantage of providing readers with sufficient detail to draw their own conclusions, rather than be forced to rely on someone else's interpretation of the information. Some of these articles represent research that has stood the test of time and are generally regarded as *classics* in the field; the second reading found in each chapter is such an article.

Finally, the last type of article found in each chapter is labeled *contemporary*. These articles are fairly recent examples of research currently being conducted in social psychology. As noted in the Preface, these articles can be particularly challenging to read but are significant in terms of what they represent about the field of social psychology.

The format of each chapter is the same. Each opens with a brief introduction to the chapter topic; one general, one classic, and one contemporary article are then presented, in that order. Each article begins with an introduction written by me, which serves to focus your perspective before reading. Every article is then followed by Critical Thinking Questions. In some cases, these questions directly refer to information contained in the articles; in others, the questions are more speculative, asking you to go beyond the data presented. The classic articles also contain Additional Related Readings. The references included here are either recent articles that address the same issues discussed in the classic article (a way of updating the current status of research on the topic) or a topic similar to the one discussed in the original. In either case, the interested student can use these references to find more information on the topic. Finally, each chapter concludes with a section called Chapter Integration Questions. These questions relate the articles to one another, usually by having you identify a theme or themes that cut across them. Considering these questions provides another way of seeing the articles in the larger context of the topic, rather than as isolated pieces of research.

Before reading the articles in this book, it might be worthwhile to review the fundamentals of research tactics. Having such a basic understanding will help you understand even the most complex articles.

Research studies in social psychology (or indeed, in any scientifically based discipline) fall into two broad categories: correlational studies and experimental studies. A *correlation* is a finding that two variables are somehow related; that is, as one variable changes, so does the other one. For example, consider the relationship between the amount of violent content that children watch on television and their subsequent aggressive behavior. A correlation may show that the more aggressive programs a child watches, the more aggressive he or she is in playing with other children. Would such a correlation mean that watching the aggressive shows makes children more aggressive? Not necessarily. The children may be more aggressive for other reasons (e.g., maybe they eat too much candy while watching the shows), or perhaps children who are innately more aggressive are more attached to violent programs. In short, all that a correlation tells us is that two variables are related. It does *not* tell us that one variable causes the other one.

What, then, is the value of a correlation if it does not allow us to make cause–effect connections? One major value is that a correlation allows us to *predict*. That is, knowing that two variables are correlated allows us to predict the value of one when we only know the other is present. Again, using the violent programs example, if we know that there is a strong correlation between the amount of time children spend watching violent television and their subsequent aggressive behavior, then simply knowing how much violent television a child watches will allow us to predict the likelihood of his or her being aggressive.

In addition to making predictions, sometimes we want research to determine *why* something happens. In other words, we may want to determine a cause-and-effect relationship. The established way to do so is to use *experimental* research. The goal of all experimental research is to determine causation. No matter how complex a study's research design, the underlying logic of experimental research is fundamentally the same and fairly straightforward.

To understand the logic behind experimental research, along with its commonly used terms, let's look again at the example of aggressive television programming and children's behavior. Suppose we want to determine if exposure to violent television makes children more aggressive. First of all, we will need two groups of children—one watching violent television and the other watching something else—so that we can compare one group to another. But how will we form the two groups of children? We could ask the children which type of programming they prefer to watch and then group them accordingly. The problem with this approach is that we will not know if children already prone to aggression are more likely to prefer watching violent television programs.

The solution to this problem is actually quite simple: We will use *random assignment* to put the children into the groups. In other words, we will use pure chance, such as the results of a coin toss, to determine to which group each child is assigned. Why? By using chance, we are essentially creating two equal groups at the beginning of the study. For each child who is aggressive and is assigned to the one group, by chance, there will be another aggressive child assigned to the other group. In other words, individual differences cancel themselves out when we use random assignment.

Let's get back to our study design. Suppose we start out with, say, 100 children of the same age and randomly assign them to the two groups. Half of these children are assigned to a group that will watch violent television programs. This group is called the *experimental group,* since it involves the variable we are investigating—namely, exposure to violent programs. The other half of the children are assigned to a group that will watch nonviolent programs. This latter group is called the *control group,* and it will be our comparison group.

Another term you need to understand is *independent variable.* The independent variable is what the researcher is manipulating. In our example, the independent variable is whether or not the child is exposed to violent television programs. It is called *independent* because the experimenter is free to manipulate it as he or she wishes.

Let's pause for a second to look at the design of our experiment thus far. We started out with a group of children and randomly assigned them to two groups. Doing so resulted in our starting out with two equal groups. Next, we treated the two groups the same except for one thing: the independent variable. That is, half the children watched violent shows, and the other half watched nonviolent shows. Next, following exposure to the independent variable, we need some sort of way to measure the children's aggression. This outcome measure is known as the *dependent variable.* The two groups were identical to begin with (due to our random assignment), but what if we now find they are different after exposure to the independent variable? The answer is that the difference must be due to the only difference between the two groups—namely, exposure to the independent variable. Thus, a cause-and-effect relationship can be established, demonstrating that exposure to violent television programming causes children to become more aggressive.

No matter how complex a study's research design is (and you will encounter some very complex designs in the studies that follow), the logic of experimental research is the same as outlined in our experiment: Identical groups are created through random assignment, they are exposed to different conditions (the independent variable), and the outcomes are measured (the dependent variable). If a difference is observed in the dependent variable, then it must be due to the different treatments that the subjects received.

The reality of conducting research and drawing warranted conclusions obviously is a bit more complicated than our discussion would indicate. Nonetheless, if you keep in mind the basics of experimental design, you will find it easier to understand the studies that you read.

All of the articles in this collection are reprinted in their entirety. Not a word has been abridged or altered. (Again, the only exception is Article 14, which has been abbreviated due to a copyright restriction.) For the general articles, this should not be a problem for anyone. However, if this is the first time that you are reading journal articles from their primary sources, some assistance might be in order. First of all, do not allow yourself to be overwhelmed or intimidated. New students often are confused by some of the terminology that is used and are left totally dumbfounded by the detailed statistics that are usually part of such articles. Approached in the right way, these articles need not be intimidating and should be comprehensible to any reader willing to expend a little effort.

In reading a research article, I would like to make the following suggestions:

■ Most articles begin with an Abstract or end with a Summary. If these are provided, begin by carefully reading them; they will give you an overview of why the study was conducted, what was done, and what the results were.

■ Next, read the Introduction fairly carefully; this is where the authors describe previous research in the area and develop the logic for why they are conducting the experiment in the first place.

■ The Methods section describes in detail the techniques used by the researchers to conduct their study; read this section thoroughly in order to understand exactly what was done.

■ The next section, Results, is where the authors describe what was found in the study. This is often the most technically difficult part of the article; from your standpoint, you might want to skim over this part, focusing only on the sections that verbally describe what the results were. Do not worry about the detailed statistical analyses that are presented.

■ Finally, you might want to read the Discussion section in some detail; here, the authors discuss the findings and implications of the study and perhaps suggest avenues for further study.

To summarize: Each article is fairly straightforward to comprehend, provided that you do not allow yourself to get too bogged down in the details and thus frustrated. The journey may seem difficult at times, but the end result—an appreciation and understanding of the complex issues of human social behavior—will be worth it. Enjoy!

W.L.

Chapter One

THE FIELD OF SOCIAL PSYCHOLOGY

An INTRODUCTION TO a course such as social psychology often includes a section on research methods. Nonmajors confronting this topic often wonder why they need to know about research methods when in all likelihood they will never actually conduct research. Whether you are majoring in psychology or not, familiarity with research methods will benefit you, for several reasons.

First, it will help you understand the studies that make up the knowledge base of social psychology. Familiarity with methodology will allow you to make informed decisions about the conclusions drawn by various studies. Second, and perhaps more important, some knowledge of research issues will allow you to be an intelligent consumer of research information. Results of studies often are reported to the general public in newspapers and magazines. Knowing something about the methods used to produce these results will better prepare you to decide whether the conclusions drawn are warranted. Finally, it is useful to fully appreciate why the results of experimental data are needed instead of just relying on common sense. Article 1 provides some basic guidelines for making sense of the various research results we encounter on a regular basis. "How to Be a Wise Consumer of Psychological Research" gives some invaluable tools for how best to draw valid conclusions from studies. While the focus of the article is on psychological research, many of the concepts really can be applied to a variety of other science and social science disciplines as well.

Research is the basic underpinning of psychological science. Given the subject matter of social psychology, it is often difficult, if not impossible, to get unbiased results if subjects know what is being observed. For that reason, psychologists, in general, and social psychologists, in particular, often have relied on deception as a means of obtaining naive subjects. But what ethical issues are involved in the use of deception? And what if deception is so widely used that subjects expect to be deceived whenever they participate in a research study? What, if any, are the alternatives to the use of deception? These are some of the questions addressed in Article 2, "Human Use of Human Subjects: The Problem of Deception in Social Psychological Experiments."

Finally, Article 3 deals with how much weight scientific evidence actually has on influencing people's beliefs with regard to paranormal claims. "Social Influences on Paranormal Belief: Popular Versus Scientific Support" demonstrates that scientific evidence may not be as strong as we might think it is in influencing people's thinking. While the article deals with paranormal beliefs in particular, there may be larger issues regarding trust in scientific findings in general.

ARTICLE 1 _____

Anyone who reads a newspaper or magazine or watches the news constantly encounters the results of some study or another reporting on what people think about certain issues (the war in Iraq, for example) or what factors are most associated with certain behaviors (that violent video games increase real-life aggressive tendencies, for example). Often we hear only of the conclusions of a particular study, but not necessarily the details of what the study entailed. Unfortunately, as the saying goes, "the devil is in the details." Knowing exactly what was done in a study, or who was surveyed in an opinion poll, is an important part in determining how much confidence (if any) we can have in the reported findings. While it might be assumed that anyone conducting research would know how to properly do research and thus minimize problems, such is not always the case. Even the best-intentioned researcher may have methodological issues in their studies that may impact on their findings.

While a truer appreciation of the complexities of conducting valid research usually is acquired by taking a course or courses in research methodology and statistics, not everyone will have the opportunity to do so. Yet, to be an intelligent consumer of the research results that we routinely encounter in our lives, some understanding of the issues pertaining to research studies is important. The following article published by the American Psychological Association provides suggestions for how to become a wise consumer of psychological research. An understanding of these concepts will help readers maximize their appreciation of the remaining articles in this book as well as the research results they see reported in their daily lives.

How to Be a Wise Consumer of Psychological Research

It is difficult to turn the pages of a newspaper without coming across a story that makes an important claim about human nature. News stories report the latest findings regarding what causes divorce, how men and women differ psychologically, or how work-related stress influences physical illness. Other stories summarize the results of surveys designed to tell us how people will vote in an upcoming election or what proportion of Americans routinely wear seat belts. Flip to the advertisements and you will be exposed to claims about everything from how to improve your memory by listening to subliminal tapes to how to become more popular. Being able to evaluate research claims objectively is an important skill. Separating the scientific wheat from the chaff can influence how you vote, whether you adopt a new diet, or whether you decide to get professional help for a child with a learning disorder. With this in mind, this short essay is devoted to the topic of being a wise consumer of psychological research. As consumers of both products and ideas, we all need to know the difference between carefully conducted and poorly conducted research. **This essay can help you evaluate research-based claims and make you a better consumer of many of the products and services that shape your daily life.**

SHOW ME THE DATA! LOOKING AT EVIDENCE

Perhaps the most important lesson about being a wise consumer of psychological research is that, from a scientific perspective, all claims require **evidence**, not just opinions. Scientists who evaluate research claims behave like ideal jury members who are asked to evaluate claims made by prosecuting attorneys. They begin with the skeptical assumption that all claims are false (the defendant is innocent until proven guilty; the diet plan is ineffective; testosterone plays no role in aggression). Only after considering the strengths and weaknesses of the evidence relevant to a claim do jurors and scientists decide whether to accept the claims of those doing the claiming (for example, prosecuting attorneys, advertisers, scientists). This decision to accept or reject a claim is best made by paying careful attention to the methods that served as the basis for a specific claim. Behavioral scientists have hundreds of tools in their methodological toolboxes, but as it turns out, two of these tools turn out to be much more important than any others. Understanding the nature and purpose of these two tools is thus the first step to becoming an educated consumer of psychological research. In short, sound research methods lead to more valid research conclusions. The two tools that lie at the heart of sound research methods are random sampling and experimental manipulation based on random assignment.

SAYS WHO? RANDOM SAMPLING

When behavioral scientists want to assess the attitudes or preferences of very large groups of people (e.g., American voters, Asian-American college students, human beings), they face a seemingly insurmountable problem. It is usually impossible to ask every member of a very large group what he or she thinks, feels, or does. However, behavioral scientists have solved this tricky problem by developing a technique called **random sampling**. When survey researchers use random sampling, they select a very small proportion of the people from within a very large sample (e.g., 1,000 out of 50 million registered voters). They **then estimate** what the entire population is like on the basis of the responses of those sampled. The key to getting an accurate estimate is the use of random sampling. Random sampling refers to selecting people from a population so that everyone in the entire population (e.g., all registered voters in the U.S.) has an equal chance of being selected. This turns out to be an incredibly powerful technique. If every person in a group of 50 million voters really does have an equal chance of being selected into a national survey, then the results of the survey based on 1,000 people will almost always prove to resemble the results for the total population.

An excellent example of the importance of random sampling can be found in the 1936 U.S. Presidential election. Prior to that election, the *Literary Digest* sent postcards to more than 10 million Americans, asking them to report who they planned to vote for in the upcoming election. Among the 2 million Americans who returned the postcards, Alf Landon was the overwhelming favorite. In contrast, a much smaller survey conducted by the recently-formed Gallup group yielded very different results. Based on the responses of only a few thousand likely voters, the Gallup poll suggested that Franklin D. Roosevelt would be the winner. If you pull a dime out of your pocket, and look to see whose face is there, you'll see that the Gallup pollsters were correct. FDR won in a landslide, and Alf Landon faded into obscurity. How did the Gallup poll, based on many fewer people outperform the enormous *Literary Digest* poll? The Gallup pollsters came very close to performing a true random sample of likely voters. In contrast, the *Literary Digest* sampled people by taking names from automobile registrations and telephone listings. In 1936, people who owned cars and phones were usually pretty wealthy—and wealthy people overwhelming preferred Alf Landon.

The lesson of the *Literary Digest* error is that whenever you hear the results of any survey, you should ask yourself how the surveyed people were sampled. Were those sampled really like the pool of people (e.g., American voters, African American children) whose attitudes and behavior the researcher would like to describe?

Even when a researcher makes careful use of random sampling, it is also useful to pay attention to a different form of sampling bias, known as **non-response bias**. If only a small percentage of randomly sampled people agree to respond to a survey, it is quite likely that those who did respond will be different than those who refused. Modern pollsters have long mastered the science of random sampling. These days, most of the error in most scientific polls is based on the fact that it can be hard to get very high response rates (or hard to know who to sample in the first place). For example, if you randomly sampled all those eligible to vote in a state gubernatorial race, and you only got a 30% response rate, you would have to worry about whether those who refused to be surveyed would vote the same way as the eager 30% who agreed. Moreover, even if everyone agreed to be surveyed, you'd have to worry about whether the sub sample of all eligible voters who actually showed up at the polls on election day had the same preferences as those who either didn't bother to vote or were unable to do so.

It is also important to note that random sampling helps you describe only the population of people from whom you sampled (and not other populations). For example, if researchers randomly sampled registered voters, but only did so in North Carolina, they might get a great idea of what North Carolinians believe, but it would be very risky to generalize these results to other Americans. This is why people sometimes criticize the results of surveys taken of college students, who differ markedly from older adults. On the other hand, if surveyors wanted to know the opinions of college students, it would make little sense to sample anyone else. The key issue might be exactly which college students. A random sample of 1,000 American college students would tell us much more than a random sample of 1,000 students at Vassar College. Of course, if we cared only about Vassar College students, we would want to sample Vassarians at random. The key issue in sampling is to pay careful attention to who was sampled and to make certain that those sampled are the same kind of people about whom a researcher has made a claim (a claim about what the evidence shows).

HOW TO ASK WHY: EXPERIMENTAL MANIPULATIONS AND RANDOM ASSIGNMENT

When a researcher moves from descriptive research to experimental research, random sampling is still important, but it begins to take a back seat to a second major technique. This second technique is random assignment, and it is the cornerstone of the experimental method. Unlike random sampling, which is a technique for deciding who to study, **random assignment** can take place only **after people** have already been selected into a study. Random assignment is a technique for assigning people to different specific conditions in an experiment, and random assignment occurs only when everyone in the study has an equal chance of serving in any specific condition. In the same way that random sampling guarantees that the people sampled in a study will be as similar as possible to those who were not sampled, random assignment guarantees that those assigned to one experimental condition will be as similar as possible to those assigned to a different condition. This is crucial because the whole idea of an experiment is to identify two identical groups of people and then to **manipulate** something. One group gets an experimental treatment, and one does not. If the group that gets the treatment (e.g., a drug, exposure to a violent videogame) behaves differently than the control group that did not get the treatment, we can attribute the difference to the treatment—but only if we can rest assured that the two groups were similar prior to the treatment.

Another way to put this is that if we wish to identify the causes of human behavior, we must usually perform experiments in which we manipulate one thing, or a few factors, at a time. We can only do this by making use of random assignment. Suppose a researcher at Cornell University developed a new technique for teaching foreign language. If the researcher could do so, he might persuade all of his colleagues in the Spanish department to start using this new technique. After a year of instruction using the new technique, suppose that the professor documented that the average student who completed one year of Spanish at Cornell performed well above the national average in a test of Spanish fluency (relative to students at other universities who had also completed a year of Spanish). Can we attribute this performance advantage to the new instruction technique? Given how difficult it is to get admitted to Cornell in the first place, it is likely that students at Cornell would have performed well above the national norm even if they had been taught using a new technique. If the researcher really wanted to know if his teaching technique was superior, he would have needed to randomly assign some Cornell students to receive the new form of instruction while randomly assigning others to receive a traditional form of instruction (this would be hard to do, but that is a detail).

Consider a more important question. Do seatbelts save lives? One way to find out would be to obtain records of thousands of serious automobile accidents. To simplify things, suppose a researcher focused exclusively on drivers (rather than passengers) and found an accurate way to determine whether drivers were wearing their seatbelts at the time of each crash. The researcher then obtained accurate records of whether the driver in each crash survived. Imagine that drivers wearing seatbelts were much more likely to have survived. Can

we safely assume that seatbelts are the reason? Not on the basis of this study alone. The problem is that, for ethical reasons, the people in this hypothetical study were not randomly assigned to different seatbelt conditions. As it turns out, those who do and do not routinely wear seatbelts differ in many important ways. Compared with habitual non-users of seatbelts, habitual users are older, more educated, and less likely to speed or drink and drive. These additional factors are also likely to influence survival in a serious accident, and they are all confounded with seatbelt use. On the basis of this study and this study alone, we cannot tell whether it is seatbelts or other safe driving practices that are responsible for the greater survival rates among seatbelt users.

If we were to conduct a large-scale experiment on seatbelt use (by determining habitual seatbelt use on the basis of coin flips), we could completely eliminate all of these confounds in one simple step. Random assignment would create two identical groups of people, exactly half of whom were forced to use seatbelts at all times, and exactly half of whom were forbidden from doing so during the experimental period. Of course, this hypothetical experiment would be unethical. Thus, researchers interested in seatbelt use have had to do a lot of other things to document the important role that seatbelts play in saving people's lives (including laboratory crash tests and studies that used sophistical statistical techniques to separate the effects of seatbelt use from other effects). The point is not that seatbelts don't save lives. They clearly do. The point is that it has taken a lot of time and effort to document this fact because of the impossibility of conducting an experiment on this topic. If you want to conduct a single study to figure out what causes something, you will almost always need to conduct an experiment in which you make use of random assignment. As a consumer of psychological research, you must thus ask yourself whether a research claim was based on the results of a careful experiment, or whether a researcher may have compared two groups of people who differed in more than one way at the beginning of the study.

LONGITUDINAL RESEARCH

Sometimes a researcher can bypass the use of random assignment by comparing people with themselves—by conducting a **longitudinal study** or a study with a **pretest** and a **post-test**. Although such studies can be very informative, these studies often come with their own special kinds of confounds. Many of these confounds boil down to the fact that people can and do change over time, for many reasons. For example, consider GRE prep courses. When a student who scores poorly on the GRE takes a preparation course and then takes the GRE again, such a student will often do better the second time around, sometimes a lot better! This would seem to show that the prep course is effective. However, another very effective way to improve the performance of a group of students who have recently performed poorly on a test is to give them the test again without any intervention. In most cases, such students will do better on the test the second time around (including a different version of the same test). (The reason why low scorers tend to improve in the absence of training is known as "regression toward the mean", but its details are beyond the scope of this short essay.) The key issue is that it is always important to have a control group if you want to assess the impact of a treatment.

SOME FINAL THOUGHTS

There are many other ways in which research can go astray. Did Dr. Snittle word his survey questions fairly? Were participants reporting their attitudes honestly? Did those carrying out the research bias answers by subtly communicating to participants what they hoped to find? Was the size of the sample large enough to draw meaningful comparisons? For example, if you read that 4 out of 5 doctors use Brand X, were only five doctors surveyed? Were those who conducted the research strongly motivated to produce a specific result? For example, if those studying the effects of a drug were paid by a pharmaceutical company to do the research, could this conflict of interest distort the way they collect or interpret their data? The list continues. Specific issues such as these aside, however, the two concerns that should come to mind first when evaluating any research claim have to do with proper sampling and proper experimental control. First, were those studied truly representative of the people about whom we would like to draw conclusions? Second, did the researchers isolate the variables they studied by disentangling them from other confounded variables? It is not always easy to get answers to these questions, but if you get in the habit of asking them you will gradually become a better shopper for psychological truths.

CRITICAL THINKING QUESTIONS

1. Opinion surveys often are conducted via telephone. The technology of communication has changed considerably in recent times (e.g., cell phones, answering machines). Do you think these technological changes have had an impact on who may or may not be sampled for a given study, or who may choose to respond to a given survey? Explain.

2. *External validity* refers to how generalizable the results of one particular study are to other settings. A large number of social psychology experiments tend to use college students as subjects. Is this a problem? Why or why not?

3. Develop a list of what you consider the most important questions that social psychology should try to answer. As you go through the course, keep track of which of these questions have been investigated and what the findings were. If a question you listed has not been investigated, why do you think that may be the case?

4. Find the results of a study related to a social psychology topic that is reported in a recent newspaper or magazine. Based on the points raised in this article, as a wise consumer of psychological research what are the questions you should be asking about that reported study? What information that you consider to be important in reaching valid conclusions is not reported in the article?

ARTICLE 2 _____

Have you ever participated in a social psychology experiment? What were you thinking while you were participating? Were you accepting of the situation and the explanation you were given by the researcher, or were you trying to figure out the real purpose of the experiment? If you were doing the latter, you would be in good company, as many people have come to associate psychological research (and in particular, social psychology research) with the use of deception.

Deception has always been a staple in the research conducted in the field. But what exactly is *deception?* Is it simply another term for *lying?* In practice, deception in research can be located on a continuum from simply withholding from the subjects the true nature of the experiment to actively creating a cover story to try to keep the subjects from determining the actual purpose of the study. Deception is largely based on the assumption that if subjects knew the true nature of the experiment (the hypothesis being tested, that is), then they would not act naturally and hence contaminate the results.

This next classic article by Herbert C. Kelman explores the use of deception in social psychological experiments. After discussing some of the ethical issues involved in the use of deception, Kelman goes on to suggest how the use of deception should be handled as well as alternatives to deception. In the years since the publication of this article in 1967, many changes in the ethical guidelines for the treatment of human subjects have been made. For example, it is now standard policy for institutions to have ethical review boards for the approval of any study involving human subjects. Nonetheless, deception in one form or another is still a common feature in social psychological research.

Human Use of Human Subjects
The Problem of Deception in Social Psychological Experiments[1]
■ Herbert C. Kelman

Though there is often good reason for deceiving Ss in social psychological experiments, widespread use of such procedures has serious (a) ethical implications (involving not only the possibility of harm to S, but also the quality of the E-S relationship), (b) methodological implications (relating to the decreasing naïveté of Ss), and (c) implications for the future of the discipline. To deal with these problems, it is necessary (a) to increase active awareness of the negative implications of deception and use it only when clearly justified, not as a matter of course; (b) to explore ways of counteracting and minimizing negative consequences of deception when it is used; and (c) to develop new experimental techniques that dispense with deception and rely on S's positive motivations.

In 1954, in the pages of the *American Psychologist,* Edgar Vinacke raised a series of questions about experiments—particularly in the area of small groups—in which "the psychologist conceals the true purpose and conditions of the experiment, or positively misinforms the subjects, or exposes them to painful, embarrassing, or worse, experiences, without the subjects' knowledge of what is going on [p. 155]." He summed up his concerns by asking,

"What . . . is the proper balance between the interests of science and the thoughtful treatment of the persons who, innocently, supply the data? [p. 155]." Little effort has been made in the intervening years to seek answers to the questions he raised. During these same years, however, the problem of deception in social psychological experiments has taken on increasingly serious proportions.[2]

The problem is actually broader, extending beyond the walls of the laboratory. It arises, for example, in various field studies in which investigators enroll as members of a group that has special interest for them so that they can observe its operations from the inside. The pervasiveness of the problem becomes even more apparent when we consider that deception is built into most of our measurement devices, since it is important to keep the respondent unaware of the personality or attitude dimension that we wish to explore. For the present purposes, however, primarily the problem of deception in the context of the social psychological experiment will be discussed.

The use of deception has become more and more extensive, and it is now a commonplace and almost standard feature of social psychological experiments. Deception has been turned into a game, often played with great skill and virtuosity. A considerable amount of the creativity and ingenuity of social psychologists is invested in the development of increasingly elaborate deception situations. Within a single experiment, deception may be built upon deception in a delicately complex structure. The literature now contains a fair number of studies in which second- or even third-order deception was employed.

One well-known experiment (Festinger & Carlsmith, 1959), for example, involved a whole progression of deceptions. After the subjects had gone through an experimental task, the investigator made it clear—through word and gesture—that the experiment was over and that he would now "like to explain what this has been all about so you'll have some idea of why you were doing this [p. 205]." This explanation was false, however, and was designed to serve as a basis for the true experimental manipulation. The manipulation itself involved asking subjects to serve as the experimenter's accomplices. The task of the "accomplice" was to tell the next "subject" that the experiment in which he had just participated (which was in fact a rather boring experience) had been interesting and enjoyable. He was also asked to be on call for unspecified future occasions on which his services as accomplice might be needed because "the regular fellow couldn't make it, and we had a subject scheduled [p. 205]." These newly recruited "accomplices," of course, were the true subjects, while the "subjects" were the experimenter's true accomplices. For their presumed services as "accomplices," the true subjects were paid in advance—half of them receiving $1, and half $20. When they completed their service, however, the investigators added injury to insult by asking them to return their hard-earned cash. Thus, in this one study, in addition to receiving the usual misinformation about the purpose of the experiment, the subject was given feedback that was really an experimental manipulation, was asked to be an accomplice who was really a subject, and was given a $20 bill that was really a will-o'-the-wisp. One wonders how much further in this direction we can go. Where will it all end?

It is easy to view this problem with alarm, but it is much more difficult to formulate an unambiguous position on the problem. As a working experimental social psychlogist, I cannot conceive the issue in absolutist terms. I am too well aware of the fact that there are good reasons for using deception in many experiments. There are many significant problems that probably cannot be investigated without the use of deception, at least not at the present level of development of our experimental methodology. Thus, we are always confronted with a conflict of values. If we regard the acquisition of scientific knowledge about human behavior as a positive value, and if an experiment using deception constitutes a significant contribution in such knowledge which could not very well be achieved by other means, then we cannot unequivocally rule out this experiment. The question for us is not simply whether it does or does not use deception, but whether the amount and type of deception are justified by the significance of the study and the unavailability of alternative (that is, deception-free) procedures.

I have expressed special concern about second-order deceptions, for example, the procedure of letting a person believe that he is acting as experimenter or as the experimenter's accomplice when he is in fact serving as the subject. Such a procedure undermines the relationship between experimenter and subject even further than simple misinformation about the purposes of the experiment; deception does not merely take place *within* the experiment, but encompasses the whole definition of the relationship between the parties involved. Deception that takes place while the person is within the role of subject for which he has contracted can, to some degree, be isolated, but deception about the very nature of the contract itself is more likely to suffuse the experimenter-subject relationship as a whole and to remove the possibility of mutual trust. Thus, I would be inclined to take a more absolutist stand with regard to such second-order deceptions—but even here the issue turns out to be more complicated. I am stopped short when I think, for example, of the ingenious studies on experimenter bias by Rosenthal and his associates (e.g., Rosenthal & Fode, 1963; Rosenthal, Persinger, Vikan-Kline, & Fode, 1963; Rosenthal, Persinger, Vikan-Kline, & Mulry, 1963). These experiments employed second-order deception in that subjects were led to believe that they were the experimenters. Since these were experiments about experiments, however, it is very hard to conceive of any alternative procedures that the investigators might have used. There is no question in my mind that these are significant studies; they provide fundamental inputs to present efforts at reexamining the social psychology of the experiment. These studies, then, help to underline even further the point that we are confronted with a conflict of values that cannot be resolved by fiat.

I hope it is clear from these remarks that my purpose in focusing on this problem is not to single out specific studies performed by some of my colleagues and to point a finger at them. Indeed, the finger points at me as well. I too have used deception, and have known the joys of applying my skills and ingenuity to the creation of elaborate experimental situations that the subjects would not be able to decode. I am now making active attempts to find alternatives to deception, but still I have not forsworn the use of deception under any and all circumstances. The questions I am raising, then, are addressed to myself as well as to my colleagues. They are questions with which all of us who are committed to social psychology must come to grips, lest we leave their resolution to others who have no understanding of what we are trying to accomplish.

What concerns me most is not so much that deception is used, but precisely that it is used without question. It has now become standard operating procedure in the social psychologist's laboratory. I sometimes feel that we are training a generation of students who do not know that there is any other way of doing experiments in our field—who feel that deception is as much de rigueur as significance at the .05 level. Too often deception is used not as a last resort, but as a matter of course. Our attitude seems to be that if you can deceive, why tell the truth? It is this unquestioning acceptance, this routinization of deception, that really concerns me.

I would like to turn now to a review of the bases for my concern with the problem of deception, and then suggest some possible approaches for dealing with it.

IMPLICATIONS OF THE USE OF DECEPTION IN SOCIAL PSYCHOLOGICAL EXPERIMENTS

My concern about the use of deception is based on three considerations: the ethical implications of such procedures, their methodological implications, and their implications for the future of social psychology.

1. *Ethical implications.* Ethical problems of a rather obvious nature arise in the experiments in which deception has potentially harmful consequences for the subject. Take, for example, the brilliant experiment by Mulder and Stemerding (1963) on the effects of threat on attraction to the group and need for strong leadership. In this study—one of the very rare examples of an experiment conducted in a natural setting—independent food merchants in a number of Dutch towns were brought together for group meetings, in the course of which they were informed that a large organization was planning to open up a series of supermarkets in the Netherlands. In the High Threat condition, subjects were told that there was a high probability that their town would be selected as a site for such markets, and that the advent of these markets would cause a considerable drop in their business. On the advice of the executives of the shopkeepers' organizations, who had helped to arrange the group meetings, the investigators did not reveal the experimental manipulations to their subjects. I have been worried about these Dutch merchants ever since I heard about this study for the first time. Did some of them go out of business in anticipation of the heavy competition? Do some of them have an anxiety reaction every time they see a bulldozer? Chances are that they soon forgot about this threat (unless, of course, supermarkets actually did move into town) and that it became just one of the many little moments of anxiety that must occur in every shopkeeper's life. Do we have a right, however, to add to life's little anxieties and to risk the possibility of more extensive anxiety purely for the purposes of our experiments, particularly since deception deprives the subject of the opportunity to choose whether or not he wishes to expose himself to the risks that might be entailed?

The studies by Bramel (1962, 1963) and Bergin (1962) provide examples of another type of potentially harmful effects arising from the use of deception. In the Bramel studies, male undergraduates were led to believe that they were homosexually aroused by photographs of men. In the Bergin study, subjects of both sexes were given discrepant information about their level of masculinity or femininity; in one experimental condition, this information was presumably based on an elaborate series of psychological tests in which the subjects had participated. In all of these studies, the deception was explained to the subject at the end of the experiment. One wonders, however, whether such explanation removes the possibility of harmful effects. For many persons in this age group, sexual identity is still a live and sensitive issue, and the self-doubts generated by the laboratory experience may take on a life of their own and linger on for some time to come.

Yet another illustration of potentially harmful effects of deception can be found in Milgram's (1963, 1965) studies of obedience. In these experiments, the subject was led to believe that he was participating in a learning study and was instructed to administer increasingly severe shocks to another person who after a while began to protest vehemently. In fact, of course, the victim was an accomplice of the experimenter and did not receive any shocks. Depending on the conditions, sizable proportions of the subjects obeyed the experimenter's instructions and continued to shock the other person up to the maximum level, which they believed to be extremely painful. Both obedient and defiant subjects exhibited a great deal of stress in this situation. The complexities of the issues surrounding the use of deception become quite apparent when one reads the exchange between Baumrind (1964) and Milgram (1964) about the ethical implications of the obedience research. There is clearly room for disagreement, among honorable people, about the evaluation of this research from an ethical point of view. Yet, there is good reason to believe that at least some of the obedient subjects came away from this experience with a lower self-esteem, having to live with the realization that they were willing to yield to destructive authority to the point of inflicting extreme pain on a fellow human being. The fact that this may have provided, in Milgram's (1964) words, "an opportunity to learn something of importance about themselves, and more generally, about the conditions of human action [p. 850]" is beside the point. If this were a lesson from life, it would indeed constitute an instructive confrontation and provide a valuable insight. But do we, for the purpose of experimentation, have the right to provide such potentially disturbing insights to subjects who do not know that this is what they are coming for? A similar question can be raised about the Asch (1951) experiments on group pressure, although the stressfulness of the situation and the implications for the person's self-concept were less intense in that context.

While the present paper is specifically focused on social psychological experiments, the problem of deception and its possibly harmful effects arises in other areas of psychological experimentation as well. Dramatic illustrations are provided by two studies in which subjects were exposed, for experimental purposes, to extremely stressful conditions. In an experiment designed to study the establishment of a conditioned response in a situation that is traumatic but not painful, Campbell, Sanderson, and Laverty (1964) induced—through the use of a drug—a temporary interruption of respiration in their subjects. "This has no permanently harmful physical consequences but is nonetheless a severe stress which is not in itself painful . . . [p. 628]." The subjects' reports confirmed that this was a "horrific" experience for them. "All the subjects in the standard series said that they thought they were dying [p. 631]." Of course the subjects, "male alcoholic patients who volunteered for the experiment when they were told that it was connected with a possible therapy for alcoholism [p. 629]," were not warned in advance about the effect of the drug, since this information would have reduced the traumatic impact of the experience.[3] In a series of studies on the effects of psychological stress, Berkun, Bialek, Kern, and Yagi (1962) devised a number of ingenious experimental situations designed to convince the subject that his life was actually in danger. In one situation, the subjects, a group of Army recruits, were actually "passengers aboard an apparently stricken plane which was being forced to 'ditch' or crash-land [p. 4]." In another experiment, an isolated subject in a desolate area learned that a sudden emergency had arisen (accidental nuclear radiation in the area, or a sudden forest fire, or misdirected artillery shells—depending on the experimental condition) and that he could be rescued only if he reported his position over his radio transmitter, "which has quite suddenly failed [p. 7]." In yet another situation, the subject was led to believe that he was responsible for an explosion that seriously injured another soldier. As the authors pointed out, reactions in these situations are more likely to approximate reactions to combat experiences or to naturally occurring disasters than are reactions to various laboratory stresses, but is the experimenter justified in exposing his subjects to such extreme threats?

So far, I have been speaking of experiments in which deception has potentially harmful consequences. I am equally concerned, however, about the less obvious cases, in which there is little danger of harmful effects, at least in the conventional sense of the term. Serious ethical issues are raised by deception per se and the kind of use of human beings that it implies. In our other interhuman relationships, most of us would never think of doing the kinds of things that we do to our subjects—exposing others to lies and tricks, deliberately misleading them about the purposes of the interaction or withholding pertinent information, making promises or giving assurances that we intend to disregard. We would view such behavior as a violation of the respect to which all fellow humans are entitled and of the whole basis of our relationship with them. Yet we seem to forget that the experimenter-subject relationship—whatever else it is—is a *real* interhuman relationship, in which we have responsibility toward the subject as another human

being whose dignity we must preserve. The discontinuity between the experimenter's behavior in everyday life and his behavior in the laboratory is so marked that one wonders why there has been so little concern with this problem, and what mechanisms have allowed us to ignore it to such an extent. I am reminded, in this connection, of the intriguing phenomenon of the "holiness of sin," which characterizes certain messianic movements as well as other movements of the true-believer variety. Behavior that would normally be unacceptable actually takes on an aura of virtue in such movements through a redefinition of the situation in which the behavior takes place and thus of the context for evaluating it. A similar mechanism seems to be involved in our attitude toward the psychological experiment. We tend to regard it as a situation that is not quite real, that can be isolated from the rest of life like a play performed on stage, and to which, therefore, the usual criteria for ethical interpersonal conduct become irrelevant. Behavior is judged entirely in the context of the experiment's scientific contribution and, in this context, deception—which is normally unacceptable—can indeed be seen as a positive good.

The broader ethical problem brought into play by the very use of deception becomes even more important when we view it in the light of present historical forces. We are living in an age of mass societies in which the transformation of man into an object to be manipulated at will occurs "on a mass scale, in a systematic way, and under the aegis of specialized institutions deliberately assigned to this task [Kelman, 1965]." In institutionalizing the use of deception in psychological experiments, we are, then, contributing to a historical trend that threatens values most of us cherish.

2. Methodological implications. A second source of my concern about the use of deception is my increasing doubt about its adequacy as a methodology for social psychology.

A basic assumption in the use of deception is that a subject's awareness of the conditions that we are trying to create and of the phenomena that we wish to study would affect his behavior in such a way that we could not draw valid conclusions from it. For example, if we are interested in studying the effects of failure on conformity, we must create a situation in which the subjects actually feel that they have failed, and in which they can be kept unaware of our interest in observing conformity. In short, it is important to keep our subjects naïve about the purposes of the experiment so that they can respond to the experimental inductions spontaneously.

How long, however, will it be possible for us to find naïve subjects? Among college students, it is already very difficult. They may not know the exact purpose of the particular experiment in which they are participating, but at least they know, typically, that it is not what the experimenter says it is. Orne (1962) pointed out that the use of deception "on the part of psychologists is so widely known in the college population that even if a psychologist is honest with the subject, more often than not he will be distrusted." As one subject pithily put it, "'Psychologists always lie!'" Orne added that "This bit of paranoia has some support in reality [pp. 778–779]." There are, of course, other sources of human subjects that have not been tapped, and we could turn to them in our quest for naïveté. But even there it is only a matter of time. As word about psychological experiments gets around in whatever network we happen to be using, sophistication is bound to increase. I wonder, therefore, whether there is any future in the use of deception.

If the subject in a deception experiment knows what the experimenter is trying to conceal from him and what he is really after in the study, the value of the deception is obviously nullified. Generally, however, even the relatively sophisticated subject does not know the exact purpose of the experiment; he only has suspicions, which may approximate the true purpose of the experiment to a greater or lesser degree. Whether or not he knows the true purpose of the experiment, he is likely to make an effort to figure out its purpose, since he does not believe what the experimenter tells him, and therefore he is likely to operate in the situation in terms of his own hypothesis of what is involved. This may, in line with Orne's (1962) analysis, lead him to do what he thinks the experimenter wants him to do. Conversely, if he resents the experimenter's attempt to deceive him, he may try to throw a monkey wrench into the works; I would not be surprised if this kind of Schweikian game among subjects became a fairly well-established part of the culture of sophisticated campuses. Whichever course the subject uses, however, he is operating in terms of his own conception of the nature of the situation, rather than in terms of the conception that the experimenter is trying to induce. In short, the experimenter can no longer assume that the conditions that he is trying to create are the ones that actually define the situation for the subject. Thus, the use of deception, while it is designed to give the experimenter control over the subject's perceptions and motivations, may actually produce an unspecifiable mixture of intended and unintended stimuli that make it difficult to know just what the subject is responding to.

The tendency for subjects to react to unintended cues—to features of the situation that are not part of the experimenter's design—is by no means restricted to experiments that involve deception. This problem has concerned students of the interview situation for some time, and more recently it has been analyzed in detail in the writings and research of Riecken, Rosenthal, Orne, and Mills. Subjects enter the experiment with their own aims, including attainment of certain rewards, divination of the experimenter's true purposes, and favorable self-presentation (Riecken, 1962). They are therefore responsive to demand characteristics of the situation (Orne, 1962), to unintended communications of the experimenter's expectations (Rosenthal, 1963), and to the role of the experimenter within the social system that experimenter and subject jointly constitute (Mills,

1962). In any experiment, then, the subject goes beyond the description of the situation and the experimental manipulation introduced by the investigator, makes his own interpretation of the situation, and acts accordingly.

For several reasons, however, the use of deception especially encourages the subject to dismiss the stated purposes of the experiment and to search for alternative interpretations of his own. First, the continued use of deception establishes the reputation of psychologists as people who cannot be believed. Thus, the desire "to penetrate the experimenter's inscrutability and discover the rationale of the experiment [Riecken, 1962, p. 34]" becomes especially strong. Generally, these efforts are motivated by the subject's desire to meet the expectations of the experimenter and of the situation. They may also be motivated, however, as I have already mentioned, by a desire to outwit the experimenter and to beat him at his own game, in a spirit of genuine hostility or playful one-upmanship. Second, a situation involving the use of deception is inevitably highly ambiguous since a great deal of information relevant to understanding the structure of the situation must be withheld from the subject. Thus, the subject is especially motivated to try to figure things out and likely to develop idiosyncratic interpretations. Third, the use of deception, by its very nature, causes the experimenter to transmit contradictory messages to the subject. In his verbal instructions and explanations he says one thing about the purposes of the experiment; but in the experimental situation that he has created, in the manipulations that he has introduced, and probably in covert cues that he emits, he says another thing. This again makes it imperative for the subject to seek his own interpretation of the situation.

I would argue, then, that deception increases the subject's tendency to operate in terms of his private definition of the situation, differing (in random or systematic fashion) from the definition that the experimenter is trying to impose; moreover, it makes it more difficult to evaluate or minimize the effects of this tendency. Whether or not I am right in this judgment, it can, at the very least, be said that the use of deception does not resolve or reduce the unintended effects of the experiment as a social situation in which the subject pursues his private aims. Since the assumptions that the subject is naïve and that he sees the situation as the experimenter wishes him to see it are unwarranted, the use of deception no longer has any special obvious advantages over other experimental approaches. I am not suggesting that there may not be occasions when deception may still be the most effective procedure to use from a methodological point of view. But since it raises at least as many methodological problems as any other type of procedure does, we have every reason to explore alternative approaches and to extend our methodological inquiries to the question of the effects of using deception.

3. *Implications for the future of social psychology.* My third concern about the use of deception is based on its long-run

implications for our discipline and combines both the ethical and methodological considerations that I have already raised. There is something disturbing about the idea of relying on massive deception as the basis for developing a field of inquiry. Can one really build a discipline on a foundation of such research?

From a long-range point of view, there is obviously something self-defeating about the use of deception. As we continue to carry out research of this kind, our potential subjects become more and more sophisticated, and we become less and less able to meet the conditions that our experimental procedures require. Moreover, as we continue to carry out research of this kind, our potential subjects become increasingly distrustful of us, and our future relations with them are likely to be undermined. Thus, we are confronted with the anomalous circumstance that the more research we do, the more difficult and questionable it becomes.

The use of deception also involves a contradiction between our experimental procedures and our long-range aims as scientists and teachers. In order to be able to carry out our experiments, we are concerned with maintaining the naïveté of the population from which we hope to draw our subjects. We are all familiar with the experimenter's anxious concern that the introductory course might cover the autokinetic phenomenon, need achievement, or the Asch situation before he has had a chance to complete his experimental runs. This perfectly understandable desire to keep procedures secret goes counter to the traditional desire of the scientist and teacher to inform and enlighten the public. To be sure, experimenters are interested only in temporary secrecy, but it is not inconceivable that at some time in the future they might be using certain procedures on a regular basis with large segments of the population and thus prefer to keep the public permanently naïve. It is perhaps not too fanciful to imagine, for the long run, the possible emergence of a special class, in possession of secret knowledge—a possibility that is clearly antagonistic to the principle of open communication to which we, as scientists and intellectuals, are so fervently committed.

DEALING WITH THE PROBLEM OF DECEPTION IN SOCIAL PSYCHOLOGICAL EXPERIMENTS

If my concerns about the use of deception are justified, what are some of the ways in which we, as experimental social psychologists, can deal with them? I would like to suggest three steps that we can take: increase our active awareness of the problem, explore ways of counteracting and minimizing the negative effects of deception, and give careful attention to the development of new experimental techniques that dispense with the use of deception.

1. Active awareness of the problem. I have already stressed that I would not propose the complete elimination of deception

under all circumstances, in view of the genuine conflict of values with which the experimenter is confronted. What is crucial, however, is that we always ask ourselves the question whether deception, in the given case, is necessary and justified. How we answer the question is less important than the fact that we ask it. What we must be wary of is the tendency to dismiss the question as irrelevant and to accept deception as a matter of course. Active awareness of the problem is thus in itself part of the solution for it makes the use of deception a matter for discussion, deliberation, investigation, and choice. Active awareness means that, in any given case, we will try to balance the value of an experiment that uses deception against its questionable or potentially harmful effects. If we engage in this process honestly, we are likely to find that there are many occasions when we or our students can forego the use of deception—either because deception is not necessary (that is, alternative procedures that are equally good or better are available), because the importance of the study does not warrant the use of an ethically questionable procedure, or because the type of deception involved is too extreme (in terms of the possibility of harmful effects or of seriously undermining the experimenter-subject relationship).

2. Counteracting and minimizing the negative effects of deception. If we do use deception, it is essential that we find ways of counteracting and minimizing its negative effects. Sensitizing the apprentice researcher to this necessity is at least as fundamental as any other part of research training.

In those experiments in which deception carries the potential of harmful effects (in the more usual sense of the term), there is an obvious requirement to build protections into every phase of the process. Subjects must be selected in a way that will exclude individuals who are especially vulnerable; the potentially harmful manipulation (such as the induction of stress) must be kept at a moderate level of intensity; the experimenter must be sensitive to danger signals in the reactions of his subjects and be prepared to deal with crises when they arise; and, at the conclusion of the session, the experimenter must take time not only to reassure the subject, but also to help him work through his feelings about the experience to whatever degree may be required. In general, the principle that a subject ought not to leave the laboratory with greater anxiety or lower self-esteem than he came with is a good one to follow. I would go beyond it to argue that the subject should in some positive way be enriched by the experience, that is, he should come away from it with the feeling that he has learned something, understood something, or grown in some way. This, of course, adds special importance to the kind of feedback that is given to the subject at the end of the experimental session.

Postexperimental feedback is, of course, the primary way of counteracting negative effects in those experiments in which the issue is deception as such, rather than possible threats to the subject's well-being. If we do deceive the subject, then it is our obligation to give him a full and detailed explanation of what we have done and of our reasons for using this type of procedure. I do not want to be absolutist about this, but I would suggest it as a good rule of thumb to follow: Think very carefully before undertaking an experiment whose purposes you feel unable to reveal to the subjects even after they have completed the experimental session. It is, of course not enough to give the subject a perfunctory feedback, just to do one's duty. Postexperimental explanations should be worked out with as much detail as other aspects of the procedure and, in general, some thought ought to be given to ways of making them meaningful and instructive for the subject and helpful for rebuilding his relationship with the experimenter. I feel very strongly that to accomplish these purposes, we must keep the feedback itself inviolate and under no circumstance give the subject false feedback or pretend to be giving him feedback while we are in fact introducing another experimental manipulation. If we hope to maintain any kind of trust in our relationship with potential subjects, there must be no ambiguity that the statement "The experiment is over and I shall explain to you what it was all about" means precisely that and nothing else. If subjects have reason to suspect even that statement, then we have lost the whole basis for a decent human relationship with our subjects and all hope for future cooperation from them.

3. *Development of new experimental techniques.* My third and final suggestion is that we invest some of the creativity and ingenuity, now devoted to the construction of elaborate deceptions, in the search for alternative experimental techniques that do not rely on the use of deception. The kind of techniques that I have in mind would be based on the principle of eliciting the subject's positive motivations to contribute to the experimental enterprise. They would draw on the subject's active participation and involvement in the proceedings and encourage him to cooperate in making the experiment a success—not by giving the results he thinks the experimenter wants, but by conscientiously taking the roles and carrying out the tasks that the experimenter assigns to him. In short, the kind of techniques I have in mind would be designed to involve the subject as an active participant in a joint effort with the experimenter.

Perhaps the most promising source of alternative experimental approaches are procedures using some sort of role playing. I have been impressed, for example, with the role playing that I have observed in the context of the Inter-Nation Simulation (Guetzkow, Alger, Brody, Noel, & Snyder, 1963), a laboratory procedure involving a simulated world in which the subjects take the roles of decision-makers of various nations. This situation seems to create a high level of emotional involvement and to elicit motivations that have a real-life quality to them. Moreover, within this situation—which is highly complex and generally permits only gross experimental manipulations—it is possible to test specific theoretical hypotheses by using data based on repeated measurements as interaction between the simulated nations develops. Thus, a study carried out at the Western Behavioral Sciences Institute provided, as an extra, some interesting opportunities for testing hypotheses derived from balance theory, by the use of mutual ratings made by decision-makers of Nations A, B, and C, before and after A shifted from an alliance with B to an alliance with C.

A completely different type of role playing was used effectively by Rosenberg and Abelson (1960) in their studies of cognitive dilemmas. In my own research program, we have been exploring different kinds of role-playing procedures with varying degrees of success. In one study, the major manipulation consisted in informing subjects that the experiment to which they had just committed themselves would require them (depending on the condition) either to receive shocks from a fellow subject, or to administer shocks to a fellow subject. We used a regular deception procedure, but with a difference: We told the subjects before the session started that what was to follow was make-believe, but that we wanted them to react as if they really found themselves in this situation. I might mention that some subjects, not surprisingly, did not accept as true the information that this was all make-believe and wanted to know when they should show up for the shock experiment to which they had committed themselves. I have some questions about the effectiveness of this particular procedure. It did not do enough to create a high level of involvement, and it turned out to be very complex since it asked subjects to role-play subjects, not people. In this sense, it might have given us the worst of both worlds, but I still think it is worth some further exploration. In another experiment, we were interested in creating differently structured attitudes about an organization by feeding different kinds of information to two groups of subjects. These groups were then asked to take specific actions in support of the organization, and we measured attitude changes resulting from these actions. In the first part of the experiment, the subjects were clearly informed that the organization and the information that we were feeding to them were fictitious, and that we were simply trying to simulate the conditions under which attitudes about new organizations are typically formed. In the second part of the experiment, the subjects were told that we were interested in studying the effects of action in support of an organization on attitudes toward it, and they were asked (in groups of five) to role-play a strategy meeting of leaders of the fictitious organization. The results of this study were very encouraging. While there is obviously a great deal that we need to know about the meaning of this situation to the subjects, they did react differentially to the experimental manipulations and these reactions followed an orderly pattern, despite the fact that they knew it was all make-believe.

There are other types of procedures, in addition to role playing, that are worth exploring. For example, one might design field experiments in which, with the full cooperation of the subjects, specific experimental variations are introduced. The advantages of dealing with motivations at a real-life level of intensity might well outweigh the disadvantages of subjects' knowing the general purpose of the experiment. At the other extreme of ambitiousness, one might explore the effects of modifying standard experimental procedures slightly by informing the subject at the beginning of the experiment that he will not be receiving full information about what is going on, but asking him to suspend judgment until the experiment is over.

Whatever alternative approach we try, there is no doubt that it will have its own problems and complexities. Procedures effective for some purposes may be quite ineffective for others, and it may well turn out that for certain kinds of problems there is no adequate substitute for the use of deception. But there *are* alternative procedures that, for many purposes, may be as effective or even more effective than procedures built on deception. These approaches often involve a radically different set of assumptions about the role of the subject in the experiment: They require us to *use* the subject's motivation to cooperate rather than to bypass it; they may even call for increasing the sophistication of potential subjects, rather than maintaining their naïveté. My only plea is that we devote some of our energies to active exploration of these alternative approaches.

REFERENCES

Asch, S. E. Effects of group pressure upon the modification and distortion of judgments. In H. Guetzkow (Ed.), *Groups, leadership, and men.* Pittsburgh: Carnegie Press, 1951. Pp. 117–190.

Baumrind, D. Some thoughts on ethics of research: After reading Milgram's "Behavioral Study of Obedience." *American Psychologist,* 1964, 19, 421–423.

Bergin, A. E. The effect of dissonant persuasive communications upon changes in a self-referring attitude. *Journal of Personality,* 1962, 30, 423–438.

Berkun, M. M., Bialek, H. M., Kern, R. P., & Yagi, K. Experimental studies of psychological stress in man. *Psychological Monographs,* 1962, 76(15, Whole No. 534).

Bramel, D. A dissonance theory approach to defensive projection. *Journal of Abnormal and Social Psychology,* 1962, 64, 121–129.

Bramel, D. Selection of a target for defensive projection. *Journal of Abnormal and Social Psychology,* 1963, 66, 318–324.

Campbell, D., Sanderson, R. E., & Laverty, S. G. Characteristics of a conditioned response in human subjects during extinction trials following a single traumatic conditioning trial. *Journal of Abnormal and Social Psychology,* 1964, 68, 627–639.

Festinger, L., & Carlsmith, J. M. Cognitive consequences of forced compliance. *Journal of Abnormal and Social Psychology,* 1959, 58, 203–210.

Guetzkow, H., Alger, C. F., Brody, R. A., Noel, R. C., & Snyder, R. C. *Simulation in international relations.* Englewood Cliffs, N.J.: Prentice-Hall, 1963.

Kelman, H. C. Manipulation of human behavior: An ethical dilemma for the social scientist. *Journal of Social Issues,* 1965, 21(2), 31–46.

Milgram, S. Behavioral study of obedience. *Journal of Abnormal and Social Psychology,* 1963, 67, 371–378.

Milgram, S. Issues in the study of obedience: A reply to Baumrind. *American Psychologist,* 1964, 19, 848–852.

Milgram, S. Some conditions of obedience and disobedience to authority. *Human Relations,* 1965, 18, 57–76.

Mills, T. M. A sleeper variable in small groups research: The experimenter. *Pacific Sociological Review,* 1962, 5, 21–28.

Mulder, M., & Stemerding, A. Threat, attraction to group, and need for strong leadership. *Human Relations,* 1963, 16, 317–334.

Orne, M. T. On the social psychology of the psychological experiment: With particular reference to demand characteristics and their implications. *American Psychologist,* 1962, 17, 776–783.

Riecken, H. W. A program for research on experiments in social psychology. In N. F. Washburne (Ed.), *Decisions, values and groups.* Vol. 2. New York: Pergamon Press, 1962. Pp. 25–41.

Rosenberg, M. J., & Abelson, R. P. An analysis of cognitive balancing. In M. J. Rosenberg et al., *Attitude organization and change.* New Haven: Yale University Press, 1960. Pp. 112–163.

Rosenthal, R. On the social psychology of the psychological experiment: The experimenter's hypothesis as unintended determinant of experimental results. *American Scientist,* 1963, 51, 268–283.

Rosenthal, R., & Fode, K. L. Psychology of the scientist: V. Three experiments in experimenter bias. *Psychological Reports,* 1963, 12, 491–511. (Monogr. Suppl. 3-V12)

Rosenthal, R., Persinger, G. W., Vikan-Kline, L., & Fode, K. L. The effect of early data returns on data subsequently obtained by outcome-biased experimenters. *Sociometry,* 1963, 26, 487–498.

Rosenthal, R., Persinger, G. W., Vikan-Kline, L., & Mulry, R. C. The role of the research assistant in the mediation of experimenter bias. *Journal of Personality,* 1963, 31, 313–335.

Vinacke, W. E. Deceiving experimental subjects. *American Psychologist,* 1954, 9, 155.

ENDNOTES

1. Paper read at the symposium on "Ethical and Methodological Problems in Social Psychological Experiments," held at the meetings of the American Psychological Association in Chicago, September 3, 1965. This paper is a product of a research program on social influence and behavior change supported by United States Public Health Service Research Grant MH-07280 from the National Institute of Mental Health.

2. In focusing on deception in *social* psychological experiments, I do not wish to give the impression that there is no serious problem elsewhere. Deception is widely used in most studies involving human subjects and gives rise to issues similar to those discussed in this paper. Some examples of the use of deception in other areas of psychological experimentation will be presented later in this paper.

3. The authors reported, however, that some of their other subjects were physicians familiar with the drug; "they did not suppose they were dying but, even though they knew in a general way what to expect, they too said that the experience was extremely harrowing [p. 632]." Thus, conceivably, the purposes of the experiment might have been achieved even if the subjects had been told to expect the temporary interruption of breathing.

CRITICAL THINKING QUESTIONS

1. Which of the studies mentioned in the article involves the greatest ethical issues? Why? Select one of the studies cited in this article, and suggest an alternative to the type of deception that was employed.

2. Should the use of deception be banned? Why or why not? If not, under what conditions should it be allowed? What impact would such a limitation have on social psychological research? Defend your position.

3. Who should determine what constitutes an ethically appropriate experiment? Professors? Students? Outside laypeople? Explain your answer. What would be the ideal composition of a board charged with reviewing research proposals? Why?

4. Obtain a copy of the current "American Psychological Association Guide for the Ethical Treatment of Human Subjects." Review these guidelines, considering how comprehensive they are. What criteria should be used in determining what is in the best interests of the subjects of an experiment?

5. What do you think of Kelman's position on "second-order" deception? Do you agree that it is of even greater concern than standard ("first-order") deception practices? Why or why not?

6. What do you think of Kelman's suggestions for the development of new experimental techniques as an alternative to deception? Find a research study that tried such a technique in lieu of deception. Alternatively, find a research study reported in this book of readings and suggest an alternative to the deception that was used. In either case, what might be lost and what might be gained by not deceiving subjects? Explain your answer.

ADDITIONAL RELATED READINGS

Hertwig, R., & Ortmann, A. (2008). Deception in experiments: Revisiting the arguments in its defense. *Ethics & Behavior, 18*(1), 59–92.

Oczak, M., & Niedźwieńska, A. (2007). Debriefing in deceptive research: A proposed new procedure. *Journal of Empirical Research on Human Research Ethics, 2*(3), 49–59.

ARTICLE 3 ———————————————

How do we acquire the many beliefs we have about the world? Perhaps some of them are original thoughts based upon our own unique experiences. For example, you may believe that eating eggs will make you sick because of having eaten them in the past and having become ill. That belief was based on a personal experience and not necessarily on what other people told us. Yet much of what we do believe is at least in part influenced by external sources of information. There are many such sources of information (books, television, etc.), but let's look at just one of them: What do other people think about something? Of course, what does "other people" mean? On the one hand, other people can simply be individuals that we know (family, friends) or it can be people in general (e.g., as in "a blockbuster movie that obviously was liked by many people"). On the other hand, "other people" can also refer to someone with particular expertise on a given topic. One such source of evidence based upon expertise might be what scientists tell us.

So which source of influence (other people in general or scientific opinion) has a greater influence on our belief systems? That may depend on what the belief is about. For example, if your friends think smoking doesn't really have any impact on health, yet you know that overwhelming scientific evidence shows that smoking is harmful in many ways, who are you most likely going to believe? It would seem that the latter might have a bigger impact on your beliefs, yet that might not necessarily be the case. Consider how many people continue to smoke or start to smoke even though they are fully aware of the scientific evidence as to how harmful smoking is. How other people influence our belief systems is known as *social influence,* a topic more fully addressed in Chapter 9.

The following article by Heather Ridolfo, Amy Baxter, and Jeffrey W. Lucas examines how belief in the paranormal is influenced by either popular support or scientific support for it. Paranormal beliefs include phenomena such as extrasensory perception (ESP), psychic or spiritual healing, clairvoyance, and ghosts. Whatever your beliefs are on these topics, how likely are your beliefs to be influenced by what other people in general think of those topics, and how likely are your beliefs to be influenced by what the scientific evidence maintains for those topics? This article explores how these two sources of information impact people's belief systems regarding the paranormal. While this article specifically deals with paranormal beliefs, the underlying issues that it addresses, such as the public's trust in scientific findings, are an important topic in social psychology and in science in general.

Social Influences on Paranormal Belief: Popular Versus Scientific Support

■ Heather Ridolfo, Amy Baxter, and Jeffrey W. Lucas

ABSTRACT

Paranormal claims enjoy relatively widespread popular support despite by definition being rejected by the scientific community. We propose that belief in paranormal claims is influenced by how popular those claims are as well as by dominant scientific views on the claims. We additionally propose that individuals will be most likely to be positively influenced by the views of science when claims are unpopular. An experimental study varied instructions to participants in a 2 × 2 design which informed participants that

a particular paranormal belief/claim (ESP) was very popular or not and was rejected by science or not. Participants then watched a brief video that appeared to present evidence of ESP. As predicted, participants became more likely to believe in ESP when claims were more popular. Contrary to predictions, participants appeared to react against the views of science when evaluating claims, particularly when they believed those claims were unpopular. This finding may reflect decreasing trust in the institution of science.

Ridolfo, H.; Baxter, A.; & Lucas, J.W. (2010). Social influences on paranormal belief: Popular versus scientific support. *Current Research in Social Psychology, 15*(3), 33–41. Used with permission of the author.

INTRODUCTION

Belief in paranormal claims has increased markedly in the United States in recent decades. For example, a 2001 Gallup Poll found significant (greater than 5%) increases in belief for seven paranormal claims since 1990, and a significant decrease in only one polled belief (Moore 2005).[1] Further, the overall percent of Americans believing in paranormal claims is high. According to the 2001 Gallup Poll, for example, half or more of Americans believe in psychic or spiritual healing (54% believed, 26% did not believe) and in extrasensory perception (ESP) (50% believed, 27% did not believe). Belief in paranormal claims in student populations is similarly high (Duncan, Donnelly, Nicholson, and Hees 1992; Messer and Griggs 1989). These findings are troubling to educators who value and teach an approach of appropriating belief according to evidence. In that belief in paranormal claims by definition requires one to disregard existing bodies of knowledge, paranormal beliefs may reflect an inability or unwillingness to link conclusions to evidence.[2] Consistent with this, belief in the paranormal tends to be associated with lower cognitive ability and academic performance (Blackmore and Troscianko 1985; Musch and Ehrenberg 2002; Tobacyk 1984).

Belief in paranormal claims has increased alongside decreasing trust in social institutions. Evidence of malfeasance in organizations such as Enron, WorldCom, Halliburton, and Tyco led to a significant loss of trust in the integrity of the U.S. corporate sector, and particularly of corporate leadership (Alsop 2004; Gosschalk and Hyde 2005; Leeds 2003). This declining trust has also extended to the institution of science (Bloom and Rosovsky 2001; Hanley and Shogren 2005). Surveys indicate that trust in science in general seems to be declining (Nowotny 2005).

It may be a coincidence that increasing belief in paranormal claims appears to have coincided with decreasing trust in science. The correspondence, however, raises interesting questions. Basic social psychology indicates that individuals will become more likely to believe claims that are more popular. We also expect people to generally adhere to the dominant views of science. What happens when the popularity of beliefs conflicts with the views of science is the focus of the research reported here.

We conducted an experimental study in which participants watched a videotape manipulated to appear to show a person demonstrate ESP. Study instructions varied to participants in a 2 × 2 experimental design. Half of participants were told that public belief in ESP is high, half that it is low. Additionally, instructions told half of participants that science rejects the possibility of ESP, while half were told that scientists recognize ESP as a possibility. Results were in the direction of popularity increasing belief and scientific support *decreasing* belief. We also found a significant interaction indicating that individuals were especially likely to react against the views of science when claims were unpopular.

THEORETICAL DEVELOPMENT

Features of individuals play a significant role in the likelihoods that they will believe in paranormal claims. For example, individuals lower in critical thinking ability are more likely to accept paranormal claims as true than are individuals higher in critical thinking ability (Wierzbicki 1985). Our focus, however, is on social factors that influence belief in the paranormal. At least since Asch's (1951) classic research on conformity, social psychological research has demonstrated that individuals will change their beliefs in a direction consistent with group standards. As a result, we should expect that beliefs in paranormal claims will be affected by perceptions of social acceptance of those claims.[3]

Markovsky and Thye (2001) demonstrated in an experimental study the malleability of paranormal beliefs to social pressures. In their study, participants became significantly more likely to believe they had witnessed a paranormal phenomenon when a confederate who witnessed the same phenomenon claimed to believe the phenomenon to be true. Furthermore, confederates who were not present were just as highly influential as sources who were present. In Asch's research, larger groups were more influential in producing conformity than were smaller groups. And, subsequent research (Campbell and Fairey 1989) found that increasing group size had larger effects when normative influence processes, as opposed to information influence, were operating. From this body of research, we should expect perceptions of beliefs in society in general to have significant effects on an individual's likelihood to believe in a paranormal claim. We thus make the following prediction:

Hypothesis 1: Participants will be more likely to accept a paranormal explanation for an unusual event when they believe the paranormal explanation is more widely popular compared to when they believe it is less popular.

We also anticipate that individuals will be influenced by the views of science in their acceptance of paranormal claims. Although trust in science is declining, scientists remain more trusted than politicians and those in other public institutions (Nowotny 2005). A 2009 poll by the Pew Research Center (2009) found that an overwhelming majority of Americans (84%) believed that science has had a positive effect on society and that science has made life easier for most people. Further, those polled held scientists in high regard. In rating professions by their contributions to society's well-being, scientists were rated lower than only teachers and members of the military and ahead of medical doctors, journalists, and lawyers among other professions. We predict the following:

Hypothesis 2: Participants will be more likely to accept a paranormal explanation for an unusual event when they believe that the scientific community is accepting of the paranormal explanation than when they believe that the scientific community rejects it.

Although trust in science remains generally high, Americans are willing to depart from dominant views of science on particular issues such as evolution and global warming (Lang 2005). The 2009 Pew poll which found that trust in science remains high also found increasing skepticism about science. When asked America's greatest achievement in the prior 50 years, 47% of Americans in 1999 listed a scientific achievement. In 2009, only 27% of Americans listed a scientific achievement in response to the same question. The growing acceptance of paranormal claims combined with a decreased trust in science and willingness to depart from science on particular issues leads us to predict that individuals will selectively adhere to dominant views of science. We predict that individuals will attend to the views of science when claims are unpopular but will tend to disregard the views of science for popular claims:

Hypothesis 3: Popularity and scientific acceptance will interact such that participants will become less likely to believe paranormal claims rejected by the scientific community when belief in those claims is unpopular but not when belief is popular.

Our goal in carrying out our research was not to test for levels of paranormal belief in the population at-large. The prevalence of belief in the paranormal among Americans is well-documented. Instead, our objective was to test the above predictions on how dominant belief systems affect individual beliefs. To test our predictions, we carried out an experimental study with college student volunteers as participants. Details of the study are described below.

METHODS

Participants were undergraduate students at a large public university. Upon arriving for the study, participants first completed an information form containing standard demographic items. They also answered a question indicating the extent to which they believed that ESP is a real phenomenon. Instructions said that the investigators were interested in studying how individuals respond to evidence of ESP. The study contained four conditions in a 2 × 2 design that varied popularity of ESP and the perspective of science on ESP. The four conditions of the study were as follows:

Condition 1: Participants read that 25% of the American public believes in ESP and that the scientific community rejects the possibility of ESP.
Condition 2: Participants read that over 90% of the American public believes in ESP and that the scientific community rejects the possibility of ESP.
Condition 3: Participants read that 25% of the American public believes in ESP and that the scientific community is becoming more open to the possibility of ESP.
Conditions 4: Participants read that 90% of the American public believes in ESP and that the scientific community becoming more open to the possibility of ESP.

Thus, participants were told that either 25% or 90% of the public believes in ESP (in fact, about 50% of Americans believe

in ESP) and that the scientific community either rejects or accepts the possibility of ESP (in fact, the scientific community overwhelmingly rejects the possibility of ESP). The text of instructions participants received was as follows:

"ESP is particularly relevant to study in today's society because there has been a dramatic increase in the proportion of the United States' population that believes in ESP. A recent Gallup Poll found that [about 25%] [more than 90%] of Americans believe that some persons possess ESP, a figure up significantly from just 10 years ago. [While more and more Americans are believing in ESP, the overwhelming majority of the scientific community still rejects the possibility of ESP, arguing that it violates certain irrefutable scientific principles] [Along with the American public increasingly believing in ESP, the scientific community is becoming more open to the idea as well—many scientists now believe that ESP is at least possible]."

After reading instructions particular to their conditions, participants watched a short video in which an individual completes a card-guessing task. The individual in the video performs much better than would be predicted by chance (unknown to participants, the individual in the video was informed of answers by someone off-camera). After watching the video, participants completed a number of questionnaire items, including whether the participants believed in ESP and whether they thought the individual in the video displayed ESP in her guesses. We predict that as participants believe that a greater proportion of the American public believes in ESP, they will become more likely to believe (i.e., greater belief in Condition 2 than in Condition 1 and in Condition 4 than in Condition 3). We further predict that as participants believe that the scientific community is more open to the possibility of ESP, they will become more likely to believe (i.e., greater belief in Condition 3 than in Condition 1 and in Condition 4 than in Condition 2). We also predict an interaction between public and scientists' beliefs such that the effect of the views of science is greater when beliefs are less popular in the public at large.

RESULTS

Forty participants completed each experimental condition for a total of 160 participants. We rejected data from an additional five participants who did not believe the video was authentic or did not believe the study instructions were truthful.

We predicted that participants would become more accepting of paranormal explanations when they believed the explanation had high public support or support from the scientific community. We also predicted that effects of public and scientific support would interact such that effects of science would be greater for less popular claims. We tested our hypotheses by comparing results on a dependent variable that asked participants the extent to which they believed in ESP after watching the video presentation. We measured the item on a

7-point scale with the top end of the scale reflecting high levels of belief in ESP.

Following are mean scores on the belief in ESP scale across conditions:

Condition 1 (25% of public believes; science rejects): 4.58 (SD = 1.92)

Condition 2 (90% of public believes; science rejects): 4.50 (SD = 1.60)

Condition 3 (25% of public believes; science accepts): 3.58 (SD = 1.84)

Condition 4 (90% of public believes; science accepts): 4.80 (SD = 1.70)

Mean differences show a pattern that is difficult to interpret. The most noteworthy finding appears to be that individuals are especially likely to reject claims that are unpopular but accepted by science. We conducted an ANOVA to test for main effects of scientific and public support as well as the interaction between the two, while controlling for participant gender, age, and race. ANOVA results showed a significant main effect for public support ($F = 7.077$, $p = .009$). When participants believed that claims were more popular, they became more likely to accept them. The main effect for the views of science was not significant ($F = 1.162$, $p = .283$).

Participants were not significantly affected by the views of science. The interaction between public and scientific views was significant ($F = 6.786 = .010$). The interaction, however, operated differently than we predicted. We expected the views of science to carry less weight for more popular claims. This was the case. However, the effect of science for unpopular claims was in the opposite direction of what we expected: When claims were unpopular, individuals reacted against the views of science in their beliefs.

DISCUSSION

We found relatively strong evidence that individuals are more likely to accept paranormal claims as true when they believe such claims have popular support. This finding contributes to and extends research that has found significant effects of social influences on belief in the paranormal. We found no effects indicating that science rejecting a claim led individuals to be less likely to believe the claim. In fact, when participants believed that science rejected a claim, they moved in the direction of being *more* likely to accept the claim as true. This finding ran counter to our expectations but is consistent with findings that trust in science is decreasing.

We predicted that effects of science and popularity would interact such that individuals would be most likely to look to the views of science when evaluating unpopular claims. The effects of science were largest when beliefs were unpopular, but the effects were in the opposite direction of what we predicted. When participants believed that ESP had widespread support, participants indicated generally high belief irrespective of information on the views of science. When participants believed that ESP had less popular support, they were more likely to believe when they were told science rejected ESP than when they were told that science accepted the possibility of ESP. Comparing means across conditions, participants expressed similar levels of belief in three of the four conditions—both conditions in which ESP had high popular support and the condition in which ESP did not have widespread popular support and science rejected the possibility of ESP. In the fourth condition, in which participants were instructed that belief in ESP is not popular but science accepts ESP as a possibility, mean belief scores dropped significantly.

A possible explanation for the set of means across conditions is that participants first may have looked to the popularity of claims when determining belief. If claims were popular, then participants were generally likely to believe. When claims were unpopular, however, participants might have considered the views of science and moved away from dominant scientific thought. Another explanation is that the condition with anomalous findings is the only condition that presented a set of information likely to be inconsistent with any of the participants' prior experiences. Claims not being widely accepted and being rejected by science go hand in hand, as do claims being widely believed and accepted by science. Beliefs being popular but rejected by science (e.g., spiritual healing) also often complement each other. However, it is difficult to think of claims rejected by three quarters of the public at large but accepted by scientists as true. Perhaps other conditions triggered cognitive processes that led to expressions of belief in some participants, whereas the condition with inconsistent information did not. These potential explanations are purely speculative, and this issue would benefit from further investigation.

Overall, our research demonstrated that individuals responded positively to perceptions of the popularity of paranormal claims when making decisions about belief in those claims. Results also suggest that participants reacted *against* the views of science in making decisions about paranormal claims. These findings may be due to individuals seeing paranormal belief as a matter of faith rather than evidence and therefore reacting against science. Alternatively, perhaps endorsement from peers provides a stronger source of legitimacy for paranormal beliefs than authorization from a higher authority. Or, the findings may result from a decreasing trust in the institution of science.

REFERENCES

Alsop, Ronald J. 2004. "Corporate Reputation: Anything but Superficial—The Deep but Fragile Nature of Corporate Reputation." *Journal of Business Strategy* 25: 21–29.

Asch, Solomon E. 1951. "Effects of Group Pressure Upon the Modification and Distortion of Judgments." Pp. 178–190 in H. Guetzkow (Ed.), *Groups, Leadership, and Men.* Pittsburgh, PA: Carnegie Press.

Blackmore, Susan, and Tom Troscianko. 1985. "Belief in the Paranormal: Probability Judgments, Illusory Control, and the 'Chance Baseline Shift'." *British Journal of Psychology* 76: 459–468.

Bloom, David E., and Henry Rosovsky. 2001. "Higher Education and International Development." *Current Science* 81: 252–256.

Campbell, Jennifer D., and Patricia J. Fairey. 1989. "Informational and Normative Routes to Conformity: The Effect of Faction Size as a Function of Norm Extremity and Attention to the Stimulus." *Journal of Personality and Social Psychology* 57: 457–468.

Duncan, David F., William J. Donnelly, Thomas Nicholson, and Alice J. Hees. 1992. "Cultural Diversity, Superstitions, and Pseudoscientific Beliefs among Allied Health Students." *College Student Journal* 26: 525–530.

Gosschalk, Brian, and Allan Hyde. 2005. "The Business World will Never be the Same: The Contribution of Research to Corporate Governance Post-Enron." *International Journal of Market Research* 47: 29–44.

Hanley, Nick, and Jason F. Shogren. 2005. "Is Cost-Benefit Analysis Anomaly-Proof?" *Environmental and Resource Economics* 32: 13–34.

Lang, Graeme. 2005. " 'Democratic Ignorance' and the Politics of Knowledge." *International Review of Sociology* 15: 203–206.

Leeds, Roger. 2003. "Breach of Trust: Leadership in a Market Economy." *Harvard International Review* 25: 76–82.

Markovsky, Barry, and Shane R. Thye. 2001. "Social Influence on Paranormal Beliefs." *Sociological Perspectives* 44: 21–44.

Messer, Wayne S., and Richard A. Griggs. 1989. "Student Belief and Involvement in the Paranormal and Performance in Introductory Psychology." *Teaching of Psychology* 16: 187–191.

Moore, David A. 2005. *Three in Four Americans Believe in Paranormal.* Princeton: Gallup News Service.

Musch, Jochen, and Katja Ehrenberg. 2002. "Probability Misjudgment, Cognitive Ability, and Belief in the Paranormal." *British Journal of Social Psychology* 93: 169–177.

Nowotny, Helga. 2005. "High- and Low-Cost Realities for Science and Society." *Science* 20: 1117–1118.

Pew Research Center. 2009. "Public Praises Science: Scientists Fault Public, Media." Published July 7, 2009. Retrieved July 26, 2009 at http://pewresearch.org/pubs/ 1276/science-survey.

Tobacyk, Jermone. 1984. "Paranormal Belief and College Grade Point Average." *Psychological Reports* 54: 217–218.

Wierzbicki, Michael. 1985. "Reasoning Errors and Belief in the Paranormal." *The Journal of Social Psychology* 125: 489–494.

ENDNOTES

1. Paranormal beliefs showing significant increases from 1990 to 2001 included haunted houses, ghosts, witches, communication with the dead, psychic or spiritual healing, that extraterrestrials have visited earth, and clairvoyance. Demonic possession showed a significant decrease in belief.

2. Following Markovsky and Thye (2001), we adopt a broad definition of "paranormal." For our purposes, claims are paranormal if they violate widely accepted scientific principles (such as perpetual motion machines), if they are very unlikely given existing knowledge (such as Bigfoot), or if they are outside the realm of natural explanations (such as astrology).

3. Beliefs may be conscious or unconscious, controllable or not. By "belief," we mean here conscious representations of beliefs.

CRITICAL THINKING QUESTIONS

1. According to the article, public trust in social institutions and in science has been decreasing over the years. Based on your experiences and observations, do you think that there has been a decrease in trust in science? Social institutions? Explain your position.

2. Talk to some people about their beliefs in various paranormal claims. Can you ascertain where their beliefs come from? In other words, was it direct experience? Something someone told them about? Something they read somewhere? A scientific report that they encountered? Try to determine if there is any pattern in the responses you observed.

3. The article mentions some of the potential reasons that public support of social institutions has decreased. What are some of the reasons that you might give? Give specific examples to support your position.

4. Look at the pattern of findings from this study. Are there any other areas of belief or behavior that might follow a similar pattern of results? Explain your reasoning.

CHAPTER INTEGRATION QUESTIONS

1. All three articles in this chapter relate to aspects of research: how to be a wise consumer of psychological research, the problems of deception in research, and how scientific evidence may (or may not) influence people's beliefs. Identify one or more themes common to all three articles.

2. Based on these articles, what are the major issues confronting an individual embarking on a career in social psychology research?

3. In *How to Lie with Statistics,* Darrell Huff states, "Statistics are like people. Torture them enough and they will tell you anything." What does this quotation mean to you? Do you agree or disagree with it? Why?

Chapter Two

SOCIAL PERCEPTION

HOW DO WE form impressions of other people? What information do we use in forming those impressions? How important are first impressions? How do we make judgments about why people act the way they do? These are some of the questions addressed by the readings in this chapter on social perception.

When we interact with another person, we are literally bombarded with information. What the person looks like, what he or she is saying, and how he or she is acting comprise but a fraction of the information available to us that we may use in forming an impression of the individual. One judgment we may make about another individual concerns his or her overall character. In other words, we want to know how honest, trustworthy, likeable, or good the person is. But exactly what are we looking for? And are some of us better than others at making accurate judgments?

One topic of study in this area is how long it takes for us to form an impression of someone. Do we do so almost immediately, or do we hold off until we know more about him or her? Furthermore, how accurate are our first impressions? Is a first impression formed after less than a minute of interaction with a stranger any less accurate than an impression formed after knowing someone for a much longer period of time? These and other questions pertaining to the power of first impressions are examined in Article 4, "The Once-Over: Can You Trust First Impressions?"

Another topic of interest is whether all the information available about someone is equally relevant in forming our impressions of him or her. In other words, are some factors more important than others? Article 5, "The Warm-Cold Variable in First Impressions of Persons," examines some of the important factors that influence our judgments of other people. This classic article is a fine example of the power of first impressions and the impact that they have on how we relate to others.

Finally, Article 6, "Indirect Detection of Deception: Looking for Change," offers a contemporary look at research on one particular aspect of impression formation: the ability to detect when someone is lying. As the article indicates, people are very poor at detecting lies, even when they are in a profession where lie detection may be especially critical (e.g., law enforcement). However, this inaccuracy may be due to the incorrect stereotypes people are using to detect deception. The article explores how other, more indirect, methods for detecting deception might actually improve the accuracy of lie detection.

ARTICLE 4

What information do we use in forming impressions of other people? When meeting someone for the first time, we rely on a variety of information, such as how he or she acts, looks, and dresses and what he or she says. Some of this information is nonverbal. We pay a lot of attention to facial expressions, for example, as well as body postures and movements. Most of us have some sort of intuitive rules for decoding nonverbal behavior. For example, what does it mean when someone is standing upright with his or her arms folded across the chest? Is that person being defensive? Not very warm and open? Some popularizations of psychology maintain that certain nonverbal cues have specific meanings, such as in the example just given. However, the example used might also mean nothing more than that the person was cold or that he or she habitually stands that way. Regardless of any supposedly clear-cut meanings of nonverbal behavior, we all have our own intuitive means for making judgments about the people we meet.

Although we may have confidence in our own judgments, the concept known as the *fundamental attribution error* suggests that we only see what we want to see. According to this concept, we have a basic tendency to make global, personality generalizations based upon observations made in specific situations. For example, if we meet someone at a party who seems warm, outgoing, and confident, we assume that this is what his or her personality is like in other situations, as well. In other words, we think that we know the real person and ignore or downplay the fact that he or she may act quite differently in other situations. Worse yet, once we form this initial impression, it may be hard to change, since we may persist in only seeing what is consistent with our initial judgment.

So, how long does it take for us to make a judgment about someone? An hour? Fifteen minutes? Two seconds? The following article by Carlin Flora discusses research that shows that people make judgments about others in a remarkably short period of time. Furthermore, these quick judgments tend to be amazingly similar to those made by people interacting over a much longer time period or even by trained interviewers. But the question is this: How accurate are the judgments made by *any* of these people?

The Once-Over

Can You Trust First Impressions?

■ Carlin Flora

Bill and Hillary Clinton often tell the story of how they met: They locked eyes across Yale's law library, until Hillary broke the silent flirtation and marched straight over to Bill. "Look, if you're going to keep staring at me, and I'm going to keep staring back, we might as well be introduced. I'm Hillary Rodham. What's your name?" Bill has said he couldn't remember his own name. It was quite a first impression, one so powerful that it sparked a few chapters of U.S. history. Initial encounters are emotionally concentrated events that can overwhelm us—even convince us that the room is spinning. We walk away from them with a first impression that is like a Polaroid picture—a head-to-toe image that develops instantly and never entirely fades. Often, that snapshot captures important elements of the truth.

Consider one study in which untrained subjects were shown 20- to 32-second videotaped segments of job applicants greeting interviewers. The subjects then rated the applicants on attributes such as self-assurance and likability. Surprisingly, their assessments were very close to those of trained interviewers who spent at least 20 minutes with each applicant. What semblance of a person—one with a distinct appearance, history and complex personality—could have been captured in such a fleeting moment?

The answer lies in part in how the brain takes first-impression Polaroids—creating a composite of all the signals given off by a new experience. Psychologists agree that snap judgments are a holistic phenomenon in which clues (mellifluous voice, Rolex watch, soggy handshake, hunched shoulders) hit us all at once and form an impression larger than their sum.

We do search for one particular sign on a new face: a smile. "We can pick up a smile from 30 meters away," says Paul Ekman, professor of psychology at the University of California Medical School in San Francisco, and a pioneer of research on facial expressions. "A smile lets us know that we're likely to get a positive reception, and it's hard not to reciprocate."

By the time we flash that return grin, our Polaroid shutter will have already closed. Just three seconds are sufficient to make a conclusion about fresh acquaintances. Nalini Ambady, professor of psychology at Tufts University in Medford, Massachusetts, studies first impressions carved from brief exposure to another person's behavior, what she calls "thin slices" of experience. She says humans have developed the ability to quickly decide whether a new person will hurt or enrich us—judgments that had lifesaving ramifications in an earlier era.

She believes that thin slices are generated in the most primitive area of the brain, where feelings are also processed, which accounts for the emotional punch of some first encounters. Immediate distrust of a certain car salesman or affinity for a prospective roommate originates in the deepest corners of the mind.

The ability to interpret thin slices evolved as a way for our ancestors to protect themselves in an eat-or-be-eaten world, whereas modern-day threats to survival often come in the form of paperwork (dwindling stock portfolios) or intricate social rituals (impending divorce). The degree to which thin slices of experience help us navigate modern encounters—from hitchhikers to blind dates—is up for debate.

Ekman says that people excel at reading facial expressions quickly, but only when a countenance is genuine. Most people cannot tell if someone is feigning an emotion, he says, "unless their eyes have been trained to spot very subtle expressions that leak through." Consider anger: When we are boiling mad, our lips narrow—an expression we can't make on demand when we're pretending.

And the accuracy of a snap judgment always depends on what exactly we're sizing up. Ekman doesn't think we can use a thin slice of behavior to judge, say, if someone is smart enough to be our study partner or generous enough to lend us a bus token. "But we can pretty easily distinguish one emotion from another, particularly if it's on the face for a second or more." Spending more time with a genuine person, he says, won't yield a more accurate sense of that person's emotional state.

First impressions are not merely hardwired reactions—we are also taught how to judge others, holding our thin slices up to the light of social stereotypes. Brian Nosek, professor of psychology at the University of Virginia, studies the implicit attitudes that enter into our calculations. Just because someone carries an ACLU membership card or makes a point to invite their senior-citizen friends to dance-club outings doesn't mean they don't have prejudices bubbling under the surface. Nosek and colleagues administer a quick online test that reveals the beliefs people either can't or won't report.

Called the Implicit Association Test, it asks participants to pair concepts, such as "young" with "good," or "elderly" with "good." If, in some part of his mind, "old" is more closely related to "bad" than to "good," the test taker will respond more quickly to the first pairing of words than to the second. In versions of these tests, small differences in response times are used to determine if someone is biased toward youth over the elderly, African-Americans over Caucasians or for President Bush over President Kennedy. "When I took the test," says Nosek, "I showed a bias toward whites. I was shocked. We call it unconsciousness-raising, in contrast to the consciousness-raising of the 1960s."

As subtle as implicit attitudes are, they can cause serious real-world damage. If an angry person stumbles upon someone of a different race or religion, he is likely to perceive that person negatively, according to recent research. Anger incites instinctive prejudiced responses toward "outsiders," a finding that has important implications for people in law enforcement and security.

Street-Corner Psychologists: From Store Manager to Police Officer, Certain Professions Rely on Making the Right Snap Judgment

—Jeff Grossman, Neil Parmar, Jammie Salagubang, and Susan A. Smith

Jeff Ayers, novelty-store manager

To spot a thief, check for eye contact, says New York-based Ayers. Persistent looking around or eyes that dart from left to right should raise suspicion. Ayers also watches people with "forced body language." They pace purposefully up and down aisles. "Sometimes the best-dressed [are the culprits]; they're on a shopping spree with someone else's credit card. The ones I can't [pick out] are those I've been friendly with. One guy would jibber-jabber, then bend down to tie his shoes and stick $300 worth of stuff in his bag."

Gerald Scott, police officer

Scott has been a New York City police officer for 10 years. He says he can easily spot bad apples on the street because they "tend to stay in a certain space for long periods of time. They're not really doing anything, they're just watching everybody. They're never reading the paper or anything. They're worried about everything going on around them. Just look at their eyes. There's a lot of nervousness. You can tell they're trying to figure out if you're a cop or not."

Eric McMullen, cardsharp

In the gritty gambling locales of Harlem, McMullen is better known as "DOC," or the Dealer of Cards. "If I don't cheat, I don't eat," says the amateur magician turned master cardsharp. "Amateurs have shifty eyes. They look around the table and try to talk to everyone. Let's say the sharp wants to switch the whole deck. He'll get a little fidgety—that's a telltale sign for cheating." Subtlety is the secret behind flawless moves. "Always make gestures and jokes, look people in the eye and don't look at the deck."

John Breen, retired detective

"I'm not claiming to be Sherlock Holmes, but there are a number of behavioral interviewing techniques taught in the police academy that can help tell you when someone is lying," says Breen, a former police lieutenant in Arizona. "A suspect might put her hand up to her mouth or she may cross her arms over her chest. Whereas someone who is more receptive, open and forthcoming won't cross her arms. But you can't take that as gospel. You have to [measure up] the individual and determine what her normal reactions might be."

Sudha Chinniah, high-end salesperson

"You can never tell who's going to spend on clothing," says Chinniah, who works at the Bergdorf Goodman department store in New York. But "how you look is an extension of [how you feel]. The wealthiest guy may be dressed casually, but he carries himself with confidence. A customer's wallet, watch and shoes approximate her financial background. Right now there's a trend toward slim shoes with elongated toes, which defines a customer who's absolutely current."

David Boyle, county prosecutor

Every nuance counts for a trial lawyer, who must quickly convince a group of strangers that his version of the facts is the truth. "Everything you do is being judged—the way you dress, the way you talk," says Boyle, a prosecutor in Walton County, Georgia. If he wants jurors to listen to a friendly witness, Boyle positions himself at the far end of the jury box, forcing the witness to look straight at the jury and speak loud enough for everyone to hear. During harmful testimony, he'll study his files or consult with his partner to indicate complete disinterest.

Certain physical features consistently prompt our brains to take first-impression Polaroids with a distorting filter. People who have a "baby face," characterized by a round shape, large eyes and small nose and chin, give off the impression of trustworthiness and naiveté—on average, a false assumption. A pretty face also leads us astray: Our tendency is to perceive beautiful people as healthier and just plain better than others.

Leslie Zebrowitz, professor of psychology at Brandeis University in Massachusetts, argues that we overgeneralize in the presence of baby mugs and homely visages. Humans are hardwired to recognize a baby as an innocent, weak creature who requires protection. By the same token, mating with someone who is severely deformed, and thereby unattractive, may keep your DNA from spreading far and wide. But we overgeneralize these potentially helpful built-in responses, coddling adults with babyish miens who in fact don't need our care and shunning unattractive people who may not meet our standards of beauty but certainly don't pose an imminent threat to our gene pool.

Zebrowitz has found that many baby-faced grown-ups, particularly young men, overcompensate for misperceptions by cultivating tougher-than-average personalities in an attempt to ward off cheek-pinching aunts. Think of the sweet-faced rapper Eminem, who never cracks a smile, or the supermodel-juggling, hard-partying actor Leonardo DiCaprio.

Not every observer is equally likely to draw unwarranted conclusions about a smooth-cheeked man or a woman with stunning, symmetrical features. People who spend time cultivating relationships are more likely to make accurate snap judgments.

"A good judge of personality isn't just someone who is smarter—it's someone who gets out and spends time with people," says David Funder, a professor of psychology at the University of California at Riverside, who believes in the overall accuracy of snap judgments. Funder has found that two observers often reach a consensus about a third person, and the assessments are accurate in that they match the third person's assessment of himself. "We're often fooled, of course, but we're more often right."

On the other side of the equation, some people are simpler to capture at first glance than others. "The people who are easiest to judge are the most mentally healthy," says Randy Colvin, associate professor of psychology at Northeastern University in Boston. "With mentally healthy individuals," Colvin theorizes, "exterior behavior mimics their internal views of themselves. What you see is what you get."

LEARN MORE ABOUT IT

First Impressions Valerie White and Ann Demarais *(Bantam, 2004)*
Emotions Revealed: Recognizing Faces and Feelings to Improve Communication and Emotional Life Paul Ekman *(Times Books, 2003)*
How to Make People Like You in 90 Seconds or Less Nicholas Boothman *(Workman, 2000)*
Implicit Association Test (http://implicit.harvard.edu.implicit/)

How to Make a Great First Impression

Curb Conversational Narcissism

He's talking about his new Subaru, which reminds you of the battle you waged—and won—with that smarmy Hertz-rental-car dealer in Miami last month. This "faux segue" is a big no-no, says psychologist and business consultant Valerie White. "We are tempted to share impressive things about ourselves, but the one idea you should keep in mind is 'How am I making the other person feel?'" Actively encourage others to talk about themselves, and respond genuinely—without bringing it back to you.

Don't Betray Your Anxiety

"If you're not quick-witted or well-versed in certain subjects, you can still make a great impression," White says. Just focus on the other person. This in turn will take the pressure off you. However, avoid interrogating a new acquaintance. If you're jittery, control movements such as leg twitching. And remember to speak slowly—nervousness makes us talk too fast.

Fake a Sunny Mood

"Be yourself" is solid first-impression advice from cognitive scientists and self-help gurus alike. But it's worth suppressing a bad mood when you meet someone new. While you know you are just experiencing a momentary state, a new acquaintance will take you for a full-time complainer. "There is a contagion effect," says White. "A bad mood will bring the other person down, too. Try to start off well, and then share what's bothering you."

The Eyes Have It

If you want to get to know a stranger, break with body language conventions by catching her eye for more than a second. When you first meet someone, author and lecturer Nicholas Boothman says, focus on your eye contact, your smile and your posture. "If you notice somebody's eye color, and you say 'great' to yourself, you will actually be smiling, and you will give off a super mood."

Get in Sync

Adjusting your posture, voice, words and gestures to match those of a new acquaintance is critical, says Boothman, because we are attracted to others who are just like us. "People respond when you speak at their pace," agrees White. To establish an instant rapport, mirror your new friend's head nods and tilts.

Use Flattery, Sparingly

"People like to be flattered," says White. "Even if they suspect you are brownnosing, they still like it." But use flattery judiciously—focus on the other person's accomplishments or achievements. This works best when a person believes you don't say ingratiating things to just anyone.

The Do-Over

You arrive at a party fuming over a parking ticket. A cheery guest introduces herself, but you brush her off and head for the bar. You've made a bad impression, but you can recover if you demonstrate self-awareness, says White. Pull her aside and say, "I wasn't myself earlier." Show your sense of humor: "I see you met my evil twin." And remember to cut others slack if they make a bad impression on you.

CRITICAL THINKING QUESTIONS

1. In everyday situations, what can be done to help minimize the power of first impressions? Or is it even possible not to *form* first impressions? Defend your position with data regarding impression formation and impression management.

2. What advice have you received from others about how to make a good first impression? How consistent (or inconsistent) is that advice with the information contained in this article?

3. How might the findings in this article about the power of first impressions be applicable to jury trials? Dating situations? Job interviews? Is the process involved in forming a first impression fundamentally the same in all situations, or does it depend on the context in which the impression is being made? Defend your position.

4. Is it feasible to teach people to be more aware of the first impressions they make? Is it possible to teach people how to interpret such impressions more accurately? How might either or both of these goals be accomplished? Explain your answers.

5. "You cannot *not* communicate." Discuss what this statement means in terms of impression formation.

ARTICLE 5 _____

A variety of sources of information may be available for use in forming an impression of a person. However, that does not mean that all of the information will be used or hold equal value. Some sources of information may carry more weight than others. For example, we may notice how the person acts, or we may have heard something about him or her from someone else. How do we use this information to develop an impression of the person?

Building on the classic work of S. E. Asch, Harold H. Kelley examines what can be called a *central organizing trait,* one that is important in influencing the impressions that we form. By examining the effect of changing just one adjective in describing a person (i.e., *warm* versus *cold*), the study demonstrates that this initial difference influenced how the subjects actually rated the person. Even more interesting is that these differences in initial impression carried over into how the subjects interacted with the person. The implication is that perhaps our initial impressions lead us to act in certain ways toward others, perhaps creating a self-fulfilling prophecy by giving us what we expected to see in the first place.

The Warm-Cold Variable in First Impressions of Persons
■ Harold H. Kelley

This experiment is one of several studies of first impressions (3), the purpose of the series being to investigate the stability of early judgments, their determinants, and the relation of such judgments to the behavior of the person making them. In interpreting the data from several nonexperimental studies on the stability of first impressions, it proved to be necessary to postulate inner-observer variables which contribute to the impression and which remain relatively constant through time. Also some evidence was obtained which directly demonstrated the existence of these variables and their nature. The present experiment was designed to determine the effects of one kind of inner-observer variable, specifically, *expectations* about the stimulus person which the observer brings to the exposure situation. That prior information or labels attached to a stimulus person make a difference in observers' first impressions is almost too obvious to require demonstration. The expectations resulting from such preinformation may restrict, modify, or accentuate the impressions he will have. The crucial question is: What changes in perception will accompany a given expectation? Studies of stereotyping, for example, that of Katz and Braly (2), indicate that from an ethnic label such as "German" or "Negro," a number of perceptions follow which are culturally determined. The present study finds its main significance in relation to a study by Asch (1) which demonstrates that certain crucial labels can transform the entire impression of the person, leading to attributions which are related to the label on a broad cultural basis or even, perhaps, on an autochthonous basis.

Asch read to his subjects a list of adjectives which purportedly described a particular person. He then asked them to characterize that person. He found that the inclusion in the list of what he called *central* qualities, such as "warm" as opposed to "cold," produced a widespread change in the entire impression. This effect was not adequately explained by the halo effect since it did not extend indiscriminately in a positive or negative direction to all characteristics. Rather, it differentially transformed the other qualities, for example, by changing their relative importance in the total impression. Peripheral qualities (such as "polite" versus "blunt") did not produce effects as strong as those produced by the central qualities.[1]

The present study tested the effects of such central qualities upon the early impressions of *real* persons, the same qualities, "warm" vs. "cold," being used. They were introduced as preinformation about the stimulus person before his actual appearance; so presumably they operated as expectations rather than as part of the stimulus pattern during the exposure period. In addition, information was obtained about the effects of the expectations upon the observers' behavior toward the stimulus person. An earlier study in this series has indicated that the more incompatible the observer initially perceived the stimulus person to be, the less the observer initiated interaction with him thereafter. The second purpose of the present experiment, then, was to provide a better controlled study of this relationship.

No previous studies reported in the literature have dealt with the importance of first impressions for behavior. The most

From "The warm-cold variable in first impressions of persons," Kelly H. H., *Journal of Personality, 18*(4), 431–439. Blackwell Publishers. Used with permission.

relevant data are found in the sociometric literature, where there are scattered studies of the relation between choices among children having some prior acquaintance and their interaction behavior. For an example, see the study by Newstetter, Feldstein, and Newcomb (8).

PROCEDURE

The experiment was performed in three sections of a psychology course (Economics 70) at the Massachusetts Institute of Technology.[2] The three sections provided 23, 16, and 16 subjects respectively. All 55 subjects were men, most of them in their third college year. In each class the stimulus person (also a male) was completely unknown to the subjects before the experimental period. One person served as stimulus person in two sections, and a second person took this role in the third section. In each case the stimulus person was introduced by the experimenter, who posed as a representative of the course instructors and who gave the following statement:

> *Your regular instructor is out of town today, and since we of Economics 70 are interested in the general problem of how various classes react to different instructors, we're going to have an instructor today you've never had before, Mr. _____. Then, at the end of the period, I want you to fill out some forms about him. In order to give you some idea of what he's like, we've had a person who knows him write up a little biographical note about him. I'll pass this out to you now and you can read it before be arrives. Please read these to yourselves and don't talk about this among yourselves until the class is over so that he won't get wind of what's going on.*

Two kinds of these notes were distributed, the two being identical except that in one the stimulus person was described among other things as being "rather cold" whereas in the other form the phrase "very warm" was substituted. The content of the "rather cold" version is as follows:

> *Mr. _____ is a graduate student in the Department of Economics and Social Science here at M.I.T. He has had three semesters of teaching experience in psychology at another college. This is his first semester teaching Ec. 70. He is 26 years old, a veteran, and married. People who know him consider him to be a rather cold person, industrious, critical, practical, and determined.*

The two types of preinformation were distributed randomly within each of the three classes and in such a manner that the students were not aware that two kinds of information were being given out. The stimulus person then appeared and led the class in a twenty-minute discussion. During this time the experimenter kept a record of how often each student participated in the discussion. Since the discussion was almost totally leader-centered, this participation record indicates the number of times each student initiated verbal interaction with the instructor. After the discussion period, the stimulus person left the room, and the experimenter gave the following instructions:

> *Now, I'd like to get your impression of Mr. _____. This is not a test of you and can in no way affect your grade in this course. This material will not be identified as belonging to particular persons and will be kept strictly confidential. It will be of most value to us if you are completely honest in your evaluation of Mr. _____. Also, please understand that what you put down will not be used against him or cause him to lose his job or anything like that. This is not a test of him but merely a study of how different classes react to different instructors.*

The subjects then wrote free descriptions of the stimulus person and finally rated him on a set of 15 rating scales.

RESULTS AND DISCUSSION

1. *Influence of warm-cold variable on first impressions.* The differences in the ratings produced by the warm-cold variable were consistent from one section to another even where different stimulus persons were used. Consequently, the data from the three sections were combined by equating means (the S.D.'s were approximately equal) and the results for the total group are presented in Table 1. Also in this table is presented that part of Asch's data which refers to the qualities included in our rating scales. From this table it is quite clear that those given the "warm" preinformation consistently rated the stimulus person more favorably than those given the "cold" preinformation. Summarizing the statistically significant differences, the "warm" subjects rated the stimulus person as more considerate of others, more informal, more sociable, more popular, better natured, more humorous, and more humane. These findings are very similar to Asch's for the characteristics common to both studies. He found more frequent attribution to his hypothetical "warm" personalities of sociability, popularity, good naturedness, generosity, humorousness, and humaneness. So these data strongly support his finding that such a central quality as "warmth" can greatly influence the total impression of a personality. This effect is found to be operative in the perception of real persons.

This general favorableness in the perceptions of the "warm" observers as compared with the "cold" ones indicates that something like a halo effect may have been operating in these ratings. Although his data are not completely persuasive on this point, Asch was convinced that such a general effect was *not* operating in his study. Closer inspection of the present data makes it clear that the "warm-cold" effect cannot be explained altogether on the basis of simple halo effect. In Table 1 it is evident that the "warm-cold" variable produced differential effects from one rating scale to another. The size of this effect seems to depend upon the closeness of relation between the

TABLE 1 / Comparison of "Warm" and "Cold" Observers in Terms of Average Ratings Given Stimulus Persons

Item	Low End of Rating Scale	High End of Rating Scale	Average Rating		Level of Significance of Warm-Cold Difference	Asch's Data: Percent of Group Assigning Quality at Low End of Our Rating Scale*	
			Warm N = 7	Cold N = 28		Warm	Cold
1	Knows his stuff	Doesn't know his stuff	3.5	4.6			
2	Considerate of others	Self-centered	6.3	9.6	1%		
3†	Informal	Formal	6.3	9.6	1%		
4†	Modest	Proud	9.4	10.6			
5	Sociable	Unsociable	5.6	10.4	1%	91%	38%
6	Self-assured	Uncertain of himself	8.4	9.1			
7	High intelligence	Low intelligence	4.8	5.1			
8	Popular	Unpopular	4.0	7.4	1%	84%	28%
9†	Good natured	Irritable	9.4	12.0	5%	94%	17%
10	Generous	Ungenerous	8.2	9.6		91%	08%
11	Humorous	Humorless	8.3	11.7	1%	77%	13%
12	Important	Insignificant	6.5	8.6		88%	99%
13†	Humane	Ruthless	8.6	11.0	5%	86%	31%
14†	Submissive	Dominant	13.2	14.5			
15	Will go far	Will not get ahead	4.2	5.8			

*Given for all qualities common to Asch's list and this set of rating scales.

†These scales were reversed when presented to the subjects.

specific dimension of any given rating scale and the central quality of "warmth" or "coldness." Even though the rating of intelligence may be influenced by a halo effect, it is not influenced to the same degree to which considerateness is. It seems to make sense to view such strongly influenced items as considerateness, informality, good naturedness, and humaneness as dynamically more closely related to warmth and hence more perceived in terms of this relation than in terms of a general positive or negative feeling toward the stimulus person. If first impressions are normally made in terms of such general dimensions as "warmth" and "coldness," the power they give the observer in making predictions and specific evaluations about such disparate behavior characteristics as formality and considerateness is considerable (even though these predictions may be incorrect or misleading).

The free report impression data were analyzed for only one of the sections. In general, there were few sizable differences between the "warm" and "cold" observers. The "warm" observers attributed more nervousness, more sincerity, and more industriousness to the stimulus person. Although the frequencies of comparable qualities are very low because of the great variety of descriptions produced by the observers, there is considerable agreement with the rating scale data.

Two important phenomena are illustrated in these free description protocols, the first of them having been noted by Asch. *Firstly,* the characteristics of the stimulus person are interpreted in terms of the precognition of warmth or coldness. For example, a "warm" observer writes about a rather shy and retiring stimulus person as follows: "He makes friends slowly but they are lasting friendships when formed." In another instance, several "cold" observers described him as being, " . . . intolerant: would be angry if you disagree with his view . . . "; while several "warm" observers put the same thing this way: "Unyielding in principle, not easily influenced or swayed from his original attitude." *Secondly,* the preinformation about the stimulus person's warmth or coldness is evaluated and interpreted in the light of the direct behavioral data about him. For example, "He has a slight inferiority complex which leads to his coldness," and "His conscientiousness and industriousness might be mistaken for coldness." Examples of these two phenomena occurred rather infrequently, and there was no way to evaluate the relative strengths of these countertendencies. Certainly some such evaluation is necessary to determine the conditions under which behavior which is contrary to a stereotyped label resists distortion and leads to rejection of the label.

A comparison of the data from the two different stimulus persons is pertinent to the last point in so far as it indicates the interaction between the properties of the stimulus person and the label. The fact that the warm-cold variable generally produced differences in the same direction for the two stimulus persons, even though they are very different in personality, behavior, and mannerisms, indicates the strength of this variable. However, there were some exceptions to this tendency as well as marked differences in the *degree* to which the experimental variable was able to produce differences. For example, stimulus person A typically appears to be anything but lacking in self-esteem and on rating scale 4 he was generally at the "proud" end of the scale. Although the "warm" observers tended to rate him as they did the other stimulus person (i.e., more "modest"), the difference between the "warm" and "cold" means for stimulus person A is very small and not significant as it is for stimulus person B. Similarly, stimulus person B was seen as "unpopular" and "humorless," which agrees with his typical classroom behavior. Again the "warm" observers rated him more favorably on these items, but their ratings were not significantly different from those of the "cold" observers, as was true for the other stimulus person. Thus we see that the strength or compellingness of various qualities of the stimulus person must be reckoned with. The stimulus is not passive to the forces arising from the label but actively resists distortion and may severely limit the degree of influence exerted by the preinformation.[3]

2. *Influence of warm-cold variable on interaction with the stimulus person.* In the analysis of the frequency with which the various students took part in the discussion led by the stimulus person, a larger proportion of those given the "warm" preinformation participated than of those given the "cold" preinformation. Fifty-six per cent of the "warm" subjects entered the discussion, whereas only 32 per cent of the "cold" subjects did so. Thus the expectation of warmth not only produced more favorable early perceptions of the stimulus person but led to greater initiation of interaction with him. This relation is a low one, significant at between the 5 per cent and 10 percent level of confidence, but it is in line with the general principle that social perception serves to guide and steer the person's behavior in his social environment.

As would be expected from the foregoing findings, there was also a relation between the favorableness of the impression and whether or not the person participated in the discussion. Although any single item yielded only a small and insignificant relation to participation, when a number are combined the trend becomes clear cut. For example, when we combine the seven items which were influenced to a statistically significant degree by the warm-cold variable, the total score bears considerable relation to participation, the relationship being significant as well beyond the 1 per cent level. A larger proportion of those having favorable total impressions participated than of those having unfavorable impressions, the bi-serial correlation between these variables being .34. Although this relation may be interpreted in several ways, it seems most likely that the unfavorable perception led to a curtailment of interaction. Support for this comes from one of the other studies in this series (3). There it was found that those persons having unfavorable impressions of the instructor at the end of the first class meeting tended less often to initiate interactions with him in the succeeding four meetings than did those having favorable first impressions. There was also some tendency in the same study for those persons who interacted least with the instructor to change least in their judgments of him from the first to later impressions.

It will be noted that these relations lend some support to the autistic hostility hypothesis proposed by Newcomb (7). This hypothesis suggests that the possession of an initially hostile attitude toward a person leads to a restriction of communication and contact with him which in turn serves to preserve the hostile attitude by preventing the acquisition of data which could correct it. The present data indicate that a restriction of interaction is associated with unfavorable preinformation and an unfavorable perception. The data from the other study support this result and also indicate the correctness of the second part of the hypothesis, that restricted interaction reduces the likelihood of change in the attitude.

What makes these findings more significant is that they appear in the context of a discussion class where there are numerous *induced* and *own* forces to enter the discussion and to interact with the instructor. It seems likely that the effects predicted by Newcomb's hypothesis would be much more marked in a setting where such forces were not present.

SUMMARY

The warm-cold variable had been found by Asch to produce large differences in the impressions of personality formed from a list of adjectives. In this study the same variable was introduced in the form of expectations about a real person and was found to produce similar differences in first impressions of him in a classroom setting. In addition, the differences in first impressions produced by the different expectations were shown to influence the observers' behavior toward the stimulus person. Those observers given the favorable expectation (who, consequently, had a favorable impression of the stimulus person) tended to interact more with him than did those given the unfavorable expectation.

REFERENCES

Asch, S. E. Forming impressions of personality. *J. Abnorm. Soc. Psychol.,* 1946, 41, 258–290.

Katz, D., and Braly, K. W. Verbal stereotypes and racial prejudice. In New-comb, T. M. and Hartley, E. L. (eds.), *Readings in social psychology.* New York: Holt, 1947. Pp. 204–210.

Kelley, H. H. First impressions in interpersonal relations. Ph.D. thesis, Massachusetts Institute of Technology, Cambridge, Mass. Sept., 1948.

Krech, D., and Crutchfield, R. S. *Theory and problems of social psychology.* New York: McGraw-Hill, 1948.

Luchins, A. S. Forming impressions of personality: A critique. *J. Abnorm. Soc. Psychol.,* 1948, 43, 318–325.

Mensch, I. N., and Wishner, J. Asch on "Forming impressions of personality": further evidence. *J. Personal.,* 1947, 16, 188–191.

Newcomb, T. M. Autistic hostility and social reality. *Hum. Relations.,* 1947, 1, 69–86.

Newstetter, W. I., Feldstein, M. H., and Newcomb, T. M. *Group adjustment: A study in experimental sociology.* Cleveland: Western Reserve University, 1938.

ENDNOTES

1. Since the present experiment was carried out, Mensch and Wishner (6) have repeated a number of Asch's experiments because of dissatisfaction with his sex and geographic distribution. Their data substantiate Asch's very closely. Also, Luchins (5) has criticized Asch's experiments for their artificial methodology, repeated some of them, and challenged some of the kinds of interpretations Asch made from his data. Luchins also briefly reports some tantalizing conclusions from a number of studies of first impressions of actual persons.

2. Professor Mason Haire, now of the University of California, provided valuable advice and help in executing the experiment.

3. We must raise an important question here: Would there be a tendency for "warm" observers to distort the perception in the favorable direction regardless of how much the stimulus deviated from the expectation? Future research should test the following hypothesis, which is suggested by Gestalt perception theory (4, pp. 95–98): If the stimulus differs but slightly from the expectation, the perception will tend to be *assimilated* to the expectation; however, if the difference between the stimulus and expectation is too great, the perception will occur by contrast to the expectation and will be distorted in the opposite direction.

CRITICAL THINKING QUESTIONS

1. Reread the information that was presented to the subjects to manipulate the warm-cold variable. The manipulation obviously produced a significant effect on the subjects' subsequent evaluations of the teacher. Do you feel that the manipulation was realistic? For example, how realistic is it to have a guest teacher described as "rather cold" in a brief biographical sketch? Could this particular manipulation have resulted in any experimental demand characteristics? Address the issue of the relative importance of experimental versus mundane realism as it pertains to this study.

2. How long lasting do you think first impressions are? For example, would they persist over the course of a semester or even longer? How could you test this?

3. What are the practical implications of this study? If you were working in a setting where you were interviewing and hiring applicants for a job, how could you use this information to help you make better, more accurate decisions?

4. The warm-cold information was provided by the instructor of the course, a person who presumably had high credibility. Do you think the credibility of the source of the information would affect how influenced the individuals were? How could you test this?

ADDITIONAL RELATED READINGS

Kervyn, N., Dolderer, M., Mahieu, T., & Yzerbyt, V. Y. (2010). Atypicality and the two fundamental dimensions: Applying the negativity effect on warmth to group perception. *European Journal of Social Psychology, 40*(3), 484–489.

Olivola, C. Y. & Todorov, A. (2010). Fooled by first impressions? Reexamining the diagnostic value of appearance-based inferences. *Journal of Experimental Social Psychology, 46*(2), 315–324.

ARTICLE 6 _____

As discussed in Article 4 on first impressions, we use a variety of information in forming judgments of other people. Yet this process also seems to occur quite quickly. In fact, as that article points out, we often draw conclusions about people we meet in as little as three seconds!

Some of the information that we use in forming initial impressions of people is based on stereotypes of what they look like or whom they remind us of, but even more information is obtained from watching their nonverbal cues. Why is this the case? Simply put, many of the things that people do are under their direct control. For example, the words that we choose to speak are subject to our conscious influence and hence can be readily manipulated. But our nonverbal behavior, such as the body movements that accompany our words, are somewhat less under conscious control. Furthermore, while we are better able to select the words we speak, we may be less aware of—and thus able to control—changes in our speech patterns (known as *paralanguage*), such as pausing, pitch of voice, and rate of speech. An observer may give the nonverbal and paralanguage cues more weight than what we actually say because those cues may seem a more honest reflection of what we are really all about.

One obvious practical application of the use of nonverbal and paralanguage cues is to detect deception. Being able to tell when someone is lying to us has real advantages. Research suggests that lying is a fairly common part of human interaction. Occasionally, these falsehoods take the form of bold-faced lies, such as making up a story to get out of trouble for something we have done. More commonly, however, we use so-called white lies to skirt the truth and perhaps not hurt someone's feelings ("Yes, dear, I really loved the vacuum cleaner you gave me for Christmas").

But how accurate are most of us in detecting such deceptions? Furthermore, are trained professionals, such as police and customs agents, better at detecting deception than the average person? A good deal of research suggests that most people, including law-enforcment professionals, are not particularly accurate in determining when someone is lying.

What may account for this? One possibility is that people, including law-enforcement personnel, may be looking at the wrong things when they are trying to determine if someone is lying. For instance, perhaps they are looking at the stereotypes that they have for how people behave when they are lying, and in fact these stereotypes may be inaccurate. The following article by Christian L. Hart, Derek G. Fillmore, and James D. Griffith looks at the possibility that lie detection may be more accurate when people are asked to simply look at how a person's behavior, mannerisms, or speech *changed* (what the authors call *indirect deception*) rather than being asked to determine whether or not the person was lying.

Indirect Detection of Deception: Looking for Change

■ Christian L. Hart, Derek G. Fillmore, and James D. Griffith

ABSTRACT

In this study, we examined the effectiveness of using indirect methods to detect liars. College students viewed a video in which half of the people told some lies and half of the people were entirely truthful. Participants were either asked to detect the liars in the video or they were asked to identify people in the video whose behavior, mannerisms, or speech changed. Participants using the indirect lie detection method of looking for behavioral change were more accurate in their categorizations of liars and non-liars than were participants who were directly and explicitly looking for liars.

INTRODUCTION

In his analysis of the historical definitions of lying in the scientific literature, Vrij (2000) used the terms lie and deception interchangeably and defined them as "a successful or unsuccessful deliberate attempt, without forewarning, to create in another

From "Indirect detection of deception: Looking for change," Hart, C. L.; Fillmore, D. G.; & Griffith, J. D., *Current Research in Social Psychology*, *14*(9), 134–142. Reprinted with permission of Christian L. Hart, Ph.D.

a belief which the communicator believes to be untrue." Telling lies and other forms of deception is a consistent feature of human social behavior. Research on the self-reported frequency of lying indicates that in the course of their normal daily activities people lie in about 25% of their interactions with others (DePaulo & Bell, 1996; DePaulo & Kashy, 1998; Kashy & DePaulo, 1996). While it is obviously advantageous to detect lies, most of the empirical research on the detection of deception indicates that people lack any special skills or abilities to detect when others are lying (see Vrij, 2004 for a review). In fact, it seems that humans perform only slightly better than chance when attempting to detect who is lying and who is telling the truth. In a recent meta-analysis, Bond and DePaulo (2006) examined the accuracy rates of lie detectors in 206 studies. They found that, on average, people were accurate in only 54% of their lie-truth judgments, whereas one would expect 50% accuracy by chance alone. Understanding the subtle indications of lying would certainly benefit anyone wishing to detect lying and deception in others.

Despite the rather unimpressive success most people have at lie detection, scientific investigations have uncovered a few noteworthy approaches to detecting deception. There is a rather long history of using physiological measures such as the polygraph to detect evidence of deception (Larson, 1927; Marston, 1917). More recently, researchers have attempted to use measures of brain activity to identify liars (see Langleben, 2008 for a review). It should be noted that physiological measures are only indirect measures of lying and therefore questions about the validity of using them to detect deception remain (Honts, 1994; National Research Council, 2002; Spence, 2008).

Researchers have examined verbal communication cues of deception. Speech cues such as pauses, voice pitch, interruptions, hesitations, latency to respond, and response length have been used to detect deception (Vrij, 1995; Vrij, Edward, & Bull, 2001; Vrij, Edward, Roberts, & Bull, 2000). The contents of speech such as descriptions of feelings, reproductions of speech, amount of detail, logical inconsistencies, and spontaneous corrections have also been found to vary with the veracity of statements (DePaulo, Lindsay, Malone, Muhlenbruck, Charlton, and Cooper, 2003; Vrij, Edward, Roberts, & Bull, 2000). The validity concerns previously noted with physiological measures also exist with the measures of speech cues. While certain variables of speech may change when one lies, those changes can and do occur for other reasons not tied to deception.

Historically, humans have looked to non-verbal behavior for indications of another's honesty or mendacity. Three major themes currently exist to explain the presence of non-verbal indicators of deception, each with its own unique contribution (Vrij, 2000). First, the emotional arousal hypothesis suggests that deception produces various emotional states which may influence non-verbal signals. For example, liars may experience fear, which may contribute to nervous movements or fidgeting. Second, the cognitive hypothesis focuses on the mental work load of deception and proposes that lying requires more cognitive effort which detracts from the liar's ability to behave normally. Thirdly, the behavioral control hypothesis suggests that liars may attempt to counteract any potential signs of their deception, but in the process come off as unnatural. Thus, if a liar is trying to manage several possible verbal and non-verbal cues to their deception simultaneously, their behavior may actually appear less natural and spontaneous due to their own heightened behavioral awareness and control.

Although stereotypes about the non-verbal behavior of liars are numerous, researchers have failed to identify many reliable cues (DePaulo, Lindsay, Malone, Muhlenbruck, Charlton, & Cooper, 2003; Vrij, 2004). Some researchers have reported changes in posture, eye contact, and eye blinks when people lie, yet others have failed to find these changes. Behavioral cues such as hand, arm, foot, and leg movements have been consistently linked to deception, but as with the physiological and verbal cues, these non-verbal behavioral cues are not entirely reliable and valid indicators of lying.

Although researchers have identified potentially useful cues to indicate deception, many people erroneously rely on an entirely different set of cues to identify liars. For instance, researchers have found that many people believe that liars make less eye contact, increase their fidgeting, and shift their posture (Akehurst, Kohnken, Vrij, and Bull, 1996; Hart, Hudson, Fillmore, & Griffith, 2006). Furthermore, research also suggests that many of these inaccurate perceptions are held by both lay persons and more highly trained lie detectors, such as law enforcement officers (Vrij & Semin, 1996; Akehurst, et al., 1996). The confidence that people have in their ability to detect deception, has been examined in a number of studies and further supports the notion that people are poor lie detectors. In a meta-analysis of this literature, DePaulo, Charlton, Cooper, Lindsay, and Muhlenbruck (1997) examined the relationship between confidence and accuracy and found that the overall correlation between confidence and accuracy of detection was very small, suggesting that confidence is largely independent of accuracy. Clearly, people hold incorrect beliefs about the behavior of liars yet confidently make social judgments based on these beliefs.

The source of the many misconceptions people have about liars' behaviors is unclear. Stromwall, Granhag, and Hartwig (2004) suggested that for laypersons, the likely factors resulting in these wrongful beliefs include several psychological factors. First, the representativeness heuristic, or our tendency to assume that a sample or incident is an exemplar of the overall population, could lead people to generalize from a small set of experiences in which liars are exposed. Second, confirmation bias, the tendency to look for confirming instead of disconfirming evidence, could explain how certain misconceptions are propagated by people not looking for evidence that their beliefs are wrong. Thirdly, it is also possible that feedback plays a crucial role in our many misconceptions. For feedback to be corrective of misconceptions, it should take place often, be consistent, and happen promptly (Allwood & Granhag, 1999; Ekman, 2001). By contrast, many judgments about deception never receive any feedback whatsoever. Lastly, in the past, professionals responsible for detecting deception have been trained with incorrect and inaccurate procedures that continue to circulate within the unique cultures of these professions (Stromwall, Granhag, and Hartwig, 2004). For example, police interrogation manuals have historically included unsubstantiated claims which, nonetheless, are passed on from one generation of law enforcement to the next. Ultimately, these and other factors may explain the pervasiveness or firmness of peoples' many false beliefs about deception.

Because people may be searching for invalid behavioral or verbal cues when attempting to determine if someone is lying, it is perhaps not surprising that direct attempts to detect deception lead to such low accuracy rates. One novel approach to detecting deception is to avoid the biases held by most people by having them engage in indirect lie detection tasks. Indirect approaches to lie detection involve having people search for particular verbal and non-verbal behavioral patterns, rather than explicitly directing them to look for evidence that another person is lying. This indirect method has been referred to as indirect or implicit lie detection and the body of research supporting it is growing and diverse (see Granhag, 2006 for a review).

A number of researchers have, in the context of their research, identified clear evidence that people are, at times, more accurate when using indirect rather than direct methods of detecting deception. For instance, researchers found that the indirect technique of having participants identify speakers who looked like they were "thinking hard" yielded more accurate lie/truth categorizations than explicit attempts at lie detection (Vrij, Edwards, and Bull, 2001). In another study, Anderson, DéPaulo, and Ansfield (2002) found that when simply asked to indicate whether speakers appeared to feel comfortable or not, participants were more accurate at categorizing liars and truth tellers than other participants who were explicitly attempting to distinguish liars from truth tellers.

Others have investigated indirect detection methods that relied on implicit cognitive processes. Hurd and Noller (1988) asked participants to explicitly identify whether a statement was a lie or the truth, but participants thought aloud during the decision making process. Interestingly, when deliberating about a statement that was a lie, subjects were more likely to speculate that the scenario indeed might be deceptive, despite what their final explicit decision may have been. Still other

interesting research by Anderson (1999) investigated direct and indirect detection in heterosexual romantic partnerships. Of note, compared to strangers, romantic partners performed more poorly using direct detection, but were better than strangers when using indirect methods. These studies seem to provide evidence that indirect approaches to lie-detection help participants bypass the many biases and stereotypes that have historically led to such abysmal accuracy rates in lie detection studies.

A review of the lie detection literature reveals that the behavior of liars does not change in some predictable and customary manner (see Vrij, 2000 for a review); however, it is conceivable that the behavior of each individual liar does vary in some unique and minor ways when he or she lies. Given this possibility, it may be that looking for a typical set of cues to lying in people will not be as productive as simply looking for changes in individual behavioral patterns. When asked how they spot liars, people often describe seeking out behavioral evidence based on inaccurate and stereotyped ideas about the behavior of liars (Akehurst, Köhnken, Vrij, & Bull, 1996; Hart, Hudson, Fillmore & Griffith, 2006). These stereotypes likely draw attention away from valid and individualized indications of a person's deception.

The aim of the present study was to further investigate the effectiveness of indirect compared to direct methods of detecting deception. Specifically, this study evaluated the relative effectiveness of a novel indirect method of lie detection involving the detection of change in behavioral patterns. As mentioned previously, there are theoretical themes underlying the behavioral variation thought to correspond with lying. Specifically, it is thought that liars may experience emotional arousal and increased cognitive work load and may attempt to control their behavior. If this is accurate, then one might assume that behavior would change when a person lies. However, the precise nature of the behavioral change is not specified by these theoretical approaches. Thus, simply looking for changes in behavior might be more productive as a lie detection strategy than looking for any specific set of behaviors thought to be associated with lying. The hypothesis was that indirect lie detection methods would result in greater accuracy than direct attempts to detect deception.

METHOD

Participants

Participants were 104 (53 males, 51 females) undergraduate students at a small coeducational university in the southern United States. We recruited participants from psychology classes. All participants were given extra credit in their courses in exchange for their participation.

Stimulus Materials

The stimulus for this investigation was a video consisting of brief interviews of twenty (10 male and 10 female) people. The video was recorded prior to the study using male and female volunteers ranging in age from 19 to 61. Before being interviewed, each volunteer completed a fifteen question autobiographical survey. The volunteers sat for the interview, and their entire head to toe image was captured on the recording. While the voices of both the interviewer and volunteers were recorded, the interviewer was located off screen. In the videotaped interview, each of the interviewees answered the same four biographical questions: 1) *Can you tell me about any pets you have?* 2) *Tell me about where you grew up.* 3) *Would you tell me a little about where you work?* 4) *Let's talk about your family. Do you have any brothers or sisters?* None of the interviewees were aware of the specific interview questions prior to appearing on the video. Immediately before the interview began, half of the interviewees were instructed to lie in response to any questions about their family (the fourth interview question), and the other half were asked to answer honestly. While there was no way of ascertaining whether the interviewees' responses were actually truthful or lies, the researchers did address this issue. After the interview concluded, the researchers examined the biographical information provided in the interviewees' surveys in order to verify that the information provided in the supposed truthful interviewee statements corresponded with the information provided in their survey responses. The researchers also verified that the supposed deceptive responses did not correspond with information provided on the surveys. The presentation order of the ten liars and ten non-liars in the video was randomized. The same video recording was presented to all participants.

Procedure

The researchers collected data from groups of ten to twenty participants at a time. Each group was assigned to one of the experimental conditions (direct lie detection vs. indirect lie detection). Each group of participants was given one of two sets of instructions prior to viewing the videos. The direct lie detection instruction asked participants to determine whether each individual in the video was lying or telling the truth when answering the fourth interview question. The indirect lie detection instruction asked participants to determine whether each individual in the video exhibited a "change in behavior, body language, or speech changes" when answering the fourth question. These two sets of instructions comprised the two levels of the independent variable. To avoid contamination, all students in a group were given the same set of instructions.

Participants viewed the 20 video clips of people answering interview questions. After viewing each interviewee, the video was briefly paused and participants were asked to make their determinations about the interviewee's response to the fourth question (lie vs. truth, or change vs. no change). Participants indicated their responses on a form. Furthermore, each participant provided a rating of their confidence for each of their judgments on a seven point Likert type rating scale where 1 indicated very low confidence and 7 indicated very high confidence. After participants finished viewing the video and completing their ratings of each clip, they were debriefed by the researcher.

RESULTS

A t-test was used to determine if the two groups differed significantly in their ability to accurately distinguish between liars and non-liars in the video. We found that participants in the indirect detection group were significantly more accurate in classifying liars ($M = 55.2\%$, $SD = 20.2$) than those in the direct detection group ($M = 49.4\%$, $SD = 14.2$) were ($t(1,102) = 1.688$, $p < .05$). An accuracy rate of 50% would have been expected by chance alone. A one sample t-test revealed that those in the indirect detection category performed significantly better than chance levels ($t(1,51) = 1.859$, $p < .05$), while those in the direct detection group did not ($t(1,51) = 0.293$, $p = .39$). Furthermore, the results of a t-test showed that those in the indirect detection group had more confidence in their decisions ($M = 5.23$, $SD = .73$) than those in the direct detection group ($M = 4.90$, $SD = .77$) when judging liars ($t(1,102) = 2.194$, $p < .05$).

A similar set of analyses was used to determine whether or not the two groups differed in their ability to classify truthful responses. While there were small differences in accuracy between the indirect detection group ($M = 57.5\%$, $SD = 20.2$) and the direct detection group ($M = 59.8\%$, $SD = 17.2$), these differences were not statistically significant ($t(1,102) = .627$, $p = .27$). However, both the indirect and direct groups performed significantly better than chance levels ($t(1,51) = 2.680$, $p < .005$ and $t(1,51) = 4.110$, $p < .001$). There was no significant difference in the confidence expressed by the indirect detection group ($M = 5.12$, $SD = .87$) and the direct detection group ($M = 4.94$, $SD = .95$) ($t(1,102) = .995$, $p = .16$).

DISCUSSION

The results of this study are consistent with previous studies indicating that those trying to directly or explicitly detect liars typically perform at near chance levels (Bond & DePaulo, 2006). In this study, the attempted direct detection of lying resulted in very poor accuracy. However, we did find that the use of an indirect method resulted in more accurate categorization of liars and truth-tellers. The indirect detection method that was utilized in this study involved having participants simply look for changes in behavior. Previous researchers have failed to identify a consistent pattern of behaviors associated with lying (Vrij,

2000). While it may be the case that liars do not universally exhibit or inhibit any specific behavior or set of behaviors, it is conceivable that the behavior of most liars does change when they lie. It might be that, when lying, each liar's behavior changes in some subtle and rather unique ways. Therefore, searching for some elusive, universal set of cues to deception may not be as fruitful as identifying the changes that particular individuals evince when deceiving as compared to their baseline behaviors exhibited when not lying.

In this study, the participants indirectly detected liars by looking for changes in behavior without knowing that lying was a central aspect of the study. When primed to search for liars, many people report engaging in search and detection strategies based on stereotyped or faulty schemas of lying behaviors (Akehurst, Köhnken, Vrij, & Bull, 1996; Hart, Hudson, Fillmore & Griffith, 2006). Thus, relying on stereotypes about liars engaging in less eye contact and more fidgeting may pull attention away from accurate, subtle, and varied behavioral indications of lying. It may be that ignorance about the aim of this study prevented our subjects from focusing on the irrelevant and stereotypical behavioral cues that seem to sidetrack many people engaged in lie detection.

One of the significant limitations of this study is that it utilized a very low-stakes deception scenario. The individuals in the video were asked to lie about biographical information, but there were no serious consequences associated with failure to produce a believable lie. In many real-world contexts, the consequences associated with failed lies can be quite severe, thus anxiety and fear may lead to more exaggerated behavioral and verbal changes in those contexts. Also, the external validity of this study is limited by the fact that participants evaluated people in a video rather than in a face-to-face format. It seems likely that the social dynamics of interacting with a live person differ considerably from those associated with viewing people in a video. Finally, participants only viewed the truthful baseline behavior of people for several seconds before deceptive behavior was presented. It might be that longer exposure to the baseline behavior would have increased the participants' abilities to spot changes in behaviors among liars.

The present study adds to a growing body of evidence that indirect lie detection strategies may offer some advantages in accuracy over more direct behavioral detection of deception (Anderson, 1999; Anderson, DePaulo, & Ansfield, 2002; Granhag, 2006; Hurd & Noller, 1988; Vrij, Edwards, & Bull, 2001). This growing body of evidence suggests that if people can be disengaged from their stereotype-driven deception detection strategies, they might detect important and meaningful behavioral cues that would have otherwise gone unnoticed. For future research, it will be vital to explore the variety of indirect approaches that might yield better detection of liars. It will also be important to examine these strategies in more realistic and high stakes scenarios.

REFERENCES

Akehurst, L., Köhnken, G., Vrij, A., & Bull, R. (1996). Lay persons' and police officers' beliefs regarding deceptive behaviour. *Applied Cognitive Psychology, 10*(6), 461–471.

Allwood, C. M., & Granhag, P. A. (1999). Feelings of confidence and the realism of confidence judgments in everyday life. In P. Juslin, & H. Montgomery (Eds.), *Judgment and decision making: Neo-brunswikian and process-tracing approaches.* (pp. 123–146). Mahwah, NJ, US: Lawrence Erlbaum Associates Publishers.

Anderson, D. E., DePaulo, B. M., & Ansfield, M. E. (2002). The development of deception detection skill: A longitudinal study of same-sex friends. *Personality and Social Psychology Bulletin, 28*(4), 536–545.

Anderson, D. E. (1999). *Cognitive and motivational processes underlying truth bias. (deception detection, romantic relationships).* US: ProQuest Information & Learning.

Bond, C. F. J., & DePaulo, B. M. (2006). Accuracy of deception judgments. *Personality and Social Psychology Review, 10*(3), 214–234.

DePaulo, B. M., & Bell, K. L. (1996). Truth and investment: Lies are told to those who care. *Journal of Personality and Social Psychology, 71*(4), 703–716.

DePaulo, B. M., Charlton, K., Cooper, H., Lindsay, J. J., & Muhlenbruck, L. (1997). The accuracy-confidence correlation in the detection of deception. *Personality and Social Psychology Review, 1*(4), 346–357.

DePaulo, B. M., & Kashy, D. A. (1998). Everyday lies in close and casual relationships. *Journal of Personality and Social Psychology, 74*(1), 63–79.

DePaulo, B. M., Lindsay, J. J., Malone, B. E., Muhlenbruck, L., Charlton, K., & Cooper, H. (2003). Cues to deception. *Psychological Bulletin, 129*(1), 74–118.

Ekman, P. (2001). *Telling lies: Clues to deceit in the marketplace, politics, and marriage.* New York: W W Norton & Co.

Granhag, P. A. (2006). Rethinking implicit lie detection. *Journal of Credibility Assessment and Witness Psychology, 7*(3), 180–190.

Hart, C. L., Hudson, L. P., Fillmore, D. G., & Griffith, J. D. (2006). Managerial beliefs about the behavioral cues of deception. *Individual Differences Research, 4*, 176–184.

Honts, C. R. (1994). Psychophysiological detection of deception. *Current Directions in Psychological Science, 3*(3), 77–82.

Hurd, K., & Noller, P. (1988). Decoding deception: A look at the process. *Journal of Nonverbal Behavior, 12*(3), 217–233.

Kashy, D. A., & DePaulo, B. M. (1996). Who lies? *Journal of Personality and Social Psychology, 70*(5), 1037–1051.

Langleben, D. D. (2008). Detection of deception with fMRI: Are we there yet? *Legal and Criminological Psychology, 13*, 1–9.

Larson, J. A. (1927). The polygraph and deception. *Welfare Magazine, 18*, 646–669.

Marston, W. M. (1917). Systolic blood pressure symptoms of deception. *Journal of Experimental Psychology, 2*(2), 117–163.

National Research Council (2002). National Research Council, Committee to Review the Scientific Evidence of the Polygraph, Division of Behavioral and Social Sciences and Education. Washington, DC: The National Academies Press.

Spence, S. A. (2008). Playing devil's advocate: The case against fMRI lie detection. *Legal and Criminological Psychology, 13*, 11–25.

Strömwall, L. A., Granhag, P. A., & Hartwig, M. (2004). Practitioners' beliefs about deception. In P. Granhag, & L. Strömwall (Eds.), *The detection of deception in forensic contexts.* (pp. 229–250). New York: Cambridge University Press.

Vrij, A. (1995). Behavioral correlates of deception in a simulated police interview. *Journal of Psychology: Interdisciplinary and Applied, 129*(1), 15–28.

Vrij, A. (2000). *Detecting lies and deceit: The psychology of lying and the implications for professional practice.* New York: John Wiley & Sons, Ltd.

Vrij, A. (2004). Why professionals fail to catch liars and how they can improve. *Legal and Criminological Psychology, 9*(2), 159–181.

Vrij, A., Edward, K., & Bull, R. (2001). People's insight into their own behaviour and speech content while lying. *British Journal of Psychology, 92*(2), 373–389.

Vrij, A., Edward, K., Roberts, K. P., & Bull, R. (2000). Detecting deceit via analysis of verbal and nonverbal behavior. *Journal of Nonverbal Behavior, 24*(4), 239–263.

Vrij, A., & Semin, G. R. (1996). Lie experts' beliefs about nonverbal indicators of deception. *Journal of Nonverbal Behavior, 20*(1), 65–80.

Authors' Note: We wish to thank Laura Katherine Cowan, M.A. for her considerable help in editing this manuscript.

CRITICAL THINKING QUESTIONS

1. Compare the conclusions in this article with those presented in Article 4. What similarities do you see in their findings? What differences? Can any of the information presented in this article (Article 6) be generalized to the issues of impression formation presented in Article 4 or vice versa? Explain your answer.

2. What implications does the information presented in this article have for situations such as therapy sessions and courtroom proceedings? For instance, is it feasible to teach people to be more aware of the nonverbal and verbal messages they send when they are lying or telling the truth? Can people learn how to interpret such messages more accurately? How might either or both of these goals be accomplished? Explain your answers.

3. From the information contained in this article, how (if at all) can people be trained to be more accurate in detecting deception? In other words, what would you train them to look for?

4. How useful are the findings from the present study for detecting deception in real-world settings? Include in your answer the implications for police settings as well as non-law enforcement settings.

5. Reread the last two sentences of the article. What do you think may be some of the other "indirect approaches that might yield better detection of liars?" How can these strategies be examined in "more realistic and high stakes scenarios?" Explain your answers.

CHAPTER INTEGRATION QUESTIONS

1. Do any common themes emerge from the three articles in this chapter? If so, what are they?

2. Using the information from these articles, what advice could you give on how to make the most positive first impression on others? Also, how can we more accurately form first impressions of other people?

3. Spanish philosopher Santayana wrote, "People often see what they believe rather than believe what they see." What does this quotation mean to you? Do you agree or disagree with it? Why?

4. How can you relate the Santayana quotation to the chapter themes that you identified in Question 1?

Chapter Three

SOCIAL COGNITION

THE WORLD AROUND us presents a complex array of information. Due simply to sheer volume, it is humanly impossible to pay attention to all the information available to us. So, given all of this information, how do we make sense of it? This chapter on social cognition examines some of the ways that people process information about themselves and others in order to make judgments.

A major interest of social psychologists is how people mentally process the information they receive. Decisions are not always based on a thorough analysis of the information at hand. Instead, people sometimes rely on mental shortcuts or intuition in reaching decisions. These mental shortcuts, or *heuristics,* are commonly employed strategies that people use for making sense of the world. The problem is these mental strategies often get us into trouble by shading how we interpret events in the world around us. Article 7, "Some Systematic Biases of Everyday Judgment," examines how heuristics and other forms of cognitive bias may hinder effective decision making.

Social cognition also deals with how we make sense of ourselves. One interesting line of research has addressed the relationship between cognition and emotion. Specifically, do our mental processes influence what we feel, or do our feelings shape our mental processes? Article 8, "Cognitive, Social, and Physiological Determinants of Emotional State," is a classic investigation of the relationship between thought processes and emotion. The methods and findings of the study make interesting reading, but its implications are even more important: Is it possible to change the emotions we experience simply by changing the cognitive labels that we attach to them?

The last article in this chapter is related to the previously mentioned article. Specifically, it too deals with how we make sense of ourselves, in this case concerning the memories we have of our experiences. Article 9, "Lasting False Beliefs and Their Behavioral Consequences," examines how memories of events that did not really happen can be created and how these "false memories" in turn may influence actual behavior.

ARTICLE 7 _____

Social cognition is concerned with the processes that people use to make sense of the social world. One finding from research in this area is that people tend to be *cognitive misers;* that is, all things being equal, people prefer to think as little as possible in reaching decisions. To help them achieve this goal, they employ cognitive strategies such as *heuristics* (i.e., mental shortcuts for understanding the world).

For example, why are some people afraid of flying? If you asked them whether they know that statistics show that airplane travel actually is safer than other modes of transportation, the majority undoubtedly would say that yes, they know that. Yet their fear persists. Why? One contributing factor may be the *availability heuristic,* a mental shortcut that involves judging the probability of something happening by how easily it comes to mind. We all can vividly recall the images of airplane crashes that appear in the media every time an accident occurs. The pictures are terrifying, so they readily come to mind. Even though automobile accidents are more common, how often do we see detailed (and repeated) images of car crashes? Rarely. So even though airplane crashes occur much less frequently than fatal automobile accidents, it is easier to recall images of the former. Hence, we have a greater tendency to fear them, as well.

We use many types of heuristics to help us explain and understand our world. What all of these mental shortcuts do, however, are create biases in how we interpret the events around us. Many of these biases involve inconsequential events, and no harm comes from believing them. But in other situations, using this biased information processing to make important decisions about our lives may lead to problems.

The following article by Thomas Gilovich examines some of the biases in everyday judgment that cloud our ability for accurate, critical thinking.

Some Systematic Biases of Everyday Judgment

■ Thomas Gilovich

Skeptics have long thought that everyday judgment and reasoning are biased in predictable ways. Psychological research on the subject conducted during the past quarter century largely confirms these suspicions. Two types of explanations are typically offered for the dubious beliefs that are dissected in *Skeptical Inquirer.* On one hand, there are motivational causes: Some beliefs are comforting, and so people embrace that comfort and convince themselves that a questionable proposition is true. Many types of religious beliefs, for example, are often explained this way. On the other hand, there are cognitive causes: faulty processes of reasoning and judgment that lead people to misevaluate the evidence of their everyday experience. The skeptical community is convinced that everyday judgment and reasoning leave much to be desired.

Why are skeptics so unimpressed with the reasoning abilities and habits of the average person? Until recently, this pessimism was based on simple observation, often by those with a particularly keen eye for the foibles of human nature. Thus, skeptics often cite such thinkers as Francis Bacon, who stated:

> . . . *all superstition is much the same whether it be that of astrology, dreams, omens, retributive judgment, or the like . . .*

> *[in that] the deluded believers observe events which are fulfilled, but neglect or pass over their failure, though it be much more common. (Bacon 1899/1620)*

John Stuart Mill and Bertrand Russell are two other classic scholars who, along with Bacon, are often quoted for their trenchant observations on the shortcomings of human judgment. It is also common to see similar quotes of more recent vintage—in *Skeptical Inquirer* and elsewhere—from the likes of Richard Feynman, Stephen Jay Gould, and Carl Sagan. During the past twenty-five years, a great deal of psychological research has dealt specifically with the quality of everyday reasoning, and so it is now possible to go beyond simple observation and arrive at a truly rigorous assessment of the shortcomings of everyday judgment. In so doing, we can determine whether or not these scholars we all admire are correct. Do people misevaluate evidence in the very ways and for the very reasons that Bacon, Russell, and others have claimed? Let us look at the research record and see.

Reprinted from *The Skeptical Inquirer*, March 13, 1997, 18 (2), p. 31. Copyright © 1997. CSICOP, Inc. Reprinted with permission.

THE "COMPARED TO WHAT?" PROBLEM

Some of the common claims about the fallibility of human reasoning stand up well to empirical scrutiny. For example, it is commonly argued that people have difficulty with what might be called the "compared to what" problem. That is, people are often overly impressed with an absolute statistic without recognizing that its true import can only be assessed by comparison to some relevant baseline.

For instance, a 1986 article in *Discover* magazine (cited in Dawes 1988) urges readers who fly in airplanes to "know where the exits are and rehearse in your mind exactly how to get to them." Why? The article approvingly notes that someone who interviewed almost two hundred survivors of fatal airline accidents found that " . . . more than 90% had their escape routes mentally mapped out beforehand." Good for them, but note that whoever did the study cannot interview anyone who perished in an airplane crash. Air travel being as scary as it is to so many people, perhaps 90 percent or more of those who died in airline crashes rehearsed their escape routes as well. Ninety percent sounds impressive because it is so close to 100 percent. But without a more pertinent comparison, it really does not mean much.

Similarly, people are often impressed that, say, 30 percent of all infertile couples who adopt a child subsequently conceive. That is great news for that 30 percent to be sure, but what percentage of those who do not adopt likewise conceive? People likewise draw broad conclusions from a cancer patient who goes into remission after steadfastly practicing mental imagery. Again, excellent news for that individual, but might the cancer have gone into remission even if the person had not practiced mental imagery?

This problem of failing to invoke a relevant baseline of comparison is particularly common when the class of data that requires inspection is inherently difficult to collect. Consider, for example, the commonly expressed opinion, "I can always tell that someone is wearing a hairpiece." Are such claims to be believed, or is it just that one can tell that someone is wearing a hairpiece . . . when it is obvious that he is wearing a hairpiece? After all, how can one tell whether some have gone undetected? The goal of a good hairpiece is to fool the public, and so the example is one of those cases in which the confirmations speak loudly while the disconfirmations remain silent.

A similar asymmetry should give pause to those who have extreme confidence in their "gaydar," or their ability to detect whether someone is gay. Here, too, the confirmations announce themselves. When a person for whatever reason "seems gay" and it is later determined that he is, it is a salient triumph for one's skill at detection. But people who elude one's gaydar rarely go out of their way to announce, "By the way, I fooled you: I'm gay."

At any rate, the notion that people have difficulty invoking relevant comparisons has received support from psychological research. Studies of everyday reasoning have shown that the logic and necessity of control groups, for example, is often lost on a large segment of even the educated population (Boring 1954; Einhorn and Hogarth 1978; Nisbett and Ross 1980).

THE "SEEK AND YE SHALL FIND" PROBLEM

Another common claim that stands up well to empirical research is the idea that people do not assess hypotheses even-handedly. Rather, they tend to seek out confirmatory evidence for what they suspect to be true, a tendency that has the effect of "seek and ye shall find." A biased search for confirmatory information frequently turns up more apparent support for a hypothesis than is justified.

This phenomenon has been demonstrated in numerous experiments explicitly designed to assess people's hypothesis-testing strategies (Skov and Sherman 1986; Snyder and Swann 1978). But it is so pervasive that it can also be seen in studies designed with an entirely different agenda in mind. One of my personal favorites is a study in which participants were given the following information (Shafir 1993):

> Imagine that you serve on the jury of an only-child sole-custody case following a relatively messy divorce. The facts of the case are complicated by ambiguous economic, social, and emotional considerations, and you decide to base your decision entirely on the following few observations. To which parent would you award sole custody of the child?

> **Parent A:**
> *average income*
> *average health*
> *average working hours*
> *reasonable rapport with the child*
> *relatively stable social life*

> **Parent B:**
> *above-average income*
> *minor health problems*
> *lots of work-related travel*
> *very close relationship with the child*
> *extremely active social life*

Faced with this version of the problem, the majority of respondents chose to award custody to Parent B, the "mixed bag" parent who offers several advantages (above-average income), but also some disadvantages (health problems), in comparison to Parent A. In another version of the problem, however, a different group is asked to which parent they would deny custody of the child. Here, too, a majority selects Parent B. Parent B, then, is paradoxically deemed both more and less worthy of caring for the child.

The result is paradoxical, that is, unless one takes into account people's tendencies to seek out confirming information.

Asked which parent should be awarded the child, people look primarily for positive qualities that warrant being awarded the child—looking less vigilantly for negative characteristics that would lead one to favor the other parent. When asked which parent should be denied custody, on the other hand, people look primarily for negative qualities that would disqualify a parent. A decision to award or deny, of course, should be based on a comparison of the positive and negative characteristics of the two parents, but the way the question is framed channels respondents down a narrower path in which they focus on information that would confirm the type of verdict they are asked to render.

The same logic often rears its head when people test certain suppositions or hypotheses. Rumors of some dark conspiracy, for example, can lead people to search disproportionately for evidence that supports the plot and neglect evidence that contradicts it.

THE SELECTIVE MEMORY PROBLEM

A third commonly sounded complaint about everyday human thought is that people are more inclined to remember information that fits their expectations than information at variance with their expectations. Charles Darwin, for example, said that he took great care to record any observation that was inconsistent with his theories because "I had found by experience that such facts and thoughts were far more apt to escape from the memory than favourable ones" (cited in Clark 1984).

This particular criticism of the average person's cognitive faculties is in need of revision. Memory research has shown that often people have the easiest time recalling information that is inconsistent with their expectations or preferences (Bargh and Thein 1985; Srull and Wyer 1989). A little reflection indicates that this is particularly true of those "near misses" in life that become indelibly etched in the brain. The novelist Nicholson Baker (1991) provides a perfect illustration:

> [I] told her my terrible story of coming in second in the spelling bee in second grade by spelling keep "c-e-e-p" after successfully tossing off microphone, and how for two or three years afterward I was pained every time a yellow garbage truck drove by on Highland Avenue and I saw the capitals printed on it, "Help Keep Our City Clean," with that impossible irrational K that had made me lose so humiliatingly. . . .

Baker's account, of course, is only an anecdote, possibly an apocryphal one at that. But it is one that, as mentioned above, receives support from more systematic studies. In one study, for example, individuals who had bet on professional football games were later asked to recall as much as they could about the various bets they had made (Gilovich 1983). They recalled significantly more information about their losses—outcomes

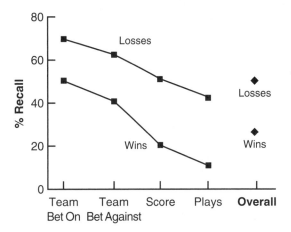

FIGURE 1 / Gamblers' Recall of Information about Bets Won and Lost. (From Gilovich 1983.)

they most likely did not expect to have happen and certainly did not prefer to have happen (see Figure 1).

Thus, the simple idea that people remember best that which they expect or prefer needs modification. Still, there is something appealing and seemingly true about the idea, and it should not be discarded prematurely. When considering people's belief in the accuracy of psychic forecasts, for example, it certainly seems to be fed by selective memory for successful predictions. How then can we reconcile this idea with the finding that often inconsistent information is better recalled? Perhaps the solution lies in considering when an event is eventful. With respect to their capacity to grab attention, some events are one-sided and others two-sided. Two-sided events are those that stand out and psychologically register as events regardless of how they turn out. If you bet on a sporting event or an election result, for example, either outcome—a win or a loss—has emotional significance and is therefore likely to emerge from the stream of everyday experience and register as an event. For these events, it is doubtful that confirmatory information is typically better remembered than disconfirmatory information.

In contrast, suppose you believe that "the telephone always rings when I'm in the shower." The potentially relevant events here are one-sided. If the phone happens to ring while showering, it will certainly register as an event, as you experience great stress in deciding whether to answer it, and you run dripping wet to the phone only to discover that it is someone from AT&T asking if you are satisfied with your long-distance carrier. When the phone does not ring when you are in the shower, on the other hand, it is a non-event. Nothing happened. Thus, with respect to the belief that the phone always rings while you are in the shower, the events are inherently one-sided: Only the confirmations stand out.

Perhaps it is these one-sided events to which Bacon's and Darwin's comments best apply. For one-sided events, as I discuss below, it is often the outcomes consistent with expectations that stand out and are more likely to be remembered. For two-sided events, on the other hand, the two types of outcomes are likely to be equally memorable; or, on occasion, events inconsistent with expectations may be more memorable.

But what determines whether an event is one- or two-sided? There are doubtless several factors. Let's consider two of them in the context of psychic predictions. First, events relevant to psychic predictions are inherently one-sided in the sense that such predictions are disconfirmed not by any specific event, but by their accumulated failure to be confirmed. Thus, the relevant comparison here is between confirmations and non-confirmations, or between events and non-events. It is no surprise, surely, that events are typically more memorable than non-events.

In one test of this idea, a group of college students read a diary purportedly written by another student, who described herself as having an interest in the prophetic nature of dreams (Madey 1993). To test whether there was any validity to dream prophecy, she decided to record each night's dreams and keep a record of significant events in her life, and later determine if there was any connection between the two. Half of the dreams (e.g., "I saw lots of people being happy") were later followed by events that could be seen as fulfilling ("My professor cancelled our final, which produced cheers throughout the class"). The other half went unfulfilled.

After reading the entire diary and completing a brief "filler" task, the participants were asked to recall as many of the dreams as they could. As Figure 2 shows, they recalled many more of the prophecies that were fulfilled than those that were not

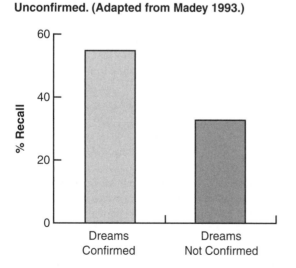

FIGURE 2 / Participants' Recall of Dream Prophecies That Were Either Confirmed or Unconfirmed. (Adapted from Madey 1993.)

(see Figure 2). This result is hardly a surprise, of course, because the fulfillment of a prophecy reminds one of the original prediction, whereas a failure to fulfill it is often a non-event. The relevant outcomes are therefore inherently one-sided, and the confirmations are more easily recalled. The end result is that the broader belief in question—in this case, dream prophecy—receives spurious support.

The events relevant to psychic predictions are one-sided in another way as well. Psychic predictions are notoriously vague about when the prophesied events are supposed to occur. "A serious misfortune will befall a powerful leader" is a more common prophecy than "The President will be assassinated on March 15th." Such predictions are temporally unfocused, in that there is no specific moment to which interested parties are to direct their attention. For such predictions, confirmatory events are once again more likely to stand out because confirmations are more likely to prompt a recollection of the original prophecy. The events relevant to temporally unfocused expectations, then, tend to be one-sided, with the confirmations typically more salient and memorable than disconfirmations.

Temporally focused expectations, on the other hand, are those for which the timing of the decisive outcome is known in advance. If one expects a particular team to win the Super Bowl, for example, one knows precisely when that expectation will be confirmed or refuted—at the end of the game. As a result, the events relevant to temporally focused expectations tend to be two-sided because one's attention is focused on the decisive moment, and both outcomes are likely to be noticed and remembered.

In one study that examined the memory implications of temporally focused and unfocused expectations, participants were asked to read the diary of a student who, as part of an ESP experiment, was required to try to prophesy an otherwise unpredictable event every week for several weeks (Madey and Gilovich 1993). The diary included the student's weekly prophecy as well as various passages describing events from that week. There were two groups of participants in the experiment. In the temporally unfocused condition, the prophecies made no mention of when the prophesied event was likely to occur ("I have a feeling that I will get into an argument with my Psychology research group"). In the temporally focused condition, the prediction identified a precise day on which the event was to occur ("I have a feeling that I will get into an argument with my Psychology research group on Friday"). For each group, half of the prophecies were confirmed (e.g., "Our professor assigned us to research groups, and we immediately disagreed over our topic") and half were disconfirmed (e.g., "Our professor assigned us to research groups, and we immediately came to a unanimous decision on our topic"). Whether confirmed or disconfirmed, the relevant

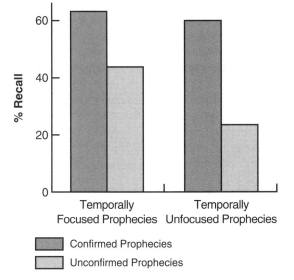

FIGURE 3 / Participants' Recall of Prophecies That Were Confirmed or Disconfirmed, as a Function of Whether or Not the Prophecies Specified When the Critical Events Were to Occur. (Adapted from Madey and Gilovich 1993.)

event was described in the diary entry for the day prophesied in the temporally focused condition. After reading the diary and completing a short distracter task, the participants were asked to recall as many prophecies and relevant events as they could.

Knowing when the prophesied events were likely to occur helped the respondents' memories, but only for those prophecies that were disconfirmed (see Figure 3). Confirmatory events were readily recalled whether temporally focused or not. Disconfirmations, on the other hand, were rarely recalled unless they disconfirmed a temporally focused prediction. When one considers that most psychic predictions are temporally unfocused, the result, once again, is that the evidence for psychic predictions can appear more substantial than it is.

CONCLUSION

There is, of course, much more psychological research on the quality of everyday judgment than that reviewed here (see, for example, Baron 1988; Dawes 1988; Gilovich 1991; Nisbett and Ross 1980; Kahneman, Slovic, and Tversky 1982). But even this brief review is sufficient to make it clear that some of the reputed biases of everyday judgment turn out to be real, verifiable shortcomings. Systematic research by and large supports the suspicions of much of the skeptical community that everyday judgment is not to be trusted completely. At one level, this should not come

as a surprise: It is precisely because everyday judgment cannot be trusted that the inferential safeguards known as the scientific method were developed. It is unfortunate that those safeguards are not more widely taught or more generally appreciated.

REFERENCES

Bacon, F. 1899. *Advancement of Learning and the Novum Organum* (rev. ed.). New York: Colonial Press. (Original work published 1620).

Baker, N. 1991. *Room Temperature.* New York: Vintage.

Bargh, J. A., and R. D. Thein. 1985. Individual construct accessibility, person memory, and the recall-judgment link: The case of information overload. *Journal of Personality and Social Psychology* 49: 1129–1146.

Baron, J. 1988. *Thinking and Deciding.* New York: Cambridge University Press.

Boring, E. G. 1954. The nature and history of experimental control. *American Journal of Psychology* 67: 573–589.

Clark, R. W. 1984. *The Survival of Charles Darwin: A Biography of a Man and an Idea.* New York: Random House.

Dawes, R. M. 1988. *Rational Choice in an Uncertain World.* San Diego, Calif.: Harcourt Brace Jovanovich.

Einhorn, H. J., and R. M. Hogarth. 1978. Confidence in judgment: Persistence in the illusion of validity. *Psychological Review* 85: 395–416.

Gilovich, T. 1983. Biased evaluation and persistence in gambling. *Journal of Personality and Social Psychology* 44: 1110–1126.

————.1991. *How We Know What Isn't So: The Fallibility of Human Reason in Everyday Life.* New York: Free Press.

Kahneman, D., P. Slovic, and A. Tversky. 1982. *Judgment under Uncertainty: Heuristics and Biases.* Cambridge: Cambridge University Press.

Madey, S. F. 1993. Memory for expectancy-consistent and expectancy-inconsistent information: An investigation of one-sided and two-sided events. Unpublished doctoral dissertation, Cornell University.

Madey, S. F., and T. Gilovich. 1993. Effect of temporal focus on the recall of expectancy-consistent and expectancy-inconsistent information. *Journal of Personality and Social Psychology* 65: 458–468.

Nisbett, R. E., and L. Ross. 1980. *Human Inference: Strategies and Shortcomings of Social Judgment.* Englewood Cliffs, N.J.: Prentice-Hall.

Shafir, E. 1993. Choosing versus rejecting: Why some options are both better and worse than others. *Memory and Cognition* 21: 546–556.

Skov, R. B., and S. J. Sherman. 1986. Information-gathering processes: Diagnosticity, hypothesis-confirmatory strategies, and perceived hypothesis confirmation. *Journal of Experimental Social Psychology* 22: 93–121.

Synder, M., and W. B. Swann. 1978. Hypothesis-testing processes in social interaction. *Journal of Personality and Social Psychology* 36: 1202–1212.

Srull, T. K., and R. S. Wyer. 1989. Person memory and judgment. *Psychological Review* 9: 58–83.

CRITICAL THINKING QUESTIONS

1. Find sources from various media that illustrate the "compared to what" problem discussed in the article. Discuss how your examples illustrate erroneous reasoning.

2. The article states that "Studies of everyday reasoning have shown that the logic and necessity of control groups, for example, is often lost on a large segment of even the educated population." Explain what is meant by the "logic and necessity of control groups."

3. Do you agree or disagree with the concept expressed in the quote in Question 2 that many people have poor critical-thinking skills? If you agree, what suggestions do you have for how people can handle life's issues most effectively? If you disagree, defend your position.

4. Give a personal example of some sort of biased thinking that you have witnessed. What bias or biases were involved?

5. Check your horoscope at the beginning of the day to see what it says is in store for you. Then record events at the end of the day that either confirm or disconfirm the predictions in your horoscope. Use the information contained in the article to discuss your findings.

ARTICLE 8 _____

How do you know what emotion you are experiencing? Ask that question of someone who has just learned that he or she has won the lottery, and the answer would undoubtedly be "thrilled," "excited," "overjoyed," or some such adjective to describe a very positive emotional state. Ask if it is actually anger that the winner is feeling, and he or she probably would look at you as if you were crazy. But how does that person *know* what emotion he or she is feeling?

The work that follows by Schachter and Singer is a classic study that addresses what determines a person's emotional state. Briefly, the authors' findings suggest that what we call *emotion* is partly due to some sort of physiological arousal. However, what we feel is also determined by the cognitive label that we attach to that physiological arousal. According to this approach, a person who experiences some sort of physiological arousal might subjectively experience one of two very different emotional states, either anger or euphoria, depending on how he or she labeled the experience. The article discusses the process as well as some of the conditions that result when this process occurs.

While reading the article, think of its implications: Is cognition a necessary part of emotion? Without it, what (if anything) would we feel? What about newborn children? Since their cognitive abilities are not yet fully developed, does that mean that they don't experience emotions?

Cognitive, Social, and Physiological Determinants of Emotional State[1]

■ Stanley Schachter and Jerome E. Singer

The problem of which cues, internal or external, permit a person to label and identify his own emotional state has been with us since the days that James (1890) first tendered his doctrine that "the bodily changes follow directly the perception of the exciting fact, and that our feeling of the same changes as they occur *is* the emotion" (p. 449). Since we are aware of a variety of feeling and emotion states, it should follow from James' proposition that the various emotions will be accompanied by a variety of differentiable bodily states. Following James' pronouncement, a formidable number of studies were undertaken in search of the physiological differentiators of the emotions. The results, in these early days, were almost uniformly negative. All of the emotional states experimentally manipulated were characterized by a general pattern of excitation of the sympathetic nervous system but there appeared to be no clear-cut physiological discriminators of the various emotions. This pattern of results was so consistent from experiment to experiment that Cannon (1929) offered, as one of the crucial criticisms of the James-Lange theory, the fact that "the same visceral changes occur in very different emotional states and in non-emotional states" (p. 351).

More recent work, however, has given some indication that there may be differentiators. Ax (1953) and Schachter (1957) studied fear and anger. On a large number of indices both of

these states were characterized by a similarly high level of autonomic activation but on several indices they did differ in the degree of activation. Wolf and Wolff (1947) studied a subject with a gastric fistula and were able to distinguish two patterns in the physiological responses of the stomach wall. It should be noted, though, that for many months they studied their subject during and following a great variety of moods and emotions and were able to distinguish only two patterns.

Whether or not there are physiological distinctions among the various emotional states must be considered an open question. Recent work might be taken to indicate that such differences are at best rather subtle and that the variety of emotion, mood, and feeling states are by no means matched by an equal variety of visceral patterns.

This rather ambiguous situation has led Ruckmick (1936), Hunt, Cole, and Reis (1958), Schachter (1959) and others to suggest that cognitive factors may be major determinants of emotional states. Granted a general pattern of sympathetic excitation as characteristic of emotional states, granted that there may be some differences in pattern from state to state, it is suggested that one labels, interprets, and identifies this stirred-up state in terms of the characteristics of the precipitating situation and one's apperceptive mass. This suggests, then, that an emotional state may be considered a function of a state of

Cognitive, social, and physiological determinants of emotional state. Schachter, Stanley; Singer, Jerome. *Psychological Review*, 69(5), Sep 1962, 379–399.

physiological arousal[2] and of a cognition appropriate to this state of arousal. The cognition, in a sense, exerts a steering function. Cognitions arising from the immediate situation as interpreted by past experience provide the framework within which one understands and labels his feelings. It is the cognition which determines whether the state of physiological arousal will be labeled as "anger," "joy," "fear," or whatever.

In order to examine the implications of this formulation let us consider the fashion in which these two elements, a state of physiological arousal and cognitive factors, would interact in a variety of situations. In most emotion inducing situations, of course, the two factors are completely interrelated. Imagine a man walking alone down a dark alley; a figure with a gun suddenly appears. The perception-cognition "figure with a gun" in some fashion initiates a state of physiological arousal; this state of arousal is interpreted in terms of knowledge about dark alleys and guns and the state of arousal is labeled "fear." Similarly a student who unexpectedly learns that he has made Phi Beta Kappa may experience a state of arousal which he will label "joy."

Let us now consider circumstances in which these two elements, the physiological and the cognitive, are, to some extent, independent. First, is the state of physiological arousal alone sufficient to induce an emotion? Best evidence indicates that it is not. Marañon[3] (1924), in a fascinating study (which was replicated by Cantril & Hunt, 1932, and Landis & Hunt, 1932), injected 210 of his patients with the sympathomimetic agent adrenalin and then simply asked them to introspect. Seventy-one percent of his subjects simply reported their physical symptoms with no emotional overtones; 29% of the subjects responded in an apparently emotional fashion. Of these the great majority described their feelings in a fashion that Marañon labeled "cold" or "as if" emotions, that is, they made statements such as "I feel *as if* I were afraid" or "*as if* I were awaiting a great happiness." This is a sort of emotional "déjà vu" experience; these subjects are neither happy nor afraid, they feel "as if" they were. Finally a very few cases apparently reported a genuine emotional experience. However, in order to produce this reaction in most of these few cases, Marañon (1924) points out:

> One must suggest a memory with strong affective force but not so strong as to produce an emotion in the normal state. For example, in several cases we spoke to our patients before the injection of their sick children or dead parents and they responded calmly to this topic. The same topic presented later, during the adrenal commotion, was sufficient to trigger emotion. This adrenal commotion places the subject in a situation of "affective imminence." (pp. 307–308)

Apparently, then, to produce a genuinely emotional reaction to adrenalin, Marañon was forced to provide such subjects with an appropriate cognition.

Though Marañon (1924) is not explicit on his procedure, it is clear that his subjects knew that they were receiving an injection and in all likelihood knew that they were receiving adrenalin and probably had some order of familiarity with its effects. In short, though they underwent the pattern of sympathetic discharge common to strong emotional states, at the same time they had a completely appropriate cognition or explanation as to why they felt this way. This, we would suggest, is the reason so few of Marañon's subjects reported any emotional experience.

Consider now a person in a state of physiological arousal for which no immediately explanatory or appropriate cognitions are available. Such a state could result were one covertly to inject a subject with adrenalin or, unknown to him, feed the subject a sympathomimetic drug such as ephedrine. Under such conditions a subject would be aware of palpitations, tremor, face flushing, and most of the battery of symptoms associated with a discharge of the sympathetic nervous system. In contrast to Marañon's (1924) subjects he would, at the same time, be utterly unaware of why he felt this way. What would be the consequence of such a state?

Schachter (1959) has suggested that precisely such a state would lead to the arousal of "evaluative needs" (Festinger, 1954), that is, pressures would act on an individual in such a state to understand and label his bodily feelings. His bodily state grossly resembles the condition in which it has been at times of emotional excitement. How would he label his present feelings? It is suggested, of course, that he will label his feelings in terms of his knowledge of the immediate situation.[4] Should he at the time be with a beautiful woman, he might decide that he was wildly in love or sexually excited. Should he be at a gay party, he might, by comparing himself to others, decide that he was extremely happy and euphoric. Should he be arguing with his wife, he might explode in fury and hatred. Or, should the situation be completely inappropriate, he could decide that he was excited about something that had recently happened to him or, simply, that he was sick. In any case, it is our basic assumption that emotional states are a function of the interaction of such cognitive factors with a state of physiological arousal.

This line of thought, then, leads to the following propositions:

1. Given a state of physiological arousal for which an individual has no immediate explanation, he will "label" this state and describe his feelings in terms of the cognitions available to him. To the extent that cognitive factors are potent determiners of emotional states, it could be anticipated that precisely the same state of physiological arousal could be labeled "joy" or "fury" or "jealousy" or any of a great diversity of emotional labels depending on the cognitive aspects of the situation.

2. Given a state of physiological arousal for which an individual has a completely appropriate explanation (e.g., "I feel this way because I have just received an injection of adrenalin") no evaluative needs will arise and the individual is unlikely to label his feelings in terms of the alternative cognitions available.

Finally, consider a condition in which emotion inducing cognitions are present but there is no state of physiological arousal. For example, an individual might be completely aware that he is in great danger but for some reason (drug or surgical) remain in a state of physiological quiescence. Does he experience the emotion "fear"? Our formulation of emotion as a joint function of a state of physiological arousal and an appropriate cognition, would, of course, suggest that he does not, which leads to our final proposition.

3. Given the same cognitive circumstances, the individual will react emotionally or describe his feelings as emotions only to the extent that he experiences a state of physiological arousal.[5]

PROCEDURE

The experimental test of these propositions requires (a) the experimental manipulation of a state of physiological arousal, (b) the manipulation of the extent to which the subject has an appropriate or proper explanation of his bodily state, and (c) the creation of situations from which explanatory cognitions may be derived.

In order to satisfy the first two experimental requirements, the experiment was cast in the framework of a study of the effects of vitamin supplements on vision. As soon as a subject arrived, he was taken to a private room and told by the experimenter:

> In this experiment we would like to make various tests of your vision. We are particularly interested in how certain vitamin compounds and vitamin supplements affect the visual skills. In particular, we want to find out how the vitamin compound called "Suproxin" affects your vision.
>
> What we would like to do, then, if we can get your permission, is to give you a small injection of Suproxin. The injection itself is mild and harmless; however, since some people do object to being injected we don't want to talk you into anything. Would you mind receiving a Suproxin injection?

If the subject agrees to the injection (and all but 1 of 185 subjects did) the experimenter continues with instructions we shall describe shortly, then leaves the room. In a few minutes a physician enters the room, briefly repeats the experimenter's instructions, takes the subject's pulse and then injects him with Suproxin.

Depending upon condition, the subject receives one of two forms of Suproxin—epinephrine or a placebo.

Epinephrine or adrenalin is a sympathomimetic drug whose effects, with minor exceptions, are almost a perfect mimicry of a discharge of the sympathetic nervous system. Shortly after injection systolic blood pressure increases markedly, heart rate increases somewhat, cutaneous blood flow decreases, while muscle and cerebral blood flow increase, blood sugar and lactic acid concentration increase, and respiration rate increases slightly. As far as the subject is concerned the major subjective symptoms are palpitation, tremor, and sometimes a feeling of flushing and accelerated breathing. With a subcutaneous injection (in the dosage administered to our subjects), such effects usually begin within 3–5 minutes of injection and last anywhere from 10 minutes to an hour. For most subjects these effects are dissipated within 15–20 minutes after injection.

Subjects receiving epinephrine received a subcutaneous injection of 1/2 cubic centimeter of a 1:1000 solution of Winthrop Laboratory's Suprarenin, a saline solution of epinephrine bitartrate.

Subjects in the placebo condition received a subcutaneous injection of 1/2 cubic centimeter of saline solution. This is, of course, completely neutral material with no side effects at all.

Manipulating an Appropriate Explanation

By "appropriate" we refer to the extent to which the subject has an authoritative, unequivocal explanation of his bodily condition. Thus, a subject who had been informed by the physician that as a direct consequence of the injection he would feel palpitations, tremor, etc. would be considered to have a completely appropriate explanation. A subject who had been informed only that the injection would have no side effects would have no appropriate explanation of his state. This dimension of appropriateness was manipulated in three experimental conditions which shall be called: Epinephrine Informed (Epi Inf), Epinephrine Ignorant (Epi Ign), and Epinephrine Misinformed (Epi Mis).

Immediately after the subject had agreed to the injection and before the physician entered the room, the experimenter's spiel in each of these conditions went as follows:

Epinephrine Informed. *I should also tell you that some of our subjects have experienced side effects from the Suproxin. These side effects are transitory, that is, they will only last for about 15 or 20 minutes. What will probably happen is that your hand will start to shake, your heart will start to pound, and your face may get warm and flushed. Again these are side effects lasting about 15 or 20 minutes.*

While the physician was giving the injection, she told the subject that the injection was mild and harmless and repeated this description of the symptoms that the subject could expect as a consequence of the shot. In this condition, then, subjects have a completely appropriate explanation of their bodily state. They know precisely what they will feel and why.

Epinephrine Ignorant

In this condition, when the subject agreed to the injection, the experimenter said nothing more relevant to side effects and simply left the room. While the physician was giving the injection, she told the subject that the injection was mild and harmless and would have no side effects. In this condition, then, the subject has no experimentally provided explanation for his bodily state.

Epinephrine Misinformed. *I should also tell you that some of our subjects have experienced side effects from the Suproxin. These side effects are transitory, that is, they will only last for about 15 or 20 minutes. What will probably happen is that your feet will feel numb, you will have an itching sensation over parts of your body, and you may get a slight headache. Again these are side effects lasting 15 or 20 minutes.*

And again, the physician repeated these symptoms while injecting the subject.

None of these symptoms, of course, are consequences of an injection of epinephrine and, in effect, these instructions provide the subject with a completely inappropriate explanation of his bodily feelings. This condition was introduced as a control condition of sorts. It seemed possible that the description of side effects in the Epi Inf condition might turn the subject introspective, self-examining, possibly slightly troubled. Differences on the dependent variable between the Epi Inf and Epi Ign conditions might, then, be due to such factors rather than to differences in appropriateness. The false symptoms in the Epi Mis condition should similarly turn the subject introspective, etc., but the instructions in this condition do not provide an appropriate explanation of the subject's state.

Subjects in all of the above conditions were injected with epinephrine. Finally, there was a placebo condition in which subjects, who were injected with saline solution, were given precisely the same treatment as subjects in the Epi Ign condition.

Producing an Emotion Inducing Cognition

Our initial hypothesis has suggested that given a state of physiological arousal for which the individual has no adequate explanation, cognitive factors can lead the individual to describe his feelings with any of a diversity of emotional labels. In order to test this hypothesis, it was decided to manipulate emotional states which can be considered quite different—euphoria and anger.

There are, of course, many ways to induce such states. In our own program of research, we have concentrated on social determinants of emotional states and have been able to demonstrate in other studies that people do evaluate their own feelings by comparing themselves with others around them (Schachter 1959; Wrightsman 1960). In this experiment we have attempted again to manipulate emotional state by social means. In one set of conditions, the subject is placed together with a stooge who has been trained to act euphorically. In a second set of conditions the subject is with a stooge trained to act in an angry fashion.

Euphoria

Immediately[6] after the subject had been injected, the physician left the room and the experimenter returned with a stooge whom he introduced as another subject, then said:

> Both of you have had the Suproxin shot and you'll both be taking the same tests of vision. What I ask you to do now is just wait for 20 minutes. The reason for this is simply that we have to allow 20 minutes for the Suproxin to get from the injection site into the bloodstream. At the end of 20 minutes when we are certain that most of the Suproxin has been absorbed into the bloodstream, we'll begin the tests of vision.

The room in which this was said had been deliberately put into a state of mild disarray. As he was leaving, the experimenter apologetically added:

> The only other thing I should do is to apologize for the condition of the room. I just didn't have time to clean it up. So, if you need any scratch paper or rubber bands or pencils, help yourself. I'll be back in 20 minutes to begin the vision tests.

As soon as the experimenter had left, the stooge introduced himself again, made a series of standard icebreaker comments, and then launched his routine. For observation purposes, the stooge's act was broken into a series of standard units, demarcated by a change in activity or a standard comment. In sequence, the units of the stooge's routine were the following:

1. Stooge reaches for a piece of paper and starts doodling saying, "They said we could use this for scratch, didn't they?" He doodles a fish for some 30 seconds, then says:
2. "This scrap paper isn't even much good for doodling" and crumples paper and attempts to throw it into wastebasket in far corner of the room. He misses but this leads him into a "basketball game." He crumples up other sheets of paper, shoots a few baskets, says "Two points" occasionally. He gets up and does a jump shot saying, "The old jump shot is really on today."
3. If the subject has not joined in, the stooge throws a paper basketball to the subject saying, "Here, you try it."
4. Stooge continues his game saying, "The trouble with paper basketballs is that you don't really have any control."
5. Stooge continues basketball, then gives it up saying, "This is one of my good days. I feel like a kid again. I think I'll make a plane." He makes a paper airplane saying, "I guess I'll make one of the longer ones."
6. Stooge flies plane. Gets up and retrieves plane. Flies again, etc.
7. Stooge throws plane at subject.
8. Stooge, flying plane, says, "Even when I was a kid, I was never much good at this."
9. Stooge tears off part of plane saying, "Maybe this plane can't fly but at least it's good for something." He wads up paper and making a slingshot of a rubber band begins to shoot the paper.

10. Shooting, the stooge says, "They [paper ammunition] really go better if you make them long. They don't work right if you wad them up."
11. While shooting, stooge notices a sloppy pile of manila folders on a table. He builds a tower of these folders, then goes to the opposite end of the room to shoot at the tower.
12. He misses several times, then hits and cheers as the tower falls. He goes over to pick up the folders.
13. While picking up, he notices, behind a portable blackboard, a pair of hula hoops which have been covered with black tape with a few wires sticking out of the tape. He reaches for these, taking one for himself and putting the other aside but within reaching distance of the subject. The stooge tries the hula hoop, saying, "This isn't as easy as it looks."
14. Stooge twirls hoop wildly on arm, saying, "Hey, look at this—this is great."
15. Stooge replaces the hula hoop and sits down with his feet on the table. Shortly thereafter the experimenter returns to the room.

This routine was completely standard, though its pace, of course, varied depending upon the subject's reaction, the extent to which he entered into this bedlam and the extent to which he initiated activities of his own. The only variations from this standard routine were those forced by the subject. Should the subject originate some nonsense of his own and request the stooge to join in, he would do so. And, he would, of course, respond to any comments initiated by the subject.

Subjects in each of the three "appropriateness" conditions and in the placebo condition were submitted to this setup. The stooge, of course, never knew in which condition any particular subject fell.

Anger

Immediately after the injection, the experimenter brought a stooge into the subject's room, introduced the two and after explaining the necessity for a 20 minute delay for "the Suproxin to get from the injection site into the bloodstream" he continued, "We would like you to use these 20 minutes to answer these questionnaires." Then handing out the questionnaires, he concludes with, "I'll be back in 20 minutes to pick up the questionnaires and begin the tests of vision."

Before looking at the questionnaire, the stooge says to the subject,

I really wanted to come for an experiment today, but I think it's unfair for them to give you shots. At least, they should have told us about the shots when they called us; you hate to refuse, once you're here already.

The questionnaires, five pages long, start off innocently requesting face sheet information and then grow increasingly personal and insulting. The stooge, sitting directly opposite the subject, paces his own answers so that at all times subject and stooge are working on the same question. At regular points in the questionnaire, the stooge makes a series of standardized comments about the questions. His comments start off innocently enough, grow increasingly querulous, and finally he ends up in a rage. In sequence, he makes the following comments.

1. Before answering any items, he leafs quickly through the questionnaire saying, "Boy, this is a long one."
2. Question 7 on the questionnaire requests, "List the foods that you would eat in a typical day." The stooge comments, "Oh for Pete's sake, what did I have for breakfast this morning?"
3. Question 9 asks, "Do you ever hear bells? _____ How often? _____" The stooge remarks, "Look at Question 9. How ridiculous can you get? I hear bells every time I change classes."
4. Question 13 requests, "List the childhood diseases you have had and the age at which you had them" to which the stooge remarks, "I get annoyed at this childhood disease question. I can't remember what childhood diseases I had, and especially at what age. Can you?"
5. Question 17 asks, "What is your father's average annual income?" and the stooge says, "This really irritates me. It's none of their business what my father makes. I'm leaving that blank."
6. Question 25 presents a long series of items such as "Does not bathe or wash regularly," "Seems to need psychiatric care," etc. and requests the respondent to write down for which member of his immediate family each item seems most applicable. The question specifically prohibits the answer "None" and each item must be answered. The stooge says, "I'll be damned if I'll fill out Number 25. 'Does not bathe or wash regularly'—that's a real insult." He then angrily crosses out the entire item.
7. Question 28 reads: "How many times each week do you have sexual intercourse?" 0–1 _____ 2–3 _____ 4–6 _____ 7 and over _____. The stooge bites out, "The hell with it! I don't have to tell them all this."
8. The stooge sits sullenly for a few moments then he rips up his questionnaire, crumples the pieces and hurls them to the floor, saying, "I'm not wasting any more time. I'm getting my books and leaving" and he stamps out of the room.
9. The questionnaire continues for eight more questions ending with: "With how many men (other than your father) has your mother had extramarital relationships?" 4 and under _____; 5–9 _____; 10 and over _____.

Subjects in the Epi Ign, Epi Inf and Placebo conditions were run through this "anger" inducing sequence. The stooge, again, did not know to which condition the subject had been assigned.

In summary, this is a seven condition experiment which, for two different emotional states, allows us (a) to evaluate the effects of "appropriateness" on emotional inducibility and (b) to begin to evaluate the effects of sympathetic activation on emotional inducibility. In schematic form the conditions are the following:

Euphoria	Anger
Epi Inf	Epi Inf
Epi Ign	Epi Ign
Epi Mis	Placebo
Placebo	

The Epi Mis condition was not run in the Anger sequence. This was originally conceived as a control condition and it was felt that its inclusion in the Euphoria conditions alone would suffice as a means of evaluating the possible artifactual effect of the Epi Inf instructions.

Measurement

Two types of measures of emotional state were obtained. Standardized observation through a one-way mirror was the technique used to assess the subject's behavior. To what extent did he act euphoric or angry? Such behavior can be considered in a way as a "semi-private" index of mood for as far as the subject was concerned, his emotional behavior could be known only to the other person in the room—presumably another student. The second type of measure was self-report in which, on a variety of scales, the subject indicated his mood of the moment. Such measures can be considered "public" indices of mood for they would, of course, be available to the experimenter and his associates.

Observation

Euphoria

For each of the first 14 units of the stooge's standardized routine an observer kept a running chronicle of what the subject did and said. For each unit the observer coded the subject's behavior in one or more of the following categories:

Category 1: Joins in activity.If the subject entered into the stooge activities, e.g., if he made or flew airplanes, threw paper basketballs, hula hooped, etc., his behavior was coded in this category.

Category 2: Initiates new activity.A subject was so coded if he gave indications of creative euphoria, that is, if, on his own, he initiated behavior outside of the stooge's routine. Instances of such behavior would be the subject who threw open the window and, laughing, hurled paper basketballs at passersby; or, the subject who jumped on a table and spun one hula hoop on his leg and the other on his neck.

Categories 3 and 4: Ignores or watches stooge. Subjects who paid flatly no attention to the stooge or who, with or without comment, simply watched the stooge without joining in his activity were coded in these categories.

For any particular unit of behavior, the subject's behavior was coded in one or more of these categories. To test reliability of coding two observers independently coded two experimental sessions. The observers agreed completely on the coding of 88% of the units.

Anger

For each of the units of stooge behavior, an observer recorded the subject's responses and coded them according to the following category scheme:

Category 1: Agrees.In response to the stooge the subject makes a comment indicating that he agrees with the stooge's standardized comment or that he, too, is irked by a particular item on the questionnaire. For example, a subject who responded to the stooge's comment on the "father's income" question by saying, "I don't like that kind of personal question either" would be so coded (scored +2).

Category 2: Disagrees.In response to the stooge's comment, the subject makes a comment which indicates that he disagrees with the stooge's meaning or mood; e.g., in response to the stooge's comment on the "father's income" question, such a subject might say, "Take it easy, they probably have a good reason for wanting the information" (scored –2).

Category 3: Neutral.A noncommittal or irrelevant response to the stooge's remark (scored 0).

Category 4: Initiates agreement or disagreement. With no instigation by the stooge, a subject, so coded, would have volunteered a remark indicating that he felt the same way or, alternatively, quite differently than the stooge. Examples would be "Boy I hate this kind of thing" or "I'm enjoying this" (scored +2 or –2).

Category 5: Watches.The subject makes no verbal response to the stooge's comment but simply looks directly at him (scored 0).

Category 6: Ignores.The subject makes no verbal response to the stooge's comment nor does he look at him; the subject, paying no attention at all to the stooge, simply works at his own questionnaire (scored –1).

A subject was scored in one or more of these categories for each unit of stooge behavior. To test reliability, two observers independently coded three experimental sessions. In order to get a behavioral index of anger, observation protocol was scored according to the values presented in parentheses after each of the above definitions of categories. In a unit-by-unit comparison, the two observers agreed completely on the scoring of 71% of the units jointly observed. The scores of the two observers differed by a value of 1 or less for 88% of the units coded and in not a single case did the two observers differ in the direction of their scoring of a unit.

Self-Report of Mood and Physical Condition

When the subject's session with the stooge was completed, the experimenter returned to the room, took pulses and said:

> Before we proceed with the vision tests, there is one other kind of information which we must have. We have found, as you can probably imagine, that there are many things beside Suproxin that affect how well you see in our tests. How hungry you are, how tired you are, and even the mood you're in at the time—whether you feel happy or irritated at the time of testing will affect how well you see. To understand the data we collect on you, then, we must be able to figure out which effects are due to causes such as these and which are caused by Suproxin.
>
> The only way we can get such information about your physical and emotional state is to have you tell us. I'll hand out these questionnaires and ask you to answer them as accurately as possible. Obviously our data on the vision tests will only be as accurate as your description of your mental and physical state.

In keeping with this spiel, the questionnaire that the experimenter passed out contained a number of mock questions about hunger, fatigue, etc., as well as questions of more immediate relevance to the experiment. To measure mood or emotional state the following two were the crucial questions:

1. How irritated, angry or annoyed would you say you feel at present?

I don't feel at all irritated or angry (0)	I feel a little irritated and angry (1)	I feel quite irritated and angry (2)	I feel very irritated and angry (3)	I feel extremely irritated and angry (4)

2. How good or happy would you say you feel at present?

I don't feel at all happy or good (0)	I feel a little happy and good (1)	I feel quite happy and good (2)	I feel very happy and good (3)	I feel extremely happy and good (4)

To measure the physical effects of epinephrine and determine whether or not the injection had been successful in producing the necessary bodily state, the following questions were asked:

1. Have you experienced any palpitation (consciousness of your own heart beat)?

Not at all (0)	A slight amount (1)	A moderate amount (2)	An intense amount (3)

2. Did you feel any tremor (involuntary shaking of the hands, arms or legs)?

Not at all (0)	A slight amount (1)	A moderate amount (2)	An intense amount (3)

To measure possible effects of the instructions in the Epi Mis condition, the following questions were asked:

1. Did you feel any numbness in your feet?
2. Did you feel any itching sensation?
3. Did you experience any feeling of headache?

To all three of these questions was attached a four-point scale running from "Not at all" to "An intense amount."

In addition to these scales, the subjects were asked to answer two open-end questions on other physical or emotional sensations they may have experienced during the experimental session. A final measure of bodily state was pulse rate which was taken by the physician or the experimenter at two times—immediately before the injection and immediately after the session with the stooge.

When the subjects had completed these questionnaires, the experimenter announced that the experiment was over, explained the deception and its necessity in detail, answered any questions, and swore the subjects to secrecy. Finally, the subjects answered a brief questionnaire about their experiences, if any, with adrenalin and their previous knowledge or suspicion of the experimental setup. There was no indication that any of the subjects had known about the experiment beforehand but 11 subjects were so extremely suspicious of some crucial feature of the experiment that their data were automatically discarded.

Subjects

The subjects were all male, college students taking classes in introductory psychology at the University of Minnesota. Some 90% of the students in these classes volunteer for a subject pool for which they receive two extra points on their final exam for every hour that they serve as experimental subjects. For this study the records of all potential subjects were cleared with the Student Health Service in order to insure that no harmful effects would result from the injections.

Evaluation of the Experimental Design

The ideal test of our propositions would require circumstances which our experiment is far from realizing. First, the proposition that: "A state of physiological arousal for which an individual has no immediate explanation will lead him to label this state in terms of the cognitions available to him" obviously requires conditions under which the subject does not and cannot have a proper explanation of his bodily state. Though we toyed with such fantasies as ventilating the experimental room with vaporized adrenalin, reality forced us to rely on the disguised injection of Suproxin—a technique which was far from ideal for no matter what the experimenter told them, some subjects would inevitably attribute their feelings to the injection. To the extent that subjects did so, differences between the several appropriateness conditions should be attenuated.

Second, the proposition that: "Given the same cognitive circumstances the individual will react emotionally only to the extent that he experiences a state of physiological arousal" requires for its ideal test the manipulation of states of physiological arousal and of physiological quiescence. Though there is no question that epinephrine effectively produces a state of arousal, there is also no question that a placebo does not prevent physiological arousal. To the extent that the experimental situation effectively produces sympathetic stimulation in placebo subjects, the proposition is difficult to test, for such a factor would attenuate differences between epinephrine and placebo subjects.

Both of these factors, then, can be expected to interfere with the test of our several propositions. In presenting the results of this study, we shall first present condition by condition results and then evaluate the effect of these two factors on experimental differences.

RESULTS

Effects of the Injections on Bodily State

Let us examine first the success of the injections at producing the bodily state required to examine the propositions at test. Does the injection of epinephrine produce symptoms of sympathetic discharge as compared with the placebo injection? Relevant data are presented in Table 1 where it can be immediately seen that on all items subjects who were in epinephrine conditions show considerably more evidence of sympathetic

activation than do subjects in placebo conditions. In all epinephrine conditions pulse rate increases significantly when compared with the decrease characteristic of the placebo conditions. On the scales it is clear that epinephrine subjects experience considerably more palpitation and tremor than do placebo subjects. In all possible comparisons on these symptoms, the mean scores of subjects in any of the epinephrine conditions are greater than the corresponding scores in the placebo conditions at better than the .001 level of significance. Examination of the absolute values of these scores makes it quite clear that subjects in epinephrine conditions were, indeed, in a state of physiological arousal, while most subjects in placebo conditions were in a relative state of physiological quiescence.

The epinephrine injection, of course, did not work with equal effectiveness for all subjects; indeed for a few subjects it did not work at all. Such subjects reported almost no palpitation or tremor, showed no increase in pulse and described no other relevant physical symptoms. Since for such subjects the necessary experimental conditions were not established, they were automatically excluded from the data and all further tabular presentations will not include such subjects. Table 1, however, does include the data of these subjects. There were four such subjects in euphoria conditions and one of them in anger conditions.

In order to evaluate further data on Epi Mis subjects it is necessary to note the results of the "numbness," "itching," and "headache" scales also presented in Table 1. Clearly the subjects in the Epi Mis condition do not differ on these scales from subjects in any of the other experimental conditions.

Effects of the Manipulations on Emotional State

Euphoria

Self-Report   The effects of the several manipulations on emotional state in the euphoria conditions are presented in Table 2. The scores recorded in this table are derived, for each

TABLE 1 / Effects of the Injections on Bodily State

Condition	N	Pulse		Self-Rating of				
		Pre	Post	Palpitation	Tremor	Numbness	Itching	Headache
Euphoria								
Epi Inf	27	85.7	88.6	1.20	1.43	0	0.16	0.32
Epi Ign	26	84.6	85.6	1.83	1.76	0.15	0	0.55
Epi Mis	26	82.9	86.0	1.27	2.00	0.06	0.08	0.23
Placebo	26	80.4	77.1	0.29	0.21	0.09	0	0.27
Anger								
Epi Inf	23	85.9	92.4	1.26	1.41	0.17	0	0.11
Epi Ign	23	85.0	96.8	1.44	1.78	0	0.06	0.21
Placebo	23	84.5	79.6	0.59	0.24	0.14	0.06	0.06

TABLE 2 / Self-Report of Emotional State in the Euphoria Conditions

Condition	N	Self-Report Scales	Comparison	p
Epi Inf	25	0.98	Epi Inf vs. Epi Mis	< .01
Epi Ign	25	1.78	Epi Inf vs. Epi Ign	.02
Epi Mis	25	1.90	Placebo vs. Epi Mis, Ign, or Inf	ns
Placebo	26	1.61		

All *p* values reported throughout paper are two-tailed.

subject, by subtracting the value of the point he checks on the irritation scale from the value of the point he checks on the happiness scale. Thus, if a subject were to check the point "I feel a little irritated and angry" on the irritation scale and the point "I feel very happy and good" on the happiness scale, his score would be +2. The higher the positive value, the happier and better the subject reports himself as feeling. Though we employ an index for expositional simplicity, it should be noted that the two components of the index each yield results completely consistent with those obtained by use of this index.

Let us examine first the effects of the appropriateness instructions. Comparison of the scores for the Epi Mis and Epi Inf conditions makes it immediately clear that the experimental differences are not due to artifacts resulting from the informed instructions. In both conditions the subject was warned to expect a variety of symptoms as a consequence of the injection. In the Epi Mis condition, where the symptoms were inappropriate to the subject's bodily state the self-report score is almost twice that in the Epi Inf condition where the symptoms were completely appropriate to the subject's bodily state. It is reasonable, then, to attribute differences between informed subjects and those in other conditions to differences in manipulated appropriateness rather than to artifacts such as introspectiveness or self-examination.

It is clear that, consistent with expectations, subjects were more susceptible to the stooge's mood and consequently more euphoric when they had no explanation of their own bodily states than when they did. The means of both the Epi Ign and Epi Mis conditions are considerably greater than the mean of the Epi Inf condition.

It is of interest to note that Epi Mis subjects are somewhat more euphoric than are Epi Ign subjects. This pattern repeats itself in other data shortly to be presented. We would attribute this difference to differences in the appropriateness dimension. Though, as in the Epi Ign condition, a subject is not provided

with an explanation of his bodily state, it is, of course, possible that he will provide one for himself which is not derived from his interaction with the stooge. Most reasonably he could decide for himself that he feels this way because of the injection. To the extent that he does so he should be less susceptible to the stooge. It seems probable that he would be less likely to hit on such an explanation in the Epi Mis condition than in the Epi Ign condition for in the Epi Mis condition both the experimenter and the doctor have told him that the effects of the injection would be quite different from what he actually feels. The effect of such instructions is probably to make it more difficult for the subject himself to hit on the alternative explanation described above. There is some evidence to support this analysis. In open-end questions in which subjects described their own mood and state, 28% of the subjects in the Epi Ign condition made some connection between the injection and their bodily state compared with the 16% of subjects in the Epi Mis condition who did so. It could be considered, then, that these three conditions fall along a dimension of appropriateness, with the Epi Inf condition at one extreme and the Epi Mis condition at the other.

Comparing the placebo to the epinephrine conditions, we note a pattern which will repeat itself throughout the data. Placebo subjects are less euphoric than either Epi Mis or Epi Ign subjects but somewhat more euphoric than Epi Inf subjects. These differences are not, however, statistically significant. We shall consider the epinephrine-placebo comparisons in detail in a later section of this paper following the presentation of additional relevant data. For the moment, it is clear that, by self-report manipulating appropriateness has had a very strong effect on euphoria.

Behavior   Let us next examine the extent to which the subject's behavior was affected by the experimental manipulations. To the extent that his mood has been affected, one should expect that the subject will join in the stooge's whirl of manic activity and initiate similar activities of his own. The relevant data are presented in Table 3. The column labeled "Activity Index" presents summary figures on the extent to which the subject joined in the stooge's activity. This is a weighted index which reflects both the nature of the activities in which the subject engaged and the amount of time he was active. The index was devised by assigning the following weights to the subject's activities: 5—hula hooping; 4—shooting with slingshot; 3—paper airplanes; 2—paper basketballs; 1—doodling; 0—does nothing. Pretest scaling on 15 college students ordered these activities with respect to the degree of euphoria they represented. Arbitrary weights were assigned so that the wilder the activity, the heavier the weight. These weights are multiplied by an estimate of the amount of time the subject spent in each activity and the summed products make up the activity index for each subject. This

TABLE 3 / Behavioral Indications of Emotional State in the Euphoria Conditions

Condition	N	Activity Index	Mean Number of Acts Initiated
Epi Inf	25	12.72	.20
Epi Ign	25	18.28	.56
Epi Mis	25	22.56	.84
Placebo	26	16.00	.54

p value

Comparison	Activity Index	Initiates
Epi Inf vs. Epi Mis	.05	.03
Epi Inf vs. Ipi Ign	ns	.08
Plac vs. Epi Mis. Ign. or Inf	ns	ns

Tested by χ^2 comparison of the proportion of subjects in each condition initiating new acts.

TABLE 4 / Self-Report of Emotional State in the Anger Conditions

Condition	N	Self-Report Scales	Comparison	p
Epi Inf	22	1.91	Epi Inf vs. Epi Ign	.08
Epi Ign	23	1.39	Placebo vs. Epi Ign or Inf	ns
Placebo	23	1.63		

index may be considered a measure of behavioral euphoria. It should be noted that the same between-condition relationships hold for the two components of this index as for the index itself.

The column labeled "Mean number of acts initiated" presents the data on the extent to which the subject deviates from the stooge's routine and initiates euphoric activities of his own.

On both behavioral indices, we find precisely the same pattern of relationships as those obtained with self-reports. Epi Mis subjects behave somewhat more euphorically than do Epi Ign subjects who in turn behave more euphorically than do Epi Inf subjects. On all measures, then, there is consistent evidence that a subject will take over the stooge's euphoric mood to the extent that he has no other explanation of his bodily state.

Again it should be noted that on these behavioral indices, Epi Ign and Epi Mis subjects are somewhat more euphoric than placebo subjects but not significantly so.

Anger

Self-Report   Before presenting data for the anger conditions, one point must be made about the anger manipulation. In the situation devised, anger, if manifested, is most likely to be directed at the experimenter and his annoyingly personal questionnaire. As we subsequently discovered, this was rather unfortunate, for the subjects, who had volunteered for the experiment for extra points on their final exam, simply refused to endanger these points by publicly blowing up, admitting their irritation to the experimenter's face or spoiling the questionnaire. Though as the reader will see, the subjects were quite willing to manifest anger when they were alone with the

stooge, they hesitated to do so on material (self-ratings of mood and questionnaire) that the experimenter might see and only after the purposes of the experiment had been revealed were many of these subjects willing to admit to the experimenter that they had been irked or irritated.

This experimentally unfortunate situation pretty much forces us to rely on the behavioral indices derived from observation of the subject's presumably private interaction with the stooge. We do, however, present data on the self-report scales in Table 4. These figures are derived in the same way as the figures presented in Table 2 for the euphoria conditions, that is, the value checked on the irritation scale is subtracted from the value checked on the happiness scale. Though, for the reasons stated above, the absolute magnitude of these figures (all positive) is relatively meaningless, we can, of course, compare condition means within the set of anger conditions. With the happiness-irritation index employed, we should, of course, anticipate precisely the reverse results from those obtained in the euphoria conditions; that is, the Epi Inf subjects in the anger conditions should again be less susceptible to the stooge's mood and should, therefore, describe themselves as in a somewhat happier frame of mind than subjects in the Epi Ign condition. This is the case; the Epi Inf subjects average 1.91 on the self-report scales while the Epi Ign subjects average 1.39.

Evaluating the effects of the injections, we note again that, as anticipated, Epi Ign subjects are somewhat less happy than Placebo subjects but, once more, this is not a significant difference.

Behavior   The subject's responses to the stooge, during the period when both were filling out their questionnaires, were systematically coded to provide a behavioral index of anger. The coding scheme and the numerical values attached to each of the categories have been described in the methodology section. To arrive at an "Anger index" the numerical value assigned to a subject's responses to the stooge is summed together for the several units of stooge behavior. In the coding scheme used, a positive value to this index indicates that the subject agrees with the stooge's comment and is growing angry. A negative value indicates that the subject either disagrees with the stooge or ignores him.

The relevant data are presented in Table 5. For this analysis, the stooge's routine has been divided into two phases—the first

TABLE 5 / Behavioral Indications of Emotional State in the Anger Conditions

Condition	N	Neutral Units	Anger Units
Epi Inf	22	+0.07	−0.18
Epi Ign	23	+0.30	+2.28
Placebo	22[a]	−0.09	+0.79

Comparison for Anger Units	p
Epi Inf vs. Epi Ign	< .01
Epi Ign vs. Placebo	< .05
Placebo vs. Epi Inf	ns

[a]For one subject in this condition the sound system went dead and the observer could not, of course, code his reactions.

two units of his behavior (the "long" questionnaire and "What did I have for breakfast?") are considered essentially neutral revealing nothing of the stooge's mood; all of the following units are considered "angry" units for they begin with an irritated remark about the "bells" question and end with the stooge's fury as he rips up his questionnaire and stomps out of the room. For the neutral units, agreement or disagreement with the stooge's remarks is, of course, meaningless as an index of mood and we should anticipate no difference between conditions. As can be seen in Table 5, this is the case.

For the angry units, we must, of course, anticipate that subjects in the Epi Ign condition will be angrier than subjects in the Epi Inf condition. This is indeed the case. The Anger index for the Epi Ign condition is positive and large, indicating that these subjects have become angry, while in the Epi Inf condition the Anger index is slightly negative in value indicating that these subjects have failed to catch the stooge's mood at all. It seems clear that providing the subject with an appropriate explanation of his bodily state greatly reduces his tendency to interpret his state in terms of the cognitions provided by the stooge's angry behavior.

Finally, on this behavioral index, it can be seen that subjects in the Epi Ign condition are significantly angrier than subjects in the Placebo condition. Behaviorally, at least, the injection of epinephrine appears to have led subjects to an angrier state than comparable subjects who received placebo shots.

Conformation of Data to Theoretical Expectations

Now that the basic data of this study have been presented, let us examine closely the extent to which they conform to theoretical expectations. If our hypotheses are correct and if this experimental design provided a perfect test for these hypotheses, it should be anticipated that in the euphoria conditions the degree of experimentally produced euphoria should vary in the following fashion:

$$\text{Epi Mis} \geq \text{Epi Ign} > \text{Epi Inf} = \text{Placebo}$$

And in the anger conditions, anger should conform to the following pattern:

$$\text{Epi Ign} > \text{Epi Inf} = \text{Placebo}$$

In both sets of conditions, it is the case that emotional level in the Epi Mis and Epi Ign conditions is considerably greater than that achieved in the corresponding Epi Inf conditions. The results for the Placebo condition, however, are ambiguous for consistently the Placebo subjects fall between the Epi Ign and the Epi Inf subjects. This is a particularly troubling pattern for it makes it impossible to evaluate unequivocally the effects of the state of physiological arousal and indeed raises serious questions about our entire theoretical structure. Though the emotional level is consistently greater in the Epi Mis and Epi Ign conditions than in the Placebo condition, this difference is significant at acceptable probability levels only in the anger conditions.

In order to explore the problem further, let us examine the experimental factors identified earlier, which might have acted to restrain the emotional level in the Epi Ign and Epi Mis conditions. As was pointed out earlier, the ideal test of our first two hypotheses requires an experimental setup in which the subject has flatly no way of evaluating his state of physiological arousal other than by means of the experimentally provided cognitions. Had it been possible to physiologically produce a state of sympathetic activation by means other than injection, one could have approached this experimental ideal more closely than in the present setup. As it stands, however, there is always a reasonable alternative cognition available to the aroused subject—he feels the way he does because of the injection. To the extent that the subject seizes on such an explanation of his bodily state, we should expect that he will be uninfluenced by the stooge. Evidence presented in Table 6 for the anger condition and in Table 7 for the euphoria conditions indicates that this is, indeed, the case.

As mentioned earlier, some of the Epi Ign and Epi Mis subjects in their answers to the open-end questions clearly attributed their physical state to the injection, e.g., "the shot gave me the shivers." In Tables 6 and 7 such subjects are labeled "Self-informed." In Table 6 it can be seen that the self-informed subjects are considerably less angry than are the remaining subjects; indeed, they are not angry at all. With these self-informed subjects eliminated the difference between the Epi Ign and the Placebo conditions is significant at the .01 level of significance.

TABLE 6 / The Effects of Attributing Bodily State to the Injection on Anger in the Anger Epi Ign Condition

Condition	N	Index	Anger p
Self-informed subjects	3	−1.67	ns
Others	20	+2.88	ns
Self-informed vs. Others			.05

TABLE 7 / The Effects of Attributing Bodily State to the Injection on Euphoria in the Euphoria Epi Ign and Epi Mis Conditions

	Epi Ign		
	N	Activity Index	p
Self-informed subjects	8	11.63	ns
Others	17	21.14	ns
Self-informed vs. Others			.05

	Epi Mis		
	N	Activity Index	p
Self-informed subjects	5	12.40	ns
Others	20	25.10	ns
Self-informed vs. Others			.10

Precisely the same pattern is evident in Table 7 for the euphoria conditions. In both the Epi Mis and the Epi Ign conditions, the self-informed subjects have considerably lower activity indices than do the remaining subjects. Eliminating self-informed subjects, comparison of both of these conditions with the Placebo condition yields a difference significant at the .03 level of significance. It should be noted, too, that the self-informed subjects have much the same score on the activity index as do the experimental Epi Inf subjects (Table 3).

It would appear, then, that the experimental procedure of injecting the subjects, by providing an alternative cognition, has, to some extent, obscured the effects of epinephrine. When account is taken of this artifact, the evidence is good that the state of physiological arousal is a necessary component of an emotional experience for when self-informed subjects are removed, epinephrine subjects give consistent indications of greater emotionality than do placebo subjects.

Let us examine next the fact that consistently the emotional level, both reported and behavioral, in Placebo conditions is greater than that in the Epi Inf conditions. Theoretically, of course, it should be expected that the two conditions will be equally low, for by assuming that emotional state is a joint function of a state of physiological arousal and of the appropriateness of a cognition we are, in effect, assuming a multiplicative function, so that if either component is at zero, emotional level is at zero. As noted earlier this expectation should hold if we can be sure that there is no sympathetic activation in the Placebo conditions. This assumption, of course, is completely unrealistic for the injection of placebo does not prevent sympathetic activation. The experimental situations were fairly dramatic and certainly some of the placebo subjects gave indications of physiological arousal. If our general line of reasoning is correct, it should be anticipated that the emotional level of subjects who give indications of sympathetic activity will be greater than that of subjects who do not. The relevant evidence is presented in Tables 8 and 9.

TABLE 8 / Sympathetic Activation and Euphoria in the Euphoria Placebo Condition

Subjects Whose:	N	Activity Index	p
Pulse decreased	14	10.67	ns
Pulse increased or remained same	12	23.17	ns
Pulse decrease vs. pulse increase or same			.02

As an index of sympathetic activation we shall use the most direct and unequivocal measure available—change in pulse rate. It can be seen in Table 1 that the predominant pattern in the Placebo condition is a decrease in pulse rate. We shall assume, therefore, that those subjects whose pulse increases or remains the same give indications of sympathetic activity while those subjects whose pulse decreases do not. In Table 8, for the euphoria condition, it is immediately clear that subjects who give indications of sympathetic activity are considerably more euphoric than are subjects who show no sympathetic activity. This relationship is, of course, confounded by the fact that euphoric subjects are considerably more active than non-euphoric subjects—a factor which independent of mood could elevate pulse rate. However, no such factor operates in the anger condition where angry subjects are neither more active nor talkative than calm subjects. It can be seen in Table 9 that Placebo subjects who show signs of sympathetic activation give indications of considerably more anger than do subjects who show no such signs. Conforming to expectation, sympathetic activation accompanies an increase in emotional level.

It should be noted, too, that the emotional levels of subjects showing no signs of sympathetic activity are quite comparable to the emotional level of subjects in the parallel Epi Inf conditions (see Table 3 and 5). The similarity of these sets of scores and their uniformly low level of indicated emotionality would certainly make it appear that both factors are essential to an emotional state. When either the level of sympathetic arousal is low or a completely appropriate cognition is available, the level of emotionality is low.

TABLE 9 / Sympathetic Activation and Anger in Anger Placebo Condition

Subjects Whose:	N[a]	Activity Index	p
Pulse decreased	13	+0.15	ns
Pulse increased or remained same	8	+1.69	ns
Pulse decrease vs. pulse increase or same			.01

[a]*N* reduced by two cases owing to failure of sound system in one case and experimenter's failure to take pulse in another.

DISCUSSION

Let us summarize the major findings of this experiment and examine the extent to which they support the propositions offered in the introduction of this paper. It has been suggested, first, that given a state of physiological arousal for which an individual has no explanation, he will label this state in terms of the cognitions available to him. This implies, of course, that by manipulating the cognitions of an individual in such a state we can manipulate his feelings in diverse directions. Experimental results support this proposition for following the injection of epinephrine, those subjects who had no explanation for the bodily state thus produced, gave behavioral and self-report indications that they had been readily manipulable into the disparate feeling states of euphoria and anger.

From this first proposition, it must follow that given a state of physiological arousal for which the individual has a completely satisfactory explanation, he will not label this state in terms of the alternative cognitions available. Experimental evidence strongly supports this expectation. In those conditions in which subjects were injected with epinephrine and told precisely what they would feel and why, they proved relatively immune to any effects of the manipulated cognitions. In the anger condition, such subjects did not report or show anger; in the euphoria condition, such subjects reported themselves as far less happy than subjects with an identical bodily state but no adequate knowledge of why they felt the way they did.

Finally, it has been suggested that given constant cognitive circumstances, an individual will react emotionally only to the extent that he experiences a state of physiological arousal. Without taking account of experimental artifacts, the evidence in support of this proposition is consistent but tentative. When the effects of "self-informing" tendencies in epinephrine subjects and of "self-arousing" tendencies in placebo subjects are partialed out, the evidence strongly supports the proposition.

The pattern of data, then, falls neatly in line with theoretical expectations. However, the fact that we were forced, to some extent, to rely on internal analyses in order to partial out the effects of experimental artifacts inevitably makes our conclusions somewhat tentative. In order to further test these propositions on the interaction of cognitive and physiological determinants of emotional state, a series of additional experiments, published elsewhere, was designed to rule out or overcome the operation of these artifacts. In the first of these, Schachter and Wheeler (1962) extended the range of manipulated sympathetic activation by employing three experimental groups—epinephrine, placebo, and a group injected with the sympatholytic agent, chlorpromazine. Laughter at a slapstick movie was the dependent variable and the evidence is good that amusement is a direct function of manipulated sympathetic activation.

In order to make the epinephrine-placebo comparison under conditions which would rule out the operation of any self-informing tendency, two experiments were conducted on rats. In one of these Singer (1961) demonstrated that under fear inducing conditions, manipulated by the simultaneous presentation of a loud bell, a buzzer, and a bright flashing light, rats injected with epinephrine were considerably more frightened than rats injected with a placebo. Epinephrine-injected rats defecated, urinated, and trembled more than did placebo-injected rats. In nonfear control conditions, there were no differences between epinephrine and placebo groups, neither group giving any indication of fear. In another study, Latané and Schachter (1962) demonstrated that rats injected with epinephrine were notably more capable of avoidance learning than were rats injected with a placebo. Using a modified Miller-Mowrer shuttle-box, these investigators found that during an experimental period involving 200 massed trials, 15 rats injected with epinephrine avoided shock an average of 101.2 trials while 15 placebo-injected rats averaged only 37.3 avoidances.

Taken together, this body of studies does give strong support to the propositions which generated these experimental tests. Given a state of sympathetic activation, for which no immediately appropriate explanation is available, human subjects can be readily manipulated into states of euphoria, anger, and amusement. Varying the intensity of sympathetic activation serves to vary the intensity of a variety of emotional states in both rats and human subjects.

Let us examine the implications of these findings and of this line of thought for problems in the general area of the physiology of the emotions. We have noted in the introduction that the numerous studies on physiological differentiators of emotional states have, viewed en masse, yielded quite inconclusive results. Most, though not all, of these studies have indicated no differences among the various emotional states. Since as human beings, rather than as scientists, we have no difficulty identifying, labeling, and distinguishing among our feelings, the results of these studies have long seemed rather puzzling and paradoxical. Perhaps because of this, there has been a persistent tendency to discount such results as due to ignorance or methodological inadequacy and to pay far more attention to the very few studies which demonstrate *some* sort of physiological differences among emotional states than to the very many studies which indicate no differences at all. It is conceivable, however, that these results should be taken at face value and that emotional states may, indeed, be generally characterized by a high level of sympathetic activation with few if any physiological distinguishers among the many emotional states. If this is correct, the findings of the present study may help to resolve the problem. Obviously this study does *not* rule out the possibility of physiological differences among the emotional states. It is the case, however, that given precisely the same state of epinephrine-induced sympathetic activation, we have, by means of cognitive manipulations, been able to produce in our subjects the very disparate states of euphoria and anger. It may indeed be the case that cognitive factors are major determiners of the emotional labels we apply to a common state of sympathetic arousal.

Let us ask next whether our results are specific to the state of sympathetic activation or if they are generalizable to other states of physiological arousal. It is clear that from our experiments proper, it is impossible to answer the question for our studies have been concerned largely with the effects of an epinephrine created state of sympathetic arousal. We would suggest, however, that our conclusions are generalizable to almost any pronounced internal state for which no appropriate explanation is available. This suggestion receives some support from the experiences of Nowlis and Nowlis (1956) in their program of research on the effects of drugs on mood. In their work the Nowlises typically administer a drug to groups of four subjects who are physically in one another's presence and free to interact. The Nowlises describe some of their results with these groups as follows:

> *At first we used the same drug for all 4 men. In those sessions seconal, when compared with placebo, increased the checking of such words as expansive, forceful, courageous, daring, elated, and impulsive. In our first statistical analysis we were confronted with the stubborn fact that when the same drug is given to all 4 men in a group, the N that has to be entered into the analysis is 1, not 4. This increases the cost of an already expensive experiment by a considerable factor, but it cannot be denied that the effects of these drugs may be and often are quite contagious. Our first attempted solution was to run tests on groups in which each man had a different drug during the same session, such as 1 on seconal, 1 on benzedrine, 1 on dramamine, and 1 on placebo. What does seconal do? Cooped up with, say, the egotistical benzedrine partner, the withdrawn, indifferent dramamine partner, and the slightly bored lactose man, the seconal subject reports that he is distractible, dizzy, drifting, glum, defiant, languid, sluggish, discouraged, dull, gloomy, lazy, and slow! This is not the report of mood that we got when all 4 men were on seconal. It thus appears that the moods of the partners do definitely influence the effect of seconal. (p. 350)*

It is not completely clear from this description whether this "contagion" of mood is more marked in drug than in placebo groups, but should this be the case, these results would certainly support the suggestion that our findings are generalizable to internal states other than that produced by an injection of epinephrine.

Finally, let us consider the implications of our formulation and data for alternative conceptualizations of emotion. Perhaps the most popular current conception of emotion is in terms of "activation theory" in the sense employed by Lindsley (1951) and Woodworth and Schlosberg (1958). As we understand this theory, it suggests that emotional states should be considered as at one end of a continuum of activation which is defined in terms of degree of autonomic arousal and of electroencephalographic measures of activation. The results of the experiment described in this paper do, of course, suggest that such a formulation is not completely adequate. It is possible to have very high degrees of activation without a subject either appearing to be or describing himself as "emotional." Cognitive factors appear to be indispensable elements in any formulation of emotion.

SUMMARY

It is suggested that emotional states may be considered a function of a state of physiological arousal and of a cognition appropriate to this state of arousal. From this follows these propositions:

1. Given a state of physiological arousal for which an individual has no immediate explanation, he will label this state and describe his feelings in terms of the cognitions available to him. To the extent that cognitive factors are potent determiners of emotional states, it should be anticipated that precisely the same state of physiological arousal could be labeled "joy" or "fury" or "jealousy" or any of a great diversity of emotional labels depending on the cognitive aspects of the situation.
2. Given a state of physiological arousal for which an individual has a completely appropriate explanation, no evaluative needs will arise and the individual is unlikely to label his feelings in terms of the alternative cognitions available.
3. Given the same cognitive circumstances, the individual will react emotionally or describe his feelings as emotions only to the extent that he experiences a state of physiological arousal.

An experiment is described which, together with the results of other studies, supports these propositions.

REFERENCES

Ax, A. F. Physiological differentiation of emotional states. *Psychosom. Med.,* 1953, *15,* 435–442.

Cannon, W. B. *Bodily changes in pain, hunger, fear and rage.* (2nd ed.) New York: Appleton, 1929.

Cantril, H., & Hunt, W. A. Emotional effects produced by the injection of adrenalin. *Amer. J. Psychol.,* 1932, *44,* 300–307.

Festinger, L. A theory of social comparison processes. *Hum. Relat.,* 1954, *7,* 114–140.

Hunt, J. McV., Cole, M. W., & Reis, E. E. Situational cues distinguishing anger, fear, and sorrow. *Amer. J. Psychol.,* 1958, *71,* 136–151.

James, W. *The principles of psychology.* New York: Holt, 1890.

Landis, C., & Hunt, W. A. Adrenalin and emotion. *Psychol. Rev.,* 1932, *39,* 467–485.

Latané, B., & Schachter, S. Adrenalin and avoidance learning. *J. Comp. Physiol. Psychol.,* 1962, *65,* 369–372.

Lindsley, D. B. Emotion. In S. S. Stevens (Ed.), *Handbook of experimental psychology.* New York: Wiley, 1951. Pp. 473–516.

Marañon, G. Contribution à l'étude de l'action émotive de l'adrénaline. *Rev. Francaise Endocrinol.,* 1924, *2,* 301–325.

Nowlis, V., & Nowlis, H. H. The description and analysis of mood. *Ann. N. Y. Acad. Sci.,* 1956, *65,* 345–355.

Ruckmick, C. A. *The psychology of feeling and emotion.* New York: McGraw-Hill, 1936.

Schachter, J. Pain, fear, and anger in hypertensives and normotensives: A psychophysiologic study. *Psychosom. Med.,* 1957, *19,* 17–29.

Schachter, S. *The psychology of affiliation.* Stanford, CA: Stanford Univer. Press, 1959.

Schachter, S., & Wheeler, L. Epinephrine, chlorpromazine, and amusement. *J. Abnorm. Soc. Psychol.,* 1962, *65,* 121–128.

Singer, J. E. The effects of epinephrine, chlorpromazine and dibenzyline upon the fright responses of rats under stress and non-stress conditions. Unpublished doctoral dissertation, University of Minnesota, 1961.

Wolf, S., & Wolff, H. G. *Human gastric function.* New York: Oxford Univer. Press, 1947.

Woodworth, R. S., & Schlosberg, H. *Experimental psychology.* New York: Holt, 1958.

Wrightsman, L. S. Effects of waiting with others on changes in level of felt anxiety. *J. Abnorm. Soc. Psychol.,* 1960, *61,* 216–222.

ENDNOTES

1. This experiment is part of a program of research on cognitive and physiological determinants of emotional state which is being conducted at the Department of Social Psychology at Columbia University under PHS Research Grant M-2584 from the National Institute of Mental Health, United States Public Health Service. This experiment was conducted at the Laboratory for Research in Social Relations at the University of Minnesota.

The authors wish to thank Jean Carlin and Ruth Hase, the physicians in the study, and Bibb Latané and Leonard Weller who were the paid participants.

2. Though our experiments are concerned exclusively with the physiological changes produced by the injection of adrenalin, which appear to be primarily the result of sympathetic excitation, the term physiological arousal is used in preference to the more specific "excitation of the sympathetic nervous system" because there are indications, to be discussed later, that this formulation is applicable to a variety of bodily states.

3. Translated copies of Marañon's (1924) paper may be obtained by writing to the senior author.

4. This suggestion is not new for several psychologists have suggested that situational factors should be considered the chief differentiators of the emotions. Hunt, Cole, and Reis (1958) probably make this point most explicitly in their study distinguishing among fear, anger, and sorrow in terms of situational characteristics.

5. In his critique of the James-Lange theory of emotion, Cannon (1929) also makes the point that sympathectomized animals and patients do seem to manifest emotional behavior. This criticism is, of course, as applicable to the above proposition as it was to the James-Lange formulation. We shall discuss the issues involved in later papers.

6. It was, of course, imperative that the sequence with the stooge begin before the subject felt his first symptoms for otherwise the subject would be virtually forced to interpret his feelings in terms of events preceding the stooge's entrance. Pretests had indicated that, for most subjects, epinephrine-caused symptoms began within 3–5 minutes after injection. A deliberate attempt was made then to bring in the stooge within 1 minute after the subject's injection.

CRITICAL THINKING QUESTIONS

1. In order to conduct the experiment, the researchers deceived the subjects. What ethical issues are involved in this type of research? The obvious deception was not telling the subjects the true nature of the experiment. Does the use of injections of a drug that had a physiological impact on the subjects prompt additional ethical considerations? Explain your answer.

2. This study examines the effects of just one drug, epinephrine, which has excitatory effects on people. Would you expect a similar pattern of results for other classes of drugs? Why or why not? Which ones might be interesting to study?

3. What might the implications of this study be for people who use drugs in a social setting? Would the feelings that they associate with using drugs be due to how others around them responded? Explain your answer. How could you test this possibility?

4. Do you think it is possible to change the emotion you are experiencing by changing the label of the emotion? For example, if you were afraid of public speaking, could you change your emotion from a negative one (fear) to a positive one (excitement) by changing the label given to your physiological arousal? Have you had any personal experience with something like this that may have occurred or a situation when you were aware of how other people influenced how you interpreted the situation? Explain your answer.

ADDITIONAL RELATED READINGS

Carlo, G., Mestre, M. V., Samper, P., Tur, A., & Armenta, B. E. (2010). Feelings or cognitions? Moral cognitions and emotions as longitudinal predictors of prosocial and aggressive behaviors. *Personality and Individual Differences, 48*(8), 872–877.

Lazarus, R. S. (1984). On the primacy of cognition. *American Psychologist, 39,* 124–129.

Zajonc, R. B. (1984). On the primacy of affect. *American Psychologist, 39,* 117–123.

ARTICLE 9 _____

Social cognition, the topic of this chapter, deals with how people make sense of the world around them, as well as understanding themselves. How we make sense of all of this depends on a variety of factors, including the ways in which we tend to process information. Some of the ways that we tend to process information are subject to certain biases, some of which were discussed in Article 7 in this chapter. However, another important source of information that we use in making judgments about ourselves and the world around us is our memories. Our recollections of how someone treated us or some experience we've had not only help to shape our memories of those events but also influence how we understand ourselves and the world at present. For example, if you recalled that someone treated you very badly in the past it stands to reason that how you deal with them in the present may be influenced by that memory.

But how accurate are our memories of past events? Most of us take for granted that our memories are accurate recollections of those events, much like a photograph is a visual representation of a scene. Yet research shows that memories are dynamic, not static, things and undergo changes and distortions as time goes by. Nonetheless, even though we may intellectually acknowledge that our memories might not be "perfect" recollections of the past, we still might feel that they are fairly accurate recollections of those events.

Yet what if the memory you so clearly have is not accurate at all? In fact, that it is a totally false recollection that you nonetheless feel is true? If such *false memories* are possible, how might we acquire them? Over the past years, a good amount of media attention was given to people who had what was termed "recovered memories," that is, memories that had long been forgotten but somehow had been recovered, usually in the process of therapy. These recovered memories could be about anything, but often centered on some long-forgotten (or repressed) traumatic memory, such as concerning sexual abuse or physical abuse. Based on these recovered memories, individuals have been motivated to take the alleged wrongdoers to court to address the abuse.

But just because a memory is "recovered" in the process of therapy, does that mean that that memory is true? It may be, but then again it may have developed in response to "suggestion" on the part of the therapist. There has been a growing body of literature on false memories that has demonstrated that totally false memories can be suggested to participants, who in turn internalize these memories as true. A pioneer in the field, Elizabeth Loftus, has demonstrated that various memories of events that never happened, such as being lost in a shopping mall or hospitalized when as a child, can be incorporated by the individual as a real memory of the event.

The following article by Elke Geraerts, Daniel M. Bernstein, Harald Merckelbach, Christel Linders, Linsey Raymackers, and Elizabeth F. Loftus continues the exploration of the development of false beliefs. Additionally, this article also explores how these false beliefs may have behavioral consequences. In other words, not only is the event recalled as being true (even though it is not) but that supposed event also affects how people respond now and in the future to similar situations.

Lasting False Beliefs and Their Behavioral Consequences

■ Elke Geraerts, Daniel M. Bernstein, Harald Merckelbach, Christel Linders, Linsey Raymaekers, and Elizabeth F. Loftus

ABSTRACT

False beliefs and memories can affect people's attitudes, at least in the short term. But can they produce real changes in behavior? This study explored whether falsely suggesting to subjects that they had experienced a food-related event in their childhood would lead to a change in their behavior shortly after the suggestion and up to 4 months later. We falsely suggested to 180 subjects that, as children, they had gotten ill after eating egg salad. Results showed that, after this manipulation, *a significant minority of subjects came to believe they had experienced this childhood event even though they had initially denied having experienced it. This newfound autobiographical belief was accompanied by the intent to avoid egg salad, and also by significantly reduced consumption of egg-salad sandwiches, both immediately and 4 months after the false suggestion. The false suggestion of a childhood event can lead to persistent false beliefs that have lasting behavioral consequences.*

Geraerts, E.; Bernstein, D.M; Merckelbach, H; Linders, C; Raymackers, L; & Loftus E.F. *Psychological Science*, 19:8, pp. 749–753.
Copyright © 2008 by the Association for Psychological Science. Reprinted by permission of SAGE Publications.

Laboratory research has demonstrated that human memory can be remarkably fragile and even inventive. Studies on false memories and beliefs, for example, have compellingly shown that misleading information can lead to the creation of recollections of entire events that have not occurred (Loftus, 2005). In one of the first studies on this issue, subjects were led to believe that when they were children, they had been lost in the shopping mall for an extended period of time before being reunited with their parents (Loftus & Pickrell, 1995). In subsequent work, subjects falsely remembered even more unusual or upsetting events, such as spilling a punch bowl at a wedding (Hyman, Husband, & Billings, 1995), having a ride in a hot-air balloon (Wade, Garry, Read, & Lindsay, 2002), or even having been hospitalized as a child (Raymaekers, 2005).

Salient real-life examples of misremembering the past are cases in which people have falsely recovered memories of childhood sexual abuse, often instigated by suggestive therapeutic techniques (Geraerts et al., 2007; Loftus & Davis, 2006). People also claim to have recovered memories of more inconceivable experiences, including memories involving satanicritual abuse (Scott, 2001), previous lives (Peters, Horselenberg, Jelicic, & Merckelbach, 2007), and abduction by space aliens (Clancy, 2005), and such memories are often recovered during suggestive therapy as well. Even though such memories may not be real, they sometimes cause emotional pain similar to that of people who have experienced a traumatic event (McNally et al., 2004). This can have behavioral consequences, such as suing the alleged perpetrator after recovering memories of childhood abuse.

Strikingly, although a clear link between beliefs and behavior has been found repeatedly (Ajzen, 2005), laboratory research, until now, has not examined the possible effects of false memories on behavior. Can false beliefs be sufficiently strong to alter behavior? If one develops false memories in the laboratory, might they have an influence on one's short- and long-term attitudes and actions? Recently, Bernstein, Laney, Morris, and Loftus (2005a, 2005b) took the first steps toward answering this question by developing a procedure for examining the effects of false childhood memories and beliefs. Their subjects received the false suggestion that they had become ill after eating a certain food (e.g., hard-boiled eggs, strawberry ice cream) when they were children. The false suggestion increased subjects' confidence that the critical event had occurred. Moreover, the false belief resulted in decreased self-reported preference for the target food and increased anticipated behavioral avoidance of that food.

These findings clearly demonstrate that false beliefs can influence attitudes. A remaining question, though, is whether false beliefs or memories produce real changes in behavior. The current study explored whether falsely suggesting to subjects that they had experienced a food-related event in their childhood would lead to a quantifiable change in their behavior. Moreover, we examined whether lasting false beliefs can have long-term consequences with respect to particular eating habits.

We falsely suggested to subjects that, as children, they had become ill after eating egg salad. We then examined whether this suggestion increased their confidence that this event had occurred and whether they avoided the target food, in both the short and the long term (i.e., after 4 months).

METHOD

Subjects

The subjects were 180 first-year undergraduates (135 women, 45 men; average age = 20.99, SD = 2.76) at Maastricht University in The Netherlands. Subjects were all screened to ensure that they did not have eating disorders. We randomly assigned subjects to one of two groups: Subjects in the egg-salad group (n = 120) received the false suggestion that they had gotten sick after eating egg salad as a child. The remaining 60 subjects were in the control group and did not receive this false suggestion. All instructions were given in Dutch.

Materials and Procedure

Subjects initially signed up for a study called "Food and Personality." After 4 months, they were recontacted by a different experimenter, who asked them to enroll in an allegedly separate study.

During the first session, subjects completed a 24-item food-history inventory (Bernstein et al., 2005b) containing the critical event, "got sick after eating egg salad." They rated whether or not each event on this inventory happened to them before their 10th birthday, using a scale ranging from 1 (*definitely did not happen*) to 8 (*definitely did happen*). Subjects also completed a questionnaire about their food preferences, rating how much they liked to eat 62 different foods, including egg salad. Finally, subjects imagined being at a party with a variety of foods and beverages available and indicated their likelihood of consuming each of 20 options, including the critical item, egg salad.

During the second session, which occurred exactly 1 week later, subjects received false feedback about their responses to the questionnaires that they had completed during the first session. We falsely told subjects that we had entered their responses into a computer that had then generated a profile of their early childhood experiences with certain foods. We told subjects that, as young children, they disliked Brussels sprouts, enjoyed eating pizza, and felt happy when a classmate brought sweets to school. Additionally, subjects in the egg-salad group were told, "You got sick after eating egg salad." To ensure that subjects in this group thought about this feedback, we told them that the computer randomly selected one feedback item for them to elaborate on, and that the item was egg salad (for a detailed description of the materials and procedure, see Bernstein et al., 2005a). Control subjects responded to a filler item.

After this elaboration phase, subjects again completed the food-history inventory, food-preferences questionnaire, and party-behavior questionnaire. Responses on these questionnaires were used to determine whether there were changes in (a) subjects' confidence that the critical event had happened in their childhood and (b) their avoidance of the critical item. Subjects also completed a memory-belief form with questions pertaining to three events from the food-history inventory, including the critical item. They were asked to indicate whether they had a specific belief or memory of each of these events from before age 10. If they had a specific memory of an event, they wrote "M" and gave as many details as possible, and if they believed the event happened but had no specific memory of it, they wrote "B" and explained why they believed the event happened. If they were positive that the event did not happen, they wrote "P" and explained why they were so sure that the event did not happen.

Finally, subjects were taken in small groups to another room, where they received a bogus debriefing. In the beginning of this 15-min period, subjects were told that the researchers wanted to thank them for their participation by providing a treat, and a catering company brought in drinks and sandwiches with five different fillings: egg salad (critical item), tuna salad, chicken salad, cheese, and ham. While the alleged debriefing was given, the experimenter, who did not know the group to which each subject had been assigned, recorded what type of sandwiches the subjects chose.

After 4 months, another experimenter recontacted the subjects to recruit them for an allegedly separate study at another laboratory at Maastricht University. In total, 153 (85%) subjects agreed to participate. They were told that this study (in reality, the third session) involved a taste test designed to examine people's preferences for certain types of food. The procedure of this taste test was adapted from the methods of Herman and Polivy (1980).

Subjects were asked to evaluate five different types of fruit-flavored water (lime, raspberry, tropical punch, apple, and tangerine) and five types of sandwiches (ham, cheese, chicken salad, tuna salad, and egg salad), using 8-point scales to rate them for appearance, smell, flavor, and food preference. While preserving quantity, we ensured that the sandwiches had a different appearance than in the second session so as not to remind subjects of that session. Next, subjects were instructed to complete three (filler) questionnaires. They were also told that the residual food would be thrown away, and that they should feel free to consume as much as they wanted. After 15 min, the food was removed. Subjects then again completed the food-history inventory, food-preferences questionnaire, party-behavior questionnaire, and memory-belief form. We changed the layout of all these questionnaires so as to disguise the link with the previous sessions.

After completing the questionnaires, subjects were asked what they thought the purpose of the new study was and whether they thought the third session was a study separate from the first two sessions. Only 5 subjects (1 in the egg-salad group, 4 in the control group) reported that the study was about memory, and no subjects reported that the study was about false memories.[1] Thus, the contributions of social desirability to the results were minimized.[2] All subjects thought the sessions were unrelated. Finally, subjects were debriefed about the entire research project. They were also asked whether we could verify with their parents if they might have truly gotten sick from eating egg salad as a child.

RESULTS

Subjects were considered to have arguably true memories (a) if they both scored above the midpoint for the critical item on the food-history inventory during the first session and reported a belief or memory for the critical egg-salad event or (b) if their parents confirmed that they had gotten sick after eating egg salad as a child. Five subjects met these criteria[3] and were excluded from analyses. After these subjects were excluded, the remaining sample consisted of 117 subjects in the experimental group and 58 subjects in the control group. Next, in the egg-salad group, we identified subjects who were believers ($n = 41$) and nonbelievers ($n = 58$; see Morris, Laney, Bernstein, & Loftus, 2006). Subjects were considered believers if they met two criteria: Their confidence that the critical event happened had to increase after they received the false feedback, and they had to report a memory or belief related to the critical event on the memory-belief form (3 believers, 7%, reported a memory, rather than a belief). Nonbelievers were subjects whose confidence that the critical egg-salad event had happened remained the same or decreased after they received the false feedback. Of the 153 subjects who returned to the lab for the third session, 35 were believers, 54 were nonbelievers, and 50 were control subjects.

Confidence and Preference

Results for the attitudinal measures replicated previous findings (e.g., Bernstein et al., 2005a): Although responses to the food-history inventory showed no group differences in subjects' initial confidence that the critical egg-salad event had happened, responses in both the second and the third sessions, after subjects in the egg-salad group had received the false feedback, indicated that believers were significantly more confident that they had gotten sick from eating egg salad than nonbelievers and control subjects were, all ts > 11.73, all ps < .001 (see Figure 1a). Between the first and second sessions, believers' confidence that they had experienced this event increased an average of 3.29 points on the 8-point scale, $t(40) = 11.95$, $p < .001$, $d = 2.32$.

Also, in both sessions after the false feedback, believers reported significantly less preference for egg salad on the food-preferences and party-behavior questionnaires than did nonbelievers and

FIGURE 1A / Subjects' mean confidence that they had gotten ill after eating egg salad as a child, as a function of session. Session 1 was before the false suggestion, Session 2 was 1 week later, and Session 3 was 4 months later. Results are shown separately for subjects who believed the false suggestion, subjects who did not believe the false suggestion, and control subjects (who were not exposed to the false suggestion). Error bars represent standard errors of the means.

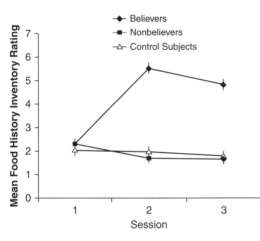

FIGURE 2A / Mean number of egg-salad sandwiches consumed by believers, nonbelievers, and control subjects in the second and third sessions. Error bars represent standard errors of the means.

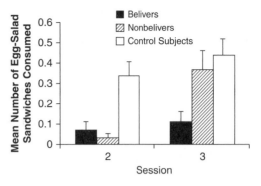

control subjects. Finally, during the taste testing in the third session, believers gave the egg-salad sandwiches lower ratings for appearance and flavor than did nonbelievers and control subjects.[4]

EATING BEHAVIOR

The critical findings concerned whether the false suggestion affected actual eating behavior. In fact, the groups differed in the number of egg-salad sandwiches eaten in the second session, $F(2, 154) = 12.45$, $p < .001$, $\eta^2 = .14$, and in the third session, $F(2, 136) = 3.55$, $p = .031$, $\eta^2 = .05$. Specifically, in the second session, believers and nonbelievers both ate fewer egg-salad sandwiches than did control subjects, $t(97) = 3.10$, $p = .003$, $d = 0.63$, and $t(114) = 4.32$, $p < .001$, $d = 0.81$, respectively, but the numbers of egg-salad sandwiches eaten by believers and nonbelievers did not differ significantly ($t < 1$). In the third session, believers ate fewer egg-salad sandwiches than did both nonbelievers, $t(87) = 2.08$, $p = .041$, $d = 0.44$, and control subjects, $t(83) = 3.02$, $p = .003$, $d = 0.66$ (see Figure 2a). In both sessions, the three groups did not differ in their consumption of the other types of sandwiches, all Fs < 1.38, ps > .25.

DISCUSSION

This study shows that falsely suggesting that a person experienced a childhood event can change that person's behavior considerably, in both the short and the longer term. We falsely

suggested to subjects that, as children, they had become ill after eating egg salad. After this manipulation, a significant minority of our subjects came to believe they had experienced this event. More important, this newfound autobiographical belief was accompanied by significantly reduced consumption of egg-salad sandwiches, both immediately and 4 months after the false suggestion.

Our findings show that, at least in the short term, simply having received the false feedback deterred both believers and nonbelievers from actually eating egg salad. Thus, they exhibited a *contagion effect* (Rozin & Fallon, 1987). That is, all subjects who received the false feedback must have been reminded of what it must feel like to become ill after eating egg salad. This finding also indicates that suggestions about the past may have more persistent effects on behavior than on self-reports, at least in the short term. Such a dissociation between behavior and self-reports is a well-known phenomenon in social psychology (Greenwald et al., 2002).

However, in the third session, we found a significant difference between believers and nonbelievers in their consumption of egg-salad sandwiches. That is, the false feedback that was given 4 months earlier did not seem to have had a lasting effect on nonbelievers, who ate more egg-salad sandwiches than believers did at this session. It is possible that believers had been contemplating the egg-salad event and had consequently created memories about having gotten ill after eating egg salad as a child.

Of course, we cannot prove the falseness of the reports subjects provided. One could definitely claim that the manipulation triggered true memories rather than creating false ones. However, because we sought corroboration from subjects' parents, we can be fairly certain that the subjects whose data we analyzed did not experience the critical event when they were children.

Our findings demonstrate that it is possible, in at least a significant minority of adult subjects, to induce lasting false beliefs that have consequences not only for attitudes, but also for behavior (see also Scoboria, Mazzoni, & Jarry, 2008). Scholars should consider this when conducting research on false beliefs, because some subjects might experience adverse outcomes from an experimentally induced false belief. These findings also have important implications for people's food and dieting choices. That is, possibly people could learn to avoid certain foods, and thus have healthier eating habits, by believing that they had negative childhood experiences with unhealthy foods. With overweight and obesity having reached epidemic levels around the world (Ogden et al., 2006), the influence of false beliefs on eating behavior seems an essential topic for future work, which should explore whether the consequences of actually having gotten sick after eating a food are similar to the consequences of having a false belief that one has experienced this event. Also, it would be interesting to investigate whether certain individual differences (e.g., suggestibility) may mediate or explain the effects on short- and long-term behavior that we found in this study. In any case, this study clearly demonstrates that false suggestions about childhood events can profoundly change people's attitudes and behavior.

ACKNOWLEDGMENTS

Elke Geraerts was supported by a grant from the Netherlands Organization for Scientific Research (NWO 451 07 004).

REFERENCES

Ajzen, I. (2005). *Attitudes, personality, and behavior* (2nd ed.). Milton-Keynes, England: Open University Press/McGraw-Hill.

Bernstein, D.M., Laney, C., Morris, E.K., & Loftus, E.F. (2005a). False beliefs about fattening foods can have healthy consequences. *Proceedings of the National Academy of Sciences, USA, 102,* 13724–13731.

Bernstein, D.M., Laney, C., Morris, E.K., & Loftus, E.F. (2005b). False memories about food can lead to food avoidance. *Social Cognition, 23,* 11–34.

Clancy, S.A. (2005). *Abducted: How people come to believe they were kidnapped by aliens.* Cambridge, MA: Harvard University Press.

Geraerts, E., Schooler, J., Merckelbach, H., Jelicic, M., Hauer, B.J.A., & Ambadar, Z. (2007). The reality of recovered memories: Corroborating continuous and discontinuous memories of childhood sexual abuse. *Psychological Science, 18,* 564–568.

Greenwald, A.G., Banaji, M.R., Rudman, L.A., Farnham, S.D., Nosek, B.A., & Mellott, D.S. (2002). A unified theory of implicit attitudes, stereotypes, self-esteem, and self-concept. *Psychological Review, 109,* 3–25.

Herman, C.P., & Polivy, J. (1980). Experimental and clinical aspects of restrained eating. In A. Stunkard (Ed.), *Obesity: Basic mechanisms and treatment* (pp. 208–225). Philadelphia: W.B. Saunders.

Hyman, I.E., Husband, T.H., & Billings, F.J. (1995). False memories of childhood experiences. *Applied Cognitive Psychology, 9,* 181–195.

Laney, C., Bowman Fowler, N., Nelson, K.J., Bernstein, D.M., & Loftus, E.F. (in press). The persistence of false beliefs. *Acta Psychologica.*

Loftus, E.F. (2005). Planting misinformation in the human mind: A 30-year investigation of the malleability of memory. *Learning and Memory, 12,* 361–366.

Loftus, E.F., & Davis, D. (2006). Recovered memories. *Annual Review of Clinical Psychology, 2,* 469–498.

Loftus, E.F., & Pickrell, J.E. (1995). The formation of false memories. *Psychiatric Annals, 25,* 720–725.

McNally, R.J., Lasko, N.B., Clancy, S.A., Macklin, M.L., Pitman, R.K., & Orr, S.P. (2004). Psychophysiological responding during script-driven imagery in people reporting abduction by space aliens. *Psychological Science, 15,* 493–497.

Morris, E.K., Laney, C., Bernstein, D.M., & Loftus, E.F. (2006). Susceptibility to memory distortion: How do we decide it has occurred? *American Journal of Psychology, 119,* 255–276.

Ogden, C.L., Carroll, M.D., Curtin, L.R., McDowell, M.A., Tabak, C.J., & Flegal, K.M. (2006). Prevalence of overweight and obesity in the United States, 1999–2004. *Journal of the American Medical Association, 295,* 1549–1555.

Peters, M.J.V., Horselenberg, R., Jelicic, M., & Merckelbach, H. (2007). The false fame illusion in people with memories about a previous life. *Consciousness and Cognition, 16,* 162–169.

Raymaekers, L. (2005). *Using doctored photographs to study false memories for neutral/positive and negative events.* Unpublished bachelor's thesis, Maastricht University, Maastricht, The Netherlands.

Rozin, P., & Fallon, A.E. (1987). A perspective on disgust. *Psychological Review, 94,* 23–41.

Scoboria, A., Mazzoni, G., & Jarry, J.L. (2008). Suggesting childhood food illness results in reduced eating behavior. *Acta Psychologica, 128,* 304–309.

Scott, S. (2001). *The politics and experience of ritual abuse: Beyond disbelief.* Buckingham, England: Open University Press.

Wade, K., Garry, M., Read, J.D., & Lindsay, D.S. (2002). A picture is worth a thousand lies: Using false photographs to create false childhood memories. *Psychonomic Bulletin & Review, 9,* 597–603.

ENDNOTES

[1] Excluding these subjects from analyses did not change the results. Note that no subjects had yet completed courses on memory or false memory.

[2] Previous findings showed that social desirability could not account for significant variance in effects of false beliefs on attitudes (e.g., Laney, Bowman Fowler, Nelson, Bernstein, & Loftus, in press).

[3] The egg-salad memories of all 5 subjects who met the first criterion were also confirmed by their parents.

[4] Complete reports of the analyses are available from the first author.

CRITICAL THINKING QUESTIONS

1. As the study reported, a "significant minority" of subjects came to believe the event that did not actually happen to them. Speculate on the possible reasons why only some subjects were incorporated this false memory. Explain your reasoning.
2. The article suggests that there may be some possible implications of the findings of this study for real-world food and dieting choices. Design a procedure that might lead to food preference changes based on the development of false memories. Are there any ethical issues that such a procedure might entail? Explain.
3. According to the article, " . . . some subjects might experience adverse outcomes from an experimentally induced false belief." Research other articles that have created false beliefs. What false memories did they create? What possible adverse outcomes might the creation of those false beliefs entail? Would the types of debriefing of the subjects minimize or eliminate negative outcomes? Explain.
4. People differ in their levels of suggestibility, which in turn may have an impact on whether false beliefs are internalized as true beliefs. Why do you think that some people are more suggestible than others? Is there any way that suggestibility can be increased or decreased? Explain your answer.

CHAPTER INTEGRATION QUESTIONS

1. What do you see as a common theme or themes across all of the articles in this chapter?
2. Mark Twain said, "My life has been filled with terrible misfortunes—most of which never happened. Life does not consist mainly—or even largely—of facts and happenings. It consists mainly of the storm of thoughts that is forever blowing through one's head." What does this quotation mean to you? Do you agree or disagree with it? Defend your answer.
3. Relate the quotation from Twain to the overall theme or themes that you identified for this chapter in Question 1.

Chapter Four

ATTITUDES

T HE STUDY OF attitudes is considered by many social psychologists to be the core issue in understanding human behavior. The way we act in any given situation is the product of the attitudes that we have formed, which in turn are based on the experiences we have had.

Whether or not we believe that attitudes constitute the core of social psychology, the study of attitudes and attitude change has been prominent in social psychological research from the beginning. Part of this interest has been theoretically driven. How attitudes are formed and how they can be changed, as well as what factors make some attitudes so resistant to change, are but a few of the topics that theorists have studied. However, there is also a more pragmatic, applied reason for this interest in attitudes: Principles of attitude change and attitude measurement have a direct bearing on several major industries and even psychotherapy. For example, survey organizations and advertising agencies focus on attitudes, measuring what they are, how they change over time, as well as how best to change them. Likewise, a major goal of both therapy and health promotion might be viewed as modifying people's dysfunctional or health-endangering attitudes and behaviors. Theoretical research has often provided the foundation for the principles applied by clinicians, health professionals, and advertisers.

The readings in this chapter relate to various aspects of attitudes and attitude change. Article 10, "Changing Behaviors by Degrees," relates an extremely serious issue—global warming and other environmental changes— to some of the social psychological knowledge on how attitudes—and behaviors—are effectively changed. Moreover, the article also addresses some behavioral change strategies that actually not only don't work but in fact could produce behavior changes in an undesired direction.

Article 11, "Cognitive Consequences of Forced Compliance," is a classic demonstration of a powerful theoretical model in social psychology known as *cognitive dissonance*. It is an excellent example of how commonsense predictions are often exactly opposite of what actually occurs.

Finally, Article 12, "The Origins of Cognitive Dissonance: Evidence from Children and Monkeys," is a contemporary article that elaborates on an aspect of cognitive dissonance presented in Chapter 11. Article 12 investigates the intriguing possibility that cognitive dissonance processes do not just occur in higher cognitively functioning creatures (i.e., adult humans) but in fact may occur in children and even in monkeys as well.

ARTICLE 10 _____

Obviously, attitudes are formed in a great variety of ways. Some are the result of direct experience. For instance, we meet someone from a certain country and, based on that limited experience, form an attitude (or stereotype) about people from that country. In other words, we generalize our experience to form an attitude. In many other cases, however, we do not experience the person, situation, or event directly but rather indirectly. These so-called *secondhand attitudes* are the result of information we received from someone else, such as our parents or friends. In fact, this kind of information is a major source of our beliefs.

Typically, attitudes are comprised of three components. First, there is a *cognitive* or *belief* component, which is what we believe is or should be true. Second, there is an *affective* or *emotional* component, where we not only believe something to be true, but we also feel very strongly about it. Finally, an attitude may also include a *behavior tendency*: We strongly tend to avoid doing things that violate our belief and affective components.

Based on an accumulating body of evidence from a variety of fields, there is a growing awareness that human activities result in significant, and potentially catastrophic, changes in the climate. The overwhelming scientific consensus is that if we continue doing what we have been doing, then we might wreak havoc on the world in which we live. But many of these experts also believe that even if we can't totally undo the damage already done, we can at least mitigate our negative impact on the environment.

How people respond to this growing environmental crisis is influenced by their attitudes, which, as mentioned earlier, have belief, emotional, and behavioral components. That is, the way people respond to the environment is determined by their beliefs about various environmental issues, how emotionally invested they are in those issues, and ultimately how they behave toward the environment. Psychology has accumulated a great amount of knowledge about how attitudes and behaviors are effectively changed. The following article by Michael Price discusses how some of these psychological principles might be employed to change people's awareness of and behavior toward their environment.

Changing Behaviors by Degrees

■ Michael Price

With the polar ice caps melting at alarming rates, temperatures rising worldwide and tropical storms becoming more violent, all signs point to global peril. Yet Earth's fate may depend on the globe atop your shoulders.

Psychologists are becoming increasingly aware of their role in curbing the devastating effects of global warming, and the best solution to climate change is behavior change, they say.

"With any problem of society that involves human behavior, such as global climate change, psychologists have a role to play in that," says APA President Alan E. Kazdin, PhD, of Yale University. Kazdin argues that if global warming is indeed due to human influence—as most scientists think—then changing human behavior is the most important step toward correcting the problem. "And that's wildly right in the middle of psychology," he says.

Kazdin chose to make Psychology's Contributions to the Grand Challenges of Society one of his priorities during his term as president. Effecting positive change in people's attitudes toward the natural world is a large part of this priority, he says.

And it's also an opportunity for psychologists to showcase tangible effects of their skills, he adds.

"Let's show the public we can make a real contribution," Kazdin says. "We have the knowledge—there's no question about that—but we need to show we can get some things done."

SPREADING THE WORD

For starters, that means convincing people to reduce their energy consumption.

The American Geophysical Union, a scientific society composed of more than 50,000 earth scientists, teachers and students, issued a statement in January emphasizing that climate change is intimately tied to human energy use, and that successfully reducing our energy usage will depend upon the willingness of scientists, industries, governments and the public to work together.

According to the U.S. Environmental Protection Agency and the Department of Energy, if every household in the country replaced a single normal light bulb with an energy-efficient compact fluorescent light bulb, it would reduce greenhouse gas emissions by an amount equivalent to that produced by 800,000 cars.

But convincing large numbers of people to act in concert is not easy. For one thing, there's a lot of confusion and misinformation out there, says Christie Manning, PhD, a visiting cognitive psychology professor at Macalester College in St. Paul, Minn., who also contributes to a Web site, www.teachgreenpsych.com, dedicated to helping instructors incorporate conservation topics in the classroom.

"People actually aren't aware of the extent to which their actions are contributing to environmental problems," she says. For example, people don't realize that eating a meat-heavy diet contributes more to climate change than not recycling, says Manning. And while recycling is well and good, she says, a more effective way to help the environment would be to eat less meat—a message that isn't as firmly entrenched in the public consciousness.

Responsibility for getting the word out about effective environmental solutions doesn't fall exclusively to psychologists, but they can and should do their part, says Britain Scott, PhD, a psychologist at the University of St. Thomas in St. Paul. Scott, who founded www.teachgreenpsych.com, advises academic psychologists to teach their students about the importance of sustainability.

"We have the opportunity—and the responsibility—to educate tomorrow's conservation scientists, policymakers and grassroots activists about the fundamental connections between human behavior and the environmental crisis," she says. Scott's St. Thomas colleague Elise Amel, PhD, encourages psychologists to hold seminars for the public and for teachers in other disciplines to help them bring conservation into their classrooms, too.

Manning urges psychologists to reach out to their communities by helping local "green" organizations to fine tune their messages.

PEER PRESSURE

But even when people do have all the right information, they still don't often act on it. "Information by itself is not enough," says Robert Cialdini, PhD.

"You have to motivate people to use it."

Cialdini, an Arizona State University psychology professor who studies the science of persuasion, is putting his research to work for the planet. One of the most effective motivators he's found is a positive version of the classic adage "If everyone jumped off a bridge, would you?" By manipulating what people perceive as social norms, Cialdini says, you can achieve remarkable behavioral changes.

In a 2007 study, for example, Cialdini experimented with the wording on door-hanger notices encouraging people to conserve energy. One notice urged residents to think about their effect on the environment. Another informed them how much money they could save by using fans instead of their air conditioning. A third implored them to consider future gener-

ations. The fourth and final notice told residents that most of their neighbors actively conserved energy. Cialdini and his team distributed these door hangers randomly, then waited to see what, if any, the effects on energy conservation would be.

The first three notices—the appeals to the environment, money and future generations—all fell flat, achieving essentially no energy conservation. The final one, though, made a big difference. On average, those households dropped their energy usage by nearly two kilowatt-hours per day—a 10 percent reduction in daily power usage.

The study results reinforce mounting evidence for the theory that people, as social beings, rely far more on social cues than informational ones.

"There's an evolutionary explanation for it," Cialdini says. "The most primitive way we've developed to make decisions is to watch what other people in similar situations are doing."

These subtle cues can, of course, swing both ways. Well-intentioned environmental messages can have negative effects if they hype the idea that many people are contributing to the problem, he says. A public service announcement that proclaims, "So many people today are littering that the aluminum cans lying on our streets would stretch to the moon and back" would do more harm than good because it normalizes littering, Cialdini says. Instead, psychologists should make litterers feel as if they're in the minority, he advises.

Cialdini is publishing these findings not just in psychology journals, but in hotel-management publications, consumer research journals and popular-magazines—for anyone who will listen, basically.

OVERCOMING OBSTACLES

Psychologists can also address shortcomings where the potential for positive change exists but people, for whatever reason, are hesitant to embrace that potential. Raymond Nickerson, PhD, offers e-mail as an example of an environmental promise yet to deliver. Nickerson, a psychologist at Tufts University whose 2003 book "Psychology and Environmental Change" discusses these topics, says that despite the Internet Age's ability to reduce our paper consumption, people are still using just as much paper as ever—and possibly even more, according to some studies.

"This so-called 'paperless society' we've heard about hasn't really worked out," Nickerson says. "Ironically, it may have done the opposite. People prefer to read things on paper as opposed to a computer screen, and e-mail and the Internet have made it easier to just print it off."

Psychologists are investigating whether this is just a generational thing—Nickerson suspects younger people who've grown up reading on the computer might be less averse to electronic displays—or if the displays themselves are the problem.

This disconnect between innovation and environmental intention illustrates an important point: You can't predict exactly how people are going to use new technologies, Nickerson says. Just because an industry produces an environmentally friendly product doesn't mean that it will be used that way.

"If the technology gives you the promise but no one wants to use it, that's a tough obstacle," Nickerson says. "That's a psychological issue."

Like Cialdini, Nickerson believes psychologists play a big part in understanding why people might be averse to positive behaviors and that they can help cobble together strategies to make those behaviors more palatable.

Of course, psychologists can't do it alone. They, like the rest of the world, rely largely on the research of climate scientists, oceanographers, geologists and other physical scientists whose job it is to assess what behaviors are causing damage, and the risks associated with them. But Cialdini considers psychologists to be the arbiters of this information, charged with turning that research into action when it hits the public.

"We know how to most powerfully craft and transmit a message," he says. "We can be a lever for change."

A PIVOTAL MOMENT

These changes need to come quickly, though. Global warming is not something scientists can debate anymore, says psychologist Rep. Brian Baird, PhD (D-Wash.), who in January traveled to Antarctica, the Great Barrier Reef and an Australian rainforest to witness firsthand the effects of climate change. One disconcerting sight, Baird reports, was seeing the devastation to the expansive coral reefs off the northeast Australian coast. In response to rising ocean temperatures and increased ocean acidification, the reefs are losing the unicellular algae that they rely upon for photosynthesis. There's about a 50 percent probability that all of the world's coral reefs could die within 50 years, Baird says.

He likens the immobile coral's predicament to our own: The reef can't get up and move to a new climate, and we can't move off this planet. We have to live in the environment around us.

So if we're not going anywhere, we need to work to make here a better place. Changing public policy is one way to get people to be more environmentally conscientious, says Baird, who chairs the U.S. House of Representatives Subcommittee on Research and Science Education. Industry regulations and financial motivation will eventually have to reflect a greener outlook on production if we expect any lasting changes. But adjusting policy takes time and is largely dependent on the ebb and flow of politics—not really an option when catastrophic consequences loom low on the horizon.

To that end, the field of ecopsychology promotes a less egocentric mode of thinking in favor of a more eco-centric one. By encouraging humans to rethink their position in the natural world, some psychologists believe they can influence people to be more responsible stewards of nature.

"Attitudes toward nature are very important," Nickerson says.

For instance, hikers and snowmobilers both use mountains recreationally, but hiking is generally less damaging to the ecosystem, he says. A hobby like hiking, ecopsychologists say, fosters a positive, self-inclusive attitude toward nature that reflects in other behaviors, as well. It's one more tool psychologists can use to promote environmental responsibility.

Baird recognizes that behavioral and attitudinal change is ultimately what's going to make or break the planet, and that's where psychologists need to step up their game.

"If psychologists just spend their time talking to each other about esoteric topics," says Baird, "they'll have no impact whatsoever. But if they realize they need to be active in their own communities, go to town hall meetings, craft a strategy and become activists, then they can make a difference."

Kazdin agrees, saying APA can serve as a sort of clearinghouse for pro-environmental psychological approaches. Members can talk with staff of APA's directorates and devise a plan for how their individual talents map onto the overarching goals of conservation and sustainability. Kazdin believes APA's depth of experience and diversity makes it a natural choice for coordinating joint research projects between different fields and then disseminating information.

"By mobilizing our own group and bringing in diverse people, we can provide a science-based technology for effecting change," he says.

CRITICAL THINKING QUESTIONS

1. According to the article, "By encouraging humans to rethink their position in the natural world, some psychologists believe they can influence people to be more responsible stewards of nature." Using information from this article as well as other thoughts you may have, how might this be effectively accomplished?
2. Identify one behavior on campus that relates to an environmental-impact issue. Design a procedure for trying to change that behavior in a more environmentally conscious way. Be sure to discuss *why* your methods might be likely to succeed.
3. The article identifies several examples of approaches to changing attitudes toward the environment that might not only be ineffective but may actually result in a change in the undesired direction. What are they? Can you find any examples from the media or from your own personal experiences that might be ineffective attempts at attitude and/or behavior change?
4. Discuss two beliefs or behaviors regarding the environment that have changed over the course of your lifetime. When and why did each of these beliefs or behaviors change? Is there any particular reason each changed when it did rather than, say, 50 years before? Explain your answers.

ARTICLE 11 _____

Suppose someone asked you to publicly say something that contradicted your privately held beliefs and then offered you either a small reward (say, $1) or a large reward ($20) for doing so. Under which of those conditions would you be most likely to actually change your privately held belief to bring it more into the realm of what you just said? If you guessed that would be most likely to happen in the $20 condition, you would have guessed wrong.

A major theory in social psychology is known as *cognitive dissonance.* Briefly stated, this theory says that people feel a tension when they are aware of an inconsistency either between two attitudes or between an attitude and a behavior. Moreover, the theory asserts that such tension produces some type of change to reduce the state of dissonance. The resulting outcome is often counterintuitive to what common sense would predict. The exact conditions under which cognitive dissonance operates and how it is reduced have been investigated in many experiments over the years.

The following article by Leon Festinger and James M. Carlsmith is *the* classic study on dissonance theory. The hypothesis being tested is a simple yet powerful and nonobvious one. Aside from the outcomes, of particular interest is the elaborate design of the experiment. While reading the article, put yourself in the shoes of the subjects and try to imagine how their thinking might account for the obtained results.

Cognitive Consequences of Forced Compliance

■ Leon Festinger and James M. Carlsmith

What happens to a person's private opinion if he is forced to do or say something contrary to that opinion? Only recently has there been any experimental work related to this question. Two studies reported by Janis and King (1954; 1956) clearly showed that, at least under some conditions, the private opinion changes so as to bring it into closer correspondence with the overt behavior the person was forced to perform. Specifically, they showed that if a person is forced to improvise a speech supporting a point of view with which he disagrees, his private opinion moves toward the position advocated in the speech. The observed opinion change is greater than for persons who only hear the speech or for persons who read a prepared speech with emphasis solely on elocution and manner of delivery. The authors of these two studies explain their results mainly in terms of mental rehearsal and thinking up new arguments. In this way, they propose, the person who is forced to improvise a speech convinces himself. They present some evidence, which is not altogether conclusive, in support of this explanation. We will have more to say concerning this explanation in discussing the results of our experiment.

Kelman (1953) tried to pursue the matter further. He reasoned that if the person is induced to make an overt statement contrary to his private opinion by the offer of some reward, then the greater the reward offered, the greater should be the subsequent opinion change. His data, however, did not support this idea. He found, rather, that a large reward produced less subsequent opinion change than did a smaller reward. Actually, this finding by Kelman is consistent with the theory we

will outline below but, for a number of reasons, is not conclusive. One of the major weaknesses of the data is that not all subjects in the experiment made an overt statement contrary to their private opinion in order to obtain the offered reward. What is more, as one might expect, the percentage of subjects who complied increased as the size of the offered reward increased. Thus, with self-selection of who did and who did not make the required overt statement and with varying percentages of subjects in the different conditions who did make the required statement, no interpretation of the data can be unequivocal.

Recently, Festinger (1957) proposed a theory concerning cognitive dissonance from which come a number of derivations about opinion change following forced compliance. Since these derivations are stated in detail by Festinger (1957, Ch. 4), we will here give only a brief outline of the reasoning.

Let us consider a person who privately holds opinion "X" but has, as a result of pressure brought to bear on him, publicly stated that he believes "not X."

1. This person has two cognitions which, psychologically, do not fit together: one of these is the knowledge that he believes "X," the other the knowledge that he has publicly stated that he believes "not X." If no factors other than his private opinion are considered, it would follow, at least in our culture, that if he believes "X" he would publicly state "X." Hence, his cognition of his private belief is dissonant with his cognition concerning his actual public statement.

Cognitive consequences of forced compliance. Festinger, L., & Carlsmith, J. M. *Journal of Abnormal Psychology*, (1959), 58, 203–210.

2. Similarly, the knowledge that he has said "not X" is consonant with (does fit together with) those cognitive elements corresponding to the reasons, pressures, promises of rewards and/or threats of punishment which induced him to say "not X."

3. In evaluating the total magnitude of dissonance, one must take account of both dissonances and consonances. Let us think of the sum of all the dissonances involving some particular cognition as "D" and the sum of all the consonances as "C." Then we might think of the total magnitude of dissonance as being a function of "D" divided by "D" plus "C."

Let us then see what can be said about the total magnitude of dissonance in a person created by the knowledge that he said "not X" and really believes "X." With everything else held constant, this total magnitude of dissonance would decrease as the number and importance of the pressures which induced him to say "not X" increased. Thus, if the overt behavior was brought about by, say, offers of reward or threats of punishment, the magnitude of dissonance is maximal if these promised rewards or threatened punishments were just barely sufficient to induce the person to say "not X." From this point on, as the promised rewards or threatened punishment become larger, the magnitude of dissonance becomes smaller.

4. One way in which the dissonance can be reduced is for the person to change his private opinion so as to bring it into correspondence with what he has said. One would consequently expect to observe such opinion change after a person has been forced or induced to say something contrary to his private opinion. Furthermore, since the pressure to reduce dissonance will be a function of the magnitude of the dissonance, the observed opinion change should be greatest when the pressure used to elicit the overt behavior is just sufficient to do it.

The present experiment was designed to test this derivation under controlled, laboratory conditions. In the experiment we varied the amount of reward used to force persons to make a statement contrary to their private views. The prediction [from 3 and 4 above] is that the larger the reward given to the subject, the smaller will be the subsequent opinion change.

PROCEDURE

Seventy-one male students in the introductory psychology course at Stanford University were used in the experiment. In this course, students are required to spend a certain number of hours as subjects (Ss) in experiments. They choose among the available experiments by signing their names on a sheet posted on the bulletin board which states the nature of the experiment. The present experiment was listed as a two-hour experiment dealing with "Measures of Performance."

During the first week of the course, when the requirement of serving in experiments was announced and explained to the students, the instructor also told them about a study that the psychology department was conducting. He explained that, since they were required to serve in experiments, the department was conducting a study to evaluate these experiments in order to be able to improve them in the future. They were told that a sample of students would be interviewed after having served as Ss. They were urged to cooperate in these interviews by being completely frank and honest. The importance of this announcement will become clear shortly. It enabled us to measure the opinions of our Ss in a context not directly connected with our experiment and in which we could reasonably expect frank and honest expressions of opinion.

When the S arrived for the experiment on "Measures of Performance" he had to wait for a few minutes in the secretary's office. The experimenter (E) then came in, introduced himself to the S and, together, they walked into the laboratory room where the E said:

This experiment usually takes a little over an hour but, of course, we had to schedule it for two hours. Since we have that extra time, the introductory psychology people asked if they could interview some of our subjects. [Offhand and conversationally.] Did they announce that in class? I gather that they're interviewing some people who have been in experiments. I don't know much about it. Anyhow, they may want to interview you when you're through here.

With no further introduction or explanation the S was shown the first task, which involved putting 12 spools onto a tray, emptying the tray, refilling it with spools, and so on. He was told to use one hand and to work at his own speed. He did this for one-half hour. The E then removed the tray and spools and placed in front of the S a board containing 48 square pegs. His task was to turn each peg a quarter turn clockwise, then another quarter turn, and so on. He was told again to use one hand and to work at his own speed. The S worked at this task for another half hour.

While the S was working on these tasks, the E sat, with a stop watch in his hand, busily making notations on a sheet of paper. He did so in order to make it convincing that this was what the E was interested in and that these tasks, and how the S worked on them, was the total experiment. From our point of view the experiment had hardly started. The hour which the S spent working on the repetitive, monotonous tasks was intended to provide, for each S uniformly, an experience about which he would have a somewhat negative opinion.

After the half hour on the second task was over, the E conspicuously set the stop watch back to zero, put it away, pushed his chair back, lit a cigarette, and said:

O.K. Well, that's all we have in the experiment itself. I'd like to explain what this has been all about so you'll have some idea of why you were doing this. [E pauses.] Well, the way the experiment is set up is this. There are actually two groups in the experiment. In one, the group you were in, we bring the subject in and give him essentially no introduction to the experiment. That is, all we tell him is what he needs to know in order to do the tasks, and he has no idea of what the experiment is all about, or what it's going to be like, or anything like that. But in the other group, we have a student that we've hired that works for us regularly, and what I do is take him into the next room where the subject is waiting—the same room you were waiting in before—and I introduce him as if he had just finished being a subject in the experiment. That is, I say: "This is so-and-so, who's just finished the experiment and I've asked him to tell you a little of what it's about before you start." The fellow who works for us then, in conversation with the next subject, makes these points: [The E then produced a sheet headed "For Group B" which had written on it: It was very enjoyable, I had a lot of fun, I enjoyed myself, it was very interesting, it was intriguing, it was exciting. The E showed this to the S and then proceeded with his false explanation of the purpose of the experiment.] Now, of course, we have this student do this, because if the experimenter does it, it doesn't look as realistic, and what we're interested in doing is comparing how these two groups do on the experiment—the one with this previous expectation about the experiment, and the other, like yourself, with essentially none.

Up to this point the procedure was identical for *S*s in all conditions. From this point on they diverged somewhat. Three conditions were run, Control, One Dollar, and Twenty Dollars, as follows:

Control Condition

The *E* continued:

Is that fairly clear? [Pause.] Look, that fellow [looks at watch] I was telling you about from the introductory psychology class said he would get here a couple of minutes from now. Would you mind waiting to see if he wants to talk to you? Fine. Why don't we go into the other room to wait? [The E left the S in the secretary's office for four minutes. He then returned and said:] O.K. Let's check and see if he does want to talk to you.

One and Twenty Dollar Conditions

The *E* continued:

Is that fairly clear how it is set up and what we're trying to do? [Pause.] Now, I also have a sort of strange thing to ask you. The thing is this. [Long pause, some confusion and uncertainty in the following, with a degree of embarrassment on the part of the E. The manner of the E contrasted strongly with the preceding unhesitant and assured false explanation of the experiment. The point was to make it seem to the S that this was the first time the E had done this and that he felt unsure of himself.] The

fellow who normally does this for us couldn't do it today—he just phoned in, and something or other came up for him—so we've been looking around for someone that we could hire to do it for us. You see, we've got another subject waiting [looks at watch] who is supposed to be in that other condition. Now Professor _____, who is in charge of this experiment, suggested that perhaps we could take a chance on your doing it for us. I'll tell you what we had in mind: the thing is, if you could do it for us now, then of course you would know how to do it, and if something like this should ever come up again, that is, the regular fellow couldn't make it, and we had a subject scheduled, it would be very reassuring to us to know that we had somebody else we could call on who knew how to do it. So, if you would be willing to do this for us, we'd like to hire you to do it now and then be on call in the future, if something like this should ever happen again. We can pay you a dollar (twenty dollars) for doing this for us, that is, for doing it now and then being on call. Do you think you could do that for us?

If the *S* hesitated, the *E* said things like, "It will only take a few minutes," "The regular person is pretty reliable; this is the first time he has missed," or "If we needed you we could phone you a day or two in advance; if you couldn't make it, of course, we wouldn't expect you to come." After the *S* agreed to do it, the *E* gave him the previously mentioned sheet of paper headed "For Group B" and asked him to read it through again. The *E* then paid the *S* one dollar (twenty dollars), made out a hand-written receipt form, and asked the *S* to sign it. He then said:

O.K., the way we'll do it is this. As I said, the next subject should be here by now. I think the next one is a girl. I'll take you into the next room and introduce you to her, saying that you've just finished the experiment and that we've asked you to tell her a little about it. And what we want you to do is just sit down and get into a conversation with her and try to get across the points on that sheet of paper. I'll leave you alone and come back after a couple of minutes. O.K.?

The *E* then took the *S* into the secretary's office where he had previously waited and where the next *S* was waiting. (The secretary had left the office.) He introduced the girl and the *S* to one another saying that the *S* had just finished the experiment and would tell her something about it. He then left saying he would return in a couple of minutes. The girl, an undergraduate hired for this role, said little until the *S* made some positive remarks about the experiment and then said that she was surprised because a friend of hers had taken the experiment the week before and had told her that it was boring and that she ought to try to get out of it. Most *S*s responded by saying something like "Oh, no, it's really very interesting. I'm sure you'll enjoy it." The girl listened quietly after this, accepting and agreeing to everything the *S* told her.

The discussion between the *S* and the girl was recorded on a hidden tape recorder.

After two minutes the *E* returned, asked the girl to go into the experimental room, thanked the *S* for talking to the girl, wrote down his phone number to continue the fiction that we might call on him again in the future and then said: "Look, could we check and see if that fellow from introductory psychology wants to talk to you?"

From this point on, the procedure for all three conditions was once more identical. As the *E* and the *S* started to walk to the office where the interviewer was, the *E* said: "Thanks very much for working on those tasks for us. I hope you did enjoy it. Most of our subjects tell us afterward that they found it quite interesting. You get a chance to see how you react to the tasks and so forth." This short persuasive communication was made in all conditions in exactly the same way. The reason for doing it, theoretically, was to make it easier for anyone who wanted to persuade himself that the tasks had been, indeed, enjoyable.

When they arrived at the interviewer's office, the *E* asked the interviewer whether or not he wanted to talk to the *S*. The interviewer said yes, the *E* shook hands with the *S*, said good-bye, and left. The interviewer, of course, was always kept in complete ignorance of which condition the *S* was in. The interview consisted of four questions, on each of which the *S* was first encouraged to talk about the matter and was then asked to rate his opinion or reaction on an 11-point scale. The questions are as follows:

1. Were the tasks interesting and enjoyable? In what way? In what way were they not? Would you rate how you feel about them on a scale from −5 to +5 where −5 means they were extremely dull and boring, +5 means they were extremely interesting and enjoyable, and zero means they were neutral, neither interesting nor uninteresting.

2. Did the experiment give you an opportunity to learn about your own ability to perform these tasks? In what way? In what way not? Would you rate how you feel about this on a scale from 0 to 10 where 0 means you learned nothing and 10 means you learned a great deal.

3. From what you know about the experiment and the tasks involved in it, would you say the experiment was measuring anything important? That is, do you think the results may have scientific value? In what way? In what way not? Would you rate your opinion on this matter on a scale from 0 to 10 where 0 means the results have no scientific value or importance and 10 means they have a great deal of value and importance.

4. Would you have any desire to participate in another similar experiment? Why? Why not? Would you rate your desire to participate in a similar experiment again on a scale from −5 to +5, where −5 means you would definitely dislike to participate, +5 means you would definitely like to participate, and 0 means you have no particular feeling about it one way or the other.

As may be seen, the questions varied in how directly relevant they were to what the *S* had told the girl. This point will be discussed further in connection with the results.

At the close of the interview the *S* was asked what he thought the experiment was about and, following this, was asked directly whether or not he was suspicious of anything and, if so, what he was suspicious of. When the interview was over, the interviewer brought the *S* back to the experimental room where the *E* was waiting together with the girl who had posed as the waiting *S*. (In the control condition, of course, the girl was not there.) The true purpose of the experiment was then explained to the *S* in detail, and the reasons for each of the various steps in the experiment were explained carefully in relation to the true purpose. All experimental *S*s in both One Dollar and Twenty Dollar conditions were asked, after this explanation, to return the money they had been given. All *S*s, without exception, were quite willing to return the money.

The data from 11 of the 71 *S*s in the experiment had to be discarded for the following reasons:

1. Five *S*s (three in the One Dollar and two in the Twenty Dollar condition) indicated in the interview that they were suspicious about having been paid to tell the girl the experiment was fun and suspected that that was the real purpose of the experiment.
2. Two *S*s (both in the One Dollar condition) told the girl that they had been hired, that the experiment was really boring but they were supposed to say it was fun.
3. Three *S*s (one in the One Dollar and two in the Twenty Dollar condition) refused to take the money and refused to be hired.
4. One *S* (in the One Dollar condition), immediately after having talked to the girl, demanded her phone number saying he would call her and explain things, and also told the *E* he wanted to wait until she was finished so he could tell her about it.

These 11 *S*s were, of course, run through the total experiment anyhow and the experiment was explained to them afterwards. Their data, however, are not included in the analysis.

Summary of Design

There remain, for analysis, 20 *S*s in each of the three conditions. Let us review these briefly: 1. *Control condition.* These *S*s were treated identically in all respects to the *S*s in the experimental conditions, except that they were never asked to, and never did, tell the waiting girl that the experimental tasks were enjoyable and lots of fun. 2. *One Dollar condition.* These *S*s were hired for one dollar to tell a waiting *S* that tasks, which were really rather dull and boring, were interesting, enjoyable, and lots of fun. 3. *Twenty Dollar condition.* These *S*s were hired for twenty dollars to do the same thing.

RESULTS

The major results of the experiment are summarized in Table 1 which lists, separately for each of the three experimental conditions, the average rating which the *S*s gave at the end of each question on the interview. We will discuss each of the questions on the interview separately, because they were intended to measure different things. One other point before we proceed to examine the data. In all the comparisons, the Control condition should be regarded as a baseline from which to evaluate the results in the other two conditions. The Control condition gives us, essentially, the reactions of *S*s to the tasks and their opinions about the experiment as falsely explained to them, without the experimental introduction of dissonance. The data from the other conditions may be viewed, in a sense, as changes from this baseline.

How Enjoyable the Tasks Were

The average ratings on this question, presented in the first row of figures in Table 1, are the results most important to the experiment. These results are the ones most directly relevant to the specific dissonance which was experimentally created. It will be recalled that the tasks were purposely arranged to be rather boring and monotonous. And, indeed, in the Control condition the average rating was −.45, somewhat on the negative side of the neutral point.

In the other two conditions, however, the *S*s told someone that these tasks were interesting and enjoyable. The resulting dissonance could, of course, most directly be reduced by persuading themselves that the tasks were, indeed, interesting and enjoyable. In the One Dollar condition, since the magnitude of dissonance was high, the pressure to reduce this

TABLE 1 / Average Ratings on Interview Questions for Each Condition

Question on Interview	Experimental Condition		
	Control (N = 20)	One Dollar (N = 20)	Twenty Dollars (N = 20)
How enjoyable tasks were (rated from −5 to +5)	−.45	+1.35	−.05
How much they learned (rated from 0 to 10)	3.08	2.80	3.15
Scientific importance (rated from 0 to 10)	5.60	6.45	5.18
Participate in similar exp. (rated from −5 to +5)	−.62	+1.20	−.25

dissonance would also be high. In this condition, the average rating was +1.35, considerably on the positive side and significantly different from the Control condition at the .02 level[1] (*t* = 2.48).

In the Twenty Dollar condition, where less dissonance was created experimentally because of the greater importance of the consonant relations, there is correspondingly less evidence of dissonance reduction. The average rating in this condition is only −.05, slightly and not significantly higher than the Control condition. The difference between the One Dollar and Twenty Dollar conditions is significant at the .03 level (*t* = 2.22). In short, when an *S* was induced, by offer of reward, to say something contrary to his private opinion, this private opinion tended to change so as to correspond more closely with what he had said. The greater the reward offered (beyond what was necessary to elicit the behavior) the smaller was the effect.

Desire to Participate in a Similar Experiment

The results from this question are shown in the last row of Table 1. This question is less directly related to the dissonance that was experimentally created for the *S*s. Certainly, the more interesting and enjoyable they felt the tasks were, the greater would be their desire to participate in a similar experiment. But other factors would enter also. Hence, one would expect the results on this question to be very similar to the results on "how enjoyable the tasks were" but weaker. Actually, the results, as may be seen in the table, are in exactly the same direction, and the magnitude of the mean differences is fully as large as on the first question. The variability is greater, however, and the differences do not yield high levels of statistical significance. The difference between the One Dollar condition (+1.20) and the Control condition (−.62) is significant at the .08 level (*t* = 1.78). The difference between the One Dollar condition and the Twenty Dollar condition (−.25) reaches only the .15 level of significance (*t* = 1.46).

The Scientific Importance of the Experiment

This question was included because there was a chance that differences might emerge. There are, after all, other ways in which the experimentally created dissonance could be reduced. For example, one way would be for the *S* to magnify for himself the value of the reward he obtained. This, however, was unlikely in this experiment because money was used for the reward and it is undoubtedly difficult to convince oneself that one dollar is more than it really is. There is another possible way, however. The *S*s were given a very good reason, in addition to being paid, for saying what they did to the waiting girl. The *S*s were told it was necessary for the experiment. The dissonance could, consequently, be reduced by magnifying the importance of this cognition. The more scientifically important they considered the experiment to be, the less was the total magnitude of dissonance. It is possible, then, that the results on this question, shown in the third row of figures in Table 1, might reflect dissonance reduction.

The results are weakly in line with what one would expect if the dissonance were somewhat reduced in this manner. The One Dollar condition is higher than the other two. The difference between the One and Twenty Dollar conditions reaches the .08 level of significance on a two-tailed test ($t = 1.79$). The difference between the One Dollar and Control conditions is not impressive at all ($t = 1.21$). The result that the Twenty Dollar condition is actually lower than the Control condition is undoubtedly a matter of chance ($t = 0.58$).

How Much They Learned from the Experiment

The results on this question are shown in the second row of figures in Table 1. The question was included because, as far as we could see, it had nothing to do with the dissonance that was experimentally created and could not be used for dissonance reduction. One would then expect no differences at all among the three conditions. We felt it was important to show that the effect was not a completely general one but was specific to the content of the dissonance which was created. As can be readily seen in Table 1, there are only negligible differences among conditions. The highest t value for any of these differences is only 0.48.

DISCUSSION OF A POSSIBLE ALTERNATIVE EXPLANATION

We mentioned in the introduction that Janis and King (1954; 1956) in explaining their findings, proposed an explanation in terms of the self-convincing effect of mental rehearsal and thinking up new arguments by the person who had to improvise a speech. Kelman (1953), in the previously mentioned study, in attempting to explain the unexpected finding that the persons who complied in the moderate reward condition changed their opinion more than in the high reward condition, also proposed the same kind of explanation. If the results of our experiment are to be taken as strong corroboration of the theory of cognitive dissonance, this possible alternative explanation must be dealt with.

Specifically, as applied to our results, this alternative explanation would maintain that perhaps, for some reason, the Ss in the One Dollar condition worked harder at telling the waiting girl that the tasks were fun and enjoyable. That is, in the One Dollar condition they may have rehearsed it more mentally, thought up more ways of saying it, may have said it more convincingly, and so on. Why this might have been the case is, of course, not immediately apparent. One might expect

that, in the Twenty Dollar condition, having been paid more, they would try to do a better job of it than in the One Dollar condition. But nevertheless, the possibility exists that the Ss in the One Dollar condition may have improvised more.

Because of the desirability of investigating this possible alternative explanation, we recorded on a tape recorder the conversation between each S and the girl. These recordings were transcribed and then rated, by two independent raters, on five dimensions. The ratings were, of course done in ignorance of which condition each S was in. The reliabilities of these ratings, that is, the correlations between the two independent raters, ranged from .61 to .88, with an average reliability of .71. The five ratings were:

1. The content of what the S said *before* the girl made the remark that her friend told her it was boring. The stronger the S's positive statements about the tasks, and the more ways in which he said they were interesting and enjoyable, the higher the rating.
2. The content of what the S said *after* the girl made the above-mentioned remark. This was rated in the same way as for the content before the remark.
3. A similar rating of the overall content of what the S said.
4. A rating of how persuasive and convincing the S was in what he said and the way in which he said it.
5. A rating of the amount of time in the discussion that the S spent discussing the tasks as opposed to going off into irrelevant things.

The mean ratings for the One Dollar and Twenty Dollar conditions, averaging the ratings of the two independent raters, are presented in Table 2. It is clear from examining the table that, in all cases, the Twenty Dollar condition is slightly higher. The differences are small, however, and only on the

TABLE 2 / Average Ratings of Discussion between Subject and Girl

Dimensions Rated	Condition		
	One Dollar	Twenty Dollars	Value of t
Content before remark by girl (rated from 0 to 5)	2.26	2.62	1.08
Content after remark by girl (rated from 0 to 5)	1.63	1.75	0.11
Over-all content (rated from 0 to 5)	1.89	2.19	1.08
Persuasiveness and conviction (rated from 0 to 10)	4.79	5.50	0.99
Time spent on topic (rated from 0 to 10)	6.74	8.19	1.80

rating of "amount of time" does the difference between the two conditions even approach significance. We are certainly justified in concluding that the *S*s in the One Dollar condition did not improvise more nor act more convincingly. Hence, the alternative explanation discussed above cannot account for the findings.

SUMMARY

Recently, Festinger (1957) has proposed a theory concerning cognitive dissonance. Two derivations from this theory are tested here. These are:

1. If a person is induced to do or say something which is contrary to his private opinion, there will be a tendency for him to change his opinion so as to bring it into correspondence with what he has done or said.
2. The larger the pressure used to elicit the overt behavior (beyond the minimum needed to elicit it) the weaker will be the above-mentioned tendency.

A laboratory experiment was designed to test these derivations. Subjects were subjected to a boring experience and then paid to tell someone that the experience had been interesting and enjoyable. The amount of money paid the subject was varied. The private opinions of the subjects concerning the experiences were then determined.

The results strongly corroborate the theory that was tested.

REFERENCES

Festinger, L. *A theory of cognitive dissonance.* Evanston, Ill.: Row Peterson, 1957.

Janis, I. L., & King, B. T. The influence of role-playing on opinion change. *Journal of Abnormal and Social Psychology,* 1954, *49,* 211–218.

Kelman, H. Attitude change as a function of response restriction. *Human Relations,* 1953, *6,* 185–214.

King, B. T., & Janis, I. L. Comparison of the effectiveness of improvised versus non-improvised role-playing in producing opinion changes. *Human Relations,* 1956, *9,* 177–186.

ENDNOTE

1. All statistical tests referred to in this paper are two-tailed.

CRITICAL THINKING QUESTIONS

1. Using the concept of dissonance theory, select an attitude or belief that you might want to change and design a procedure that could be effective in producing change in the desired direction.
2. This study was cited in Article 2 as an example of some of the ethical issues in social psychological research. What do you see as the ethical issues present in this experiment? Do you see any alternative to deception in this type of study? Why or why not?
3. Based on personal experience, have you ever suspected that cognitive dissonance was operating in some change that came about in your own attitudes? Elaborate on how that may have occurred.
4. Festinger and Carlsmith discuss a possible alternative explanation for the obtained results. What is your position on this alternative explanation? Discuss any other possible explanations for the findings of the study.
5. Might cognitive dissonance be operating in many real-life situations? For example, consider the initiation process (known as *hazing*) used in some social groups, such as fraternities, or the procedures used in the military as part of basic training. How might cognitive dissonance be operating in these or other situations to account for the outcomes of the experience?

ADDITIONAL RELATED READINGS

Chen, M. K., & Risen, J. L. (2010). How choice affects and reflects preferences: Revisiting the free-choice paradigm. *Journal of Personality and Social Psychology,* 99(4), 573–594.

Heitland, K., & Bohner, G. (2010). Reducing prejudice via cognitive dissonance: Individual differences in preference for consistency moderate the effects of counter-attitudinal advocacy. *Social Influence,* 5(3), 164–181.

ARTICLE 12 _____

In the years since publication of Festinger and Carlsmith's classic study (Article 11), many experiments have been conducted to test dissonance theory and to elaborate on the conditions necessary for its operation. As it turns out, there are many different causes of dissonance. For example, dissonance may be aroused when an individual puts a great deal of effort into a given activity, as though he or she needs to justify expending so much effort to obtain a certain goal. This is sort of a "suffering leads to liking" effect. Dissonance will also likely be aroused when an individual has the freedom to choose whether to do (or not do) something. There is little reason to experience dissonance when you are forced to do something. You know why you did it: Someone *made* you do it. Finally, issues such as self-esteem may influence the arousal (and subsequent reduction) of cognitive dissonance. People with high levels of self-esteem may actually be *more* likely to engage in dissonance reduction than those with low levels of self-esteem when they see their behavior as inconsistent with their beliefs.

The central premise of cognitive dissonance theory is that people are motivated to avoid or reduce any tension produced by a perceived inconsistency between two attitudes or between an attitude and a behavior. So, what would happen when someone encounters a persuasive argument that is contrary to his or her own privately held beliefs? Dissonance theory suggests that this person will be motivated to reduce the internal tension generated by that perceived inconsistency, which can be accomplished in several ways. For example, he or she simply might not pay attention to the opposing viewpoint, distort the message to make it more consistent with his or her own beliefs, or avoid the message altogether.

But why does cognitive dissonance exist in the first place? Is it a mental process that we learn as we mature and a reflection of our increasing complex cognitive abilities? Or is it something fundamentally more basic that occurs earlier in life? In fact, is it possible that even some nonhuman primates are capable of engaging in cognitive dissonance reduction processes? The following article by Louisa C. Egan, Laurie R. Santos, and Paul Bloom addresses this issue of the origins of cognitive dissonance and whether such processes may be found not only in children but also in monkeys. The developmental and evolutionary implications of their findings are interesting.

The Origins of Cognitive Dissonance
Evidence from Children and Monkeys
■ Louisa C. Egan, Laurie R. Santos, and Paul Bloom

ABSTRACT

In a study exploring the origins of cognitive dissonance, preschoolers and capuchins were given a choice between two equally preferred alternatives (two different stickers and two differently colored M&M's®, respectively). On the basis of previous research with adults, this choice was thought to cause dissonance because it conflicted with subjects' belief that the two options were equally valuable. We therefore expected subjects to change their attitude toward the unchosen alternative, deeming it less valuable. We then presented subjects with a choice between the unchosen option and an option that was originally as attractive as both options in the first choice. Both groups preferred the novel over the unchosen option in this experimental condition, but not in a control condition in which they did not take part in the first decision. These results provide the first evidence of decision rationalization in children and nonhuman primates. They suggest that the mechanisms underlying cognitive-dissonance reduction in human adults may have originated both developmentally and evolutionarily earlier than previously thought.

Cognitive dissonance is one of the most heavily studied phenomena in the history of psychology. The term *cognitive dissonance* describes a psychological state in which an individual's cognitions—beliefs, attitudes, and behaviors—are at odds (Festinger, 1957). People experience cognitive dissonance as aversive (Elliot & Devine, 1994), and are motivated to resolve the inconsistency between their discrepant cognitions. Psychologists have long been interested in the nature of cognitive dissonance, as this phenomenon has implications for many areas

Egan, L.C.; Santos, L.R.; & Bloom, P. (2007). *Psychological Science*, 18(11), 978–983. Copyright © 2007 by Association for Psychological Science. Reprinted by Permission of SAGE Publications.

of psychology, including attitudes and prejudice (e.g., Leippe & Eisenstadt, 1994), moral cognition (e.g., Tsang, 2002), decision making (e.g., Akerlof & Dickens, 1982), happiness (e.g., Lyubomirsky & Ross, 1999), and therapy (Axsom, 1989).

Unfortunately, despite long-standing interest in cognitive dissonance, there is still little understanding of its origins—both developmentally over the life course and evolutionarily as the product of human phylogenetic history. Does cognitive-dissonance reduction begin to take hold only after much experience with the aversive consequences of dissonant cognitions, or does it begin earlier in development? Similarly, are humans unique in their drive to avoid dissonant cognitions, or is this process older evolutionarily, perhaps shared with nonhuman primate species?

To date, little research has investigated whether children or nonhuman primates experience and strive to reduce dissonance. In one welcome exception in the developmental literature, Aronson and Carlsmith (1963) found that 4-year-old children who obeyed an experimenter's mild warning not to play with an attractive toy later liked the toy less than did children who had obeyed an experimenter's severe warning not to play with the toy. Aronson and Carlsmith interpreted this result in terms of cognitive dissonance: Because children seek to make their attitudes consistent with their behaviors, when they followed the warning and avoided the toy, their liking for the toy decreased. This effect, however, relied on an induced behavior—obedience to an adult's admonition—rather than on more self-driven decisions on the part of the children. We believe that a demonstration that children shift their attitudes because of counterattitudinal self-driven behavior would provide clearer evidence that they are motivated to resolve cognitive dissonance in their everyday lives.

There is also relatively limited work on cognitive-dissonance reduction in other species, despite the fact that Festinger himself wondered about the extent to which animals experience dissonance. Indeed, Lawrence and Festinger (1962) postulated that cognitive dissonance could explain patterns of extinction across different reward conditions. In line with this suggestion, work on cognitive dissonance in nonhuman animals has exclusively employed variants of the effort-justification paradigm (see Aronson & Mills, 1959, for a version of this paradigm with human subjects). This research has led to mixed results. Lewis (1964), for example, demonstrated that rats who pulled a weight harder to obtain a food pellet ran faster to retrieve the pellet after the work was completed. Although Lewis explained these results in terms of cognitive dissonance, other researchers have argued that they could have been due to a simple transfer-of-effort effect: A rat who has just pulled a heavy weight may run faster than a rat who has pulled a light weight because it is physiologically aroused, not necessarily because it experiences greater anticipation of the reward (see Armus, 2001). In a study supporting this view, Armus (2001)

observed no differential preferences for food pellets when one food was given in response to much work and another was given in response to limited work. This negative result suggests that rats may not strive to reduce cognitive dissonance, at least in the context of effort justification.

Other nonhuman species—particularly birds—have demonstrated effects similar to dissonance reduction in the context of effort-justification paradigms (*Stumus vulgaris:* Kacelnik & Marsh, 2002; *Columba livia:* Clement, Feltus, Kaiser, & Zentall, 2000; DiGian, Friedrich, & Zentall, 2004; Friedrich, Clement, & Zentall, 2004). Friedrich and Zentall (2004), for example, demonstrated that pigeons prefer to eat from a feeder that is associated with greater rather than lesser effort. The authors explained these results in terms of relative contrast effects: Pigeons who receive a piece of food after pecking many times experience a larger shift in relative hedonic status than those who simply receive a piece of food after pecking once (Friedrich & Zentall, 2004). Thus, the results of effort-justification studies of animals may be attributed to changes in the relative hedonic value of the reward, rather than changes to the animals' attitudes per se.[1]

In the study reported here, we used a combined comparative-developmental approach to investigate both the developmental and the evolutionary origins of cognitive-dissonance reduction (see Hauser & Spelke, 2004). More specifically, we tested two populations—human children and nonhuman primates—on similar tasks to address the questions of how adult mechanisms for cognitive-dissonance reduction originate and when these mechanisms originated phylogenetically. This type of combined comparative-developmental approach has been used to investigate questions of origins in numerous domains of psychological inquiry, such as theory of mind (Tomasello, Call, & Hare, 2003; Tomasello, Carpenter, Call, Behne, & Moll, 2005), numerical cognition (Feigenson, Dehaene, & Spelke, 2004), and core physics knowledge (Hauser & Spelke, 2004; Spelke, 2000). In the present study, our goal was to examine whether children and nonhuman primates, like human adults, would shift their attitudes to fall in line with their decisions.

We hoped to develop a method that not only could be used with both children and monkeys, but also would provide an especially simple and direct test of cognitive-dissonance reduction—a test in which changes in behavior could clearly be attributed to attitude change per se, rather than alternative phenomena. To do this, we modified the free-choice paradigm pioneered by Brehm (1956). In the traditional free-choice paradigm, individuals rate the attractiveness of a variety of items. They are then given a choice between two items that they have rated as equally attractive. This choice is thought to induce dissonance because a decision to avoid the unchosen alternative conflicts with the many positive, preferred aspects of that alternative. After making the choice, subjects are asked to rerate all items. Typically, subjects will rerate items that they have chosen as more attractive, and items that they did not choose as less attractive, apparently changing their attitudes to fit with their choices. This rating pattern suggests that subjects change their present attitudes to be in line with their past decisions.

Adapting this free-choice methodology for use with nonverbal populations, we first assessed individuals' preferences for similar objects and determined three (A, B, and C) that were equally attractive. Next, subjects received a choice between A and B (Phase 1) and then a second choice between whatever they did not select (either A or B) and C (Phase 2). We predicted that if subjects experienced dissonance in choosing one equally preferred item over the other, then they would change their attitude toward the unchosen item, liking it less because of their decision. Therefore, in Phase 2, when they had a choice between it and another (originally equally preferred) option, they would choose the unchosen item less. Subjects also participated in a control condition in which we removed the intentional-choice phase: Rather than choose intentionally between A and B in Phase 1, subjects simply received one of the two alternatives from the experimenter. In this condition, subjects were not expected to experience dissonance—as they themselves never made a choice between the two items—and therefore were not expected to show a preference in Phase 2.

METHOD

Child Study

Subjects

Thirty 4-year-olds (M = 53.8 months, SD = 2.45; 14 girls, 16 boys) participated in this study. Four other children began the study but did not complete it because of inability to understand the procedure or fatigue during testing. Children were recruited from a database of potential child subjects and from preschools and day-care centers in the New Haven, Connecticut, area. They were tested in the laboratory or in their preschools while seated on a carpeted floor across from the experimenter.

Procedure

The experimenter assessed children's preferences for different stickers using a smiley-face rating scale that included six faces, corresponding to six levels of liking (see Fig. 1). We used commercially available adhesive foam stickers of various shapes (e.g., dolphin, dragonfly, ladybug). Stickers are often used in preschools as rewards for good behavior, and the children were enthusiastic about playing with the stickers. The experimenter first familiarized the children with the rating scale, explaining that the face with the large smile corresponded to great liking, the face with a straight line for a mouth corresponded to no liking, and the intermediate faces corresponded to liking that increased as the degree of smile increased. Children's comprehension of the scale was confirmed by appropriate responses to the experimenter's three queries: "Let's say I like a sticker a whole lot/not very much at all/somewhere in the middle. Which face should I put it with?" Two children from the original sample were replaced because they had difficulty understanding the rating scale, as indicated by repeated failures to match stickers to appropriate faces.

After the children demonstrated their understanding of the scale, they were asked to match a series of stickers to the faces on it. They continued performing these ratings until they appeared to become fatigued. Each child included in the sample rated stickers until the experimenter was able to identify at least two triads of stickers for which the child had equal liking (i.e., stickers the child had matched to the same face on the scale). Two children from the original sample became fatigued before two full triads could be identified, and were replaced.

Once a child had rated the stickers, the experimenter randomly labeled the stickers in each triad as A, B, and C. The child was then given choices involving each triad of stickers. Each child participated in one of two conditions, either the *choice* condition or the *no-choice* condition. In the choice condition, the child was given one choice between A and B. The experimenter displayed A in one hand and B in the other and said, "Now, you get to choose a sticker to take home." Next, the child was given a similar choice between the unchosen alternative (i.e., either A or B, depending on which option the child had chosen) and C (i.e., the novel yet equally preferred alternative). The experimenter continued with other triads of stickers until all available triads were exhausted.

In the no-choice condition, each child received either A or B. The experimenter displayed A and B as in the choice condition and said, "Now, I'm going to give you a sticker to take home." The experimenter then randomly gave the child one of the

FIGURE 1 / Schematic of the smiley-face rating scale used with child subjects to assess their liking for stickers.

two stickers. After receiving this sticker, the child was given a choice between the unreceived alternative (again, either A or B, depending on which one the experimenter had just given the child) and the equally preferred alternative, C.

At least two triads were used with each child, and the data were averaged across trials for each child.

Capuchin Study

Subjects

We tested 6 capuchins (*Cebus apella*) from the Comparative Cognition Laboratory at Yale University. This group included 4 adults and 2 adolescents. The monkeys were tested using M&M® candies as stimuli.

Procedure

We first assessed the monkeys' existing preferences for M&M's of different colors by timing how long they took to retrieve individual M&M's. For each monkey, preferences for at least nine different M&M colors were assessed. As each preference test began, the monkey was inside its home cage, just outside a testing chamber, and was allowed to watch as the experimenter placed one colored M&M on a tray outside the other side of the chamber. The door to the testing chamber was opened, and the monkey was allowed to enter when it wished to retrieve the M&M. We measured how quickly the monkey entered the testing chamber to retrieve the M&M. Preferences for each color were assessed across 20 trials per monkey; trials for each color spanned two experimental sessions.

After preference testing, we performed analyses of variance to determine whether each monkey had statistically significant preferences. We identified triads of equally preferred colors (all $ps > .05$), and designated the items within each triad as choices A, B, and C (choices were specific to each individual monkey); although there were no significant differences in preferences across the three M&M colors within a triad, we conservatively used each subject's least preferred color of the three (i.e., the one the monkey took longest to obtain during preference testing) as option C.

Each monkey was given four tests conceptually similar to those presented to the children. The monkeys were tested inside a familiar testing enclosure (82.5 cm × 82.5 cm × 82.5 cm) that had one wall with two openings (5 cm high × 9 cm long) spaced such that the subjects could not reach through both of the openings at the same time (see Fig. 2). Each monkey received one choice session followed by a no-choice session, and then either a second choice session followed by a second no-choice session or a second no-choice session followed by a choice session (counterbalanced across monkeys). Each session consisted of 1 choice trial (Phase 1) and 10 test trials (Phase 2).

A given monkey's first two sessions involved the same triad of M&M colors; that is, a monkey that liked red, blue, and yellow equally was tested using that triad of colors in both the choice and the no-choice conditions. The first choice and no-choice test sessions were separated by 2 months. The received alternative in this first no-choice session was whichever color the monkey had originally selected in the choice session. Two different triads of M&M colors were used for the third and fourth sessions. In the second no-choice session, the unreceived M&M color was chosen at random, but was never the M&M color that the subject least preferred within the triad because, as noted, we conservatively reserved the M&M color that was least preferred within the triad for use as option C. We emphasize, though, that although the monkeys took longest to obtain option C during preference testing, A and B were not significantly preferred over C.

In the choice condition, each monkey was initially presented with a choice trial involving a decision between two M&M colors (A and B). At the beginning of this trial (see Fig. 2a), M&M's A and B were presented on a tray that was outside the

FIGURE 2 / The experimental setup used with capuchin subjects. First (a), the tray was presented outside the monkey's reach so that it could see the two options, but not reach them. The tray was then lowered, and the monkey either (b) was allowed to make a choice between the options (choice condition) or (c) could not obtain one of the foods (because one of the openings was closed) and therefore was not given a choice between them (no-choice condition).

testing chamber and just beyond the monkey's reach. The experimenter placed the tray such that the monkey was able to see the two M&M's on the tray, but could not access them. After the monkey saw both items, the experimenter lowered the tray so that the monkey could choose one but not both of the options (see Fig. 2b). Immediately after the monkey made a choice, the tray was removed in order to prevent the monkey from gaining access to the other alternative. Then, the 10 test trials were presented; each provided a choice between the unchosen option (either A or B, depending on the monkey's choice) and the novel yet equally preferred option, C. The position of the chosen and novel options was randomized across the 10 test trials.

The no-choice condition was identical to the choice condition except for the initial choice trial. In the no-choice condition, the monkey had no choice between the two initially presented options; instead, the experimenter kept one of the two openings closed during the choice period (see Fig. 2c), allowing the monkey to take only one of the M&M's (either A or B). The experimenter then presented the monkey with 10 test trials involving decisions between the unreceived alternative and the novel option, C, as described for the choice condition.

RESULTS

We first analyzed the children's performance on the rating task. On average, children tested in the choice condition and those tested in the no-choice condition completed ratings for the same total number of triads (*ns* = 4.13 and 4.40 triads, respectively).

Next, for each child we computed a percentage preference for the novel option, C, over the unchosen (choice condition) or unreceived (no-choice condition) option A or B (e.g., a child who chose C for four out of five triads would have a percentage preference score of 80%). We then compared the mean percentage preference for C across the choice and no-choice conditions. An unpaired *t* test revealed a reliable difference between the two conditions, *t*(28) = 2.03, *p* = .05, two-tailed. As depicted in Figure 3, children in the choice condition were more likely to prefer option C (mean percentage choice of C = 63.0%) than were children in the no-choice condition (mean percentage choice of C = 47.2%). Average choice of C in the choice condition differed reliably from chance, according to a one-sample *t* test with a hypothesized mean of 50%, *t*(14) = 2.28, *p* = .04, two-tailed. This was not true for the no-choice condition, *t*(14) = 0.53, *p* = .60, two-tailed.

We performed similar analyses on the monkeys' percentage choice of option C. A repeated measures analysis of variance with condition (choice and no-choice) and order (first two sessions or second two sessions) as within-subjects variables revealed only a significant main effect of condition, *F*(1, 5) = 32.5, *p* = .002. The monkeys chose option C (mean percentage choice of C = 60.0%) more in the choice condition than in the no-choice condition

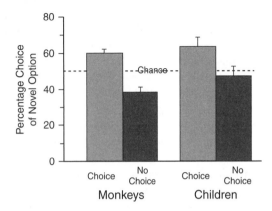

FIGURE 3 / Mean percentage of choices of the novel but equally preferred option (C) in the choice and no-choice conditions, for monkeys and children. Error bars indicate standard errors.

(mean percentage choice of C = 38.3%; see Fig. 3). This pattern was confirmed by nonparametric analyses (paired sign: *p* = .03). In addition, the percentage of trials on which the monkeys chose C differed from chance in both conditions. A one-sample *t* test revealed that in the choice condition, the monkeys showed a significant preference for option C, *t*(5) = 5.48, *p* = .003. They showed the opposite preference in the no-choice condition, significantly preferring the unreceived over the novel option, *t*(5) = 4.18, *p* = .009. We did not anticipate this effect, but believe it may be attributable to the methodology of the no-choice condition: The monkeys saw the experimenter keep one option and give them the other. They may have interpreted this behavior as the experimenter choosing the better option for herself and offering them the inferior alternative. Such an interpretation may have caused them to inflate the value of the alternative "chosen" by the experimenter (see Lyons & Santos, 2007, for a similar finding).

DISCUSSION

Both children and capuchins demonstrated a decrease in preference for one of two equally preferred alternatives after they had chosen against it—but not when the experimenter had chosen against it. These results suggest that children and monkeys change their current preferences to fit with their past decisions. Like adult humans tested in similar paradigms, children and monkeys seem to derogate alternatives they have chosen against, changing their current attitudes and preferences to more closely match the choices they made in previous decisions.

Our present findings fit with those of previous studies involving preference changes in both children and nonhuman species. Previous studies using the forbidden-toy paradigm demonstrated that children change their attitude toward a toy that is associated with a potential mild punishment (Aronson & Carlsmith, 1963). Similarly, previous work showed that a number of bird species prefer items that are obtained with more effort (e.g., Clement et al., 2000; DiGian et al., 2004; Friedrich & Zentall, 2004; Friedrich et al., 2004). Unfortunately, the results of these latter studies can be interpreted without attributing dissonance reduction to the birds, as they may have preferred the option that required more work because of hedonic-contrast effects. The present study was better able to isolate the reasons for both children's and animals' attitude change because the only feature that differed between the experimental and control conditions was whether or not subjects made an intentional choice. Our subjects' attitude changes had to be due to the fact that they made a cognitive-dissonance-inducing decision, one that was discordant with their previous assessment that the two options were of equal value. The present study thus provides what we feel is a simpler and more direct demonstration of dissonance reduction per se than work performed previously. Moreover, we used nearly identical methods to demonstrate similar attitude changes in children and primates.

Our findings for young children challenge the idea that people's extensive experience with the negative consequences of their decisions teaches them to change their discordant attitudes. Because young children have relatively little experience with decision making, it is unlikely that the motivation to reduce cognitive dissonance can be attributed solely to past cognitive history. We recognize, of course, that 4-year-olds have some prior experience with the consequences of dissonant cognitions (though surely less than adults). For this reason, future studies with infants, who have virtually no experience with such cognitions, can clarify the extent to which experience plays a role in the development of dissonance-reduction mechanisms.

The fact that both children and nonhuman primates derogate unchosen alternatives raises the possibility that the drive to reduce dissonance is an aspect of human psychology that emerges without the need for much experience. Indeed, behavioral similarities between young human subjects and closely related primates are a signature of cognitive systems that are typically thought to be constrained across development, maybe even emerging innately. Such *core-knowledge* mechanisms have been proposed in other areas of cognition, such as the domains of numerical understanding (Feigenson et al., 2004; Wynn, 1992) and object cognition (Spelke, 2000), but have, to our knowledge, never before been proposed in the domain of attitude formation and change. The present results raise an interesting possibility: There may be some core aspects of cognition that give rise to cognitive dissonance as well. Our findings hint that some of the mechanisms that drive cognitive-dissonance-reduction processes in human adults may emerge as a result of developmentally and evolutionarily constrained systems that are consistent across cultures, ages, and even species.

The speculation that cognitive-dissonance reduction relies on core processes leads to other speculations concerning the nature of the mechanisms that drive it. Many core-knowledge mechanisms seem to operate in the absence of higher-level capacities that human adults possess, including language capacities, and also in the absence of social factors such as extensive teaching and socialization. It follows, then, that cognitive-dissonance reduction may not require these higher-level processes. One might further speculate that cognitive-dissonance reduction may be more automatic than has been previously suspected (see Lieberman, Ochsner, Gilbert, & Schacter, 2001, for support of this view). The exact mechanisms behind cognitive-dissonance reduction have long been debated within social psychology: Whereas some researchers believe that dissonance is experienced as a threat to a cognitively and motivationally complex self (e.g., Steele & Liu, 1983), others argue that dissonance is due to much simpler processes (e.g., Bem, 1967; Festinger, 1957). If cognitive-dissonance reduction occurs in creatures that lack language and complex senses of self, then one must either accept that these processes are mechanistically simpler than previously thought or ascribe richer motivational complexity to populations that are thought to be less cognitively sophisticated than human adults, namely, monkeys and children.

Our study also has what we feel is an important methodological implication. Specifically, our work examining cognitive-dissonance reduction in monkeys and children illustrates the utility of incorporating comparative-developmental data in studying adult human social psychology and social psychological mechanisms. We hope that this study will pave the way for a more thorough investigation of the origins of some of the classic social psychological phenomena. Such an approach will allow researchers not only to determine the foundations of these phenomena in human development and evolution, but also to constrain hypotheses about the mechanisms underlying these phenomena.

ACKNOWLEDGMENTS

The authors would like to thank Justin Bellamy, Jeffrey Brown, Christina Jacovides, Elizabeth Moore, and Jessica Thomas for their help running the experiments and Geoffrey Cohen and Richard Eibach for helpful feedback on experimental design. This work was supported by Yale University, was approved by the Yale Institutional University Care Animal Committee, and conforms to federal guidelines for the use of animals in research.

REFERENCES

Akerlof, G.A., & Dickens, W.T. (1982). The economic consequences of cognitive dissonance. *American Economic Review, 72*, 307–319.

Armus, H.L. (2001). Effect of response effort on the reward value of distinctively flavored food pellets. *Psychological Reports, 88*, 1031–1034.

Aronson, E., & Carlsmith, J.M. (1963). Effect of severity of threat on the valuation of forbidden behavior. *Journal of Abnormal and Social Psychology, 66*, 584–588.

Aronson, E., & Mills, J. (1959). The effect of severity of initiation on liking for a group. *Journal of Abnormal and Social Psychology, 59*, 177–181.

Axsom, D. (1989). Cognitive dissonance and behavior change in psychotherapy. *Journal of Experimental Social Psychology, 25*, 234–252.

Bem, D.J. (1967). Self-perception: An alternative interpretation of cognitive dissonance phenomena. *Psychological Review, 74*, 183–200.

Brehm, J.W. (1956). Postdecision changes in the desirability of alternatives. *Journal of Abnormal and Social Psychology, 52*, 384–389.

Clement, T.S., Feltus, J.R., Kaiser, D.H., & Zentall, T.R. (2000). "Work ethic" in pigeons: Reward value is directly related to the effort or time required to obtain the reward. *Psychonomic Bulletin & Review, 7*, 100–106.

DiGian, K.A., Friedrich, A.M., & Zentall, T.R. (2004). Discriminative stimuli that follow a delay have added value for pigeons. *Psychonomic Bulletin & Review, 11*, 889–895.

Elliot, A.J., & Devine, P.G. (1994). On the motivational nature of cognitive dissonance: Dissonance as psychological discomfort. *Journal of Personality and Social Psychology, 67*, 382–394.

Feigenson, L., Dehaene, S., & Spelke, E.S. (2004). Origins and endpoints of the core systems of number: Reply to Fias and Verguts. *Trends in Cognitive Sciences, 8*, 448–449.

Festinger, L. (1957). *A theory of cognitive dissonance.* Stanford, CA: Stanford University Press.

Friedrich, A.M., Clement, T.S., & Zentall, T.R. (2004). Functional equivalence in pigeons involving a four-member class. *Behavioral Processes, 67*, 395–403.

Friedrich, A.M., & Zentall, T.R. (2004). Pigeons shift their preference toward locations of food that take more effort to obtain. *Behavioral Processes, 67*, 405–415.

Hauser, M., & Spelke, E. (2004). Evolutionary and developmental foundations of human knowledge: A case study of mathematics.

In M.S. Gazzaniga (Ed.), *The cognitive neurosciences* (3rd ed., pp. 853–864). Cambridge, MA: MIT Press.

Kacelnik, A., & Marsh, B. (2002). Cost can increase preference in starlings. *Animal Behavior, 63*, 245–250.

Lawrence, D.H., & Festinger, L. (1962). *Deterrents and reinforcements: The psychology of insufficient reward.* Stanford, CA: Stanford University Press.

Leippe, M.R., & Eisenstadt, D. (1994). Generalization of dissonance reduction: Decreasing prejudice through induced compliance. *Journal of Personality and Social Psychology, 67*, 395–413.

Lewis, M. (1964). Some nondecremental effects of effort. *Journal of Comparative and Physiological Psychology, 57*, 367–373.

Lieberman, M.D., Ochsner, K.N., Gilbert, D.T., & Schacter, D.L. (2001). Do amnesics exhibit cognitive dissonance reduction? The role of explicit memory and attention in attitude change. *Psychological Science, 12*, 135–140.

Lyons, D., & Santos, L.R. (2007). *Capuchin monkeys* (Cebus apella) *discriminate between intentional and unintentional human actions.* Manuscript submitted for publication.

Lyubomirsky, S., & Ross, L. (1999). Changes in attractiveness of elected, rejected, and precluded alternatives: A comparison of happy and unhappy individuals. *Journal of Personality and Social Psychology, 76*, 988–1007.

Spelke, E.S. (2000). Core knowledge. *American Psychologist, 55*, 1233–1243.

Steele, C.M., & Liu, T.J. (1983). Dissonance processes as self-affirmation. *Journal of Personality and Social Psychology, 45*, 5–19.

Tomasello, M., Call, J., & Hare, B. (2003). Chimpanzees understand psychological states—the question is which ones and to what extent. *Trends in Cognitive Sciences, 7*, 153–156.

Tomasello, M., Carpenter, M., Call, J., Behne, T., & Moll, H. (2005). Understanding and sharing intentions: The origins of cultural cognition. *Behavioral and Brain Sciences, 28*, 675–691.

Tsang, J. (2002). Moral rationalization and the integration of situational factors and psychological processes in immoral behavior. *Review of General Psychology, 6*, 25–50.

Wynn, K. (1992). Addition and subtraction by human infants. *Nature, 358*, 749–750.

ENDNOTE

1. Friedrich and Zentall (2004) noted that this same hedonic-contrast effect may more parsimoniously explain human effort-justification effects as well.

CRITICAL THINKING QUESTIONS

1. Can the results of the present study be used to produce dissonance and hence change in real-world applications with adults? For example, suppose you want to reduce smoking by inducing dissonance in participants. Design a study for doing so.

2. Are there any practical applications for the findings of this study for a parent or teacher who wants to change the behavior of a young child? Give an example of how such behavior change might be brought about.

3. According to the article, "We hope that this study will pave the way for a more thorough investigation of the origins of some of the classic social psychological phenomena." What are two such areas of social

psychological phenomena that might be investigated from a developmental and/or evolutionary standpoint? Explain your reasoning.

4. Question 3 in Article 11 asked, "Based on personal experience, have you ever suspected that cognitive dissonance was operating in some change that came about in your own attitudes?" Elaborate on your answer by including information from the present article on the level at which dissonance might actually be operating.

CHAPTER INTEGRATION QUESTIONS

1. Articles 11 and 12 both dealt with aspects of cognitive dissonance. How does this concept also relate to the content of Article 10?

2. Integrate the findings of all three articles into one or two themes. Discuss the practical application of your theme or themes.

3. "Only the most intelligent and most stupid do not change," according to Confucius, a Chinese philosopher. In light of the information presented in this chapter on attitudes and attitude change, do you agree or disagree with this quotation? Be sure to defend your position.

Chapter Five

SOCIAL IDENTITY

THE MAJORITY OF readings that you will encounter in this book focus on what might be called *situational variables:* particular circumstances that elicit predictable patterns of behavior in people. But do all people respond the same way in identical situations? Of course not. We each bring to every situation a set of experiences and characteristics that may influence how we act. Certainly, each of us has had unique life experiences that may be influential; biological dispositions, perhaps present from birth, may also play a role in determining behavior. Another influential factor is the personality of the individual.

But what is *personality?* Many theories have been developed to try to explain what this concept means. Some are *global theories* of personality, which attempt a total comprehensive portrait of an individual (e.g., Freud's), while others are *microtheories,* focusing on narrower, more particular dimensions of personality. Certainly, one major part of personality is *social identity*—the part of personality that is our internalized representation of how we view ourselves as being part of our social world. Two major parts of social identity—the *self* and *gender identity*—are addressed in the readings in this chapter.

Article 13, "The Many Me's of the Self-Monitor," looks at the sense of self that each of us has and asks whether that is comprised of a single sense of self or perhaps a number of selves, depending on the situation.

Article 14, "The Measurement of Psychological Androgyny," is a classic article that challenges the common-sense wisdom that the most appropriate gender-typed behavior is for a male to be masculine and a female, feminine. Perhaps masculinity and femininity are not mutually exclusive ends of a continuum after all.

Finally the contemporary reading found in Article 15, "Reducing Narcissistic Aggression by Buttressing Self-Esteem: An Experimental Field Study," examines how a central part of our sense of self—our self-esteem—may be related to aggression. An interesting aspect of this article is that it reports that increasing self-esteem might not lead to decreased aggression, a finding that is contrary to what many people intuitively believe. The method used in this study offers an intriguing way that aggression might be reduced—not by *increasing* self-esteem, but by *reaffirming* it.

ARTICLE 13 _____

Think about who you are. Do you have a stable sense of self, of knowing what you feel, believe, and want? Or do you have many selves, depending on when and in what situation you try to answer this question?

Now think about your behavior. Do you act consistently across many different situations? Or does your behavior depend on the specific situation in which you find yourself?

These questions are indeed intriguing. At one extreme may be individuals who consistently act the same way in every situation, even when doing so might not be appropriate. At the other extreme are people who modify their behavior to fit each situation, showing little consistency across contexts. These are the two extremes on a continuum of what is known as *self-monitoring.*

Self-monitoring refers to the extent to which an individual is aware of and able to control the impressions that he or she conveys to others. A high self-monitoring individual is very attuned to the situation and modifies his or her behavior according to the demands of the context. A low self-monitoring individual tends to behave more in accordance with internal dispositions than with the demands of the situation.

What are the consequences of these two styles of behaving? Does a high self-monitoring person actually have many different selves, while a low self-monitoring person has but a single self? The relationship between self-monitoring and the sense of self is but one of the issues addressed in the following article by Mark Snyder.

The Many Me's of the Self-Monitor

■ Mark Snyder

The image of myself which I try to create in my own mind in order that I may love myself is very different from the image which I try to create in the minds of others in order that they may love me.
—*W. H. Auden*

The concept of the self is one of the oldest and most enduring in psychological considerations of human nature. We generally assume that people are fairly consistent and stable beings: that a person who is generous in one situation is also likely to be generous in other situations, that one who is honest is honest most of the time, that a person who takes a liberal stance today will favor the liberal viewpoint tomorrow.

It's not always so: each of us, it appears, may have not one but many selves. Moreover, much as we might like to believe that the self is an integral feature of personal identity, it appears that, to a greater extent, the self is a product of the individual's relationships with other people. Conventional wisdom to the contrary, there may be striking gaps and contradictions—as Auden suggests—between the public appearances and private realities of the self.

Psychologists refer to the strategies and techniques that people use to control the impressions they convey to others as "impression management." One of my own research interests has been to understand why some individuals are better at impression management than others. For it is clear that some people are particularly sensitive to the ways they express and present themselves in social situations—at parties, job interviews, professional meetings, in confrontations of all kinds where one might choose to create and maintain an appearance, with or without a specific purpose in mind. Indeed, I have found that such people have developed the ability to carefully monitor their own performances and to skillfully adjust their performances when signals from others tell them that they are not having the desired effect. I call such persons "high self-monitoring individuals," and I have developed a 25-item measure—the Self-Monitoring Scale—that has proved its ability to distinguish high self-monitoring individuals from low self-monitoring individuals (see box [p. 86]). Unlike the high self-monitoring individuals, low self-monitoring individuals are not so concerned about taking in such information; instead, they tend to express what they feel, rather than mold and tailor their behavior to fit the situation.

My work on self-monitoring and impression management grew out of a long-standing fascination with explorations of reality and illusion in literature and in the theater. I was struck by the contrast between the way things often appear to be and the reality that lurks beneath the surface—on the stage, in novels, and in people's actual lives. I wanted to know how this world of appearances in social relationships was built and maintained, as well as what its effects were on the individual personality. But I was also interested in exploring the older,

From "The Many Me's of the Self-Monitor," Mark Snyder, *Psychology Today*, 1980, 13, pp. 33–40. Reprinted with permission of Mark Snyder.

more philosophical question of whether, beneath the various images of self that people project to others, there is a "real me." If we are all actors in many social situations, do we then retain in any sense an essential self, or are we really a variety of selves?

SKILLED IMPRESSION MANAGERS

There are striking and important differences in the extent to which people can and do control their self-presentation in social situations: some people engage in impression management more often—and with greater skill—than others. Professional actors, as well as many trial lawyers, are among the best at it. So are successful salespeople, confidence artists, and politicians. The onetime mayor of New York, Fiorello LaGuardia, was particularly skilled at adopting the expressive mannerisms of a variety of ethnic groups. In fact, he was so good at it that in watching silent films of his campaign speeches, it is easy to guess whose vote he was soliciting.

Of course, such highly skilled performances are the exception rather than the rule. And people differ in the extent to which they can and do exercise control over their self-presentations. It is high self-monitoring individuals among us who are particularly talented in this regard. When asked to describe high self-monitoring individuals, their friends say that they are good at learning which behavior is appropriate in social situations, have good self-control of their emotional expression, and can effectively use this ability to create the impression they want. They are particularly skilled at intentionally expressing and accurately communicating a wide variety of emotions both vocally and facially. As studies by Richard Lippa of California State University at Fullerton have shown, they are usually such polished actors that they can effectively adopt the mannerisms of a reserved, withdrawn, and introverted individual and then do an abrupt about-face and portray, just as convincingly, a friendly, outgoing, and extroverted personality.

High self-monitoring individuals are also quite likely to seek out information about appropriate patterns of self-presentation. They invest considerable effort in attempting to "read" and understand others. In an experiment I conducted with Tom Monson (then one of my graduate students), various cues were given to students involved in group discussions as to what was socially appropriate behavior in the situation. For example, some of them thought that their taped discussions would be played back to fellow students; in those circumstances, I assumed they would want their opinions to appear as autonomous as possible. Others believed that their discussions were completely private; there, I assumed they would be most concerned with maintaining harmony and agreement in the group. High self-monitoring individuals were keenly attentive to these differences; they conformed with the group when conformity was the most appropriate behavior and did not conform when they knew that the norms of the larger student audience would favor autonomy

in the face of social pressure. Low self-monitoring individuals were virtually unaffected by the differences in social setting: presumably, their self-presentations were more accurate reflections of their personal attitudes and dispositions. Thus, as we might have guessed, people who are most skilled in the arts of impression management are also most likely to practice it.

Although high self-monitoring individuals are well skilled in the arts of impression management, we should not automatically assume that they necessarily use these skills for deceptive or manipulative purposes. Indeed, in their relationships with friends and acquaintances, high self-monitoring individuals are eager to use their self-monitoring abilities to promote smooth social interactions.

We can find some clues to this motive in the way high self-monitoring individuals tend to react to, and cope with, unfamiliar and unstructured social settings. In a study done at the University of Wisconsin, psychologists William Ickes and Richard Barnes arranged for pairs of strangers to spend time together in a waiting room, ostensibly to wait for an experiment to begin. The researchers then recorded the verbal and nonverbal behavior of each pair over a five-minute period, using video and audio tapes. All possible pairings of same-sex undergraduates at high, moderate, and low levels of self-monitoring were represented. Researchers scrutinized the tapes for evidence of the impact of self-monitoring on spontaneous encounters between strangers.

In these meetings, as in so many other aspects of their lives, high self-monitoring individuals suffered little or no shyness. Soon after meeting the other person, they took an active and controlling role in the conversation. They were inclined to talk first and to initiate subsequent conversational sequences. They also felt, and were seen by their partners to have, a greater need to talk. Their partners also viewed them as having been the more directive member of the pair. It was as if high self-monitoring individuals were particularly concerned about managing their behavior in order to create, encourage, and maintain a smooth flow of conversation. Perhaps this quality may help self-monitoring people to emerge as leaders in groups, organizations, and institutions.

DETECTING IMPRESSION MANAGEMENT IN OTHERS

High self-monitoring individuals are also adept at detecting impression management in others. To demonstrate this finely tuned ability, three communications researchers at the University of Minnesota made use of videotaped excerpts from the television program "To Tell the Truth." On this program, one of the three guest contestants (all male in the excerpts chosen for the study) is the "real Mr. X." The other two who claim to be the real Mr. X are, of course, lying. Participants in the study watched each excerpt and then tried to identify the real Mr. X. High self-monitoring

Monitor Your Self

On the scale I have developed to measure self-monitoring, actors are usually high scorers, as are many obese people, who tend to be very sensitive about the way they appear to others. For much the same reason, politicians and trial lawyers would almost certainly be high scorers. Recent immigrants eager to assimilate, black freshmen in a predominantly white college, and military personnel stationed abroad are also likely to score high on the scale.

The Self-Monitoring Scale measures how concerned people are with the impression they are making on others, as well as their ability to control and modify their behavior to fit the situation. I believe that it defines a distinct domain of personality that is quite different from the traits probed by other standard scales.

Several studies show that skill at self-monitoring is not associated with exceptional intelligence or with a particular social class. Nor is it related, among other things, to being highly anxious or extremely self-conscious, to being an extrovert, or to having a strong need for approval.

They may be somewhat power-oriented or Machiavellian, but high self-monitoring individuals do not necessarily have high scores on the "Mach" scale, a measure of Machiavellianism developed by Richard Christie of Columbia University. (Two items from the scale: "The best way to handle people is to tell them what they want" and "Anyone who completely trusts anyone else is asking for trouble.") The steely-eyes Machiavellians are more manipulative, detached, and amoral than high self-monitoring individuals.

The Self-Monitoring Scale describes a unique trait and has proved to be both statistically valid and reliable, in tests on various samples.

Below is a 10-item abbreviated version of the Self-Monitoring Scale that will give readers some idea of whether they are low or high self-monitoring individuals. If you would like to test your self-monitoring tendencies, follow the instructions and then consult the scoring key.

—M. S.

These statements concern personal reactions to a number of different situations. No two statements are exactly alike, so consider each statement carefully before answering. If a statement is true, or mostly true, as applied to you, circle the T. If a statement is false, or not usually true, as applied to you, circle the F.

1. I find it hard to imitate the behavior of other people.   T   F
2. I guess I put on a show to impress or entertain people.   T   F
3. I would probably make a good actor.   T   F
4. I sometimes appear to others to be experiencing deeper emotions than I actually am.   T   F
5. In a group of people I am rarely the center of attention.   T   F
6. In different situations and with different people, I often act like very different persons. T   F
7. I can only argue for ideas I already believe.   T   F
8. In order to get along and be liked, I tend to be what people expect me to be rather than anything else.   T   F
9. I may deceive people by being friendly when I really dislike them.   T   F
10. I'm not always the person I appear to be.   T   F

SCORING: Give yourself one point for each of questions 1, 5, and 7 that you answered F. Give yourself one point for each of the remaining questions that you answered T. Add up your points. If you are a good judge of yourself and scored 7 or above, you are probably a high self-monitoring individual; 3 or below, you are probably a low self-monitoring individual.

---

individuals were much more accurate than their low self-monitoring counterparts in correctly identifying the real Mr. X and in seeing through the deception of the other two contestants.

Not only are high self-monitoring individuals able to see beyond the masks of deception successfully but they are also keenly attentive to the actions of other people as clues to their underlying intentions. E. E. Jones and Roy Baumeister of Princeton University had college students watch a videotaped

discussion between two men who either agreed or disagreed with each other. The observers were aware that one man (the target person) had been instructed either to gain the affection or to win the respect of the other. Low self-monitoring observers tended to accept behavior at face value. They found themselves attracted to the agreeable person, whether or not he was attempting to ingratiate himself with his discussion partner. In contrast, high self-monitoring observers were acutely sensitive to the motivational context within which the target person operated. They liked the target better if he was disagreeable when trying to ingratiate himself. But when he sought respect, they were more attracted to him if he chose to be agreeable. Jones and Baumeister suggest that high self-monitoring observers regarded agreeableness as too blatant a ploy in gaining affection and autonomy as an equally obvious route to respect. Perhaps the high self-monitoring individuals felt that they themselves would have acted with greater subtlety and finesse.

Even more intriguing is Jones's and Baumeister's speculation—and I share their view—that high self-monitoring individuals prefer to live in a stable, predictable social environment populated by people whose actions consistently and accurately reflect their true attitudes and feelings. In such a world, the consistency and predictability of the actions of others would be of great benefit to those who tailor and manage their own self-presentation in social situations. From this perspective, it becomes quite understandable that high self-monitoring individuals may be especially fond of those who avoid strategic posturing. Furthermore, they actually may prefer as friends those comparatively low in self-monitoring.

How can we know when strangers and casual acquaintances are engaged in self-monitoring? Are there some channels of expression and communication that are more revealing than others about a person's true, inner "self," even when he or she is practicing impression management?

Both scientific and everyday observers of human behavior have suggested that nonverbal behavior—facial expressions, tone of voice, and body movements—reveals meaningful information about a person's attitudes, feelings, and motives. Often, people who engage in self-monitoring for deceptive purposes are less skilled at controlling their body's expressive movements. Accordingly, the body may be a more revealing source of information than the face for detecting those who engage in self-monitoring and impression management.

More than one experiment shows how nonverbal behavior can betray the true attitude of those attempting impression management. Shirley Weitz of the New School for Social Research reasoned that on college campuses where there are strong normative pressures supporting a tolerant and liberal value system, all students would avoid saying anything that would indicate racial prejudice—whether or not their private attitudes supported such behavior. In fact, she found that among "liberal" white males at Harvard University, the most prejudiced students (as determined by behavioral measures of actual attempts to avoid interaction with blacks) bent over backwards to *verbally* express liking and friendship for a black in a simulated interracial encounter. However, their *nonverbal* behaviors gave them away. Although the prejudiced students made every effort to say kind and favorable things, they continued to do so in a cool and distant tone of voice. It was as if they knew the words but not the music: they knew *what* to say, but not *how* to say it.

Another way that prejudice can be revealed is in the physical distance people maintain between themselves and the target of their prejudice. To demonstrate this phenomenon, psychologist Stephen Morin arranged for college students to be interviewed about their attitudes toward homosexuality. Half the interviewers wore "Gay and Proud" buttons and mentioned their association with the Association of Gay Psychologists. The rest wore no buttons and simply mentioned that they were graduate students working on theses. Without the students' knowledge, the distance they placed their chairs from the interviewer was measured while the interviews were going on. The measure of social distance proved to be highly revealing. When the student and the interviewer were of the same sex, students tended to establish almost a foot more distance between themselves and the apparently gay interviewers. They placed their chairs an average of 32 inches away from apparently gay interviewers, but only 22 inches away from apparently nongay interviewers. Interestingly, most of the students expressed tolerant, and at times favorable, attitudes toward gay people in general. However, the distances they chose to put between themselves and the interviewers they thought gay betrayed underlying negative attitudes.

William James on the Roles We Play

A man has as many social selves as there are individuals who recognize him and carry an image of him in their mind. . . . But as the individuals who carry the images form naturally into classes, we may practically say that he has as many different social selves as there are distinct *groups* of persons about whose opinions he cares. He generally shows a different side of himself to each of these different groups. Many a youth who is demure enough before his parents and teachers swears and swaggers like a pirate among his "tough" young friends. We do not show ourselves to our children as to our club companions, to our masters and employers as to our intimate friends. From this there results what practically is a division of the man into several selves; and this may be a discordant splitting, as where one is afraid to let one set of his acquaintances know him as he is elsewhere; or it may be a perfectly harmonious division of labor, as where one tender to his children is stern to the soldiers or prisoners under his command.

—William James
The Principles of Psychology, 1890

IMPRESSION MANAGERS' DILEMMAS

The well-developed skills of high self-monitoring individuals ought to give them the flexibility to cope quickly and effectively with a diversity of social roles. They can choose with skill and grace the self-presentation appropriate to each of a wide variety of social situations. But what happens when the impression manager must effectively present a true and honest image to other people?

Consider the case of a woman on trial for a crime that she did not commit. Her task on the witness stand is to carefully present herself so that everything she does and says communicates to the jurors clearly and unambiguously her true innocence, so that they will vote for her acquittal. Chances are good, however, that members of the jury are somewhat skeptical of the defendant's claims of innocence. After all, they might reason to themselves, the district attorney would not have brought this case to trial were the state's case against her not a convincing one.

The defendant must carefully manage her verbal and nonverbal behaviors so as to ensure that even a skeptical jury forms a true impression of her innocence. In particular, she must avoid the pitfalls of an image that suggests that "she doth protest her innocence too much and therefore must be guilty." To the extent that our defendant skillfully practices the art of impression management, she will succeed in presenting herself to the jurors as the honest person that she truly is.

It often can take as much work to present a truthful image as to present a deceptive one. In fact, in this case, just being honest may not be enough when facing skeptical jurors who may bend over backwards to interpret any and all of the defendant's behavior—nervousness, for example—as a sign of guilt.

The message from research on impression management is a clear one. Some people are quite flexible in their self-presentation. What effects do these shifts in public appearance have on the more private realities of self-concept? In some circumstances, we are persuaded by our own appearances: we become the persons we appear to be. This phenomenon is particularly likely to occur when the image we present wins the approval and favor of those around us.

In an experiment conducted at Duke University by psychologists E. E. Jones, Kenneth Gergen, and Keith Davis, participants who had been instructed to win the approval of an interviewer presented very flattering images of themselves. Half the participants (chosen at random) then received favorable reactions from their interviewers; the rest did not. All the participants later were asked to estimate how accurately and honestly their self-descriptions had mirrored their true personalities.

Those who had won the favor of their interviewers considered their self-presentations to have been the most honest of all. One interpretation of this finding is that those people were operating with rather pragmatic definitions of self-concept: that which produced the most positive results was considered to be an accurate reflection of the inner self.

The reactions of other people can make it all the more likely that we become what we claim to be. Other people may accept our self-presentations at face value; they may then treat us as if we really were the way we pretend to be. For example, if I act as if I like Chris, chances are Chris will like me. Chris will probably treat me in a variety of friendly ways. As a result of Chris's friendliness, I may come to like Chris, even though I did not in the first place. The result, in this case, may be beneficial to both parties. In other circumstances, however, the skilled impression manager may pay an emotional price.

High self-monitoring orientation may be purchased at the cost of having one's actions reflect and communicate very little about one's private attitudes, feelings, and dispositions. In fact, as I have seen time and again in my research with my former graduate students Beth Tanke and Bill Swann, correspondence between private attitudes and public behavior is often minimal for high self-monitoring individuals. Evidently, the words and deeds of high self-monitoring individuals may reveal precious little information about their true inner feelings and attitudes.

Yet, it is almost a canon of modern psychology that a person's ability to reveal a "true self" to intimates is essential to emotional health. Sidney Jourard, one of the first psychologists to hold that view, believed that only through self-disclosure could we achieve self-discovery and self-knowledge: "Through my self-disclosure, I let others know my soul. They can know it, really know it, only as I make it known. In fact, I am beginning to suspect that I can't even know *my own soul* except as I disclose it. I suspect that I will know myself 'for real' at the exact moment that I have succeeded in making it known through my disclosure to another person."

Only low self-monitoring individuals may be willing or able to live their lives according to Jourard's prescriptions. By contrast, high self-monitoring individuals seem to embody Erving Goffman's view of human nature. For him, the world of appearances appears to be all, and the "soul" is illusory. Goffman defines social interactions as a theatrical performance in which each individual acts out a "line." A line is a set of carefully chosen verbal and nonverbal acts that express one's self. Each of us, in Goffman's view, seems to be merely the sum of our various performances.

What does this imply for the sense of self and identity associated with low and high self-monitoring individuals?

I believe that high self-monitoring individuals and low self-monitoring individuals have very different ideas about what constitutes a self and that their notions are quite well-suited to how they live. High self-monitoring individuals regard themselves as rather flexible and adaptive people who tailor their social behavior shrewdly and pragmatically to fit appropriate conditions. They believe that a person is whoever he appears to be in any particular situation: "I am me, the me I am right now."

This self-image fits well with the way high self-monitoring individuals present themselves to the world. It allows them to act in ways that are consistent with how they believe they should act.

By contrast, low self-monitoring individuals have a firmer, more single-minded idea of what a self should be. They value and strive for congruence between "who they are" and "what they do" and regard their actions as faithful reflections of how they feel and think. For them, a self is a single identity that must not be compromised for other people or in certain situations. Indeed, this view of the self parallels the low self-monitoring individual's consistent and stable self-presentation.

What is important in understanding oneself and others, then, is not the elusive question of whether there is a quintessential self, but rather, understanding how different people define those attributes of their behavior and experience that they regard as "me." Theory and research on self-monitoring have attempted to chart the processes by which beliefs about the self are actively translated into patterns of social behavior that reflect self-conceptions. From this perspective, the processes of self-monitoring are the processes of self—a system of operating rules that translate self-knowledge into social behavior.

CRITICAL THINKING QUESTIONS

1. Self-monitoring can be measured along a continuum. What are the advantages and disadvantages for someone who scores very high on this dimension (i.e., a high self-monitoring individual)? Very low (i.e., a low self-monitoring individual)?

2. How might high versus low self-monitoring individuals act differently in an intimate situation such as dating? Give examples to support your answer.

3. How do you think differences in self-monitoring develop? In other words, why might some people be attuned to external factors while others are not? In your opinion, what level of self-monitoring might be best overall for healthy functioning? Explain your answers.

4. Articles 11 and 12 dealt with the concept of cognitive dissonance. Based on your understanding of the concept, do you think that dissonance arousal in a given situation may be influenced by the level of self-monitoring used by the person? How so?

ARTICLE 14 _____

Let's do a quick exercise. Make a list of words or adjectives that you would use to describe someone that you think of as being feminine. Make another list of masculine descriptors. Next, compare the lists. Does one set of characteristics seem better than the other or just different? Could it be that the different stereotypical characteristics associated with masculinity and femininity might each be important, depending on the situation?

Masculine characteristics are generally considered *instrumental,* meaning that they are useful in task- or goal-oriented situations. Feminine characteristics tend to be more *expressive,* meaning that they focus more on the affective concern of the welfare of others. Typically, American society socializes its members to believe that males should act masculine and females, feminine and that each gender should suppress the characteristics of its opposite.

The following classic article by Sandra L. Bem postulates that when males are only allowed to act masculine and females are only allowed to act feminine, each gender is, in a sense, limited in what it can do. Masculine males are thus good in situations that call for instrumental, get-the-job-done traits, whereas feminine females are good in settings where concern for the feelings of others is important. But what about the person of either gender who has both masculine *and* feminine characteristics? Might he or she not be more adaptive and flexible to a greater variety of human experiences? In short, might not this person be better adjusted than the more rigidly defined masculine males and feminine females? Besides attempting to answer these questions, Bem's article is also a good example of how an instrument designed to measure a dimension of behavior characteristics is developed.

The Measurement of Psychological Androgyny[1]

■ Sandra L. Bem

This article describes the development of a new sex-role inventory that treats masculinity and femininity as two independent dimensions, thereby making it possible to characterize a person as masculine, feminine, or "androgynous" as a function of the difference between his or her endorsement of masculine and feminine personality characteristics. Normative data are presented, as well as the results of various psychometric analyses. The major findings of conceptual interest are: (a) the dimensions of masculinity and femininity are empirically as well as logically independent; (b) the concept of psychological androgyny is a reliable one; and (c) highly sex-typed scores do not reflect a general tendency to respond in a socially desirable direction, but rather a specific tendency to describe oneself in accordance with sex-typed standards of desirable behavior for men and women.

Both in psychology and in society at large, masculinity and femininity have long been conceptualized as bipolar ends of a single continuum; accordingly, a person has had to be either masculine or feminine, but not both. This sex-role dichotomy has served to obscure two very plausible hypotheses: first, that many individuals might be "androgynous"; that is, they might be *both* masculine and feminine, *both* assertive and yielding,

both instrumental and expressive—depending on the situational appropriateness of these various behaviors; and conversely, that strongly sex-typed individuals might be seriously limited in the range of behaviors available to them as they move from situation to situation. According to both Kagan (1964) and Kohlberg (1966), the highly sex-typed individual is motivated to keep his behavior consistent with an internalized sex-role standard, a goal that he presumably accomplishes by suppressing any behavior that might be considered undesirable or inappropriate for his sex. Thus, whereas a narrowly masculine self-concept might inhibit behaviors that are stereotyped as feminine, and a narrowly feminine self-concept might inhibit behaviors that are stereotyped as masculine, a mixed, or androgynous, self-concept might allow an individual to freely engage in both "masculine" and "feminine" behaviors.

The current research program is seeking to explore these various hypotheses, as well as to provide construct validation for the concept of androgyny (Bem, 1974). Before the research could be initiated, however, it was first necessary to develop a new type of sex-role inventory, one that would not automatically build in an inverse relationship between masculinity and femininity. This article describes that inventory.

TABLE 1 / Sample of Items on the Masculinity, Femininity, and Social Desirability Scales of the BSRI

Masculine Items	Feminine Items	Neutral Items
Aggressive	Tender	Friendly
Competitive	Affectionate	Conscientious

Note: This table includes only a few samples of the items found in the BSRI. For the full list of items in each category, see the original source.

Source: Reproduced by special permission of the Publisher, Mind Garden, Inc., 855 Oak Grove Ave., Suite 215, Menlo Park, CA 94025 USA www.mindgarden.com from the **Bem Sex Role Inventory** by Sandra Bem. Copyright 1978 by Consulting Psychologists Press, Inc. All rights reserved. Further reproduction is prohibited without the Publisher's written consent.

The Bem Sex-Role Inventory (BSRI) contains a number of features that distinguish it from other, commonly used, masculinity-femininity scales, for example, the Masculinity-Femininity scale of the California Psychological Inventory (Gough, 1957). First, it includes both a Masculinity scale and a Femininity scale, each of which contains 20 personality characteristics. These characteristics are listed in the first and second columns of Table 1, respectively. Second, because the BSRI was founded on a conception of the sex-typed person as someone who has internalized society's sex-typed standards of desirable behavior for men and women, these personality characteristics were selected as masculine or feminine on the basis of sex-typed social desirability and not on the basis of differential endorsement by males and females as most other inventories have done. That is, a characteristic qualified as masculine if it was judged to be more desirable in American society for a man than for a woman, and it qualified as feminine if it was judged to be more desirable for a woman than for a man. Third, the BSRI characterizes a person as masculine, feminine, or androgynous as a function of the difference between his or her endorsement of masculine and feminine personality characteristics. A person is thus sex typed, whether masculine or feminine, to the extent that this difference score is high, the androgynous, to the extent that this difference score is low. Finally, the BSRI also includes a Social Desirability scale that is completely neutral with respect to sex. This scale now serves primarily to provide a neutral context for the Masculinity and Femininity scales, but it was utilized during the development of the BSRI to insure that the inventory would not simply be tapping a general tendency to endorse socially desirable traits. The 20 characteristics that make up this scale are listed in the third column of Table 1.

ITEM SELECTION

Both historically and cross-culturally, masculinity and femininity seem to have represented two complementary domains of *positive* traits and behaviors (Barry, Bacon, & Child, 1957;

Erikson, 1964; Parsons & Bales, 1955). In general, masculinity has been associated with an instrumental orientation, a cognitive focus on "getting the job done"; and femininity has been associated with an expressive orientation, an affective concern for the welfare of others.

Accordingly, as a preliminary to item selection for the Masculinity and Femininity scales, a list was compiled of approximately 200 personality characteristics that seemed to the author and several students to be both positive in value and either masculine or feminine in tone. This list served as the pool from which the masculine and feminine characteristics were ultimately chosen. As a preliminary to item selection for the Social Desirability scale, an additional list was compiled of 200 characteristics that seemed to be neither masculine nor feminine in tone. Of these "neutral" characteristics, half were positive in value and half were negative.

Because the BSRI was designed to measure the extent to which a person divorces himself from those characteristics that might be considered more "appropriate" for the opposite sex, the final items were selected for the Masculinity and Femininity scales if they were judged to be more desirable in American society for one sex than for the other. Specifically, judges were asked to utilize a 7-point scale, ranging from 1 ("Not at all desirable") to 7 ("Extremely desirable"), in order to rate the desirability in American society of each of the approximately 400 personality characteristics mentioned above. (E.g., "In American society, how desirable is it for a man to be truthful?" "In American society, how desirable is it for a woman to be sincere?") Each individual judge was asked to rate the desirability of all 400 personality characteristics either "for a man" or "for a woman." No judge was asked to rate both. The judges consisted of 40 Stanford undergraduates who filled out the questionnaire during the winter of 1972 and an additional 60 who did so the following summer. In both samples, half of the judges were male and half were female.

A personality characteristic qualified as masculine if it was independently judged by both males and females in both samples to be significantly more desirable for a man than for a woman ($p < .05$).[2] Similarly, a personality characteristic qualified as feminine if it was independently judged by both males and females in both samples to be significantly more desirable for a woman than for a man ($p < .05$). Of those characteristics that satisfied these criteria, 20 were selected for the Masculinity scale and 20 were selected for the Femininity scale (see the first and second columns of Table 1, respectively).

A personality characteristic qualified as neutral with respect to sex and hence eligible for the Social Desirability scale (a) if it was independently judged by both males and females to be no more desirable for one sex than for the other ($t < 1.2$, $p > .2$) and (b) if male and female judges did not differ significantly in their overall desirability judgments of that trait ($t < 1.2$, $p > .2$). Of those items that satisfied these several criteria, 10 positive and 10

TABLE 2 / Mean Social Desirability Ratings of the Masculine, Feminine, and Neutral Items

Item	Male Judges			Female Judges		
	Masculine Item	Feminine Item	Neutral Item	Masculine Item	Feminine Item	Neutral Item
For a man	5.59	3.63	4.00	5.83	3.74	3.94
For a woman	2.90	5.61	4.08	3.46	5.55	3.98
Difference	2.69	1.98	.08	2.37	1.81	.04
t	14.41*	12.13*	.17	10.22*	8.28*	.09

*$*p < .001$.

negative personality characteristics were selected for the BSRI Social Desirability scale in accordance with Edwards' (1964) finding that an item must be quite positive or quite negative in tone if it is to evoke a social desirability response set. (The 20 neutral characteristics are shown in the third column of Table 1.)

After all of the individual items had been selected, mean desirability scores were computed for the masculine, feminine, and neutral items for each of the 100 judges. As shown in Table 2, for both males and females, the mean desirability of the masculine and feminine items was significantly higher for the "appropriate" sex than for the "inappropriate" sex, whereas the mean desirability of the neutral items was no higher for one sex than for the other. These results are, of course, a direct consequence of the criteria used for item selection.

Table 3 separates out the desirability ratings of the masculine and feminine items for male and female judges rating their *own* sex. These own-sex ratings seem to best represent the desirability of these various items as perceived by men and women when they are asked to describe *themselves* on the inventory. That is, the left-hand column of Table 3 represents the phenomenology of male subjects taking the test and the right-hand column represents the phenomenology of female subjects taking the test. As can be seen in Table 3, not only are "sex-appropriate" characteristics more desirable for both males and females than "sex-inappropriate" characteristics, but the phenomenologies of male and female subjects are almost perfectly symmetric: that is, men and women are nearly equal in their perceptions of the desirability of sex-appropriate characteristics, sex-inappropriate characteristics, and the difference between them (*t* < 1 in all three comparisons).

TABLE 3 / Mean Social Desirability Ratings of the Masculine and Feminine Items for One's Own Sex

Item	Male Judges for a Man	Female Judges for a Woman
Masculine	5.59	3.46
Feminine	3.63	5.55
Difference	1.96	2.09
t	11.94*	8.88*

*$*p < .001$.

SCORING

The BSRI asks a person to indicate on a 7-point scale how well each of the 60 masculine, feminine, and neutral personality characteristics describes himself. The scale ranges from 1 ("Never or almost never true") to 7 ("Always or almost always true") and is labeled at each point. On the basis of his responses, each person receives three major scores: a Masculinity score, a Femininity score and, most important, an Androgyny score. In addition, a Social Desirability score can also be computed.

The Masculinity and Femininity scores indicate the extent to which a person endorses masculine and feminine personality characteristics as self-descriptive. Masculinity equals the mean self-rating for all endorsed masculine items, and Femininity equals the mean self-rating for all endorsed feminine items. Both can range from 1 to 7. It will be recalled that these two scores are logically independent. That is, the structure of the test does not constrain them in any way, and they are free to vary independently.

The Androgyny score reflects the relative amounts of masculinity and femininity that the person includes in his or her self-description, and, as such, it best characterizes the nature of the person's total sex role. Specifically, the Androgyny score is defined as Student's *t* ratio for the difference between a person's masculine and feminine self-endorsement; that is, the Androgyny score is the difference between an individual's masculinity and femininity normalized with respect to the standard deviations of his or her masculinity and femininity scores. The use of a *t* ratio as the index of androgyny—rather than a simple difference score—has two conceptual advantages: first, it allows us to ask whether a person's endorsement of masculine attributes differs significantly from his or her endorsement of feminine attributes and, if it does (*t* ≥ 2.025, *df* = 38, *p* < .05), to classify that person as significantly sex typed; and second, it allows us to compare different populations in terms of the percentage of significantly sex-typed individuals present within each.[3]

It should be noted that the greater the absolute value of the Androgyny score, the more the person is sex typed or sex reversed, with high positive scores indicating femininity and high negative scores indicating masculinity. A "masculine" sex role thus represents not only the endorsement of masculine attributes but the simultaneous rejection of feminine attributes. Similarly, a "feminine" sex role represents not only the endorsement of feminine attributes but the simultaneous rejection of masculine attributes. In contrast, the closer the Androgyny score is to zero, the more the person is androgynous. An "androgynous" sex role thus represents the equal endorsement of both masculine and feminine attributes.

The Social Desirability score indicates the extent to which a person describes himself in a socially desirable direction on items that are neutral with respect to sex. It is scored by reversing the self-endorsement ratings for the 10 undesirable items and then calculating the subject's mean endorsement score across all 20 neutral personality characteristics. The Social Desirability score can thus range from 1 to 7, with 1 indicating a strong tendency to describe oneself in a socially undesirable direction and 7 indicating a strong tendency to describe oneself in a socially desirable direction.

PSYCHOMETRIC ANALYSES

Subjects

During the winter and spring of 1973, the BSRI was administered to 444 male and 279 female students in introductory psychology at Stanford University. It was also administered to an additional 117 male and 77 female paid volunteers at Foothill Junior College. The data that these students provided represent the normative data for the BSRI, and, unless explicitly noted, they serve as the basis for all of the analyses that follow.

Internal Consistency

In order to estimate the internal consistency of the BSRI, coefficient alpha was computed separately for the Masculinity, Femininity and Social Desirability scores of the subjects in each of the two normative samples (Nunnally, 1967). The results showed all three scores to be highly reliable, both in the Stanford sample (Masculinity a = .86; Femininity a = .80; Social Desirability a = .75) and in the Foothill sample (Masculinity a = .86; Femininity a = .82; Social Desirability

a = .70). Because the reliability of the Androgyny t ratio could not be calculated directly, coefficient alpha was computed for the highly correlated Androgyny difference score, Femininity-Masculinity, using the formula provided by Nunnally (1967) for linear combinations. The reliability of the Androgyny difference score was .85 for the Stanford sample and .86 for the Foothill sample.

Relationship between Masculinity and Femininity

As indicated earlier, the Masculinity and Femininity scores of the BSRI are logically independent. That is, the structure of the test does not constrain them in any way, and they are free to vary independently. The results from the two normative samples reveal them to be empirically independent as well (Stanford male $r = .11$, female $r = -.14$; Foothill male $r = -.02$, female $r = -.07$). This finding vindicates the decision to design an inventory that would not artifactually force a negative correlation between masculinity and femininity.

Social Desirability Response Set

It will be recalled that a person is sex typed on the BSRI to the extent that his or her Androgyny score reflects the greater endorsement of "sex-appropriate" characteristics than of "sex-inappropriate" characteristics. However, because of the fact that the masculine and feminine items are all relatively desirable, even for the "inappropriate" sex, it is important to verify that the Androgyny score is not simply tapping a social desirability response set.

Accordingly, product-moment correlations were computed between the Social Desirability score and the Masculinity, Femininity, and Androgyny scores for the Stanford and Foothill samples separately. They were also computed between the Social Desirability score and the absolute value of the Androgyny score. These correlations are displayed in Table 4. As expected, both Masculinity and Femininity were correlated with Social Desirability. In contrast, the near-zero correlations between Androgyny and Social Desirability confirm that the Androgyny score is not measuring a general

TABLE 4 / Correlation of Masculinity, Femininity, and Androgyny with Social Desirability

Sample	Masculinity with Social Desirability		Femininity with Social Desirability		Androgyny with Social Desirability		|Androgyny| with Social Desirability	
	Males	Females	Males	Females	Males	Females	Males	Females
Stanford	.42	.19	.28	.26	.12	.03	.08	−.10
Foothill	.23	.19	.15	.15	−.07	.06	−.12	−.09
Stanford and Foothill combined	.38	.19	.28	.22	.08	.04	.03	−.10

TABLE 5 / Correlation of the Masculinity-Femininity Scales of the California Psychological Inventory (CPI) and Guilford-Zimmerman Scale with the Masculinity, Femininity, and Androgyny Scales of the BSRI

| | CPI | | Guilford-Zimmerman | |
Scale	Males	Females	Males	Females
BSRI Masculinity	−.42	−.25	.11	.15
BSRI Femininity	.27	.25	.04	−.06
BSRI Androgyny	.50	.30	−.04	−.06

Note: The CPI scale is keyed in the feminine direction, whereas the Guilford-Zimmerman scale is keyed in the masculine direction.

tendency to respond in a socially desirable direction. Rather, it is measuring a very specific tendency to describe oneself in accordance with sex-typed standards of desirable behavior for men and women.

Test-Retest Reliability

The BSRI was administered for a second time to 28 males and 28 females from the Stanford normative sample. The second administration took place approximately four weeks after the first. During this second administration, subjects were told that we were interested in how their responses on the test might vary over time, and they were explicitly instructed not to try to remember how they had responded previously. Product-moment correlations were computed between the first and second administrations for the Masculinity, Femininity, Androgyny, and Social Desirability scores. All four scores proved to be highly reliable over the four-week interval (Masculinity $r = .90$; Femininity $r = .90$; Androgyny $r = .93$; Social Desirability $r = .89$).

Correlations with Other Measures of Masculinity-Femininity

During the second administration of the BSRI, subjects were also asked to fill out the Masculinity-Femininity scales of the California Psychological Inventory and the Guilford-Zimmerman Temperament Survey, both of which have been utilized rather frequently in previous research on sex roles. Table 5 presents the correlations between these two scales and the Masculinity, Femininity, and Androgyny scales of the BSRI. As can be seen in the table, the Guilford-Zimmerman scale is not at all correlated with any of the three scales of the BSRI, whereas the California Psychological Inventory is moderately correlated with all three. It is not clear why the BSRI should be more highly correlated with the CPI than with the Guilford-Zimmerman scale, but the fact that none of the correlations is particularly high indicates that the BSRI is measuring an aspect of sex roles which is not directly tapped by either of these two scales.

NORMS

Table 6 presents the mean Masculinity, Femininity, and Social Desirability scores separately by sex for both the Stanford and the Foothill normative samples. It also presents

TABLE 6 / Sex Differences on the BSRI

| | Stanford University | | | Foothill Junior College | | |
| | Males | Females | | Males | Females | |
Scale Score	(n = 444)	(n = 279)	t	(n = 117)	(n = 77)	t
Masculinity						
M	4.97	4.57		4.96	4.55	
SD	.67	.69	7.62*	.71	.75	3.86*
Femininity						
M	4.44	5.01		4.62	5.08	
SD	.55	.52	13.88*	.64	.58	5.02*
Social Desirability						
M	4.91	5.08		4.88	4.89	
SD	.50	.50	4.40*	.50	.53	ns
Androgyny t Ratio						
M	−1.28	1.10		−.80	1.23	
SD	1.99	2.29	14.33*	2.23	2.42	5.98*
Androgyny Difference Score						
M	−0.53	.43		−.34	.53	
SD	.82	.93	14.28*	.97	.97	6.08*

*$p < .001$.

TABLE 7 / Percentage of Subjects in the Normative Samples Classified as Masculine, Feminine, or Androgynous

	Stanford University		Foothill Junior College	
	Males	Females	Males	Females
Item	($n = 444$)	($n = 279$)	($n = 117$)	($n = 77$)
% feminine ($t \geq 2.025$)	6	34	9	40
% near feminine ($1 < t < 2.025$)	5	20	9	8
% androgynous ($-1 \leq t \leq +1$)	34	27	44	38
% near masculine ($-2.025 \leq t \leq -1$)	19	12	17	7
% masculine ($t \leq -2.025$)	36	8	22	8

means for both the Androgyny t ratio and the Androgyny difference score. As can be seen in the table, males scored significantly higher than females on the Masculinity scale, and females scored significantly higher than males on the Femininity scale in both samples. On the two measures of androgyny, males scored on the masculine side of zero and females scored on the feminine side of zero. This difference is significant in both samples and for both measures. On the Social Desirability scale, females scored significantly higher than males at Stanford but not at Foothill. It should be noted that the size of this sex difference is quite small, however, even in the Stanford sample.

Table 7 presents the percentage of subjects within each of the two normative samples who qualified as masculine, feminine, or androgynous as a function of the Androgyny t ratio. Subjects are classified as sex typed, whether masculine or feminine, if the androgyny t ratio reaches statistical significance ($| t | \geq 2.025$, $df = 38$, $p < .05$), and they are classified as androgynous if the absolute value of the t ratio is less than or equal to one. Table 7 also indicates the percentage of subjects who fall between these various cutoff points. It should be noted that these cut-off points are somewhat arbitrary and that other investigators should feel free to adjust them in accordance with the characteristics of their particular subject populations.

CONCLUDING COMMENT

It is hoped that the development of the BSRI will encourage investigators in the areas of sex differences and sex roles to question the traditional assumption that it is the sex-typed individual who typifies mental health and to begin focusing on the behavioral and societal consequences of more flexible sex-role self-concepts. In a society where rigid sex-role differentiation has already outlived its utility, perhaps the androgynous person will come to define a more human standard of psychological health.

REFERENCES

Barry, H., Bacon, M. K., & Child, I. L. A cross-cultural survey of some sex differences in socialization. *Journal of Abnormal and Social Psychology,* 1957, *55,* 327–332.

Bem, S. L. Sex-role adaptability: One consequence of psychological androgyny. *Journal of Personality and Social Psychology,* 1974, in press.

Edwards, A. L. The measurement of human motives by means of personality scales. In D. Levine (Ed.), *Nebraska symposium on motivation: 1964.* Lincoln: University of Nebraska Press, 1964.

Erikson, E. H. Inner and outer space: Reflections on womanhood. In R. J. Lifton (Ed.), *The woman in America.* Boston: Houghton Mifflin, 1964.

Gough, H. G. *Manual for the California Psychological Inventory.* Palo Alto, Calif.: Consulting Psychologists Press, 1957.

Kagan, J. Acquisition and significance of sex-typing and sex-role identity. In M. L. Hoffman & L. W. Hoffman (Eds.), *Review of child development research.* Vol. 1. New York: Russell Sage Foundation, 1964.

Kohlberg, L. A cognitive-developmental analysis of children's sex-role concepts and attitudes. In E. E. Maccoby (Ed.), *The development of sex differences.* Stanford, Calif.: Stanford University Press, 1966.

Nunnally, J. C. *Psychometric theory.* New York: McGraw-Hill, 1967.

Parsons, T., & Bales, R. F. *Family, socialization, and interaction process.* New York: Free Press of Glencoe, 1955.

ENDNOTES

1. This research was supported by IROIMH 21735 from the National Institute of Mental Health. The author is grateful to Carol Korula, Karen Rook, Jenny Jacobs, and Odile van Embden for their help in analyzing the data.

2. All significance levels in this article are based on two-tailed t tests.

3. A Statistical Package for the Social Sciences (SPSS) computer program for calculating individual t ratios is available on request from the author. In the absence of computer facilities, one can utilize the simple Androgyny difference score, Femininity-Masculinity, as the index of androgyny. Empirically, the two indices are virtually identical ($r = .98$), and one can approximate the t-ratio value by multiplying the Androgyny difference score by 2.322. This conversion factor was derived empirically from our combined normative sample of 917 students at two different colleges.

CRITICAL THINKING QUESTIONS

1. Examine the sample items in Table 1 that are categorized as masculine, feminine, or neutral. Since this article was written in 1974, these items were selected over three decades ago. Do you think that these items are still applicable today, or are some of them dated and perhaps even controversial? Have notions of masculinity and femininity changed over time? Explain.

2. The BSRI (Bem Self-Role Inventory) is a self-report instrument. Do you think the way someone describes his or her characteristics on paper is necessarily an accurate portrayal of the way he or she really acts? In what way? How could you test this possibility?

3. What do you think of the concept of *androgyny?* Would society be better off if more people were androgynous rather than being either masculine *or* feminine? Why or why not?

4. Based on the information in the article, describe specific situations where an androgynous individual might be better suited than either a masculine or feminine individual. In what, if any, situations would someone only capable of masculine behaviors be more appropriate? What about someone only capable of feminine behaviors? Explain your answers.

5. After reading the article, you should have a good grasp of the concept of androgyny. If you explained this concept to others, do you think that most people would agree that they would be better off if they were androgynous rather than either masculine or feminine? Why or why not?

ADDITIONAL RELATED READINGS

Shin, K.H., Yang, J.A., & Edwards, C.E. (2010). Gender role identity among Korean and American college students: Links to gender and academic achievement. *Social Behavior and Personality, 38*(2), 267–272.

Wolfram, H.-J., Mohr, G., & Borchert, J. (2009). Gender role self-concept, gender-role conflict, and well-being in male primary school teachers. *Sex Roles, 60*(1–2), 114–127.

ARTICLE 15 _____

We could argue that one of the major differences separating we humans from nonhumans is our ability to self-reflect. Indeed, we spend a tremendous amount of time and energy thinking about ourselves and who we are. And while we look at and evaluate many different aspects of ourselves, perhaps the most central is that of *self-concept*. Briefly stated, our self-concept is our organized set of beliefs and feelings about ourselves. It is the totality of who we are as we see it.

Think about that for a second. If someone asked you to tell who you are, how would you describe yourself? What qualities would you mention—and not mention? However you answer, these questions will give you (and the other person) insight into your self-concept.

Even though self-concept is the centralized and organized set of images we have about ourselves, many other important aspects of the self also influence how we feel and how we act. For example, *self-esteem* is the affective evaluation we make about ourselves. That is, do we feel worthwhile, good, capable, and desirable—all characteristics of high self-esteem? Or do we not feel particularly good about ourselves—that we do not quite measure up to other people—as is the case with low self-esteem?

Most people believe that having high self-esteem is better than having low self-esteem. After all, it would seem reasonable that individuals with a better view of themselves would not only feel better about themselves but also act better than their lower self-esteem counterparts. Indeed, many parental and school-based philosophies encourage the development of high self-esteem in youth, believing that such interventions would produce a happier and better-behaved child. However, that might not actually be the case. Take aggression as an example. As it turns out, aggressive people do not necessarily have lower self-esteem. Instead, they often have an inflated view of themselves, what might be considered "normal" (as opposed to pathological) narcissism. Such narcissistic individuals, with their inflated sense of self, may be particularly vulnerable to threats to their ego and respond to such threats by lashing out aggressively.

The following article by Sander Thomaes, Brad J. Bushman, Bram Orobio de Castro, Geoffrey L. Cohen, and Jaap J.A. Denissen reports on a study designed to reduce aggression in narcissistic youth not by increasing their self-esteem but rather by buttressing their self-esteem. Buttressing self-esteem refers to reaffirming one's self-esteem rather than increasing it. How the researchers accomplished this and the implications for people who work with adolescents in particular are noteworthy.

Reducing Narcissistic Aggression by Buttressing Self-Esteem
An Experimental Field Study

■ Sander Thomaes, Brad J. Bushman, Bram Orobio de Castro, Geoffrey L. Cohen, and Jaap J.A. Denissen

ABSTRACT

Narcissistic individuals are prone to become aggressive when their egos are threatened. We report a randomized field experiment that tested whether a social-psychological intervention designed to lessen the impact of ego threat reduces narcissistic aggression. A sample of 405 young adolescents (mean age = 13.9 years) were randomly assigned to complete either a short self-affirmation writing assignment (which allowed them to reflect on their personally important values) or a control writing assignment. We expected that the self-affirmation would temporarily attenuate the ego-protective motivations that normally drive narcissists' aggression. As expected, the self-affirmation writing assignment reduced narcissistic aggression for a period of a school week, that is, for a period up to 400 times the duration of the intervention itself. These results provide the first empirical demonstration that buttressing self-esteem (as opposed to boosting self-esteem) can be effective at reducing aggression in at-risk youth.

Aggression in schools is a serious problem worldwide. Children are exposed to physical violence, verbal assaults, and psychological abuse at their schools on a daily basis (Kochenderfer-Ladd & Ladd, 2001; Nishina & Juvonen, 2005). Many current

Thomaes, S.; Bushman, B.J.; Orobio de Castro, B.; Cohen, G.L.; & Denissen, J.J.A. *Psychological Science*, 20(12), 1536–1542.

intervention programs rely on "boosting self-esteem" to reduce aggression (e.g., Kusché & Greenberg, 1994; Ringwalt, Graham, Paschall, Flewelling, & Browne, 1996). However, contrary to popular wisdom, aggressive people do not typically have low self-esteem. Instead, they often have grandiose, inflated, narcissistic self-views. Narcissistic individuals—both adults and children—are especially likely to lash out and become aggressive when their egos are threatened (e.g., Bushman & Baumeister, 1998; Stucke & Sporer, 2002; Thomaes, Bushman, Stegge, & Olthof, 2008). Thus, there are no compelling theoretical or empirical reasons to suggest that boosting self-esteem will be effective in reducing aggression. "Buttressing self-esteem" (i.e., making self-esteem less vulnerable to ego threat) should be more effective, at least in narcissistic individuals. Interventions aimed at buttressing self-esteem lessen the psychological impact of ego threat by focusing individuals on the core traits that define them as a person. Such interventions do not artificially raise, or inflate, self-esteem (Crocker, Niiya, & Mischkowski, 2008). The study we report here tested whether a short self-affirmation writing exercise known to temporarily buttress individuals' self-esteem can reduce narcissistic aggression.

INTERVENING WITH NARCISSISTIC AGGRESSION

Normal narcissism (i.e., narcissism viewed as a continuous trait, not a personality disorder) involves grandiose but simultaneously vulnerable self-views that are found in general child and adult populations (Raskin & Terry, 1988; Thomaes, Stegge, Bushman, Olthof, & Denissen, 2008). Research shows that narcissistic self-views are highly contingent on evaluations by others (Morf & Rhodewalt, 2001). Narcissists crave admiration and respect from others, and they are quick to engage in self-regulatory strategies to protect their self-views when they need to. Accordingly, researchers have explained narcissists' aggressive reactions to ego threat as defensive attempts to maintain self-worth (Bushman & Baumeister, 1998; Morf & Rhodewalt, 2001).

Thus, intervention techniques able to buffer people's self-views against ego threat should reduce narcissistic aggression. One such technique is to allow individuals to reaffirm their sense of self (Sherman & Cohen, 2006; Steele, 1988). Self-affirmation theory holds that an individual's overall sense of self is based on multiple domains of functioning, and that a threat to one domain of functioning can be compensated for by reflecting on the personal importance of a different domain (such as a self-defining skill or interest). Previous research has shown that self-affirmations buttress self-esteem, and thereby reduce the psychological impact of threatening feedback and social-evaluative stress both in the laboratory (Creswell et al., 2005; Koole, Smeets, Van Knippenberg, & Dijksterhuis, 1999; Sherman & Cohen, 2002) and in actual classroom settings (Cohen, Garcia, Apfel, & Master, 2006).

THE PRESENT STUDY

The present study tested whether a self-affirmation intervention can reduce narcissistic aggression in the "real world." Participants were 12 to 15 years old. We studied children this age for four reasons. First, ego threat is more frequently experienced in early adolescence than in any other developmental period. Children this age are increasingly concerned about blows to their self-esteem (Harter, 2006; Nishina & Juvonen, 2005; Rosenberg, 1986). Second, ego threat is particularly consequential in early adolescence, because children this age—in contrast to young children—are able to make global negative evaluations of the self (e.g., "I am a worthless person") that make ego-threatening experiences potentially harmful (Ferguson, Stegge, & Damhuis, 1991). Third, the extent to which children engage in serious aggressive and violent behavior increases steeply in early adolescence (Dodge, Coie, & Lynam, 2006). Fourth, it seems important to try to intervene with individuals' self-views in a developmental period when self-views start to take a relatively mature form, but have not yet become deeply ingrained in patterns of maladaptive behavior that may be hard to change.

We conducted a randomized field experiment in which participants completed either a short (15-min) self-affirmation or a control writing exercise in their classes (Cohen et al., 2006). In the affirmation condition, participants wrote about their most important values and why these values are important to them. In the control condition, participants wrote about their least important values and why these values may be important to other people. Peer reports of aggressive behavior in the schools served as an ecologically valid measure of aggression. We also obtained reports of state self-esteem, a continuous measure of experienced ego threat. Low state self-esteem is the key experiential component of ego threat (Baumeister, Smart, & Boden, 1996). Narcissism was measured along with trait self-esteem 3 weeks before the self-affirmation intervention. Aggression and state self-esteem were measured in the week before the self-affirmation (Assessment 1), in the week after the self-affirmation (Assessment 2), in the week after a second self-affirmation (Assessment 3), and again 3 weeks later (Assessment 4). On the basis of previous laboratory experiments (e.g., Bushman & Baumeister, 1998; Stucke & Sporer, 2002; Thomaes, Bushman, et al., 2008), we predicted that narcissistic youth would behave aggressively, but only when they reported having low state self-esteem (i.e., when they experienced high levels of ego threat). More important, we predicted that our self-affirmation intervention would reduce aggression in narcissistic youth having low state self-esteem. Our short-term longitudinal design permitted us to test the directionality of effects, and we conducted lagged-effects analyses to establish that the intervention indeed influenced narcissists' aggression after they experienced low state self-esteem (as predicted), rather than narcissists' experience of low self-esteem after they behaved aggressively.

METHOD

Participants

Participants were 405 sixth and seventh graders (52% boys, 48% girls) recruited from two public middle schools serving middle-class neighborhoods in The Netherlands (parental consent rate = 96%). They ranged in age from 12 to 15 (mean age = 13.9 years, SD = 0.7). Most participants were Caucasian (90%); 10% had other (e.g., Turkish, Dutch Antillean, mixed) cultural-ethnic backgrounds.

Self-View Measures

Three weeks before the start of the experiment, students completed self-report measures of narcissism and trait self-esteem in their classrooms. Trait self-esteem was measured to examine the possibility that low trait self-esteem contributes to real-world aggression, as has been suggested by some researchers (Donnellan, Trzesniewski, Robins, Moffitt, & Caspi, 2005). Trait self-esteem was measured using the 5-item Global Self-Worth subscale of the Self-Perception Profile for Adolescents (Harter, 1988; Cronbach's α = .76). This reliable and valid scale assesses adolescents' overall perception of worth as a person (e.g., "Some kids like the kind of person they are. How much are you like these kids?"). Items are rated along a 4-point scale (0 = *not at all*, 3 = *exactly*). Narcissism was measured using the 10-item Childhood Narcissism Scale (Thomaes, Stegge, et al., 2008; Cronbach's α = .77). This scale assesses grandiose, entitled views of self and adversarial interpersonal attitudes (e.g., "Without me, our class would be much less fun" and "Kids like me deserve something extra"). Items are rated along a 4-point scale (0 = *not at all true*, 3 = *completely true*). The Childhood Narcissism Scale is a reliable, one-dimensional measure of stable individual differences in childhood narcissism. Research indicates that childhood narcissism has psychological and interpersonal correlates very similar to those of adult narcissism (Thomaes, Stegge, et al., 2008).

Procedure

State self-esteem and aggression were first measured at Assessment 1, which was completed on Friday afternoon in the week prior to the first self-affirmation intervention. To measure state self-esteem, we presented students with a pictorial scale showing a very small figure at one end and a very large figure at the other end (the scale was taken from Bradley & Lang's, 1994, Self-Assessment Manikin). The small figure was labeled "very unsatisfied with myself in the past week," and the large figure was labeled "very satisfied with myself in the past week." Students indicated which figure on the 9-point scale best reflected how they felt about themselves in the past week. Next, students completed a peer-nomination aggression measure developed in a pilot study (see Aggression Measure Pilot Study

in the Supporting Information available on-line—see p. 1542). The measure contained 1 item for physical aggression ("Who kicked, pushed, or hit another student at school in the past week?"), 1 item for direct verbal aggression ("Who called another student names, or said mean things to another student at school in the past week?"), 1 item for relational aggression ("Who spread rumors or lies about another student, or excluded another student from the group at school in the past week?"), and 4 positively worded filler items (e.g., "Who seemed very happy in the past week?"). Students circled the names of all classmates (on a class roster with order randomized) for whom each item applied. For each student, the number of received nominations was summed across the 3 aggression items and divided by the number of classmates to yield a weekly aggression score (Cronbach's α = .74 at Assessment 1).

The following Monday morning, participants completed the intervention exercises in their classrooms. Each individual was randomly assigned to either the self-affirmation condition or the control condition. In each class, there were approximately equal numbers of participants in the two conditions, and the gender distribution was also approximately equal (53% boys and 47% girls in the self-affirmation condition; 52% boys and 48% girls in the control condition). Following standard procedures (Cohen et al., 2006), students were given a list of 12 values (i.e., athletic ability, being good at art, being smart or getting good grades, being creative, being independent, living in the moment, belonging to a social group, music, politics, relationships with friends or family, religious values, sense of humor). In the self-affirmation condition, students selected 2 or 3 of their most important values and then wrote a short paragraph about why these values were important to them. In the control condition, students selected 2 or 3 of their least important values and then wrote about why these values may be important to other people. To reinforce the manipulation, we also asked students to indicate their level of agreement with several statements about the values they chose (e.g., "I care about these values" in the self-affirmation condition and "Some people care about these values" in the control condition). Students worked on the exercises quietly and independently, and returned their work in a sealed envelope after they finished. The exercises took approximately 15 min to complete. Students who were not present on Monday (n = 9; 2%) completed the intervention exercises the first day they reentered school.

On Friday afternoon in the same week (i.e., 1 school week after the first intervention), Assessment 2 of state self-esteem and aggression was completed. The measures were identical to the ones completed at baseline (Cronbach's α = .76 for Assessment 2 aggression). To keep students motivated, we held a raffle for a CD or DVD among the participants in each class.

Five weeks later on Monday morning, students completed a second intervention exercise (or "booster shot affirmation"—Cohen et al., 2006). They were assigned to the same condition to which they were assigned previously. The exercises and procedures were the same as for the first intervention. On Friday afternoon in the same week (i.e., 6 school weeks after the first intervention and 1 school week after the second), Assessment 3 of state self-esteem and aggression was completed (Cronbach's α = .82 for Assessment 3 aggression). Finally, 3 weeks later on Friday afternoon (i.e., 9 school weeks after the first intervention and 4 school weeks after the second), students completed Assessment 4 of state self-esteem and aggression (Cronbach's α = .77 for Assessment 4 aggression).

RESULTS

Preliminary Analyses

Narcissism, trait self-esteem, baseline state self-esteem, baseline aggression, gender distribution, and age did not differ between groups (ps > .39, $p_{rep}s$ < .58). Thus, random assignment to the self-affirmation and control groups was successful. (Table S1 in the Supporting Information available online provides descriptive statistics and correlations.)

Primary Analyses

The data were analyzed using hierarchical linear modeling (SPSS mixed). They were organized to account for their hierarchical structure, with four assessment occasions (with an autoregressed AR1 covariance structure) nested within students. We tested two models with aggression as the dependent variable. Gender and trait self-esteem were included as covariates. Narcissism and state self-esteem were included as predictor variables. In addition, three dummy variables were included as predictor variables: one indicating group assignment (0 = control condition, 1 = self-affirmation condition), one indicating the short-term intervention effect (0 = control condition 1 school week ago, 1 = self-affirmation condition 1 school week ago), and one indicating the long-term intervention effect (0 = control condition 4 to 6 school weeks ago, 1 = self-affirmation condition 4 to 6 school weeks ago). Finally, we included the two-way interaction of narcissism and state self-esteem and (to analyze the predicted effects of the self-affirmation) two three-way interactions: the interaction of narcissism, state self-esteem, and the short-term intervention dummy variable and the interaction of narcissism, state self-esteem, and the long-term intervention dummy variable.[1] Continuous covariate and predictor variables were standardized to reduce multicollinearity and facilitate the interpretation of effect-size estimates (Aiken & West, 1991; Jaccard & Turrisi, 2003).

In Model 1, aggression was predicted by concurrent levels of state self-esteem (see Table 1). There was a significant interaction between narcissism and state self-esteem, b = –0.09, p < .001, p_{rep} > .98. More important, this two-way interaction was qualified by the predicted three-way interaction of narcissism, state self-esteem, and the short-term intervention dummy variable, b = 0.10, p < .02, p_{rep} > .93. To interpret this significant three-way interaction, we examined the two-way interactions between narcissism and state self-esteem separately for the control and self-affirmation conditions. In the control condition, the standard pattern found in previous laboratory research emerged. Narcissism was associated with increased aggression when students had a low level of state self-esteem (1 *SD* below the mean; Aiken & West, 1991), b = 0.35, p < .01, p_{rep} > .95, but not when students had a high level of state self-esteem (1 *SD* above the mean), b = 0.05, p > .68, p_{rep} < .37 (see Fig. 1). Thus, we generalized existing laboratory findings to the real world. By contrast, in the self-affirmation condition, narcissism was *not* associated with increased aggression, regardless of whether students had low or high state self-esteem, b = 0.15, p > .22, p_{rep} < .70, and b = –0.22, p > .07, p_{rep} < .86, respectively (see Fig. 1). Thus, these analyses indicate that a 15-min self-affirmation writing exercise reduces narcissistic aggression for a period of 1 school week. There was no significant three-way interaction effect involving the long-term intervention dummy variable, b = 0.05, p > .31, p_{rep} < .64; this result indicates that intervention effects dissipated over time. In addition, no effects were found for trait self-esteem. Boys were more aggressive than girls, b = –0.42, p < .001, p_{rep} > .98.

In Model 2, we included the same predictors as in Model 1, with the exception that we instead used the state self-esteem

FIGURE 1 / Results of the analysis testing the intervention effect after one school week. The graph shows the aggression levels of students with low (1 SD below the mean) and high (1 SD above the mean) narcissism and low (1 SD below the mean) and high (1 SD above the mean) concurrent state self-esteem, separately for the self-affirmation and the no-affirmation (control) conditions.

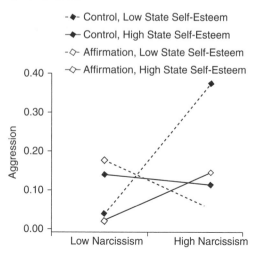

TABLE 1 / Results of Hierarchical Linear Modeling Analyses

Parameter	Model 1			Model 2			Model 3		
	b	*SE*	95% confidence interval	b	*SE*	95% confidence interval	b	*SE*	95% confidence interval
Intercept	0.20**	0.07	0.06, 0.34	0.17*	0.07	0.03, 0.32	0.09†	0.06	−0.02, 0.20
Self-affirmation condition	0.03	0.09	−0.15, 0.20	0.03	0.09	−0.14, 0.21	−0.01	0.07	−0.16, 0.13
Narcissim	0.06	0.04	−0.02, 0.15	0.06	0.04	−0.03, 0.14	−0.02	0.03	−0.08, 0.05
Trait self-esteem	−0.02	0.04	−0.11, 0.06	−0.04	0.04	−0.13, 0.04	0.42**	0.03	0.35, 0.48
Female gender	−0.42	0.09	−0.59, −0.25	−0.41	0.09	−0.58, −0.24	−0.19**	0.07	−0.32, −0.06
STI	0.00	0.04	−0.08, 0.08	0.03	0.04	−0.05, 0.11	0.01	0.05	−0.09, 0.12
LTI	−0.01	0.05	−0.10, 0.08	−0.02	0.04	−0.10, 0.07	0.00	0.06	−0.11, 0.11
IV	−0.03	0.02	−0.08, 0.01	0.02	0.02	−0.02, 0.06	0.00	0.02	−0.04, 0.05
Narcissism × IV	−0.09	0.02	−0.14, −0.04	−0.04†	0.03	−0.09, 0.01	−0.05	0.03	−0.10, 0.00
Narcissism × IV × STI	0.10	0.04	0.01, 0.19	0.09*	0.04	0.01, 0.17	0.04	0.04	−0.05, 0.12
Narcissism × IV × LTI	0.05	0.05	−0.05, 0.14	−0.02	0.04	−0.10, 0.07	0.02	0.05	−0.08, 0.12

Note: Mode I predicted aggression from concurrent self-esteem, and Model 2 predicted aggression from self-esteem at the previous assessment; Model 3 predicted self-esteem from aggression at the previous assessment. STI = short-term intervention dummy; LTI = long-term intervention dummy; IV = independent variable.

†$p < .10$.   *$p < .05$.   **$p < .01$.

level of the previous assessment (i.e., a lagged predictor) as the predictor of aggression (see Table 1). Because we also included an autoregressive term (covariance estimate = .36, $p < .001$, $p_{rep} > .98$), this predictor can be interpreted as the effect of the initial level of state self-esteem on changes in aggression. The results from Model 2 were very similar to the results from Model 1. The two-way interaction between narcissism and state self-esteem did not reach conventional levels of significance, $b = −0.04$, $p = .09$, $p_{rep} = .83$. However, the predicted three-way interaction of narcissism, state self-esteem, and the short-term intervention dummy variable remained significant, $b = 0.09$, $p < .03$, $p_{rep} > .90$. In the control condition, narcissism was associated with increased aggression when students had low but not high levels of lagged state self-esteem, $b = 0.37$, $p < .01$, $p_{rep} > .95$, and $b = 0.05$, $p > .70$, $p_{rep} < .36$, respectively. In the self-affirmation condition, narcissism was not significantly related to aggression, either for students with low lagged state self-esteem, $b = 0.09$, $p > .47$, $p_{rep} < .53$, or for students with high levels of lagged state self-esteem, $b = −0.24$, $p > .06$, $p_{rep} < .87$. Aggression again showed a significant gender effect, $b = −0.41$, $p < .001$, $p_{rep} > .98$. In summary, the results from Model 2 extend those from Model 1 by showing that narcissistic aggression follows from initially experienced ego threat, a link that can be temporarily attenuated by means of a self-affirmation exercise. Again, no effects involving the long-term intervention dummy variable or trait self-esteem were found.

To compare the direction of effects for state self-esteem and aggression, we ran an additional model in which state self-esteem was predicted by the aggression level at the previous assessment. In other words, Model 2 showed that state self-esteem was asso-

ciated with subsequent changes in aggression, and Model 3 tested whether the reverse was also true (Table 1). Not surprisingly, trait self-esteem predicted the average level of state self-esteem (intercept), $b = 0.42$, $p < .001$, $p_{rep} > .98$. In addition, a two-way interaction between narcissism and lagged (previous assessment) aggression emerged, $b = −0.05$, $p < .04$, $p_{rep} > .89$; narcissistic children tended to react to previous aggression with decreases in self-esteem, perhaps because their self-esteem is sensitive to negative interpersonal encounters (Morf & Rhodewalt, 2001; Thomaes et al., in press). There were no significant effects involving the short-term and long-term intervention dummy variables, a result supporting our prediction that the self-affirmation would influence narcissists' aggressive responses to lowered self-esteem (rather than narcissists' self-esteem responses to aggression). A significant gender effect was also found, $b = −0.19$, $p < .001$, $p_{rep} > .98$; girls had lower levels of state self-esteem than boys did.

DISCUSSION

This randomized field experiment tested whether a self-affirmation intervention can reduce narcissistic aggression in youth. We generalized existing laboratory findings to the real world by showing that narcissistic individuals (not individuals with low self-esteem) behave aggressively when they experience ego threat. More important, we found that this standard pattern was temporarily changed with a short self-affirmation writing exercise. This exercise prevented narcissists from behaving aggressively when they experienced ego threat. Lagged-effects analyses confirmed the predicted direction of effects: The intervention reduced narcissists' aggression following ego threat (rather than vice versa). The effect of the intervention lasted for a period of 1 school week (i.e., for a period of up to 400 times the duration of the intervention itself).

What accounted for the effectiveness of the seemingly minor self-affirmation in our study? We propose that the self-affirmation temporarily attenuated the ego-protective motivations that normally drive narcissists' aggression. Previous research has shown that self-affirmations buttress self-esteem. People who are reminded of values that are important to them become less vulnerable to experiences of ego threat, presumably because they realize that their worth as a person does not hinge upon one particular domain of functioning (Creswell et al., 2005; Koole et al., 1999; Sherman & Cohen, 2002). Because vulnerability to ego threat is the key cause of narcissists' aggressive inclinations (Morf & Rhodewalt, 2001), this previous research suggests that we lessened the motivational source of narcissists' aggression. Note that the intervention did not raise students' self-esteem. Trajectories of state self-esteem did not differ following the self-affirmation and control writing assignments. Rather, the intervention made students behave in a less defensive, less aggressive manner when they experienced ego threat.

The developmental timing of the intervention may also have contributed to its effectiveness. Early adolescence is a time when children become increasingly motivated to develop an autonomous identity (Collins & Steinberg, 2006; Erikson, 1968). The intervention allowed the students to reflect on the core values that define them as a person, and so it may have been particularly effective in this developmental period. Finally, small interventions can have strong effects if they interrupt negative cycles of events that would otherwise occur (Cohen et al., 2006). This may well have been the case in our study. Aggressive behaviors rarely are isolated events of one-directional hostility, but often set in motion a sequence of interpersonal hostilities (e.g., Perry, Perry, & Kennedy, 1992; Phelps, 2001). By inhibiting initial outbursts of narcissistic aggression, the intervention may have prevented subgroups of individuals from becoming entrapped in peer conflicts marked by repeated aggressive behaviors.

Our results are consistent with a basic tenet of self-affirmation theory (Sherman & Cohen, 2006; Steele, 1988), namely, that activities that remind people of "who they are" can have strong behavioral benefits. We have provided the first evidence that those benefits extend to the domain of aggressive behavior. In addition, our results contribute to the debate on the role of low self-esteem that has dominated aggression research for more than a decade (e.g., Baumeister et al., 1996; Donnellan et al., 2005). The weak and inconsistent evidence for a link between low trait self-esteem and aggression has occasionally been attributed to the frequent use of laboratory aggression measures that may not generalize outside the laboratory (Donnellan et al., 2005). Our study examined real-world aggression and still contradicts the view that low trait self-esteem underlies aggression.

The applied relevance of this study is that it provides the first empirical demonstration that buttressing self-esteem can be effective at reducing narcissistic aggression. Two cautions are needed, though. First, the self-affirmation procedure that we used should not be seen as a ready-to-use intervention strategy. We found no evidence for a sustained reduction in aggression longer than a school week. Furthermore, the impact of the intervention was relatively small. It reduced but did not eliminate narcissistic aggression. Future research is needed to generalize our findings to other applied settings, and to explore more powerful self-affirmation intervention procedures that can have longer-lasting effects. Second, the intervention was effective in aggressive youth with narcissistic tendencies, not in aggressive youth in general. Thus, self-affirmation procedures are not likely to be effective as universal, classroom-based aggression interventions.

In conclusion, we hope our study will encourage the development of theory- and evidence-based aggression interventions that target children's self-views. Many current intervention programs focus on boosting self-esteem, but there are no clear theoretical or empirical reasons why boosting self-esteem should reduce aggression. Self-affirmations buttress self-esteem and buffer people against ego threat, thereby contributing to reducing narcissistic violence and aggression in schools.

REFERENCES

Aiken, L.S., & West, S.G. (1991). *Multiple regression: Testing and interpreting interactions.* Newbury Park, CA: Sage.

Baumeister, R.F., Smart, L., & Boden, J.M. (1996). Relation of threatened egotism to violence and aggression: The dark side of high self-esteem. *Psychological Review, 103,* 5–33.

Bradley, M.M., & Lang, P.J. (1994). Measuring emotion: The Self-Assessment Manikin and the semantic differential. *Journal of Behavior Therapy and Experimental Psychiatry, 25,* 49–59.

Bushman, B.J., & Baumeister, R.F. (1998). Threatened egotism, narcissism, self-esteem, and direct and displaced aggression: Does self-love or self-hate lead to violence? *Journal of Personality and Social Psychology, 75,* 219–229.

Cohen, G.L., Garcia, J., Apfel, N., & Master, A. (2006). Reducing the racial achievement gap: A social-psychological intervention. *Science, 313,* 1307–1310.

Collins, W.A., & Steinberg, L. (2006). Adolescent development in interpersonal context. In W. Damon & R.M. Lerner (Series Eds.) & N. Eisenberg (Vol. Ed.), *Handbook of child psychology: Vol. 3. Social, emotional, and personality development* (6th ed., pp. 1003–1067). New York: Wiley.

Creswell, J.D., Welch, W., Taylor, S.E., Sherman, D.K., Gruenewald, T., & Mann, T. (2005). Affirmation of personal values buffers neuroendocrine and psychological stress responses. *Psychological Science, 16,* 846–851.

Crocker, J., Niiya, Y., & Mischkowski, D. (2008). Why does writing about important values reduce defensiveness? Self-affirmation and the role of positive other-directed feelings. *Psychological Science, 19*, 740–747.

Dodge, K.A., Coie, J.D., & Lynam, D. (2006). Aggression and antisocial behavior in youth. In W. Damon & R.M. Lerner (Series Eds.) & N. Eisenberg (Vol. Ed.), *Handbook of child psychology: Vol. 3. Social, emotional, and personality development* (6th ed., pp. 719–788). New York: Wiley.

Donnellan, M.B., Trzesniewski, K.H., Robins, R.W., Moffitt, T.E., & Caspi, A. (2005). Low self-esteem is related to aggression, antisocial behavior, and delinquency. *Psychological Science, 16*, 328–335.

Erikson, E.H. (1968). *Identity: Youth and crisis.* New York: Norton.

Ferguson, T.J., Stegge, H., & Damhuis, I. (1991). Children's understanding of guilt and shame. *Child Development, 62*, 827–839.

Harter, S. (1988). *Manual for the self-perception profile for adolescents.* Denver, CO: University of Denver.

Harter, S. (2006). The self. In W. Damon & R.M. Lerner (Series Eds.) & N. Eisenberg (Vol. Ed.), *Handbook of child psychology: Vol. 3. Social, emotional, and personality development* (6th ed., pp. 505–570). New York: Wiley.

Jaccard, J., & Turrisi, R. (2003). *Interaction effects in multiple regression* (2nd ed.). Newbury Park, CA: Sage.

Kochenderfer-Ladd, B., & Ladd, G.W. (2001). Variations in peer victimization: Relations to children's maladjustment. In J. Juvonen & S. Graham (Eds.), *Peer harassment in school: The plight of the vulnerable and victimized* (pp. 25–48). New York: Guilford.

Koole, S.L., Smeets, K., Van Knippenberg, A., & Dijksterhuis, A. (1999). The cessation of rumination through self-affirmation. *Journal of Personality and Social Psychology, 77*, 111–125.

Kusché, C., & Greenberg, M. (1994). *PATHS: Promoting alternative thinking strategies.* South Deerfield, MA: Developmental Research Programs.

Morf, C.C., & Rhodewalt, F. (2001). Unraveling the paradoxes of narcissism: A dynamic self-regulatory processing model. *Psychological Inquiry, 12*, 177–196.

Nishina, A., & Juvonen, J. (2005). Daily reports of witnessing and experiencing peer harassment in middle school. *Child development, 76*, 435–450.

Perry, D.G., Perry, L.C., & Kennedy, E. (1992). Conflict and the development of antisocial behavior. In C.U. Shantz & W.W. Hartup (Eds.), *Conflict in child and adolescent development* (pp. 301–329). New York: Cambridge University Press.

Phelps, C.E.R. (2001). Children's responses to overt and relational aggression. *Journal of Clinical Child Psychology, 30*, 240–252.

Raskin, R., & Terry, H. (1988). A principal-components analysis of the Narcissistic Personality Inventory and further evidence of its construct validation. *Journal of Personality and Social Psychology, 54*, 890–902.

Ringwalt, C.L., Graham, L.A., Paschall, M.J., Flewelling, R.L., & Browne, D.C. (1996). Supporting adolescents with guidance and employment (SAGE). *American Journal of Preventive Medicine, 12*, 31–38.

Rosenberg, M. (1986). Self-concept from middle childhood through adolescence. In J. Suls & A. Greenwald (Eds.), *Psychological perspectives on the self* (pp. 107–135). Hillsdale, NJ: Erlbaum.

Sherman, D.K., & Cohen, G.L. (2002). Accepting threatening information: Self-affirmation and the reduction of defensive biases. *Current Directions in Psychological Science, 11*, 119–123.

Sherman, D.K., & Cohen, G.L. (2006). The psychology of self-defense: Self-affirmation theory. In M.P. Zanna (Ed.), *Advances in experimental social psychology* (Vol. 38, pp. 183–242). San Diego, CA: Academic Press.

Steele, C.M. (1988). The psychology of self-affirmation: Sustaining the integrity of the self. In L. Berkowitz (Ed.), *Advances in experimental social psychology* (Vol. 21, pp. 261–302). New York: Academic Press.

Stucke, T.S., & Sporer, S.L. (2002). When a grandiose self-image is threatened: Narcissism and self-concept clarity as predictors of negative emotions and aggression following ego threat. *Journal of Personality, 70*, 509–532.

Thomaes, S., Bushman, B.J., Stegge, H., & Olthof, T. (2008). Trumping shame by blasts of noise: Narcissism, self-esteem, shame, and aggression in young adolescents. *Child Development, 79*, 1792–1801.

Thomaes, S., Reijntjes, A., Orobio de Castro, B., Bushman, B.J., Poorthuis, A., & Telch, M.J. (in press). I like me if you like me: On the interpersonal modulation and regulation of preadolescents' state self-esteem. *Child Development.*

Thomaes, S., Stegge, H., Bushman, B.J., Olthof, T., & Denissen, J. (2008). Development and validation of the Childhood Narcissism Scale. *Journal of Personality Assessment, 90*, 382–391.

ENDNOTE

1. We also modeled the trajectories of state self-esteem and aggression across the study period by including linear and quadratic time effects. Because these effects were nonsignificant, they were excluded from the subsequent models.

CRITICAL THINKING QUESTIONS

1. Have you ever known someone who had high self-esteem yet seemed to engage in socially unacceptable behaviors such as aggression or something else? Using information from this article and other sources as well, how would you explain that behavior?

2. Are there any practical implications from the findings of this article that can be used by parents? If so, what might they be and why might they work? If not, why don't you think those findings are applicable to parenting?

3. According to the article, " . . . a basic tenet of self-affirmation theory . . . (is) that activities that remind people of "who they are" can have strong behavioral benefits." What are some other activities that might remind someone of "who they are"? Explain why you think those activities might be successful.

4. The article concludes with some limitations to the findings of the study. What are they? Design a study that might overcome some of those limitations.

5. This study involved young adolescents. Do you think similar findings might occur with other populations as well? Why or why not?

CHAPTER INTEGRATION QUESTIONS_____

1. The three articles in this chapter dealt with different aspects of social identity, namely self-monitoring, gender, and self-esteem. How might these concepts be related to one another?
2. Might different styles of self-monitoring be related to masculine, feminine, and androgynous orientations? What about self-monitoring and aggression? Explain your reasoning.
3. Psychologist Nathaniel Branden said, "Of all the judgments that we pass in life, none is as important as the one we pass on ourselves." Do you agree or disagree with this quotation? Explain your reasoning. How does this quotation relate to an overall theme in this chapter?

Chapter Six

PREJUDICE
AND DISCRIMINATION

PREJUDICE. THINK OF the implications of that word. It is so negative that even people who are highly prejudiced are often reluctant to use that term to describe themselves. Instead, prejudiced people may say that their opinions about members of certain groups are accurate and well founded, perhaps even that these groups deserve disdain.

Although the words *prejudice* and *discrimination* are often used interchangeably, they actually refer to two different things. *Prejudice* is an attitude, a set of beliefs about a member of a group based just on membership in that group. *Discrimination,* on the other hand, is a behavior, the differential treatment of a person based on membership in a particular group. You do not need to look far for the results of prejudiced attitudes and discriminatory behaviors: History is full of suffering that has been inflicted on people due solely to their membership in particular groups.

During the last several decades of the twentieth century, many great strides were made in the area of social justice. Overt discrimination against various groups was outlawed and, in many cases, was reduced significantly. Consider the overtly stated opinions of people that you hear from day to day. The amount of racism, for example, is less noticeable than it would have been only 20 or 30 years ago.

So, does this mean that the level of prejudiced thinking has, indeed, decreased over time? Not necessarily. It may be that people just *express* these prejudices more subtlety than they did in the past. In fact, prejudiced thinking may be rooted in how our minds process information. Article 16, "Unmasking 'Racial Micro Aggressions'," examines how prejudices manifest themselves in many small (yet significant) ways. It turns out that prejudice may be expressed in more subtle ways than most of us realize.

Article 17, "Attitudes vs. Actions," deals with the consistency between people's attitudes and behaviors, or, more specifically, the consistency between prejudice and discrimination. Do we always act in accordance with our prejudiced attitudes? Or do we sometimes contradict what we say we believe? This classic article was one of the first to address the issue of whether prejudice and discrimination necessarily occur together.

Finally, Article 18, "Interracial Roommate Relationships: An Experimental Field Test of the Contact Hypothesis," addresses a consideration raised in Article 16: specifically, that there may be a difference between explicitly expressed prejudices (which are relatively easy to control) and more underlying and subtle forms of prejudice (which are harder to control). Most studies on prejudice tend to use explicitly stated measures of prejudice. This study used interracial college roommate relationships as its focus, and over the course of a term examined changes in both the student's explicitly stated measures of prejudice and those aspects of prejudice that are automatically activated and hence harder to control.

ARTICLE 16

Just about anyone, by virtue of membership in a particular group, can be a target of prejudice and discrimination. The standard scenario is that a person is prejudged and reacted to not as an individual but as a member of some group, such that the presumed general characteristics of the group are automatically attributed to the individual. This process is known as *stereotyping*.

Stereotyping is an everyday fact of life. Although we may hope that we judge every person as an individual, the cognitive strategies we use to make sense of our world, as discussed in Chapter 3, suggest otherwise. In particular, when confronted with a member of an identifiable group, we may rely on a stereotype as a sort of decision-making shortcut, rather than consider the person on his or her own merits. How we feel about the person and how we treat him or her will be based on the stereotype, not the individual. As such, stereotypes frequently underlie prejudiced attitudes and discriminatory behaviors.

Are people less prejudiced today than in the past? In attempting to answer this question, it may be useful to distinguish between the various ways in which prejudice can be expressed. At one extreme are legalized forms of discrimination, such as the so-called Jim Crow laws of the past, which institutionalized discrimination against African Americans, and current laws that restrict women from combat roles in the U.S. military. At the other extreme are subtle types of differential treatment, such as how people are addressed and even how much eye contact they receive. Although subtle, these types of behaviors may have a huge impact on the people against whom they are directed. Furthermore, while it is relatively easy to control what we say (e.g., not making racist remarks), it is much more difficult to control the nonverbal cues that may betray our underlying feelings (e.g., moving away from someone).

The following article by Tori DeAngelis examines some very subtle forms of racism, so subtle, in fact, that neither the performer nor the recipient of that behavior may understand exactly what is going on. These *racial microaggressions* may send subtle yet powerful negative messages which are very difficult to deal with precisely because they operate at a very subtle, and most likely unconscious, level.

Unmasking "Racial Micro Aggressions"

■ Tori DeAngelis

Two colleagues—one Asian-American, the other African-American—board a small plane. A flight attendant tells them they can sit anywhere, so they choose seats near the front of the plane and across the aisle from each another so they can talk.

At the last minute, three white men enter the plane and take the seats in front of them. Just before takeoff, the flight attendant, who is white, asks the two colleagues if they would mind moving to the back of the plane to better balance the plane's load. Both react with anger, sharing the same sense that they are being singled out to symbolically "sit at the back of the bus." When they express these feelings to the attendant, she indignantly denies the charge, saying she was merely trying to ensure the flight's safety and give the two some privacy.

Were the colleagues being overly sensitive, or was the flight attendant being racist?

For Teachers College, Columbia University psychologist Derald Wing Sue, PhD—the Asian-American colleague on the plane, incidentally—the onus falls on the flight attendant. In his view, she was guilty of a "racial microaggression"—one of the "everyday insults, indignities and demeaning messages sent to people of color by well-intentioned white people who are unaware of the hidden messages being sent to them," in Sue's definition.

In other words, she was acting with bias—she just didn't know it, he says.

Sue and his team are developing a theory and classification system to describe and measure the phenomenon to help people of color understand what is going on and perhaps to educate white people as well, Sue says.

"It's a monumental task to get white people to realize that they are delivering microaggressions, because it's scary to them," he contends. "It assails their self-image of being good, moral, decent human beings to realize that maybe at an unconscious level they have biased thoughts, attitudes and feelings that harm people of color."

To better understand the type and range of these incidents, Sue and other researchers are also exploring the concept among specific groups and documenting how a regular dose of these psychological slings and arrows may erode people's mental health, job performance and the quality of social experience.

AVERSIVE RACISM

The term racial microaggressions was first proposed by psychiatrist Chester M. Pierce, MD, in the 1970s, but psychologists have significantly amplified the concept in recent years.

In his landmark work on stereotype threat, for instance, Stanford University psychology professor Claude Steele, PhD, has shown that African-Americans and women perform worse on academic tests when primed with stereotypes about race or gender. Women who were primed with stereotypes about women's poor math performance do worse on math tests. Blacks' intelligence test scores plunge when they're primed with stereotypes about blacks' inferior intelligence.

Meanwhile, social psychologists Jack Dovidio, PhD, of Yale University, and Samuel L. Gaertner, PhD, of the University of Delaware, have demonstrated across several studies that many well-intentioned whites who consciously believe in and profess equality unconsciously act in a racist manner, particularly in ambiguous circumstances. In experimental job interviews, for example, whites tend not to discriminate against black candidates when their qualifications are as strong or as weak as whites'. But when candidates' qualifications are similarly ambiguous, whites tend to favor white over black candidates, the team has found. The team calls this pattern "aversive racism," referring in part to whites' aversion to being seen as prejudiced, given their conscious adherence to egalitarian principles.

Sue adds to these findings by naming, detailing and classifying the actual manifestations of aversive racism. His work illuminates the internal experiences of people affected by microaggressions—a new direction, since past research on prejudice and discrimination has focused on whites' attitudes and behaviors, notes Dovidio.

"The study of microaggressions looks at the impact of these subtle racial expressions from the perspective of the people being victimized, so it adds to our psychological understanding of the whole process of stigmatization and bias," Dovidio says.

Research shows that uncertainty is very distressing to people, Dovidio adds. "It's the uncertainty of microaggressions that can have such a tremendous impact on people of color," including on the job, in academic performance and even in therapy, he and others find.

CREATING A VOCABULARY

Sue first proposed a classification of racial microaggressions in a 2007 article on how they manifest in clinical practice in the *American Psychologist* (Vol. 2, No. 4). There, he notes three types of current racial transgressions:

- **Microassaults:** Conscious and intentional actions or slurs, such as using racial epithets, displaying swastikas or deliberately serving a white person before a person of color in a restaurant.
- **Microinsults:** Verbal and nonverbal communications that subtly convey rudeness and insensitivity and demean a person's racial heritage or identity. An example is an employee who asks a colleague of color how she got her job, implying she may have landed it through an affirmative action or quota system.
- **Microinvalidations:** Communications that subtly exclude, negate or nullify the thoughts, feelings or experiential reality of a person of color. For instance, white people often ask Asian-Americans where they were born, conveying the message that they are perpetual foreigners in their own land.

Sue focuses on microinsults and microinvalidations because of their less obvious nature, which puts people of color in a psychological bind, he asserts: While the person may feel insulted, she is not sure exactly why, and the perpetrator doesn't acknowledge that anything has happened because he is not aware he has been offensive.

"The person of color is caught in a Catch-22: If she confronts the perpetrator, the perpetrator will deny it," Sue says.

In turn, that leaves the person of color to question what actually happened. The result is confusion, anger and an overall sapping of energy, he says.

REFINING THE CONCEPT

While Sue's 2007 *American Psychologist* article mainly laid out his theory and an initial taxonomy of microaggressions, his team is now examining how these subtle communications vary among different populations. In a qualitative study in the June *Professional Psychology: Research and Practice* (Vol. 39, No. 3), Sue and his colleagues conducted focus groups with 13 African-Americans who discussed their perceptions of, reactions to and interpretations of microaggressions, as well as the emotional toll they take. Participants, age 22 to 32, all lived in the New York metropolitan area and were either graduate students or worked in higher education.

Respondents agreed that these backhanded communications can make them feel as if they don't belong, that they are abnormal or that they are untrustworthy. Some described the terrible feeling of being watched suspiciously in stores as if they were about to steal something, for instance. Some reported anticipating the impact of their race by acting preemptively: One man noted how he deliberately relaxes his body while in close quarters with white women so he doesn't frighten them.

Others cited the pressure to represent their group in a positive way. One woman said she was constantly vigilant about her work performance because she was worried that any slipups would negatively affect every black person who came after her.

A similar study in the January 2007 *Cultural Diversity and Ethnic Minority Psychology* (Vol. 13, No. 1) found that many Asian-Americans cited the experience of people asking them where they were born or telling them they "spoke good English," which gave them the message that they are "aliens." Others described classroom experiences where teachers or students assumed they were great in math, which led to feelings of being trapped in a stereotype that wasn't necessarily true. Female participants complained that white men interested in dating them assumed they would be subservient sexual partners who would take care of their every need.

"These incidents may appear small, banal and trivial, but we're beginning to find they assail the mental health of recipients," Sue says.

Other researchers are showing the harm of racial microaggressions in a variety of arenas, though research in the area is still sparse, Sue acknowledges. For instance, in a 2007 article in *American Behavioral Scientist* (Vol. 51, No. 4), University of Utah social psychologist William A. Smith, PhD, and colleagues conducted focus groups with 36 black male students on five elite campuses, including Harvard and the University of Michigan.

Participants reported experiencing racial microaggressions in academic, social and public settings. For instance, some participants reported that when they went to their school's computer lab to do schoolwork, white students would call security to make sure they weren't there to cause trouble. When security arrived, they would check the students' IDs, sometimes asking them to provide a second one to prove the first was valid.

In another case, fraternity students who had gathered for practice found themselves surrounded by police vehicles, the result of someone calling in a concern about gang activity, Smith notes.

Meanwhile, in therapy, the more likely black people are to perceive their therapist using racial microaggressions, the weaker the therapeutic bond and the lower their reported satisfaction, finds a 2007 study in the *Journal of Counseling Psychology* (Vol. 54, No. 1). Sue and other researchers are beginning to study the impact of racial microaggressions on other groups as well, including people of various ethnic groups, people with disabilities, and gay, lesbian, bisexual and transgendered individuals.

What Will Obama's Election Mean for Race Relations in America?

Like millions of Americans, racism researcher Derald Wing Sue, PhD, felt a surge of pride as he witnessed the country electing its first president of color. But alongside those feelings, Sue maintains a social scientist's perspective: Why did a majority white country elect Barack Obama? And what might his presidency mean for race relations in this country?

In terms of the election itself, the Teachers College, Columbia University psychologist believes the event represented a rare constellation of events that likely overrode rather than canceled out some people's latent racial biases. Those factors include Obama's immense talent and charisma; the fact that he came on the heels of several major crises and an unpopular Republican president; and in a more psychological sense, that some white Americans voted for Obama because he doesn't represent a "typical" black person.

"There's no way for me to prove this, but I think it's possible that [some white] people voted for Obama because he represents their unconscious view that he is an *exception* to most black Americans," Sue says, "and at the same time cling to the belief that black Americans as a group are not as capable and qualified as white Americans"—in essence, a microaggression, or subtle form of unconscious bias that is a major focus of Sue's research (see main article).

Sue also plans to watch for the appearance of another microaggressive phenomenon his research has found: that white people hold minority and female leaders to higher standards than they do white male leaders.

"All studies indicate that you have to be a super minority to achieve what you achieve, and that when you achieve it, the standards are much higher," he notes.

On the plus side, Sue posits that as Americans get a regular dose of the Obamas—at least via TV and the Web—bias may fall, in accord with research showing that having intimate contact with those different from us and receiving accurate information in place of stereotypes can help dispel prejudice.

For people of color, the Obama presidency is clearly a cause for hope and pride, Sue adds. That said, he is concerned about what may happen when reality sets in and people realize that some of the inequities that existed before Obama took office—in education, health care and employment, for example—remain.

"Barack Obama is a symbol of what this nation could be, but it would be unfair to place all of the responsibility on one person," he says. "That responsibility resides with all of us."

—T. Deangelis

MOUNTAIN OR MOLE HILL?

Not everyone agrees that microaggressions are as rampant or destructive as Sue says they are. In rebuttal letters to the 2007 *American Psychologist* article, respondents accuse Sue of blowing the phenomenon out of proportion and advancing an unnecessarily negative agenda.

"Implementing his theory would restrict rather than promote candid interaction between members of different racial groups," maintains Kenneth R. Thomas, PhD, of the University of Wisconsin–Madison, one of the critics. In the therapy relationship, for example, having to watch every word "potentially discourages therapist genuineness and spontaneity," says Thomas, who is white.

Likewise, aspects of Sue's theory enforce a victim mentality by creating problems where none exist, Thomas asserts. "The theory, in general, characterizes people of color as weak and vulnerable, and reinforces a culture of victimization instead of a culture of opportunity," he says.

Kenneth Sole, PhD, whose consulting firm Sole & Associates Inc., trains employees on team communication, agrees with Sue that microaggressions are pervasive and potentially damaging.

Indeed, clients talk about them all of the time, he says. But instead of encouraging their anger, he works with them on ways to frame the incidents so they feel empowered rather than victimized, he notes.

"My own view is that we don't serve ourselves well in the hundreds of ambiguous situations we experience by latching onto the definition of the experience that gives us the greatest pain"—particularly in one-time encounters where one can't take more systemic action, he says.

For instance, if a white person makes a potentially offensive remark to a person of color, the person could choose either to get angry and see the person as a bigot or to perceive the person as ignorant and move on, he says.

For Sue's part, he believes it's important to keep shining a light on the harm these encounters can inflict, no matter how the person of color decides to handle a given encounter.

"My hope is to make the invisible visible," he says. "Microaggressions hold their power because they are invisible, and therefore they don't allow us to see that our actions and attitudes may be discriminatory."

CRITICAL THINKING QUESTIONS

1. After reading this article, how optimistic or pessimistic are you that prejudice can be eliminated from society? Specifically, can people overcome their prejudiced behaviors, including the microaggressions discussed in the article? Support your position.

2. The article describes three types of current racial transgressions: microassaults, microinsults, and microinvalidations. Can you give at least one example of each of these microaggressions that you have seen directed at your or someone else based on an identifiable membership in a particular group (such as, but not limited to, race, gender, sexual orientation, and ethnic identity)?

3. As described in the article, how common is *aversive racism*? Do you think aversive racism in whites is something that has increased, decreased, or stayed the same over the years? Explain your answer.

4. Many studies on prejudice involve asking subjects about their attitudes toward particular groups. What do the findings of this article suggest about the validity of such self-reporting techniques? What may be a more accurate way of assessing prejudiced attitudes? Explain your answer.

5. According to the article, "Not everyone agrees that microaggressions are as rampant or destructive as Sue says they are." What is your position on the prevalence of microaggressions as well as their negative impact on people? Are they common or not? Defend your position.

ARTICLE 17 _____

As mentioned in the introduction to this chapter, the terms *prejudice* and *discrimination* are often used interchangeably, but, in fact, they refer to two different concepts. Prejudice is an *attitude,* whereby a particular person is judged based solely on his or her membership in a particular group. Discrimination refers to the *behavior* of treating people differently based upon their membership in a group.

While the two terms do, indeed, refer to different things, do they occur together in the real world? It stands to reason that if you have negative beliefs about a particular group of people, then you would act in a negative fashion toward them. Or does it? Are we always consistent in our attitudes and behaviors?

Sometimes there is a strong consistency between what people say about their beliefs and how they act. For example, surveys are usually accurate in predicting outcomes of elections based upon asking people about their attitudes toward the candidates. In other cases, such consistency simply does not exist.

"Attitudes vs. Actions" is a classic work in the field that addresses the issue of attitude–behavior consistency. Before LaPiere's publication of this study in 1934, attitude research on prejudice involved asking respondents to give hypothetical responses to hypothetical situations (e.g., Would you serve a person of a given race at your restaurant?). LaPiere measured the number of times that a Chinese couple was actually refused lodging or food and then followed up with a questionnaire to the same establishments six months later, asking if they would serve Chinese persons. In doing so, LaPiere claimed to demonstrate the lack of consistency between what people say and what they actually do. Even though the study does have some methodological flaws, it is a good example of pioneering research in the field. It also provides an interesting microcosm of prejudice and discrimination issues that existed in the United States over a half-century ago.

Attitudes vs. Actions

■ Richard T. LaPiere

By definition, a social attitude is a behaviour pattern, anticipatory set or tendency, predisposition to specific adjustment to designated social situations, or, more simply, a conditioned response to social stimuli.[1] Terminological usage differs, but students who have concerned themselves with attitudes apparently agree that they are acquired out of social experience and provide the individual organism with some degree of preparation to adjust, in a well-defined way, to certain types of social situations if and when these situations arise. It would seem, therefore, that the totality of the social attitudes of a single individual would include all his socially acquired personality which is involved in the making of adjustments to other human beings.

But by derivation social attitudes are seldom more than a verbal response to a symbolic situation. For the conventional method of measuring social attitudes is to ask questions (usually in writing) which demand a verbal adjustment to an entirely symbolic situation. Because it is easy, cheap, and mechanical, the attitudinal questionnaire is rapidly becoming a major method of sociological and socio-psychological investigation. The technique is simple. Thus from a hundred or a thousand responses to the question "Would you get up to give an Armenian woman your seat in a street-car?" the investigator derives the "attitude" of non-Armenian males toward Armenian females. Now the question may be constructed with elaborate skill and hidden with consummate cunning in a maze of supplementary or even irrelevant questions yet all that has been obtained is a symbolic response to a symbolic situation. The words "Armenian woman" do not constitute an Armenian woman of flesh and blood, who might be tall or squat, fat or thin, old or young, well or poorly dressed—who might, in fact, be a goddess or just another old and dirty hag. And the questionnaire response, whether it be "yes" or "no," is but a verbal reaction and this does not involve rising from the seat or stolidly avoiding the hurt eyes of the hypothetical woman and the derogatory stares of other street-car occupants. Yet, ignoring these limitations, the diligent investigator will jump briskly from his factual evidence to the unwarranted conclusion that he has measured the "anticipatory behavior patterns" of non-Armenian males toward Armenian females encountered on street cars. Usually he does not stop here, but proceeds to deduce certain general conclusions regarding the social relationships between Armenians and non-Armenians. Most of us have applied the questionnaire technique with greater caution, but not I fear with any greater certainty of success.

Some years ago I endeavored to obtain comparative data on the degree of French and English antipathy towards dark-skinned peoples.[2] The informal questionnaire technique was used, but, although the responses so obtained were exceedingly consistent, I supplemented them with what I then considered an index to overt behavior. The hypothesis as then stated *seemed* entirely logical. "Whatever our attitude on the validity of 'verbalization' may be, it must be recognized that any study of attitudes through direct questioning is open to serious objection, both because of the limitations of the sampling method and because in classifying attitudes the inaccuracy of human judgment is an inevitable variable. In this study, however, there is corroborating evidence on these attitudes in the policies adopted by hotel proprietors. Nothing could be used as a more accurate index of color prejudice than the admission or non-admission of colored people to hotels. For the proprietor must reflect the group attitude in his policy regardless of his own feelings in the matter. Since he determines what the group attitude is towards Negroes through the expression of that attitude in overt behavior and over a long period of actual experience, the results will be exceptionally free from those disturbing factors which inevitably affect the effort to study attitudes by direct questioning."

But at that time I overlooked the fact that what I was obtaining from the hotel proprietors was still a "verbalized" reaction to a symbolic situation. The response to a Negro's request for lodgings might have been an excellent index of the attitude of hotel patrons towards living in the same hotel as a Negro. Yet to ask the proprietor "Do you permit members of the Negro race to stay here?" does not, it appears, measure his potential response to an actual Negro.

All measurement of attitudes by the questionnaire technique proceeds on the assumption that there is a mechanical relationship between symbolic and non-symbolic behavior. It is simple enough to prove that there is no *necessary* correlation between speech and action, between response to words and to the realities they symbolize. A parrot can be taught to swear, a child to sing "Frankie and Johnny" in the Mae West manner. The words will have no meaning to either child or parrot. But to prove that there is no *necessary* relationship does not prove that such a relationship may not exist. There need be no relationship between what the hotel proprietor says he will do and what he actually does when confronted with a colored patron. Yet there may be. Certainly we are justified in assuming that the verbal response of the hotel proprietor would be more likely to indicate what he would actually do than would the verbal response of people whose personal feelings are less subordinated to economic expediency. However, the following study indicates that the reliability of even such responses is very small indeed.

Beginning in 1930 and continuing for two years thereafter, I had the good fortune to travel rather extensively with a young Chinese student and his wife.[3] Both were personable, charming, and quick to win the admiration and respect of those they had the opportunity to become intimate with. But they were foreign-born Chinese, a fact that could not be disguised. Knowing the general "attitude" of Americans towards the Chinese as indicated by the "social distance" studies which have been made, it was with considerable trepidation that I first approached a hotel clerk in their company. Perhaps the clerk's eyebrows lifted slightly, but he accommodated us without a show of hesitation. And this in the "best" hotel in a small town noted for its narrow and bigoted "attitude" towards Orientals. Two months later I passed that way again, phoned the hotel and asked if they would accommodate "an important Chinese gentleman." The reply was an unequivocal "No." That aroused my curiosity and led to this study.

In something like ten thousand miles of motor travel, twice across the United States, up and down the Pacific Coast, we met definite rejection from those asked to serve us just once. We were received at 66 hotels, auto camps, and "Tourist Homes," refused at one. We were served in 184 restaurants and cafes scattered throughout the country and treated with what I judged to be more than ordinary consideration in 72 of them. Accurate and detailed records were kept of all these instances. An effort, necessarily subjective, was made to evaluate the overt response of hotel clerks, bell boys, elevator operators, and waitresses to the presence of my Chinese friends. The factors entering into the situations were varied as far and as often as possible. Control was not, of course, as exacting as that required by laboratory experimentation. But it was as rigid as is humanly possible in human situations. For example, I did not take the "test" subjects into my confidence fearing that their behavior might become self-conscious and thus abnormally affect the response of others towards them. Whenever possible I let my Chinese friend negotiate for accommodations (while I concerned myself with the car or luggage) or sent them into a restaurant ahead of me. In this way I attempted to "factor" myself out. We sometimes patronized high-class establishments after a hard and dusty day on the road and stopped at inferior auto camps when in our most presentable condition.

In the end I was forced to conclude that those factors which most influenced the behavior of others towards the Chinese had nothing at all to do with race. Quality and condition of clothing, appearance of baggage (by which, it seems, hotel clerks are prone to base their quick evaluations), cleanliness and neatness were far more significant for person to person reaction in the situations I was studying than skin pigmentation, straight black hair, slanting eyes, and flat noses. And yet an air of self-confidence might entirely offset the "unfavorable" impression made by dusty clothes and the usual disorder to appearance consequent upon some hundred miles of motor travel. A supercilious desk clerk in a hotel of noble aspirations could not refuse his master's hospitality to people who appeared to take their request as a perfectly normal and conventional thing, though they might look like tin-can tourists and two of them belong to the racial category "Oriental." On the other hand, I became rather adept at approaching hotel clerks with that peculiar crab-wise manner which is so effective in provoking a somewhat scornful disregard. And then a bland smile would serve to reverse the entire situation. Indeed, it appeared that a genial smile was the most effective password to acceptance. My Chinese friends were skillful smilers, which may account, in part, for the fact that we received but one rebuff in all our experience. Finally, I was impressed with the fact that even where some tension developed due to the strangeness for the Chinese it would evaporate immediately when they spoke in unaccented English.

The one instance in which we were refused accommodations is worth recording here. The place was a small California town, a rather inferior auto-camp into which we drove in a very dilapidated car piled with camp equipment. It was early evening, the light so dim that the proprietor found it somewhat difficult to decide the genus *voyageur* to which we belonged. I left the car and spoke to him. He hesitated, wavered, said he was not sure that he had two cabins, meanwhile edging towards our car. The realization that the two occupants were Orientals turned the balance or, more likely, gave him the excuse he was looking for. "No," he said, "I don't take Japs!" In a more pretentious establishment we secured accommodations, and with an extra flourish of hospitality.

To offset this one flat refusal were the many instances in which the physical peculiarities of the Chinese served to heighten curiosity. With few exceptions this curiosity was considerably hidden behind an exceptional interest in serving us. Of course, outside of the Pacific Coast region, New York, and Chicago, the Chinese physiognomy attracts attention. It is different, hence noticeable. But the principal effect this curiosity has upon the behavior of those who cater to the traveler's needs is to make them more attentive, more responsive, more reliable. A Chinese companion is to be recommended to the white traveling in his native land. Strange features when combined with "human" speech and action seems, at times, to heighten sympathetic response, perhaps on the same principle that makes us uncommonly sympathetic toward the dog that has a "human" expression in his face.

What I am trying to say is that in only one out of 251 instances in which we purchased goods or services necessitating intimate human relationships did the fact that my companions were Chinese adversely affect us. Factors entirely unassociated with race were, in the main, the determinant of significant variations in our reception. It would appear reasonable to conclude that the "attitude" of the American people, as reflected in the behavior of those who are for pecuniary reasons presumably most sensitive to the antipathies of their white clientele, is anything but negative towards the Chinese. In terms of "social distance" we might conclude that native

Caucasians are not averse to residing in the same hotels, auto-camps, and "Tourist Homes" as Chinese and will with complacency accept the presence of Chinese at an adjoining table in restaurant or cafe. It does not follow that there is revealed a distinctly "positive" attitude towards the Chinese, that whites prefer the Chinese to other whites. But the facts as gathered certainly preclude the conclusion that there is an intense prejudice towards the Chinese.

Yet the existence of this prejudice, very intense, is proven by a conventional "attitude" study. To provide a comparison of symbolic reaction to symbolic social situations with actual reaction to real social situations, I "questionnaired" the establishments which we patronized during the two year period. Six months were permitted to lapse between the time I obtained the overt reaction and the symbolic. It was hoped that the effects of the actual experience with Chinese guests, adverse or otherwise, would have faded during the intervening time. To the hotel or restaurant a questionnaire was mailed with an accompanying letter purporting to be a special and personal plea for response. The questionnaires all asked the same question, "Will you accept members of the Chinese race as guests in your establishment?" Two types of questionnaire were used. In one this question was inserted among similar queries concerning Germans, French, Japanese, Russians, Armenians, Jews, Negroes, Italians, and Indians. In the other the pertinent question was unencumbered. With persistence, completed replies were obtained from 128 of the establishments we had visited; 81 restaurants and cafes and 47 hotels, auto-camps, and "Tourist Homes." In response to the relevant question 92 per cent of the former and 91 per cent of the latter replied "No." The remainder replied "Uncertain; depend upon circumstances." From the woman proprietor of a small auto-camp I received the only "Yes," accompanied by a chatty letter describing the nice visit she had had with a Chinese gentleman and his sweet wife during the previous summer.

A rather unflattering interpretation might be put upon the fact that those establishments who had provided for our needs so graciously were, some months later, verbally antagonistic towards hypothetical Chinese. To factor this experience out responses were secured from 32 hotels and 96 restaurants located in approximately the same regions, but uninfluenced by this particular experience with Oriental clients. In this, as in the former case, both types of questionnaires were used. The results indicate that neither the type of questionnaire nor the fact of previous experience had important bearing upon the symbolic response to symbolic social situations.

It is impossible to make direct comparison between the reactions secured through questionnaires and from actual experience. On the basis of the above data it would appear foolhardy for a Chinese to attempt to travel in the United States. And yet, as I have shown, actual experience indicates that the American people, as represented by the personnel of hotels, restaurants, etc., are not at all averse to fraternizing with

TABLE 1 / Distribution of Results from Questionnaire Study of Establishment "Policy" Regarding Acceptance of Chinese as Guests
   Replies are to the question: "Will you accept members of the Chinese race as guests in your establishment?"

	Hotels, Etc. Visited		Hotels, Etc. Not Visited		Restaurants, Etc. Visited		Restaurants, Etc. Not Visited	
Total	*47*		*32*		*81*		*96*	
	1*	2*	1	2	1	2	1	2
Number replying	22	25	20	12	43	38	51	45
No	20	23	19	11	40	35	37	41
Undecided: depend upon circumstances	1	2	1	1	3	3	4	3
Yes	1	0	0	0	0	0	0	1

*Column (1) indicates in each case those responses to questionnaires which concerned Chinese only. The figures in column (2) are from the questionnaires in which the above was inserted among questions regarding Germans, French, Japanese, etc.

Chinese within the limitations which apply to social relationships between Americans themselves. The evaluations which follow are undoubtedly subject to the criticism which any human judgment must withstand. But the fact is that, although they began their travels in this country with considerable trepidations, my Chinese friends soon lost all fear that they might receive a rebuff. At first somewhat timid and considerably dependent upon me for guidance and support, they came in time to feel fully self-reliant and would approach new social situations without the slightest hesitation.

The conventional questionnaire undoubtedly has significant value for the measurement of "political attitudes." The presidential polls conducted by the *Literary Digest* have proven that. But a "political attitude" is exactly what the questionnaire can be justly held to measure; a verbal response to a symbolic situation. Few citizens are ever faced with the necessity of adjusting themselves to the presence of the political leaders whom, periodically, they must vote for—or against. Especially is this true with regard to the president, and it is in relation to political attitudes towards presidential candidates that we have our best evidence. But while the questionnaire may indicate what the voter will do when he goes to vote, it does not and cannot reveal what he will do when he meets Candidate Jones on the street, in his office, at his club, on the golf course, or wherever two men may meet and adjust in some way one to the other.

The questionnaire is probably our only means of determining "religious attitudes." An honest answer to the question "Do you believe in God?" reveals all there is to be measured. "God" is a symbol; "belief" a verbal expression. So here, too, the questionnaire is efficacious. But if we would know the emotional responsiveness of a person to the spoken or written word "God"

some other method of investigation must be used. And if we would know the extent to which that responsiveness restrains his behavior it is to his behavior that we must look, not to his questionnaire response. Ethical precepts are, I judge, something more than verbal professions. There would seem little to be gained from asking a man if his religious faith prevents him from committing sin. Of course it does—on paper. But "moral attitudes" must have a significance in the adjustment to actual situations or they are not worth the studying. Sitting at my desk in California I can predict with a high degree of certainty what an "average" business man in an average Mid-Western city will reply to the question "Would you engage in sexual intercourse with a prostitute in a Paris brothel?" Yet no one, least of all the man himself, can predict what he would actually do should he by some misfortune find himself face to face with the situation in question. His moral "attitudes" are no doubt already stamped into his personality. But just what those habits are which will be invoked to provide him with some sort of adjustment to this situation is quite indeterminate.

It is highly probable that when the "Southern Gentleman" says he will not permit Negroes to reside in his neighborhood we have a verbal response to a symbolic situation which reflects the "attitudes" which would become operative in an actual situation. But there is no need to ask such a question of the true "Southern Gentleman." We knew it all the time. I am inclined to think that in most instances where the questionnaire does reveal non-symbolic attitudes the case is much the same. It is only when we cannot easily observe what people do in certain types of situations that the questionnaire is resorted to. But it is just here that the danger in the questionnaire technique arises. If Mr. A adjusts himself to Mr. B in a specified way we can

TABLE 2 / Distribution of Results Obtained from Actual Experience in the Situation Symbolized in the Questionnaire Study

Conditions	Hotels, Etc.		Restaurants, Etc.	
	Accompanied by investigator	Chinese not so accompanied at inception of situation*	Accompanied by investigator	Chinese not so accompanied at inception of situation
Total	55	12	165	19
Reception very much better than investigator would expect to have received had he been alone, but under otherwise similar circumstances	6	19	63	9
Reception different only to extent of heightened curiosity, such as investigator might have incurred were he alone but dressed in manner unconventional to region yet not incongruous	3	22	76	6
Reception "normal"	2	9	21	3
Reception perceptibly hesitant and not to be explained on other than "racial" grounds	1	3	4	1
Reception definitely, though temporarily, embarrassing	0	1	1	0
Not accepted	0	1	0	0

*When the investigator was not present at the inception of the situation the judgments were based upon what transpired after he joined the Chinese. Since intimately acquainted with them it is probable that errors in judgment were no more frequent under these conditions than when he was able to witness the inception as well as results of the situation.

deduce from his behavior that he has a certain "attitude" towards Mr. B and, perhaps, all of Mr. B's class. But if no such overt adjustment is made it is impossible to discover what A's adjustment would be should the situation arise. A questionnaire will reveal what Mr. A writes or says when confronted with a certain combination of words. But not what he will do when he meets Mr. B. Mr. B is a great deal more than a series of words. He is a man and he acts. His action is not necessarily what Mr. A "imagines" it will be when he reacts verbally to the symbol "Mr. B."

No doubt a considerable part of the data which the social scientist deals with can be obtained by the questionnaire method. The census reports are based upon verbal questionnaires and I do not doubt their basic integrity. If we wish to know how many children a man has, his income, the size of his home, his age, and the condition of his parents, we can reasonably ask him. These things he has frequently and conventionally converted into verbal responses. He is competent to report upon them, and will do so accurately, unless indeed he wishes to do otherwise. A careful

investigator could no doubt even find out by verbal means whether the man fights with his wife (frequently, infrequently, or not at all), though the neighbors would be a more reliable source. But we should not expect to obtain by the questionnaire method his "anticipatory set or tendency" to action should his wife pack up and go home to Mother, should Elder Son get into trouble with the neighbor's daughter, the President assume the status of a dictator, the Japanese take over the rest of China, or a Chinese gentleman come to pay a social call.

Only a verbal reaction to an entirely symbolic situation can be secured by the questionnaire. It may indicate what the responder would actually do when confronted with the situation symbolized in the question, but there is no assurance that it will. And so to call the response a reflection of a "social attitude" is to entirely disregard the definition commonly given for the phrase "attitude." If social attitudes are to be conceptualized as partially integrated habit sets which will become operative under specific circumstances and lead to a particular pattern of adjustment they must, in the main, be derived from a study of humans behaving in actual social situations. They must not be imputed on the basis of questionnaire data.

The questionnaire is cheap, easy, and mechanical. The study of human behavior is time consuming, intellectually fatiguing, and depends for its success upon the ability of the investigator. The former method gives quantitative results, the latter mainly qualitative. Quantitative measurements are quantitatively accurate; qualitative evaluations are always subject to the errors of human judgment. Yet it would seem far more worth while to make a shrewd guess regarding that which is essential than to accurately measure that which is likely to prove quite irrelevant.

ENDNOTES

1. See Daniel D. Droba, "Topical Summaries of Current Literature," *The American Journal of Sociology,* 1934, p. 513.
2. "Race Prejudice: France and England," *Social Forces,* September 1928, pp. 102–111.
3. The results of this study have been withheld until the present time out of consideration for their feelings.

CRITICAL THINKING QUESTIONS

1. A central thesis of the LaPiere article was that the method of directly asking people about their attitudes has certain limitations in terms of accuracy and consistency. What are these limitations? How could they be overcome, other than in the ways suggested by the author?
2. LaPiere maintained that there is little consistency between responses to attitude surveys and actual behavior. If that is the case, then what is the value (if any) of the multitude of attitude surveys that are regularly administered in the United States? Support your position.
3. Did the study involve any ethical issues? For example, what do you think about the fact that the author did not tell his Chinese friends that they were part of a study he was conducting? Are there any other ethical considerations? Explain your answers.
4. The article ended by making a distinction between *quantitative results,* such as those obtained by questionnaires, and *qualitative results,* such as those obtained by the author in his visits to the establishments. LaPiere obviously favors qualitative methods, arguing that although they are prone to errors of human judgment, such methods are preferred because it is better to "make a shrewd guess regarding what is essential than to accurately measure that which is likely quite irrelevant." Are the results of attitude questionnaires "likely quite irrelevant"? Why or why not?
5. If you were to conduct the study, what methodological improvements would you make to reduce the subjectivity of the measures?
6. A major conclusion of the study was that responses to hypothetical questions do not necessarily predict actual behavior. Is this evidence for a lack of consistency between attitudes and behavior? In answering this, think of the specific methodology that was employed. Was there anything wrong with it, given the conclusions that were drawn? What methodology could be used to more directly assess the consistency between attitudes and behavior? Explain your answers.
7. LaPiere made the observation that factors such as clothing, cleanliness, and smiles were more important than was skin color in determining whether the couple was served. Design a study that would experimentally test this observation.

ADDITIONAL RELATED READINGS

Pearson, M. R. (2010). How "undocumented workers" and "illegal aliens" affect prejudice toward Mexican immigrants. *Social Influence, 5*(2), 118–132.

Pettigrew, T. F. (2009). Probing the complexity of intergroup prejudice. *International Journal of Psychology, 44*(1), 40–42.

ARTICLE 18 _____

Why are people prejudiced? Any social psychology text will list a number of reasons that account for prejudiced attitudes and discriminatory behaviors. For example, social learning approaches will focus on the attitudes a person learns in his or her environment, particularly at home, to account for prejudice. The realistic group conflict approach will focus on the competition between groups for scarce resources as a cause of prejudice. Yet other approaches will try to identify a personality type that might be related to prejudice—for instance, the authoritarian personality.

Over the past several decades, the amount of overtly discriminatory behavior based on race has decreased significantly in the United States. This may be due to changes in laws that make certain previously accepted forms of discrimination illegal. It may also be due to changes in attitudes and beliefs regarding prejudice. Regardless, one thing that is certain is that in most quarters today, the expression of overt racism is not nearly as common as it might have been a half-century ago. But does that mean that racial prejudice has indeed decreased? Or has it perhaps just become more subtle?

In answering these questions, it may be useful to distinguish between *explicit* and *implicit* racial prejudice. *Explicit* racial prejudice refers to overt expressions of prejudice, of which we are consciously aware. Saying that you would never live next door to a person of a certain race is an example of explicit racial prejudice. *Implicit* racial prejudice, on the other hand, comprises more subtle forms of prejudice, which typically operate out of conscious awareness. Taking longer to respond to a member of another race and unconsciously associating a certain race with undesirable characteristics are both examples of implicit racial prejudice. A crucial distinction between explicit and implicit racial prejudice is that the former can be consciously controlled (and hence is subject to social desirability), whereas the latter is very difficult to control.

The following article by Natalie J. Shook and Russell H. Fazio examines how contact with members of another group may impact both explicit and implicit (or automatically activated) prejudice. Previous research had found that equal-status contact tended to reduce prejudice. However, most of that research involved explicit prejudice measures, which are easier to control. This study looked at changes over time in explicit as well as implicit measures of prejudice in White dormitory students assigned to either a White or African American roommate.

Interracial Roommate Relationships
An Experimental Field Test of the Contact Hypothesis
■ Natalie J. Shook and Russell H. Fazio

ABSTRACT

This study investigated how automatically activated racial attitudes are affected by relatively long-term interracial relationships. A natural field experiment was conducted in a college dormitory system. Participants were White freshmen who had been randomly assigned to either a White or an African American roommate. Students participated in two sessions during the first 2 and last 2 weeks of their first quarter on campus. During these sessions, they answered questions about their satisfaction and involvement with their roommates and completed an inventory of intergroup anxiety and an implicit measure of racial attitudes.

Participants in interracial rooms reported less satisfaction and less involvement with their roommates than did participants in same-race rooms. However, automatically activated racial attitudes and intergroup anxiety improved over time among students in interracial rooms, but not among students in same-race rooms. Thus, the results suggest that interracial roommate relationships, although generally less satisfying and involving than same-race roommate relationships, do produce benefits.

Prejudice is a major social issue faced by many groups. As a result, much research over the past few decades has focused on prejudice and the reduction of intergroup conflict. A primary

Shook, N.J. & and Fazio, R.H. *Psychological Science*, 19(7), 717–723. Copyright © 2008 by the Association for Psychological Science. Reprinted by permission of SAGE Publications.

theory regarding prejudice reduction is the *contact hypothesis* (Allport, 1954; Pettigrew, 1998). The underlying assumption of this theory is that prejudice stems from a lack of knowledge and exposure. Thus, increased interaction with members of different groups should allow individuals to gain information about other groups and should lead to a reduction in hostility and prejudice (for reviews, see Brewer & Brown, 1998; Pettigrew, 1998; Pettigrew & Tropp, 2000).

Investigators have conducted a great deal of research to test the contact hypothesis and determine the optimal conditions for successful intergroup contact (see Pettigrew, 1998, for a review). A recent meta-analysis of more than 500 studies found that intergroup contact is generally beneficial (Pettigrew & Tropp, 2006). However, an important issue that has been raised recently concerns the appropriateness of the measures used to assess prejudice in intergroup-contact research (for relevant discussions, see Aberson, Shoemaker, & Tomolillo, 2004; Henry & Hardin, 2006; Vonofakou, Hewstone, & Voci, 2007). Most research in this area has relied on explicit reports of attitudes toward different groups. There are, of course, many interpretational problems inherent to self-report measures (Schwarz, 1999). However, the very topic on which intergroup-contact researchers ask participants to report presents a particular concern. Self-presentational concerns and motivational factors may lead individuals not to respond truthfully on scales measuring explicit racial bias and prejudice (Dovidio & Gaertner, 1991; Dunton & Fazio, 1997).

The MODE (Motivation and Opportunity as Determinants) model (Fazio, 1990; Fazio & Towles-Schwen, 1999) posits that when individuals have the motivation and opportunity (i.e., time and resources), their behavior, including their verbal reports, may be guided by a more deliberative process rather than by their automatically activated attitudes. With regard to prejudice, various motivational factors, such as a desire to appear egalitarian or to avoid dispute, can prompt individuals to correct for the influence of their automatically activated attitudes when behaving or responding to an attitudinal query (Dunton & Fazio, 1997; Plant & Devine, 1998). Several experiments have demonstrated a discordance between automatically activated racial attitudes and behavior that increases with the extent to which individuals are motivated to control prejudiced reactions (see Olson & Fazio, in press, for a review). Thus, it is difficult to interpret expressions of positivity toward a specific group on explicit measures of racial attitudes. Generally, individuals have the opportunity to monitor their responses on a self-report measure if they are so motivated. Consequently, positive, non-prejudiced responses may be indicative not of a person's automatically activated attitude, but of a motivational goal not to be considered prejudiced. Explicit measures of prejudice are not necessarily accurate indicators of individuals' automatically activated attitudes.

Placing individuals into a situation in which they are to consider, or interact with, a member of a different group may make salient and strengthen motivations to control prejudiced behaviors. Consequently, the benefits of intergroup contact documented via explicit measures may stem from an increased salience of motivational factors, rather than from a reduction in prejudice at the level of automatic attitude activation. Implicit measures of attitudes would provide a clearer assessment of individuals' spontaneous evaluations of a given group, avoid the issue of motivational factors influencing self-reports, and, hence, better address the extent of prejudice reduction yielded by contact. Thus, the purpose of the current study was to experimentally test the effect of intergroup contact on automatically activated racial attitudes.

In Allport's (1954) original conception, various conditions were deemed optimal for successful intergroup contact and prejudice reduction: equal status, cooperation, common goals, and support of authorities. Equal status between the interacting groups is presumed to decrease the effect of negative stereotypes often associated with a lower-status group (Cook, 1978). Intergroup cooperation and common goals are important in overcoming competition between groups and encourage members of the groups to rely on one another to achieve their shared goals (Sherif, Harvey, White, Hood, & Sherif, 1961). Finally, the support of authorities facilitates intergroup contact by defining social norms and serving as a means of influencing individuals' behavior (Deutsch & Collins, 1951).

Two additional factors that have been highlighted more recently are intimacy and friendship. Personal, intimate interaction between individual group members allows for self-disclosure and social comparison and is thought to contribute to reductions in intergroup prejudice (Amir, 1976; Brewer & Miller, 1984; Miller, 2002). Similarly, the formation of friendships (Pettigrew, 1998) is a critical contributor to the positive change in prejudice that emerges from intergroup contact. Pettigrew's (1997) structural equation analyses of cross-sectional data indicate that the path from friendship to reduced prejudice is stronger than the reverse path, that is, the path from prejudice to fewer intergroup friends. Thus, providing a situation in which interaction is intimate and friendships can easily form should increase the effectiveness of intergroup contact in reducing prejudice.

A real-life context that meets many of these conditions, and has been used to explore intergroup contact, is dormitory housing (Nesdale & Todd, 1998, 2000; Van Laar, Levin, Sinclair, & Sidanius, 2005). Many students are randomly assigned to their college roommates, which leads to some being assigned to roommates from other groups and others being assigned to roommates from their own group. Students sharing a room are generally considered to be of equal status. A dormitory room is ideally a cooperative environment, with individuals working together to achieve a suitable living situation. The university may be seen as an authority that supports the intergroup contact; representatives of the institution assigned students to their rooms and oversee the housing system. Finally, the dormitory situation involves a very intimate setting in which frequent and personal interactions may occur, thus providing an ideal opportunity for friendship formation.

In addition, studying dormitory roommates can circumvent several shortcomings of intergroup-contact research that have been noted in the literature (see Brewer & Gaertner, 2004; Dovidio, Gaertner, & Kawakami, 2003; Miller, 2002; Pettigrew, 1998; Pettigrew & Tropp, 2006). Random assignment eliminates potential concerns about self-selection, allowing for a natural field experiment. The college housing situation also allows for longitudinal research, as students generally live together for an extended period of time. Therefore, the consequences of long-term intergroup contact can be explored, unlike in most laboratory situations, which involve more limited interactions.

In a recent exploration of intergroup contact within university dormitories, students were tracked over a 5-year span (Van Laar et al., 2005). Starting the summer before their freshman year of college and continuing each subsequent spring quarter, participants completed surveys about the ethnicity of their roommates, friends, and dating partners, as well as questions assessing their own bias and prejudice. Generally, students who were placed in an interracial room earlier in their academic career reported more positive affect toward different ethnic groups and more heterogeneity in their friendships. Overall, interracial dormitory relationships proved to be beneficial, so the results support the contact hypothesis. However, the study involved only self-report measures (as is also true of work by Nesdale & Todd, 1998, 2000). The extent to which motivational factors contributed to the positive outcomes observed on the explicit measures remains unknown, as does the potential impact of intergroup contact on automatically activated attitudes. Living with a roommate of a different race may have strengthened individuals' motivation to control prejudiced reactions without affecting their automatically activated attitudes. Such a result would still represent a notable consequence of interracial contact, but there is a substantial difference between being motivated to respond without prejudice (when such motivation is evoked and one has the opportunity to monitor and control behavior) and not experiencing automatic activation of a negative attitude.

Presumably, a key contributor to the results observed by Van Laar et al. (2005) was that the interracial roommate relationships were themselves successful, positive experiences. That is, roommates presumably developed a cooperative and satisfying living situation, possibly even becoming close friends. However, are such successful interracial relationships to be expected? To the contrary, some research indicates that interracial dormitory relationships are less satisfying and more problematic than same-race dormitory relationships (Phelps et al., 1998; Towles-Schwen & Fazio, 2006).

Phelps et al. (1998) found that White freshmen randomly assigned to an African American roommate believed that they were less compatible with their roommate than did White freshmen randomly assigned to a White roommate. Towles-Schwen and Fazio (2006) found that White freshmen randomly assigned to an African American roommate spent less time with their roommate, experienced less social involvement between their social network and their roommate's social network, and were less likely to continue living with that roommate for the duration of the academic semester than were White freshmen randomly assigned to another White freshman. If interracial relationships dissolve quickly, or are viewed as incompatible, the likelihood of friendships forming would not be high. Thus, the potential benefits of contact may not come to fruition.

The goals of the study reported in this article were to assess the nature of interracial relationships and test the effect of intergroup contact on automatically activated attitudes in a real-life situation. The research took advantage of random assignment to college dormitory rooms, which allowed for a natural, long-term field experiment. Concerns regarding self-selection were reduced not only by initial random assignment, but also by the fact that the university housing system was experiencing a "housing crunch." That is, there was a room shortage on campus, which required that students maintain their assigned living situation for at least a quarter, until other housing arrangements could be made. As a result, the dormitory situation was all the more ideal for testing the long-term effects of contact. Even more important, the study used an implicit measure of racial attitudes to eliminate any concern about motivational factors influencing participants' verbal responses and, hence, to permit an experimental test of the long-term consequences of interracial contact on automatically activated attitudes.

METHOD

Participants

White freshmen randomly assigned to a White (*n* = 136) or African American (*n* = 126) freshman roommate were recruited in the beginning of the autumn quarter of two consecutive academic years. Students were contacted via e-mail or telephone and asked to participate in a two-session study concerning adjustment to college life. As compensation for their time, they received either $25 or research-experience credit for an introductory psychology course. Two students from same-race rooms and 4 students from interracial rooms did not return for the second session. Of the participants who returned for the second session, 97% continued to share a room with the roommate to whom they were originally assigned. Only 3 students in same-race rooms and 5 students in interracial rooms experienced a change in their roommate.

Measures

The participants completed a 1-hr experimental session within the first 2 weeks of their first quarter of college and a second 1-hr experimental session within the last 2 weeks of the same quarter. During each session, they answered questionnaires regarding their satisfaction with their roommate, joint activities with their roommate, time spent together with their roommate, and the degree to which they and their roommate were involved in and comfortable with each other's social networks (see Towles-Schwen & Fazio, 2006, for details). They also completed a standard inventory of intergroup anxiety toward African Americans (Britt, Boniecki, Vescio, Biernat, & Brown, 1996) and an evaluative priming procedure designed to assess racial attitudes unobtrusively (Fazio, Jackson, Dunton, & Williams, 1995).[1]

The priming procedure involved five phases. During the first phase, positive and negative adjectives were presented on a computer monitor one at a time, and participants were asked to indicate as quickly as possible whether each word was good or bad. Response times in this phase served as a baseline measure of latency. During each trial, the adjective appeared in the center of the screen until the participant responded, or until 1.75 s had elapsed. Participants completed two blocks of 24 trials, with all 24 adjectives presented in random order during each block.

The second and third phases of the priming procedure served to bolster the cover story that this computer task assessed multitasking ability. In the second phase, faces were presented on the computer screen, and participants were told to study the faces because their recall would be tested in the next phase. Participants were presented with 20 faces that varied in ethnicity and gender. In the third phase, participants were presented with 20 faces split across two blocks and told to indicate either "yes," they had seen the face in the second phase, or "no," they had not seen the face. Half of the faces were target faces from the previous phase, and half were filler faces. Each face was presented on the computer monitor until the participant responded, or until 5 s had elapsed.

The fourth phase combined the first two phases, presumably as an assessment of multitasking ability. This was the phase of interest. On any given trial, an African American, White, Asian, or Hispanic face was presented for 315 ms, followed by a 135-ms interval and then presentation of a target adjective from the first phase. Each adjective appeared on the computer screen until participants indicated whether the adjective was positive or negative, or until 1.75 s had elapsed. Participants finished a short practice block before completing four 48-trial blocks. In each experimental block, 16 African American faces and 16 White faces, matched for level of attractiveness, were presented. The other 16 faces were fillers. The same 48 faces were presented in random order in each block. However, each time a given face appeared, it was followed by a different adjective. Each face was followed by two positive adjectives and two negative adjectives.

The fifth phase was included, again, simply to bolster the cover story. Faces were presented on the computer screen, and participants were asked to indicate whether they had seen each face in the preceding phase.

Procedure

When participants arrived for the first session, they were told that the project concerned college experiences and adjustment to college life. After providing informed consent, they completed the priming procedure, which was presented as a measure of their multitasking abilities. So that the priming procedure would fit the cover story, participants were told that a person's ability to multitask is an important predictor of success in college. After completing this task, participants were provided with questionnaire packets that contained the roommate-relationship questions and the intergroup anxiety scale, along with a variety of filler items concerning college life. At the end of the session, participants were paid $10 or given 1 hr of research-experience credit for their time.

During the last 2 weeks of the autumn quarter, participants were asked to return to the lab for the second session. The procedure was identical to that for the first session. Participants were reminded that the information they provided was confidential and that their participation was voluntary. They completed the priming measure and the questionnaire packet. Then, they were debriefed and informed of the true nature of the project. Any questions or concerns that they had were addressed. Finally, they were paid $15 or given 1.5 hr of research credit for completing the second session.

RESULTS

Assessment of Roommate Relationships

Differences between students in same-race and interracial rooms were evident across all of the relationship measures at both the beginning and the end of the autumn quarter (see Tables 1 and 2 for means and *t* values). Overall, interracial roommate relationships were less satisfying, less socially involving, and less comfortable than were White-White relationships.

Across time, there were a number of reliable changes in the roommate-relationship variables within each of the two-room types, as well as significant between-condition differences in the extent of change (see Table 3 for means and *t* values). Strikingly, most of the relationship evaluations of students in same-race rooms declined significantly over time; the only variable that improved significantly was the roommate's presumed comfort with the participant's friends. Among students in interracial rooms, some of the evaluations also declined, but the declines were less likely to be significant and were not as extreme. Students in interracial rooms did report increases in time spent together with the roommate in the dormitory room and in their roommate's comfort with their friends.

Racial Attitudes

The latency data from the priming measure were used to calculate an estimate of automatically activated racial attitudes for each participant (see Fazio et al., 1995, for details regarding the calculation of the attitude scores). Given the scoring procedure, more negative scores reflect more automatically activated negativity in response to photographs of African American faces relative to photographs of White faces. At the first experimental session, there were no differences in automatically activated racial attitudes between the students in the two room types, $p > .10$. Of primary interest, though, was how racial

TABLE 1 / Relationship Evaluations at the First Session: Means and Tests of Differences Between Same-Race and Interracial Rooms

Variable	Same-race room	Interracial room	t (261)
Satisfaction with roommate	6.05	4.83	4.96***
Joint activity with roommate	3.38	2.41	5.01***
Time spent with roommate	2.69	1.54	5.58**
In room	3.24	2.10	5.55***
Outside room	2.14	0.98	4.29***
Involvement between participant's and roommate's social networks	2.96	2.61	3.51***
Participant's comfort with roommate's friends	6.85	5.71	4.82***
Roommate's comfort with participant's friends	6.71	6.10	2.71**

Note: Satisfaction with roommate, time spent with roommate, participant's comfort with roommate's friends, and roommate's comfort with participant's friends were assessed on scales from 0 to 9. Joint activity with roommate was assessed on a scale from 0 to 8. Involvement between the participant's and roommate's social networks was assessed on a scale from 0 to 6.
**$p < .01$.   ***$p < .001$.

TABLE 2 / Relationship Evaluations at the Second Session: Means and Tests of Differences Between Same-Race and Interracial Rooms

Variable	Same-race room	Interracial room	t (255)
Satisfaction with roommate	5.70	4.65	3.56***
Joint activity with roommate	2.98	2.24	3.79***
Time spent with roommate	2.38	1.64	3.51**
In room	3.22	2.36	3.74***
Outside room	1.54	0.92	2.44*
Involvement between participant's and roommate's social networks	2.81	2.44	3.43***
Participant's comfort with roommate's friends	6.91	5.90	3.87***
Roommate's comfort with participant's friends	7.02	6.40	2.62**

Note: Satisfaction with roommate, time spent with roommate, participant's comfort with roommate's friends, and roommate's comfort with participant's friends were assessed on scales from 0 to 9. Joint activity with roommate was assessed on a scale from 0 to 8. Involvement between the participant's and roommate's social networks was assessed on a scale from 0 to 6.
*$p < .05$.   **$p < .01$.   ***$p < .001$.

TABLE 3 / Mean Difference Scores for the Relationship Evaluations and Tests of Differences Between Same-Race and Interracial Rooms

Variable	Same-race room	Interracial room	t (255)
Satisfaction with roommate	−0.34*	−0.16	0.87
Joint activity with roommate	−0.40**	−0.18*	1.77†
Time spent with roommate	−0.31*	0.09	2.57*
In room	−0.04	0.23*	1.40
Outside room	−0.57**	−0.06	2.53**
Involvement between participant's and roommate's social networks	−0.13*	−0.13*	0.01
Participant's comfort with roommate's friends	0.07	0.26	0.74
Roommate's comfort with participant's friends	0.34*	0.39*	0.20

Note: Asterisks after difference scores indicate a significant difference from zero; asterisks after *t* values indicate a significant difference between the two room types.

†$p < .08$.   *$p < .05$.   **$p < .01$.

attitudes changed over time as a function of room type. An analysis of covariance (ANCOVA) was conducted to assess the effect of room type on automatically activated racial attitudes at the end of the autumn quarter, controlling for attitudes at the beginning of the quarter. There was a significant effect of room type, $F(1, 236) = 4.33$, $p_{rep} = .90$, $\eta^2 = .02$. The results supported the contact hypothesis: White freshmen in interracial rooms exhibited significantly more positive automatically activated racial attitudes at the second session ($M = 0.03$) than at the first session ($M = -0.06$), $t(113) = 2.51$, $p_{rep} = .94$, $d = 0.47$, whereas the automatically activated racial attitudes of freshmen in same-race rooms did not change ($Ms = -0.02$ and -0.05 for the first and second sessions, respectively), $t < 1$.

Intergroup Anxiety

A similar ANCOVA was conducted to assess intergroup anxiety toward African Americans. There was a marginally significant effect of room type, $F(1, 255) = 2.91$, $p_{rep} = .83$, $\eta^2 = .01$. Participants in interracial rooms exhibited a significant reduction in intergroup anxiety ($Ms = 1.50$ and 1.42 for the first and second sessions, respectively), $t(121) = 1.92$, $p_{rep} = .87$, $d = 0.35$, whereas participants in same-race rooms showed no change ($Ms = 1.44$ and 1.46 for the first and second sessions, respectively), $t < 1$. That is, White freshmen with African American roommates reported increased comfort interacting with African Americans at the end of the quarter.[2]

DISCUSSION

The results of this research indicate that interracial roommate relationships are generally less agreeable to Whites than are same-race roommate relationships, which is consistent with previous findings (Phelps et al., 1998; Towles-Schwen & Fazio, 2006). White freshmen randomly assigned to an African American roommate were generally less satisfied, less socially involved, and less comfortable with their roommates than were White freshmen randomly assigned to a White roommate. These more negative assessments were reported at both the beginning and the end of the fall quarter. Thus, overall, interracial relationships were evaluated more negatively than were same-race relationships.

However, the novel contribution of the present research stems from the observed benefits of the intergroup living situation. That is, despite the deficits in White students' relationships with African American roommates, the automatically activated racial attitudes of White students in interracial rooms became more positive toward African Americans, whereas the attitudes of White students in same-race rooms did not change. Participants in interracial rooms also reported decreased intergroup anxiety toward African Americans at the end of the quarter, whereas participants in same-race rooms did not exhibit any change on this measure. Thus, it appears that the opportunity for intergroup contact experienced by students in the interracial rooms did have positive consequences.[3]

Notably, the benefits of interracial contact were found in real-life rooming situations, and because the experiment focused on students who had been randomly paired with either an African American or a White roommate, this research is characterized by all the advantages of random assignment to condition. The dormitory setting also provided a situation in which the interracial contact occurred for an extended period of time. Thus, the interaction was both more natural and more extensive than is typical for laboratory studies, and therefore allowed for a better assessment of the consequences of contact. An important feature of this study is that it incorporated an implicit measure of attitudes. Therefore, unlike studies that use explicit measures, it avoided concerns that the results might have been influenced by participants' motivations to not be perceived as prejudiced.

In light of the study's design features, the observed reduction in prejudice, especially in students' automatically activated racial attitudes, provides striking and noteworthy support for the contact hypothesis. This positive outcome was found despite interracial roommate relationships being evaluated much more negatively than same-race roommate relationships. Living with an African American roommate for a single academic quarter (3 months), even though not as satisfying, on average, as rooming with a fellow White student, led to change in participants' spontaneous reactions to African Americans as a group and to a reduction in intergroup anxiety. Presumably, having exposure to and opportunity to interact with the African American roommates (and possibly their friends) led to the attitude change. Participants in same-race rooms simply did not have the same opportunities and, thus, did not exhibit any change in their racial attitudes.

In the future, this line of research should be extended to explore the effects of an interracial roommate relationship on African American students. Recent work has suggested that intergroup contact is less effective for minority than for majority group members (Tropp & Pettigrew, 2005) and that minority members' experiences during an intergroup interaction are quite different from majority group members' experiences (Shelton, Richeson, & Salvatore, 2005). It would be interesting to compare African American and White students' perceptions of their interracial roommate relationships and to determine whether the experience benefits African American students.

Another direction for future work is to extend the time period studied. Prejudice was found to be reduced after the first academic quarter. It would be worthwhile to determine whether automatically activated attitudes continue to improve over a longer period and at what point the improvement might reach an asymptote. Following students after their 1st year and after they are no longer living with their roommate would provide evidence regarding the persistence of any prejudice reduction. Van Laar et al. (2005) did find benefits of interracial dormitory housing in self-report measures after students had left the interracial roommate relationship, which suggests that intergroup contact has a long-term value. It would be valuable to determine whether automatically activated racial attitudes also continue to improve after a specific interracial relationship has ended. It would also be informative to examine how interracial roommate relationships progress beyond a single academic quarter. Although racial attitudes improved after one academic quarter, the roommate relationships were not generally assessed more positively. However, there were some small indications in the reports of the interracial roommate relationships that there was improvement over time. With a longer study period, it may be possible to observe larger changes in assessments of interracial roommate relationships.

ACKNOWLEDGMENTS

This research was conducted under the supervision of Russell H. Fazio as part of a dissertation by Natalie J. Shook. The authors thank Suzanne Miller, Melissa Keeley, Beth Bayham, and Brandon Cordes for their assistance with data collection and especially thank Ron Kochendoerfer of the University Housing Office for his assistance in identifying potential participants and for his support throughout the project.

REFERENCES

Aberson, C.L., Shoemaker, C., & Tomolillo, C. (2004). Implicit bias and contact: The role of interethnic friendships. *The Journal of Social Psychology, 144,* 335–347.

Allport, G.W. (1954). *The nature of prejudice.* Reading, MA: Addison-Wesley.

Amir, Y. (1976). The role of intergroup contact in change of prejudice and race relations. In P.A. Katz (Ed.), *Towards the elimination of racism* (pp. 245–280). New York: Pergamon.

Brewer, M.B., & Brown, R.J. (1998). Intergroup relations. In D.T. Gilbert, S.T. Fiske, & G. Lindzey (Eds.), *The handbook of social psychology* (Vol. 2, pp. 554–594). Boston: McGraw-Hill.

Brewer, M.B., & Gaertner, S.L. (2004). Toward reduction of prejudice: Intergroup contact and social categorization. In M.B. Brewer & M. Hewstone (Eds.), *Self and social identity* (pp. 298–318). Malden, MA: Blackwell.

Brewer, M.B., & Miller, N. (1984). Beyond the contact hypothesis: Theoretical perspectives on desegregation. In N. Miller & M.B. Brewer (Eds.), *Groups in contact: The psychology of desegregation* (pp. 281–302). Orlando, FL: Academic Press.

Britt, T.W., Boniecki, K.A., Vescio, T.K., Biernat, M., & Brown, L.M. (1996). Intergroup anxiety: A person x situation approach. *Personality and Social Psychology Bulletin, 22,* 1177–1188.

Cook, S.W. (1978). Interpersonal and attitudinal outcomes in cooperating interracial groups. *Journal of Research and Development in Education, 12,* 97–113.

Deutsch, M., & Collins, M.E. (1951). *Interracial housing: A psychological evaluation of a social experiment.* Minneapolis: University of Minnesota Press.

Dovidio, J.F., & Gaertner, S.L. (1991). Changes in the nature and expression of racial prejudice. In H. Knopke, J. Norrell, & R. Rogers (Eds.), *Opening doors: An appraisal of race relations in contemporary America* (pp. 201–241). Tuscaloosa: University of Alabama Press.

Dovidio, J.F., Gaertner, S.L., & Kawakami, K. (2003). Intergroup contact: The past, present, and future. *Group Processes & Intergroup Relations, 6,* 5–21.

Dunton, B.C., & Fazio, R.H. (1997). An individual difference measure of motivation to control prejudiced reactions. *Personality and Social Psychology Bulletin, 23,* 316–326.

Fazio, R.H. (1990). Multiple processes by which attitudes guide behavior: The MODE model as an integrative framework. In M.P. Zanna (Ed.), *Advances in experimental social psychology* (Vol. 23, pp. 75–109). San Diego, CA: Academic Press.

Fazio, R.H., Jackson, J.R., Dunton, B.C., & Williams, C.J. (1995). Variability in automatic activation as an unobtrusive measure of racial attitudes: A bona fide pipeline? *Journal of Personality and Social Psychology, 69,* 1013–1027.

Fazio, R.H., & Towles-Schwen, T. (1999). The MODE model of attitude-behavior processes. In S. Chaiken & Y. Trope (Eds.), *Dual process theories in social psychology* (pp. 97–116). New York: Guilford.

Henry, P.J., & Hardin, C.D. (2006). The contact hypothesis revisited: Status bias in the reduction of implicit prejudice in the United States and Lebanon. *Psychological Science, 17,* 862–868.

Miller, N. (2002). Personalization and the promise of contact theory. *Journal of Social Issues, 58,* 387–410.

Nesdale, D., & Todd, P. (1998). Intergroup ratio and the contact hypothesis. *Journal of Applied Social Psychology, 28,* 1196–1217.

Nesdale, D., & Todd, P. (2000). Effect of contact on intercultural acceptance: A field study. *International Journal of Intercultural Relations, 24,* 341–360.

Olson, M.A., & Fazio, R.H. (in press). Implicit and explicit measures of attitudes: The perspective of the MODE model. In R.E. Petty, R.H. Fazio, & P. Briñol (Eds.), *Attitudes: Insights from the new implicit measures.* New York: Psychology Press.

Pettigrew, T.F. (1997). Generalized intergroup contact effects on prejudice. *Personality and Social Psychology Bulletin, 23,* 173–185.

Pettigrew, T.F. (1998). Intergroup contact theory. *Annual Review of Psychology, 49,* 65–85.

Pettigrew, T.F., & Tropp, L.R. (2000). Does intergroup contact reduce prejudice: Recent meta-analytic findings. In S. Oskamp (Ed.), *Reducing prejudice and discrimination* (pp. 93–114). Mahwah, NJ: Erlbaum.

Pettigrew, T.F., & Tropp, L.R. (2006). A meta-analytic test of intergroup contact theory. *Journal of Personality and Social Psychology, 90,* 751–783.

Phelps, R.E., Altschul, D.B., Wisenbaker, J.M., Day, J.F., Cooper, D., & Potter, C.G. (1998). Roommate satisfaction and ethnic identity in mixed-race and white university roommate dyads. *Journal of College Student Development, 39,* 194–203.

Plant, E.A., & Devine, P.G. (1998). Internal and external motivation to respond without prejudice. *Journal of Personality and Social Psychology, 75,* 811–832.

Schwarz, N. (1999). Self-reports: How the questions shape the answers. *American Psychologist, 54,* 93–105.

Shelton, J.N., Richeson, J.A., & Salvatore, J. (2005). Expecting to be the target of prejudice: Implications for interethnic interactions. *Personality and Social Psychology Bulletin, 31,* 1189–1202.

Sherif, M., Harvey, O.J., White, B.J., Hood, W.R., & Sherif, C.W (1961). *Intergroup conflict and cooperation: The Robbers Cave Experiment.* Norman: University of Oklahoma Book Exchange.

Shook, N.J. (2007). *Interracial contact: Consequences for attitudes, relationships, and well-being.* Unpublished doctoral dissertation, Ohio State University, Columbus.

Towles-Schwen, T., & Fazio, R.H. (2006). Automatically activated racial attitudes as predictors of the success of interracial roommate relationships. *Journal of Experimental Social Psychology, 42,* 698–705.

Tropp, L.R., & Pettigrew, T.F. (2005). Relationships between intergroup contact and prejudice among minority and majority status groups. *Psychological Science, 16,* 951–957.

Van Laar, C., Levin, S., Sinclair, S., & Sidanius, J. (2005). The effect of university roommate contact on ethnic attitudes and behavior. *Journal of Experimental Social Psychology, 41,* 329–345.

Vonofakou, C., Hewstone, M., & Voci, A. (2007). Contact with out-group friends as a predictor of meta-attitudinal strength and accessibility of attitudes toward gay men. *Journal of Personality and Social Psychology, 92,* 804–820.

ENDNOTES

1. Many studies now attest to the predictive validity of this measure (see Olson & Fazio, in press, for a review). Of most relevance to the present concerns is the fact that it predicted the longevity of interracial roommate relationships among people who were randomly paired with their roommates (Towles-Schwen & Fazio, 2006); more negative attitudes were associated with earlier dissolution of the relationship.

2. Change in interpersonal anxiety was uncorrelated with change in automatically activated attitudes, which suggests that interracial contact had independent influences on these two measures. This finding is consistent with the often-advanced argument that the effects of contact on prejudice reduction are likely to be mediated by multiple mechanisms (e.g., Pettigrew, 1998).

3. As noted earlier, our focus in this report centers on experimental effects, that is, differences observed as a function of assignment to an African American or a White roommate. Readers interested in the prospective relations between racial attitudes and relationship assessments will find an extensive series of such analyses in Shook (2007).

CRITICAL THINKING QUESTIONS

1. According to the article, "Recent work has suggested that intergroup contact is less effective for minority than for majority group members . . . and that minority members' experiences during an intergroup interaction are quite different from majority group members' experiences." Do you agree that intergroup contact is less effective for minority members? Why or why not? In what ways, if any, might their experiences be different than majority members' experiences? Explain your reasoning.

2. This article used a particular methodology to measure automatically activated prejudiced attitudes. In what other ways can automatically active prejudice be manifested and/or measured? Be specific.

3. Using the information from this article as well as your own reasoning, describe how people can be made more aware of their automatically activated prejudices. How can automatically activated prejudices be reduced?

4. Can you think of a personal example of an automatically activated prejudice that you experienced? In other words, some thought or feeling that you immediately had toward another person, yet might never have overtly acted upon it? Explain your experience in relation to the information from this article.

5. According to the *contact hypothesis*, " . . . prejudice stems from a lack of knowledge and exposure." Does increased knowledge of and exposure to other groups automatically lead to reductions in prejudices? Why or why not?

CHAPTER INTEGRATION QUESTIONS

1. Søren Kirkegaard, existential philosopher, said, "When you label me, you negate me." What does this quote mean to you? Explain.

2. How would you relate the Kirkegaard quote to each of the articles in this chapter?

3. Is there a common theme among the articles to which this quotation also applies? Discuss.

4. Have you ever felt that you were being judged based on having been assigned some label? Explain how this quotation may be applicable to experiences from your life.

Chapter Seven

INTERPERSONAL ATTRACTION

D o "Birds of a feather flock together," or do "Opposites attract"? Both of these folk wisdoms, as contradictory as they are, attempt to answer an age-old question: To whom are we attracted and why?

The research on *interpersonal attraction* has gone in various directions in an attempt to answer this question. *Attraction* here is defined not in the narrow sense of romantic attraction but as attraction to anyone with whom we may associate—a friend, a coworker, or even a child. Many factors have been identified as important determinants of interpersonal attraction, but perhaps the most widely investigated factor (and the one with the most distressing findings) is that of *physical attractiveness.* Study after study seem to demonstrate that how someone looks is a major determinant of how he or she is viewed and treated by other people.

"Why I Hate Beauty," Article 19, examines how our perceptions of beauty have been markedly influenced by our almost constant exposure to media images of attractiveness. We are all aware of how we are confronted with very attractive people just about any time we look at television, watch a movie, or pick up a magazine. But what is the cumulative impact of our exposure to attractive people? This article explores the possibility that such exposure may not only have an impact on our satisfaction with our current partners but even on the possibility of our divorcing them later on.

Our judgment of physical attractiveness is not just limited to selecting potential partners, however. It may also influence what other characteristics we ascribe to people based solely on their looks. Article 20, "What Is Beautiful Is Good," is a classic demonstration of how positive stereotypes are associated with physical attractiveness. Given the pervasiveness of the effect of physical attractiveness, it has real implications for how we deal with and judge others in our daily lives.

Article 21, however, suggests that while physical attractiveness is a cue that is obviously noticeable upon first encounters, other factors affecting attraction may also be operating even in the earliest moments of meeting someone. "The Ability to Judge the Romantic Interest of Others" examined how accurate males and females are in determining the romantic interest of people they are observing. Why as a group female interest is harder to "read" and why some people are able to pick up on interest cues more readily than others are but two of the observations discussed in this article.

ARTICLE 19 _____

Imagine that you are living a thousand years ago in just about any part of the world. If you were like the vast majority of people who lived then, you would be living in a small village and your exposure to other people would be pretty much limited to those living nearby. Without a means of rapid transportation, you most likely would not have ventured beyond a few miles of your birthplace during the course of your lifetime. Even if you were among the more adventurous of your group, you may have traveled only a few hundred miles, and even then, you mostly would have encountered people of similar background to your own. Given this situation, in deciding on a mate, to whom are you going to be most attracted? Will the looks of the other person matter? Research suggests that it will. But what will influence what you consider to be *beautiful?*

Our perceptions of what is beautiful are partly innate and partly learned. For example, research indicates that young infants, well before they have been exposed to media or cultural stereotypes of beauty, spend more time gazing at more attractive faces than less attractive faces. *Sociobiology,* the field that examines the biological or evolutionary underpinnings of our social behaviors, suggests that there is a biological reason we are drawn to attractive people. For example, in evolutionary terms, young, attractive women may suggest health and thus fertility to men seeking to carry on their genes. Sociobiological research even indicates that there are some universal factors associated with beauty, such as facial and body symmetry, which transcend specific cultural ideals of attractiveness. So, there may indeed be at least a partial biological reason as to why we have such a strong preference for beautiful people.

But what is considered physically attractive? While there may be some underlying biological reasons we prefer the more attractive to the less attractive, the specifics of what we may be attracted to are based on what we see around us. Take the opening scenario in the first paragraph. Living long ago, you most likely would have been exposed to a very small number of people in your lifetime. Given the diversity of human appearance, only a very small number of the people you may have encountered in your lifetime might be described as very physically attractive. So, what you as an individual might consider to be attractive would be based on the relative ratings of the people you saw around you. In other words, if you only very rarely (if ever) encountered a highly attractive person, you might consider the normal people surrounding you as more attractive than if you were constantly exposed to many highly attractive people.

Fast forward to the present time: The mass media has done many things to us and the world around us. One thing that it certainly has done, however, is to expose us to a large number of highly attractive people in ways that previously were simply not possible. On a daily basis, we are bombarded with images of young, highly attractive people, be it in advertising, the movies, or television shows. Moreover, people around the world get these same images of highly attractive people, over and over again.

Does this constant exposure to images of highly attractive people affect our perceptions of the real people around us? The following article by Michael Levine and Hara Estroff Marano suggests that it does. As the research described by the authors suggests, such constant exposure to mass media images of beauty actually may impact not only our choices of mates but also our satisfaction with our current mates and even the possibility of our divorcing them.

Why I Hate Beauty

■ Michael Levine with Hara Estroff Marano

Poets rave about beauty. Brave men have started wars over beauty. Women the world over strive for it. Scholars devote their lives to deconstructing our impulse to obtain it. Ordinary mortals erect temples to beauty. In just about every way imaginable, the world honors physical beauty. But I hate beauty.

I live in what is likely the beauty capital of the world and have the enviable fortune to work with some of the most beautiful women in it. With their smooth bodies and supple waists, these women are the very picture of youth and attractiveness. Not only are they exemplars of nature's design for detonating desire in men, but they stir yearnings for companionship that date back to ancestral mating dances. Still, beauty is driving me nuts, and although I'm a successful red-blooded American male, divorced and available, it is beauty alone that is keeping me single and lonely.

It is scant solace that science is on my side. I seem to have a confirmed case of the contrast effect. It doesn't make me any happier knowing it's afflicting lots of others too.

As an author of books on marketing, I have long known about the contrast effect. It is a principle of perception whereby the differences between two things are exaggerated depending on the order in which those things ore presented. If you lift a light object and then a heavy object, you will judge the second object heavier than if you had lifted it first or solo.

Psychologists Sara Gutierres, Ph.D., and Douglas Kenrick, Ph.D., both of Arizona State University, demonstrated that the contrast effect operates powerfully in the sphere of person-to-person attraction as well. In a series of studies over the past two decades, they have shown that, more than any of us might suspect, judgments of attractiveness (of ourselves and of others) depend on the situation in which we find ourselves. For example, a woman of average attractiveness seems a lot less attractive than she actually is if a viewer has first seen a highly attractive woman. If a man is talking to a beautiful female at a cocktail party and is then joined by a less attractive one, the second woman will seem relatively unattractive.

The contrast principle also works in reverse. A woman of average attractiveness will seem more attractive than she is if she enters a room of unattractive women. In other words, context counts.

In their very first set of studies, which have been expanded and refined over the years to determine the exact circumstances under which the findings apply and their effects on both men and women, Gutierres and Kenrick asked male college dormitory residents to rate the photo of a potential blind date. (The photos had been previously rated by other males to be of average attractiveness.) If the men were watching an episode of *Charlie's Angels* when shown the photo, the blind date was rated less desirable than she was by males watching a different show. The initial impressions of romantic partners—women who were actually available to them and likely to be interested in them—were so adversely affected that the men didn't even want to bother.

Since these studies, the researchers have found that the contrast effect influences not only our evaluations of strangers but also our views of our own mates. And it sways self-assessments of attractiveness too.

Most recently, Kenrick and Gutierres discovered that women who are surrounded by other attractive women, whether in the flesh, in films or in photographs, rate themselves as less satisfied with their attractiveness—and less desirable as a marriage partner. "If there are a large number of desirable members of

one's own sex available, one may regard one's own market value as lower," the researchers reported in the *Personality and Social Psychology Bulletin.*

If you had to pick ground zero for the contrast effect, it would be Hollywood. To feed the film industry's voracious appetite for attractive faces, it lures especially beautiful women from around the world. And for those who don't arrive already at the pinnacle of perfection, whole industries exist here to render it attainable, to reshape faces and bodies to the prevailing standard of attractiveness.

There's an extraordinarily high concentration of gorgeous females in Los Angeles, and courtesy of the usually balmy weather and lifestyle, they tend to be highly visible—and not just locally. The film and television industries project their images all over the world, not to mention all the supporting media dealing with celebrities and gossip that help keep them professionally viable.

As the head of a public relations agency, I work with these women day and night. You might expect that to make me feel good, as we normally like being around attractive people. But my exposure to extreme beauty is ruining my capacity to love the ordinarily beautiful women of the real world, women who are more likely to meet my needs for deep connection and partnership of the soul.

The contrast effect doesn't apply just to strangers men have yet to meet who might be most suitable for them. In ongoing studies, Gutierres and Kenrick have found that it also affects men's feelings about their current partner. Viewing pictures of attractive women weakens their commitment to their mates. Men rate themselves as being less in love with their partner after looking at *Playboy* centerfolds than they did before seeing the pictures of beautiful women.

This finding is all the more surprising because getting someone aroused normally boosts their attraction to their partner. But seeing beautiful models wiped out whatever effect the men might have experienced from being sexually aroused.

The strange thing is, being bombarded with visions of beautiful women (or for women, socially powerful men) doesn't make us think our partners are less physically attractive. It doesn't change our perception of our partner. Instead, by some sleight of mind, it distorts our idea of the pool of possibilities.

These images make us think there's a huge field of alternatives. It changes our estimate of the number of people who are available to us as potential mates. In changing our sense of the possibilities, it prods us to believe we could always do better, keeping us continually unsatisfied.

"The perception of the comparison pool is changed," says Gutierres. "In this context our partner doesn't look so great." Adds Kenrick: "You think, 'Yes, my partner's fine—but why do I have to settle for fine when there are just so many great people out there?'" All you have to do is turn on the TV or look at the covers of magazines in the supermarket checkout line to be convinced there are any number of incredibly beautiful women available.

Kenrick puts it in evolutionary perspective. Like us, he says, our ancestors were probably designed to make some estimation of the possible pool of alternatives and some estimation of their own worth relative to the possibilities.

The catch is they just didn't see that many people, and certainly not many beautiful people. They lived in a little village of maybe 30. Even if you counted distant third cousins, our ancestors might have been exposed to a grand total of 500 people in their lifetime. And among those 500, some were old, some were young, but very few were very attractive.

Today anyone who turns on the TV or looks at a magazine can easily see 500 beautiful people in an hour, certainly in an evening. "My pool includes the people I see in my everyday life," explains Kenrick. "I don't consciously think that the people I see through movies, TV and magazines are artificial. Still, seeing Juliette Binoche all the time registers in my brain."

Our minds have not caught up. They haven't evolved to correct for MTV. "Our research suggests that our brains don't discount the women on the cover of *Cosmo* even when subjects know these women are models. Subjects judge an average attractive woman as less desirable as a date after just having seen models," Kenrick says.

Part of the problem is we're built to selectively remember the really beautiful. They stand out. "That's what you're drawn to," says Kenrick. "It feels good on the brain." And any stimulus that's vivid becomes readily available to memory, encouraging you to overestimate the true frequency of beautiful women out there.

So the women men count as possibilities are not real possibilities for most of them. That leads to a lot of guys sitting at home alone with their fantasies of unobtainable supermodels, stuck in a secret, sorry state that makes them unable to access real love for real women. Or, as Kenrick finds, a lot of guys on college campuses whining, "There are no attractive women to date." Under a constant barrage of media images of beautiful women, these guys have an expectation of attractiveness that is unusually high—and that makes the real people around them, in whom they might really be interested, seem lackluster, even if they are quite good-looking.

The idea that beauty could make so many men so miserable has acquired hard-nosed mathematical proof. In the world of abstract logic, marriage is looked on as a basic matching problem with statistical underpinnings in game theory. Logic says that everybody wants to do as well as they possibly can in selecting a life partner. And when people apply varied criteria for choosing a mate, everybody ends up with a partner with whom they are more or less satisfied. Not everybody gets his or her No. 1 choice, but everybody winds up reasonably content.

But the world has changed since mathematicians first tackled the matching of people with mates in the early 1960s.

Films, television and magazines have not only given beauty a commanding presence in our lives but have also helped standardize our vision of attractiveness. Enter Guido Caldarelli, Ph.D., of the University of Rome, and Andrea Capocci, Ph.D., of the University of Fribourg in Switzerland. Once they introduced into their mating equations what they call the "*Vogue* factor"—a measure of the influence of beauty—they found that people become dissatisfied with their sexual partners.

"When the concept of 'most beautiful' people in the world tends to be the same for everyone, it becomes more and more difficult to make more people happy," say the researchers. The same few beautiful people top everyone's list of desired partners—clearly an impossibility—and no one comes close to being matched with any of their choices. So people become unhappy with their partner possibilities.

Alas, it's not simply a theoretical issue. Sociologist Satoshi Kanazawa, Ph.D., finds that real-life consequences of the contrast effect exist, such as divorce. The contrast effect not only undermines marriages; it then keeps men single—and miserable.

Kanazawa, assistant professor of sociology at Indiana University of Pennsylvania, wondered: "If men found themselves being less attracted to their mates after being exposed to eight or 16 pictures in a half-hour experiment, what would be the effect if that happened day in, day out, for 20 years?" It immediately occurred to him that high school and college teachers would be prime candidates for a study; they are constantly surrounded by young women in their reproductive prime. The only other occupation he could think of where the overwhelming majority of people men come in contact with are young women, was Hollywood movie directors, as well as producers and actors—a group not known for their stable marriages. But there was not an available body of data on them like there was on teachers, from a general population survey.

What Kanazawa found was summed up in the title of his report published last year in *Evolution and Human Behavior:* "Teaching May Be Hazardous to Your Marriage." Men are generally less likely to be currently divorced or separated than women, and overall teachers are particularly unlikely to be divorced or separated. But being a male teacher or professor wiped out that advantage. And not just any male teacher is at risk. Male kindergarten and grade school teachers were contentedly monogamous. "There appears to be something about male teachers who come in daily contact with teenage women that increases the likelihood of being currently divorced or separated," Kanazawa says. He adds that these men remain unmarried because any adult women they might meet and date after their divorce would pale in comparison to the pretty young things constantly around them.

"Most real-life divorces happen because one or the other spouse is dissatisfied with their mate," says Kanazawa. "The contrast effect can explain why men might unconsciously become dissatisfied. They don't know why they suddenly find their middle-aged wives not appealing anymore; their exposure to young women might be a reason."

It would be blissfully easy to point a finger and claim that such infatuation with the young and the beautiful is the fault of the media and its barrage of nubile bodies. But it would also be incorrect. They're just giving us what we are naturally interested in.

All the evidence indicates that we are wired to respond to beauty. It's more than a matter of mere aesthetics; beauty is nature's shorthand for healthy and fertile, for reproductive capacity, a visible cue that a woman has the kind of prime partner potential that will bestow good genes on future generations. One of the prime elements of beauty, for example, is symmetry of body features. Research suggests that symmetrical people are physically and psychologically healthier than their less symmetrical counterparts.

If we're now all reeling from a surfeit of images of attractiveness, well, it's a lot like our dietary love affair with sugar.

"We want it. We need it. And our ancestors didn't have enough of it," observes Kenrick. "They were more concerned with starving. As a result, we have very hypersensitive detectors for it. And modern technology packages it and sends us doses that are way too large for our health."

There are, of course, beautiful women in other parts of the country. But L.A. is a mecca, attracting the most beautiful. Women don't look like this anywhere else in the country, and certainly not in the quantity they do here.

L.A. is an adopted city for me, as it is for many. Born in New York, I wonder from time to time what shape my life would have taken if I hadn't moved here in the 1970s. Whatever else, I would not have been saturated with the sight of so many beautiful women on a daily basis. But then I remember; these are the women whose images are broadcast all over the globe. While most people do not live in L.A., they visit it every day when they turn on the TV or go to the movies. It is safe to say that, to one degree or another, we all live in the shadow of the Hollywood sign.

CRITICAL THINKING QUESTIONS

1. This article suggests that we are exposed to very attractive people almost constantly in the media. What specific images of attractiveness are presented today in the media? Find media images of physical attractiveness from the 1950s and 1960s. What is the difference, if any, between the images presented then and the images presented now? Would the contrast effect work the same, regardless of the specific images of beauty being portrayed in the media? Explain.

2. Obesity among Americans recently has been described as a major health problem, second only to smoking as being preventable. At the same time, people have complained about the images of the very thin models and media figures that appear all around us. How do you reconcile this modeling of thinness as the ideal of beauty with the fact that Americans are increasingly overweight? In other words, why hasn't the media image of thinness resulted in people losing weight, when the opposite actually seems to have occurred? Explain.

3. This article deals with the issue of the contrast effect and how constant exposure to images of very attractive people may leave us less satisfied with our real-life peers. Besides beauty, what other images conveyed by the media may produce contrast effects, resulting in us being less happy with what we actually have and desirous of what we constantly see in the media?

4. Mass media images of beauty are disseminated worldwide via mechanisms such as movies and magazines. Many, but not all, of these images originate in the United States. Do you think the same contrast effect occurs in cultures that are very dissimilar to that of the United States? For that matter, would the same contrast effect occur even within the various subgroups that comprise the United States? Explain.

5. A common stereotype is that men rate the physical attractiveness of women as more important than women rate the physical attractiveness of men. In fact, much of the research on physical attractiveness focuses on the effects of female beauty on males. Design a study to determine how the contrast effect impacts females who are exposed to male media stereotypes of physical attractiveness.

ARTICLE 20 _____

It may seem obvious that looks matter when it comes to dating and mate selection. While many people would argue that physical attractiveness is not the only thing that they look for in a potential partner, few would argue that they are oblivious to appearance. Furthermore, according to Article 19—which considered how people's beauty preferences might have biological roots—there is fairly strong agreement as to what features people find attractive.

So, what is life like for people who happen to have the features that others find attractive? Are their lives significantly different from those of individuals who do not possess such good looks? Furthermore, do looks have any impact on people's lives outside the areas of dating and mating popularity? For example, compared to a less attractive counterpart, will an attractive person more likely be successful in the work world? Be a better parent? Be a happier person overall? The following classic article by Karen Dion, Ellen Berscheid, and Elaine Walster was one of the first studies to investigate the "What is beautiful is good" effect. As indicated in the article, attractiveness may convey a great many benefits to those people who possess it.

What Is Beautiful Is Good[1]
■ Karen Dion, Ellen Berscheid, and Elaine Walster

A person's physical appearance, along with his sexual identity, is the personal characteristic that is most obvious and accessible to others in social interaction. The present experiment was designed to determine whether physically attractive stimulus persons, both male and female, are (a) assumed to possess more socially desirable personality traits than physically unattractive stimulus persons and (b) expected to lead better lives (e.g., be more competent husbands and wives, be more successful occupationally, etc.) than unattractive stimulus persons. Sex of Subject × Sex of Stimulus Person interactions along these dimensions also were investigated. The present results indicate a "what is beautiful is good" stereotype along the physical attractiveness dimension with no Sex of Judge × Sex of Stimulus interaction. The implications of such a stereotype on self-concept development and the course of social interaction are discussed.

A person's physical appearance, along with his sexual identity, is the personal characteristic most obvious and accessible to others in social interaction. It is perhaps for this reason that folk psychology has always contained a multitude of theorems which ostensibly permit the forecast of a person's character and personality simply from knowledge of his outward appearance. The line of deduction advanced by most physiognomic theories is simply that "What is beautiful is good . . . [Sappho, Fragments, No. 101]," and that "Physical beauty is the sign of an interior beauty, a spiritual and moral beauty . . . [Schiller, 1882]."

Several processes may operate to make the soothsayers' prophecies more logical and accurate than would appear at first glance. First, it is possible that a correlation between inward character and appearance exists because certain personality traits influence one's appearance. For example, a calm, relaxed person may develop fewer lines and wrinkles than a tense, irritable person. Second, cultural stereotypes about the kinds of personalities appropriate for beautiful or ugly people may mold the personalities of these individuals. If casual acquaintances invariably assume that attractive individuals are more sincere, noble, and honest than unattractive persons, then attractive individuals should be habitually regarded with more respect than unattractive persons. Many have noted that one's self-concept develops from observing what others think about oneself. Thus, if the physically attractive person is consistently treated as a virtuous person, he may become one.

The above considerations pose several questions: (a) Do individuals in fact have stereotyped notions of the personality traits possessed by individuals of varying attractiveness? (b) To what extent are these stereotypes accurate? (c) What is the cause of the correlation between beauty and personality if, in fact, such a correlation exists?

Some observers, of course, deny that such stereotyping exists, and thus render Questions *b* and *c* irrelevant. Chief among these are rehabilitation workers (cf. Wright, 1960) whose clients possess facial and other physical disabilities. These researchers, however, may have a vested interest in believing that physical beauty is a relatively unimportant determinant of the opportunities an individual has available to him.

Dion, K., Berscheid, E., & Walster, E. (1972). What is beautiful is good. Journal of Personality and Social Psychology, 24, 285–290.

Perhaps more interestingly, it has been asserted that other researchers also have had a vested interest in retaining the belief that beauty is a peripheral characteristic. Aronson (1969), for example, has suggested that the fear that investigation might prove this assumption wrong has generally caused this to be a taboo area for social psychologists:

> *As an aside, I might mention that physical attractiveness is rarely investigated as an antecedent of liking—even though a casual observation (even by us experimental social psychologists) would indicate that we seem to react differently to beautiful women than to homely women. It is difficult to be certain why the effects of physical beauty have not been studied more system-atically. It may be that, at some levels, we would hate to find evidence indicating that beautiful women are better liked than homely women—somehow this seems undemocratic. In a democracy we like to feel that with hard work and a good deal of motivation, a person can accomplish almost anything. But, alas (most of us believe), hard work cannot make an ugly woman beautiful. Because of this suspicion perhaps most social psychologists implicitly prefer to believe that beauty is indeed only skin deep—and avoid the investigation of its social impact for fear they might learn otherwise [p. 160].*

The present study was an attempt to determine if a physical attractiveness stereotype exists and, if so, to investigate the content of the stereotype along several dimensions. Specifically, it was designed to investigate (*a*) whether physically attractive stimulus persons, both male and female, are assumed to possess more *socially desirable personality traits* than unattractive persons and (*b*) whether they are expected to *lead better lives* than unattractive individuals. With respect to the latter, we wished to determine if physically attractive persons are generally expected to be better husbands and wives, better parents, and more successful socially and occupationally than less attractive persons.

Because it seemed possible that jealousy might attenuate these effects (if one is jealous of another, he may be reluctant to accord the other the status that he feels the other deserves), and since subjects might be expected to be more jealous of attractive stimulus persons of the same sex than of the opposite sex, we examined the Sex of Subject × Sex of Stimulus Person interactions along the dimensions described above.

METHOD

Subjects

Sixty students, 30 males and 30 females, who were enrolled in an introductory course in psychology at the University of Minnesota participated in this experiment. Each had agreed to participate in return for experimental points to be added to their final exam grade.

Procedure

When the subjects arrived at the designated rooms, they were introduced to the experiment as a study of accuracy in person perception. The experimenter stated that while psychological studies have shown that people do form detailed impressions of others on the basis of a very few cues, the variables determining the extent to which these early impressions are generally accurate have not yet been completely identified. The subjects were told that the purpose of the present study was to compare person perception accuracy of untrained college students with two other groups who had been trained in vari-ous interpersonal perception techniques, specifically graduate students in clinical psychology and clinical psychologists. The experimenter noted his belief that person perception accuracy is a general ability varying among people. Therefore, according to the experimenter, college students who are high on this ability may be as accurate as some professional clinicians when making first-impression judgments based on noninterview material.

The subjects were told that standard sets of photographs would be used as the basis for personality inferences. The indi-viduals depicted in the photographs were said to be part of a group of college students currently enrolled at other universities who were participating in a longitudinal study of personality development scheduled to continue into adulthood. It would be possible, therefore, to assess the accuracy of each subject's judg-ments against information currently available on the stimulus persons and also against forthcoming information.

Stimulus Materials Following the introduction, each subject was given three envelopes. Each envelope contained one photo of a stimulus person of approximately the subject's own age. One of the three envelopes that the subject received contained a photograph of a physically attractive stimulus person; another contained a photograph of a person of average attractiveness; and the final envelope contained a photograph of a relatively unattractive stimulus person.[2] Half of our subjects received three pictures of girls; the remainder received pictures of boys.

To increase the generalizability of our findings and to insure that the general dimension of attractiveness was the characteristic responded to (rather than unique characteristics such as hair color, etc.), 12 different sets of three pictures each were prepared. Each subject received and rated only 1 set. Which 1 of the 12 sets of pictures the subject received, the order in which each of the three envelopes in the set were presented, and the ratings made of the person depicted, were all randomly determined.

Dependent Variables The subjects were requested to record their judgments of the three stimulus persons in several booklets.[3] The first page of each booklet cautioned the subjects that this study was an investigation of accuracy of person perception and that we were not interested in the subjects' tact, politeness, or other factors usually important in social situations. It was stressed that it was important for the subject to rate the stimulus persons frankly.

The booklets tapped impressions of the stimulus person along several dimensions. First, the subjects were asked to open the first envelope and then to rate the person depicted on 27 different *personality traits* (which were arranged in random order).[4] The subjects' ratings were made on 6-point scales, the ends of which were labeled by polar opposites (i.e., exciting–dull). When these ratings had been computed, the subject was asked to open the second envelope, make ratings, and then open the third envelope.

In a subsequent booklet, the subjects were asked to assess the stimulus persons on five additional personality traits.[5] These ratings were made on a slightly different scale. The subjects were asked to indicate which stimulus person possessed the "most" and "least" of a given trait. The stimulus person thought to best represent a positive trait was assigned a score of 3; the stimulus person thought to possess an intermediate amount of the trait was assigned a score of 2; and the stimulus person thought to least represent a trait was assigned a score of 1.

In a previous experiment (see Endnote 3), a subset of items was selected to comprise an index of the *social desirability* of the personality traits assigned to the stimulus person. The subjects' ratings of each stimulus person on the appropriate items were simply summed to determine the extent to which the subject perceived each stimulus person as socially desirable.

In order to assess whether or not attractive persons are expected to lead happier and more successful lives than unattractive persons, the subjects were asked to estimate which of the stimulus persons would be most likely, and which least likely, to have a number of different life experiences. The subjects were reminded again that their estimates would eventually be checked for accuracy as the lives of the various stimulus persons evolved. The subjects' estimates of the stimulus person's probable life experiences formed indexes of the stimulus person's future happiness in four areas: (*a*) marital happiness (Which stimulus person is most likely to ever be divorced?); (*b*) parental happiness (Which stimulus person is most likely to be a good parent?); (*c*) social and professional happiness (Which stimulus person is most likely to experience deep personal fulfillment?); and (*d*) total happiness (sum of Indexes *a*, *b*, and *c*).

A fifth index, an occupational success index, was also obtained for each stimulus person. The subjects were asked to indicate which of the three stimulus persons would be most likely to engage in 30 different occupations. (The order in which the occupations were presented and the estimates made was randomized.) The 30 occupations had been chosen such that three status levels of 10 different general occupations were represented, three

examples of which follow: Army sergeant (low status); Army captain (average status); Army colonel (high status). Each time a high-status occupation was foreseen for a stimulus person, the stimulus person was assigned a score of 3; when a moderate status occupation was foreseen, the stimulus person was assigned a score of 2; when a low-status occupation was foreseen, a score of 1 was assigned. The average status of occupations that a subject ascribed to a stimulus person constituted the score for that stimulus person in the occupational status index.

RESULTS AND DISCUSSION

Manipulation Check

It is clear that our manipulation of the relative attractiveness of the stimulus persons depicted was effective. The six unattractive stimulus persons were seen as less attractive than the average stimulus persons, who, in turn, were seen as less attractive than the six attractive stimulus persons. The stimulus persons' mean rankings on the attractiveness dimension were 1.12, 2.02, and 2.87, respectively. These differences were statistically significant ($F = 939.32$).[6]

Test of Hypotheses

It will be recalled that it was predicted that the subjects would attribute more socially desirable personality traits to attractive individuals than to average or unattractive individuals. It also was anticipated that jealousy might attenuate these effects. Since the subjects might be expected to be more jealous of stimulus persons of the same sex than of the opposite sex, we blocked both on sex of subject and sex of stimulus person. If jealousy attenuated the predicted main effect, a significant Sex of Subject × Sex of Stimulus Person interaction should be secured in addition to the main effect.

All tests for detection of linear trend and interaction were conducted via a multivariate analysis of variance. (This procedure is outlined in Hays, 1963.)

The means relevant to the hypothesis that attractive individuals will be perceived to possess more socially desirable personalities than others are reported in Table 1. Analyses reveal that attractive individuals were indeed judged to be more socially desirable than are unattractive ($F = 29.61$) persons. The Sex of Subject × Sex of Stimulus Person interaction was insignificant (interaction $F = .00$). Whether the rater was of the same or the opposite sex as the stimulus person, attractive stimulus persons were judged as more socially desirable.[7]

Furthermore, it was also hypothesized that the subjects would assume that attractive stimulus persons are likely to secure more prestigious jobs than those of lesser attractiveness, as well as experiencing happier marriages, being better parents, and enjoying more fulfilling social and occupational lives.

TABLE 1 / Traits Attributed to Various Stimulus Others

Trait Ascription[a]	Unattractive Stimulus Person	Average Stimulus Person	Attractive Stimulus Person
Social desirability of the stimulus person's personality	56.31	62.42	65.39
Occupational status of the stimulus person	1.70	2.02	2.25
Marital competence of the stimulus person	.37	.71	1.70
Parental competence of the stimulus person	3.91	4.55	3.54
Social and professional happiness of the stimulus person	5.28	6.34	6.37
Total happiness of the stimulus person	8.83	11.60	11.60
Likelihood of marriage	1.52	1.82	2.17

[a]The higher the number, the more socially desirable, the more prestigious an occupation, etc., the stimulus person is expected to possess.

The means relevant to these predictions concerning the estimated future life experiences of individuals of varying degrees of physical attractiveness are also depicted in Table 1. As shown in the table, there was strong support for all of the preceding hypotheses save one. Attractive men and women were expected to attain more prestigious occupations than were those of lesser attractiveness ($F = 42.30$), and this expectation was expressed equally by raters of the same or the opposite sex as the stimulus person (interaction $F = .25$).

The subjects also assumed that attractive individuals would be more competent spouses and have happier marriages than those of lesser attractiveness ($F = 62.54$). (It might be noted that there is some evidence that this may be a correct perception. Kirkpatrick and Cotton (1951), reported that "well-adjusted" wives were more physically attractive than "badly adjusted" wives. "Adjustment," however, was assessed by friends' perceptions, which may have been affected by the stereotype evident here.)

According to the means reported in Table 1, it is clear that attractive individuals were not expected to be better parents ($F = 1.47$). In fact, attractive persons were rated somewhat lower than any other group of stimulus persons as potential parents, although no statistically significant differences were apparent.

As predicted, attractive stimulus persons were assumed to have better prospects for happy, social, and professional lives ($F = 21.97$). All in all, the attractive stimulus persons were expected to have more total happiness in their lives than those of lesser attractiveness ($F = 24.20$).

The preceding results did not appear to be attenuated by a jealousy effect (Sex of Subject × Stimulus Person interaction Fs = .01, .07, .21, and .05, respectively).

The subjects were also asked to estimate the likelihood that the various stimulus persons would marry early or marry at all. Responses were combined into a single index. It is evident that the subjects assumed that the attractive stimulus persons were more likely to find an acceptable partner than those of lesser attractiveness ($F = 35.84$). Attractive individuals were expected to marry earlier and to be less likely to remain single. Once again, these conclusions were reached by all subjects, regardless of whether they were of the same or opposite sex of the stimulus person (interaction $F = .01$).

The results suggest that a physical attractiveness stereotype exists and that its content is perfectly compatible with the "What is beautiful is good" thesis. Not only are physically attractive persons assumed to possess more socially desirable personalities than those of lesser attractiveness, but it is presumed that their lives will be happier and more successful.

The results also suggest that the physical attractiveness variable may have a number of implications for a variety of aspects of social interaction and influence. For example, it is clear that physically attractive individuals may have even more advantages in the dating market than has previously been assumed. In addition to an aesthetic advantage in marrying a beautiful spouse (cf. Josselin de Jong, 1952), potential marriage partners may also assume that the beautiful attract all of the world's material benefits and happiness. Thus, the lure of an attractive marriage partner should be strong indeed.

We do not know, of course, how well this stereotype stands up against contradictory information. Nor do we know the extent to which it determines the pattern of social interaction that develops with a person of a particular attractiveness level. Nevertheless, it would be odd if people did not behave toward others in accordance with this stereotype. Such behavior has been previously noted anecdotally. Monahan (1941) has observed that

Even social workers accustomed to dealing with all types often find it difficult to think of a normal, pretty girl as being guilty of a crime. Most people, for some inexplicable reason, think of crime in terms of abnormality in appearance, and I must say that beautiful women are not often convicted [p. 103].

A host of other familiar social psychological dependent variables also should be affected in predictable ways.

In the above connection, it might be noted that if standards of physical attractiveness vary widely, knowledge of the content of the physical attractiveness stereotype would be of limited usefulness in predicting its effect on social interaction and the development of the self-concept. The present study was not designed to investigate the degree of variance in perceived beauty. (The physical attractiveness ratings of the stimulus materials were made by college students of a similar background to those who participated in this study.) Preliminary evidence (Cross & Cross, 1971) suggests that such differences in perceived beauty may not be as severe as some observers have suggested.

REFERENCES

Aronson, E. Some antecedents of interpersonal attraction. In W. J. Arnold & D. Levine (Eds.), *Nebraska Symposium on Motivation*, 1969, *17*, 143–177.

Cross, J. F., & Cross, J. Age, sex, race, and the perception of facial beauty. *Developmental Psychology*, 1971, *5*, 433–439.

Hays, W. L. *Statistics for psychologists*. New York: Holt, Rinehart & Winston, 1963.

Josselin de Jong, J. P. B. *Lévi-Strauss' theory on kinship and marriage*. Leiden, Holland: Brill, 1952.

Kirkpatrick, C., & Cotton, J. Physical attractiveness, age, and marital adjustment. *American Sociological Review*, 1951, *16*, 81–86.

Monahan, F. *Women in crime*. New York: Ives Washburn, 1941.

Schiller, J. C. F. *Essays, esthetical and philosophical, including the dissertation on the "Connexions between the animal and the spiritual in man."* London: Bell, 1882.

Wright, B. A. *Physical disability—A psychological approach*. New York: Harper & Row, 1960.

ENDNOTES

1. This research was financed in part by National Institute of Mental Health Grants MH 16729 to Berscheid and MH 16661 to Walster.

2. The physical attractiveness rating of each of the pictures was determined in a preliminary study. One hundred Minnesota undergraduates rated 50 yearbook pictures of persons of the opposite sex with respect to physical attractiveness. The criteria for choosing the 12 pictures to be used experimentally were (*a*) high-interrater agreement as to the physical attractiveness of the stimulus (the average interrater correlation for all of the pictures was .70); and (*b*) pictures chosen to represent the very attractive category and very unattractive category were not at the extreme ends of attractiveness.

3. A detailed report of the items included in these booklets is available. Order Document No. 01972 from the National Auxiliary Publication Service of the American Society for Information Science, c/o CCM Information Services, Inc., 909 3rd Avenue, New York, New York 10022. Remit in advance $5.00 for photocopies or $2.00 for microfiche and make checks payable to: Research and Microfilm Publications, Inc.

4. The subjects were asked how altruistic, conventional, self-assertive, exciting, stable, emotional, dependent, safe, interesting, genuine, sensitive, outgoing, sexually permissive, sincere, warm, sociable, competitive, obvious, kind, modest, strong, serious, sexually warm, simple, poised, bold, and sophisticated each stimulus person was.

5. The subjects rated stimulus persons on the following traits: friendliness, enthusiasm, physical attractiveness, social poise, and trustworthiness.

6. Throughout this report, $df = 1/55$.

7. Before running the preliminary experiment to determine the identity of traits usually associated with a socially desirable person (see Endnote 3), we had assumed that an exciting date, a nurturant person, and a person of good character would be perceived as quite different personality types. Conceptually, for example, we expected that an exciting date would be seen to require a person who was unpredictable, challenging, etc., while a nurturant person would be seen to be predictable and unthreatening. It became clear, however, that these distinctions were not ones which made sense to the subjects. There was almost total overlap between the traits chosen as representative of an exciting date, of a nurturant person, and a person of good or ethical character. All were strongly correlated with social desirability. Thus, attractive stimulus persons are assumed to be more exciting dates ($F = 39.97$), more nurturant individuals ($F = 13.96$), and to have better character ($F = 19.57$) than persons of lesser attractiveness.

CRITICAL THINKING QUESTIONS

1. The study used college students, presumably most of them of ages 18 to 22. Do you think that the age of the subjects might influence the results? Why or why not?

2. The study used photographs as stimulus materials. Do you think that the "What is beautiful is good" effect would also occur in face-to-face encounters? Or might the judgments made in person somehow be different than those made by looking at photographs? How could you test this possibility?

3. The study indicated that physically attractive people are perceived as having more socially desirable traits and are expected to be more successful in life than their less attractive counterparts. Do you think that attractive people *actually* are more desirable and more successful in life? Why or why not?

4. This article suggests that ample positive attributions are made for attractive people. In what ways might being attractive actually be a liability, instead of an asset? Explain your reasoning.

ADDITIONAL RELATED READINGS

Johnson, S. K., Podratz, K. E., Dipboye, R. L., & Gibbons, E. (2010). The physical attractiveness biases in ratings of employment suitability: Tracking down the "beauty is beastly" effect. *Journal of Social Psychology, 150*(3), 301–318.

Toma, C. L., & Hancock, J. T. (2010). Looks and lies: The role of physical attractiveness in online dating self-presentation and deception. *Communication Research, 37*(3), 335–351.

ARTICLE 21

Both of the preceding articles looked at the important role that physical attractiveness plays in interpersonal attraction. Article 19 focused on the effects of constant media exposure to highly attractive people and the subsequent impact of such exposure on our perceptions of the people surrounding us. Article 20 demonstrated that we place great importance on physical attractiveness in deciding whom we want to date and that we associate all sorts of positive and desirable characteristics with people we find attractive. This "what is beautiful is good" effect may bestow significant benefits on people deemed physically attractive in a given society.

A great deal of the research that has investigated the relationship between physical attractiveness and attraction has used photographs of people as stimuli. In the typical research model, the subject views a photograph of an attractive or unattractive (or at least less attractive) stimulus person. Then either the subject is asked to make judgments about that stimulus person or the study determines how exposure to that stimulus person affects the subject's perceptions of his or her own partners or other real-world people.

However, when we encounter real people in the real world, their physical appearance is but one piece of the information available to us. Have you ever had the experience of seeing a very attractive person but, once you started to talk with him or her, found yourself not all that attracted? Or maybe you have, over time, become attracted to someone whom you found likeable but not physically attractive at first. Obviously, our being attracted to other individuals depends on more than just how they look.

So when you do meet someone for the first time, how quickly do you form an impression of whether this is someone you'd like to get to know better? And how quickly (and accurately!) are you able to determine if the other person is interested in you? There are compelling arguments that men, and especially women, have motivations to both quickly and accurately determine the interest levels of others if for no other reason than to not spend time on an unlikely prospect. This ability to "read" the interest levels of someone else toward us may also be related to how good we are in determining the interest levels of others toward each other. This article by Skyler S. Place, Peter M. Todd, Lars Penke, and Jens B. Asendorpf had people observe the interactions of people toward each other in a speed-dating situation. Their findings as to how accurate people are in correctly determining such interest, as well as to whether or not that accuracy applied equally to males and females, provide further insights into the earliest aspects of interpersonal attraction.

The Ability to Judge the Romantic Interest of Others

■ Skyler S. Place, Peter M. Todd, Lars Penke, and Jens B. Asendorpf

ABSTRACT

The ability to judge another individual's romantic interest level— both toward oneself and toward others—is an adaptively important skill when choosing a suitable mate to pursue. We tested this ability using videos of individuals on speed dates as stimuli. Male and female observers were equally good at predicting interest levels, but they were more accurate when predicting male interest: Predictions of female interest were just above chance. Observers predicted interest successfully using stimuli as short as 10 s, and they performed best when watching clips of the middle or end of the speed date. There was considerable variability between daters, with some being very easy to read and others apparently masking their true intentions. Variability between observers was also found.

The results suggest that the ability to read nonverbal behavior quickly in mate choice is present not only for individuals in the interaction, but also for third-party observers.

It is adaptively important for an individual to be able to evaluate the interest level of a potential mate. Choosing a mate is a key component of gene promotion, and it is one of the most central decisions concerning reproduction across species (Andersson, 1994). Accurately appraising interest minimizes wasted time and resources and allows for a greater chance of success in a competitive mating market (Wiegmann & Angeloni, 2007). In terms of evolutionary life-history theory, it is thus fundamental for an efficient allocation of mating effort (Kaplan & Gangestad, 2005). Correctly perceiving interest is useful not only for choosing a

Place, S.S.; Todd, P.M.; Penke, L.; & Asenforpf, J.B. *Psychological Science*, 20(1), 22–26. Copyright © 2009 by the Association for Psychological Science. Reprinted by permission of SAGE Publications.

mate but also for determining one's own mate value (Simão & Todd, 2002), which is important for future mating decisions (Penke, Todd, Lenton, & Fasolo, 2007; Penke & Denissen, 2008). Thus, it is beneficial for humans to be able to pick up on cues that allow them to excel at such appraisals. These cues could include information available through language content and tone of voice, as well as nonverbal behaviors such as body language, social signaling, and eye contact (Ambady & Rosenthal, 1992; Penke & Asendorpf, 2008).

In addition to evaluating a potential mate's level of interest in oneself, it is advantageous to be able to evaluate levels of interest between others via observed interactions. This is important for building knowledge of the surrounding social network (Pentland, 2007), including the availability and desirability of future potential mates (Simão & Todd, 2002; see also the literature on mate copying in animals—e.g., Dugatkin, 1992, 2000—and in humans—e.g., Jones, DeBruine, Little, Buriss, & Feinberg, 2007). Observer perception in general has been a fruitful field for social psychologists: Kenny and colleagues (Kenny, 1994; Kenny & Albright, 1987; Kenny, Bond, Mohr, & Horn, 1996) studied "third-party metaperceptions," with participants observing interactions between pairs of individuals, and found that people performed above chance at predicting who feels friendly toward whom. This and other social perceptions can be made accurately with limited information (see Ambady & Rosenthal, 1992, for a review).

Given the results on accurate observer predictions regarding friendship, along with the adaptive need for an efficient mechanism to predict interest in mate choice, we hypothesized that individuals will be able to accurately predict others' interest in themselves and in third parties. Here we focus on the latter, third-party metaperceptions of how romantically interested other people are in each other. To be adaptive in everyday situations, the ability to determine this should require only a limited amount of information, suggesting that performance should not be hindered by shortened stimuli-presentation times. Furthermore, because women face greater risks during mate choice due to their inevitably higher minimal parental investment in potentially resulting offspring (Trivers, 1972), we predicted that they would behave more cautiously, covertly, and ambiguously during initial interactions, making their intentions more difficult to read than those of men (Grammer, Kruck, Juette, & Fink, 2000; Haselton & Buss, 2000). Finally, we also investigated the observers' relationship status as a potentially confounding factor.

To test these ideas, we needed a set of mate-choice-relevant interactions that observers could watch and judge, and for which there was information on actual romantic interest so we could assess the observer's accuracy. Videos of speed dating interactions fulfilled these requirements and also allowed us to limit the information available to our judges by presenting them with clips of various durations.

METHOD

Participants

The study included 54 participants—28 women (mean age = 19.8 years, SD = 3.8 years; 14 in relationships) and 26 men (mean age = 19.5, SD = 1.1 years; 9 in relationships). Participants were recruited from the Indiana University psychology participant pool and were compensated with research credits required for undergraduate coursework. Participants were screened to be over 18 years old, to be heterosexual, and to have no knowledge of the German language (because the stimuli were in German; see next section).

Stimuli

The videos of mate-choice situations were gathered during a series of laboratory-based speed dating sessions run at Humboldt University in Berlin, Germany. Speed dating is a paradigm designed to allow singles to meet a large number of possible mates in a short period of time (Finkel & Eastwick, 2008). The individuals who participated in the Berlin Speed Dating Study (BSDS) were recruited using advertising and publicity in media outlets; in exchange for free speed dating, they agreed to have their interactions videotaped and to provide additional data on themselves. Seventeen sessions of speed dating were run as part of the study, for a total of 382 participants.

The "dates" took place in separated booths, and each lasted for 3 min, at the end of which each individual wrote down whether he or she was interested in seeing that date again (an "offer"). Pairs making mutual offers were given each other's contact information after the session so they could meet again. The videos of these interactions were the stimuli used in our experiment. Each of the two individuals in a speed date was filmed with a separate over-the-shoulder camera, and these two videos (with audio in German) were shown in a synchronized side-by-side combination to our participants. These combined video presentations, which we refer to as a video clip, allowed a naturalistic view of the date. Videos of 24 interactions were used in this experiment, randomly selected from two different sessions comprising speed daters in their 20s; each person appeared in only one video. This sample matched the entire population of interactions from the BSDS sessions with regard to offer rates from men (41%) and women (33%), as well as rates of mutual interest between individuals (15%).

Participants watched shortened video clips that were either 10 s or 30 s long and came from the beginning, middle, or end of the date (three temporal locations). For each of the 24 interactions we used, each participant saw four clips (in randomized order, both within and across interactions): 10-s clips from all three locations and one 30-s clip from a location that was randomized across interactions. The experimental design was therefore a 2 (observer sex: male, female) × 2 (relationship status: single, in relationship) × 3 (clip location: beginning, middle, end) × 2 (clip length: 10 s, 30 s) mixed factorial design.

Procedure

Participants first provided their age, sex, ethnicity, and relationship status. Our dependent measure was the observing participant's perception of the interest within each speed dating interaction they watched. Observers answered two questions after each video clip: "Do you think the man was interested in the woman?" and "Do you think the woman was interested in the man?" Their binary "yes" or "no" answers were then compared to the binary decisions of the actual speed daters.

RESULTS

The first question posed was whether observers could predict romantic or dating interest between others accurately. Figure 1 presents the results for prediction of male interest and for prediction of female interest separately, collapsing across all within-subjects conditions. A paired-sample t test

FIGURE 1 / Overall accuracy in predicting romantic interest of videotaped speed-dating participants. Dashed lines indicate chance performance levels for predicting interest for daters of each sex. Error bars show standard errors of the means.

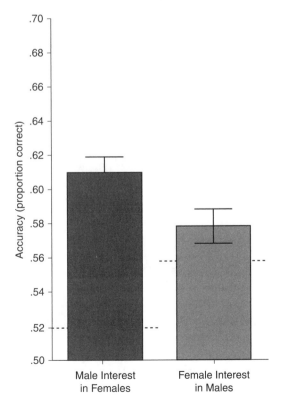

showed a significant difference between the two measures, $t(53) = 3.64$, $p_{rep} = .986$, $d = 1.00$. It is important to note that observers could achieve a chance accuracy above 50% in this task if they had knowledge of the fact that daters make offers less than half the time (see above), and they could have had such knowledge through past dating experience (participants were not explicitly informed of the interest rates prior to the start of the experiment). If they took account of the actual offer prevalence rates, the best that observers could do at chance would be 52% ($.41 × .41 +$ $[1 − .41] × [1 − .41]$) for predicting male interest and 56% ($.33 × .33 + [1 − .33] × [1 − .33]$) for predicting female interest, calculated using the base rates of interest present in the stimuli set.

Observer performance on both of the dependent measures was significantly better than these adjusted chance levels for predicting male interest, $t(53) = 10.76$, $p_{rep} = .986$, $d = 2.94$, but was just above chance for predicting female interest, $t(53) = 2.24$, $p_{rep} = .908$, $d = 0.62$. (See Ambady & Rosenthal, 1992, for similar accuracy ranges for other thin-slice social perceptions.)

Each dependent measure was analyzed for contributing factors using a mixed-factor analysis of variance (ANOVA). For predicting male interest in females, there was no effect of sex. There was an effect of relationship status, such that individuals in relationships outperformed individuals who were single, $F(1, 50) = 6.18$, $p_{rep} = .935$, $\eta_p^2 = .11$. The length of the video clip presented had no effect on accuracy. There was, however, an effect of video-clip location, $F(2, 100) = 16.86$, $p_{rep} = .986$, $\eta_p^2 = .25$. None of the possible interactions reached significance. For predicting female interest in males, sex, relationship status, and video presentation length were all not significant. As in the male-interest data, there was a significant effect of video-clip location, $F(2, 100) = 16.18$, $p_{rep} = .986$, $\eta_p^2 = .41$.

We further analyzed the within-subjects factor of location using a single-factor ANOVA (with levels beginning, middle, and end), revealing a significant difference of location for predicting both male interest in females, $F(2, 106) = 29.35$, $p_{rep} = .986$, $\eta_p^2 = .36$, and female interest in males, $F(2, 106) = 36.52$, $p_{rep} = .986$, $\eta_p^2 = .41$. Figure 2 shows that the best performance at judging interest came from viewing clips from the middle and end of the interaction. Post hoc comparisons using the Bonferroni correction showed significant differences between the beginning clip and both the middle and end clips for both male interest and female interest.

To look at how "readable" individual speed daters were, the data were further analyzed at the per-dater level (see Fig. 3). Daters were sorted from most-accurately predicted (mean accuracy across all observers) to least. This was done by individual, not by interaction—a single video could include a woman who was very easy to read (yielding high accuracy) and a difficult-to-read man (yielding low accuracy), and we assessed readability

FIGURE 2 / Accuracy in predicting romantic interest of speed-dating participants by video-clip location. Error bars show standard errors of the means.

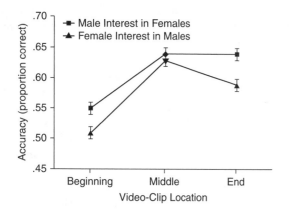

performance based on guessing. The simulation generated a set of responses for each observer, for each video, for each of the four partial clips. Predictions of interest in each case were chosen randomly according to the interest-judgment rates (~60%) of observers. The simulation was run 1,000 times, and the responses were averaged within each observer for each dater in the videos and then averaged across observers. The results rank-ordered across daters (Fig. 3, dashed lines) have a slope that is less steep than that of the experimental data. Both the male and the female human-observer data fall clearly above the 95% confidence intervals of the Monte Carlo simulation in the 11 daters who were easiest to predict. In addition, the five women daters who were the hardest for observers to read fall below the 95% confidence intervals, showing that observers were systematically fooled in these cases.

of these two individuals separately. In fact, being accurate at predicting the dating interest of one sex does not help in predicting the interest level of the other: The correlation between accuracy in predicting male interest and accuracy in predicting female interest in the same video was zero, $r = .00$, $p_{rep} = .083$.

The solid lines in Figure 3 show participants' mean accuracy at predicting all males and all females. The steep downward slope of both lines indicates the wide range in observers' ability to predict the interest level of different individuals. To find out if these results are different from those expected by chance, we ran a Monte Carlo simulation designed to determine chance-level

DISCUSSION

The data supported our two main hypotheses: Observers were able to assess the dating interest of others at above-chance levels, and the length of time required to do so was brief. For both sexes, accurately perceiving romantic interest both of and toward potential mates holds evolutionary benefits through the efficient allocation of mating effort. Our results suggest that men and women possess this adaptive ability. Whether it is the result of a domain-specific adaptation or a more general ability for social perception remains to be determined. Furthermore, as predicted, it was on average easier for observers to gauge men's

FIGURE 3 / Accuracy in predicting each dater's interest, comparing human judges with Monte Carlo simulations. Error bars for observed data show standard errors of the means. Error bars for simulated expected data show 95% confidence intervals. Open circles indicate daters who were not interested; closed circles indicate daters who were interested.

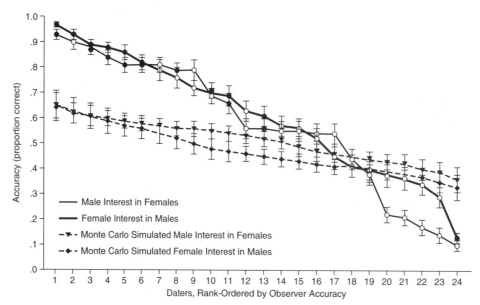

intentions than it was to gauge women's intentions (though there was high variance in observers' performance levels across individual daters of both sexes). The lower overall accuracy concerning women's intentions was not due to observers guessing or performing at chance but to a systematic overperception of female daters' interest (Fig. 3)—surpassing 80% erroneous interest predictions for the five hardest-to-read women.

This dramatic rate of incorrect perception supports our hypothesis that women are harder to read, presumably because they mask their true intentions: As Grammer et al. (2000) argued, the biologically deep-rooted sex inequality in parental investment (Trivers, 1972) puts greater risks on the females of a species during mate choice. As a result, females, including women in speed dating (Todd, Penke, Fasolo, & Lenton, 2007), are much more critical and picky when making mate-choice decisions. And, in order to evaluate potential mates longer without signaling their true intentions, women behave more covertly and ambiguously during initial interactions with the opposite sex. Men, in contrast, face lower risks and consequently should be less likely to hide their intentions. In our study, observers only saw an individual interacting on one date, but perhaps if multiple dates with the same individual were presented, observers would be better able to differentiate instances of deceptive and true interest from that individual.

Whereas the degree of observer accuracy seems to depend heavily on the individual dater being watched, the length of time spent watching has almost no effect. However, a systematic difference in observer performance appears when comparing across video-clip locations: In our study, the best observer judgment performance came for video clips taken from the middle and end of the dates. This may arise because daters are using the information they gather throughout their brief encounter to make their ultimate decisions, so that their decisions are not fully determined, and therefore not fully readable by others, until later in the encounter. If true, this would counter a major critique of speed dating as a method of finding a long-term partner: that people are using only physical attractiveness to make their dating decisions because they do not have the time to assess much else (Eastwick & Finkel, 2008; Kurzban & Weeden, 2005; Todd et al., 2007). Other data are needed to determine whether daters are using multiple cues over time or just taking time to register an attractiveness-driven decision.

Some observers also appear to be better at using the available information for making some judgments. Whereas we did not aim to identify the individual differences underlying good observers (see Funder, 2001), we did find that observers who indicated they were currently in a relationship did better at predicting male interest than did those who were currently single. This suggestive finding could stem in part from learning through relationship experiences. Alternatively, it is possible that the social skills necessary to succeed in finding and maintaining a relationship also support the ability to correctly perceive romantic interest. Studying younger observers before they have much relationship experience could help to disentangle these (and potentially other) hypotheses.

The results of this study add to the body of findings on the abilities of naive observers to make quick and accurate judgments, demonstrating that this ability extends to assessments of romantic interest in the mate-choice domain as well. We have shown this through a novel method that provides a strong criterion against which the observer judgments were evaluated: unambiguously stated, consequential mate-choice decisions of actual partner-seeking singles meeting available potential mates while speed dating. With limited information, observers can make accurate judgments of mate-choice decisions, though their abilities may be hampered by the desire of some daters to mask their true intentions.

ACKNOWLEDGMENTS

This research was supported by Grant As 59/15 of the German Research Foundation (DFG), awarded to Jens Asendorpf. We would like to thank Marie-Luise Haupt, Karsten Krauskopf, Harald Schneider, and Sebastian Teubner for their help with the Berlin Speed Dating Study. Lars Penke is supported by the United Kingdom Medical Research Council (Grant No. 82800) and is part of the University of Edinburgh Centre for Cognitive Ageing and Cognitive Epidemiology. Funding from the Biotechnology and Biological Sciences Research Council, Engineering and Physical Sciences Research Council, Economic and Social Research Council, and Medical Research Council is gratefully acknowledged.

REFERENCES

Ambady, N., & Rosenthal, R. (1992). Thin slices of expressive behavior as predictors of interpersonal consequences: A metaanalysis. *Psychological Bulletin, 111*, 256–274.

Andersson, M.B. (1994). *Sexual selection.* Princeton, NJ: Princeton University Press.

Dugatkin, L.A. (1992). Sexual selection and imitation: Females copy the mate choice of others. *American Naturalist, 139*, 1384–1389.

Dugatkin, L.A. (2000). *The imitation factor: Evolution beyond the gene.* New York: Free Press.

Eastwick, P.W., & Finkel, E.J. (2008). Sex differences in mate preferences revisited: Do people know what they initially desire in a romantic partner? *Journal of Personality and Social Psychology, 94*, 245–264.

Finkel, E.J., & Eastwick, P.W. (2008). Speed-dating. *Current Directions in Psychological Science, 17*, 193–197.

Funder, D.C. (2001). Accuracy in personality judgment: Some research and theory concerning an obvious question. In B. Roberts & R. Hogan (Eds.), *Personality psychology in the workplace* (pp. 121–140). Washington, DC: American Psychological Association.

Grammer, K., Kruck, K., Juette, A., & Fink, B. (2000). Non-verbal behavior as courtship signals: The role of control and choice in selecting partners. *Evolution and Human Behavior, 21*, 371–390.

Haselton, M.G., & Buss, D.M. (2000). Error management theory: A new perspective on biases in cross-sex mind reading. *Journal of Personality and Social Psychology, 78*, 81–91.

Jones, B., DeBruine, L., Little, A., Burriss, R., & Feinberg, D. (2007). Social transmission of face preferences among humans. *Proceedings of the Royal Society B: Biological Sciences, 274*, 899–903.

Kaplan, H.S., & Gangestad, S.W. (2005). Life history theory and evolutionary psychology. In D.M. Buss (Ed.), *The handbook of evolutionary psychology* (pp. 68–95). New York: Wiley.

Kenny, D.A. (1994). *Interpersonal perception: A social relations analysis.* New York: Guilford Press.

Kenny, D.A., & Albright, L. (1987). Accuracy in interpersonal perception: A social relations analysis. *Psychological Bulletin, 102*, 390–402.

Kenny, D.A., Bond, C.F., Jr., Mohr, C.D., & Horn, E.M. (1996). Do we know how much people like one another? *Journal of Personality and Social Psychology, 71*, 928–936.

Kurzban, R., & Weeden, J. (2005). HurryDate: Mate preferences in action. *Evolution and Human Behavior, 26*, 227–244.

Penke, L., & Asendorpf, J.B. (2008). Beyond global sociosexual orientations: A more differentiated look at sociosexuality and its effects on courtship and romantic relationships. *Journal of Personality and Social Psychology, 95*, 1113–1135.

Penke, L., & Denissen, J.J.A. (2008). Sex differences and lifestyle-dependent shifts in the attunement of self-esteem to self-perceived mate value: Hints to an adaptive mechanism? *Journal of Research in Personality, 42*, 1123–1129.

Penke, L., Todd, P.M., Lenton, A.P., & Fasolo, B. (2007). How self-assessments can guide human mating decisions. In G. Geher & G. Miller (Eds.), *Mating intelligence: Sex, relationships, and the mind's reproductive system* (pp. 37–75). Mahwah, NJ: Erlbaum.

Pentland, A. (2007). On the collective nature of human intelligence. *Adaptive Behavior, 15*, 189–198.

Simão, J., & Todd, P.M. (2002). Modeling mate choice in monogamous mating systems with courtship. *Adaptive Behavior, 10*, 113–136.

Todd, P.M., Penke, L., Fasolo, B., & Lenton, A.P. (2007). Different cognitive processes underlie human mate choices and mate preferences. *Proceedings of the National Academy of Sciences, USA, 104*, 15011–15016.

Trivers, R.L. (1972). Parental investment and sexual selection. In B. Campbell (Ed.), *Sexual selection and the descent of man* (pp. 136–179). Chicago: Aldine-Atherton.

Wiegmann, D.D., & Angeloni, L.M. (2007). Mate choice and uncertainty in the decision process. *Journal of Theoretical Biology, 249*, 654–666.

CRITICAL THINKING QUESTIONS

1. Do you agree with the reasoning presented in the article as to why observers found it easier to determine a male's interest than a female's? Can you think of any other possible reasons to explain this finding? Explain your answer.

2. Based on your own observations of others, what are the cues that people may exhibit that would show an interest in another person? Are there gender differences in the cues that are used? Are those cues consciously controlled or unconsciously determined?

3. According to the findings of this study, women's interest in another is much harder to read than male interest. The method employed in this study involved "speed dating," characterized by very brief interactions. Do you think this difference would persist over time? If so, how might you expect it to change? Explain your reasoning.

4. The study found a lot of variability between the participants in the dating sessions and the observers, with some people being easier to "read" and some people being better "readers." What do you think may account for these differences in both the participants and the observers?

CHAPTER INTEGRATION QUESTIONS_____

1. Articles 19 and 20 are both concerned with the importance placed on physical attractiveness, whereas Article 21 seems to suggest that physical attractiveness might only be part of the process of attraction even upon first meeting. Taken together, what implications do these articles have for the way attractiveness affects us? Do the articles suggest how the impact of attractiveness can be minimized? If so, how?

2. What factors besides physical beauty may affect our attraction to other people? Might these factors, in turn, affect how physically attractive we find others? Explain.

3. "Beauty is in the eye of the beholder," according to an old proverb. In light of the information presented in the articles in this chapter, discuss whether this proverb is true or false or both.

Chapter Eight

CLOSE RELATIONSHIPS

Of ALL THE interactions that occur between human beings, perhaps none is more capable of producing such intense feelings as love. If we look at how often love is portrayed in the popular media, we get the definite impression that it is a major concern, almost a preoccupation, of most people. However, if we look at the literature in social psychology, we might get a very different impression. Until recently, the topic of love was largely ignored in the research literature.

A specific subject of interest to many people is the failure of love and the dissolution of relationships. Anyone who has been through a divorce or has witnessed its effects on someone close to him or her knows that the ending of a marriage is usually an extremely painful ordeal. Yet in spite of the pain involved in splitting up, nearly half of all marriages end up in divorce. What goes wrong? More importantly, what can be done earlier in a relationship to decrease the likelihood of divorce later on? Article 22, "Great Expectations," examines the types of unrealistic expectations that people today have for marriage as well as the origins of such beliefs. Perhaps having more realistic expectations for marriage is a key component to having a successful relationship.

After meeting someone who catches your attention, and then deciding that you would like to get to know him or her better, comes a big step: asking the person out. So you take the chance and ask for a date. Which response to your request would increase your liking of the recipient of your request the most: The person enthusiastically accepts your offer, or the person first plays "hard to get" and then later accepts your invitation? Much folk wisdom would suggest the value of not appearing too eager. But does that hard-to-get strategy actually work? Article 23, "Playing Hard to Get," is an amusing classic article that addresses this dating dilemma.

Finally, Article 24, "Does a Long-Term Relationship Kill Romantic Love?," examines the possibility that romantic love, which includes feelings of intensity with the other, engagement with each other, and sexual interest in his or her partner, can exist in long-term relationships. Many people, and indeed many researchers and therapists, tend to believe that passionate love in a long-term relationship is an unrealistic expectation and one that few people ever achieve. The findings reported in this article may suggest otherwise.

ARTICLE 22 _____

The high divorce rate in the United States is of social concern to a large number of Americans. Current statistics indicate that nearly half of all marriages will end in divorce. And while the number of divorces has decreased slightly in the last few years, it still remains around the 50% mark. Whether the high rates of divorce seen over the last few decades will remain the same, increase, or decrease remains to be seen. Nonetheless, the prevalence of divorce is certainly characteristic of contemporary U.S. society.

In spite of the 50/50 odds that a marriage will not last, nearly 95% of the adult U.S. population will marry at least once in their lifetimes. Marriage obviously holds a strong attraction for most people. Even among those who divorce, many will remarry, further pointing to the importance that most people place on the institution of marriage. It probably is a rare couple who marry with the thought that they will divorce. Indeed, most people take to heart the wedding vows of "For better or worse, in sickness and in health, until death do us part," believing that the dire divorce statistics apply to other couples, not them.

So, why has the divorce rate risen and continued to hover around the 50% mark? And for those married people today who have not divorced, are they less satisfied with their marriages than were their counterparts in the past? The answers to both of these questions are quite complex. However, one common denominator may lie in the reasons that people now have for getting married. If you are not married, take a moment and ask yourself (or someone else who is not married) why you want to get married. If you are married, why did you choose to do so? Chances are, the most common answer is for love, with the implication being that marriage provides people with unique happiness and satisfaction. Yet surveys of young adults a century ago found that the majority wanted to get married for much more pragmatic reasons, such as to have children and to own a home.

What does getting married for love (or happiness) have to do with the higher divorce rate? The problem is not marrying for love per se but rather entering a marriage with certain expectations. If a person marries for love and the love he or she experiences after marriage does not conform to his or her expectations, then the logical conclusion may be that he or she made a mistake. That is the thinking of many people today. We live in a culture that highly promotes individual happiness and fulfillment. Such an attitude suggests that individual happiness and fulfillment are paramount and should take precedence over all else. Thus, divorce is seen as an acceptable way to pursue individual happiness and fulfillment.

As mentioned earlier, a major part of the problem may be the unrealistic expectations that people today bring with them to marriage. These expectations may be impossible to meet and thus undoubtedly result in unhappiness in the relationship. The following article by Polly Shulman examines the types of unrealistic expectations that people today have for marriage as well as the sources of such expectations. Perhaps having more realistic views of courtship and marriage can provide a major antidote to the high rate of divorce.

Great Expectations

■ Polly Shulman

Marriage is dead! The twin vises of church and law have relaxed their grip on matrimony. We've been liberated from the grim obligation to stay in a poisonous or abusive marriage for the sake of the kids or for appearances. The divorce rate has stayed constant at nearly 50 percent for the last two decades. The ease with which we enter and dissolve unions makes marriage seem like a prime-time spectator sport, whether it's Britney Spears in Vegas or bimbos chasing after the Bachelor.

Long live the new marriage! We once prized the institution for the practical pairing of a cash-producing father and a home-building mother. Now we want it all—a partner who reflects our taste and status, who sees us for who we are, who loves us for all the "right" reasons, who helps us become the person we want to be. We've done away with a rigid social order, adopting instead an even more onerous obligation: the mandate to find a perfect match. Anything short of this ideal prompts us to ask: Is this all there is? Am I as happy as I should be? Could there be somebody out there who's better for me? As often as not, we answer yes to that last question and fall victim to our own great expectations.

That somebody is, of course, our soul mate, the man or woman who will counter our weaknesses, amplify our strengths and provide the unflagging support and respect that is the essence of a contemporary relationship. The reality is that few marriages or partnerships consistently live up to this ideal. The result is a commitment limbo, in which we care deeply for our partner but keep one stealthy foot out the door of our hearts. In so doing, we subject the relationship to constant review: Would I be happier, smarter, a *better person* with someone else? It's a painful modern quandary. "Nothing has produced more unhappiness than the concept of the soul mate," says Atlanta psychiatrist Frank Pittman.

Consider Jeremy, a social worker who married a businesswoman in his early twenties. He met another woman, a psychologist, at age 29, and after two agonizing years, left his wife for her. But it didn't work out—after four years of cohabitation, and her escalating pleas to marry, he walked out on her, as well. Jeremy now realizes that the relationship with his wife was solid and workable but thinks he couldn't have seen that 10 years ago, when he left her. "There was always someone better around the corner—and the safety and security of marriage morphed into boredom and stasis. The allure of willing and exciting females was too hard to resist," he admits. Now 42 and still single, Jeremy acknowledges, "I hurt others, and I hurt myself."

Like Jeremy, many of us either dodge the decision to commit or commit without fully relinquishing the right to keep looking—opting for an arrangement psychotherapist Terrence Real terms "stable ambiguity."

"You park on the border of the relationship, so you're in it but not of it," he says. There are a million ways to do that: You can be in a relationship but not be sure it's really the right one, have an eye open for a better deal or something on the side, choose someone impossible or far away.

Yet commitment and marriage offer real physical and financial rewards. Touting the benefits of marriage may sound like conservative policy rhetoric, but nonpartisan sociological research backs it up: Committed partners have it all over singles, at least on average. Married people are more financially stable, according to Linda Waite, a sociologist at the University of Chicago and a coauthor of *The Case for Marriage: Why Married People Are Happier, Healthier and Better Off.* Both married men and married women have more assets on average than singles; for women, the differential is huge.

The benefits go beyond the piggy bank. Married people, particularly men, tend to live longer than people who aren't married. Couples also live better: When people expect to stay together, says Waite, they pool their resources, increasing their individual standard of living. They also pool their expertise—in cooking say, or financial management. In general, women improve men's health by putting a stop to stupid bachelor tricks and bugging their husbands to exercise and eat their vegetables. Plus, people who aren't comparing their partners to someone else in bed have less trouble performing and are more emotionally satisfied with sex. The relationship doesn't have to be wonderful for life to get better, says Waite: The statistics hold true for mediocre marriages as well as for passionate ones.

The pragmatic benefits of partnership used to be foremost in our minds. The idea of marriage as a vehicle for self-fulfillment and happiness is relatively new, says Paul Amato, professor of sociology, demography and family studies at Penn State University. Surveys of high school and college students 50 or 60 years ago found that most wanted to get married in order to have children or own a home. Now, most report that they plan to get married for love. This increased emphasis on emotional fulfillment within marriage leaves couples ill-prepared for the realities they will probably face.

Because the early phase of a relationship is marked by excitement and idealization, "many romantic, passionate couples expect to have that excitement forever," says Barry McCarthy, a clinical psychologist and coauthor—with his wife, Emily McCarthy—of *Getting It Right the First Time: How to Build a Healthy Marriage.* Longing for the charged energy of the early days, people look elsewhere or split up.

Flagging passion is often interpreted as the death knell of a relationship. You begin to wonder whether you're really right for each other after all. You're comfortable together, but you don't really connect the way you used to. Wouldn't it be more honest—and braver—to just admit that it's not working and call it off? "People are made to feel that remaining in a marriage that doesn't make you blissfully happy is an act of existential cowardice," says Joshua Coleman, a San Francisco psychologist.

Coleman says that the constant cultural pressure to have it all—a great sex life, a wonderful family—has made people ashamed of their less-than-perfect relationships and question whether such unions are worth hanging on to. Feelings of dissatisfaction or disappointment are natural, but they can seem intolerable when standards are sky-high. "It's a recent historical event that people expect to get so much from individual partners," says Coleman, author of *Imperfect Harmony,* in which he advises couples in lackluster marriages to stick it out—especially if they have kids. "There's an enormous amount of pressure on marriages to live up to an unrealistic ideal."

Michaela, 28, was drawn to Bernardo, 30, in part because of their differences: She'd grown up in European boarding schools, he fought his way out of a New York City ghetto. "Our backgrounds made us more interesting to each other," says Michaela. "I was a spoiled brat and he'd been supporting himself from the age of 14, which I admired." Their first two years of marriage were rewarding, but their fights took a toll.

"I felt that because he hadn't grown up in a normal family, he didn't grasp basic issues of courtesy and accountability," says Michaela. They were temperamental opposites: He was a screamer, and she was a sulker. She recalls, "After we fought, I needed to be drawn out of my corner, but he took that to mean that I was a cold bitch." Michaela reluctantly concluded that the two were incompatible.

In fact, argue psychologists and marital advocates, there's no such thing as true compatibility.

"Marriage is a disagreement machine," says Diane Sollee, founder of the Coalition for Marriage, Family and Couples Education. "All couples disagree about all the same things. We have a highly romanticized notion that if we were with the right person, we wouldn't fight." Discord springs eternal over money, kids, sex and leisure time, but psychologist John Gottman has shown that long-term, happily married couples disagree about these things just as much as couples who divorce.

"There is a mythology of 'the wrong person,'" agrees Pittman. "All marriages are incompatible. All marriages are between people from different families, people who have a different view of things. The magic is to develop binocular vision, to see life through your partner's eyes as well as through your own."

The realization that we're not going to get everything we want from a partner is not just sobering, it's downright miserable. But it is also a necessary step in building a mature relationship, according to Real, who has written about the subject in *How Can I Get Through to You: Closing the Intimacy Gap Between Men and Women.* "The paradox of intimacy is that our ability to stay close rests on our ability to tolerate solitude inside a relationship," he says. "A central aspect of grown-up love is grief. All of us long for—and think we deserve—perfection."

We can hardly be blamed for striving for bliss and self-fulfillment in our romantic lives—our inalienable right to the pursuit of happiness is guaranteed in the first blueprint of American society.

This same respect for our own needs spurred the divorce-law reforms of the 1960s and 1970s. During that era, "The culture shifted to emphasize individual satisfaction, and marriage was part of that," explains Paul Amato, who has followed more than 2,000 families for 20 years in a long-term study of marriage and divorce. Amato says that this shift did some good by freeing people from abusive and intolerable marriages. But it had an unintended side effect: encouraging people to abandon relationships that may be worth salvaging.

In a society hell-bent on achievement and autonomy, working on a difficult relationship may get short shrift, says psychiatrist Peter Kramer, author of *Should You Leave?*

"So much of what we learn has to do with the self, the ego, rather than giving over the self to things like a relationship," Kramer says. In our competitive world, we're rewarded for our individual achievements rather than for how we help others.

We value independence over cooperation, and sacrifices for values like loyalty and continuity seem foolish. "I think we get the divorce rate that we deserve as a culture."

The steadfast focus on our *own* potential may turn a partner into an accessory in the quest for self-actualization, says Maggie Robbins, a therapist in New York City. "We think that this person should reflect the beauty and perfection that is the inner me—or, more often, that this person should compensate for the yuckiness and mess that is the inner me," says Robbins. "This is what makes you tell your wife, 'Lose some weight—you're making me look bad,' not 'Lose some weight, you're at risk for diabetes.'"

Michaela was consistently embarrassed by Bernardo's behavior when they were among friends. "He'd become sullen and withdrawn—he had a shifty way of looking off to the side when he didn't want to talk. I felt like it reflected badly on me," she admits. Michaela left him and is now dating a wealthy entrepreneur. "I just thought there had to be someone else out there for me."

The urge to find a soul mate is not fueled just by notions of romantic manifest destiny. Trends in the workforce and in the media create a sense of limitless romantic possibility. According to Scott South, a demographer at SUNY-Albany, proximity to potential partners has a powerful effect on relationships. South and his colleagues found higher divorce rates among people living in communities or working in professions where they encounter lots of potential partners—people who match them in age, race and education level. "These results hold true not just for unhappy marriages but also for happy ones," says South.

The temptations aren't always living, breathing people. According to research by psychologists Sara Gutierres and Douglas Kenrick, both of Arizona State University, we find reasonably attractive people less appealing when we've just seen a hunk or a hottie—and we're bombarded daily by images of gorgeous models and actors. When we watch *Lord of the Rings,* Viggo Mortensen's kingly mien and Liv Tyler's elfin charm can make our husbands and wives look all too schlumpy.

Kramer sees a similar pull in the narratives that surround us. "The number of stories that tell us about other lives we could lead—in magazine articles, television shows, books—has increased enormously. We have an enormous reservoir of possibilities," says Kramer.

And these possibilities can drive us to despair. Too many choices have been shown to stymie consumers . . . and an array of alternative mates is no exception. In an era when marriages were difficult to dissolve, couples rated their marriages as more satisfying than do today's couples, for whom divorce is a clear option, according to the National Opinion Research Center at the University of Chicago.

While we expect marriage to be "happily ever after," the truth is that for most people, neither marriage nor divorce seem to have a decisive impact on happiness. Although Waite's research shows that married people are happier than their single counterparts, other studies have found that after a couple years of marriage, people are just about as happy (or unhappy) as they were before settling down. And assuming that marriage will automatically provide contentment is itself a surefire recipe for misery.

"Marriage is not supposed to make you happy. It is supposed to make you married," says Pittman. "When you are all the way in your marriage, you are free to do useful things, become a better person." A committed relationship allows you to drop pretenses and seductions, expose your weaknesses, be yourself—and know that you will be loved, warts and all. "A real relationship is the collision of my humanity and yours, in all its joy and limitations," says Real.

"How partners handle that collision is what determines the quality of their relationship."

Such a down-to-earth view of marriage is hardly romantic, but that doesn't mean it's not profound: An authentic relationship with another person, says Pittman, is "one of the first steps toward connecting with the human condition—which is necessary if you're going to become fulfilled as a human being." If we accept these humble terms, the quest for a soul mate might just be a noble pursuit after all.

LEARN MORE ABOUT IT

101 Things I Wish I Knew When I Got Married Linda and Charlie Bloom (New World Library, 2004)

CRITICAL THINKING QUESTIONS

1. "Nothing has produced more unhappiness than the concept of the soul mate." Discuss this quote from the article, giving specific examples to support why you do or do not agree with it.

2. Do an informal survey of people to find out what they think is the most important factor in a successful marriage. Chances are, "good communication" will most often be cited. How does this factor (or whatever factor your survey finds most important) relate to the information contained in the article? Discuss.

3. List five things that you learned from this article that may decrease your chance of getting divorced. Which of these factors would be the easiest to change or control? Which would be the most difficult? Explain your answers.

4. How are love and marriage portrayed in the movies? Identify specific films, and discuss each in terms of whether it portrays a realistic or unrealistic view of love and marriage. What, if any, problems are associated with the general media portrayals of love and marriage?

5. Article 19 discussed the concept of the contrast effect and how being exposed to very attractive people might make us less attracted to our actual partners. Beyond physical attractiveness, how else might the contrast effect be working to the detriment of successful marriages?

ARTICLE 23 _____

Wanting to love and be loved is perhaps the most profound and universal human longing. As personal experience teaches us, love is not only a highly desired and sought-after state, but it may actually also be necessary for our very well-being. Yet exactly what love means and how it is expressed and felt may be something that differs in each of us.

Let's back up a step. Before talking about a deep and profound love for another person, what about the initial stages that may precede it? In other words, what factors are involved in the initial attraction to another potential romantic partner? People vary considerably in what they find attractive and desirable in another person, but there are common dimensions that seem to be fairly universal—the importance of physical attractiveness and certain personality traits such as intelligence, for instance.

Suppose that you have just met someone who has caught your attention. You are interested enough that you want to ask the person out on a date. Whether you are the initiator or the recipient of the request, a date often creates a set of mixed feelings. On one hand, the potential pleasure that one can have in a successful relationship is highly desirable. On the other hand, most people do not like rejection, and any such beginning also carries with it the possibility of an end.

All right, so he finally asks her out. (Although females certainly initiate dates, research still shows that males typically take this first step in U.S. culture.) How does she respond to his request? Obviously, she can say no. If she says yes, however, there are many ways that it can be said. Which do you think would be most favorably received by the man—someone who enthusiastically and without hesitation says "Yes. I thought you'd never ask" or someone who plays hard to get, ultimately accepting the invitation but only after some hesitation or convincing?

Folk advice going back thousands of years states that playing hard to get might be the way to proceed. As this classic article by Elaine Hatfield, G. William Walster, Jane Piliavin, and Lynn Schmidt indicates, however, that might not be the best advice to follow.

"Playing Hard to Get"
Understanding an Elusive Phenomenon
■ Elaine Hatfield, G. William Walster, Jane Piliavin, and Lynn Schmidt

According to folklore, the woman who is hard to get is a more desirable catch than the woman who is too eager for an alliance. Five experiments were conducted to demonstrate that individuals value hard-to-get dates more than easy-to-get ones. All five experiments failed. In Experiment VI, we finally gained an understanding of this elusive phenomenon. We proposed that two components contribute to a woman's desirability: (a) how hard the woman is for the subject to get and (b) how hard she is for other men to get. We predicted that the selectively hard-to-get woman (i.e., a woman who is easy for the subject to get but hard for all other men to get) would be preferred to either a uniformly hard-to-get woman, a uniformly easy-to-get woman, or a woman about which the subject has no information. This hypothesis received strong support. The reason for the popularity of the selective woman was evident. Men ascribe to her all of the assets of uniformly hard-to-get and the uniformly easy-to-get women and none of their liabilities.

According to folklore, the woman who is hard to get is a more desirable catch than is the woman who is overly eager for alliance. Socrates, Ovid, Terence, the *Kama Sutra,* and Dear Abby all agree that the person whose affection is easily won is unlikely to inspire passion in another. Ovid, for example, argued:

> *Fool, if you feel no need to guard your girl for her own sake, see that you guard her for mine, so I may want her the more. Easy things nobody wants, but what is forbidden is tempting. . . . Anyone who can love the wife of an indolent cuckold, I should suppose, would steal buckets of sand from the shore.* (pp. 65–66)

When we first began our investigation, we accepted cultural lore. We assumed that men would prefer a hard-to-get woman. Thus, we began our research by interviewing college men as to why they preferred hard-to-get women. Predictably, the men responded to experimenter demands. They explained that they preferred hard-to-get women because the elusive woman is almost inevitably a valuable woman. They pointed out that a woman can only afford to be "choosy" if she is popular—and a woman is popular for some reason. When a woman is hard to get, it is usually a tip-off that she is especially pretty, has a good personality, is sexy, etc. Men also were intrigued by the challenge that the elusive woman offered. One can spend a great deal of time fantasizing about what it would be like to date such a woman. Since the hard-to-get woman's desirability is well recognized, a man can gain prestige if he is seen with her.

An easy-to-get woman, on the other hand, spells trouble. She is probably desperate for a date. She is probably the kind of woman who will make too many demands on a person; she might want to get serious right away. Even worse, she might have a "disease."

In brief, nearly all interviewees agreed with our hypothesis that a hard-to-get woman is a valuable woman, and they could supply abundant justification for their prejudice. A few isolated men refused to cooperate. These dissenters noted that an elusive woman is not always more desirable than an available woman. Sometimes the hard-to-get woman is not only hard to get—she is *impossible* to get, because she is misanthropic and cold. Sometimes a woman is easy to get because she is a friendly, outgoing woman who boosts one's ego and insures that dates are "no hassle." We ignored the testimony of these deviant types.

We then conducted five experiments designed to demonstrate that an individual values a hard-to-get date more highly than an easy-to-get date. All five experiments failed.

THEORETICAL RATIONALE

Let us first review the theoretical rationale underlying these experiments.

In Walster, Walster, and Berscheid (1971) we argued that if playing hard to get does increase one's desirability, several psychological theories could account for this phenomenon:

1. Dissonance theory predicts that if a person must expend great energy to attain a goal, one is unusually appreciative of the goal (see Aronson and Mills, 1959; Gerard and Mathewson, 1966; Zimbardo, 1965). The hard-to-get date requires a suitor to expend more effort in her pursuit than he would normally expend. One way for the suitor to justify such unusual effort is by aggrandizing her.

2. According to learning theory, an elusive person should have two distinct advantages: (a) Frustration may increase the suitor's drive—by waiting until the suitor has achieved a high sexual drive state, heightening his drive level by introducing momentary frustration, and then finally rewarding him, the hard-to-get woman can maximize the impact of the sexual reward she provides (see Kimball, 1961, for evidence that frustration does energize behavior and does increase the impact of appropriate rewards). (b) Elusiveness and value may be associated—individuals may have discovered through frequent experience that there is more competition for socially desirable dates than for undesirable partners. Thus, being "hard to get" comes to be associated with "value." As a consequence, the conditional stimulus (CS) of being hard to get generates a fractional antedating goal response and a fractional goal response, which leads to the conditioned response of liking.

3. In an extension of Schachterian theory, Walster (1971) argued that two components are necessary before an individual can experience passionate love; (a) He must be physiologically aroused; and (b) the setting must make it appropriate for him to conclude that his aroused feelings are due to love. On both counts, the person who plays hard to get might be expected to generate unusual passion. Frustration should increase the suitor's physiological arousal, and the association of "elusiveness" with "value" should increase the probability that the suitor will label his reaction to the other as "love."

From the preceding discussion, it is evident that several conceptually distinct variables may account for the hard-to-get phenomenon. In spite of the fact that we can suggest a plethora of reasons as to why the playing hard-to-get strategy might be an effective strategy, all five studies failed to provide any support for the contention that an elusive woman is a desirable woman. Two experiments failed to demonstrate that outside observers perceive a hard-to-get individual as especially "valuable." Three experiments failed to demonstrate that a suitor perceives a hard-to-get date as especially valuable.

Walster, Walster, and Berscheid (1971) conducted two experiments to test the hypothesis that teenagers would deduce that a hard-to-get boy or girl was more socially desirable than was a teenager whose affection could be easily obtained. In these experiments high school juniors and seniors were told that we were interested in finding out what kind of first impression various teenagers made on others. They were shown pictures and biographies of a couple. They were told how romantically interested the stimulus person (a boy or girl) was in his partner after they had met only four times. The stimulus person was said to have liked the partner "extremely much," to have provided no information to us, or to have liked the partner "not particularly much." The teenagers were then asked how socially desirable both teenagers seemed (i.e., how likable, how physically attractive, etc.). Walster, Walster, and Berscheid, of course, predicted that the more romantic interest the stimulus person expressed in a slight acquaintance, the less socially desirable that stimulus person would appear to an outside observer. The results were diametrically opposed to those predicted. The more romantic interest the stimulus person expressed in an acquaintance, the *more* socially desirable teenagers judged him to be. Restraint does not appear to buy respect. Instead, it appears that "All the world *does* love a lover."

Lyons, Walster, and Walster (1971) conducted a field study and a laboratory experiment in an attempt to demonstrate that men prefer a date who plays hard to get. Both experiments were conducted in the context of a computer matching service. Experiment III was a field experiment. Women who signed up for the computer matching program were contacted and hired as experimenters. They were then given precise instructions as to how to respond when their computer match called them for a date. Half of the time they were told to pause and think for 3 seconds before accepting the date. (These women were labeled "hard to get.") Half of the time they were told to accept the date immediately. (These women are labeled "easy to get.") The data indicated that elusiveness had no impact on the man's liking for his computer date.

Experiment IV was a laboratory experiment. In this experiment, Lyons et al. hypothesized that the knowledge that a woman is elusive gives one indirect evidence that she is socially desirable. Such indirect evidence should have the biggest impact when a man has no way of acquiring *direct* evidence about a coed's value or when he has little confidence in his own ability to assess value. When direct evidence is available, and the man possesses supreme confidence in his ability to make correct judgments, information about a woman's elusiveness should have little impact on a man's reaction to her. Lyons et al. thus predicted that when men lacked direct evidence as to a woman's desirability, a man's self-esteem and the woman's elusiveness should interact in determining his respect and liking for her. Lyons et al. measured males' self-esteem via Rosenberg's (1965) measure of self-esteem, Rosenfeld's (1964) measure of fear of rejection, and Berger's (1952) measure of self-acceptance.

The dating counselor then told subjects that the computer had assigned them a date. They were asked to telephone her from the office phone, invite her out, and then report their first impression of her. Presumably the pair would then go out on a date and eventually give us further information about how successful our computer matching techniques had been. Actually, all men were assigned a confederate as a date. Half of the time the woman played hard to get. When the man asked her out she replied:

Mmm [slight pause] No, I've got a date then. It seems like I signed up for that Date Match thing a long time ago and I've met more people since then—I'm really pretty busy all this week.

She paused again. If the subject suggested another time, the confederate hesitated only slightly, then accepted. If he did not suggest another time, the confederate would take the initiative of suggesting: "How about some time next week—or just meeting for coffee in the Union some afternoon?" And again, she accepted the next invitation. Half of the time, in the easy-to-get condition, the confederate eagerly accepted the man's offer of a date.

Lyons et al. predicted that since men in this blind date setting lacked direct evidence as to a woman's desirability, low-self-esteem men should be more receptive to the hard-to-get woman than were high-self-esteem men. Although Lyons et al.'s manipulation checks indicate that their manipulations were successful and their self-esteem measure was reliable, their hypothesis was not confirmed. Elusiveness had no impact on liking, regardless of subject's self-esteem level.

Did we give up our hypothesis? Heavens no. After all, it had only been disconfirmed four times.

By Experiment V, we had decided that perhaps the hard-to-get hypothesis must be tested in a sexual setting. After all, the first theorist who advised a woman to play hard to get was Socrates; his pupil was Theodota, a prostitute. He advised:

They will appreciate your favors most highly if you wait till they ask for them. The sweetest meats, you see, if served before they are wanted seem sour, and to those who had enough they are positively nauseating; but even poor fare is very welcome when offered to a hungry man. [Theodota inquired] And how can I make them hungry for my fare? [Socrates' reply] Why, in the first place, you must not offer it to them when they have had enough—but prompt them by behaving as a model of Propriety, by a show of reluctance to yield, and by holding back until they are as keen as can be; and then the same gifts are much more to the recipient than when they're offered before they are desired. (see Xenophon, p. 48)

Walster, Walster, and Lambert (1971) thus proposed that a prostitute who states that she is selective in her choice of customers will be held in higher regard than will be the prostitute who admits that she is completely unselective in her choice of partners.

In this experiment, a prostitute served as the experimenter. When the customer arrived, she mixed a drink for him; then she delivered the experimental manipulation. Half of the time, in the hard-to-get condition, she stated, "Just because I see you this time it doesn't mean that you can have my phone number or see me again. I'm going to start school soon, so I won't have much time, so I'll only be able to see the people that I like the best." Half of the time, in the easy-to-get condition, she did not communicate this information. From this point on, the prostitute and the customer interacted in conventional ways.

The client's liking for the prostitute was determined in two ways: First, the prostitute estimated how much the client had seemed to like her. (Questions asked were, for example, How much did he seem to like you? Did he make arrangements to return? How much did he pay you?) Second, the experimenter recorded how many times within the next 30 days the client arranged to have sexual relations with her.

Once again we failed to confirm the hard-to-get hypothesis. If anything, those clients who were told that the prostitute did not take just anyone were *less* likely to call back and liked the prostitute less than did other clients.

At this point, we ruefully decided that we had been on the wrong track. We decided that perhaps all those practitioners who advise women to play hard to get are wrong. Or perhaps it is only under very special circumstances that it will benefit one to play hard to get.

Thus, we began again. We reinterviewed students—this time with an open mind. This time we asked men to tell us about the advantages *and* disadvantages of hard-to-get and easy-to-get women. This time replies were more informative. According to reports, choosing between a hard-to-get woman and an easy-to-get woman was like choosing between Scylla and Charybdis—each woman was uniquely desirable and uniquely frightening.

Although the elusive woman was likely to be a popular prestige date, she presented certain problems. Since she was not particularly enthusiastic about you, she might stand you up or humiliate you in front of your friends. She was likely to be unfriendly, cold, and to possess inflexible standards.

The easy-to-get woman was certain to boost one's ego and to make a date a relaxing, enjoyable experience, but . . . Unfortunately, dating an easy woman was a risky business. Such a woman might be easy to get, but hard to get rid of. She might "get serious." Perhaps she would be so oversexed or over-affectionate in public that she would embarrass you. Your buddies might snicker when they saw you together. After all, they would know perfectly well why you were dating *her.*

The interlocking assets and difficulties envisioned when they attempted to decide which was better—a hard-to-get or an easy-to-get woman—gave us a clue as to why our previous experiments had not worked out. The assets and liabilities of the elusive and the easy dates had evidently generally balanced out. On the average, then, both types of women tended to be equally well liked. When a slight difference in liking did appear, it favored the easy-to-get woman.

It finally impinged on us that there are *two* components that are important determinants of how much a man likes a woman: (*a*) How hard or easy she is for him to get, and (*b*) how hard or easy she is for *other men* to get. So long as we were examining the desirability of women who were hard or easy for everyone to get, things balanced out. The minute we examined other possible configurations, it became evident that there is one type of woman who can transcend the limitations of the uniformly hard-to-get or the uniformly easy-to-get

woman. If a woman has a reputation for being hard to get, but for some reason she is easy for the subject to get, she should be maximally appealing. Dating such a woman should insure one of great prestige; she is, after all, hard to get. Yet, since she is exceedingly available to the subject, the dating situation should be a relaxed, rewarding experience. Such a *selectively* hard-to-get woman possesses the assets of both the easy-to-get and the hard-to-get women, while avoiding all of their liabilities.

Thus, in Experiment VI, we hypothesized that a selectively hard-to-get woman (i.e., a woman who is easy for the subject to get but very hard for any other man to get) will be especially liked by her date. Women who are hard for everyone—including the subject—to get, or who are easy for everyone to get—or control women, about whom the subject had no information—will be liked a lesser amount.

METHOD

Subjects were 71 male summer students at the University of Wisconsin. They were recruited for a dating research project. This project was ostensibly designed to determine whether computer matching techniques are in fact more effective than is random matching. All participants were invited to come into the dating center in order to choose a date from a set of five potential dates.

When the subject arrived at the computer match office, he was handed folders containing background information on five women. Some of these women had supposedly been "randomly" matched with him; others had been "computer matched" with him. (He was not told which women were which.)

In reality, all five folders contained information about fictitious women. The first item in the folder was a "background questionnaire" on which the woman had presumably described herself. This questionnaire was similar to one the subject had completed when signing up for the match program. We attempted to make the five women's descriptions different enough to be believable, yet similar enough to minimize variance. Therefore, the way the five women described themselves was systematically varied. They claimed to be 18 or 19 years old; freshmen or sophomores; from a Wisconsin city, ranging in size from over 500,000 to under 50,000; 5 feet 2 inches to 5 feet 4 inches tall; Protestant, Catholic, Jewish or had no preference; graduated in the upper 10 to 50 percent of their high school class; and Caucasians who did not object to being matched with a person of another race. The women claimed to vary on a political spectrum from "left of center" through "moderate" to "near right of center"; to place little or no importance on politics and religion; and to like recent popular movies. Each woman listed four or five activities she liked to do on a first date (i.e., go to a movie, talk in a quiet place, etc.).

In addition to the background questionnaire, three of the five folders contained five "date selection forms." The experimenter explained that some of the women had already been able to come in, examine the background information of their matches, and indicate their first impression of them. Two of the subject's matches had not yet come in. Three of the women had already come in and evaluated the subject along with her four other matches. These women would have five date selection forms in their folders. The subject was shown the forms, which consisted of a scale ranging from "definitely do *not* want to date" (−10) to "definitely want to date" (+10). A check appeared on each scale. Presumably the check indicated how much the woman had liked a given date. (At this point, the subject was told his identification number. Since all dates were identified by numbers on the forms, this identification number enabled him to ascertain how each date had evaluated both him and her four other matches.)

The date selection forms allowed us to manipulate the elusiveness of the woman. One woman appeared to be uniformly hard to get. She indicated that though she was willing to date any of the men assigned to her, she was not enthusiastic about any of them. She rated all five of her date choices from +1 to +2, including the subject (who was rated 1.75).

One woman appeared to be uniformly easy to get. She indicated that she was enthusiastic about dating all five of the men assigned to her. She rated her desire to date all five of her date choices +7 to +9. This included the subject, who was rated 8.

One woman appeared to be easy for the subject to get but hard for anyone else to get (i.e., the selectively hard-to-get woman). She indicated minimal enthusiasm for four of her date choices, rating them from +2 to +3, and extreme enthusiasm (+8) for the subject.

Two women had no date selection forms in their folders (i.e., no information women).

Naturally, each woman appeared in each of the five conditions.

The experimenter asked the man to consider the folders, complete a "first impression questionnaire" for each woman, and then decide which *one* of the women he wished to date. (The subject's rating of the dates constitute our verbal measure of liking; his choice in a date constitutes our behavioral measure of liking.)

The experimenter explained that she was conducting a study of first impressions in conjunction with the dating research project. The study, she continued, was designed to learn more about how good people are at forming first impressions of others on the basis of rather limited information. She explained that filling out the forms would probably make it easier for the man to decide which one of the five women he wished to date.

The first impression questionnaire consisted of three sections:

Liking for Various Dates

Two questions assessed subjects' liking for each woman: "If you went out with this girl, how well do you think you would get along?"—with possible responses ranging from "get along extremely well" (5) to "not get along at all" (1)—and "What was your overall impression of the girl?"—with possible responses ranging from "extremely favorable" (7) to "extremely unfavorable" (1). Scores on these two questions were summed to form an index of expressed liking. This index enables us to compare subjects' liking for each of the women.

Assets and Liabilities Ascribed to Various Dates

We predicted that subjects would prefer the selective woman, because they would expect her to possess the good qualities of both the uniformly hard-to-get and the uniformly easy-to-get woman, while avoiding the bad qualities of both her rivals. Thus, the second section was designed to determine the extent to which subjects imputed good and bad qualities to the various dates.

This section was comprised of 10 pairs of polar opposites. Subjects were asked to rate how friendly–unfriendly, cold–warm, attractive-unattractive, easy–going–rigid, exciting–boring, shy– outgoing, fun–loving–dull, popular–unpopular, aggressive–passive, selective–nonselective each woman was. Ratings were made on a 7-point scale. The more desirable the trait ascribed to a woman, the higher the score she was given.

Liabilities Attributed to Easy-to-Get Women

The third scale was designed to assess the extent to which subjects attributed selected negative attributes to each woman. The third scale consisted of six statements:

> She would more than likely do something to embarrass me in public.
> She probably would demand too much attention and affection from me.
> She seems like the type who would be too dependent on me.
> She might turn out to be too sexually promiscuous.
> She probably would make me feel uneasy when I'm with her in a group.
> She seems like the type who doesn't distinguish between the boys she dates. I probably would be "just another date."

Subjects were asked whether they anticipated any of the above difficulties in their relationship with each woman. They indicated their misgivings on a scale ranging from "certainly true of her" (1) to "certainly not true of her" (7).

The experimenter suggested that the subject carefully examine both the background questionnaires and the date selection forms of all potential dates in order to decide whom he wanted to date. Then she left the subject. (The experimenter was, of course, unaware of what date was in what folder.)

The experimenter did not return until the subject had completed the first impression questionnaires. Then she asked him which woman he had decided to date.

After his choice had been made, the experimenter questioned him as to what factors influenced his choice. Frequently men who chose the selectively easy-to-get woman said that

"She chose me, and that made me feel really good" or "She seemed more selective than the others." The uniformly easy-to-get woman was often rejected by subjects who complained "She must be awfully hard up for a date—she really would take anyone." The uniformly hard-to-get woman was once described as a "challenge" but more often rejected as being "snotty" or "too picky."

At the end of the session, the experimenter debriefed the subject and then gave him the names of five actual dates who had been matched with him.

RESULTS

We predicted that the selectively hard-to-get woman (easy for me but hard for everyone else to get) would be liked more than women who were uniformly hard to get, uniformly easy to get, or neutral (the no information women). We had no prediction as to whether or not her three rivals would differ in attractiveness. The results strongly support our hypothesis.

Dating Choices

When we examine the men's choices in dates, we see that the selective woman is far more popular than any of her rivals. (See Table 1.) We conducted a chi-square test to determine whether or not men's choices in dates were randomly distributed. They were not ($\chi^2 = 69.5$, $df = 4$, $p < .001$). Nearly all subjects preferred to date the selective woman. When we compare the frequency with which her four rivals (combined) are chosen, we see that the selective woman does get far more than her share of dates ($\chi^2 = 68.03$, $df = 1$, $p < .001$).

We also conducted an analysis to determine whether or not the women who are uniformly hard to get, uniformly easy to get, or whose popularity is unknown, differed in popularity. We see that they did not ($\chi^2 = 2.86$, $df = 3$).

Liking for the Various Dates

Two questions tapped the men's romantic liking for the various dates: (*a*) "If you went out with this woman, how well do you think you'd get along?"; and (*b*) "What was your overall impression of the woman?" Scores on these two indexes were summed to form an index of liking. Possible scores ranged from 2 to 12.

A contrast was then set up to test our hypothesis that the selective woman will be preferred to her rivals. The contrast that tests this hypothesis is of the form $\Gamma_1 = 4\mu$ (selectively hard to get) -1 (uniformly hard to get) -2μ (neutral). We tested the hypothesis $\Gamma_1 = 0$ against the alternative hypothesis $\Gamma_1 \neq 0$. An explanation of this basically simple procedure may be found in Hays (1963). If our hypothesis is true, the preceding contrast should be large. If our hypothesis is false, the resulting contrast should not differ significantly from 0. The data again provide strong support for the hypothesis that the selective woman is better liked than her rivals ($F = 23.92$, $df = 1/70$, $p < .001$).

Additional Data Snooping

We also conducted a second set of contrasts to determine whether the rivals (i.e., the uniformly hard-to-get woman, the uniformly easy-to-get woman, and the control woman) were differentially liked. Using the procedure presented by Morrison (1967) in chapter 4, the data indicate that the rivals are differentially liked ($F = 4.43$, $df = 2/69$). As Table 2 indicates, the uniformly hard-to-get woman seems to be liked slightly less than the easy-to-get or control woman.

In any attempt to explore data, one must account for the fact that observing the data permits the researcher to capitalize on chance. Thus, one must use simultaneous testing methods so as not to spuriously inflate the probability of attaining statistical significance. In the present situation, we are interested in comparing the means of a number of dependent measures, namely the liking for the different women in the dating situation. To perform post hoc multiple comparisons in this situation, one can use a transformation of Hotelling's t^2 statistic, which is distributed as F. The procedure is directly analogous to Scheffé's multiple-comparison procedure for independent groups, except where one compares means of a number of dependent measures.

To make it abundantly clear that the main result is that the discriminating woman is better liked than each of the other rivals, we performed an additional post hoc analysis, pitting each of the rivals separately against the discriminating woman. In these analyses, we see that the selective woman is better liked than the woman who is uniformly easy to get ($F = 3.99$, $df = 3/68$), than the woman who is uniformly hard to get ($F = 9.47$, $df = 3/68$), and finally, than the control women ($F = 4.93$, $df = 3/68$).

TABLE 1 / Men's Choices in a Date

Item	Selectively Hard to Get	Uniformly Hard to Get	Uniformly Easy to Get	No Information for No. 1	No Information for No. 2
Number of men choosing to date each woman	42	6	5	11	7

TABLE 2 / Men's Reactions to Various Dates

Item	Type of Date			
	Selectively Hard to Get	Uniformly Hard to Get	Uniformly Easy to Get	No Information
Men's liking for dates	9.41[a]	7.90	8.53	8.58
Evaluation of women's assets and liabilities				
Selective[b]	5.23	4.39	2.85	4.30
Popular[b]	4.83	4.58	4.65	4.83
Friendly[c]	5.58	5.07	5.52	5.37
Warm[c]	5.15	4.51	4.99	4.79
Easy Going[c]	4.83	4.42	4.82	4.61
Problems expected in dating	5.23[d]	4.86	4.77	4.99

[a]The higher the number, the more liking the man is expressing for the date.

[b]Traits we expected to be ascribed to the selectively hard-to-get and the uniformly hard-to-get dates.

[c]Traits we expected to be ascribed to the selectively hard-to-get and the uniformly easy-to-get dates.

[d]The higher the number the *fewer* the problems the subject anticipates in dating.

Thus, it is clear that although there are slight differences in the way rivals are liked, these differences are small, relative to the overwhelming attractiveness of the selective woman.

Assets and Liabilities Attributed to Dates

We can now attempt to ascertain *why* the selective woman is more popular than her rivals. Earlier, we argued that the selectively hard-to-get woman should occupy a unique position; she should be assumed to possess all of the virtues of her rivals, but none of their flaws.

The virtues and flaws that the subject ascribed to each woman were tapped by the polar-opposite scale. Subjects evaluated each woman on 10 characteristics.

We expected that subjects would associate two assets with a uniformly hard-to-get woman: Such a woman should be perceived to be both "selective" and "popular." Unfortunately, such a woman should also be assumed to possess three liabilities—she should be perceived to be "unfriendly," "cold," and "rigid." Subjects should ascribe exactly the opposite virtues and liabilities to the easy-to-get woman: Such a woman should possess the assets of "friendliness," "warmth," and "flexibility," and the liabilities of "unpopularity" and "lack of selectivity." The selective woman was expected to possess only assets: She should be perceived to be as "selective" and "popular" as the uniformly elusive woman, and as "friendly," "warm," and "easy-going" as the uniformly easy woman. A contrast was set up to test this specific hypothesis. (Once again, see Hays for the procedure.) This contrast indicates that our hypothesis is confirmed ($F = 62.43$, $df = 1/70$). The selective woman is rated most like the uniformly hard-to-get

woman on the first two positive characteristics and most like the uniformly easy-to-get woman on the last three characteristics.

For the reader's interest, the subjects' ratings of all five women's assets and liabilities are presented in Table 2.

Comparing the Selective and the Easy Women

Scale 3 was designed to assess whether or not subjects anticipated fewer problems when they envisioned dating the selective woman than when they envisioned dating the uniformly easy-to-get woman. On the basis of pretest interviews, we compiled a list of many of the concerns men had about easy women (e.g., "She would more than likely do something to embarrass me in public.").

We, of course, predicted that subjects would experience more problems when contemplating dating the uniformly easy woman than when contemplating dating a woman who was easy for *them* to get, but hard for anyone else to get (i.e., the selective woman).

Men were asked to say whether or not they envisioned each of the difficulties were they to date each of the women. Possible replies varied from 1 (certainly true of her) to 7 (certainly not true of her). The subjects' evaluations of each woman were summed to form an index of anticipated difficulties. Possible scores ranged from 6 to 42.

A contrast was set up to determine whether the selective woman engendered less concern than the uniformly easy-to-get woman. The data indicate that she does ($F = 17.50$, $df = 1/70$). If the reader is interested in comparing concern engendered by each woman, these data are available in Table 2.

The data provide clear support for our hypotheses: The selective woman is strongly preferred to any of her rivals. The reason for her popularity is evident. Men ascribe to her all of the assets of the uniformly hard-to-get and the uniformly easy-to-get women, and none of their liabilities.

Thus, after five futile attempts to understand the "hard-to-get" phenomenon, it appears that we have finally gained an understanding of this process. It appears that a woman can intensify her desirability if she acquires a reputation for being hard-to-get and then, by her behavior, makes it clear to a selected romantic partner that she is attracted to him.

In retrospect, especially in view of the strongly supportive data, the logic underlying our predictions sounds compelling. In fact, after examining our data, a colleague who had helped design the five ill-fated experiments noted that, "That is exactly what I would have predicted" (given his economic view of man). Unfortunately, we are all better at postdiction than prediction.

REFERENCES

Aronson, E., and Mills, J. The effect of severity of initiation on liking for a group. *Journal of Abnormal and Social Psychology,* 1959, 67, 31–36.

Berger, E. M. The relation between expressed acceptance of self and expressed acceptance of others. *Journal of Abnormal and Social Psychology,* 1952, 47, 778–782.

Gerard, H. B., and Mathewson, G. C. The effects of severity of initiation and liking for a group: A replication. *Journal of Experimental Social Psychology,* 1966, 2, 278–287.

Hays, W. L. *Statistics for psychologists.* New York: Holt, Rinehart, 1963.

Kimball, G. A. *Hilgard and Marquis' conditioning and learning.* New York: Appleton-Century-Crofts, 1961.

Lyons, J., Walster, E., and Walster, G. W. Playing hard-to-get: An elusive phenomenon University of Wisconsin, Madison: Author, 1971. (Mimeo)

Morrison, D. F. *Multivariate statistical methods.* New York: McGraw-Hill, 1967.

Ovid. *The art of love.* Bloomington: University of Indiana Press, 1963.

Rosenberg, M. *Society and the adolescent self image.* Princeton, N.J.: Princeton University Press, 1965.

Rosenfeld, H. M. Social choice conceived as a level of aspiration. *Journal of Abnormal and Social Psychology,* 1964, 68, 491–499.

Walster, E. Passionate love. In B. I. Murstein (Ed.), *Theories of attraction and love.* New York: Springer, 1971.

Walster, E., Walster, G. W., and Berscheid, E. The efficacy of playing hard-to-get. *Journal of Experimental Education,* 1971, 39, 73–77.

Walster, G. W., and Lambert, P. Playing hard-to-get: A field study. University of Wisconsin, Madison: Author, 1971. (Mimeo)

Xenophon. *Memorabilia.* London: Heinemann, 1923.

Zimbardo, P. G. The effect of effort and improvisation on self persuasion produced by role-playing. *Journal of Experimental Social Psychology,* 1965, 1, 103–120.

This research was supported in part by National Science Foundation Grants GS 2932 and GS 30822X and in part by National Institute for Mental Health Grant MH 16661.

CRITICAL THINKING QUESTIONS

1. Nonsignificant results are difficult to interpret in research. For example, if a woman playing hard to get is not viewed differently from one playing "easy," is there really no difference? Why or why not? Or is it possible that the experimental manipulation (how playing hard to get or easy were varied in the study) was not strong enough to produce an effect? Discuss this possibility by examining how playing hard to get was manipulated in the first five experiments reported in this article.

2. Are ethical issues involved in any of the studies? In particular, what are your views of Study 5, which involved the services of a prostitute?

3. This study ultimately determined that selectively hard-to-get women were most preferred by the men. Do you think the reverse is true—that most women prefer selectively hard-to-get men? Why or why not?

4. Do you think that the results of this study could be generalized to the sexual arena (i.e., when it comes to sex, a selectively hard-to-get woman would be preferred over either a hard-to-get or easy-to-get woman)? Explain.

ADDITIONAL RELATED READINGS

Finkel, E. J., & Eastwick, P. W. (2009). Arbitrary social norms influence sex differences in romantic selectivity. *Psychological Science, 20*(10), 1290–1295.

Luo, S., & Zhang, G. (2009). What leads to romantic attraction: Similarity, reciprocity, security, or beauty? Evidence from a speed-dating study. *Journal of Personality, 77*(4), 933–964.

ARTICLE 24 _____

What is love? The topic certainly has been and continues to be a popular one in the realm of philosophy, theology, and the arts. In spite of the high value that people place on the experience, social scientists did not begin to investigate this topic until recently for a variety of reasons. First and foremost is the nature of the subject matter itself. What, exactly, is love? How can someone begin to define it, let alone measure it? But there were other reasons why the question was not addressed. For one thing, many people thought that the very importance of this feeling is why it should not be addressed. Perhaps love is too private, and best left alone.

The first scientific studies of love began over a quarter of a century ago. Since then, a great deal of research had shed considerable light on the subject. Besides being embraced as a legitimate subject of study for its own sake, the investigation of love perhaps came of age because of certain changes in society. Specifically, as divorce rates began to soar, it became more urgent to understand what role love plays in the beginning (and ending) of a relationship.

Various researchers have proposed different types of love. An examination of any social psychology textbook will provide more information on some of the more widely accepted definitions of these types of love. However, regardless of the specific terminology used, one aspect of love that is of considerable interest is that of romantic love. Part of the reason for this particular interest is that romantic love is seen as being at the heart of some of our most intimate relationships. After all, isn't love the reason most people marry (at least in cultures that don't have arranged marriages)? Given the time and energy that people invest in finding an intimate partner, experiencing romantic love would seem to be a highly desirable goal for most people.

If, as most people in Western cultures do, you find someone to marry, you most likely love that person when you decide to take your vows. At least in Western cultures most would find it quite odd if you didn't. But now that you've married the person you love, will that love last over time? Or does it diminish, or perhaps transform into something other than the types of feelings you had when you first married? Many people (and some researchers) generally believe that "time kills romantic love," and that what people who've been married for many years experience, for example, is not the same later as it was in the beginning. But is this really the case, or can people maintain high levels of romantic love even many years into a marriage? The following article by Bianca P. Acevedo and Arthur Aron examines a wealth of previous research to answer this important question.

Does a Long-Term Relationship Kill Romantic Love?

■ Bianca P. Acevedo and Arthur Aron

This article examines the possibility that romantic love (with intensity, engagement, and sexual interest) can exist in long-term relationships. A review of taxonomies, theory, and research suggests that romantic love, without the obsession component typical of early stage romantic love, can and does exist in long-term marriages, and is associated with marital satisfaction, well-being, and high self-esteem. Supporting the separate roles of romantic love and obsession in long-term relationships, an analysis of a moderately large data set of community couples identified independent latent factors for romantic love and obsession and a subsample of individuals reporting very high levels of romantic love (but not obsession) even after controlling for social desirability.

Finally, a meta-analysis of 25 relevant studies found that in long- and short-term relationships, romantic love (without obsession) was strongly associated with relationship satisfaction; but obsession was negatively correlated with it in long-term and positively in short-term relationships.

> One should always be in love. That is the reason one should never marry.
>
> —Oscar Wilde

In contemporary Western culture, romantic love is deemed an important part of marriage. Many individuals view romantic love as a basis to marry (Dion & Dion, 1991) and its disappearance as grounds to terminate marriage (Simpson, Campbell, & Berscheid, 1986). Increasingly, romantic love and marriage have come to be viewed as a source of self-fulfillment and expression (Dion & Dion, 1991). Ironically though, it is widely believed that over time romantic love fades and that at best it evolves into a "warm afterglow" (Reik, 1944) of companionate love, a friendship-type love. How then, could something that is considered critical, if not the purpose of marrying, also be assumed to die out inevitably?

Psychologists, therapists, and laypeople have puzzled over the possibility of romantic love in long-term marriages. Some have assumed that very high levels of romantic love in long-term relationships might be inefficient, being metabolically costly (e.g., Fisher, 2006) and perhaps even deterring the lover from familial, work, and community obligations. Perhaps others have been swayed by media reports highlighting the dark side of love and marriage (e.g., high divorce rates, infidelity, stalking, domestic violence, etc.). Last, maintaining the assumption that romantic love cannot last allows those with good, but not stellar relationships to maintain the status quo and avoid being threatened by the possibility of high levels of love in long-term relationships. Indeed, this is perhaps a rational strategy (even if based on a myth) given that relationship well-being appears to be significantly benefited by downward social comparison with other couples (Rusbult, Van Lange, Wildschut, Yovetich, & Verette, 2000). Or perhaps, as proposed by Mitchell (2002), love could be enduring, but in an attempt to guarantee safety and minimize risks of having unrealistic assumptions about the certainty of the relationship, individuals dull romantic love over time.

Determining whether romantic love can thrive over time, and if so, what it is like in long-term relationships, is important for understanding basic relationship principles, their applications, and evolutionary foundations. For example, the possibility of romantic love in long-term relationships would suggest that the field needs to consider more than the absence of problems and conflict (the main focus of most current marital literature). The possibility of long-term romantic love may also shift therapists' and individuals' perceptions, so they set higher expectations, and so that long-term mates are less likely to seek out alternative partners or terminate relationships rather than face what has seemed like impossible challenges to achieve romantic love in their marriages. Moreover, this presumes people are willing to commit to long-term relationships at all. The assumption that time kills romantic love may undermine people's decisions even to enter into marriages.

In this article we argue that romantic love—with intensity, engagement, and sexual interest—can last. Although it does not usually include the obsessional qualities of early stage love, it does not inevitably die out or at best turn into companionate love—a warm, less intense love, devoid of attraction and sexual desire. We suggest that romantic love in its later and early

stages can share the qualities of intensity, engagement, and sexual liveliness. We briefly review relevant taxonomies, theoretical perspectives, and research; present new analyses of an existing data set of long-term couples; report a meta-analysis of the association of relationship satisfaction with romantic love in long and short-term relationships; review studies of long-term love's relation to individual well-being; and conclude with implications for theory, research, and applications.

TAXONOMIES, THEORETICAL PERSPECTIVES, AND RESEARCH

Taxonomies

Berscheid and Hatfield (1969), pioneers in the scientific exploration of love, proposed two major types of love—passionate and companionate. Passionate love, "a state of intense longing for union with another" (Hatfield & Rapson, 1993, p. 5), also referred to as "being in love" (Meyers & Berscheid, 1997), "infatuation" (Fisher, 1998), and "limerence" (Tennov, 1979), includes an obsessive element, characterized by intrusive thinking, uncertainty, and mood swings. The very widely used Passionate Love Scale (PLS; Hatfield & Sprecher, 1986) includes obsessive items (e.g., "Sometimes I feel I can't control my thoughts; they are obsessively on my partner;" "I sometimes find it difficult to concentrate on work because thoughts of my partner occupy my mind"). Companionate love, less intense than passionate love, combines attachment, commitment, and intimacy. It is defined as "the affection and tenderness we feel for those with whom our lives are deeply entwined" (Berscheid & Hatfield, 1969, p. 9); and refers to deep friendship, easy companionship, the sharing of common interests and activities, but not necessarily including sexual desire or attraction (e.g., Grote & Frieze, 1994). A widely accepted view is that over time there is a linear passage of passionate love into companionate love (Hatfield & Walster, 1978).

Another prominent taxonomy, Love Styles (Lee, 1977; Hendrick & Hendrick, 1986), delineates six basic styles of which three are directly relevant here: (a) Eros or romantic love, an intense focus, valuing, and desire for union with the beloved, without obsession; (b) Mania or obsessive love in which "The lover is jealous, full of doubt about the partner's sincerity and commitment, subject to physical symptoms such as inability to eat and sleep, experiences acute excitement alternating with debilitating depression" (Hendrick & Hendrick, 1992, p. 66); and (c) Storge or friendship love, a feeling of natural affection, a secure, trusting, friendship (often experienced toward siblings or friends) that does not involve sexual desire and is akin to companionate love. Eros and Mania together correspond to Berscheid and Hatfield's (1969) definition of passionate love and its operationalization in the PLS. Storge, corresponds to Berscheid and Hatfield's definition of companionate love. In this article, we refer to "Romantic love" as a rough equivalent to Eros (with intensity, attraction, engagement, and sexuality), without Mania (or obsession), and as distinguishable from a calmer, friendship-type attachment (companionate love or Storge).

A third influential taxonomy, Sternberg's (1986) Triangular Theory, conceptualizes love as consisting of three components—passion, intimacy, and commitment—of which different combinations result in different types of love. Passionate love is derived from a combination of intimacy and passion, without commitment; infatuated love, from passion without commitment or intimacy; and fatuous love, from passion and commitment, without intimacy. Sternberg argued that over the course of successful relationships, passion generally decreases, latent intimacy increases, and commitment increases then levels off; the rapid development of passion is generally followed by habituation in which people reach a more or less stable, low level of arousal toward their beloved.

Theoretical Perspectives

Many models of love imply that over time romantic love inevitably declines and, at best, evolves into some kind of friendship or companionate love. Social science models (e.g., Berscheid & Hatfield, 1969; Sternberg, 1986) emphasize habituation and familiarity, unavoidable interdependence conflicts, and the like. Other approaches describe mechanisms that can promote an occasional existence of romantic love in long-term relationships. Berscheid's (1983) interruption model predicts that temporary interruptions, such as brief separations and conflicts, may reignite latent passionate love (including its obsessive element). The self-expansion model (Aron & Aron, 1986) proposes that there are natural mechanisms that may promote long-term romantic love—such as shared participation in novel and challenging activities (e.g., Aron et al., 2000). Similarly, the rate of change in intimacy model (Baumeister & Bratslavsky, 1999) suggests that if couples have opportunities to increase intimacy at a rapid pace, it may also increase passion. Finally, recent evolutionary models propose that long-term romantic love may be an adaptation that promotes continued pair-bonding, keeping partners together even when problems or desirable alternatives present themselves (Buss, 2006). Other evolutionary work suggests that distinct systems evolved for mating, romantic attraction, and long-term attachments (Fisher, 1998); that in general, romantic attraction fades, but may exist in some cases serving to keep older couples energetic, optimistic, and with a companion (Fisher, 2006).

Research

Two key qualitative studies suggest that romantic love may be experienced for a long-term partner. In their classic interview study of nearly 500 American middle-class marriages of 10 years or more, Cuber and Haroff (1965) distinguished between "intrinsic" couples, who continued to enjoy deep, intimate, and affectionate connections with their partners and "utilitarian" couples, who maintained the bond for other reasons than to experience deep involvement with their spouse. Two subgroups of intrinsic couples were identified: "vital" couples, those intensely bound in important life matters with enjoyment, and "total" couples, those with many points of vital meshing shared mutually and enthusiastically. Tennov (1979) conducted hundreds of interviews with individuals reporting being intensely in love and observed that many older people in happy marriages replied affirmatively to being in love, but unlike those in "limerant" relationships, they did not report continuous and intrusive thinking. There have also been a number of relevant quantitative surveys that lead to the same conclusion, with three bearing directly on whether romantic/passionate love lasts. One interview study by Hatfield, Traupmann, and Sprecher (1984) found that women, aged 50 to 82, in long-term relationships (33 years or more) reported high levels ($M = 2.98$ on a 5-point scale) of passionate love (described as a wildly emotional state, with tender and sexual feelings, elation and pain, anxiety and relief), although slightly lower levels than compared with women in shorter relationships (<33 years, $M = 3.27$). In another study, Tucker and Aron (1993) found high levels of passionate love (PLS) across family life cycles (marriage, parenthood, and empty nest), with only slight decreases, even when controlling for marital satisfaction. Montgomery and Sorrell (1997) investigated love styles among four family life stages and found no significant differences in romantic love (Eros) from single in-love youth to those married with and without children living at home.

FACTOR ANALYSIS OF THE PASSIONATE LOVE SCALE IN LONG-TERM RELATIONSHIPS

The PLS, as we have noted, includes items that assess both romantic love and obsession. The PLS has proven itself to be a valid, reliable, and unifactorial measure in the context of new relationships (Aron et al., 2005; Hatfield & Sprecher, 1986). However, comingling romantic love and obsession may be problematic in the context of long-term relationships. To examine this issue, we assembled a data set large enough to conduct a factor analysis, consisting of Study 5 from Aron et al. (2000), plus data from three follow-up experiments (currently being prepared for submission), yielding 156 heterosexual couples (312 individuals) recruited from the Long Island, NY, community (M relationship length = 8.84 years (SD = 4.98). In each study, participants: completed a pretest including 15 items from the PLS, Hendrick's (1988) Generic Measure of Relationship Satisfaction, and seven items from Edmonds' (1967) Martial Conventionalization Scale (assesses social desirability in the marital context); participated in a joint activity that differed across studies; and completed a posttest including the remaining 15 PLS and 8 Conventionalization items. All posttest PLS and Conventionalization scores were adjusted within study for experimental condition; all pre- and posttest measures were adjusted between studies, for study.

We first conducted a factor analysis (principal components extraction) of the entire data set for adjusted PLS scores. A scree test yielded a clear two-factor solution (first six eigenvalues: 10.16, 2.24, 1.61, 1.45, 1.33, 1.26). Following varimax rotation, items on Factor 1 with very high loadings (≥.60) corresponded to romantic love or Eros (e.g., "I want my partner—physically, emotionally, and mentally," "For me, my partner is the perfect romantic partner," "I would rather be with my partner than anyone else," "I sense my body responding when my partner touches me," "My partner can make me feel effervescent and bubbly," and "I possess a powerful attraction for my partner"). Factor 2 corresponded closely to obsession or Mania (e.g., "I sometimes find it difficult to concentrate on work because thoughts of my partner occupy my mind" and "Sometimes I feel I can't control my thoughts; they are obsessively on my partner."). The factor analysis results were virtually identical in every respect when the following were analyzed separately: women and men, those together more than 2 years or together more than 4 years, whether missing values were excluded pairwise or listwise, whether principal components or principal axis factoring were used, and whether orthogonal or oblique rotations were used.

We next constructed scales from items with highest loadings on each factor (alphas .93 and .65, respectively). The correlation between these two scales was moderate ($r = .35$; controlling for relationship length and social desirability, partial $r = .27$); neither was correlated with relationship length in this data set, which included only couples married for at least a year or more ($rs = .06$ and .02, respectively; controlling for social desirability, .08 and .03). Factor 1 (romantic love) was strongly correlated with marital satisfaction ($rs = .52$ overall, .55 for women, .49 for men; controlling for social desirability and relationship length, $prs = .44, .46, .42$; all $ps < .001$); Factor 2 (obsession) was not (r and $pr = .04$). Entering both factors simultaneously, Factor 1 continued to have strong betas ($rs = .58, .60, .55$; $prs = .52, .53, .52$; all $ps < .001$). Factor 2 (obsession) displayed small to moderate, significant negative beta ($rs = -.17, -.15, -.17$: $prs = -.18, -.17, -.19$; all $ps < .05$). The correlations (and all partial correlations and betas) of the two factors with satisfaction were significantly different (all $ps < .001$).

The near-zero correlations with relationship length for romantic love further supports the idea that romantic love can exist in long-term relationships. Results from the factor analysis and correlations with satisfaction support the notion that in long-term relationships, romantic love and obsession are quite distinct: Romantic love (without obsession) is positively associated with relationship satisfaction, but the obsessive aspect is negatively associated with it.

We also examined the proportion reporting intense romantic love. We identified individuals who on each PLS factor scale rated all items as 6s (the highest possible value), even after controlling for social desirability (i.e., mean raw score residual predicting from social desirability score ≥6). (To be conservative, we only considered pretest PLS items; posttest items may have been affected by experimental condition and controls for condition make ambiguous what should count as a 6. However, results were virtually identical including posttest items.) Key result: 42 (13%) of the 312 participants gave all 6s to every romantic love (Factor 1) item, even after controlling for social desirability. Their mean relationship length (8.39 years) was virtually identical to the overall mean. For obsession (Factor 2), for which it was easier to have all 6s by chance (there were fewer items), only six individuals (2%) gave the highest possible answer to each question after controlling for social desirability; none of these six overlapped with the 42 in the first group; their time together and gender was about the same as for the extreme romantic love group and the overall sample. This additional analysis, while having its limits, adds to our confidence that intense romantic love—with engagement, centrality to life, and sexual liveliness—can and does exist in a nontrivial proportion of long-term relationships; but intense obsession is much rarer and largely unrelated to intense romantic love.

META-ANALYSIS OF LOVE TYPES AND SATISFACTION IN SHORT AND LONG-TERM RELATIONSHIPS

A recent meta-analysis (Masuda, 2003) of 33 studies, including both short and long-term relationships and various measures, found substantial correlations of romantic love with relationship satisfaction (weighted mean correlation = .64, range = .10 to .77). Masuda reported that correlations were consistent across measures and concluded that various measures of passionate and romantic love assess the same construct. These results are not surprising given the great deal of overlap between various measures of romantic love and that the meta-analysis aggregated studies with samples from dating, middle-school students to married individuals with and without children out of the nest. Thus, the present meta-analysis attempted to examine correlations of love with satisfaction *separately* by relationship stage and *separately* by constructs of love.

Method

Cross-sectional and longitudinal studies were searched that assessed both satisfaction and one of the focal types of love in samples of college age or older in a romantic relationship. Romantic love without obsession and obsessive love by itself were coded from measures including the Eros and Mania subscale, respectively, of the LAS or the similar SAMPLE (Laswell &

Laswell, 1976). Romantic love with obsession was coded from the PLS, the Passion subscale of Sternberg's (1997) Triangular Love Scale, and similar measures. Companionate love was coded, following Masuda (2003), from Rubin's (1970) Love Scale (assesses attachment, caring, and intimacy), Lund's (1985) short Love Scale, the Storge subscale of the LAS and SAMPLE, and the Triangular Love Scale Intimacy subscale. Relationship satisfaction was coded from the Dyadic Adjustment Scale (DAS; Spanier, 1976), the Relationship Assessment Scale (RAS; Hendrick, 1988), the Relationship Rating Form (RRF; Davis & Todd, 1985), Rusbult's (1983) relationship satisfaction scale, and original items (such as global items). Effect sizes were computed separately for short-term and long-term relationships. The short-term group included studies reporting on samples of college students, mostly single or dating. Studies with samples that included subsets of engaged, cohabiting, or married participants were also assigned to the short-term group if they met *all* three of the following conditions: (a) such participants comprised less than the majority of the sample, (b) the average relationship length overall was less than 4 years, and (c) participants were mostly college-age (18–23 years old). The long-term relationship group included studies assessing middle-aged participants (typically married 10 years or more). (If relationship status could not be determined or the sample was quite heterogeneous and did not report effect sizes separately by relationship stage or length, the study was not included in our meta-analysis.)

Results

Our search yielded 25 independent studies that met inclusion criteria, yielding a total of 17 short-term samples and 10 long-term samples (two studies had both short and long-term samples). Table 1a displays a summary of the effect sizes for the two groups by love type. Associations between romantic love and satisfaction were similar and large for both short and long-term groups ($Q = .21$, $p > .10$). Companionate love correlations with satisfaction were moderate (smaller than romantic love with satisfaction) and were significantly greater for the long-term than the short-term samples ($Q = 86.79$, $p < .001$). Passionate love (romantic love with obsession) had large correlations th[at] were slightly larger for the short-term group (Q = 3.62; $p < .10$).

Finally, obsessive love's correlation with satisfaction was small but positive for short-term and small but negative for long-term; these were significantly different ($Q = 7.10$, $p < .01$).

Discussion

The strong and similar association between romantic love (without obsession) and satisfaction in short and long-term relationships highlights its importance in both formation and maintenance phases. Companionate love was moderately correlated with satisfaction in short-term relationships and slightly more so in long-term relationships, highlighting the greater relevance of a calm, friendship-type, attachment to the success of long-term relationships. For Passionate love (romantic love *with* obsession), the pattern was the reverse, with short-term displaying a nearly significantly larger association with satisfaction (.55) than long-term (.46). This suggests that passionate love is closely tied with relationship satisfaction at all phases, but somewhat more so in the early stages. This may be a reflection of the undermining of passionate love scores for the long-term relationship group by its inclusion of the obsessive aspect. This idea is clearly supported by the small positive association of obsessive love with satisfaction in short-term samples but the slight negative association in the long-term samples.

LONG-TERM ROMANTIC LOVE AND WELL-BEING

If romantic love—intense, engaging, and sexual—does exist in long-term relationships (and does not just turn into companionship), is it associated with general well-being? We have seen that romantic love seems to be a good thing for the relationship. Nevertheless, is this just a folie-a-deux? Is it also good for the individuals involved and those around them? A number of studies have found that just being married is associated with subjective well-being (e.g., Diener, Suh, Lucas, & Smith, 1999). With regard to love in those marriages, studies suggest that it is also an important predictor of happiness, positive emotions, and life satisfaction (e.g., Diener & Lucas, 2000, who assessed love in general; Kim & Hatfield, 2004, who

TABLE 1A / Results of Meta-Analyses: Mean Aggregate Effect Sizes of Love Types With Relationship Satisfaction for Short-Term Relationships and Long-Term Relationships

Love type	Short-term Group				Long-term Group			
	N	k	r	SD	N	k	r	SD
Romantic love	3256	13	.55	.21	1419	7	.56	.26
Companionate love	3388	14	.26	.28	1905	9	.48	.41
Passionate love	1836	5	.55	.13	302	2	.46	.23
Mania	2958	12	.08	.13	889	6	−.02	.12

Note: N = Total sample size; k = number of independent studies; r = average effect size; SD = Standard deviation.

used the PLS). However, problems related to marriage (e.g., jealousy, control, and domestic violence) might suggest that a great deal of obsession in marriage might be maladaptive, or at the least distracting, steering a passionate couple away from fulfilling parental and occupational duties, socializing with friends, family, and the community.

Well-Being

Marital satisfaction predicts global happiness, above and beyond other types of satisfaction (e.g., Glenn & Weaver, 1981); predicts psychological well-being and physical health (e.g., Drigotas, Rusbult, Wieselquist, & Whitton, 1999); and may serve as a buffer to stressful life events (e.g., Coan, Schaefer, & Davidson, 2006; Treboux, Crowell, & Waters, 2004). Correspondingly, low quality marital bonds are predictive of depression (e.g., Beach & O'Leary, 1993) and marital dissolution (e.g., Huston et al., 2001). How much of this has to do specifically with romantic love? A study comparing normative versus distressed married couples in long-term relationships (*M* = 19 years) found that "love" (defined as a deep emotional bond, mutual caring and attraction, together with trust and closeness) ranked as the highest of 19 variables discriminating between the normative and distressed groups (Riehl-Emde, Thomas, & Willi, 2003). Other studies have also suggested strong and significant links between romantic love (even when measured with the PLS) with overall happiness in life (Aron & Henkemeyer, 1995), and lower psychological symptoms, greater life satisfaction, and better physical health (Traupmann, Eckels, & Hatfield, 1982).

Self-Esteem

Several theorists have suggested self-esteem plays an important role in relationships and specifically in relation to romantic love. For example, Hendrick and Hendrick (1992) describe Eros (romantic love) as "self-confidence and high self-esteem which allow an intense, exclusive focus on a partner but not possessiveness or jealousy" (p. 64). In contrast, Mania (obsession) is described as being full of insecurity and doubt and related to relationship turbulence, dissatisfaction, and obsession. Consistent with this idea, several studies report that self-esteem is moderately positively associated with higher Eros and lower Mania scores (e.g., Campbell, Foster, & Finkel, 2002; Dion & Dion, 1988; Hendrick & Hendrick, 1986, Hendrick, 1988). The direction of causality could be from self-esteem to love. For example, adults classified as "secure" according to attachment theory models, tend to report higher self-esteem (e.g., Feeney & Noller,1990; Treboux et al., 2004), and endorse mutual support and development (e.g., Ainsworth, 1991; Crowell, Treboux, & Waters, 2002). Thus, having the felt security that a partner is "there for you," not only makes for a smooth functioning relationship but also may facilitate feelings of romantic love. In contrast, individuals classified as insecure are less effective at using and providing a consistent secure base for their partners, have lower satisfaction and greater conflict in relationships, and also report lower self-esteem. Such events may heighten feelings of insecurity about the relationship, and could manifest as obsessive love.

GENERAL DISCUSSION

Many major theories of romantic love propose that it inevitably diminishes over time (e.g., Berscheid & Hatfield, 1969; Stermberg, 1986); other models have suggested mechanisms and functions for the maintenance of romantic love in long-term relationships (e.g., Aron & Aron, 1986; Berscheid, 1983; Buss, 2006; Fisher, 2006). The few directly relevant studies suggests that it is indeed a real phenomenon (e.g., Tucker & Aron, 1993; Hatfield et al., 1984), even when comparing romantic love between single, in-love youth with married adults (e.g., Montgomery & Sorrell, 1997). Extensive in-depth interviews also suggest that some individuals sustain deeply connected, intense, sexually alive relationships with a long-term partner, but without including obsessive elements (e.g., Cuber & Haroff, 1965; Tennov, 1979). We suggest that both a major reason for the assumption romantic love cannot exist in long-term relationships and confusion in the relevant literature is the mixing of romantic love with passionate love (defined based on new relationships) as including high obsession, uncertainty, and anxiety. By disentangling these constructs in a factor analysis, decades of research can be unraveled to suggest that romantic love—including intensity, interest, and sexuality—thrives in some enduring relationships, while obsession is much less common and unrelated to romantic love in long-term relationships.

We also explored the associations between romantic love with and without obsession and relationship satisfaction. Results from our meta-analysis of 25 studies showed that romantic love was strongly correlated with relationship satisfaction in both short and long-term relationships, whereas obsessive love was slightly correlated with relationship satisfaction in new relationships but very slightly negatively correlated with it in long-term relationships. Moreover, in no study is there evidence that romantic love is negatively associated with satisfaction. This is contrary to some views that romantic love, if it does occur in a long-term relationship, may be maladaptive. Of course, one cannot completely rule out the possibility that being highly passionate in a long-term marriage could undermine familial or social responsibilities. (Interestingly, Bataille, 1962, argued that life should be primarily about meaningful, intense engagement, and thus romantic love is a good thing that does undermine the social status quo, and for just that reason has been suppressed.)

Limitations and Future Directions

Research on love and relationships has advanced significantly in the last few decades, but several issues remain to be addressed. Most studies of long-term relationships (including the major longitudinal studies) have not even measured romantic love. The few studies that have done so have been mainly cross-sectional. Another issue is sentiment override (Weiss, 1980)—happy participants respond in positive ways to everything about their relationship. Our meta-analysis however found that effect sizes for types of love and relationship satisfaction differed across short and long-term relationship groups, suggesting that respondents do discriminate between love types and select varying degrees, not just high or low scores across the board. A related concern is social desirability. However, our reanalysis of the Long Island couple data set found that controlling for relationship-relevant social desirability minimally affected the obtained results. Nevertheless, more objective measures (implicit, physiological, neuroscience) will be a useful future direction. Finally, future research may aim to recruit more representative and culturally diverse samples, thus addressing the possibility that results are biased by self-selection of happy couples or Western values.

CONCLUSION

Contrary to what has been widely believed, long-term romantic love (with intensity, sexual interest, and engagement, but without the obsessive element common in new relationships), appears to be a real phenomenon that may be enhancing to individuals' lives—positively associated with marital satisfaction, mental health, and overall well-being. These conclusions suggest a dramatic revision of some theories and careful attention to measures of love that include or exclude obsession. In terms of real-world implications, the possibility of intense long-term romantic love sets a standard that couples (and marital therapists) can strive for that is higher than seems to have been generally considered realistic. This could also be distressing for long-term couples who have achieved a kind of contented, even happy—but not intensely romantic—status quo, assuming it is the best anyone can expect. Couples benefit from downward social comparison with other couples and will even distort their evaluation of their own relationship to an objectively unrealistically positive view (Rusbult et al., 2000). Yet, a shocking recognition of possibilities, that a long-term marriage does not necessarily kill the romance in one's relationship, may give some couples the inspiration they need, even if challenging, to make changes that will enhance their relationship quality (and thus general well being).

Could Oscar Wilde be wrong?

REFERENCES

Ainsworth, M. (1991). Attachment and other affectional bonds across the life cycle. In C. M. Parkes, J. Stevenson-Hinde, & P. Marris P (Eds.), *Attachment across the life cycle.* London: Tavistock.

Aron, A., & Aron, E. (1986). *Love and the expansion of self: Understanding attraction and satisfaction.* New York: Hemisphere.

Aron, A., Fisher, H., Mashek, D., Strong, G., Li, H., & Brown, L. (2005). Reward, motivation and emotion systems associated with early-stage intense romantic love. *Journal of Neurophysiology, 93,* 327–337.

Aron, A., & Henkemeyer, L. (1995). Marital satisfaction and passionate love. *Journal of Social and Personal Relationships, 12,* 139–146.

Aron, A., Norman, C. C., Aron, E. N., McKenna, C., & Heyman, R. (2000). Couples' shared participation in novel and arousing activities and experienced relationship quality. *Journal of Personality and Social Psychology, 78,* 273–283.

Bataille, G. (1962). *Eroticism* (M. Dalwood, Trans.). London: Calder.

Baumeister, R. F., & Bratslavsky, E. (1999). Passion, intimacy, and time: Passionate love as a function of change in intimacy. *Personality and Social Psychology Review, 3,* 49–67.

Beach, S. R., & O'Leary, K. D. (1993). Marital discord and dysphoria: For whom does this marital relationship predict Depressive symptomatology? *Journal of Social and Personal Relationships, 10,* 405–420.

Berscheid, E. (1983). Emotion. In H. H. Kelley, E. Berscheid, A. Christensen, et al. (Eds.), *Close relationships* (pp. 110–168). New York: Freeman.

Berscheid, E., & Hatfield [Walster], E. H. (1969). *Interpersonal attraction.* New York: Addison Wesley.

Buss, D. M. (2006). The evolution of love. In R. Sternberg & K. Weis (Eds.), *The new psychology of love* (pp. 65–86). New Haven: Yale University Press.

Campbell, L., Foster, C. A., & Finkel, E. J. (2002). Does self-love lead to love for others? A story of narcissistic game playing. *Journal of Personality and Social Psychology, 83,* 340–354.

Coan, J. A., Schaefer, H. S., & Davidson, R. (2006). Lending a hand: Social regulation of the neural response to threat. *Psychological Science, 17,* 1032–1039.

Crowell, J. A., Treboux, D., & Waters, E. (2002). Stability of attachment representations: The transition to marriage. *Developmental Psychology, 38,* 467–479.

Cuber, J. F., & Haroff, P. B. (1965). *The significant Americans.* New York: Appleton-Century.

Davis, K. E., & Todd, M. J. (1985). Assessing friendship: Prototypes, paradigm cases, and relationship assessment. In S. W. Duck & D. Perlman (Eds.), *Understanding personal relationships: An interdisciplinary approach* (pp. 17–34). Beverly Hills, CA: Sage.

Diener, E., & Lucas, R. (2000). Subjective emotional well-being. In M. Lewis & J. M. Haviland-Jones (Eds.), *Handbook of emotions* (2nd ed.). New York: The Guilford Press.

Diener, E., Suh, E. M., Lucas, R. E., & Smith, H. (1999). Subjective well-being: Three decades of progress—1967–1997. *Psychological Bulletin, 125,* 276–302.

Dion, K. L., & Dion, K. K. (1988). Romantic love: Individual and cultural perspectives. In R. J. Sternberg & M. L. Barnes (Eds.), *The psychology of love* (pp. 264–289). New Haven, CT: Yale University Press.

Dion, K. L., & Dion, K. K. (1991). Psychological individualism and romantic love. *Journal of Social Behavior and Personality, 6,* 17–33.

Drigotas, S. M., Rusbult, C. E., Wieselquist, J., & Whitton, S. (1999). Close partner as the sculptor of the ideal self: Behavioral affirmation and the Michaelangelo phenomenon. *Journal of Personality and Social Psychology, 77,* 293–323.

Edmonds, V. H. (1967). Marital conventionalization: Definition and measurement. *Journal of Marriage and the Family, 29,* 661–688.

Feeney, J. A., & Noller, P. (1990). Attachment style as a predictor of adult romantic relationships. *Journal of Personality and Social Psychology, 58,* 281–291.

Fisher, H. E. (1998). Lust, attraction and attachment in mammalian reproduction. *Human Nature, 9,* 23–52.

Fisher, H. E. (2006). The drive to love. In R. Sternberg & K. Weis (Eds.), *The new psychology of love* (pp. 87–115). New Haven: Yale University Press.

Glenn, N. D., & Weaver, C. N. (1981). The contribution of marital happiness to global happiness. *Journal of Marriage & the Family, 43,* 161–168.

Grote, N. K., & Frieze, I. H. (1994). The measurement of friendship-based love in intimate relationships. *Personal Relationships, 1,* 275–300.

Hatfield (Walster), E., & Walster, G. (1978). *A new look at love.* Langham, MD: University Press of America.

Hatfield, E., & Rapson, R. L. (1993). Historical and cross-cultural perspectives on passionate love and sexual desire. *Annual Review of Sex Research, 4,* 67–98.

Hatfield, E., & Sprecher, S. (1986). Measuring passionate love in intimate relationships. *Journal of Adolescence, 6,* 383–410.

Hatfield, E., Traupmann, J., & Sprecher, S. (1984). Older women's perceptions of their intimate relationships. *Journal of Social and Clinical Psychology, 2,* 108–124.

Hendrick, C., & Hendrick, S. S. (1986). A theory and method of love. *Journal of Personality and Social Psychology, 50,* 392–402.

Hendrick, S. S. (1988). A generic measure of relationship satisfaction. *Journal of Marriage and the Family, 50,* 93–98.

Hendrick, S. S., & Hendrick, C. (1992). *Romantic love.* Newbury Park, CA: Sage.

Huston, T. L., Houts, R. M., Caughlin, J. P., Smith, S. E., & George, L. J. (2001). The connubial crucible: Newlywed years as predictors of marital delight, distress, and divorce. *Journal of Personality and Social Psychology, 80,* 237–252.

Kim, J., & Hatfield, E. (2004). Love types and subjective well-being: A cross cultural study. *Social Behavior and Personality, 32,* 173–182.

Laswell, T. E., & Laswell, M. E. (1976). I love you but I'm not in love with you. *Journal of Marriage and Family Counseling, 38,* 211–224.

Lee, J. A. (1977). A typology of styles of loving. *Personality and Social Psychology Bulletin, 3,* 173–182.

Lund, M. (1985). The development of investment and commitment scales for predicting continuity of personal relationships. *Journal of Social and Personal Relationships, 2,* 3–23.

Masuda, M. (2003). Meta-analyses of love scales: Do various love scales measure the same psychological constructs? *Japanese Psychological Research, 45,* 25–37.

Mitchell, S. A. (2002). *Can love last?* New York: Norton.

Montgomery, M. J., & Sorell, G. T. (1997). Differences in love attributes across family life stages. *Family Relations, 46,* 55–61.

Meyers, S. A., & Berscheid, E. (1997). The language of love: The difference a preposition makes. *Personality and Social Psychology Bulletin, 23,* 347–362.

Reik, T. (1944). *A psychologist looks at love.* New York: Farrar & Reinhart.

Riehl-Emde, A., Thomas, V., & Willi, J. (2003). Love: An important dimension in marital research and therapy. *Family Process, 42,* 253–267.

Rubin, Z. (1970). Measurement of romantic love. *Journal of Personality and Social Psychology, 16,* 265–273.

Rusbult, C. E. (1983). A longitudinal test of the investment model: The development (and deterioration) of satisfaction and commitment in heterosexual involvement. *Journal of Personality and Social Psychology, 45,* 101–117.

Rusbult, C. E., Van Lange, P. A. M., Wildschut, T., Yovetich, N. A., & Verette, J. (2000). Perceived superiority in close relationships: Why it exists and persists. *Journal of Personality and Social Psychology, 79,* 521–545.

Simpson, J. A., Campbell, B., & Berscheid, E. (1986). The association between romantic love and marriage: Kephart (1967). Twice revisited. *Personality and Social Psychology Bulletin, 12,* 363–372.

Spanier, G. B. (1976). Measuring dyadic adjustment: New scales for assessing the quality of marriage and similar dyads. *Journal of Marriage and the Family, 32,* 15–28.

Sternberg, R. J. (1986). A triangular theory of love. *Psychological Review, 93,* 119–135.

Sternberg, R. J. (1997). Construct validation of a triangular love scale. *European Journal of Social Psychology, 27,* 313–335.

Tennov, D. (1979). *Love and limerence: The experience of being in love.* New York: Stein & Day.

Traupmann, J., Eckels, E., & Hatfield, E. (1982). *Intimacy in older women's lives. The Gerontologist, 22,* 493–498.

Treboux, D., Crowell, J. A., & Waters, E. (2004). When the "new" meets "old": Configurations of adult attachment representations and their implications for marital functioning. *Developmental Psychology, 40,* 295–314.

Tucker, P., & Aron, A. (1993). Passionate love and marital satisfaction at key transition points in the family cycle. *Journal of Social and Clinical Psychology, 12,* 135–147.

Weiss, R. L. (1980). Strategic behavioral marital therapy: Toward a model for assessment and intervention, Vol. 1. In J. P. Vincent (Ed.), *Advances in family intervention, assessment and theory* (pp. 229–271). Greenwich, CT: JAI Press.

ENDNOTE

1. Additional methods details are provided in the online Suppl., including search procedures, inclusion criteria, coding, handling multiple effect sizes within studies, and effect-size computation methods. Also included in the Suppl. are references for the included studies and tables of their sample characteristics and effect sizes. Suppl. information can be found at: http://www.psychology.sunysb.edu/gpr/Supplementary_Materials_MS_3403508.pdf

CRITICAL THINKING QUESTIONS

1. In U.S. contemporary society, what role does love play in the decision to get married? What role *should* it play? Has love always been at the core of a decision to marry? Present your personal views on the relationship between love and marriage. What about a marriage where love has gone? Is that a valid reason to get divorced? Explain your answers.

2. Take a look at the types of love described in the section labeled "Taxonomies" in the article. By examining a popular media source, such as television or the movies, what type or types of love seem to be portrayed most often? Do you think that these media portrayals of love have an impact on how people view love? Explain.

3. The article concludes that " . . . romantic love—including intensity, interest, and sexuality—thrives in some enduring relationships . . . ". What can couples do to keep romantic love alive? Use the information in the article to bolster your answer.

4. Why do so many people, including therapists, assume that romantic love decreases (or even disappears) over time? What, if anything, could change that belief? Explain your reasoning.

5. Based on your own experiences as well as your observations of others (your parents, parents of your friends, your friends, etc.), what pattern seems to be the most common in long-term relationships—romantic love continuing over time, some sort of friendship or companionate relationship evolving, or something else? Can you suggest reasons that these differences might exist in these couples? Explain your thinking.

CHAPTER INTEGRATION QUESTIONS

1. In a sense, the three articles in this chapter progress through the possible aspects of a relationship, from the initial attraction ("playing hard-to-get") to romantic love in a relationship, to divorce (but not in that order of article presentation). What similar themes run though these articles? Specifically, do any of the factors discussed about initial attraction and love affect the likelihood of being divorced later on? Explain your answer.

2. What factors identified in the articles on divorce and romantic love in long-term relationships may be useful in developing more satisfying relationships earlier on in the relationship? Explain your answers.

3. In *Keeping the Love You Find: A Guide for Singles,* the author, Harville Hendrix, said, "Love is hard—life is hard—but it's the only game in town. It's a high-stakes game, because how well you play determines how you will thrive and grow. You might as well learn to play it as well as possible as soon as possible." What does this quotation mean to you? Do you agree or disagree with it? Explain.

Chapter Nine

SOCIAL INFLUENCE

SOCIAL INFLUENCE IS the process of inducing change in other people. Sometimes social change results from direct orders to do something, such as when a military officer gives an order to a subordinate. When this happens, we call it *obedience*. Basic to situations involving obedience is some sort of power, either real or imagined, that the person giving the orders has over the person obeying him or her.

Not all social influence is due to direct orders from people in positions of authority. Instead, we may simply ask that a person do something for us. *Compliance* is when a person does something just because he or she was asked to, not because the requestor had any type of power over him or her.

Finally, social influence also operates in a very subtle way when people follow *norms,* or generally expected ways of behaving in certain situations. For example, when you are in an elevator, what do you do? Most likely, you face forward and stare at the numbers. *Conformity* occurs in many situations where norms exist for proper behavior. In a sense, conformity is the lifeblood of a society, for without conformity to rules, society could not exist.

Among the studies that address situational influences on behavior—and, in particular, in bringing out negative behavior—the two most often mentioned are the Stanford prison experiment and Stanley Milgram's study on obedience. Article 25, "Revisiting the Stanford Prison Experiment: A Lesson in the Power of Situation," is written by the person who conducted this classic study, Philip G. Zimbardo. This article describes the study and also discusses the current relevance of the experiment.

Milgram's study—considered to be a classic work on obedience and perhaps one of the most widely known studies in the field of social psychology—is found in Article 26, "Behavioral Study of Obedience." This study intended to demonstrate experimentally that the average person could be induced to harm another person simply by being ordered to by someone in a position of authority. The large number of people in this study who fully obeyed the orders surprised everyone.

Finally, Article 27, "The Constructive, Destructive, and Reconstructive Power of Social Norms," examines how social norms can be used to effectively change behavior, in this case energy usage. In particular, this article examines why attempts at such behavior change sometimes are successful and other times they are not. The key may not only be in telling a person what others are doing (a *descriptive normative message*) but also in presenting them with social approval or disapproval for that behavior (an *injunctive normative message*).

ARTICLE 25 _____

When people read about a horrendous act that has been committed, they naturally think that the person who committed it is somehow deranged or inhuman. Sometimes that is indeed the case, as when a psychotic commits an act under orders he or she has supposedly received during hallucinations. Personal pathology and mental illness are certainly involved in many of the hideous acts that people commit. But are personality or psychological factors always the cause of such behavior? Is it possible that an otherwise normal individual may commit an abnormal, sick act not because there is something wrong with him or her but because of the situation he or she might be in?

History is full of examples of normal people who have committed abnormal acts. For example, warfare has often induced otherwise normal, nonviolent people not only to kill but also to commit atrocities. Yet the suggestion that somehow anyone placed in the same situation may act the same way is repugnant. It might be a lot more personally comforting to believe that people who do bad things are somehow different from us. We, after all, are good and certainly incapable of being mass murderers. Only other people who are either sick or are somehow overly conforming could do such things. In other words, we tend to attribute others' acts to their disposition—that is, some personality or other enduring trait causes them to act that way.

The work of Stanley Milgram, which appears in Article 26, is the classic study in the field of social psychology that suggested that perhaps individual characteristics (dispositions) are less responsible for people performing terrible acts than are the situations that produce such behavior. Another classic research study that rivals Milgram's obedience study is what has come to be known as the Stanford prison experiment. In the following article, researcher Philip G. Zimbardo describes this famous study and discusses the current relevance of the work.

Revisiting the Stanford Prison Experiment
A Lesson in the Power of the Situation
■ Phillip G. Zimbardo

By the 1970s, psychologists had done a series of studies establishing the social power of groups. They showed, for example, that groups of strangers could persuade people to believe statements that were obviously false. Psychologists had also found that research participants were often willing to obey authority figures even when doing so violated their personal beliefs. The Yale studies by Stanley Milgram in 1963 demonstrated that a majority of ordinary citizens would continually shock an innocent man, even up to near-lethal levels, if commanded to do so by someone acting as an authority. The "authority" figure in this case was merely a high-school biology teacher who wore a lab coat and acted in an official manner. The majority of people shocked their victims over and over again despite increasingly desperate pleas to stop.

In my own work, I wanted to explore the fictional notion from William Golding's *Lord of the Flies* about the power of anonymity to unleash violent behavior. In one experiment from 1969, female students who were made to feel anonymous and given permission for aggression became significantly more hostile than students with their identities intact. Those and a host of other social-psychological

studies were showing that human nature was more pliable than previously imagined and more responsive to situational pressures than we cared to acknowledge. In sum, these studies challenged the sacrosanct view that inner determinants of behavior—personality traits, morality, and religious upbringing—directed good people down righteous paths.

Missing from the body of social-science research at the time was the direct confrontation of good versus evil, of good people pitted against the forces inherent in bad situations. It was evident from everyday life that smart people made dumb decisions when they were engaged in mindless groupthink, as in the disastrous Bay of Pigs invasion by the smart guys in President John F. Kennedy's cabinet. It was also clear that smart people surrounding President Richard M. Nixon, like Henry A. Kissinger and Robert S. McNamara, escalated the Vietnam War when they knew, and later admitted, it was not winnable. They were caught up in the mental constraints of cognitive dissonance—the discomfort from holding two conflicting thoughts—and were unable to cut bait even though it was the only rational strategy to save lives and face. Those examples,

From 'The Revisiting of the Stanford Prison Experiment: A Lesson of Power of the Situation', P.G. Zimbardo, *The Chronicle of Higher Education*, March 30, 2007, pp. B6–B7. Reprinted with permission of Philip Zimbardo.

however, with their different personalities, political agendas, and motives, complicated any simple conceptual attempt to understand what went wrong in these situations.

I decided that what was needed was to create a situation in a controlled experimental setting in which we could array on one side a host of variables, such as role-playing, coercive rules, power differentials, anonymity, group dynamics, and dehumanization. On the other side, we lined up a collection of the "best and brightest" of young college men in collective opposition to the might of a dominant system. Thus in 1971 was born the Stanford prison experiment, more akin to Greek drama than to university psychology study. I wanted to know who wins—good people or an evil situation—when they were brought into direct confrontation.

First we established that all 24 participants were physically and mentally healthy, with no history of crime or violence, so as to be sure that initially they were all "good apples." They were paid $15 a day to participate. Each of the student volunteers was randomly assigned to play the role of prisoner or guard in a setting designed to convey a sense of the psychology of imprisonment (in actuality, a mock prison set up in the basement of the Stanford psychology department). Dramatic realism infused the study. Palo Alto police agreed to "arrest" the prisoners and book them, and once at the prison, they were given identity numbers, stripped naked, and deloused. The prisoners wore large smocks with no underclothes and lived in the prison 24/7 for a planned two weeks; three sets of guards each patrolled eight-hour shifts. Throughout the experiment, I served as the prison "superintendent," assisted by two graduate students.

Initially nothing much happened as the students awkwardly tried out their assigned roles in their new uniforms. However, all that changed suddenly on the morning of the second day following a rebellion, when the prisoners barricaded themselves inside the cells by putting their beds against the door. Suddenly the guards perceived the prisoners as "dangerous"; they had to be dealt with harshly to demonstrate who was boss and who was powerless. At first, guard abuses were retaliation for taunts and disobedience. Over time, the guards became ever more abusive, and some even delighted in sadistically tormenting their prisoners. Though physical punishment was restricted, the guards on each shift were free to make up their own rules, and they invented a variety of psychological tactics to demonstrate their dominance over their powerless charges.

Nakedness was a common punishment, as was placing prisoners' heads in nylon stocking caps (to simulate shaved heads); chaining their legs; repeatedly waking them throughout the night for hourlong counts; and forcing them into humiliating "fun and games" activities. Let's go beyond those generalizations to review some of the actual behaviors that were enacted in the prison simulation. They are a lesson in "creative evil," in how certain social settings can transform intelligent young men into perpetrators of psychological abuse.

PRISON LOG, NIGHT 5

The prisoners, who have not broken down emotionally under the incessant stress the guards have been subjecting them to since their aborted rebellion on Day 2, wearily line up against the wall to recite their ID numbers and to demonstrate that they remember all 17 prisoner rules of engagement. It is the 1 a.m. count, the last one of the night before the morning shift comes on at 2 a.m. No matter how well the prisoners do, one of them gets singled out for punishment. They are yelled at, cursed out, and made to say abusive things to each other. "Tell him he's a prick," yells one guard. And each prisoner says that to the next guy in line. Then the sexual harassment that had started to bubble up the night before resumes as the testosterone flows freely in every direction.

"See that hole in the ground? Now do 25 push-ups [expletive] that hole! You hear me!" One after another, the prisoners obey like automatons as the guard shoves them down. After a brief consultation, our toughest guard (nicknamed "John Wayne" by the prisoners) and his sidekick devise a new sexual game. "OK, now pay attention. You three are going to be female camels. Get over here and bend over, touching your hands to the floor." When they do, their naked butts are exposed because they have no underwear beneath their smocks. John Wayne continues with obvious glee, "Now you two, you're male camels. Stand behind the female camels and *hump* them."

The guards all giggle at this double-entendre. Although their bodies never touch, the helpless prisoners begin to simulate sodomy by making thrusting motions. They are then dismissed back to their cells to get an hour of sleep before the next shift comes on, and the abuse continues.

By Day 5, five of the student prisoners have to be released early because of extreme stress. (Recall that each of them was physically healthy and psychologically stable less than a week before.) Most of those who remain adopt a zombielike attitude and posture, totally obedient to escalating guard demands.

TERMINATING THE TORMENT

I was forced to terminate the projected two-week-long study after only six days because it was running out of control. Dozens of people had come down to our "little shop of horrors," seen some of the abuse or its effects, and said nothing. A prison chaplain, parents, and friends had visited the prisoners, and psychologists and others on the parole board saw a realistic prison simulation, an experiment in action, but did not challenge me to stop it. The one exception erupted just before the time of the prison-log notation on Night 5.

About halfway through the study, I had invited some psychologists who knew little about the experiment to interview the staff and participants, to get an outsiders' evaluation of how it was going. A former doctoral student of mine, Christina

Maslach, a new assistant professor at the University of California at Berkeley, came down late Thursday night to have dinner with me. We had started dating recently and were becoming romantically involved. When she saw the prisoners lined up with bags over their heads, their legs chained, and guards shouting abuses at them while herding them to the toilet, she got upset and refused my suggestion to observe what was happening in this "crucible of human nature." Instead she ran out of the basement, and I followed, berating her for being overly sensitive and not realizing the important lessons taking place here.

"It is terrible what YOU are doing to those boys!" she yelled at me. Christina made evident in that one statement that human beings were suffering, not prisoners, not experimental subjects, not paid volunteers. And further, I was the one who was personally responsible for the horrors she had witnessed (and which she assumed were even worse when no outsider was looking). She also made clear that if this person I had become—the heartless superintendent of the Stanford prison—was the real me, not the caring, generous person she had come to like, she wanted nothing more to do with me.

That powerful jolt of reality snapped me back to my senses. I agreed that we had gone too far, that whatever was to be learned about situational power was already indelibly etched on our videos, data logs, and minds; there was no need to continue. I too had been transformed by my role in that situation to become a person that under any other circumstances I detest—an uncaring, authoritarian boss man. In retrospect, I believe that the main reason I did not end the study sooner resulted from the conflict created in me by my dual roles as principal investigator, and thus guardian of the research ethics of the experiment, and as the prison superintendent, eager to maintain the stability of my prison at all costs. I now realize that there should have been someone with authority above mine, someone in charge of oversight of the experiment, who surely would have blown the whistle earlier.

By the time Christina intervened, it was the middle of the night, so I had to make plans to terminate the next morning. The released prisoners and guards had to be called back and many logistics handled before I could say, "The Stanford prison experiment is officially closed." When I went back down to the basement, I witnessed the final scene of depravity, the "camel humping" episode. I was so glad that it would be the last such abuse I would see or be responsible for.

GOOD APPLES IN BAD BARRELS AND BAD BARREL MAKERS

The situational forces in that "bad barrel" had overwhelmed the goodness of most of those infected by their viral power. It is hard to imagine how a seeming game of "cops and robbers" played by college kids, with a few academics (our research team) watching, could have descended into what became a hellhole for many in that basement. How could a mock prison, an experimental simulation, become "a prison run by psychologists, not by the state," in the words of one suffering prisoner? How is it possible for "good personalities" to be so dominated by a "bad situation"? You had to be there to believe that human character could be so swiftly transformed in a matter of days—not only the traits of the students, but of me, a well-seasoned adult. Most of the visitors to our prison also fell under the spell. For example, individual sets of parents observing their son's haggard appearance after a few days of hard labor and long nights of disrupted sleep said they "did not want to make trouble" by taking their kid home or challenging the system. Instead they obeyed our authority and let some of their sons experience full-blown emotional meltdowns later on. We had created a dominating behavioral context whose power insidiously frayed the seemingly impervious values of compassion, fair play, and belief in a just world.

The situation won; humanity lost. Out the window went the moral upbringings of these young men, as well as their middle-class civility. Power ailed, and unrestrained power became an aphrodisiac. Power without surveillance by higher authorities was a poisoned chalice that transformed character in unpredictable directions. I believe that most of us tend to be fascinated with evil not because of its consequences but because evil is a demonstration of power and domination over others.

CURRENT RELEVANCE

Such research is now in an ethical time capsule, since institutional review boards will not allow social scientists to repeat it (although experiments like it have been replicated on several TV shows and in artistic renditions). Nevertheless, the Stanford prison experi-ment is now more popular than ever in its 36-year history. A Google search of "experiment" reveals it to be fourth among some 132 million hits, and sixth among some 127 million hits on "prison." Some of this recent interest comes from the apparent similarities of the experiment's abuses with the images of depravity in Iraq's Abu Ghraib prison—of nakedness, bagged heads, and sexual humiliation.

Among the dozen investigations of the Abu Ghraib abuses, the one chaired by James R. Schlesinger, the former secretary of defense, boldly proclaims that the landmark Stanford study "provides a cautionary tale for all military detention operations." In contrasting the relatively benign environment of the Stanford prison experiment, the report makes evident that "in military detention operations, soldiers work under stressful combat conditions that are far from benign." The implication is that those combat conditions might be expected to generate even more extreme abuses of power than were observed in our mock prison experiment.

However, the Schlesinger report notes that military leaders did not heed that earlier warning in any way. They should have—a psychological perspective is essential to understanding the transformation of human character in response to special situational forces. "The potential for abusive treatment of detainees during the Global War on Terrorism was entirely predictable based on a fundamental understanding of the principles of social psychology coupled with an awareness of numerous known environmental risk factors," the report says. "Findings from the field of social psychology suggest that the conditions of war and the dynamics of detainee operations carry inherent risks for human mistreatment, and therefore must be approached with great caution and careful planning and training." (Unfortunately this vital conclusion is buried in an appendix.)

The Stanford prison experiment is but one of a host of studies in psychology that reveal the extent to which our behavior can be transformed from its usual set point to deviate in unimaginable ways, even to readily accepting a dehumanized conception of others, as "animals," and to accepting spurious rationales for why pain will be good for them.

The implications of this research for law are considerable, as legal scholars are beginning to recognize. The criminal-justice system, for instance, focuses primarily on individual defendants and their "state of mind" and largely ignores situational forces. The Model Penal Code states: "A person is not guilty of an offense unless his liability is based on conduct that includes a voluntary act or the omission to perform an act of which he is physically capable." As my own experiment revealed, and as a great deal of social-psychological research before and since has confirmed, we humans exaggerate the extent to which our actions are voluntary and rationally chosen—or, put differently, we all understate the power of the situation. My claim is not that individuals are incapable of criminal culpability; rather, it is that, like the horrible behavior brought out by my experiment in good, normal young men, the situation and the system creating it also must share in the responsibility for illegal and immoral behavior.

If the goals of the criminal system are simply to blame and punish individual perpetrators—to get our pound of flesh—then focusing almost exclusively on the individual defendant makes sense. If, however, the goal is actually to reduce the behavior that we now call "criminal" (and its resultant suffering), and to assign punishments that correspond with culpability, then the criminal-justice system is obligated, much as I was in the Stanford prison experiment, to confront the situation and our role in creating and perpetuating it. It is clear to most reasonable observers that the social experiment of imprisoning society's criminals for long terms is a failure on virtually all levels. By recognizing the situational determinants of behavior, we can move to a more productive public-health model of prevention and intervention, and away from the individualistic medical and religious "sin" model that has never worked since its inception during the Inquisition.

The critical message then is to be sensitive about our vulnerability to subtle but powerful situational forces and, by such awareness, be more able to overcome those forces. Group pressures, authority symbols, dehumanization of others, imposed anonymity, dominant ideologies that enable spurious ends to justify immoral means, lack of surveillance, and other situational forces can work to transform even some of the best of us into Mr. Hyde monsters, without the benefit of Dr. Jekyll's chemical elixir. We must be more aware of how situational variables can influence our behavior. Further, we must also be aware that veiled behind the power of the situation is the greater power of the system, which creates and maintains complicity at the highest military and governmental levels—with evil-inducing situations, like those at Abu Ghraib and Guantánamo Bay prisons.

Philip G Zimbardo is a professor emeritus of psychology at Stanford University and author of The Lucifer Effect: Understanding How Good People Turn Evil, *published this month by Random House.*

CRITICAL THINKING QUESTIONS

1. What are the main implications of the Stanford prison experiment? Could anyone, including you, be induced to act in the same way as the prisoners or guards if put into the same situation? Do personality and perhaps free will really have nothing to do with how someone will act in such situations? Or is free will not really possible in such situations? Support your answers.

2. If bad behaviors can be induced by the techniques described in this article, does that mean that people should not be held responsible for the things they do? Would a defense of "It was the situation that made me do it" absolve an individual of personal responsibility for his or her actions? Explain your responses.

3. The article seems to suggest that given the right (or rather wrong) situation, it is fairly easy to bring out the worst in people. How could you prevent these negative effects? For example, would educating people about what happened in the Stanford prison experiment lessen the likelihood that such behaviors would recur in the future? Discuss.

4. Discuss the ethical issues surrounding the Stanford prison experiment.

5. As stated in the article, "The goals of the criminal justice system are simply to blame and punish individual perpetrators." Furthermore, "By recognizing the situational determinants of behavior, we can move to a more productive public-health model of prevention and intervention." Based on your understanding of the article, how might society and the criminal justice system be changed to address situational influences? Or is the focus on punishing individual perpetrators appropriate? Defend your position.

ARTICLE 26 _____

Stanley Milgram's article "Behavioral Study of Obedience" was one of his first describing a series of studies investigating the conditions that produce obedience to authority. This study, as well as Milgram's subsequent research, is truly classic. In fact, if you asked someone who has had only minimal exposure to the field of social psychology about landmark research, this study would perhaps come to mind.

Part of the widespread interest in Milgram's work is due to the implications it has. Basically, Milgram took a group of male volunteers from various backgrounds and ages and induced them to perform acts that appeared to harm another person. Nearly two-thirds of the subjects were fully obedient, continuing to give shocks even though it was apparent that they were harming the victim. Does that mean that just about anyone could be made to do the same? More importantly, while reading the article, keep in mind the actual situation confronting the subjects: What would have happened to them if they had refused to obey? Would the effect demonstrated by Milgram be greater for real-life situations, where there might be punishments for failing to obey?

Besides the implications of the research, Milgram's work on obedience has also attracted considerable interest over the years because of the ethical issues raised. When reading the article, try to put yourself in the shoes of the subjects: How would you feel if you volunteered for a study on learning and instead walked out of the experiment an hour later with the realization that you were willing to harm someone just because an authority figure told you to do so? Think about the ethical issues involved in the study, including the issue of debriefing subjects following an experiment.

Behavioral Study of Obedience

■ Stanley Milgram

This chapter describes a procedure for the study of destructive obedience in the laboratory. It consists of ordering a naive S to administer increasingly more severe punishment to a victim in the context of a learning experiment. Punishment is administered by means of a shock generator with thirty graded switches ranging from Slight Shock to Danger: Severe Shock. The victim is a confederate of the E. The primary dependent variable is the maximum shock the S is willing to administer before he refuses to continue further. Twenty-six Ss obeyed the experimental commands fully, and administered the highest shock on the generator. Fourteen Ss broke off the experiment at some point after the victim protested and refused to provide further answers. The procedure created extreme levels of nervous tension in some Ss. Profuse sweating, trembling and stuttering were typical expressions of this emotional disturbance. One unexpected sign of tension—yet to be explained—was the regular occurrence of nervous laughter, which in some Ss developed into uncontrollable seizures. The variety of interesting behavioral dynamics observed in the experiment, the reality of the situation for the S, and the possibility of parametric variation within the framework of the procedure, point to the fruitfulness of further study.

Obedience is as basic an element in the structure of social life as one can point to. Some system of authority is a requirement of all communal living, and it is only the man dwelling in isolation who is not forced to respond, through defiance or submission, to the commands of others. Obedience, as a determinant of behavior, is of particular relevance to our time. It has been reliably established that from 1933–1945 millions of innocent persons were systematically slaughtered on command. Gas chambers were built, death camps were guarded, daily quotas of corpses were produced with the same efficiency as the manufacture of appliances. These inhumane policies may have originated in the mind of a single person, but they could only be carried out on a massive scale if a very large number of persons obeyed orders.

Obedience is the psychological mechanism that links individual action to political purpose. It is the dispositional cement that binds men to systems of authority. Facts of recent history and observation in daily life suggest that for many persons obedience may be a deeply ingrained behavior tendency, indeed, a prepotent impulse overriding training in ethics, sympathy, and moral conduct. C. P. Snow (1961) points to its importance when he writes:

> When you think of the long and gloomy history of man, you will find more hideous crimes have been committed in the name of obedience than have ever been committed in the name of rebellion. If you doubt that, read William Shirer's "Rise and

Fall of the Third Reich." The German Officer Corps were brought up in the most rigorous code of obedience in the name of obedience they were party to, and assisted in, the most wicked large scale actions in the history of the world. (p. 24)

While the particular form of obedience dealt with in the present study has its antecedents in these episodes, it must not be thought all obedience entails acts of aggression against others. Obedience serves numerous productive functions. Indeed, the very life of society is predicated on its existence. Obedience may be ennobling and educative and refer to acts of charity and kindness, as well as to destruction.

GENERAL PROCEDURE

A procedure was devised which seems useful as a tool for studying obedience (Milgram, 1961). It consists of ordering a naive subject to administer electric shock to a victim. A simulated shock generator is used, with 30 clearly marked voltage levels that range from 15 to 450 volts. The instrument bears verbal designations that range from Slight Shock to Danger: Severe Shock. The responses of the victim, who is a trained confederate of the experimenter, are standardized. The orders to administer shocks are given to the naive subject in the context of a "learning experiment" ostensibly set up to study the effects of punishment on memory. As the experiment proceeds the naive subject is commanded to administer increasingly more intense shocks to the victim, even to the point of reaching the level marked Danger: Severe Shock. Internal resistances become stronger, and at a certain point the subject refuses to go on with the experiment. Behavior prior to this rupture is considered "obedience," in that the subject complies with the commands of the experimenter. The point of rupture is the act of disobedience. A quantitative value is assigned to the subject's performance based on the maximum intensity shock he is willing to administer before he refuses to participate further. Thus for any particular subject and for any particular experimental condition the degree of obedience may be specified with a numerical value. The crux of the study is to systematically vary the factors believed to alter the degree of obedience to the experimental commands.

The technique allows important variables to be manipulated at several points in the experiment. One may vary aspects of the source of command, content and form of command, instrumentalities for its execution, target object, general social setting, etc. The problem, therefore, is not one of designing increasingly more numerous experimental conditions, but of selecting those that best illuminate the process of obedience from the sociopsychological standpoint.

RELATED STUDIES

The inquiry bears an important relation to philosophic analyses of obedience and authority (Arendt, 1958; Friedrich, 1958;

Weber, 1947), an early experimental study of obedience by Frank (1944), studies in "authoritarianism" (Adorno, Frenkel-Brunswik, Levinson, and Sanford, 1950; Rokeach, 1961), and a recent series of analytic and empirical studies in social power (Cartwright, 1959). It owes much to the long concern with *suggestion* in social psychology, both in its normal forms (e.g., Binet, 1900) and in its clinical manifestations (Charcot, 1881). But it derives, in the first instance, from direct observation of a social fact; the individual who is commanded by a legitimate authority ordinarily obeys. Obedience comes easily and often. It is a ubiquitous and indispensable feature of social life.

METHOD

Subjects

The subjects were 40 males between the ages of 20 and 50, drawn from New Haven and the surrounding communities. Subjects were obtained by a newspaper advertisement and direct mail solicitation. Those who responded to the appeal believed they were to participate in a study of memory and learning at Yale University. A wide range of occupations is represented in the sample. Typical subjects were postal clerks, high school teachers, salesmen, engineers, and laborers. Subjects ranged in educational level from one who had not finished elementary school, to those who had doctorate and other professional degrees. They were paid $4.50 for their participation in the experiment. However, subjects were told that payment was simply for coming to the laboratory, and that the money was theirs no matter what happened after they arrived. Table 1 shows the proportion of age and occupational types assigned to the experimental condition.

Personnel and Locale

The experiment was conducted on the grounds of Yale University in the elegant interaction laboratory. (This detail is relevant to the perceived legitimacy of the experiment. In further variations, the experiment was dissociated from the university, with consequences for performance.) The role of experimenter was played by a 31-year-old high school teacher of biology. His manner was impassive, and his appearance somewhat stern throughout the experiment. He was dressed in a gray technician's coat. The victim was played by a 47-year-old accountant, trained for the role; he was of Irish-American stock, whom most observers found mild-mannered and likable.

Procedure

One naive subject and one victim (an accomplice) performed in each experiment. A pretext had to be devised that would justify the administration of electric shock by the naive subject.

TABLE 1 / Distribution of Age and Occupational Types in the Experiment

Occupations	20–29 Years n	30–39 Years n	40–50 Years n	Percentage of Total (Occupations)
Workers, skilled and unskilled	4	5	6	37.5
Sales, business, and white-collar	3	6	7	40.0
Professional	1	5	3	22.5
Percentage of total (age)	20	40	40	

Note: Total *n* = 40.

This was effectively accomplished by the cover story. After a general introduction on the presumed relation between punishment and learning, subjects were told:

> But actually, we know very little *about the effect of punishment on learning, because almost no truly scientific studies have been made of it in human beings.*
>
> For instance, we don't know how much *punishment is best for learning—and we don't know how much difference it makes as to who is giving the punishment, whether an adult learns best from a younger or an older person than himself—or many things of that sort.*
>
> So in this study we are bringing together a number of adults of different occupations and ages. And we're asking some of them to be teachers and some of them to be learners.
>
> We want to find out just what effect different people have on each other as teachers and learners, and also what effect punishment will have on learning in this situation.
>
> Therefore, I'm going to ask one of you to be the teacher here tonight and the other one to be the learner.
>
> Does either of you have a preference?

Subjects then drew slips of paper from a hat to determine who would be the teacher and who would be the learner in the experiment. The drawing was rigged so that the naive subject was always the teacher and the accomplice always the learner. (Both slips contained the word "Teacher.") Immediately after the drawing the teacher and learner were taken to an adjacent room and the learner was strapped into an "electric chair" apparatus.

The experimenter explained that the straps were to prevent excessive movement while the learner was being shocked. The effect was to make it impossible for him to escape from the situation. An electrode was attached to the learner's wrist, and electrode paste was applied "to avoid blisters and burns." Subjects were told that the electrode was attached to the shock generator in the adjoining room.

In order to improve credibility the experimenter declared, in response to a question by the learner: "Although the shocks can be extremely painful, they cause no permanent tissue damage."

Learning Task   The lesson administered by the subject was a paired-associate learning task. The subject read a series of word

pairs to the learner, and then read the first word of the pair along with four terms. The learner was to indicate which of the four terms had originally been paired with the first word. He communicated his answer by pressing one of four switches in front of him, which in turn lit up one of four numbered quadrants in an answer-box located atop the shock generator.

Shock Generator   The instrument panel consists of 30 lever switches set in a horizontal line. Each switch is clearly labeled with a voltage designation that ranges from 15 to 450 volts. There is a 15-volt increment from one switch to the next going from left to right. In addition, the following verbal designations are clearly indicated for groups of four switches going from left to right: Slight Shock, Moderate Shock, Strong Shock, Very Strong Shock, Intense Shock, Extreme Intensity Shock, Danger: Severe Shock. (Two switches after this last designation are simply marked XXX.)

Upon depressing a switch: a pilot light corresponding to each switch is illuminated in bright red; an electric buzzing is heard; an electric blue light, labeled "voltage energizer," flashes; the dial on the voltage meter swings to the right; various relay clicks are sounded.

The upper left-hand corner of the generator is labeled Shock Generator, Type ZLB, Dyson Instrument Company, Waltham, Mass. Output 15 Volts- 450 Volts.

Details of the instrument were carefully handled to insure an appearance of authenticity. The panel was engraved by precision industrial engravers, and all components were of high quality. No subject in the experiment suspected that the instrument was merely a simulated shock generator.[1]

Sample Shock   Each naive subject is given a sample shock on the shock generator, prior to beginning his run as teacher. This shock is always 45 volts, and is applied by pressing the third switch of the generator. The shock is applied to the wrist of the naive subject, and has its source in a 45-volt battery wired into the generator. This further convinces the subject of the authenticity of the generator.

Shock Instructions   The subject is told to administer a shock to the learner each time he gives a wrong response. Moreover—and this is the key command—the subject is instructed to "move one lever higher on the shock generator each time the learner flashes a wrong answer." He is also instructed to announce the voltage level before administering a shock. This serves to continually remind subjects of the increasing intensity of shocks administered to the learner.

Preliminary and Regular Run   Pretests revealed that the procedure of reading words and administering shocks requires some practice before it can be handled smoothly. Therefore, immediately preceding the regular run, the teacher is given a preliminary series of 10 words to read to the learner. There are 3 neutral words in the practice series (i.e., words that the learner answers correctly), so that shocks are administered for 7 of the words, with the maximum shock at 105 volts (moderate shock). Almost all subjects master the procedure by the time the preliminary run is over.

Subjects are then presented with a second list, and are told that the procedure is the same as for the first list; the experimenter adds, however:

When you get to the bottom of the list, repeat it over again, and continue giving shocks, until the learner has learned all the pairs correctly.

The experimenter instructs the subject to

start from 15 volts and increase the shock level one step each time the learner gives a wrong answer.

Feedback from the Victim   In all conditions the learner gives a predetermined set of responses to the word pair test, based on a schedule of approximately three wrong answers to one correct answer. In the present experimental condition no vocal response or other sign of protest is heard from the learner until Shock Level 300 is reached. When the 300-volt shock is administered, the learner pounds on the wall of the room in which he is bound to the electric chair. The pounding can be heard by the subject. From this point on, the learner's answers no longer appear on the four-way panel.

At this juncture, subjects ordinarily turn to the experimenter for guidance. The experimenter instructs the subject to treat the absence of a response as a wrong answer, and to shock the subject according to the usual schedule. He advises the subjects to allow 5-10 seconds before considering no response as a wrong answer, and to increase the shock level one step each time the learner fails to respond correctly. The learner's pounding is repeated after the 315-volt shock is administered; afterwards he is not heard from, nor do his answers reappear on the four-way signal box.

Experimenter Feedback   At various points in the experiment the subject may turn to the experimenter for advice on whether he should continue to administer shocks. Or he may indicate that he does not wish to go on. It was important to standardize the experimenter's responses to these inquiries and reactions.

If the subject indicated his unwillingness to go on, the experimenter responded with a sequence of "prods," using as many as necessary to bring the subject into line.

Prod 1: Please continue or *Please go on.*
Prod 2: The experiment requires that you continue.
Prod 3: It is absolutely essential that you continue.
Prod 4: You have no other choice, you must go on.

The prods were always made in sequence: Only if Prod 1 had been unsuccessful, could Prod 2 be used. If the subject refused to obey the experimenter after Prod 4, the experiment was terminated. The experimenter's tone of voice was at all times firm, but not impolite. The sequence was begun anew on each occasion that the subject balked or showed reluctance to follow orders.

Special Prods   If the subject asked if the learner was liable to suffer permanent physical injury, the experimenter said:

Although the shocks may be painful, there is no permanent tissue damage, so please go on. [Followed by Prods 2, 3, and 4 if necessary.]

If the subject said that the learner did not want to go on, the experimenter replied:

Whether the learner likes it or not, you must go on until he has learned all the word pairs correctly. So please go on. [Followed by Prods 2, 3, and 4 if necessary.]

Dependent Measures

The primary dependent measure for any subject is the maximum shock he administers before he refuses to go any further. In principle this may vary from 0 (for a subject who refuses to administer even the first shock) to 30 (for a subject who administers the highest shock on the generator). A subject who breaks off the experiment at any point prior to administering the thirtieth shock level is termed a *defiant* subject. One who complies with experimental commands fully, and proceeds to administer all shock levels commanded, is termed an *obedient* subject.

Further Records   With few exceptions, experimental sessions were recorded on magnetic tape. Occasional photographs were taken through one-way mirrors. Notes were kept on any unusual behavior occurring during the course of the experiments. On occasion, additional observers were directed to write objective descriptions of the subjects' behavior. The latency and duration of shocks were measured by accurate timing devices.

Interview and Dehoax   Following the experiment, subjects were interviewed; open-ended questions, projective measures, and attitude scales were employed. After the interview, procedures were undertaken to assure that the subject would leave the laboratory in a state of well being. A friendly reconciliation was arranged between the subject and the victim, and an effort was made to reduce any tensions that arose as a result of the experiment.

RESULTS

Preliminary Notions

Before giving an account of the experimental results, it is instructive to consider how persons predict others will perform when commanded to administer powerful shocks to another person. Fourteen Yale seniors, all psychology majors, were provided with a detailed description of the experimental situation. They were asked to reflect carefully on it, and to predict the behavior of 100 hypothetical subjects. More specifically, they were instructed to plot the distribution of obedience of "100 Americans of diverse occupations, and ranging in age from 20 to 50 years," who were placed in the experimental situation.

There was considerable agreement among the respondents on the expected behavior of hypothetical subjects. All respondents predicted that only an insignificant minority would go through to the end of the shock series. (The estimates ranged from 0 to 3 percent; i.e., the most "pessimistic" member of the class predicted that of 100 persons, 3 would continue through to the most potent shock available on the shock generator—450 volts.) The class mean was 1.2 percent. The question was also posed informally to colleagues of the author, and the most general feeling was that few if any subjects would go beyond the designation Very Strong Shock.

Result of Experiment 1

Subjects Accept Situation   With few exceptions subjects were convinced of the reality of the experimental situation, that they were administering shocks to another person, and the most potent shocks were extremely painful. In the post-experimental interview subjects were asked: "How painful to the learner were the last few shocks that you administered to him?" Subjects were instructed to indicate their answers on a printed 14-point scale ranging from "Not at all painful" to "Extremely painful." The modal response was 14 (Extremely painful) with the mean at 13.42.

Signs of Extreme Tension   Many subjects showed signs of nervousness in the experimental situation, and especially upon administering the more powerful shocks. In a large number of cases the degree of tension reached extremes that are rarely seen in sociopsychological laboratory studies. Subjects were observed to sweat, tremble, stutter, bite their lips, groan, and dig their fingernails into their flesh. These were characteristic rather than exceptional responses to the experiment.

One sign of tension was the regular occurrence of nervous laughing fits. Fourteen of the 40 subjects showed definite signs of nervous laughter and smiling. The laughter seemed entirely out of place, even bizarre. Full-blown, uncontrollable seizures were observed for 3 subjects. On one occasion we observed a seizure so violently convulsive that it was necessary to call a halt to the experiment. The subject, a 46-year-old encyclopedia salesman, was seriously embarrassed by his untoward and uncontrollable behavior. In the post-experimental interviews subjects took pains to point out that they were not sadistic types, and that the laughter did not mean they enjoyed shocking the victim.

Distribution of Scores   It had been conjectured that persons would not, in general, agree to administer shocks beyond the level designated as Very Strong Shock. The distribution of maximum shocks for this experiment is shown in Table 2. The obtained distribution of scores deviates radically from the prediction.

Upon command of the experimenter, each of the 40 subjects went beyond the expected breakoff point. No subject stopped prior to administering Shock Level 20. (At this level—300 volts—the victim kicks on the wall and no longer provides answers to the teacher's multiple choice questions.)

Of the 40 subjects, 5 refused to obey the experimental commands beyond the 300-volt level. Four more subjects administered one further shock, and then refused to go on. Two broke off at the 330-volt level, and 1 each at 345, 360, and 375 volts. Thus a total of 14 subjects defied the experimenter. It is instructive to reprint their remarks at the point of defiance, as transcribed from the tape recordings:

> *[0124] I think he's trying to communicate, he's knocking Well it's not fair to shock the guy these are terrific volts. I don't think this is very humane Oh, I can't go on with this; no, this isn't right. It's a hell of an experiment. The guy is suffering in there. No, I don't want to go on. This is crazy. [Subject refused to administer more shocks.]*

> *[0123] He's hanging in there. I'm gonna chicken out. I'd like to continue, but I can't do that to a man I'm sorry I can't do that to a man. I'll hurt his heart. You take your check No really, I couldn't do it.*

These subjects were frequently in a highly agitated and even angered state. Sometimes, verbal protest was at a minimum, and the subject simply got up from his chair in front of the shock generator, and indicated that he wished to leave the laboratory.

Of the 40 subjects, 26 obeyed the orders of the experimenter to the end, proceeding to punish the victim until they reached the most potent shock available on the shock generator. At that point, the experimenter called a halt to the session. (The maximum shock is labeled 450 volts, and is two steps beyond the designation: Danger: Severe Shock.) Although obedient subjects

TABLE 2 / Distribution of Breakoff Points

Verbal Designation and Voltage Indication	Number of Subjects for Whom This Was Maximum Shock
Slight Shock	
15	
30	0
45	0
60	0
Moderate Shock	
75	0
90	0
105	0
120	0
Strong Shock	
135	0
150	0
165	0
180	0
Very Strong Shock	
195	0
210	0
225	0
240	0
Intense Shock	
255	0
270	0
285	0
300	5
Extreme Intensity Shock	
315	4
330	2
345	1
360	1
Danger: Severe Shock	
375	1
390	0
405	0
420	0
XXX	
435	0
450	26

continued to administer shocks, they often did so under extreme stress. Some expressed reluctance to administer shocks beyond the 300-volt level, and displayed fears similar to those who defied the experimenter; yet they obeyed.

After the maximum shocks had been delivered, and the experimenter called a halt to the proceedings, many obedient subjects heaved sighs of relief, mopped their brows, rubbed their fingers over their eyes, or nervously fumbled cigarettes. Some shook their heads, apparently in regret. Some subjects had remained calm throughout the experiment, and displayed only minimal signs of tension from beginning to end.

DISCUSSION

The experiment yielded two findings that were surprising. The first finding concerns the sheer strength of obedient tendencies manifested in this situation. Subjects have learned from childhood that it is a fundamental breach of moral conduct to hurt another person against his will. Yet, 26 subjects abandon this tenet in following the instructions of an authority who has no special powers to enforce his commands. To disobey would bring no material loss to the subject; no punishment would ensue. It is clear from the remarks and outward behavior of many participants that in punishing the victim they are often acting against their own values. Subjects often expressed deep disapproval of shocking a man in the face of his objections, and others denounced it as stupid and senseless. Yet the majority complied with the experimental commands. This outcome was surprising from two perspectives: first, from the standpoint of predictions made in the questionnaire described earlier. (Here, however, it is possible that the remoteness of the respondents from the actual situation, and the difficulty of conveying to them the concrete details of the experiment, could account for the serious underestimation of obedience.)

But the results were also unexpected to persons who observed the experiment in progress, through one-way mirrors. Observers often uttered expressions of disbelief upon seeing a subject administer more powerful shocks to the victim. These persons had a full acquaintance with the details of the situation, and yet systematically underestimated the amount of obedience that subjects would display.

The second unanticipated effect was the extraordinary tension generated by the procedures. One might suppose that a subject would simply break off or continue as his conscience dictated. Yet, this is very far from what happened. There were striking reactions of tension and emotional strain. One observer related:

> *I observed a mature and initially poised businessman enter the laboratory smiling and confident. Within 20 minutes he was reduced to a twitching, stuttering wreck, who was rapidly approaching a point of nervous collapse. He constantly pulled on his earlobe, and twisted his hands. At one point he pushed his fist into his forehead and muttered: "Oh God, let's stop it." And yet he continued to respond to every word of the experimenter and obeyed to the end.*

Any understanding of the phenomenon of obedience must rest on an analysis of the particular conditions in which it occurs. The following features of the experiment go some distance in explaining the high amount of obedience observed in the situation.

1. The experiment is sponsored by and takes place on the grounds of an institution of unimpeachable reputation, Yale University. It may be reasonably presumed that the personnel are competent and reputable. The importance of this background authority is now being studied by conducting a series of experiments outside of New Haven, and without any visible ties to the university.

2. The experiment is, on the face of it, designed to attain a worthy purpose—advancement of knowledge about learning and memory. Obedience occurs not as an end in itself, but as an instrumental element in a situation that the subject construes as significant, and meaningful. He may not be able to see its full significance, but he may properly assume that the experimenter does.

3. The subject perceives that the victim has voluntarily submitted to the authority system of the experimenter. He is not (at first) an unwilling captive impressed for involuntary service. He has taken the trouble to come to the laboratory presumably to aid the experimental research. That he later becomes an involuntary subject does not alter the fact that, initially, he consented to participate without qualification. Thus he has in some degree incurred an obligation toward the experimenter.

4. The subject, too, has entered the experiment voluntarily, and perceives himself under obligation to aid the experimenter. He has made a commitment, and to disrupt the experiment is a repudiation of this initial promise of aid.

5. Certain features of the procedure strengthen the subject's sense of obligation to the experimenter. For one, he has been paid for coming to the laboratory. In part this is canceled out by the experimenter's statement that:

Of course, as in all experiments, the money is yours simply for coming to the laboratory. From this point on, no matter what happens, the money is yours.[2]

6. From the subject's standpoint, the fact that he is the teacher and the other man the learner is purely a chance consequence (it is determined by drawing lots) and he, the subject, ran the same risk as the other man in being assigned the role of learner. Since the assignment of positions in the experiment was achieved by fair means, the learner is deprived of any basis of complaint on this count. (A similar situation obtains in Army units, in which—in the absence of volunteers—a particularly dangerous mission may be assigned by drawing lots, and the unlucky soldier is expected to bear his misfortune with sportsmanship.)

7. There is, at best, ambiguity with regard to the prerogatives of a psychologist and the corresponding rights of his subject. There is a vagueness of expectation concerning what a psychologist may require of his subject, and when he is overstepping acceptable limits. Moreover, the experiment occurs in a closed setting, and thus provides no opportunity for the subject to remove these ambiguities by discussion with others. There are few standards that seem directly applicable to the situation, which is a novel one for most subjects.

8. The subjects are assured that the shocks administered to the subject are "painful but not dangerous." Thus they assume that the discomfort caused the victim is momentary, while the scientific gains resulting from the experiment are enduring.

9. Through Shock Level 20 the victim continues to provide answers on the signal box. The subject may construe this as a sign that the victim is still willing to "play the game." It is only after Shock Level 20 that the victim repudiates the rules completely, refusing to answer further.

These features help to explain the high amount of obedience obtained in this experiment. Many of the arguments raised need not remain matters of speculation, but can be reduced to testable propositions to be confirmed or disproved by further experiments.[3]

The following features of the experiment concern the nature of the conflict which the subject faces.

10. The subject is placed in a position in which he must respond to the competing demands of two persons: the experimenter and the victim. The conflict must be resolved by meeting the demands of one or the other; satisfaction of the victim and the experimenter are mutually exclusive. Moreover, the resolution must take the form of a highly visible action, that of continuing to shock the victim or breaking off the experiment. Thus the subject is forced into a public conflict that does not permit any completely satisfactory solution.

11. While the demands of the experimenter carry the weight of scientific authority, the demands of the victim spring from his personal experience of pain and suffering. The two claims need not be regarded as equally pressing and legitimate. The experimenter seeks an abstract scientific datum; the victim cries out for relief from physical suffering caused by the subject's actions.

12. The experiment gives the subject little time for reflection. The conflict comes on rapidly. It is only minutes after the subject has been seated before the shock generator that the victim begins his protests. Moreover, the subject perceives that he has gone through but two-thirds of the shock levels at the time the subject's first protests are heard. Thus he understands that the conflict will have a persistent aspect to it, and may well become more intense as increasingly more powerful shocks are required. The rapidity with which the conflict descends on the subject, and his realization that it is predictably recurrent may well be sources of tension to him.

13. At a more general level, the conflict stems from the opposition of two deeply ingrained behavior dispositions: first, the disposition not to harm other people, and second, the tendency to obey those whom we perceive to be legitimate authorities.

REFERENCES

Adorno, T., Frenkel-Brunswik, E., Levinson, D. J., and Sanford, R. N. *The authoritarian personality.* New York: Harper, 1950.

Arendt, H. What was authority? In C. J Friedrich (ed.), *Authority.* Cambridge: Harvard Univer. Press, 1958. Pp. 81–112.

Binet, A. *La suggestibilité.* Paris: Schleicher, 1900.

Buss, A. H. *The psychology of aggression.* New York: Wiley, 1961.

Cartwright, S. (ed.) *Studies in social power.* Ann Arbor: University of Michigan Institute for Social Research, 1959.

Charcot, J. M. *Oeuvres complètes.* Paris: Bureaux du Progrès Médical, 1881.

Frank, J. D. Experimental studies of personal pressure and resistance. *J. Gen. Psychol.* 1944, *30*, 23–64.

Freidrich, C. J. (ed.) *Authority.* Cambridge: Harvard Univer. Press, 1958.

Milgram, S. Dynamics of obedience. Washington: National Science Foundation, 25 January 1961. (Mimeo).

Milgram, S. Some conditions of obedience and disobedience to authority. *Hum. Relat.,* 1965, *18,* 57–76.

Rokeach, M. Authority, authoritarianism, and conformity. In I. A. Berg and B. M. Bass (eds.), *Conformity and deviation.* New York: Harper, 1961. Pp. 230–257.

Snow, C. P. Either-or. *Progressive,* 1961 (Feb.) 24.

Weber, M. *The theory of social and economic organization.* Oxford: Oxford Univer. Press, 1947.

ENDNOTES

1. A related technique, making use of a shock generator, was reported by Buss (1961) for the study of aggression in the laboratory. Despite the considerable similarity of technical detail in the experimental procedures, each investigator proceeded in ignorance of the other's work. Milgram provided plans and photographs of his shock generator, experimental procedure, and first results in a report to the National Science Foundation in January 1961. This report received only limited circulation. Buss reported his procedure six months later, but to a wider audience. Subsequently, technical information and reports were exchanged. The present article was first received in the editor's office on December 27, 1961; it was resubmitted with deletions on July 27, 1962.

2. Forty-three subjects, undergraduates at Yale University, were run in the experiment without payment. The results are very similar to those obtained with paid subjects.

3. A series of recently completed experiments employing the obedience paradigm is reported in Milgram (1965).

This research was supported by a grant (NSF G-17916) from the National Science Foundation. Exploratory studies conducted in 1960 were supported by a grant from the Higgins Fund at Yale University. The research assistance of Alan E. Elms and Jon Wayland is gratefully acknowledged.

CRITICAL THINKING QUESTIONS

1. What are the ethical implications of this study? In particular, are you satisfied that no lasting harm was done to the participants? Would the debriefing at the end of the experiment be sufficient to eliminate any long-term problems from participation in the study? What about short-term effects? Many of the subjects obviously suffered during the experiment. Was the infliction of this distress on the subjects justified? Support your answers. (*Note:* For a good discussion of the ethics of the study, see the Baumrind and Milgram articles cited below.)

2. What are the implications of this study for people accused of committing atrocities? Suppose that the results of this study had been known when the Nazi war criminals were put on trial in Nuremberg. Could the information have been used in their defense? Do the results remove some of the personal responsibility that people have for their actions? Explain your answers.

3. Subjects were paid a nominal amount for participation in the study. They were told that the money was theirs to keep simply because they showed up, regardless of what happened after they arrived. Do you think that this payment was partly responsible for the findings? Why or why not? Do you think that paying someone, no matter how small the amount, somehow changes the dynamics of the situation? Explain.

ADDITIONAL RELATED READINGS

Baumrind, D. (1964). Some thoughts on the ethics of research after reading Milgram's "Behavioral study of obedience." *American Psychologist, 19,* 421–423.

Burger, J. M. (2009). Replicating Milgram: Would people still obey today? *American Psychologist, 64*(1), 1–11.

Milgram, S. (1964). Issues in the study of obedience: A reply to Baumrind. *American Psychologist, 19,* 848–852.

ARTICLE 27

Conformity is a fact of life yet a behavior toward which we have decidedly ambivalent feelings. On the one hand, none of us like to think of ourselves as *conformist*. For most people, this word has a fairly negative connotation, suggesting people who mindlessly go along with the group rather than thinking for themselves. Even people who see themselves as nonconformist (e.g., in how they dress) often are just conforming to an alternative set of norms. Perhaps the best example of this is the teenager who dyes his hair blue because he wants to be "different in a conforming sort of way."

On the other hand, conformity is the very background of culture. How could we drive our cars, engage in social interactions, or do just about anything involving other people if we did not conform to what was expected of us in those situations? Without some level of conformity, total chaos would result. Even when we feel independent in the decisions we make, in fact, our choice is not *whether* to conform but rather which norms to conform to.

So, why is conformity such a vital part of the human experience? At a very basic level, it helps to promote survival of the group. After all, people are fundamentally social creatures, and without conformity, the daily interactions that make life possible would be impossible. But people conform for other reasons, as well. One such reason may be to obtain information about an otherwise ambiguous situation. For example, if you wanted to know the distance between Washington, DC, and New York City, you could look it up in a book. That information is a *fact:* an agreed-upon, accepted piece of knowledge. As such, you need only to consult the proper source to find it.

But how much of social life is about readily determinable facts? Not much. Most of the situations and questions we face are not factual but rather matters of belief, custom, or opinion. Whom should I vote for? What is the right thing to do? What is the best way to live my life? The answers to questions such as these often come from other people. Thus, another reason we conform is because other people often are able to provide us with clues for how to behave, especially when the situation is otherwise ambiguous and we are unsure of what is expected of us.

People also conform to be accepted. If you have ever deviated from the norms or beliefs of a group to which you belong, you already know the intensely uncomfortable experience of being rejected or pressured by others in the group. To be accepted by the group, we must go along with them. Thus, we sometimes conform just to be accepted and to fit into a particular group.

Of course, we sometimes conform to the actual behaviors of those around us. We see people acting in a certain way, and we do likewise. But very often, we base our behaviors not on what we actually *see* others doing but on what we *think* they are doing. Thus, we may be tempted to do something because "everyone else is doing it," even if in reality, they are not. This tendency to use social norms of what we think others are doing has been capitalized on by groups trying to change behavior in a more socially desirable direction. For example, some college campuses have used *social norms* to help reduce binge drinking by informing students as to the real rates of binge drinking on campus. The reasoning is that individuals often overestimate the frequency and amount of binge drinking, and once they correctly know that their behavior is well above the norm, they will lower their drinking accordingly. Some research supports this type of finding. But not all. The following article by P. Wesley Schultz, Jessica M. Nolan, Robert B. Cialdini, Noah J. Goldstein, and Vladus Griskevicius examines the most effective means for using social norms to change behavior.

The Constructive, Destructive, and Reconstructive Power of Social Norms

■ P. Wesley Schultz, Jessica M. Nolan, Robert B. Cialdini, Noah J. Goldstein, and Vladas Griskevicius

ABSTRACT

Despite a long tradition of effectiveness in laboratory tests, normative messages have had mixed success in changing behavior in field contexts, with some studies showing boomerang effects. To test a theoretical account of this inconsistency, we conducted a field experiment in which normative messages were used to promote *household energy conservation. As predicted, a descriptive normative message detailing average neighborhood usage produced either desirable energy savings or the undesirable boomerang effect, depending on whether households were already consuming at a low or high rate. Also as predicted, adding an injunctive message (conveying social approval or disapproval) eliminated the boomerang effect. The results offer an explanation for the mixed success of persuasive appeals based on social norms and suggest how such appeals should be properly crafted.*

After several decades of controversy over the role of norms in predicting behavior, the research has clearly established that social norms not only spur but also guide action in direct and meaningful ways (Aarts & Dijksterhuis, 2003; Cialdini, Kallgren, & Reno, 1991; Darley & Latané, 1970; Goldstein, Cialdini, & Griskevicius, 2006; Kerr, 1995; Terry & Hogg, 2001). Given this asserted power of social norms, during the past decade there has been a surge of programs that have delivered normative information as a primary tool for changing socially significant behaviors, such as alcohol consumption, drug use, disordered eating, gambling, littering, and recycling (e.g., Donaldson, Graham, & Hansen, 1994; Larimer & Neighbors, 2003; Neighbors, Larimer, & Lewis, 2004; Schultz, 1999; Schultz, Tabanico, & Rendón, in press). Such *social-norms marketing* campaigns have emerged as an alternative to more traditional approaches (e.g., information campaigns, moral exhortation, fear-inducing messages) designed to reduce undesirable conduct (Donaldson, Graham, Piccinin, & Hansen, 1995).

The rationale for the social-norms marketing approach is based on two consistent findings: (a) The majority of individuals overestimate the prevalence of many undesirable behaviors, such as alcohol use among peers (e.g., Borsari & Carey, 2003; Prentice & Miller, 1993), and (b) individuals use their perceptions of peer norms as a standard against which to compare their own behaviors (e.g., Baer, Stacy, & Larimer, 1991; Clapp & McDonell, 2000; Perkins & Berkowitz, 1986). Social-norms marketing campaigns seek to reduce the occurrence of deleterious behaviors by correcting targets' misperceptions regarding the behaviors' prevalence. The perception of prevalence is commonly referred to as the *descriptive norm* governing a behavior (Cialdini et al., 1991).

Social-norms marketing campaigns have been deemed so full of promise that nearly half of 746 U.S. colleges and universities surveyed by the Harvard School of Public Health in 2002 had adopted them in some form to combat collegiate binge drinking (Wechsler et al., 2003). However, despite the widespread adoption of social-norms marketing campaigns, evidence for the success of such programs has been surprisingly mixed. Although many studies appear to confirm the effectiveness of the social marketing approach (e.g., Agostinelli, Brown, & Miller, 1995; Haines & Spear, 1996; Neighbors et al., 2004), other studies have failed to produce substantial changes in behavior (e.g., Clapp, Lange, Russell, Shillington, & Voas, 2003; Granfield, 2005; Peeler, Far, Miller, & Brigham, 2000; Russell, Clapp, & DeJong, 2005; Werch et al., 2000). In fact,

some studies indicate that social-norms marketing campaigns have actually increased the undesirable behaviors and misperceptions they set out to decrease (e.g., Perkins, Haines, & Rice, 2005; Wechsler et al., 2003; Werch et al., 2000).

A closer analysis of social-norms theory and research provides a potential explanation for the lack of effects and suggests the possibility of boomerang effects. Descriptive norms provide a standard from which people do not want to deviate. Because people measure the appropriateness of their behavior by how far away they are from the norm, being deviant is being above *or* below the norm. For example, although the majority of college students do overestimate the prevalence of alcohol consumption on campus (see Berkowitz, 2004, for a review), a substantial proportion of them—as many as one fifth by some estimates (e.g., Perkins et al., 2005) and nearly one half by others (e.g., Wechsler & Kuo, 2000)—actually underestimate its prevalence. Because a social-norms marketing campaign provides specific descriptive normative information that can serve as a point of comparison for an individual's own behavior, the descriptive norm acts as a magnet for behavior for individuals both above and below the average. Consequently, a college campaign targeting alcohol consumption might motivate students who previously consumed less alcohol than the norm to consume more. Thus, although providing descriptive normative information may decrease an undesirable behavior among individuals who perform that behavior at a rate above the norm, the same message may actually serve to increase the undesirable behavior among individuals who perform that behavior at a rate below the norm.

Social-norms campaigns are intended to reduce problem behaviors (or increase prosocial behavior) by conveying the message that deleterious behaviors are occurring less often than most people think. But for individuals who already abstain from the undesirable behavior, such normative information can produce unintended and undesirable boomerang effects. Is there a way to eliminate them? According to the focus theory of normative conduct (Cialdini et al., 1991), there is a second type of social norm, in addition to the descriptive norm, that has a powerful influence on behavior—the *injunctive norm*. Whereas descriptive norms refer to perceptions of what is commonly done in a given situation, injunctive norms refer to perceptions of what is commonly approved or disapproved within the culture (Reno, Cialdini, & Kallgren, 1993). Focus theory predicts that if only one of the two types of norms is prominent in an individual's consciousness, it will exert the stronger influence on behavior (Cialdini & Goldstein, 2004). Thus, in situations in which descriptive normative information may normally produce an undesirable boomerang effect, it is possible that adding an injunctive message indicating that the desired behavior is approved may prevent that effect.

Schultz, P.W.; Nolan, J.M.; Cialdini, R.B.; Goldstein, N.J.; & Griskevicus, V. *Psychological Science, 18* (5), 429–434. Copyright © 2007 by the Association for Psychological Science. Reprinted by permission of SAGE Publications.

THE CURRENT RESEARCH

The purpose of the current research was to explore how normative information may differentially affect an important social behavior depending on whether the message recipients' behavior is above or below the norm. In a California community, we performed a field experiment examining the effects of normative information on household energy consumption. All households received feedback about how much energy they had consumed in previous weeks and descriptive normative information about the average consumption of other households in their neighborhood. Households were divided into two categories at each observation period: those with energy consumption above average for the community and those with energy consumption below average for the community. Households were matched on a baseline measure of energy consumption, and then half of the households were randomly assigned to receive only the descriptive normative information. The other half received the descriptive normative information plus an injunctive message conveying that their energy consumption was either approved or disapproved; specifically, households that consumed less than the average received a message displaying a positively valenced emoticon (☺), whereas those that consumed more than the average received a message displaying a negatively valenced emoticon (☹). The dependent measure was residents' subsequent actual household energy consumption.

We had three main predictions. First, we expected that descriptive normative information would decrease energy consumption in households consuming more energy than their neighborhood average. Such a result would be indicative of the constructive power of social norms, demonstrating that normative information can facilitate proenvironmental behavior. Second, we expected that descriptive normative information would increase energy consumption—that is, produce an undesirable boomerang effect—in households consuming less energy than their neighborhood average. Such a result would be indicative of the destructive power of social norms, demonstrating that a well-intended application of normative information can actually serve to decrease proenvironmental behavior. Third, we expected that providing both descriptive normative information and an injunctive message that other people approve of low-consumption behavior would prevent the undesirable boomerang effect in households consuming less energy than their neighborhood average; that is, we expected these households to continue to consume at low rates. Such a result would be indicative of the reconstructive power of injunctive messages to eliminate the untoward effects of a descriptive norm.

Method

Participants and Design

Participants were 290 households in San Marcos, CA, with visible energy meters. They were selected from three census-block groups and notified about the study through a mailed letter. (Although they were offered the opportunity not to participate, none did so.) The study was a 2 (feedback: descriptive norm only vs. descriptivee plus injunctive information) × 2 (consumption: above- vs. below-average energy consumption) × 3 (time: base-line, short-term follow-up, longer-term follow-up) mixed-factorial design. Feedback and consumption were between-participants factors, and time was a within-participants factor.

Procedure

Prior to any experimental intervention, trained research assistants read the households' electricity meters twice within a 2-week period.[1] The difference between these two readings was used to establish an initial baseline measure of daily energy usage for each household. Households were matched on this baseline measure and randomly assigned to either the descriptive-norm-only condition or the descriptive-plus-injunctive-information condition. This initial baseline energy usage was used for the descriptive normative feedback and to determine the injunctive feedback for the first written message (i.e., whether the household consumed more or less than the average). Two weeks later, researchers took a third meter reading and left written messages on residents' doors. These doorhangers reported energy consumption from the baseline period. One week after that, a second doorhanger was distributed; this message contained normative feedback that reported energy usage between the second baseline reading and distribution of the first doorhanger. Researchers also took a fourth meter reading while distributing this second doorhanger. We took a final meter reading 3 weeks after the distribution of the second feedback message.

Short-term change in electricity usage was calculated by subtracting the meter reading taken the day the first message was distributed from the reading taken the day the second message was distributed. Longer-term change in electricity usage was calculated by subtracting the meter reading taken the day of the second message from the final meter reading.

---

[1]During the training of our research team, we assessed the reliability of our meter readings. On 157 occasions, two research assistants were assigned to read the same meter. These independent readings correlated at $r = .999$. In addition, during our training period, we were able to obtain electricity-usage data from the local utility company for 92 houses in this study. The correlation between this measure and our readings was .96 and .99 on 2 separate months.

Intervention

After the baseline period, households received a total of two messages left at their doors. For households in the descriptive-norm-only condition, each message contained (a) handwritten information about how much energy (in kilowatt-hours per day) they had used in the previous week (or weeks for the second doorhanger), (b) descriptive normative information about the actual energy consumption of the average household in their neighborhood during that same period (in kilowatt-hours per day), and (c) preprinted suggestions for how to conserve energy (e.g., use fans instead of air conditioning). Households in the descriptive-plus-injunctive-information condition received the same information as did those in the descriptive-norm-only group, with one key addition: If the household had consumed less than the average for the neighborhood, the researcher drew a happy face (☺); if the household had consumed more than the average, the researcher drew a sad face (☹). The valence of the emoticon was used to communicate an injunctive message of approval or disapproval for the amount of energy being consumed. All messages were clearly identified with the university logo and a telephone number that could be used to contact our research team with questions or concerns.

Results

Of the 290 households, half were randomly assigned to receive the combined message (descriptive-norm feedback plus the injunctive emoticon), and the other half were randomly assigned to receive only the descriptive-norm feedback. Three households called to withdraw from the study following the initial normative-feedback distribution, resulting in a final sample of 287. At each measurement period, daily household energy consumption was positively skewed (M = 15.03, SD = 7.10, skew = 1.39, range = 1.63–35.88), resulting in more households below the mean than above. Although this introduced slightly unequal sample sizes for the above- and below-average groups, we used the mean as the dividing point for consumption because we believed it would provide a more meaningful number than other measures of central tendency when reported to residents.

Short-Term Change in Electricity Usage

The primary focus of our analyses was change in energy consumption, and our key interest was in the pair-wise comparison of baseline and follow-up usage in each of the four between-subjects cells (see Fig. 1a). For households that consumed more than the average during the baseline period, the descriptive-norm-only feedback produced a significant decrease in energy consumption relative to the baseline (M = 20.25, SE = 1.03 vs. baseline M = 21.47, SE = 0.89; n = 64), $t(63)$ = 2.17, p_{rep} = .93, d = 0.55. Figure 1a shows this significant change as a reduction of 1.22 kWh in daily energy consumption. Thus, the descriptive normative information led to the desired decrease in energy

FIGURE 1 / Difference between baseline daily energy consumption and daily energy consumption during the (a) short-term and (b) longer-term follow-up periods. Results are shown for the four conditions created by crossing baseline energy consumption (above vs. below average) with feedback received (descriptive normative feedback only vs. descriptive feedback combined with an injunctive message). Error bars show the 95% confidence interval of the pair-wise difference between usage during the follow-up period and during the baseline.

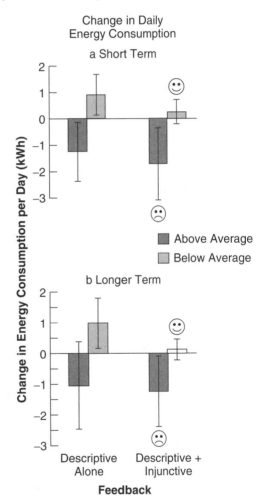

consumption for the households that were consuming more than the average for their neighborhood. This result illustrates the constructive potential of social norms.

In contrast, for households that were below the mean on baseline energy consumption, the descriptive-norm-only message produced an increase in energy consumption from baseline (M = 11.27, SE = 0.46 vs. baseline M = 10.38, SE = 0.33; n = 79), $t(78)$ = 2.28, p_{rep} = .94, d = 0.52. This change is shown in Figure la as an increase of 0.89 kWh in daily energy consumption. Thus, the descriptive normative information led to an undesired increase in energy consumption for the households that were consuming less than the average for the neighborhood—a clear example of the destructive potential of social norms.

When the injunctive message was added to the descriptive normative feedback, households that were consuming less energy than average continued to consume at the desirable low rate ($M = 10.58$, $SE = 0.38$ vs. baseline $M = 10.34$, $SE = 0.33$; $n = 81$), $t(80) = 1.04$, n.s. That is, the undesirable boomerang effect of increased usage among households low in energy consumption was eliminated when an injunctive message was added to the descriptive normative information. This result highlights the reconstructive potential of social norms. Finally, for households consuming above the average, the combined descriptive-plus-injunctive message served to decrease energy consumption ($M = 18.91$, $SE = 0.73$ vs. baseline $M = 20.63$, $SE = 0.64$; $n = 63$), $t(62) = 2.49$, $p_{rep} = .96$, $d = 0.63$.

Longer-Term Changes in Energy Consumption
Of the 287 households in the study, 41 were inconsistently above or below the average across the 2 weeks of normative feedback and were therefore excluded from the analyses of longer-term change. There were no significant differences in inconsistency rate across the four experimental conditions.

Our analyses of longer-term change followed those for short-term change, focusing primarily on planned pair-wise comparisons of baseline and follow-up energy usage. As shown in Figure lb, the outcomes were nearly identical to those for the shorter-term measure. For those households that were high in energy consumption at baseline, the descriptive-norm-only message continued to produce the (constructive) decrease in energy consumption, although the difference was not conventionally significant (baseline $M = 22.32$, $SE = 1.05$ vs. longer-term $M = 21.29$, $SE = 0.92$; $n = 52$), $t(51) = 1.45$, n.s. For those households initially low in energy consumption, the descriptive-norm-only condition produced a significant increase in electricity usage (longer-term $M = 11.13$, $SE = 0.44$ vs. baseline $M = 10.15$, $SE = 0.34$; $n = 68$), $t(67) = 2.42$, $p_{rep} = .95$, $d = 0.59$. That is, the descriptive normative message continued to produce the (destructive) boomerang effect. However, the combined injunctive-plus-descriptive message produced no change from baseline for low-consuming households (longer-term $M = 10.14$, $SE = 0.37$ vs. baseline $M = 10.04$, $SE = 0.35$; $n = 70$), $t(69) = 0.64$, n.s., again illustrating the reconstructive power of normative information when an injunctive element is added to the descriptive normative feedback. Finally, for households that initially consumed more energy than the neighborhood average, the combined descriptive-plus-injunctive feedback continued to produce a significant decrease in energy consumption relative to the baseline (baseline $M = 20.62$,

$SE = 0.64$ vs. longer-term $M = 19.39$, $SE = 0.62$; $n = 56$), $t(55) = 2.13$, $p_{rep} = .93$, $d = 0.58$. Overall, the results for both the short-term measure and the longer-term measure were consistent with predictions.

DISCUSSION
The findings of this experiment are highly consistent with predictions derived from the focus theory of normative conduct (Cialdini et al., 1991). Providing residents with descriptive normative information had a dramatically different effect depending on whether they were initially above or below the average level of energy consumption in their neighborhood. Providing high-energy-consuming households with descriptive normative information regarding the average home energy usage in their neighborhood constructively decreased energy consumption. In contrast, for households that were initially low in their base rates of energy consumption, the same descriptive message produced a destructive boomerang effect, leading to increased levels of energy consumption. However, adding an injunctive component to the message proved reconstructive by buffering this unwelcome boomerang effect. That is, for people who were initially low in energy consumption, the same descriptive normative information combined with an injunctive message of approval led to continued consumption at the desirable low rate, rather than a significant move toward the mean. Moreover, despite concerns that normative interventions have an effect for only a short time, the longer-term results indicate that the effects of the normative messages continued to be strong even 4 weeks after the initial intervention.

These findings provide a potential explanation for the mixed effects of normative messages in field contexts. Although social-norm campaigns are typically aimed at individuals whose behavior is less desirable than the norm, the widespread nature of these campaigns nearly ensures that those whose behavior is more desirable than the norm will also receive the message. Our results suggest that for those individuals who tend to engage in destructive behaviors, a descriptive normative message can be a guide to engaging in more constructive behavior; in contrast, for those individuals who already engage in the constructive behavior, a descriptive normative message can be a spur to engaging in more destructive behavior. For example, telling students that a majority of their peers drink "four or fewer drinks when they party" sends the message that abstaining from drinking is deviant. Our results demonstrate the potential for such messages to boomerang, but the results also show that an injunctive element of approval is reconstructive in its ability to ameliorate these unwanted effects.

Although the results from our field experiment are quite clear, there are several aspects that warrant additional comment. First, we should point out that the descriptive norm produced the boomerang effect among individuals who were already engaging in the desired behavior. Thus, the overall impact of a normative education campaign will depend on the distribution of the behavior in the population; a campaign could produce an increase, decrease, or no change in the behavior (the latter being most likely). For example, if the distribution of the target behavior is strongly skewed in the positive direction, such that more people are below the norm than above it, then a normative message might increase the behavior in aggregate. Second, prior research has suggested that presenting aligned descriptive and injunctive norms can result in larger behavioral changes than presenting either type of norm in isolation (Cialdini, 2003). Our results show this overall pattern, although the differences were not statistically significant. For example, in the short term, the reduction in energy usage for high-consuming households was 1.72 kWh/day in the descriptive-plus-injunctive condition, compared with 1.22 kWh/day in the descriptive-only condition. Finally, it is useful to consider potential boundary conditions that might limit the range of behaviors to which normative social influence would apply. The target behavior in this study (energy conservation) has a direct personal benefit (saving money), is private, is reoccurring (rather than a one-time action), and has widespread social approval. Although we believe that the current findings will apply to a range of other behaviors (e.g., alcohol consumption, seat-belt use, littering, consumer choices, illegal downloading of music), future research should explore the appropriate boundary conditions.

ACKNOWLEDGMENTS

Funding for this study was provided by a grant from the Hewlett Foundation (2001–7396) and by National Science Foundation Graduate Research Fellowships to the fourth and fifth authors. Our appreciation goes to Veronica Briseño, Dulcinea Contreras, Matt Dorlaque, Reginald Hartfield, Edgar Medina, Laura Murphy, Leezel Nazareno, Rene Quiroz, Ronald Tilos, Monica Tinajero, and Christina Wade. Portions of this article were presented at the annual meeting of the American Psychological Society, Los Angeles, California, May 2005.

REFERENCES

Aarts, H., & Dijksterhuis, A. (2003). The silence of the library: Environment, situational norm, and social behavior. *Journal of Personality and Social Psychology, 84,* 18–28.

Agostinelli, G., Brown, J., & Miller, W. (1995). Effects of normative feedback on consumption among heavy drinking college students. *Journal of Drug Education, 25,* 31–40.

Baer, J.S., Stacy, A., & Larimer, M. (1991). Biases in the perception of drinking norms among college students. *Journal of Studies on Alcohol, 52,* 580–586.

Berkowitz, A.D. (2004). An overview of the social norms approach. In L. Lederman & L. Stewart (Eds.), *Changing the culture of college drinking* (pp. 193–214). Cresskill, NJ: Hampton Press.

Borsari, B., & Carey, K. (2003). Descriptive and injunctive norms in college drinking: A meta-analytic integration. *Journal of Studies on Alcohol, 64,* 331–341.

Cialdini, R.B. (2003). Crafting normative messages to protect the environment. *Current Directions in Psychological Science, 12,* 105–109.

Cialdini, R.B., & Goldstein, N.J. (2004). Social influence: Compliance and conformity. *Annual Review of Psychology, 55,* 591–622.

Cialdini, R.B., Kallgren, C.A., & Reno, R.R. (1991). A focus theory of normative conduct. *Advances in Experimental Social Psychology, 24,* 201–234.

Clapp, J.D., Lange, J.E., Russell, C., Shillington, A., & Voas, R. (2003). A failed norms social marketing campaign. *Journal of Studies on Alcohol, 64,* 409–414.

Clapp, J.D., & McDonnell, A. (2000). The relationship of perceptions of alcohol promotion and peer drinking norms to alcohol problems reported by college students. *Journal of College Student Development, 41,* 19–26.

Darley, J.M., & Latané, B. (1970). Norms and normative behavior: Field studies of social interdependence. In J. Macaulay & L. Berkowitz (Eds.), *Altruism and helping behavior* (pp. 83–102). New York: Academic Press.

Donaldson, S.I., Graham, J.W., & Hansen, W.B. (1994). Testing the generalizability of intervening mechanism theories: Understanding the effects of adolescent drug use prevention interventions. *Journal of Behavioral Medicine, 17,* 195–216.

Donaldson, S.I., Graham, J.W., Piccinin, A.M., & Hansen, W.B. (1995). Resistance-skills training and the onset of alcohol use: Evidence for beneficial and potentially harmful effects in public schools and in private Catholic schools. *Health Psychology, 14,* 291–300.

Goldstein, N.J., Cialdini, R.B., & Griskevicius, V. (2006). *A room with a viewpoint: Using normative appeals to motivate environmental conservation in a hotel setting.* Manuscript submitted for publication.

Granfield, R. (2005). Alcohol use in college: Limitations on the transformation of social norms. *Addiction Research and Theory, 13,* 281–292.

Haines, M., & Spear, S. (1996). Changing the perception of the norm: A strategy to decrease binge drinking among college students. *Journal of American College Health, 45,* 134–140.

Kerr, N.L. (1995). Norms in social dilemmas. In D. Schroeder (Ed.), *Social dilemmas: Perspectives on individuals and groups* (pp. 31–48). Westport, CT: Praeger.

Larimer, M.E., & Neighbors, C. (2003). Normative misperceptions and the impact of descriptive and injunctive norms on college student gambling. *Psychology of Addictive Behaviors, 17,* 235–243.

Neighbors, C., Larimer, M., & Lewis, M. (2004). Targeting misperceptions of descriptive drinking norms: Efficacy of a computer-delivered personalized normative feedback intervention. *Journal of Consulting and Clinical Psychology, 73,* 434–447.

Peeler, C.M., Far, J., Miller, J., & Brigham, T.A. (2000). An analysis of the effects of a program to reduce heavy drinking among college students. *Journal of Alcohol and Drug Education, 45,* 39–54.

Perkins, H.W., & Berkowitz, A.D. (1986). Perceiving the community norms of alcohol use among students: Some research implications for campus alcohol education programming. *International Journal of the Addictions, 21,* 961–976.

Perkins, H.W., Haines, M.P., & Rice, R. (2005). Misperceiving the college drinking norm and related problems: A nationwide study of exposure to prevention information, perceived norms and student alcohol misuse. *Journal of Studies on Alcohol, 66,* 470–478.

Prentice, D.A., & Miller, D.T. (1993). Pluralistic ignorance and alcohol use on campus: Some consequences of misperceiving the social norm. *Journal of Personality and Social Psychology, 64,* 243–256.

Reno, R., Cialdini, R., & Kallgren, C.A. (1993). The transsituational influence of social norms. *Journal of Personality and Social Psychology. 64,* 104–112.

Russell, C., Clapp, J.D., & DeJong, W. (2005). "Done 4": Analysis of a failed social norms marketing campaign. *Health Communication, 17,* 57–65.

Schultz, P.W. (1999). Changing behavior with normative feedback interventions: A field experiment on curbside recycling. *Basic and Applied Social Psychology, 21,* 25–36.

Schultz, P.W., Tabanico, J., & Rendón, T. (in press). Normative beliefs as agents of influence: Basic process and real-world applications.

In R. Prislin & W. Crano (Eds.), *Attitudes and persuasion.* New York: Psychology Press.

Terry, D.J., & Hogg, M.A. (2001). Attitudes, behavior, and social context: The role of norms and group membership in social influence processes. In J.P. Forgas & K.D. Williams (Eds.), *Social influence: Direct and indirect processes* (pp. 253–270). Philadelphia: Psychology Press.

Wechsler, H., & Kuo, M. (2000). College students define binge drinking and estimate its prevalence: Results of a national survey. *Journal of American College Health, 49,* 57–60.

Wechsler, H., Nelson, T., Lee, J.E., Seiberg, M., Lewis, C., & Keeling, R. (2003). Perception and reality: A national evaluation of social norms marketing interventions to reduce college students' heavy alcohol use. *Quarterly Journal of Studies on Alcohol, 64,* 484–494.

Werch, C.E., Pappas, D.M., Carlson, J.M., DiClemente, C.C., Chally, P.M., & Sinder, J.S. (2000). Results of a social norm intervention to prevent binge drinking among first-year residential college students. *Journal of American College Health, 49,* 85–92.

CRITICAL THINKING QUESTIONS

1. Have you seen examples of *social norms marketing* on your campus or elsewhere? Was that campaign effective? Why or why not? Relate your answer to the points raised in this article.

2. Select a behavior that you would like to change on your campus or in the public. Using the information from this article, design a campaign to change that behavior. Be sure to incorporate the concepts of *descriptive* and *injunctive norms* in your response. Address any ethical issues that may arise in your campaign.

3. The purpose of advertising is to sell a product or idea. Examine television and print ads for alcohol advertising. What images and messages do they convey, and how might these concepts contribute to the norms, and ultimately the behaviors, of the targets of those messages?

4. The article states that the authors " . . . believe that the current findings will apply to a range of other behaviors (e.g., alcohol consumption, seat-belt use, littering, consumer choices, illegal downloading of music) . . . " Do you think the findings of this article will apply to these other behaviors? Why or why not? Are there other behaviors that you think would *not* be affected by the findings of this study? If so, what are they and why do you think these findings would not apply?

CHAPTER INTEGRATION QUESTIONS_____

1. President John F. Kennedy said, "Conformity is the jailer of freedom and the enemy of growth," and social manners writer Emily Post said, "To do exactly as your neighbors do is the only sensible rule." These two apparently contradictory quotations pertain to *conformity,* a type of social influence process. All of the articles in this chapter concern social influence processes. How do these quotes support or contradict these articles?

2. Develop an argument as to how *both* of the preceding quotes can be applied to the articles collectively. In other words, what theme from this chapter can you use to address this question?

3. Many of the chapters in this book have direct relevance in understanding a very dark period of human history: the Holocaust. Perhaps no topic is more germane in helping us understand how such a horror came to pass than that of social influence processes. How can some of the concepts on social influence be applied to the Holocaust and why did the Holocaust occur? (You can find some useful information on this topic on the website of the United States Holocaust Memorial Museum at www.ushmm.org. Click on "Online Exhibitions," some of which are permanently on display while some of which change, to address this topic.)

Chapter Ten

PROSOCIAL BEHAVIOR

HELP. IT IS something that we all need at some time in our lives, and hopefully, it is something that we all give to others. Dramatic examples of helping or failing to help are not hard to find in the mass media. Consider the various published accounts of people needing help yet receiving none versus those of people who risk their own lives to help strangers.

Why do people help or not help? Is helpfulness a personality trait, so that some people are simply helpful individuals who give assistance in a variety of settings? Or does it have more to do with the specific situation, so that a person who helps in one situation is not necessarily more likely to help in another? Or perhaps these two factors somehow interact with one another, so that people with a certain type of personality in a certain type of situation are more likely to help than others.

Article 28, "Nice by Nature?" looks at the issue of whether helping behavior is rooted in our biologic past, and if such behaviors are not limited to human beings. Knowing that human infants and certain animals are attuned to issues of fairness and are predisposed to helping others enables us to understand the origins of this behavior.

Article 29, "From Jerusalem to Jericho," is a classic example of a study that examines both situational and personality factors as influences on helping behavior. It turns out that both factors may be operating, with situational factors determining whether people will offer help in the first place and dispositional factors determining the nature of the helping response.

Finally, Article 30, "Comfortably Numb: Desensitizing Effects of Violent Media on Helping Others," examines how two forms of violent media, movies and video games, may negatively impact the likelihood of helping someone in need. Perhaps being exposed to such media might have a bigger impact than many realize. Given the preponderance of such media, the implications of this study on why people do or don't help are important.

ARTICLE 28 _____

Why do people help one another? Is their purpose pure altruism—that is, a totally unselfish concern for others without any personal benefits? Or do people help others because, in a sense, they are also doing it for themselves?

Questions like these have driven a good deal of research in social psychology that is focused on trying to determine the basic motivations for people engaging in prosocial acts. While these questions have not been definitively answered, several theories have been suggested for why people help.

The *empathy–altruism hypothesis* proposes that helpers are motivated solely by the desire to help someone in need of assistance. At the same time, the helper may feel good about having helped. Thus, the helper is deriving some personal benefit from having done a good deed. While the primary motivation may be to help another person, there may also be the secondary gain of feeling good about acting in a prosocial manner.

Another theoretical explanation for helping behavior is the *negative state relief model.* According to this model, when we see someone in distress or in need of help, we feel bad. In order to feel better, we help them. In other words, our underlying motivation for helping is to want to feel better about ourselves.

A third explanation for prosocial behavior is provided by the *empathic joy hypothesis.* It suggests that we are motivated to help others because it feels good to have a positive impact on the lives of others. How is this approach different from that of the empathy–altruism hypothesis? The empathy–altruism hypothesis includes the desire to help people in need just for the sake of helping them, whereas the empathic joy hypothesis maintains that our helping behavior is driven only by our own desire to feel good about ourselves.

You may notice that all three theories of helping behavior include at least some element of self-motivation. The model that most closely explains helping as being motivated purely by the desire to help is the empathy–altruism hypothesis. However, even that explanation suggests the possibility that while we may be motivated to help just for the sake of helping, we can also feel good about ourselves in the process.

But is helping behavior something unique to human beings? Or are other species, such as chimps, capable of exhibiting altruism as well? The following article by Sadie F. Dingfelder discusses some intriguing lines of research that suggest that helping behavior is not something only found in humans but in other creatures as well.

Nice by Nature?

■ Sadie F. Dingfelder

Pay one monkey with a delicious grape and another with a ho-hum cucumber for the same amount of work, and the monkey who got the lesser reward will probably quit working for you. He may even throw the vegetable back at you, even though monkeys are usually happy to receive cucumbers, says Sarah Brosnan, PhD, a psychology professor at Georgia State University.

That experiment by Brosnan and collaborator Frans de Waal, PhD, published in 2003 in *Nature* (Vol. 425, No. 6,955), was one of the first to show that animals may have an appreciation for fairness—a moral sense that many researchers previously thought was the sole domain of humans. Since then, a slew of intriguing results suggest that animals— particularly those that depend on cooperation for their survival—may have some of the same underpinnings of justice and altruism as we do.

For example, a chimpanzee is quick to let another chimp out of his cage, and they happily retrieve out-of-reach objects for their human handlers. Monkeys will spontaneously share rewards with others who worked toward the goal. And, in the fairness realm, dogs will quit participating in a task if they see another animal receive a better reward.

"Fairness and altruism didn't develop *de novo* in humans," Brosnan says. "It's likely something that began in social species, including primates, and evolved to us."

However, interpreting animal behavior through human eyes can be problematic, observes Marc Hauser, PhD, a Harvard psychology professor and evolutionary biologist. In the cucumber–grape. study, for example, the monkeys could have tossed the cucumbers simply because they were frustrated they didn't get a grape once they saw it. Moral outrage may never have entered the equation.

To determine which explanation makes more sense, researchers must uncover the underlying mechanisms or moral behavior, Hauser says.

"That is basically the name of the game," he says. "You are looking for behavioral or neurobiological signatures that are the same across species."

EQUAL WORK, EQUAL PAY

Research indicates that some animals—particularly ones that hunt together—divvy up the rewards of a spoil. One study even found that animals will occasionally deliver a better reward to a collaborator than they themselves receive. In a 2006 study by Brosnan and her colleagues in the *American Journal of Primatology* (Vol. 68, No. 7), two capuchin monkeys had to work together to pull a tray of food to their cages. But before they began pulling, the monkeys had to decide which one would receive a grape and which one would get a less-coveted apple slice. Instead of fighting over the grape, or always letting the dominant monkey eat it, the animals generally alternated roles across trials, so they both earned some grapes and some apple slices, Brosnan found. In the few cases where the dominant monkey hogged the good food, the other monkey tended to quit participating—she'd rather go without a reward than be paid unfairly.

That tendency to share rewards, says Brosnan, probably developed as a result of the way capuchins work together to hunt raccoon-like animals called coati. "If we are hunting, and I am not giving you much of the kill, you would be better off finding another partner," she says.

Monkeys that were sensitive to unfair situations were more likely to demand their fair share of meat, survive and ultimately reproduce, thereby passing to their offspring a genetic predisposition to seek equitable situations, Brosnan hypothesizes.

Dogs, too, go on strike if they get underpaid, according to a 2008 study in the *Proceedings of the National Academies of Science* (Vol. 106, No. 1) by Friederike Range, PhD, of the University of Vienna in Austria. In it, trained dogs were happy to "shake hands" with a human for no reward—that is, unless they saw another dog receive treats for the behavior. An intriguing result, though some criticized the study for allowing the animal's owners to be present. The owners possibly gave the dogs subtle cues—a phenomenon known as the "Clever Hans" effect, after a horse that answered math problems by stomping its hoof. The animal's owner would become tense as the horse neared the correct number of stomps, accidentally signaling it was time to stop with his posture and facial expressions.

CROSS-SPECIES COMPARISONS

No matter how methodologically sound the studies turn out to be, the animals' behavior, so far, bears only a passing resemblance to human responses to unfairness, some researchers say. In the case of the cucumber-rejecting monkeys, for example, the monkeys were only harming themselves when they passed up the food. In contrast, humans put in similar situations will take the lesser reward unless the rules of the game are set up so that, if they reject the lesser reward, they can keep the other player from a reward as well, notes Hauser.

"Some of the cases that have been coming up in the animal literature do show some of the same signs as humans and in some ways they seem different," he says.

It makes sense for species that hunt cooperatively to notice when they receive less than others, says Felix Warneken, PhD, a psychology professor at the Max Planck Institute for Evolutionary Anthropology, in Germany. However, only adult humans seem to notice when *others* get less than they deserve, he says.

"[Young] children don't mind if they get more than others," says Warneken. "But somewhere between the age of 4 and 8, children acquire these equality rules that they think everyone should receive the same."

Humans may need this advanced sense of fairness because, as a species, we occupy a tough ecological niche, says Michael Gurven, PhD, a University of California, Santa Barbara, anthropology professor. While other primates can survive off of vast amounts of relatively low-calorie roughage, humans must seek hard-to-come-by, high-calorie bonanzas—searching for honey, for example, and hunting animals that are faster than we are. As a result, it takes a lot of training and practice before people can break even on their caloric needs: Among the Ache tribe of Paraguay, a hunter-gatherer society studied by Gurven, people start hunting enough to feed themselves by the time they are 19 and they don't reach their peak productivity until age 40.

"Food sharing is crucial in human societies," says Gurven. "Human history wouldn't look anything like it does now if it weren't for the existence of widespread food exchange at a level you would never see in primates."

As a result, we've developed social rules that build on our primal inequity aversion, and we teach our children to be uncomfortable with situations where we receive more than others, Warneken says.

HAPPY TO HELP

While human standards of fairness seem to require explicit teaching, a tendency to help others may be inherent in both children and chimps, suggests research by Warneken, in a 2006 issue of *Science* (Vol. 311, No. 5,765). Warneken and his colleagues put 18-month-old infants and young primates in a variety of situations where they could assist adult humans. For example, the adults tried to grasp an out-of-reach object that the children and chimps could reach, or the adults dropped an item through a small hole in a box and unsuccessfully attempted to retrieve it, while the children or chimps could get the item by using a door in the box that the adult was unaware of.

In the easy task, both the children and the chimps spontaneously retrieved objects for the adults, but the chimps required more prompting—the experimenters had to look back and forth between the items and the chimps to request help from the animals. In the harder tasks, where it wasn't immediately clear what the adults were attempting to do, only the children pitched in.

The results, says Warneken, show that both children and chimps spontaneously assist others, though they differ in their ability to interpret situations and realize that another animal needs help.

But chimps aren't always so helpful, notes Jennifer Vonk, PhD, a psychology professor at the University of Southern Mississippi. Her research, published in 2008 in *Animal Behaviour* (Vol. 75, No. 5), gave chimps the opportunity to use a stick to knock food toward their cages and also toward another chimp's cage. After an initial learning period, the chimps often knocked food toward themselves, but they didn't use that skill to deliver food to other chimps, even as the animal begged and attempted to grasp the food.

"They just seemed indifferent," she says.

Yale psychology professor Laurie Santos, PhD, and her colleagues got a contrasting result with capuchin monkeys. In a 2008 study published in *Current Biology* (Vol. 18, No. 21), they found that, when given the choice of delivering an average or a special reward (an apple vs. a marshmallow) to a monkey in an adjacent cage, the monkeys more often chose to deliver the tasty marshmallows, for no apparent reason or reward.

The pattern of results, thus far, is perplexing, says Hauser. Why would capuchins be more generous than chimps?

"What you find is the evidence in some of these cases is on the weak side—it often shows puzzling patterns across different species and tasks," he says.

But one overarching theme is emerging: Many animals, in addition to humans, seem to act with the others' well-being in mind, Santos says.

"All pro-sociality is not unique to humans," she says. "Our close living primate relatives are very nice to each other, though perhaps not as consistently as humans."

CRITICAL THINKING QUESTIONS

1. The introduction to this article discusses several theoretical reasons why people may help. The article itself addresses how even some nonhuman species are capable of helping behavior and sharing. How does the information in the introduction relate to what is discussed in the article itself? Explain your reasoning.

2. Have you ever seen an animal engage in what might be considered helping behavior? Describe the behavior and the possible reasons it might have occurred. Are there any alternate explanations for the behavior you described other than that the animal was engaged in helping behavior?

3. On a personal level, reflect on when you have helped someone. Why did you do it? Also reflect on a situation in which you did not help but later wished you had. Why didn't you help at that time? What factors influenced your behavior in each case?

4. The article indicates that research has found that young children (and chimps) spontaneously help others. This may indicate that the tendency to help is innate. If that is the case, what may explain the vast differences in how adults differ in their willingness to help others in need? Why doesn't this innate tendency toward altruism continue on into adulthood equally for all people? Explain your reasoning.

ARTICLE 29

Many variables can potentially influence whether an individual will help someone in need. Perhaps our tendency to help (or not help) is rooted in our biologic past, as was discussed in the previous article. But what other factors may influence prosocial behavior?

Broadly speaking, two types of determinants can be considered. The first concerns *situational* factors: What circumstances surrounding the specific situation may affect helping behavior? The second variable concerns *dispositions:* To what extent are decisions to help due to relatively permanent personality factors? In other words, are some people more likely to help than others because of their unique personality makeup? Or does the situation, rather than personality, influence helping?

In "From Jerusalem to Jericho," John M. Darley and C. Daniel Batson examine both situational and dispositional variables in an experiment modeled after a biblical parable. Specifically, the study looks at helping as influenced by situational variables—whether the subjects were in a hurry and what they were thinking at the time—and dispositional variables—the religious orientations of the subjects. This classic article is interesting not only because of the methodology used but also because of the important implications of the results.

"From Jerusalem to Jericho"
A Study of Situational and Dispositional Variables in Helping Behavior
■ John M. Darley and C. Daniel Batson

The influence of several situational and personality variables on helping behavior was examined in an emergency situation suggested by the parable of the Good Samaritan. People going between two buildings encountered a shabbily dressed person slumped by the side of the road. Subjects in a hurry to reach their destination were more likely to pass by without stopping. Some subjects were going to give a short talk on the parable of the Good Samaritan, others on a nonhelping relevant topic; this made no significant difference in the likelihood of their giving the victim help. Religious personality variables did not predict whether an individual would help the victim or not. However, if a subject did stop to offer help, the character of the helping response was related to his type of religiosity.

Helping other people in distress is, among other things, an ethical act. That is, it is in act governed by ethical norms and precepts taught to children at home, in school, and in church. From Freudian and other personality theories, one would expect individual differences in internalization of these standards that would lead to differences between individuals in the likelihood with which they would help others. But recent research on bystander intervention in emergency situations (Bickman, 1969; Darley & Latané,

1968; Korte, 1969; but see also Schwartz & Clausen, 1970) has had bad luck in finding personality determinants of helping behavior. Although personality variables that one might expect to correlate with helping behavior have been measured (Machiavellianism, authoritarianism, social desirability, alienation, and social responsibility), these were not predictive of helping. Nor was this due to a generalized lack of predictability in the helping situation examined, since variations in the experimental situation, such as the availability of other people who might also help, produced marked changes in rates of helping behavior. These findings are reminiscent of Hartshorne and May's (1928) discovery that resistance to temptation, another ethically relevant act, did not seem to be a fixed characteristic of an individual. That is, a person who was likely to be honest in one situation was not particularly likely to be honest in the next (but see also Burton, 1963).

The rather disappointing correlation between the social psychologist's traditional set of personality variables and helping behavior in emergency situations suggests the need for a fresh perspective on possible predictors of helping and possible situations in which to test them. Therefore, for inspiration, we turned to the Bible, to what is perhaps the classical helping story in the Judeo-Christian tradition, the parable of the Good Samaritan. The parable proved of value in suggesting both personality and situational variables relevant to helping.

> *"And who is my neighbor?" Jesus replied, "A man was going down from Jerusalem to Jericho, and he fell among robbers, who stopped him and beat him, and departed, leaving him half dead. Now by chance a priest was going down the road; and when he saw him he passed by on the other side. So likewise a Levite, when he came to the place and saw him, passed by on the other side. But a Samaritan, as he journeyed, came to where he was; and when he saw him, he had compassion, and went to him and bound his wounds, pouring on oil and wine; then he set him on his own beast and brought him to an inn, and took care of him. And the next day he took out two dennarii and gave them to the innkeeper, saying, "Take care of him; and whatever more you spend, I will repay you when I come back." Which of these three, do you think, proved neighbor to him who fell among the robbers? He said, "The one who showed mercy on him." And Jesus said to him, "Go and do likewise." (Luke 10: 29–37 RSV)*

To psychologists who reflect on the parable, it seems to suggest situational and personality differences between the nonhelpful priest and Levite and the helpful Samaritan. What might each have been thinking and doing when he came upon the robbery victim on that desolate road? What sort of persons were they?

One can speculate on differences in thought. Both the priest and the Levite were religious functionaries who could be expected to have their minds occupied with religious matters. The priest's role in religious activities is obvious. The Levite's role, although less obvious, is equally important: The Levites were necessary participants in temple ceremonies. Much less can be said with any confidence about what the Samaritan might have been thinking, but, in contrast to the others, it was most likely not of a religious nature, for Samaritans were religious outcasts.

Not only was the Samaritan most likely thinking about more mundane matters than the priest and Levite, but, because he was socially less important, it seems likely that he was operating on a quite different time schedule. One can imagine the priest and Levite, prominent public figures, hurrying along with little black books full of meetings and appointments, glancing furtively at their sundials. In contrast, the Samaritan would likely have far fewer and less important people counting on him to be at a particular place at a particular time, and therefore might be expected to be in less of a hurry than the prominent priest or Levite.

In addition to these situational variables, one finds personality factors suggested as well. Central among these, and apparently basic to the point that Jesus was trying to make, is a distinction between types of religiosity. Both the priest and Levite are extremely "religious." But it seems to be precisely their type of religiosity that the parable challenges. At issue is the motivation for one's religion and ethical behavior. Jesus seems to feel that the religious leaders of his time, though certainly respected and upstanding citizens, may be "virtuous" for what it will get them, both in terms of the admiration of their fellowmen and in the eyes of God. New Testament scholar R. W. Funk (1966) noted that the Samaritan is at the other end of the spectrum:

> *The Samaritan does not love with side glances at God. The need of neighbor alone is made self-evident, and the Samaritan responds without other motivation. (pp. 218–219)*

That is, the Samaritan is interpreted as responding spontaneously to the situation, not as being preoccupied with the abstract ethical or organizational do's and don'ts of religion as the priest and Levite would seem to be. This is not to say that the Samaritan is portrayed as irreligious. A major intent of the parable would seem to be to present the Samaritan as a religious and ethical example, but at the same time to contrast his type of religiosity with the more common conception of religiosity that the priest and Levite represent.

To summarize the variables suggested as affecting helping behavior by the parable, the situational variables include the content of one's thinking and the amount of hurry in one's journey. The major dispositional variable seems to be differing types of religiosity. Certainly these variables do not exhaust the list that could be elicited from the parable, but they do suggest several research hypotheses.

Hypothesis 1   The parable implies that people who encounter a situation possibly calling for a helping response while thinking religious and ethical thoughts will be no more likely to offer aid than persons thinking about something else. Such a hypothesis seems to run counter to a theory that focuses on norms as determining helping behavior because a normative account would predict that the increased salience of helping norms produced by thinking about religious and ethical examples would increase helping behavior.

Hypothesis 2   Persons encountering a possible helping situation when they are in a hurry will be less likely to offer aid than persons not in a hurry.

Hypothesis 3   Concerning types of religiosity, persons who are religious in a Samaritan-like fashion will help more frequently than those religious in a priest or Levite fashion.

Obviously, this last hypothesis is hardly operationalized as stated. Prior research by one of the investigators on types of religiosity (Batson, 1971), however, led us to differentiate three distinct ways of being religious: (a) for what it will gain one (cf. Freud, 1927, and perhaps the priest and Levite), (b) for its own intrinsic value (cf. Allport & Ross, 1967), and (c) as a response to and quest for meaning in one's everyday life (cf. Batson, 1971). Both of the latter conceptions would be proposed by their exponents as related to the more Samaritanlike "true" religiosity. Therefore, depending on the theorist one follows, the third hypothesis may be stated like this: People (a) who are religious for intrinsic reasons (Allport & Ross, 1967) or (b) whose religion emerges out of questioning the meaning of their everyday lives (Batson, 1971) will be more likely to stop to offer help to the victim.

The parable of the Good Samaritan also suggested how we would measure people's helping behavior—their response to a stranger slumped by the side of one's path. The victim should appear somewhat ambiguous—dressed, possibly in need of help, but also possibly drunk or even potentially dangerous.

Further, the parable suggests a means by which the incident could be perceived as a real one rather than part of a psychological experiment in which one's behavior was under surveillance and might be shaped by demand characteristics (Orne, 1962), evaluation apprehension (Rosenberg, 1965), or other potentially artifactual determinants of helping behavior. The victim should be encountered not in the experimental context but on the road between various tasks.

METHOD

In order to examine the influence of these variables on helping behavior, seminary students were asked to participate in a study on religious education and vocations. In the first testing session, personality questionnaires concerning types of religiosity were administered. In a second individual session, the subject began experimental procedures in one building and was asked to report to another building for later procedures. While in transit, the subject passed a slumped "victim" planted in an alleyway. The dependent variable was whether and how the subject helped the victim. The independent variables were the degree to which the subject was told to hurry in reaching the other building and the talk he was to give when he arrived there. Some subjects were to give a talk on the jobs in which seminary students would be most effective, others, on the parable of the Good Samaritan.

Subjects

The subjects for the questionnaire administration were 67 students at Princeton Theological Seminary. Forty-seven of them, those who could be reached by telephone, were scheduled for the experiment. Of the 47, 7 subjects' data were not included in the analyses—3 because of contamination of the experimental procedures during their testing and 4 due

to suspicion of the experimental situation. Each subject was paid $1 for the questionnaire session and $1.50 for the experimental session.

Personality Measures

Detailed discussion of the personality scales used may be found elsewhere (Batson, 1971), so the present discussion will be brief. The general personality construct under examination was religiosity. Various conceptions of religiosity have been offered in recent years based on different psychometric scales. The conception seeming to generate the most interest is the Allport and Ross (1967) distinction between "intrinsic" versus "extrinsic" religiosity (cf. also Allen & Spilka, 1967, on "committed" versus "consensual" religion). This bipolar conception of religiosity has been questioned by Brown (1964) and Batson (1971), who suggested three-dimensional analyses instead. Therefore, in the present research, types of religiosity were measured with three instruments which together provided six separate scales; (a) a *doctrinal orthodoxy* (D-O) scale patterned after that used by Glock and Stark (1966), scaling agreement with classic doctrines of Protestant theology; (b) the Allport-Ross *extrinsic* (AR-E) scale, measuring the use of religion as a means to an end rather than as an end in itself; (c) the Allport-Ross *intrinsic* (AR-I) scale, measuring the use of religion as an end in itself; (d) the *extrinsic external* scale of Batson's Religious Life Inventory (RELI-EE), designed to measure the influence of significant others and situations in generating one's religiosity; (e) the *extrinsic internal* scale of the Religious Life Inventory (RELI-EI), designed to measure the degree of "driveness" in one's religiosity; and (f) the *intrinsic* scale of the Religious Life Inventory (RELI-I), designed to measure the degree to which one's religiosity involves a questioning of the meaning of life arising out of one's interactions with his social environment. The order of presentation of the scales in the questionnaire was RELI, AR, D-O.

Consistent with prior research (Batson, 1971), a principal-component analysis of the total scale scores and individual items for the 67 seminarians produced a theoretically meaningful, orthogonally rotated three-component structure with the following loadings:

Religion as means received a single very high loading from AR-E (.903) and therefore was defined by Allport and Ross's (1967) conception of this scale as measuring religiosity as a means to other ends. This component also received moderate negative loadings from D-O (−.400) and AR-I (−.372) and a moderate positive loading from RELI-EE (.301).

Religion as an end received high loadings from RELI-EI (.874), RELI-EE (.725), AR-I (.768), and D-O (.704). Given this configuration, and again following Allport and Ross's conceptualization, this component seemed to involve religiosity as an end in itself with some intrinsic value.

Religion as quest received a single very high loading from RELI-I (.945) and a moderate loading from RELI-EE (.75). Following Batson, this component was conceived to involve religiosity emerging out of an individual's search for meaning in his personal and social world.

The three religious personality scales examined in the experimental research were constructed through the use of complete-estimation factor score coefficients from these three components.

Scheduling of Experimental Study

Since the incident requiring a helping response was staged outdoors, the entire experimental study was run in 3 days, December 14–16, 1970, between 10 A.M. and 4 P.M. A tight schedule was used in an attempt to maintain reasonably consistent weather and light conditions. Temperature fluctuation according to the *New York Times* for the 3 days during these hours was not more than 5 degrees Fahrenheit. No rain or snow fell, although the third day was cloudy, whereas the first two were sunny. Within days the subjects were randomly assigned to experimental conditions.[1]

Procedure

When a subject appeared for the experiment, an assistant (who was blind with respect to the personality scores) asked him to read a brief statement which explained that he was participating in a study of the vocational careers of seminary students. After developing the rationale for the study, the statement read:

> What we have called you in for today is to provide us with some additional material which will give us a clearer picture of how you think than does the questionnaire material we have gathered thus far. Questionnaires are helpful, but tend to be somewhat oversimplified. Therefore, we would like to record a 3–5 minute talk you give based on the following passage. . . .

Variable 1: Message   In the task-relevant condition the passage read,

> With increasing frequency the question is being asked: What jobs or professions do seminary students subsequently enjoy most, and in what jobs are they most effective? The answer to this question used to be so obvious that the question was not even asked. Seminary students were being trained for the ministry, and since both society at large and the seminary student himself had a relatively clear understanding of what made a "good" minister, there was no need even to raise the question of for what other jobs seminary experience seems to be an asset. Today, however, neither society nor many seminaries have a very clearly defined conception of what a "good" minister is or of what sorts of jobs and professions are the best context in which to minister. Many seminary students, apparently genuinely concerned with "ministering," seem to feel that it is impossible to minister in the professional clergy. Other students, no less concerned, find the clergy the most viable profession for ministry. But are there other jobs and/or professions for which seminary experience is an asset? And, indeed, how much of an asset is it for the professional ministry? Or, even more broadly, can one minister through an "establishment" job at all?

In the helping-relevant condition, the subject was given the parable of the Good Samaritan exactly as printed earlier in this article. Next, regardless of condition, all subjects were told,

> You can say whatever you wish based on the passage. Because we are interested in how you think on your feet, you will not be allowed to use notes in giving the talk. Do you understand what you are to do? If not, the assistant will be glad to answer questions.

After a few minutes the assistant returned, asked if there were any questions, and then said:

> Since they're rather tight on space in this building, we're using a free office in the building next door for recording the talks. Let me show you how to get there [draws and explains map on 3 × 5 card]. This is where Professor Steiner's laboratory is. If you go in this door [points at map], there's a secretary right here, and she'll direct you to the office we're using for recording. Another of Professor Steiner's assistants will set you up for recording your talk. Is the map clear?

Variable 2: Hurry   In the high-hurry condition the assistant then looked at his watch and said, "Oh, you're late. They were expecting you a few minutes ago. We'd better get moving. The assistant should be waiting for you so you'd better hurry. It shouldn't take but just a minute." In the intermediate-hurry condition he said, "The assistant is ready for you, so please go right over." In the low-hurry condition, he said, "It'll be a few minutes before they're ready for you, but you might as well head on over. If you have to wait over there, it shouldn't be long."

The Incident   When the subject passed through the alley, the victim was sitting slumped in a doorway, head down, eyes closed, not moving. As the subject went by, the victim coughed twice and groaned, keeping his head down. If the subject stopped and asked if something was wrong or offered to help, the victim, startled and somewhat groggy, said, "Oh, thank you [cough]. . . . No, it's all right. [Pause] I've got this respiratory condition [cough]. . . . The doctor's given me these pills to take, and I just took one. . . . If I just sit and rest for a few minutes I'll be O.K. . . . Thanks very much for stopping though [smiles weakly]." If the subject persisted, insisting on taking the victim inside the building, the victim allowed him to do so and thanked him.

Helping Ratings   The victim rated each subject on a scale of helping behavior as follows:

> *0 = failed to notice the victim as possibly in need at all; 1 = perceived the victim as possibly in need but did not offer aid; 2 = did not stop but helped indirectly (e.g., by telling Steiner's assistant about the victim); 3 = stopped and asked if victim needed help; 4 = after stopping, insisted on taking the victim inside and then left him.*

The victim was blind to the personality scale scores and experimental conditions of all subjects. At the suggestion of the victim, another category was added to the rating scales, based on his observations of the pilot subjects' behavior:

> *5 = after stopping, refused to leave the victim (after 3–5 minutes) and/or insisted on taking him somewhere outside experimental context (e.g., for coffee or to the infirmary).*

(In some cases it was necessary to distinguish Category 0 from Category 1 by the postexperimental questionnaire and Category 2 from Category 1 on the report of the experimental assistant.)

This 6-point scale of helping behavior and a description of the victim were given to a panel of 10 judges (unacquainted with the research) who were asked to rank order the (unnumbered) categories in terms of "the amount of helping behavior displayed toward the person in the doorway." Of the 10, 1 judge reversed the order of Categories 0 and 1. Otherwise there was complete agreement with the ranking implied in the presentation of the scale above.

The Speech   After passing through the alley and entering the door marked on the map, the subject entered a secretary's office. She introduced him to the assistant who gave the subject time to prepare and privately record his talk.

Helping Behavior Questionnaire   After recording the talk, the subject was sent to another experimenter, who administered "an exploratory questionnaire on personal and social ethics." The questionnaire contained several initial questions about the interrelationship between social and personal ethics, and then asked three key questions: (a) "When was the last time you saw a person who seemed to be in need of help?" (b) "When was the last time you stopped to help someone in need?" (c) "Have you had experience helping persons in need? If so, outline briefly." These data were collected as a check on the victim's ratings of whether subjects who did not stop perceived the situation in the alley as one possibly involving need or not.

When he returned, the experimenter reviewed the subject's questionnaire, and, if no mention was made of the situation in the alley, probed for reactions to it and then phased into an elaborate debriefing and discussion session.

Debriefing

In the debriefing, the subject was told the exact nature of the study, including the deception involved, and the reasons for the deception were explained. The subject's reactions to the victim and to the study in general were discussed. The role of situational determinants of helping behavior was explained in relation to this particular incident and to other experiences of the subject. All subjects seemed readily to understand the necessity for the deception, and none indicated any resentment of it. After debriefing, the subject was thanked for his time and paid, then he left.

RESULTS AND DISCUSSION

Overall Helping Behavior

The average amount of help that a subject offered the victim, by condition, is shown in Table 1. The unequal-N analysis of variance indicates that while the hurry variable was significantly ($F = 3.56$, $df = 2.34$, $p < .05$) related to helping behavior, the message variable was not. Subjects in a hurry were likely to offer less help than were subjects not in a hurry. Whether the subject was going to give a speech on the parable of the Good Samaritan or not did not significantly affect his helping behavior on this analysis.

TABLE 1 / Means and Analysis of Variance of Graded Helping Responses

	M			
	Hurry			
Message	Low	Medium	High	Summary
Helping relevant	3.800	2.000	1.000	2.263
Task relevant	1.667	1.667	.500	1.333
Summary	3.000	1.818	.700	

Analysis of Variance				
Source	*SS*	*df*	*MS*	*F*
Message (A)	7.766	1	7.766	2.65
Hurry (B)	20.884	2	10.442	3.50*
A × B	5.237	2	2.619	.89
Error	99.633	34	2.930	

Note: $N = 40$.

*$p < .05$.

Other studies have focused on the question of whether a person initiates helping action or not, rather than on scaled kinds of helping. The data from the present study can also be analyzed on the following terms: Of the 40 subjects, 16 (40%) offered some form of direct or indirect aid to the victim (Coding Categories 2–5), 24 (60%) did not (Coding Categories 0 and 1). The percentages of subjects who offered aid by situational variable were, for low hurry, 63% offered help, intermediate hurry 45%, and high hurry 10%, for helping-relevant message 53%, task-relevant message 29%. With regard to this more general question of whether help was offered or not, an unequal-N analysis of variance (arc sine transformation of percentages of helpers, with low- and inter-mediate-hurry conditions pooled) indicated that again only the hurry main effect was significantly ($F = 5.22$, $p < .05$) related to helping behavior; the subjects in a hurry were more likely to pass by the victim than were those in less of a hurry.

Reviewing the predictions in the light of these results, the second hypothesis, that the degree of hurry a person is in determines his helping behavior, was supported. The prediction involved in the first hypothesis concerning the message content was based on the parable. The parable itself seemed to suggest that thinking pious thoughts would not increase helping. Another and conflicting prediction might be produced by a norm salience theory. Thinking about the parable should make norms for helping salient and therefore produce more helping. The data, as hypothesized, are more congruent with the prediction drawn from the parable. A person going to speak on the parable of the Good Samaritan is not significantly more likely to stop to help a person by the side of the road than is a person going to talk about possible occupations for seminary graduates.

Since both situational hypotheses are confirmed, it is tempting to stop the analysis of these variables at this point. However, multiple regression analysis procedures were also used to analyze the relationship of all of the independent variables of the study and the helping behavior. In addition to often being more statistically powerful due to the use of more data information, multiple regression analysis has an advantage over analysis of variance in that it allows for a comparison of the relative effect of the various independent variables in accounting for variance in the dependent variable. Also, multiple regression analysis can compare the effects of continuous as well as nominal independent variables on both continuous and nominal dependent variables (through the use of point biserial correlations, rpb) and shows considerable robustness to violation of normality assumptions (Cohen, 1965, 1968). Table 2 reports the results of the multiple regression analysis using both help versus no help and the graded helping scale as dependent measures. In this table the overall equation Fs show the F value of the entire regression equation as a particular row variable enters the equation. Individual variable Fs were computed with all five independent variables in the equation. Although the two situational variables, hurry and message condition, correlated more highly with the dependent measure than any of the religious dispositional variables, only hurry was a significant predictor of whether one will help or not (column 1) or of the overall amount of help given (column 2). These results corroborate the findings of the analysis of variance.[2]

Notice also that neither form of the third hypothesis, that types of religiosity will predict helping, received support from these data. No correlation between the various measures of religiosity and any form of the dependent measure ever

TABLE 2 / Stepwise Multiple Regression Analysis

| | Help vs. No Help | | | | | Graded Helping | | | |
| | Individual Variable | | Overall Equation | | | Individual Variable | | Variable Equation | |
Step	r^a	F	R	F	*Step*	r	F	R	F
1. Hurry[b]	−.37	4.537*	.37	5.884*	1. Hurry	−.42	6.665*	.42	8.196**
2. Message[c]	.25	1.495	.41	3.834*	2. Message	.25	1.719	.46	5.083*
3. Religion as quest	−.03	.081	.42	2.521	3. Religion as quest	−.16	1.297	.50	3.897*
4. Religion as means	−.03	.003	.42	1.838*	4. Religion as means	−.08	.018	.50	2.848*
5. Religion as end	.06	.000	.42	1.430	5. Religion as end	−.07	.001	.50	2.213

Note: N = 40. Helping is the dependent variable. *df* = 1/34.

[a]Individual variable correlation coefficient is a point biserial where appropriate.

[b]Variables are listed in order of entry into stepwise regression equations.

[c]Helping-relevant message is positive.

p < .05.

**p* < .01.

came near statistical significance, even though the multiple regression analysis procedure is a powerful and not particularly conservative statistical test.

Personality Difference among Subjects Who Helped

To further investigate the possible influence of personality variables, analyses were carried out using only the data from subjects who offered some kind of help to the victim. Surprisingly (since the number of these subjects was small, only 16) when this was done, one religiosity variable seemed to be significantly related to the kind of helping behavior offered. (The situational variables had no significant effect.) Subjects high on the religion as quest dimension appear likely, when they stop for the victim, to offer help of a more tentative or incomplete nature than are subjects scoring low on this dimension ($r = -.53$, $p < .05$).

This result seemed unsettling for the thinking behind either form of Hypothesis 3. Not only do the data suggest that the Allport-Ross-based conception of religion as *end* does not predict the degree of helping, but the religion as quest component is a significant predictor of offering less help. This latter result seems counterintuitive and out of keeping with previous research (Batson, 1971), which found that this type of religiosity correlated positively with other socially valued characteristics. Further data analysis, however, seemed to suggest a different interpretation of this result.

It will be remembered that one helping coding category was added at the suggestion of the victim after his observation of pilot subjects. The correlation of religious personality variables with helping behavior dichotomized between the added category (1) and all of the others (0) was examined. The correlation between religion as quest and this dichotomous helping scale was essentially unchanged ($rpb = -.54$, $p < .05$). Thus, the previously found correlation between the helping scale and religion as quest seems to reflect the tendency of those who score low on the quest dimension to offer help in the added helping category.

What does help in this added category represent? Within the context of the experiment, it represented an embarrassment. The victim's response to persistent offers of help was to assure the helper he was all right, had taken his medicine, just needed to rest for a minute or so, and, if ultimately necessary, to request the helper to leave. But the *super* helpers in this added category often would not leave until the final appeal was repeated several times by the victim (who was growing increasingly panicky at the possibility of the arrival of the next subject). Since it usually involved the subject's attempting to carry through a preset plan (e.g., taking the subject for a cup of coffee or revealing to him the strength to be found in Christ), and did not allow information from the victim to change that plan, we originally labeled this kind of helping as rigid—an interpretation supported by its increased likelihood among highly doctrinal orthodox subjects ($r = .63$, $p < .01$). It also seemed to have an inappropriate

character. If this more extreme form of helping behavior is indeed effectively less helpful, then the second form of Hypothesis 3 does seem to gain support.

But perhaps it is the experimenters rather than the super helpers who are doing the inappropriate thing; perhaps the best characterization of this kind of helping is as different rather than as inappropriate. This kind of helper seems quickly to place a particular interpretation on the situation, and the helping response seems to follow naturally from this interpretation. All that can safely be said is that one style of helping that emerged in this experiment was directed toward the presumed underlying needs of the victim and was little modified by the victim's comments about his own needs. In contrast, another style was more tentative and seemed more responsive to the victim's statements of his need.

The former kind of helping was likely to be displayed by subjects who expressed strong doctrinal orthodoxy. Conversely, this fixed kind of helping was unlikely among subjects high on the religion as quest dimension. These latter subjects, who conceived their religion as involving an ongoing search for meaning in their personal and social world, seemed more responsive to the victim's immediate needs and more open to the victim's definitions of his own needs.

CONCLUSION AND IMPLICATIONS

A person not in a hurry may stop and offer help to a person in distress. A person in a hurry is likely to keep going. Ironically, he is likely to keep going even if he is hurrying to speak on the parable of the Good Samaritan, thus inadvertently confirming the point of the parable. (Indeed, on several occasions, a seminary student going to give his talk on the parable of the Good Samaritan literally stepped over the victim as he hurried on his way!)

Although the degree to which a person was in a hurry had a clearly significant effect on his likelihood of offering the victim help, whether he was going to give a sermon on the parable or on possible vocational roles of ministers did not. This lack of effect of sermon topic raises certain difficulties for an explanation of helping behavior involving helping norms and their salience. It is hard to think of a context in which norms concerning helping those in distress are more salient than for a person thinking about the Good Samaritan, and yet it did not significantly increase helping behavior. The results were in the direction suggested by the norm salience hypothesis, but they were not significant. The most accurate conclusion seems to be that salience of helping norms is a less strong determinant of helping behavior in the present situation than many, including the present authors, would expect.

Thinking about the Good Samaritan did not increase helping behavior, but being in a hurry decreased it. It is difficult not to conclude from this that the frequently cited explanation that ethics becomes a luxury as the speed of our daily lives increases is at least an accurate description. The picture that this explanation conveys is of a person seeing another, consciously noting his distress, and consciously choosing to leave him in distress. But perhaps this is not entirely accurate, for, when a person is in a hurry, something seems to happen that is akin to Tolman's (1948) concept of the "narrowing of the cognitive map." Our seminarians in a hurry noticed the victim in that in the postexperiment interview almost all mentioned him as, on reflection, possibly in need of help. But it seems that they often had not worked this out when they were near the victim. Either the interpretation of their visual picture as a person in distress or the empathic reactions usually associated with that interpretation had been deferred because they were hurrying. According to the reflections of some of the subjects, it would be inaccurate to say that they realized the victim's possible distress, then chose to ignore it; instead, because of the time pressures, they did not perceive the scene in the alley as an occasion for an ethical decision.

For other subjects it seems more accurate to conclude that they decided not to stop. They appeared aroused and anxious after the encounter in the alley. For these subjects, what were the elements of the choice that they were making? Why were the seminarians hurrying? Because the experimenter, *whom the subject was helping* was depending on him to get to a particular place quickly. In other words, he was in conflict between stopping to help the victim and continuing on his way to help the experimenter. And this is often true of people in a hurry; they hurry because somebody depends on their being somewhere. Conflict, rather than callousness, can explain their failure to stop.

Finally, as in other studies, personality variables were not useful in predicting whether a person helped or not. But in this study, unlike many previous ones, considerable variations were possible in the kinds of help given, and these variations did relate to personality measures—specifically to religiosity of the quest sort. The clear light of hindsight suggests that the dimension of kinds of helping would have been the appropriate place to look for personality differences all along; *whether* a person helps or not is an instant decision likely to be situationally controlled. How a person helps involves a more complex and considered number of decisions, including the time and scope to permit personality characteristics to shape them.

REFERENCES

Allen, R. O., & Spilka, B. Committed and consensual religion. A specification of religion-prejudice relationships. *Journal for the Scientific Study of Religion,* 1967, *6,* 191–206.

Allport, G. W., & Ross, J. M. Personal religious orientation and prejudice. *Journal of Personality and Social Psychology,* 1967, *5,* 432–443.

Batson, C. D. Creativity and religious development: Toward a structural-functional psychology of religion Unpublished doctoral dissertation, Princeton Theological Seminary, 1971.

Bickman, L. B. The effect of the presence of others on bystander intervention in an emergency. Unpublished doctoral dissertation, City College of the City University of New York, 1969.

Brown, L. B. Classifications of religious orientation. *Journal for the Scientific Study of Religion,* 1964, *4,* 91–99.

Burton, R. V. The generality of honesty reconsidered. *Psychological Review,* 1963, *70,* 481–499.

Cohen, J. Multiple regression as a general data-analytic system. *Psychological Bulletin,* 1968, *70,* 426–443.

Cohen, J. Some statistical issues in psychological research. In B. B. Wolman (Ed.), *Handbook of clinical psychology.* New York: McGraw-Hill, 1965.

Darley, J. M., & Latané, B. Bystander intervention in emergencies: Diffusion of responsibility. *Journal of Personality and Social Psychology,* 1968, *8,* 377–383.

Freud, S. *The future of an illusion.* New York: Liveright, 1953.

Funk, R. W. *Language, hermeneutic, and word of God.* New York: Harper & Row, 1966.

Glock, C. Y., & Stark, R. *Christian beliefs and anti-Semitism.* New York: Harper & Row, 1966.

Hartshorne, H., & May, M. A. *Studies in the nature of character.* Vol. 1. *Studies in deceit.* New York: Macmillan, 1928.

Korte, C. Group effects on help-giving in an emergency. *Proceedings of the 77th Annual Convention of the American Psychological Association,* 1969, *4,* 383–384. (Summary)

Orne, M. T. On the social psychology of the psychological experiment: With particular reference to demand characteristics and their implications. *American Psychologist,* 1962, *17,* 776–783.

Rosenberg, M. J. When dissonance fails: On eliminating evaluation apprehension from attitude measurement. *Journal of Personality and Social Psychology,* 1965, *1,* 28–42.

Schwartz, S. H., & Clausen, G. T. Responsibility, norms, and helping in an emergency. *Journal of Personality and Social Psychology,* 1970, *16,* 299–310.

Tolman, E. C. Cognitive maps in rats and men. *Psychological Review,* 1948, *55,* 189–208.

ENDNOTES

1. An error was made in randomizing that increased the number of subjects in the intermediate-hurry conditions. This worked against the prediction that was most highly confirmed (the hurry prediction) and made no difference to the message variable tests.

2. To check the legitimacy of the use of both analysis of variance and multiple regression analysis, parametric analyses, on this ordinal data, Kendall rank correlation coefficients were calculated between the helping scale and the five independent variables. As expected t approximated the correlation quite closely in each case and was significant for hurry only (hurry $\tau - .38, p < .001$).

For assistance in conducting this research thanks are due Robert Wells, Beverly Fisher, Mike Shafto, Peter Sheras, Richard Detweiler, and Karen Glasser. The research was funded by National Science Foundation Grant GS-2293.

CRITICAL THINKING QUESTIONS

1. Being prompted to think of the parable of the Good Samaritan did not increase the subjects' helping behavior in this study, but being in a hurry actually decreased it. Suppose that you are in the business of soliciting money for a worthy purpose. What strategies could you use to maximize the money you receive, based on the implications of this study? Explain.

2. *Rush hour,* as the name implies, describes a time of day when people are in a hurry to get to or from work. Do you think that people would be less likely to help someone in need during rush hour than at other times of the day? What about on weekends? Design a study to test this possibility, being sure to address any ethical issues that may be involved.

3. Reading about the Good Samaritan had no impact on subsequent helping behavior. Do you think that reading an article such as this one would change people's helping behavior? Why or why not? Specifically, now that you know that being in a hurry will decrease the likelihood of your giving help, do you think that this awareness will make you more likely to give help in the future, even if you are in a hurry? Why or why not? If simply telling someone about the Good Samaritan was not enough to improve people's helping behavior, what might be more effective?

ADDITIONAL RELATED READINGS

Gillum, R. F., & Masters, K. S. (2010). Religiousness and blood donation: Findings from a national survey. *Journal of Health Psychology, 15*(2), 163–172.

Malhotra, D. (2010). (When) are religious people nicer? Religious salience and the "Sunday effect" on pro-social behavior. *Judgment and Decision Making, 5*(2), 138–143.

ARTICLE 30 _____

There were many homicides in New York City in 1964, but one of them attracted the attention of the public and the media nationally due to the circumstances surrounding that tragedy. Kitty Genovese was attacked outside of her apartment building and stabbed by her assailant. The assailant ran off, but shortly returned to the injured Genovese and murdered her at that point. What attracted the attention (and outrage) of the public was that at least 37 people in the apartment complex either heard or saw the assault and murder, and yet not one of them called the police or otherwise tried to help her. This tragic event eventually gave rise to a large body of research aimed at trying to understand why people help or don't help in emergency situations. Rather than just believing that the observers to the crime were indifferent, perhaps their inaction was due to something else.

Bibb Latane and John Darley were early pioneers in investigating why people help in emergency situations. Based on numerous studies, Latane and Darley found that there were five crucial steps that ultimately determined if someone helped or didn't help in an emergency situation. First, one must *notice* that something is happening. If one is busy or distracted, he or she might not even notice that something is happening. Second, the person must *interpret* the event as an emergency and not something else. Perhaps it isn't an assault after all, but just a loud quarrel between lovers. Third, the person must feel *personal responsibility* for helping. He or she must decide that he or she, and not someone else, needs to do something. However, even if the person decides to help, he or she might not know what to do or might not be able to do it. This *assessment of ability* determines if the person intervenes or not (the fourth step). Finally, the last step involves *deciding to help*. Factors such as fear may inhibit the person from acting even at this final stage.

There are many factors that impact the various steps mentioned earlier, and make it more or less likely that someone will help in an emergency. The following article by Brad J. Bushman and Craig A. Anderson examine how exposure to violent media (either a video game or a movie) might have an inhibiting effect on helping behavior. This may be due to something known as *desensitization*. Prior research on aggression has established that being exposed to violent media makes the viewers less sensitive to the pain and suffering of others. This desensitization, in turn, may make it less likely to help people in need.

Comfortably Numb
Desensitizing Effects of Violent Media on Helping Others
■ Brad J. Bushman and Craig A. Anderson

ABSTRACT

Two studies tested the hypothesis that exposure to violent media reduces aid offered to people in pain. In Study 1, participants played a violent or nonviolent video game for 20 min. After game play, while completing a lengthy questionnaire, they heard a loud fight, in which one person was injured, outside the lab. Participants who played violent games took longer to help the injured victim, rated the fight as less serious, and were less likely to "hear" the fight in comparison to participants who played nonviolent games. In Study 2, violent- and nonviolent-movie attendees witnessed a young woman with an injured ankle struggle to pick up her crutches outside the theater either before or after the movie. Participants who had just watched a violent movie took longer to help than participants in the other three conditions. The findings

from both studies suggest that violent media make people numb to the pain and suffering of others.

Film is a powerful medium, film is a drug, film is a potential hallucinogen—it goes into your eye, it goes into your brain, it stimulates and it's a dangerous thing—it can be a very subversive thing.

—Oliver Stone (quoted in Dworkin, 1996)

If film is a drug, then violent film content might make people "comfortably numb" (borrowing the words of Pink Floyd). Specifically, exposure to blood and gore in the media might make people numb to the pain and suffering of others—a

Bushman, B.J. & Anderson, C.A. *Psychological Science, 20*(3), 273–277. Copyright © 2009 by the Association for Psychological Science. Reprinted by permission of SAGE Publications.

process called *desensitization*. One negative consequence of such physiological desensitization is that it may cause people to be less helpful to those in need.

The link between desensitization and helping behavior is provided by a recent model that integrates the pioneering work on helping by Latané and Darley (1968) with our work on physiological desensitization to aggression, illustrated in Figure 1. Several factors must be in place before someone decides to help a victim (Latané & Darley, 1970; see Fig. 2). Three of these factors are particularly relevant here. First, the individual must notice or attend to the violent incident. However, decreased attention to violent events is likely to be one consequence of desensitization. Second, the individual must recognize the event as an emergency. However, desensitization can reduce the perceived seriousness of injury and the perception that an emergency exists. Third, the individual must feel a personal responsibility to help. However, decreased sympathy for the victim, increased belief that violence is normative, and decreased negative attitudes toward violence all decrease feelings of personal responsibility.

Although previous research has shown that violence in the media can produce desensitization-related outcomes (e.g., Linz, Donnerstein, & Adams, 1989; Molitor & Hirsch, 1994; Mullin &

Linz, 1995; Thomas, Horton, Lippincott, & Drabman, 1977), this model illuminates two gaps in the desensitization literature. First, there are no published studies testing the hypothesis that violent media stimuli known to produce physiological desensitization also reduce helping behavior. Second, there are no field experiments testing the effect of violent-entertainment media on helping an injured person. We recently found that playing a violent video game for just 20 min decreased skin conductance and heart rate while watching real scenes of violence (Carnagey, Anderson, & Bushman, 2007). We conducted two studies to help fill these gaps: a lab experiment using violent video games (Study 1) and a field study using violent movies (Study 2).

STUDY 1

Participants played a violent or a nonviolent video game. Later, they overheard a staged fight leading to injury. We predicted that playing a violent video game, in comparison to playing a nonviolent game, would decrease the likelihood of help, delay helping, decrease the likelihood of noticing an emergency (the first step in the helping process), and decrease the judged severity of the emergency (the second step in the helping process).

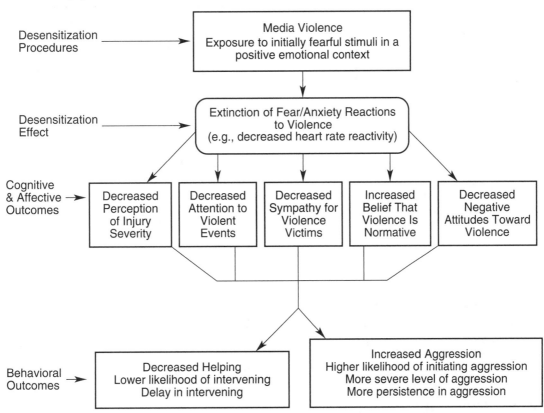

FIGURE 1 / Model of the effects of exposure to media violence. Such exposure serves as a desensitization procedure leading to increases in aggression and decreases in helping. Adapted from Carnagey, Anderson, and Bushman (2007).

FIGURE 2 / Five steps to helping. Adapted from Latané and Darley (1970).

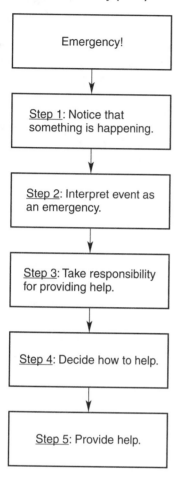

Method

Participants

Participants were 320 college students (160 men, 160 women) who received extra course credit in exchange for voluntary participation.

Procedure

Participants were tested individually. They were told that the researchers were studying what types of people liked various types of video games. After giving consent, participants played a randomly assigned violent (*Carmageddon, Duke Nukem, Mortal Kombat, Future Cop*) or nonviolent (*Glider Pro, 3D Pinball, Austin Powers, Tetra Madness*) video game. We used the same violent and nonviolent video games and the same participant pool that Carnagey et al. (2007) used to demonstrate physiological desensitization to violence.

The experimenter set a timer for 20 min, handed the participant a lengthy questionnaire, and said,

After the timer goes off, please complete this questionnaire. I need to code some data for another study, but I promise to be back in about 40 min. Please don't leave the building until I get back. I have to ask you some questions about the video game before you leave. Okay?

The experimenter then departed.

After playing the video game for 20 min, participants rated on a 10-point scale (1 = *not at all*, 10 = *extremely*) how action-packed, enjoyable, fun, absorbing, arousing, boring, entertaining, exciting, involving, stimulating, addicting, and violent the video game was. The violence rating was used as a manipulation check. The other ratings were used as possible covariates in the analyses to control for differences in video games other than violent content. After reverse-scoring boring ratings, principal components factor analysis showed that the covariates loaded on a single factor (eigenvalue = 7.21), and were therefore combined (Cronbach α = .94). Because the results were virtually identical with and without the covariates, we only report the simpler analyses that excluded the covariates.

Next, participants indicated their favorite type of video game (i.e., education, fantasy, fighting with hands or weapons, skill, or sports). They also completed a lengthy bogus questionnaire (over 200 items), ostensibly to determine what types of people prefer various types of video games. The real purpose of the questionnaire was to keep participants busy while a recording of a staged fight was played outside the lab.

Three minutes after the participant finished playing the video game, the experimenter, who was outside of the lab, played an audio recording of a staged fight between two actors. The 6-min fight was professionally recorded using experienced actors. Two parallel versions of the fight involved male actors (used for male participants) or female actors (used for female participants). In the recording, the two actors were presumably waiting to do an experiment. They began by talking about how one stole the other's girlfriend (male version) or boyfriend (female version). The discussion quickly deteriorated into a shouting match (as indicated in the following script from the male version):

FIRST ACTOR: You stole her from me. I'm right, and you know it, you loser.
SECOND ACTOR: Loser? If I'm a loser, why am I dating your ex-girlfriend?
FIRST ACTOR: Okay, that's it, I don't have to put up with this shit any longer.

When the recording reached this point, the experimenter threw a chair onto the floor, making a loud crash, and kicked the door to the participant's room twice.

SECOND ACTOR: [groans in pain]

FIRST ACTOR: Ohhhh, did I hurt you?

SECOND ACTOR: It's my ankle, you bastard. It's twisted or something.

FIRST ACTOR: Isn't that just too bad?

SECOND ACTOR: I can't even stand up!

FIRST ACTOR: Don't look to me for pity.

SECOND ACTOR: You could at least help me get off the floor.

FIRST ACTOR: You've gotta be kidding me. Help you? I'm outta here.

[slams the door and leaves]

At this point, the experimenter pressed the start button on the stopwatch to time how long it would take for participants to help the second actor—the violence victim. On the recording, the victim groaned in pain for about 1.5 min. Because the first actor had "left," there was no perceived danger to the participant in helping the second actor.

The experimenter waited 3 min after the groans of pain stopped to give participants ample time to help. If the participant left the room to help the victim, the experimenter pressed the stop button on the stopwatch and then debriefed the participant.

If the participant did not help after 3 min, the experimenter entered the room and said, "Hi, I'm back. Is everything going all right in here? I just saw someone limping down the hallway. Did something happen here?" The experimenter recorded whether the participant mentioned hearing the fight outside the room. Those who reported hearing the fight rated how serious it was on a 10-point scale (1 = *not at all serious*, 10 = *extremely serious*). As justification for rating the severity of the fight, the experimenter explained the rating was required for a formal report that needed to be filed with the campus police. Finally, the participant was fully debriefed.

We conducted a pilot study involving 50 college students (25 men, 25 women) to test whether they thought the fight was real. Only 5 of the first 10 participants in the pilot study thought the fight was real. We therefore increased the realism of the fight (e.g., knocked over a chair and pounded on the door). After making these changes, all of the remaining 40 participants thought the fight was real.

Results

Preliminary Analyses

As expected, violence ratings were higher for the violent games ($M = 7.89$) than for the nonviolent games ($M = 1.51$), $F(1, 316) = 823.13$, $p < .0001$, $p_{rep} > .99$, $d = 3.22$. We used four violent games and four nonviolent games to improve generalizability (Wells & Windschitl, 1999). Within each type of video game, we tested whether the four games produced different effects on any of the dependent variables. No significant differences were found among the four violent or the four nonviolent games. Thus, data were collapsed across exemplars of video game types for subsequent analyses.

Main Analyses

Helping Although in the predicted direction, there was no significant difference in helping rates between violent and nonviolent video game players, 21% and 25%, respectively, $z = 0.88$, $p = .38$, $p_{rep} > .59$, $\phi = -.05$. Participants who said their favorite type of video game involved "fighting with hands or weapons" were less likely to help than those who said their favorite video game was nonviolent, 11% and 26%, respectively, $z = 2.46$, $p < .02$, $p_{rep} > .92$, $\phi = -.14$.

Time to Help When people who played a violent game did decide to help, they took significantly longer ($M = 73.3$ s) to help the victim than those who played a nonviolent game ($M = 16.2$ s), $F(1, 70) = 6.70$, $p < .02$, $p_{rep} > .92$, $d = 0.61$.

Heard Fight The first step to helping is to notice the emergency. As expected, people who played a violent game were less likely to report that they heard the fight than those who played a nonviolent game, 94% and 99%, respectively, $z = 2.00$, $p < .05$, $p_{rep} > .87$, $\phi = -.11$.

Severity of Fight The second step to helping is to judge the event as an emergency. As expected, people who played a violent game thought the fight was less serious ($M = 5.91$) than did those who played a nonviolent game ($M = 6.44$), $F(1, 239) = 4.44$, $p < .04$, $p_{rep} > .89$, $d = 0.27$. Men also thought the fight was less serious ($M = 5.92$) than did women ($M = 6.49$), $F(1, 239) = 5.43$, $p < .03$, $p_{rep} > .90$, $d = 0.29$.

Discussion

Violent video games known to produce physiological desensitization in a previous study (Carnagey et al., 2006) influenced helping behavior and related perceptual and cognitive variables in theoretically expected ways in Study 1. Participants who played a violent game took significantly longer to help, over 450% longer, than participants who played a nonviolent game. Furthermore, compared to participants who played a nonviolent game, those who played a violent game were less likely to notice the fight and rated it as less serious, which are two obstacles to helping.

STUDY 2

Participants in Study 2 were adult moviegoers. Our confederate, a young woman with a wrapped ankle and crutches, "accidentally" dropped her crutches outside a movie theater and struggled to retrieve them. A researcher hidden from view timed how long it took moviegoers to retrieve the crutches for the confederate. We expected that participants who had just watched a violent movie would take longer to help the confederate than would participants who had just watched a nonviolent movie or participants who had not yet seen a movie.

Method

Participants

Participants were 162 adult moviegoers.

Procedure

A minor emergency was staged just outside theaters that were showing either a violent movie (e.g., *The Ruins*, 2008) or a nonviolent movie (e.g., *Nim's Island*, 2008). The violent movies were rated "R"; the nonviolent movies were rated "PG." Participants had the opportunity to help a young woman with a wrapped ankle who dropped her crutches just outside the theater and was struggling to retrieve them. The confederate was told to pick up her crutches after 2 min if nobody offered help, but she always received help in less than 11 s. After receiving help, she thanked the helper and then hobbled away from the theater. A researcher hidden from view timed with a stopwatch how long it took participants to help the confederate. The researcher also recorded the gender of the person offering help and the number of potential helpers in the vicinity.

The researcher flipped a coin in advance to determine whether the emergency was staged before or after the showing of a violent or nonviolent movie. Staging the emergency before the movie allowed us to test (and control) the helpfulness of people attending violent versus nonviolent movies. Staging the emergency after the movie allowed us to test the hypothesis that viewing violence inhibits helping. The confederate dropped her crutch 36 times, 9 times in each of the four experimental conditions.

Results and Discussion

Although the helping delay increased as the number of bystanders increased, and women helped less often than men, these effects were not statistically significant and were not analyzed further. The data were analyzed using a model testing approach, in which a specific contrast representing our theoretical model and the residual between-groups variance are both tested for significance. If the theoretical model adequately accounts for differences among observed means, then the specific contrast should be significant and the residual between-groups variance should be nonsignificant. As predicted, participants who had just viewed a violent movie took over 26% longer to help ($M = 6.89$ s) than participants in the other three conditions ($M = 5.46$ s), $F(1, 32) = 6.20$, $p < .01$, $p_{rep} > .95$, $d = 0.88$ (see Fig. 3). Furthermore, the residual between-groups

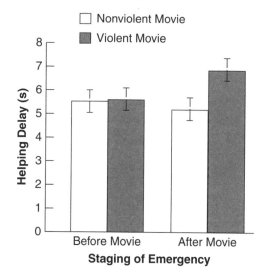

FIGURE 3 / Mean time elapsed before adults helped a confederate pick up her crutches as a function of whether they watched a violent or nonviolent movie before or after the staged emergency.

variance was not significant, $F < 1.0$, indicating that the theoretical model adequately accounted for the pattern of means. Indeed, the model accounted for 98% of the between-groups variance. The lack of a difference in helping before watching the movie rules out the possibility that less-helpful people were more likely to attend the violent movies.

GENERAL DISCUSSION

These two studies support the desensitization hypothesis linking media violence to decreased helping behavior. In Study 1, violent video games known to desensitize people caused decreases in helping-related behavior, perceptions, and cognitions. In Study 2, violent movies delayed helping in a wholly naturalistic setting. The person in need of help had an injured ankle in both studies. In Study 1, the injury resulted from interpersonal violence, whereas in Study 2, the cause of injury was unknown. The similar results across very different studies suggest that desensitization caused by media violence generalizes beyond failure to help victims of violence. Theoretically, we expect such generalization; one factor influencing helping behavior is judged severity of injury, and that judgment is influenced by one's own emotional and physiological reaction to the injury.

In sum, the present studies clearly demonstrate that violent media exposure can reduce helping behavior in precisely the way predicted by major models of helping and desensitization theory. People exposed to media violence become "comfortably numb" to the pain and suffering of others and are consequently less helpful.

ACKNOWLEDGMENTS

We thank Colleen Phillips for her help with Study 1 and Elizabeth Henley and Brad Gamache for their help with Study 2.

REFERENCES

Carnagey, N.L., Anderson, C.A., & Bushman, B.J. (2007). The effect of video game violence on physiological desensitization to real-life violence. *Journal of Experimental Social Psychology, 43,* 489–496.

Dworkin, A. (1996). *Slicing the baby in half.* Retrieved December 12, 2008, from the Times Higher Education Web site: http://www.timeshighereducation.co.uk/story.asp?storyCode=162012&section code=6.

Latané, B., & Darley, J.M. (1968). Group inhibition of bystander intervention in emergencies. *Journal of Personality and Social Psychology, 10,* 215–221.

Latané, B., & Darley, J.M. (1970). *The unresponsive bystander: Why doesn't he help?* New York: Appleton-Century-Crofts.

Linz, D., Donnerstein, E., & Adams, S.M. (1989). Physiological desensitization and judgments about female victims of violence. *Human Communication Research, 15,* 509–522.

Molitor, F., & Hirsch, K.W. (1994). Children's toleration of real-life aggression after exposure to media violence: A replication of the Drabman and Thomas studies. *Child Study Journal, 24,* 191–207.

Mullin, C.R., & Linz, D. (1995). Desensitization and resensitization to violence against women: Effects of exposure to sexually violent films on judgments of domestic violence victims. *Journal of Personality and Social Psychology, 69,* 449–459.

Thomas, M.H., Horton, R.W., Lippincott, E.C., & Drabman, R.S. (1977). Desensitization to portrayals of real life aggression as a function of television violence. *Journal of Personality and Social Psychology, 35,* 450–458.

Wells, G.L., & Windschitl, P.D. (1999). Stimulus sampling and social psychological experimentation. *Personality and Social Psychology Bulletin, 25,* 1115–1125.

CRITICAL THINKING QUESTIONS

1. Reread the quote by Oliver Stone at the beginning of the article. Do you agree or disagree with that statement? Explain your position.
2. Other than video games and movies, what other things might make people "comfortably numb" to helping others? Explain why that may be the case.
3. What types of media are young children exposed to that might have an impact on their helping behavior? Based on the findings of this study, what (if anything) should be done about such exposure to violent media? Be sure to address the issue of censorship in your response.
4. Find an example from the media of a real-life emergency situation where people failed to do anything to help. How can you apply the information presented in this article to explain this lack of helping?
5. Besides the variables described in this article, what other factors may impact people's helping behavior? Explain why you think each may influence helping behavior.

CHAPTER INTEGRATION QUESTIONS

1. "The only thing that is necessary for the triumph of evil is for good men to do nothing," according to eighteenth-century political writer Edmund Burke. Discuss why you either agree or disagree with this statement.
2. Integrate the content of the three articles in this chapter to identify one or more themes regarding helping behavior. Can Burke's quote be used to help understand the theme or themes? Explain.
3. Besides the factors covered in the articles, what else might have an impact on helping behavior? Discuss.

Chapter Eleven

AGGRESSION

PICK UP A COPY of today's newspaper. How much of it concerns acts of violence, whether from war, terrorism, homicide, or domestic violence? Aggression seems to be a fairly common part of modern life.

Now think about your own experiences. Chances are, you have not directly experienced a murder or assault. But what other types of aggressive behavior have you witnessed? Have you seen verbal aggression, where the intention was to hurt another person's feelings? Have you experienced cruelty in one form or another, where pain was experienced, even though no blood was shed?

Must aggression be part of life? Is it simply human nature and consequently something that cannot be changed? Or is it possible that the amount of aggression in the world could be reduced, if not actually eliminated?

Article 31, "Understanding Terrorism," examines some of the factors that may motivate individuals to become terrorists as well as why organized terrorism exists in the first place. An important aspect of this article is the information on effective, and not-so-effective, ways of dealing with terrorists. These ideas are particularly worthwhile given the increased threat that terrorism has become for many.

In contrast, Article 32, "Transmission of Aggression through Imitation of Aggressive Models," represents one of the earliest studies demonstrating that aggression is learned and in particular that the violence portrayed on television may contribute to aggressiveness in children. Since many behavioral patterns, such as aggression, may be learned in childhood, knowledge about what contributes to aggression can be used to help reduce those very behaviors.

Finally, Article 33, "School Violence and the Culture of Honor," provides a contemporary examination of whether certain cultural values may be related to school violence. A *culture of honor* refers to a society where aggression is viewed as an acceptable, and even expected, response when one's honor has been somehow threatened. Building on previous research that had found a relationship between the culture of honor and violent acts, including homicides, this article provides another possible explanation for the acts of school violence that have occurred over the years.

ARTICLE 31 _____

What causes aggression? Psychologists have asked that question for nearly a century now. In their search for an answer, several theoretical perspectives have emerged.

One such perspective holds that aggression is an innate tendency, something toward which people are biologically predisposed. This view, espoused by theorists such as Sigmund Freud, maintains that people periodically need to discharge a natural buildup of aggressive energy. Thus, human aggressiveness may be a normal and perhaps unavoidable fact of life.

A second view suggests that aggression is a drive to harm someone elicited by some external stimulus. In other words, certain external conditions, such as frustration, produce a tendency for people to want to harm or injure others.

Other theories of aggression maintain that aggressive behavior is purely the product of social learning. People are aggressive because they have *learned* how to be aggressive, perhaps by watching other people act in such a fashion.

The expression of aggression can take many different forms, ranging from verbal abuse to killing. One distinction that can be made about the cause of aggression is whether it is premeditated, a distinction that is also made in the law. Although unpremeditated aggression can be as harmful as premeditated aggression, a particular horror is held for acts of violence that were deliberate.

In this violent world, one particular form of aggression has become a focal point in the minds of people and in the actions of government: terrorism. People throughout the world have the images of September 11, 2001, seared into their consciousness. The images of innocent people being deliberately harmed by members of a group hoping to accomplish a social or political agenda remain with everyone old enough to remember that day. And yet terrorist acts have been with the human race for a long time before 9-11. The methods used, and the extent of the destruction and suffering, might be different, but terrorist acts have been part of the human experience almost since the beginning of recorded history.

What motivates terrorists? Why do they select the targets they do? Are terrorist acts really a form of senseless violence directed at a convenient target, or are they well-planned and deliberately executed maneuvers to further some desired end? The following article by Tori DeAngelis examines the current thinking on understanding the causes of terrorism and the ways to combat it. Given the importance of the issue of terrorism in all of our lives the findings reported in the article are of particular relevance.

Understanding Terrorism

■ Tori DeAngelis

Determining what drives people to terrorism is no easy task. For one thing, terrorists aren't likely to volunteer as experimental subjects, and examining their activities from afar can lead to erroneous conclusions. What's more, one group's terrorist is another group's freedom fighter, as the millions of Arabs who support Palestinian suicide bombers will attest.

Given these complexities, the psychology of terrorism is marked more by theory and opinion than by good science, researchers admit. But a number of psychologists are starting to put together reliable data. They're finding it is generally more useful to view terrorism in terms of political and group dynamics and processes than individual ones, and that universal psychological principles—such as our subconscious fear of death and our desire for meaning and personal significance—may

help to explain some aspects of terrorist actions and our reactions to them.

Eventually, such information could help in the complex quest to prevent terrorism. Psychologists' findings suggest that assuaging people's fear of cultural annihilation, highlighting our common humanity or demonstrating the discrepancy between the dream and reality of terrorist involvement could keep would-be terrorists from turning to violence, for instance.

In fact, the notion that terrorists could be talked out of committing violence using peaceful dialogue and a helping hand is no longer an idealist's pipe dream, but actually the aim of a growing number of "de-radicalization" programs worldwide, says social psychologist Arie Kruglanski, PhD, co-director of the National Consortium for the Study of Terrorism and

Responses to Terrorism, or START, one of several university-based Centers of Excellence established under the Homeland Security Act of 2002.

"While there is still a big need to assess these programs," says Kruglanski, who is studying some of these programs, "in some cases, there appear to be some authentic successes."

THE LURE OF TERROR

For years, psychologists examined terrorists' individual characteristics, mining for clues that could explain their willingness to engage in violence. While researchers now agree that most terrorists are not "pathological" in any traditional sense, several important insights have been gleaned though interviews with some 60 former terrorists conducted by psychologist John Horgan, PhD, who directs the Pennsylvania State University's International Center for the Study of Terrorism.

Horgan found that people who are more open to terrorist recruitment and radicalization tend to:

- Feel angry, alienated or disenfranchised.
- Believe that their current political involvement does not give them the power to effect real change.
- Identify with perceived victims of the social injustice they are fighting.
- Feel the need to take action rather than just talking about the problem.
- Believe that engaging in violence against the state is not immoral.
- Have friends or family sympathetic to the cause.
- Believe that joining a movement offers social and psychological rewards such as adventure, camaraderie and a heightened sense of identity.

Beyond the individual characteristics of terrorists, Horgan has learned that it's more fruitful to investigate *how* people change as a result of terrorist involvement than to simply ask *why* they enter in the first place. That's because asking why tends to yield pat, ideological responses, while asking how reveals important information about the processes of entry, involvement and leaving organizations, he has found. Potential areas to tap include examining the myriad ways people join organizations, whether via recruitment or personal decision; how leaders influence people's decision to adopt certain roles, for example by glorifying the role of suicide bomber; and factors that motivate people to leave.

In turn, such data could help to create plausible interventions, he says. For instance, based on what he's gleaned about why people leave organizations, a particularly promising strategy may be highlighting how the promised glamorous lifestyle never comes to pass—an experience poignantly recounted by a former terrorist now in hiding. The man told Horgan he was lured into a movement as a teen when recruiters

romanticized the cause. But he soon discovered his comrades held sectarian values, not the idealistic ones he had, and he was horrified when he killed his first victim at point-blank range.

"The reality of involvement is not what these kids are led to believe," says Horgan. "Speaking with repentant former terrorists, many with blood on their hands, offers an extraordinary opportunity to use the terrorists' own words and deeds against them."

Some psychologists believe terrorism is most accurately viewed through a political lens. Psychologist Clark McCauley, PhD, a co-investigator at START and director of the Solomon Asch Center for Study of Ethnopolitical Conflict at Bryn Mawr College, has come to see terrorism as "the warfare of the weak"—the means by which groups that lack material or political power fight what they see as oppressive forces. As such, he believes that terrorist actions and government reactions to them represent a dynamic interplay, with the moves of one group influencing those of the other. As one example, if terrorists commit an attack and a state uses extreme force to send a punishing message back, the terrorists may use that action to drum up greater anti-state sentiment among citizens, lending justification to their next actions. Yet research focuses almost solely on terrorist actions and neglects the important other side of the equation, he contends. "If you can't keep track of what we're doing in response, how can you ever hope to figure out what works better or worse?" McCauley says.

THE ROLE OF CULTURAL VALUES

Paradoxically, an unconscious fear of death may underlie much of the motivation behind terrorism and reactions to terrorism, maintains psychologist Tom Pyszczynski, PhD, of the University of Colorado at Colorado Springs. Along with colleagues Jeff Greenberg, PhD, and Sheldon Solomon, PhD, Pyszczynski developed "terror management theory," which holds that people use culture and religion to protect themselves from a fear of death that lies on the fringes of awareness.

Across dozens of studies, the team has induced thoughts of death by subliminally presenting people with death-related stimuli or by inserting a delay-and-distraction task between a reminder of death and people's assessment of its effects. This subliminal prompting induces people to psychologically defend themselves against death in ways that bear little surface relationship to the problem of death, Pyszczynski's team has found. These include clinging to their cultural identities, working hard to live up to their culture's values and going to great lengths to defend those values. (Conversely, the investigators have shown that getting people to *consciously* contemplate their mortality increases their intention to engage in life-enhancing behaviors, such as exercise.)

To test whether the theory applies to the conflict between the Middle East and the West, Pyszczynski's team conducted a set of studies in the United States, Iran and Israel. In all three countries, people who were subtly reminded of their mortality—and thus primed to cling more strongly to their group identities—were more likely to support violence against the out group. Iranians were more likely to support suicide bombing against Westerners. Americans were more likely to advocate military force to battle Islamic extremists, even if it meant killing thousands of civilians. Israelis were more likely to condone violence against Palestinians. The studies are summarized in an article in the journal *Behavioral Sciences of Terrorism & Political Aggression* (Vol. 1, No. 1).

Further research conducted by START co-director Kruglanski sheds light on the role a "collectivist mentality" may play in terrorism. His surveys of thousands of people in 15 Arab and other countries found that Muslims who have a more collectivistic mentality are more likely to support terrorist attacks against Americans than those with more individualistic leanings. The research, submitted to *Political Psychology*, also found that the lower people's reported personal success in life, the greater their tendency to endorse collectivistic ideas and to support attacks against Americans. The findings suggest that joining terrorist groups may confer a sense of security and meaning that people do not feel as individuals, Kruglanski says.

"Being part of a collectivist cause has always been a hall-mark of people willing to undergo personal sacrifices," he says.

In a more global sense, a fear of cultural annihilation may help fuel terrorist sentiments, says psychologist and terrorism expert Fathali Moghaddam, PhD, of Georgetown University's department of psychology. In "How Globalization Spurs Terrorism: The Lopsided Benefits of One World and Why That Fuels Violence" (Praeger, 2008), Moghaddam argues that rapid globalization has forced disparate cultures into contact with one another and is threatening the domination or disappearance of some groups—a cultural version of "survival of the fittest."

"You can interpret Islamic terrorism as one form of reaction to the perception that the fundamentalist way of life is under attack and is about to become extinct," he says.

Because of such beliefs, psychologists are tracking public attitudes to determine how best to promote peace. Pyszczynki, for example, has conducted as-yet-unpublished research showing that people's attitudes toward out-group violence can be changed if they are reminded of a common human problem. In two of his team's recent studies, Americans coping with the "war on terror" and Palestinians in the midst of Israeli bombings were primed to think either about a local catastrophe or global warming. Some also received reminders of their own mortality. In both studies, only those primed with thoughts of both death and global warming increased their support for peace-making activities.

"The really encouraging note is that even in the height of a conflict going on with your own people, reminders of mortality

and a common cause reduces support for war and increases support for peacemaking," Pyszczynki says.

STUDYING DE-RADICALIZATION

In the real world, psychologists also are exploring the effectiveness of initiatives taking place in countries including Egypt, Iraq, Saudi Arabia, Singapore and the United Kingdom that are seeking to soften the hearts and minds of terrorist detainees. In preliminary research, Kruglanski and colleagues note that many of these programs share:

- **An intellectual component,** often involving moderate Muslim clerics who hold dialogues with imprisoned detainees about the Qu'ran's true teachings on violence and jihad.
- **An emotional component** that defuses detainees' anger and frustration by showing authentic concern for their families, through means such as funding their children's education or offering professional training for their wives. This aspect also capitalizes on the fact that detainees are weary from their lifestyles and imprisonment.
- **A social component** that addresses the reality that detainees often re-enter societies that may rekindle their radical beliefs. A program in Indonesia, for instance, uses former militants who are now law-abiding citizens to convince former terrorists that violence against civilians compromises the image of Islam.

Some of these efforts have already shown promise, says Kruglanski. For example, Egypt's largest radical Islamic group, Al-Gama'a al-Islamiyya, renounced bloodshed in 2003, the result of a deal brokered by a Muslim attorney between the group and the Egyptian government, and a program where Muslim scholars debated with imprisoned group leaders about the true meaning of Islam. As a result, the leaders wrote 25 volumes arguing for nonviolence, and the group has perpetrated no new terrorist acts since, Kruglanski says. A second major Egyptian group, Al Jihad, renounced violence in 2007 based on a similar program.

Five other such initiatives in Northern Ireland, Yemen, Saudi Arabia, Indonesia and Colombia are being studied by Pennsylvania State University's Horgan. His not-yet-published research proposes a framework that policymakers can use to evaluate these programs, including examining how each effort conceptualizes and measures success, and evaluating the reality and practical significance of these success claims.

Given his own experience talking with former terrorists, Horgan is cautious about how much to expect from these programs. In his recent study, he discovered that some of these efforts not only lack clear criteria for establishing what constitutes "success," but also that actual de-radicalization is rarely a feature of such programs—that former terrorists may rejoin society and keep from engaging in terrorist actions, but retain their radical beliefs.

"There is no evidence to suggest that disengaging from terrorism necessarily results in de-radicalization," he contends.

Kruglanski's team promises to shed more light on the issue via an assessment instrument they are developing that will gauge attitude change in those who have undergone such programs, including gauging implicit attitude change that more accurately reads their true feelings than simply what they claim is the case.

Because of the wide variety of program types and the cultural and social conditions where they are taking place, it is imperative that successful efforts design each program on a case-by-case basis, adds terrorism researcher Max Taylor, PhD, of the University of St. Andrews, and co-editor with Horgan of "The Future of Terrorism" (Routledge, 2000).

"One big problem with terrorism policy altogether is that it tends to interpret things from our perspective, based on what makes sense to us," Taylor says. "That's not really the issue: The issue is what makes sense to people on the ground."

FURTHER READING, RESOURCES

Horgan, John. "Walking Away from Terrorism" (Routledge, 2009).

Horgan, John. "Leaving Terrorism Behind" (Routledge, 2008).

Moghaddam, F.M. (2007). *Multiculturalism and Intergroup Relations: Psychological Implications for Democracy in Global Context.* Washington, DC: APA.

Pyszczynski, T.A., Solomon, S. & Greenberg, J. (2003). *In the Wake of 911: The Psychology of Terror.* Washington, DC: APA.

Moghaddam, F.M. & Marsella, A.J. (Ed.). (2003). *Understanding Terrorism: Psychosocial Roots, Consequences and Interventions.* Washington, DC: APA.

With terrorism, labeling has implications

The words and concepts we use to discuss terrorism and counterterrorism—including the word "terrorism" itself—can have profound implications for how countries, populations and individuals behave, psychological researchers maintain.

In a paper in the December 2007 *Psychological Science in the Public Interest* (Vol. 8, No. 3), Arie Kruglanski, PhD, co-director of National Consortium for the Study of Terrorism and Responses to Terrorism, or START, and colleagues examined four metaphorical constructs that countries, organizations and academicians use to describe counterterrorist activities.

The **war metaphor** refers to a global "us against them" mentality, as in the "war on terror" concept launched by President George W. Bush in the wake of 9/11. The metaphor implies that military action should be used against a clear enemy, and that only one side may win the conflict.

The **law enforcement metaphor** focuses on apprehending individual perpetrators and on punishing individual terrorist acts, rather than on demonizing an entire group. It is more likely than the war metaphor to balance both security needs and human rights concerns, they write.

Meanwhile, the **epidemiology metaphor** suggests that terrorism is an ideological disease that needs to be fought by winning over hearts and minds, while the **prejudice-reduction metaphor** acknowledges that the conditions that spawn terrorism involve a dynamic interplay between two parties. It's the only one of the

metaphors that takes an explicitly bilateral view, and suggests that social psychological interventions such as creating positive contact between members of the conflicted groups could help to resolve their differences, the authors write.

Each of these metaphorical strategies has specific strengths, limitations and potential consequences, the authors argue. For instance, the use of military force suggested by the war metaphor could convey a country's resolve and determination, but at the same time fuel the outrage of the population targeted for military action, thus undermining the objective of winning their support in the fight. Meanwhile, negotiating with terrorists with the aim of countering their ideology may in some cases convey to terrorists that they have "won" their strategic objectives.

What's needed is a nuanced understanding and use of all of these concepts that takes into account the pluses and minuses of each—but governments are a long way from such a sophisticated approach, the authors note. One way to encourage this conversation is to expand communication between social science researchers and national security agencies, as START is now attempting to do, they say.

In another look at the power of words, Cambridge University social psychology graduate student Shahzad Shafqat is designing studies and a conceptual framework comparing the concepts of terrorism and extremism. While the two are often conflated, Shafqat believes extremism can be viewed as a broader concept that can encompass positive qualities and actions as well as negative ones. Consider people who risk their lives for a good cause, or Olympic athletes willing to take extreme physical measures to win, for example, he says.

In his dissertation, Shafqat took an empirical look at the issue by asking a sample of Cambridge students and a random sample of online browsers to describe how they felt about a man on a video who claimed to have joined an unnamed religious group and was about to embark on an unspecified task. Before watching the video, participants were primed with one of four stories describing the kind of religious group the man was entering, ranging from a peaceful monastery to a terrorist organization. He also asked participants to rate the perceived traits of the person.

The one variable that distinguished people's perception of dangerous extremists or terrorists from extremists who are not dangerous was a sense of threat, says Shafqat.

"When people feel a sense of threat in relation to someone's actions, only then do label that type of extremism as terrorism," he says.

Focusing on the broader concept of extremism may take some of punch out of the word "terrorist," which tends to be such a loaded term that it's difficult to study objectively, Shafqat adds. In his view, the only meaningful way to understand terrorism is to dissect the concept of extremism, which in turn could highlight the difference between positive and negative extremism and put terrorism into a broader and more comprehensible framework of human behavior, he says.

—*T. Deangelis*

CRITICAL THINKING QUESTIONS

1. The article offered several suggestions for how to deal with terrorists and potential terrorists. What are they, and what do you see as the advantages and disadvantages of each one?

2. The article primarily discussed how governments can respond to terrorism. What role might the media play in terrorism? Give an example of how media coverage of terrorist events could have an impact on those acts or on future acts.

3. According to a quote in this article, "There is no evidence to suggest that disengaging from terrorism necessarily results in de-radicalization . . . ." In other words, sometimes an intervention might result in a former terrorist who stops engaging in terrorism yet still maintains one's radical beliefs. Do you see this as a problem or not in terms of programs aimed at eliminating terrorism? Explain your reasoning.

4. Using the information from this article as well as from other sources, what do you think would be the best strategies in dealing with terrorism? What justifications can you provide for why your ideas might be effective?

ARTICLE 32 _____

Think of the amount of time that a typical child spends in front of the television. Do you think that what that child sees on "the tube" influences his or her behavior to a great extent? Or is television more neutral—just entertainment with no lasting effects?

A major concern of parents and social psychologists alike is the impact of one particular aspect of television on children's subsequent behavior: aggression. If you have not done so in a long time, sit down and watch the Saturday morning cartoons or other programs shown after school or in the early evening, when children are most likely to be watching. How many of these programs involve some sort of violence? What are these shows teaching children, not only in terms of behaviors but also in terms of values?

The following article by Albert Bandura, Dorothea Ross, and Sheila A. Ross was one of the earliest studies to examine the impact of televised aggression on the behavior of children. In the more than 40 years since its publication, numerous other experiments have been conducted on the same topic. These studies strongly suggest that viewing televised aggression has a direct impact on the aggressive behavior of its viewers. The research by Bandura and his colleagues helped initiate this important line of research.

Transmission of Aggression through Imitation of Aggressive Models[1]

■ Albert Bandura, Dorothea Ross, and Sheila A. Ross[2]

A previous study, designed to account for the phenomenon of identification in terms of incidental learning, demonstrated that children readily imitated behavior exhibited by an adult model in the presence of the model (Bandura & Huston, 1961). A series of experiments by Blake (1958) and others (Grosser, Polansky, & Lippitt, 1951; Rosenblith, 1959; Schachter & Hall, 1952) have likewise shown that mere observation of responses of a model has a facilitating effect on subjects' reactions in the immediate social influence setting.

While these studies provide convincing evidence for the influence and control exerted on others by the behavior of a model, a more crucial test of imitative learning involves the generalization of imitative response patterns to new settings in which the model is absent.

In the experiment reported in this paper, children were exposed to aggressive and nonaggressive adult models and were then tested for amount of imitative learning in a new situation in the absence of the model. According to the prediction, subjects exposed to aggressive models would reproduce aggressive acts resembling those of their models and would differ in this respect both from subjects who observed nonaggressive models and from [those] who had no prior exposure to any models. This hypothesis assumed that subjects had learned imitative habits as a result of prior reinforcement, and these tendencies would generalize to some extent to adult experimenters (Miller & Dollard, 1941).

It was further predicted that observation of subdued nonaggressive models would have a generalized inhibiting effect on the subjects' subsequent behavior, and this effect would be reflected in a difference between the nonaggressive and the control groups, with subjects in the latter group displaying significantly more aggression.

Hypotheses were also advanced concerning the influence of the sex of model and sex of subjects on imitation. Fauls and Smith (1956) have shown that preschool children perceive their parents as having distinct preferences regarding sex appropriate modes of behavior for their children. Their findings, as well as informal observation, suggest that parents reward imitation of sex appropriate behavior and discourage or punish sex inappropriate imitative responses, e.g., a male child is unlikely to receive much reward for performing female appropriate activities, such as cooking, or for adopting other aspects of the maternal role, but these same behaviors are typically welcomed if performed by females. As a result of differing reinforcement histories, tendencies to imitate male and female models thus acquire differential habit strength. One would expect, on this basis, subjects to imitate the behavior of a same-sex model to a greater degree than a model of the opposite sex.

Since aggression, however, is a highly masculine-typed behavior, boys should be more predisposed than girls toward imitating aggression, the difference being most marked for subjects exposed to the male aggressive model.

Bandura, A.; Ross, D.; & Ross, S.A. (1961). Transmission of aggression through imitation of aggressive models. *Journal of Abnormal and Social Psychology*, 63, 575–582.

METHOD

Subjects

The subjects were 36 boys and 36 girls enrolled in the Stanford University Nursery School. They ranged in age from 37 to 69 months, with a mean age of 52 months.

Two adults, a male and a female, served in the role of model, and one female experimenter conducted the study for all 72 children.

Experimental Design

Subjects were divided into eight experimental groups of six subjects each and a control group consisting of 24 subjects. Half the experimental subjects were exposed to aggressive models and half were exposed to models that were subdued and nonaggressive in their behavior. These groups were further subdivided into male and female subjects. Half the subjects in the aggressive and nonaggressive conditions observed same-sex models, while the remaining subjects in each group viewed models of the opposite sex. The control group had no prior exposure to the adult models and was tested only in the generalization situation.

It seemed reasonable to expect that the subjects' level of aggressiveness would be positively related to the readiness with which they imitated aggressive modes of behavior. Therefore, in order to increase the precision of treatment comparisons, subjects in the experimental and control groups were matched individually on the basis of ratings of their aggressive behavior in social interactions in the nursery school.

The subjects were rated on four five-point rating scales by the experimenter and a nursery school teacher, both of whom were well acquainted with the children. These scales measured the extent to which subjects displayed physical aggression, verbal aggression, aggression toward inanimate objects, and aggressive inhibition. The latter scale, which dealt with the subjects' tendency to inhibit aggressive reactions in the face of high instigation, provided a measure of aggression anxiety.

Fifty-one subjects were rated independently by both judges so as to permit an assessment of interrater agreement. The reliability of the composite aggression score, estimated by means of the Pearson product-moment correlation, was .89.

The composite score was obtained by summing the ratings on the four aggression scales; on the basis of these scores, subjects were arranged in triplets and assigned at random to one of two treatment conditions or to the control group.

Experimental Conditions

In the first step in the procedure subjects were brought individually by the experimenter to the experimental room and the model who was in the hallway outside the room was invited by the experimenter to come and join in the game. The experimenter then escorted the subject to one corner of the room, which was structured as the subject's play area. After seating the child at a small table, the experimenter demonstrated how the subject could design pictures with potato prints and picture stickers provided. The potato prints included a variety of geometrical forms; the stickers were attractive multicolor pictures of animals, flowers, and western figures to be pasted on a pastoral scene. These activities were selected since they had been established, by previous studies in the nursery school, as having high interest value for the children.

After having settled the subject in his corner, the experimenter escorted the model to the opposite corner of the room which contained a small table and chair, a tinker toy set, a mallet, and a 5-foot inflated Bobo doll. The experimenter explained that these were the materials provided for the model to play with and, after the model was seated, the experimenter left the experimental room.

With subjects in the *nonaggressive condition,* the model assembled the tinker toys in a quiet subdued manner totally ignoring the Bobo doll.

In contrast, with subjects in the *aggressive condition,* the model began by assembling the tinker toys but after approximately a minute had elapsed, the model turned to the Bobo doll and spent the remainder of the period aggressing toward it.

Imitative learning can be clearly demonstrated if a model performs sufficiently novel patterns of responses which are unlikely to occur independently of the observation of the behavior of a model and if a subject reproduces these behaviors in substantially identical form. For this reason, in addition to punching the Bobo doll, a response that is likely to be performed by children independently of a demonstration, the model exhibited distinctive aggressive acts which were to be scored as imitative responses. The model laid Bobo on its side, sat on it and punched it repeatedly in the nose. The model then raised the Bobo doll, picked up the mallet and struck the doll on the head. Following the mallet aggression, the model tossed the doll up in the air aggressively and kicked it about the room. This sequence of physically aggressive acts was repeated approximately three times, interspersed with verbally aggressive responses such as "Sock him in the nose . . . ," "Hit him down . . . ," "Throw him in the air . . . ," "Kick him . . . ," "Pow . . . ," and two nonaggressive comments, "He keeps coming back for more" and "He sure is a tough fella."

Thus in the exposure situation, subjects were provided with a diverting task which occupied their attention while at the same time insured observation of the model's behavior in the absence of any instructions to observe or to learn the responses in question. Since subjects could not perform the model's aggressive behavior, any learning that occurred was purely on an observational or covert basis.

At the end of 10 minutes, the experimenter entered the room, informed the subject that he would now go to another game room, and bid the model goodbye.

AGGRESSION AROUSAL

Subjects were tested for the amount of imitative learning in a different experimental room that was set off from the main nursery school building. The two experimental situations were thus clearly differentiated; in fact, many subjects were under the impression that they were no longer on the nursery school grounds.

Prior to the test for imitation, however, all subjects, experimental and control, were subjected to mild aggression arousal to insure that they were under some degree of instigation to aggression. The arousal experience was included for two main reasons. In the first place, observation of aggressive behavior exhibited by others tends to reduce the probability of aggression on the part of the observer (Rosenbaum & deCharms, 1960). Consequently, subjects in the aggressive condition, in relation both to the nonaggressive and control groups, would be under weaker instigation following exposure to the models. Second, if subjects in the nonaggressive condition expressed little aggression in the face of appropriate instigation, the presence of an inhibitory process would seem to be indicated.

Following the exposure experience, therefore, the experimenter brought the subject to an anteroom that contained these relatively attractive toys: a fire engine, a locomotive, a jet fighter plane, a cable car, a colorful spinning top, and a doll set complete with wardrobe, doll carriage, and baby crib. The experimenter explained that the toys were for the subject to play with but, as soon as the subject became sufficiently involved with the play material (usually in about 2 minutes), the experimenter remarked that these were her very best toys, that she did not let just anyone play with them, and that she had decided to reserve these toys for the other children. However, the subject could play with any of the toys that were in the next room. The experimenter and the subject then entered the adjoining experimental room.

It was necessary for the experimenter to remain in the room during the experimental session; otherwise a number of the children would either refuse to remain alone or would leave before the termination of the session. However, in order to minimize any influence her presence might have on the subject's behavior, the experimenter remained as inconspicuous as possible by busying herself with paper work at a desk in the far corner of the room and avoiding any interaction with the child.

Test for Delayed Imitation

The experimental room contained a variety of toys including some that could be used in imitative or nonimitative aggression, and others that tended to elicit predominantly nonaggressive forms of behavior. The aggressive toys included a 3-foot Bobo doll, a mallet and peg board, two dart guns, and a tether ball with a face painted on it which hung from the ceiling. The nonaggressive toys, on the other hand, included a tea set, crayons and coloring paper, a ball, two dolls, three bears, cars and trucks, and plastic farm animals.

In order to eliminate any variation in behavior due to mere placement of the toys in the room, the play material was arranged in a fixed order for each of the sessions.

The subject spent 20 minutes in this experimental room during which time his behavior was rated in terms of predetermined response categories by judges who observed the session through a one-way mirror in an adjoining observation room. The 20-minute session was divided into 5-second intervals by means of an electric interval timer, thus yielding a total number of 240 response units for each subject.

The male model scored the experimental sessions for all 72 children. Except for the cases in which he served as model, he did not have knowledge of the subjects' group assignments. In order to provide an estimate of interscorer agreement, the performances of half the subjects were also scored independently by a second observer. Thus one or the other of the two observers usually had no knowledge of the conditions to which the subjects were assigned. Since, however, all but two of the subjects in the aggressive condition performed the models' novel aggressive responses while subjects in the other conditions only rarely exhibited such reactions, subjects who were exposed to the aggressive models could be readily identified through their distinctive behavior.

The responses scored involved highly specific concrete classes of behavior and yielded high interscorer reliabilities, the product-moment coefficients being in the .90s.

Response Measures

Three measures of imitation were obtained:

Imitation of physical aggression: This category included acts of striking the Bobo doll with the mallet, sitting on the doll and punching it in the nose, kicking the doll, and tossing it in the air.
Imitative verbal aggression: Subject repeats the phrases, "Sock him," "Hit him down," "Kick him," "Throw him in the air," or "Pow."
Imitative nonaggressive verbal responses: Subject repeats, "He keeps coming back for more," or "He sure is a tough fella."

During the pretest, a number of the subjects imitated the essential components of the model's behavior but did not perform the complete act, or they directed the imitative aggressive response to some object other than the Bobo doll. Two responses of this type were therefore scored and were interpreted as partially imitative behavior.

Mallet aggression: Subject strikes objects other than the Bobo doll aggressively with the mallet.
Sits on the Bobo doll: Subject lays the Bobo doll on its side and sits on it, but does not aggress toward it.

The following additional nonimitative aggressive responses were scored:

Punched Bobo doll: Subject strikes, slaps, or pushes the doll aggressively.
Nonimitative physical and verbal aggression: This category included physically aggressive acts directed toward objects other than the Bobo doll and any hostile remarks except for those in the verbal imitation category; e.g., "Shoot the Bobo," "Cut him," "Stupid ball," "Knock over people," "Horses fighting, biting."
Aggressive gun play: Subject shoots darts or aims the guns and fires imaginary shots at objects in the room.

Ratings were also made of the number of behavior units in which subjects played nonaggressively or sat quietly and did not play with any of the material at all.

RESULT

Complete Imitation of Models' Behavior

Subjects in the aggression condition reproduced a good deal of physical and verbal aggressive behavior resembling that of the models, and their mean scores differed markedly from those of subjects in the nonaggressive and control groups who exhibited virtually no imitative aggression (see Table 1).

Since there were only a few scores for subjects in the nonaggressive and control conditions (approximately 70% of the subjects had zero scores), and the assumption of homogeneity of variance could not be made, the Friedman two-way analysis of variance by ranks was employed to test the significance of the obtained differences.

The prediction that exposure of subjects to aggressive models increases the probability of aggressive behavior is clearly confirmed (see Table 2). The main effect of treatment conditions is highly significant both for physical and verbal imitative aggression. Comparison of pairs of scores by the sign test shows that the obtained over-all differences were due almost entirely to the aggression displayed by subjects who had been exposed to the aggressive models. Their scores were significantly higher than those of either the nonaggressive or control groups, which did not differ from each other (Table 2).

TABLE 1 / Mean Aggression Scores for Experimental and Control Subjects

| | Experimental Groups | | | | |
| | Aggressive | | Nonaggressive | | |
Response Category	F Model	M Model	F Model	M Model	Control Groups
Imitative physical aggression					
Female subjects	5.5	7.2	2.5	0.0	1.2
Male subjects	12.4	25.8	0.2	1.5	2.0
Imitative verbal aggression					
Female subjects	13.7	2.0	0.3	0.0	0.7
Male subjects	4.3	12.7	1.1	0.0	1.7
Mallet aggression					
Female subjects	17.2	18.7	0.5	0.5	13.1
Male subjects	15.5	28.8	18.7	6.7	13.5
Punches Bobo doll					
Female subjects	6.3	16.5	5.8	4.3	11.7
Male subjects	18.9	11.9	15.6	14.8	15.7
Nonimitative aggression					
Female subjects	21.3	8.4	7.2	1.4	6.1
Male subjects	16.2	36.7	26.1	22.3	24.6
Aggressive gun play					
Female subjects	1.8	4.5	2.6	2.5	3.7
Male subjects	7.3	15.9	8.9	16.7	14.3

TABLE 2 / Significance of the Differences between Experimental and Control Groups in the Expression of Aggression

| | | | | Comparison of Pairs of Treatment Conditions | | |
| | | | | Aggressive vs. Nonaggressive | Aggressive vs. Control | Nonaggressive vs. Control |
Response Category	χ_r^2	Q	P	p	p	p
Imitative responses						
Physical aggression	27.17		< .001	< .001	< .001	.09
Verbal aggression	9.17		< .02	.004	.048	.09
Nonaggressive verbal responses		17.50	< .001	.004	.004	*ns*
Partial imitation						
Mallet aggression	11.06		< .01	.026	*ns*	.005
Sits on Bobo		13.44	< .01	.018	.059	*ns*
Nonimitative aggression						
Punches Bobo doll	2.87		*ns*			
Physical and verbal	8.96		< .02	.026	*ns*	*ns*
Aggressive gun play	2.75		*ns*			

Note: ns = nonsignificant.

Imitation was not confined to the model's aggressive responses. Approximately one-third of the subjects in the aggressive condition also repeated the model's nonaggressive verbal responses while none of the subjects in either the nonaggressive or control groups made such remarks. This difference, tested by means of the Cochran Q test, was significant well beyond the .001 level (Table 2).

Partial Imitation of Models' Behavior

Differences in the predicted direction were also obtained on the two measures of partial imitation.

Analysis of variance of scores based on the subjects' use of the mallet aggressively toward objects other than the Bobo doll reveals that treatment conditions are a statistically significant course of variation (Table 2). In addition, individual sign tests show that both the aggressive and the control groups, relative to subjects in the nonaggressive condition, produced significantly more mallet aggression, the difference being particularly marked with regard to female subjects. Girls who observed nonaggressive models performed a mean number of 0.5 mallet aggression responses as compared to mean values of 18.0 and 13.1 for girls in the aggressive and control groups, respectively.

Although subjects who observed aggressive models performed more mallet aggression (M = 20.0) than their controls (M = 13. 3), the difference was not statistically significant.

With respect to the partially imitative response of sitting on the Bobo doll, the over-all group differences were significant beyond the .01 level (Table 2). Comparison of pairs of scores by the sign test procedure reveals that subjects in the aggressive group reproduced this aspect of the models' behavior to a greater extent than did the nonaggressive (p = .018) or the control (p = .059) subjects. The latter two groups, on the other hand, did not differ from each other.

Nonimitative Aggression

Analyses of variance of the remaining aggression measures (Table 2) show that treatment conditions did not influence the extent to which subjects engaged in aggressive gun play or punched the Bobo doll. The effect of conditions is highly significant (χ_r^2 = 8.96, p < .02), however, in the case of the subjects' expression of nominative physical and verbal aggression. Further comparison of treatment pairs reveals that the main source of the over-all difference was the aggressive and nonaggressive groups which differed significantly from each other (Table 2), with subjects exposed to the aggressive models displaying the greater amount of aggression.

Influence of Sex of Model and Sex of Subjects on Imitation

The hypothesis that boys are more prone than girls to imitate aggression exhibited by a model was only partially confirmed. *t* tests computed for subjects in the aggressive condition reveal that boys reproduced more imitative physical aggression than girls (t = 2.50, p < .01). The groups do not differ, however, in their imitation of verbal aggression.

The use of nonparametric tests, necessitated by the extremely skewed distributions of scores for subjects in the nonaggressive and control conditions, preclude an over-all test of the influence of sex of model per se, and of the various interactions between the main effects. Inspection of the means presented in Table 1 for subjects in the aggression condition, however, clearly suggests the possibility of a Sex × Model interaction. This interaction effect is much more consistent and pronounced for the male model than for the female model. Male subjects, for example, exhibited more physical ($t = 2.07$, $p < .05$) and verbal imitative aggression ($t = 2.51$, $p < .05$), more nonimitative aggression ($t = 3.15$, $p < .025$), and engaged in significantly more aggressive gun play ($t = 2.12$, $p < .05$) following exposure to the aggressive male model than the female subjects. In contrast, girls exposed to the female model performed considerably more imitative verbal aggression and more nonimitative aggression than did the boys (Table 1). The variances, however, were equally large and with only a small N in each cell the mean differences did not reach statistical significance.

Data for the nonaggressive and control subjects provide additional suggestive evidence that the behavior of the male model exerted a greater influence than the female model on the subjects' behavior in the generalization situation.

It will be recalled that, except for the greater amount of mallet aggression exhibited by the control subjects, no significant differences were obtained between the nonaggressive and control groups. The data indicate, however, that the absence of significant differences between these two groups was due primarily to the fact that subjects exposed to the nonaggressive female model did not differ from the controls on any of the measures of aggression. With respect to the male model, on the other hand, the differences between the groups are striking. Comparison of the sets of scores by means of the sign test reveals that, in relation to the control group, subjects exposed to the nonaggressive male model performed significantly less imitative physical aggression ($p = .06$), less imitative verbal aggression ($p = .002$), less mallet aggression ($p = .003$), less nonimitative physical and verbal aggression ($p = .03$) and they were less inclined to punch the Bobo doll ($p = .07$).

While the comparison of subgroups, when some of the over-all tests do not reach statistical significance, is likely to capitalize on chance differences, nevertheless the consistency of the findings adds support to the interpretation in terms of influence by the model.

Nonaggressive Behavior

With the exception of expected sex differences, Lindquist (1956) Type III analyses of variance of the nonaggressive response scores yielded few significant differences.

Female subjects spent more time than boys playing with dolls ($p < .001$), with the tea set ($p < .001$), and coloring ($p < .05$). The boys, on the other hand, devoted significantly more time than the girls to exploratory play with the guns ($p < .01$). No sex differences were found in respect to the subjects' use of the other stimulus objects, i.e., farm animals, cars, or tether ball.

Treatment conditions did produce significant differences on two measures of nonaggressive behavior that are worth mentioning. Subjects in the nonaggressive condition engaged in significantly more nonaggressive play with dolls than either subjects in the aggressive group ($t = 2.67$, $p < .02$), or in the control group ($t = 2.57$, $p < .02$).

Even more noteworthy is the finding that subjects who observed nonaggressive models spent more than twice as much time as subjects in aggressive condition ($t = 3.07$, $p < .01$) in simply sitting quietly without handling any of the play material.

DISCUSSION

Much current research on social learning is focused on the shaping of new behavior through rewarding and punishing consequences. Unless responses are emitted, however, they cannot be influenced. The results of this study provide strong evidence that observation of cues produced by the behavior of others is one effective means of eliciting certain forms of responses for which the original probability is very low or zero. Indeed, social imitation may hasten or short-cut the acquisition of new behaviors without the necessity of reinforcing successive approximations as suggested by Skinner (1953).

Thus subjects given an opportunity to observe aggressive models later reproduced a good deal of physical and verbal aggression (as well as nonaggressive responses) substantially identical with that of the model. In contrast, subjects who were exposed to nonaggressive models and those who had no previous exposure to any models only rarely performed such responses.

To the extent that observation of adult models displaying aggression communicates permissiveness for aggressive behavior, such exposure may serve to weaken inhibitory responses and thereby to increase the probability of aggressive reactions to subsequent frustrations. The fact, however, that subjects expressed their aggression in ways that clearly resembled the novel patterns exhibited by the models provides striking evidence for the occurrence of learning by imitation.

In the procedure employed by Miller and Dollard (1941) for establishing imitative behavior, adult or peer models performed discrimination responses following which they were consistently rewarded, and the subjects were similarly reinforced whenever they matched the leaders' choice responses. While these experiments have been widely accepted as demonstrations of learning by means of imitation, in fact, they simply involve a special case of discrimination learning in which the behavior of others serves as discriminative stimuli for responses that are already part of the subject's repertoire. Auditory or visual environmental cues could easily have been substituted for the social stimuli to facilitate the discrimination learning. In contrast, the process of imitation studied in the present experiment differed in several important respects from the one investigated by Miller and Dollard in that subjects learned to combine fractional responses into relatively complex novel patterns solely by observing the performance of social models without any opportunity to perform the models' behavior in the exposure setting, and without any reinforcers delivered either to the models or to the observers.

An adequate theory of the mechanisms underlying imitative learning is lacking. The explanations that have been offered (Logan, Olmsted, Rosner, Schwartz, & Stevens, 1955; Maccoby, 1959) assume that the imitator performs the model's responses covertly. If it can be assumed additionally that rewards and punishments are self-administered in conjunction with the covert responses, the process of imitative learning could be accounted for in terms of the same principles that govern instrumental trial-and-error learning. In the early stages of the developmental process, however, the range of component responses in the organism's repertoire is probably increased through a process of classical conditioning (Bandura & Huston, 1961; Mowrer, 1950).

The data provide some evidence that the male model influenced the subjects' behavior outside the exposure setting to a greater extent than was true for the female model. In the analyses of the Sex × Model interactions, for example, only the comparisons involving the male model yielded significant differences. Similarly, subjects exposed to the nonaggressive male model performed less aggressive behavior than the controls, whereas comparisons involving the female model were consistently nonsignificant.

In a study of learning by imitation, Rosenblith (1959) has likewise found male experimenters more effective than females in influencing children's behavior. Rosenblith advanced the tentative explanation that the school setting may involve some social deprivation in respect to adult males which, in turn, enhances the male's reward value.

The trends in the data yielded by the present study suggest an alternative explanation. In the case of a highly masculine-typed behavior such as physical aggression, there is a tendency for both male and female subjects to imitate the male model to a greater degree than the female model. On the other hand, in the case of verbal aggression, which is less clearly sex linked, the greatest amount of imitation occurs in relation to the same-sex model. These trends together with the finding that boys in relation to girls are in general more imitative of physical aggression but do not differ in imitation of verbal aggression, suggest that subjects may be differentially affected by the sex of

the model but that predictions must take into account the degree to which the behavior in question is sex-typed.

The preceding discussion has assumed that maleness-femaleness rather than some other personal characteristics of the particular models involved, is the significant variable—an assumption that cannot be tested directly with the data at hand. It was clearly evident, however, particularly from boys' spontaneous remarks about the display of aggression by the female model, that some subjects at least were responding in terms of a sex discrimination and their prior learning about what is sex appropriate behavior (e.g., "Who is that lady? That's not the way for a lady to behave. Ladies are supposed to act like ladies. . . . " "You should have seen what that girl did in there. She was just acting like a man. I never saw a girl act like that before. She was punching and fighting but not swearing."). Aggression by the male model, on the other hand, was more likely to be seen as appropriate and approved by both the boys ("Al's a good socker, he beat up Bobo. I want to sock like Al.") and the girls ("That man is a strong fighter, he punched and punched and he could hit Bobo right down to the floor and if Bobo got up he said, 'Punch your nose.' He's a good fighter like Daddy.").

The finding that subjects exposed to the quiet models were more inhibited and unresponsive than subjects in the aggressive condition, together with the obtained difference on the aggression measures, suggests that exposure to inhibited models not only decreases the probability of occurrence of aggressive behavior but also generally restricts the range of behavior emitted by the subjects.

"Identification with aggressor" (Freud, 1946) or "defensive identification" (Mowrer, 1950), whereby a person presumably transforms himself from object to agent of aggression by adopting the attributes of an aggressive threatening model so as to allay anxiety, is widely accepted as an explanation of the imitative learning of aggression.

The development of aggressive modes of response by children of aggressively punitive adults, however, may simply reflect object displacement without involving any such mechanism of defensive identification. In studies of child training antecedents of aggressively antisocial adolescents (Bandura & Walters, 1959) and of young hyperaggressive boys (Bandura, 1960), the parents were found to be nonpermissive and punitive of aggression directed toward themselves. On the other hand, they actively encouraged and reinforced their sons' aggression toward persons outside the home. This pattern of differential reinforcement of aggressive behavior served to inhibit the boys' aggression toward the original instigators and fostered the displacement of aggression toward objects and situations eliciting much weaker inhibitory responses.

Moreover, the findings from an earlier study (Bandura & Huston, 1961), in which children imitated to an equal degree aggression exhibited by a nurturant and a nonnurturant model, together with the results of the present experiment in which subjects readily imitated aggressive models who were more or less neutral figures suggest that mere observation of aggression, regardless of the quality of the model-subject relationship, is a sufficient condition for producing imitative aggression in children. A comparative study of the subjects' imitation of aggressive models who are feared, who are liked and esteemed, or who are essentially neutral figures would throw some light on whether or not a more parsimonious theory than the one involved in "identification with the aggressor" can explain the modeling process.

SUMMARY

Twenty-four preschool children were assigned to each of three conditions. One experimental group observed aggressive adult models; a second observed inhibited nonaggressive models; while subjects in a control group had no prior exposure to the models. Half the subjects in the experimental conditions observed same-sex models and half viewed models of the opposite sex. Subjects were then tested for the amount of imitative as well as nonimitative aggression performed in a new situation in the absence of the models.

Comparison of the subjects' behavior in the generalization situation revealed that subjects exposed to aggressive models reproduced a good deal of aggression resembling that of the models, and that their mean scores differed markedly from those of subjects in the nonaggressive and control groups. Subjects in the aggressive condition also exhibited significantly more partially imitative and nonimitative aggressive behavior and were generally less inhibited in their behavior than subjects in the nonaggressive condition.

Imitation was found to be differentially influenced by the sex of the model with boys showing more aggression than girls following exposure to the male model, the difference being particularly marked on highly masculine-typed behavior.

Subjects who observed the nonaggressive models, especially the subdued male model, were generally less aggressive than their controls.

The implications of the findings based on this experiment and related studies for the psychoanalytic theory of identification with the aggressor were discussed.

REFERENCES

Bandura, A. Relationship of family patterns to child behavior disorders. Progress Report, 1960, Stanford University, Project No. M-1734, United States Public Health Service.

Bandura, A., & Huston, Aletha C. Identification as a process of incidental learning. *J. Abnorm. Soc. Psychol.,* 1961, *63,* 311–318.

Bandura, A., & Walters, R. H. *Adolescent aggression.* New York: Ronald, 1959.

Blake, R. R. The other person in the situation. In R. Tagiuri & L. Petrullo (Eds.), *Person perception and interpersonal behavior.* Stanford, Calif.: Stanford Univer. Press, 1958. Pp. 229–242.

Fauls, Lydia B., & Smith, W. D. Sex-role learning of five-year olds. *J. Genet. Psychol.,* 1956, *89,* 105–117.

Freud, Anna. *The ego and the mechanisms of defense.* New York: International Univer. Press, 1946.

Grosser, D., Polansky, N., & Lippitt, R. A laboratory study of behavior contagion. *Hum. Relat.,* 1951, *4,* 115–142.

Lindquist, E. F. *Design and analysis of experiments.* Boston: Houghton Mifflin, 1956.

Logan, F., Olmsted, O. L., Rosner, B. S., Schwartz, R. D., & Stevens, C. M. *Behavior theory and social science.* New Haven: Yale Univer. Press, 1955.

Maccoby, Eleanor E. Role-taking in childhood and its consequences for social learning. *Child Develpm.,* 1959, *30,* 239–252.

Miller, N. E., & Dollard, J. *Social learning and imitation.* New Haven: Yale Univer. Press, 1941.

Mowrer, O. H. (Ed.) Identification: A link between learning theory and psychotherapy. In, *Learning theory and personality dynamics.* New York: Ronald, 1950. Pp. 69–94.

Rosenbaum, M. E., & deCharms, R. Direct and vicarious reduction of hostility. *J. Abnorm. Soc. Psychol.,* 1960, *60,* 105–111.

Rosenblith, Judy F. Learning by imitation in kindergarten children. *Child Develpm.,* 1959, *30,* 69–80.

Schachter, S., & Hall, R. Group-derived restraints and audience persuasion. *Hum. Relat.,* 1952, *5,* 397–406.

Skinner, B. F. *Science and human behavior.* New York: Macmillan, 1953.

ENDNOTES

1. This investigation was supported by Research Grant M-4398 from the National Institute of Health, United States Public Health Service.

2. The authors wish to express their appreciation to Edith Dowley, Director, and Patricia Rowe, Head Teacher, Stanford University Nursery School for their assistance throughout this study.

CRITICAL THINKING QUESTIONS

1. Notice that the children's anger was aroused prior to their being placed in the situation where their aggression would be measured. Why was this done? What might have resulted had their anger not been aroused beforehand? Were there different effects, depending on whether the children experienced prior anger arousal? If so, then what are the implications for generalizing the results of this study to how violent television affects its young viewers? Explain your answers.

2. This study reported that the gender of the actor made a difference in how much physical aggression was imitated. It also mentioned that some of the children simply found it inappropriate for a female actor to act

aggressively. Over 40 years have passed since publication of this study. Do you think children today would still see physical aggression by a female as inappropriate? Support your answer.

3. Analyze the content of television shows directed toward children (including cartoons) for aggression, examining the type of aggression (physical versus verbal) and the gender of the aggressive character. Relate the findings to Question 2, mentioned earlier.

4. Examine research conducted over the last three decades that documents the impact of televised aggression on children's behavior. Given these findings, what should be done? Should laws be passed to regulate the amount of violence shown on television? Or should this form of censorship be avoided? Explain. What other alternatives might exist to reverse or prevent the potential harm of observing violence on television?

ADDITIONAL RELATED READINGS

Boxer, P., Huesmann, L. R., Bushman, B. J., O'Brien, M., & Moceri, D. (2009). The role of violent media preference in cumulative developmental risk for violence and general aggression. *Journal of Youth and Adolescence, 38*(3), 417–428.

Feshbach, S., & Tangney, J. (2008). Television viewing and aggression: Some alternative perspectives. *Perspectives on Psychological Science, 3*(5), 387–389.

ARTICLE 33 _____

An important area of research on aggression concerns its causes. Three general classes of theories have emerged: The first class, which can be called *instinct theories,* explains aggression as somehow rooted in biology. Thus, aggression stems from internally generated forces and is something that human beings are genetically programmed to do. A second type of theory, called *drive reduction,* essentially explains aggression as arising from forces outside the individual; for instance, experiencing frustration may produce readiness to engage in aggressive behavior. *Social learning* is the third theoretical explanation of aggression. Basically, this approach maintains that aggression, like many other complex social behaviors, is learned. It is not instinctive nor is it simply a reaction to a specific external event.

Each of these theoretical views attributes aggression to a different cause. It follows, then, that whichever theoretical explanation you adopt will influence how optimistic you are about the possible control of aggression. For example, if you believe that aggression is innate, a biological predisposition of sorts, then there is not much that can be done about it. It is simply human nature to be aggressive. However, if you believe that aggression is learned, then it is not inevitable that people be aggressive. After all, if aggressive behaviors can be learned, then nonaggressive behaviors can be learned, as well. And if aggression arises from forces outside the individual, then aggression can be reduced to the extent that one can control those outside forces.

Underlying our tendencies to be aggressive or not may be the particular values or beliefs that we hold. For example, in a very general sense we may believe that using violence to get something is totally acceptable. Or we may believe that it is never acceptable to do so. What helps to shape these values and beliefs are our own unique experiences in the world, including what we learn from our family and surroundings. What we learn from our family and surroundings, in turn, may be influenced by the larger culture in which we are imbedded. In short, some cultures are more accepting of aggression as a means of problem solving than are others.

One such cultural variable that may relate to aggression is the *culture of honor.* A culture-of-honor society is one that fundamentally accepts the use of aggression as an appropriate response to insults or threats to one's honor. In other words, if someone insults you or your family, it's acceptable, even expected, to hurt them in return in order to restore your honor. Such culture-of-honor values vary considerably in different groups. According to researchers, in the United States such values are more prevalent in the South and in the West than they are in the North.

As mentioned earlier, people with a culture-of-honor value system are much more likely to use violence as a response to threats to their honor. Studies have shown that indeed violent crime and homicides are more likely to occur in areas where culture-of-honor values are more prevalent. The following article by Ryan P. Brown, Lindsey L. Osterman, and Collin D. Barnes examines the issue of whether such culture-of-honor values are also related to school violence.

School Violence and the Culture of Honor

■ Ryan P. Brown, Lindsey L. Osterman, and Collin D. Barnes

ABSTRACT

We investigated the hypothesis that a sociocultural variable known as the culture of honor would be uniquely predictive of school-violence indicators. Controlling for demographic characteristics associated in previous studies with violent crime among adults, we found that high-school students in culture-of-honor states were significantly more likely than high-school students in non-culture-of-honor states to report having brought a weapon to school in the past month. Using data aggregated over a 20-year period, we also found that culture-of-honor states had more than twice as many school shootings per capita as non-culture-of-honor states. The data revealed important differences between school violence and general patterns of homicide and are consistent with the view that many acts of school violence reflect retaliatory aggression springing from intensely experienced social-identity threats.

Brown, R.P.; Osterman, L.L.; & Barnes, C.D., *Psychological Science, 20*(11), 1400–1451. Copyright © 2009 by the Association for Psychological Science. Reprinted by permission of SAGE Publications.

From the coordinated attack at Columbine High School in Colorado, to the one-man massacre at Virginia Tech, violence in schools has become a topic of increasing concern in recent years and has prompted a flurry of studies on possible precursors to gun-related aggression among youth. To date, most of these studies have utilized a focused, case-based approach, largely because of the low frequency of school shootings. This case-study approach has yielded valuable insights into certain commonalities among shooters (e.g., they tend to be interested in violent media, often have mood disorders or suicidal ideations, and are commonly the victims of taunting or rejection; Fein et al., 2002; Leary, Kowalski, Smith, & Phillips, 2003; Newman, Fox, Roth, Mehta, & Harding, 2005).

Although the focused case-study approach has illuminated important dispositional and situational variables that may contribute to school shootings, we suggest that an analysis of these incidents at a broader, cultural level might reveal additional insights into the etiology of school violence. In particular, we propose that a sociocultural variable known as the *culture of honor* might be a risk factor for school violence (the *culture-of-honor hypothesis*), just as it has been demonstrated to be for violent crimes among adults.

Societies exhibiting a culture of honor place a high premium on strength and social regard (especially among males) in connection with one's person, family, reputation, and property, presumably because economic and social factors made such priorities socially adaptive at some point in time (Nisbett, 1993). Early research on the culture of honor in the United States revealed that, compared with people living in non-culture-of-honor states, people living in culture-of-honor states were more favorable toward the death penalty and were more tolerant of, and more prone to exhibit, aggressive retaliation in response to insults and other honor threats. This tendency toward violent defense of one's honor has been demonstrated in controlled laboratory studies (Cohen, Nisbett, Bowdle, & Schwartz, 1996), as well as in archival studies on homicide and violent-crime rates in the United States (Cohen, 1998; Nisbett, Polly, & Lang, 1995). In addition to behaving aggressively, people living in culture-of-honor states endorse attitudes supportive of violence in the service of restoring or defending one's reputation, family, or property (Hayes & Lee, 2005), and they socially and legally sanction violence as sport or entertainment (Baron & Straus, 1989; Cohen, 1996). According to Nisbett and Cohen (1996), Southern and Western states in the United States are more likely to exhibit culture-of-honor qualities than are Northern and Eastern states.

In-depth case studies reported by other researchers (e.g., Leary et al., 2003; Newman et al., 2005) revealed that school violence is often preceded by social marginalization, bullying, romantic rejection, or taunting. Because such experiences represent serious threats to honor (particularly among males), we, hypothesized that the culture of honor is a significant risk factor for school violence. Some researchers have argued that the apparent relationship between adult homicide rates and culture of honor in the United States is spurious, resulting from basic demographic differences between Southern and Western states, on the one hand, and Northern and Eastern states, on the other, rather than from cultural factors per se. Specifically, culture-of-honor states are typically hotter, poorer, and more socially unstable than non-culture-of-honor states, and any of these differences might explain the apparent association between culture of honor and violence. Indeed, some early analyses of homicide rates in the Southern United States supported this contention (e.g., Anderson & Anderson, 1996), so these same state-level confounds could also explain any association discovered between the culture of honor and school violence.

In the current investigation, we attempted to link the culture of honor to indices of school violence—specifically, the percentage of high school students who reported having brought a weapon to school in the past month, as well as actual rates of school shootings over a 20-year period. To account for the most prominent confounds examined in prior research, we compiled a database on school violence, culture of honor, and variables that have been shown to covary with the culture of honor and could thus account for its possible association with school violence. These variables included measures of social and economic insecurity (e.g., divorce rates, poverty), mean state temperature, and an index of rurality.

STUDY 1

Data

In Study 1, we first examined an index of *school-violence potential*: specifically, the percentage of high school students who reported having brought a weapon to school at least once in the past month. We used data collected in 2003 and 2005 by the U.S. Centers for Disease Control and Prevention as part of the Youth Risk Behavior Surveillance System (YRBSS) and tabulated by the National Center for Education Statistics (2007). The YRBSS is an ongoing, large-scale survey that provides a representative snapshot of students in participating states. Not all states were included in the survey each year, so to increase the stability of the state-level estimates, we aggregated data across 2003 and 2005 by computing the mean across years when data for both years were available and using 1 year's data otherwise. The correlation across years for the 28 states that had survey data for both years was quite high ($r = .74$, $p < .05$). Five culture-of-honor states and 3 non-culture-of-honor states did not have any data in either year of the survey, however, leaving only 42 states for our analyses.

We also collected state-level demographics that have been associated with regional differences in violent crime in prior studies. Specifically, we included the proportion of the state population living in rural areas (U.S. Census Bureau, 2000), mean annual state temperature (National Oceanic and Atmospheric Administration, 2000), and a set of six environmental-insecurity indices determined from 2004 data (except as indicated). These latter indices included poverty levels (U.S. Census Bureau, 2006), unemployment levels (U.S. Bureau of Labor Statistics, 2005), median income (U.S. Census Bureau, 2008a), the Gini index of income inequality (computed as a rolling average across years; U.S. Census Bureau, 2005–2007), divorce rates (Munson & Sutton, 2005), and the percentage of people who lived in the same house (i.e., did not move) between 1995 and 2000 (the most recent time period available at the time of the study; U.S. Census Bureau, 2000).[1] The latter variable was included because it provides an efficient indicator of social-network stability and change.

We performed a principal-components factor analysis on the six environmental-insecurity measures, and the analysis revealed that two latent variables accounted for 67.8% of the total variance among these indices (details are available from the authors). We labeled these factors "economic insecurity" (comprising the poverty, unemployment, median income, and Gini variables) and "social insecurity" (comprising the divorce and reverse-coded housing-stability variables) and used these factors as control variables in our analyses.

Finally, most studies on regional or national trends in violent crime include some index of minority populations, particularly the African American population. We did not have a solid theoretical reason for focusing on the African American population in our studies of school shootings: As Newman et al.

(2005) have noted in their analysis of "rampage" shootings, the majority of school shooters are European American. However, the percentage of each state's population that is either Caucasian or Latino is theoretically related to the culture of honor because subgroups of the Caucasian population and many Latino cultures promote culture-of-honor values and norms in the United States (Nisbett & Cohen, 1996). We included the social demographic variable *social composition*—the percentage of state population that is Caucasian or Latino—as a covariate in our analysis along with the other state-level demographic control variables. We followed Cohen's (1998) classification of culture-of-honor states as those designated by the U.S. Census Bureau as being Southern or Western (Regions 5–9, excluding Hawaii and Alaska); the remaining states were designated as non-culture-of-honor states.

Results and Discussion

Three of the five state-level demographic control variables differed significantly between culture-of-honor and non-culture-of-honor states. Basic descriptive statistics and significance tests for these variables are displayed in Table 1[2].

As hypothesized, a higher percentage of high school students in culture-of-honor states ($M = 7.08\%$, $SD = 1.43\%$) than in non-culture-of-honor states ($M = 5.56\%$, $SD = 1.36\%$) reported having brought a weapon to school at least once in the past month, $F(1, 40) = 12.41$, $p < .01$, $d = 1.11$. When we included the state-level control variables along with culture of honor (coded as 0 for non-culture-of-honor states and 1 for culture-of-honor states) in a multiple regression analysis, the difference in weapon carrying between culture-of-honor ($M = 7.07$) and non-culture-of-honor ($M = 5.58$) states remained statistically

TABLE 1 / Comparison of Demographic Control Variables Between Culture-of-Honor and Non-Culture-of-Honor States

	Study 1				Study 2			
	Mean				Mean			
Variable	CH	Non-CH	t (40)	p	CH	Non-CH	t (48)	p
Mean temperature[a]	55.79	47.49	3.27	.002	55.74	47.45	3.70	.001
Proportion rural	0.30	0.29	0.26	.795	0.28	0.28	0.08	.940
Economic insecurity	0.38	−0.45	2.87	.007	0.38	−0.45	3.16	.003
Social insecurity	0.58	−0.49	4.03	.001	0.54	−0.63	5.06	.001
Social composition[b]	0.87	0.90	1.05	.298	0.87	0.90	1.46	.150

Note: CH = culture of honor.

[a] For Study 1 and Study 2, we used the mean annual state temperatures over the same time period, but the sample sizes differed ($N = 42$ for Study 1, $N = 50$ for Study 2).

[b]Social composition was calculated as the percentage of the state population that was Caucasian or Latino. An inverse transformation was applied to social composition prior to analysis because the distribution of this variable was strongly skewed.

significant, $\beta = .48$, $t(35) = 2.71$, $p < .01$, $d = 0.92$. Of the other state-level demographic variables included in the analysis, only proportion of the population living in rural areas was a statistically significant predictor of weapon carrying, $\beta = .39$, $t(35) = 2.84$, $p < .01$, $d = 0.96$ (Table 2)[3].

Thus, although more than 90% of high school students did not report bringing a weapon to school in the past month, students in culture-of-honor states were significantly more likely than students in non-culture-of-honor states to report having done so. Because the most deadly forms of school violence are perpetrated with weapons, this association between the culture of honor and the tendency to bring weapons to school supports the thesis that school violence might be greater in culture-of-honor states. Of course, students in culture-of-honor states might simply be more willing than students in non-culture-of-honor states to report having brought a weapon to school. Before we could infer a link between culture of honor and violence in school, we needed a violence indicator that does not rely on self-reported behaviors. The purpose of Study 2 was to obtain and assess such a violence indicator.

STUDY 2

Study 1 showed that the culture of honor is associated with an index of school-violence potential, but does the culture of honor predict actual levels of school violence? To answer this question, we compiled a database of school shootings over the past 20 years, from 1988 to 2008. We constrained our analysis to this time period for two reasons. First, a preliminary search revealed that the vast majority of school shootings on record occurred during this 20-year period. Second, the state-level demographic control variables we used were not expected to be reliable over a much longer time period, partly because some of these data were not consistently gathered and recorded by

TABLE 2 / Multiple Regression Analysis of the Percentage of High School Students Who Reported Having Brought a Weapon to School at Least Once During the Past Month (Study 1)

Predictor	β weight	t (35)	p
Culture of honor	.48	2.71	.01
Mean temperature	−.18	−1.04	.31
Proportion rural	.39	2.84	.01
Economic insecurity	−.01	−0.08	.94
Social insecurity	.16	1.05	.30
Social composition	.02	0.12	.91

Note: In the model, non-culture-of-honor states were coded as 0, and culture-of-honor states were coded as 1. R^2 for the model = 48%.

states in previous decades. We further constrained our database to include only prototypical school shootings: shootings that were not simply suicides; that did not involve a separate crime, such as a robbery; and that were perpetrated by either students or employees of the school at which the shooting occurred. Some shootings that we reviewed were actually secondary to robberies in which the attackers shot their victims because they resisted, and violence was not the central aim of the incident. Other shootings involved criminals who simply happened to be on school property when they fired their guns. We did not consider these secondary incidents as prototypical school shootings, nor did we count incidents that occurred off school property, such as gang-related drive-by shootings at a bus stop where schoolchildren were waiting, although such cases are sometimes logged by police as "school-related violence."

Data

To find cases for our analyses, we searched published case studies, government-sponsored Web sites (National School Safety Center, 2008), media reports, and other Internet databases of school violence (e.g., Know Gangs, 2008). Because our analysis was sociocultural rather than idiographic, we did not require the level of detail needed for in-depth case studies. We simply needed to know that an incident qualified as a prototypical shooting and to determine the date and location of its occurrence. We found a total of 108 incidents that qualified as prototypical school shootings. Because these incidents occurred over a 20-year period, we expanded our state-level demographic control variables to include data from both 1994 and 2004 (using the same data sources as in Study 1, except as noted). The means of 1994 and 2004 state-level poverty, median income, unemployment, divorce rate (Singh, Mathews, Clarke, Yannicos, & Smith, 1995), proportion rural, and social composition were computed. Because the Gini index of income inequality was not assessed by the U.S. Census Bureau consistently over the past 20 years, we computed the mean of 1989, 1999 (U.S. Census Bureau, 2008b), and composite 2005 to 2007 (U.S. Census Bureau, 2005–2007) levels, as these were the most relevant years for which the U.S. Census Bureau had available data. In addition, we used the same data for mean state temperature and housing stability as we used in Study 1. In Study 2, the same two factors emerged from a factor analysis using multiyear composite means as emerged using only the 2004 levels in Study 1.

Results and Discussion

As in Study 1, three of the five state-level demographic control variables differed significantly between culture-of-honor and non-culture-of-honor states (Table 1). Whereas the data from high school students used in Study 1 were anonymous, we were able to ascertain some descriptive information about most of the shooters in Study 2, although complete data were not available for the entire sample because of the brevity of reporting on many of the low-profile incidents. Among the 100 cases in which sex of perpetrator could be determined, 97% of the perpetrators were male. In the 94 cases in which age was reported, the mean perpetrator age was 18.3 years (although 50% were between 14 and 16 years old). Of the 60 cases in which race of the perpetrator could be determined from press reports or other sources, 37 perpetrators were Caucasian, 12 were Black, 5 were Asian, 2 were Native American or Alaskan, 3 were Latino, and 1 was Indian. Most (63%) of the shootings occurred at a high school, 23% occurred at an elementary or middle school, and 13% occurred on a college or university campus. The predominant motive for most of these shootings could not be reliably determined, although explicit references to bullying or teasing by peers, romantic rejection, or some form of reputation threat were made in about 28% of the cases.

Our first assessment of the relation between culture of honor and school shootings examined individual occurrences. Of the 108 prototypical shootings in our database, 75% occurred in culture-of-honor states. Thus, exactly 3 times as many school shootings occurred in culture-of-honor states as in non-culture-of-honor states. Even considering that 56.7% of the population lived in a culture-of-honor state during the period under examination, a binomial test of proportions revealed that 75% is a significantly greater proportion than expected by chance, $p < .001$. It is worth noting that when we examined the subset of school shootings in our database that were classified previously by Newman et al. (2005) as rampage shootings, we found that almost the same percentage (80%) occurred in culture-of-honor states.

To control for key demographic variables that might covary with the culture of honor, our next assessment of the culture-of-honor hypothesis involved a multiple regression analysis of the per capita number of shootings in each state. Specifically, we regressed shootings per capita on the dichotomous culture-of-honor variable, as well as on mean state temperature, social composition, proportion rural, and the economic- and social-insecurity factors described in Study 1. In this regression analysis ($R^2 = .38$), culture of honor remained a statistically significant predictor of shootings per capita, $\beta = .38$, $t(43) = 2.13$, $p < .05$, $d = 0.65$; culture-of-honor states had more school shootings ($M = 0.58$ per million residents) than did non-culture-of-honor states ($M = 0.24$ per million residents). As shown in Table 3a, both temperature, $\beta = -.43$, $t(43) = 2.35$, $p < .05$, $d = 0.72$, and social composition, $\beta = -.51$, $t(43) = 3.25$, $p < .01$, $d = 0.99$, were also significant predictors. The strength and direction of the effects of temperature and social composition were surprising, although an inspection of the zero-order associations

between these variables and shootings per capita suggested that the partial associations from the multiple regression were at least partly due to the covariances among the predictors (and to the outlier state of Alaska[4]).

The results of the multiple regression analysis increased our confidence that the raw frequency of shootings in culture-of-honor states was not simply the result of an obvious demographic difference among the states. However, this regression analysis is actually more subject to another weakness than was our analysis in Study 1. In studies that examine rare events, such as homicides, a common data-analytic problem concerns the influence of a few outliers (i.e., high frequencies) for a variable that also has a high number of zero values (for a relevant criticism of previous culture-of-honor studies, see Loftin & McDowall, 2003). The fact that 16 states in our study had zero values for shootings per capita is potentially problematic, even though the validity of the multiple regression analysis depends not on the normality of the dependent measure itself, but on the normality of the residuals from the analysis.[5] To deal with this shortcoming inherent in our rare-event data, we recoded shootings per capita into a dichotomous variable (i.e., 0 = *shootings absent*, 1 = *shootings present*) and conducted a logistic regression using all of the same predictors we used in the multiple regression model. This analysis revealed, once again, that culture of honor was a significant predictor of the likelihood of school shootings, $b = 2.46$, $SE = 1.15$, Wald statistic = 4.55, $p = .033$. The only other significant predictor of this dichotomous outcome variable was economic insecurity, $b = 1.38$, $SE = 0.64$, Wald statistic = 4.57, $p = .033$.

The results of Study 2 complement the results of Study 1 by showing that culture-of-honor predicted another measure of school violence. Study 2 built on Study 1 by using an index of school violence that did not depend on self-report and that thus could not be influenced by differences across states in the willingness to report having brought a weapon to school. Together, the data from these two studies paint a picture of a substantially increased risk of school violence in states classified as exhibiting a culture of honor.

TABLE 3 / Multiple Regression Analysis of School Shootings per Capita (Study 2)

Predictor	β weight	$t(43)$	p
Culture of honor	.38	2.13	.04
Mean temperature	−.43	−2.35	.02
Proportion rural	.21	1.61	.11
Economic insecurity	.17	1.08	.29
Social insecurity	.09	0.59	.56
Social composition	−.51	−3.25	.00

Note: R^2 for the model = 38%.

GENERAL DISCUSSION

As we hypothesized, culture of honor was significantly associated with two indices of school violence: the percentage of high school students who reported having brought a weapon to school during the past month and the prevalence of actual school shootings over a 20-year period. States classified as culture-of-honor states had higher percentages of weapon-carrying high school students and more school shootings per capita than non-culture-of-honor states did. Some researchers have suggested that the apparent relationship between general acts of violence and the culture of honor in the United States might be at least partially explained by demographic differences between Southern and Western states, on the one hand, and Northern and Eastern states, on the other, rather than being a product of cultural differences (Anderson & Anderson, 1996). Indeed, culture-of-honor states are typically hotter, more rural, and poorer than non-culture-of-honor states, and any of these differences might explain the link between culture of honor and violence.

However, the state-level demographic variables that we examined—which included temperature, rurality, social composition, and indices of economic and social insecurity—were unable to account for the association between culture of honor and our school-violence indicators, and also were inconsistent predictors of the school-violence variables across the two studies. This marks an important difference between these indicators of school violence and more general indicators of violent crime among adults, which typically show stronger and more consistent associations with temperature, rurality, and environmental-insecurity measures similar to the ones we used (Anderson, 1989; Baron & Straus, 1988; Cohen, 1996; Lee, Bankston, Hayes, & Thomas, 2007). This difference suggests that school violence is a somewhat distinct form of aggression that should not be viewed through standard lenses. That the culture of honor appears to be such a robust predictor of school violence supports the hypothesis that school violence might be partially a product of long-term or recent experiences of social marginalization, humiliation, rejection, or bullying (Leary et al., 2003; Newman et al., 2005), all of which represent honor threats with special significance to people (particularly males) living in culture-of-honor states.

We should note, of course, that even though none of the demographic variables we examined were significantly related to school violence across both of these studies, it is quite possible that our state-level analyses underestimated the potential influence of these variables. For example, as Newman et al. (2005) have shown in their examination of rampage shootings, the majority of such shootings (60%) have occurred in schools located in rural settings. Only 8% have occurred in urban settings, and the other 32% have been suburban. Therefore, the failure of our proportion-rural variable to be a statistically significant predictor of school shootings in Study 2 (despite significantly predicting weapon carrying in Study 1) should not be taken to mean that this variable does not play any role in school violence. Further studies might uncover important associations between rurality and other demographic variables in predicting similar violent occurrences, from forms of aggression that are more common than school shootings to even rarer ones, such as bombings.

These studies are the first to demonstrate an empirical association between a sociocultural variable and school violence. Additional research seems warranted, both to complement and to extend our studies. Further refinement of the culture-of-honor classification system seems particularly important, given the simple dichotomization of states we used. Surely the culture of honor is more of a continuous than a dichotomous variable, and research leading to a more nuanced classification of states might yield valuable insights into important outcomes like the ones we examined. Knowledge of how the culture of honor plays a role in school violence could also reveal ways in which educators and policymakers might identify at-risk students and understand how to address the unique psychosocial issues influencing them. Armed with such knowledge, society might keep the list of school shootings from growing at its present rate.[6]

ACKNOWLEDGMENTS

We wish to thank Paige Hoster, Justin Biggs, Joshua Buchanan, and Kirsten Brinlee for assistance in creating our database of school shootings, and Lynn Devenport for his helpful comments on an earlier draft of this article.

REFERENCES

Anderson, C.A. (1989). Temperature and aggression: Ubiquitous effects of heat on occurrence of human violence. *Psychological Bulletin, 106,* 74–96.

Anderson, C.A., & Anderson, K.B. (1996). Violent crime rate studies in philosophical context: A destructive testing approach to heat and Southern culture of violence effects. *Journal of Personality and Social Psychology, 70,* 740–756.

Baron, L., & Straus, M.A. (1988). Cultural and economic sources of homicide in the United States. *Sociological Quarterly, 29,* 371–390.

Baron, L., & Straus, M.A. (1989). *Four theories of rape in American society.* New Haven, CT: Yale University Press.

Cohen, D. (1996). Law, social policy, and violence: The impact of regional cultures. *Journal of Personality and Social Psychology, 70,* 961–978.

Cohen, D. (1998). Culture, social organization, and patterns of violence. *Journal of Personality and Social Psychology, 75,* 408–419.

Cohen, D., Nisbett, R.E., Bowdle, B.F., & Schwarz, N. (1996). Insult, aggression, and the southern culture of honor: An "experimental ethnography." *Journal of Personality and Social Psychology, 70,* 945–960.

Fein, R.A., Vossekuil, B., Pollack, W.S., Borum, R., Modzeleski, W., Reddy, M., et al. (2002). *Threat assessment in schools: A guide to managing threatening situations and to creating safe school climates.* Retrieved August 1, 2008, from U.S. Secret Service, National Threat Assessment Center Web site: http://www.ustreas.gov/usss/ntac/ssi_guide.pdf

Hayes, T.C., & Lee, M.R. (2005). The Southern culture of honor and violent attitudes. *Sociological Spectrum, 25*, 593–617.

Know Gangs. (2008). *School shooting timeline.* Retrieved November 30, 2008, from http://www.knowgangs.com/school_resources/timeline

Leary, M.R., Kowalski, R.M., Smith, L., & Phillips, S. (2003). Teasing, rejection, and violence: Case studies of the school shootings. *Aggressive Behavior, 29*, 202–214.

Lee, M.R., Bankston, W.B., Hayes, T.C., & Thomas, S.A. (2007). Revisiting the Southern culture of violence. *Sociological Quarterly, 48*, 253–275.

Loftin, C., & McDowall, D. (2003). Regional culture and patterns of homicide. *Homicide Studies: An Interdisciplinary and International Journal, 7*, 353–367.

Munson, M.L., & Sutton, P.D. (2005). *Births, marriages, divorces, and deaths: Provisional data for 2004* (National Vital Statistics Report Vol. 53, No. 21). Retrieved October 16, 2008, from http://www.cdc.gov/nchs/data/nvsr/nvsr53/nvsr53_21.pdf

National Center for Education Statistics. (2007). *Indicators of school crime and safety.* Retrieved November 20, 2008, from http://nces.ed.gov/programs/crimeindicators/crimeindicators2007/tables/table_14_2.asp

National Oceanic and Atmospheric Administration. (2000). *Average mean temperature index by month: 1971–2000.* Retrieved October 16, 2008, from http://www.cdc.noaa.gov/USclimate/tmp.state.19712000.climo

National School Safety Center. (2008). *The National School Safety Center's report on school associated violent deaths.* Retrieved November 30, 2008, from http://www.schoolsafety.us/pubfiles/savd.pdf

Newman, K.S., Fox, C., Roth, W., Mehta, J., & Harding, D. (2005). *Rampage: The social roots of school shootings.* New York: Basic Books.

Nisbett, R.E. (1993). Violence and U.S. regional culture. *American Psychologist, 48*, 441–449.

Nisbett, R.E., & Cohen, D. (1996). *Culture of honor: The psychology of violence in the South.* Boulder, CO: Westview Press.

Nisbett, R.E., Polly, G., & Lang, S. (1995). Homicide and U.S. regional culture. In B. Ruback & N. Weiner (Eds.), *Interpersonal violent behavior: Social and cultural aspects* (pp. 135–151). New York: Springer.

Singh, G.K., Mathews, T.J., Clarke, S.C., Yannicos, T., & Smith, B.L. (1995). *Annual summary of births, marriages, divorces, and deaths:*

United States, 1994 (Monthly Vital Statistics Report Vol. 43, No. 13). Retrieved October 16, 2008, from http://www.cdc.gov/nchs/data/mvsr/mv43_13.pdf

U.S. Bureau of Labor Statistics. (2005). *Unemployment rates for states, annual average rankings, year: 2004.* Retrieved October 16, 2008, from http://www.bls.gov/lau/lastrk04.htm

U.S. Census Bureau. (2000). *Census 2000 Summary File 3 (SF3)—sample data.* Retrieved October 16, 2008, and February 24, 2009, from http://factfinder.census.gov/servlet/DatasetMainPageServlet?_program=DEC&

U.S. Census Bureau. (2005–2007). *2005–2007 American Community Survey 3-year estimates.* Retrieved February 24, 2009, from http://factfinder.census.gov/servlet/DatasetMainPageServlet?_program=ACS&

U.S. Census Bureau. (2006). *POV46: Poverty status by state: 2004.* Retrieved October 16, 2008, from http://pubdb3.census.gov/macro/032005/pov/new46_100125_01.htm

U.S. Census Bureau. (2008a). *Table H-8: Median household income by state: 1984 to 2007.* Retrieved October 16, 2008, from http://www.census.gov/hhes/www/income/histinc/h08.html

U.S. Census Bureau. (2008b). *Table S4: Gini ratios by state.* Retrieved February 24, 2009, from http://www.census.gov/hhes/www/income/histinc/state/state4.html

ENDNOTES

1. For rurality and household moves, we used the *Census 2000 Summary File 3* (U.S. Census Bureau, 2000) to create tables (Tables P5 and P24) with state-level data. To obtain the Gini index of inequality, we used the *2005–2007 American Community Survey 3-Year Estimates* (U.S. Census Bureau, 2005–2007) to create Table B19083 for all states.

2. An inverse transformation was applied to social composition prior to analysis because the distribution of this variable was strongly skewed.

3. Because of the small sample size in this state-level analysis, we were concerned about violations of certain statistical assumptions, particularly the normality of the residuals from the regression. Analysis of these residuals, as well as other problem indicators (e.g., studentized deleted residuals, Cook's distance), revealed that the normality assumption was met quite well, and no data points stood out as being problematic.

4. Alaska stood out as a potentially problematic data point (e.g., Cook's distance > 0.80). When we omitted Alaska's data, the culture-of-honor effect increased in strength, $\beta = .48$, $p < .02$, but no other predictor remained significant.

5. As in Study 1, we examined the normality of the residuals from the regression analysis. This analysis, as well as other problem indicators (e.g., studentized deleted residuals, Cook's distance), revealed that the normality assumption was once again met quite well.

6. We found no evidence that incidents of school violence were becoming less frequent, contrary to what some people have claimed. Indeed, more prototypical shootings occurred in the second chronological half of our database ($n = 58$) than in the first half ($n = 50$).

CRITICAL THINKING QUESTIONS

1. Does someone you know have a culture-of-honor value system? If so, how would you describe that aspect of his or her personality? Describe any ways that this value system may be related to how you have seen them act when their "honor" has been assailed (at least in their eyes)?

2. Do you believe that there is a culture of honor that exists more strongly in some states and regions than others? If so, what do you think may account for why those differences emerged in the first place?

3. The article notes that the culture-of-honor factor occurs more often in areas that are hotter, more rural, and poorer than the non-culture-of-honor areas. How might these latter three factors (hot, rural, poor) each be a possible reason why aggression is more prevalent in those areas? Explain your answer.

4. Study 1 in this article used a self-report measure regarding bringing a weapon to school. What are the possible limitations of such self-report measures? Be sure to discuss how the culture-of-honor factor might play a role in how likely someone is to report bringing a weapon to school, regardless of whether or not he or she actually did bring it.

5. The article states, "Knowledge of how the culture of honor plays a role in school violence could also reveal ways in which educators and policymakers might identify at-risk students and understand how to address the unique psychosocial issues influencing them." Who might those "at-risk" students be, and what can be done to make them less likely to engage in school violence?

CHAPTER INTEGRATION QUESTIONS

1. Revisit the introduction to Article 31, which outlines three theoretical perspectives on aggression. Considering the three articles in this chapter together, which theoretical perspective do you feel is most supported by the data? Why?

2. Based on the information from the three articles, can you recommend one or more ways to reduce the occurrence of aggression? Explain your answer.

3. As discussed in Article 31, one major concern facing the world today is terrorism. What insights, if any, can you draw from Articles 32 and 33 regarding the causes of and potential control of terrorism? What factors other than those discussed in any of the three articles in this chapter are important in understanding the causes and control of terrorism? Explain your answers.

Chapter Twelve

GROUP BEHAVIOR

HOW MUCH OF your life is spent interacting with people in some sort of group? If we use the simple definition of a *group* as "two or more individuals that have some unifying relationship," then most likely a significant amount of your time is spent in groups, whether informal (such as two friends trying to decide what to do on a Saturday night) or formal (a work group deciding on a course of action).

Research on group behavior has gone in many directions. The three articles selected for this chapter focus on some of the most commonly investigated topics. Article 34, "Group Decision Fiascoes Continue: Space Shuttle Challenger and a Revised Groupthink Framework," uses a well-known concept, *groupthink*, to explain the decision making that resulted in a well-known tragedy, the *Challenger* disaster. Proposed by Irving Janis nearly four decades ago, groupthink helps to explain why certain types of groups may make very poor decisions, even when they may be composed of very competent individuals. Since the conditions that may contribute to groupthink are not uncommon, the implications of this article for understanding group decision making and perhaps more importantly for developing more effective group decision making extend beyond the case of the *Challenger*.

Article 35, "The Effects of Threat upon Interpersonal Bargaining," is a classic work. Think of these two possible situations: In the first situation, Party 1 has the potential to inflict harm on Party 2, but Party 2 cannot reciprocate. In the second situation, both parties have equal threat potential; that is, if Party 1 inflicts harm, Party 2 can reciprocate. Which situation would yield the best outcomes for *both* parties? As the article demonstrates, the answer is not what you might think.

Finally, Article 36, "Can High Group Cohesion Be Harmful?: A Case Study of a Junior Ice-Hockey Team," examines if *group cohesion* is necessarily a positive thing in terms of group performance. Group cohesion typically means how much the group members like one another and feel positively toward the group in general. Most people might assume that a highly cohesive group would be more functional than a less cohesive group. As the article reports, such may not always be the case. This article is also an example of how concepts like groupthink are examined in contemporary research, and it demonstrates the use of examining a case study, rather than conducting an experiment, as a means for understanding behavior.

ARTICLE 34 _____

Let us suppose that you are in a position of authority. As such, you are called on to make some very important decisions. You want to make the best possible decisions, so you turn to other people for input. You assemble the best possible set of advisors—people distinguished by their abilities and knowledge. Before making a final decision, you meet with them to discuss the options.

Following such a procedure would seem to ensure that the decision you make will be a good one. After all, with your expert resources, how can you go wrong?

Actually, it is not very hard to imagine that the procedure mentioned earlier could go wrong. Working in a group, even when that group is composed of very competent individuals, does not guarantee quality decision making. To the contrary, groups may actually make some very poor decisions. The concept of *groupthink*, a hypothesis developed by Irving L. Janis nearly four decades ago, explains how and why some groups come to make very poor decisions, not only failing to recognize that these are poor decisions but actually convincing themselves more and more that these are good decisions. In his original works, Janis explained how poor decisions from the past, such as the Bay of Pigs invasion or the escalation of the Vietnam War, could be understood as being part of the groupthink hypothesis. In subsequent years other researchers have used the concept of groupthink to explain various group decision-making processes. The following article by Gregory Moorhead, Richard Ference, and Chris P. Neck applies the groupthink concept to the ill-fated decision to launch the space shuttle *Challenger* in 1986. The implication that the ensuing tragedy could have been prevented had groupthink not prevailed in the decision to launch is indeed sobering.

Group Decision Fiascoes Continue
Space Shuttle *Challenger* and a Revised Groupthink Framework
■ Gregory Moorhead, Richard Ference, and Chris P. Neck

This paper reviews the decision situation surrounding the decision to launch the space shuttle Challenger in January 1986 in the light of the groupthink hypothesis. A revised framework is presented that proposes time and leadership style as moderators of the manner in which group characteristics lead to groupthink symptoms.

INTRODUCTION

In 1972, a new dimension was added to our understanding of group decision making with the proposal of the groupthink hypothesis by Janis (1972). Janis coined the term "groupthink" to refer to "a mode of thinking that people engage in when they are deeply involved in a cohesive in-group, when the members' striving for unanimity override their motivation to realistically appraise alternative courses of action" (Janis, 1972, p. 8). The hypothesis was supported by his hindsight analysis of several political-military fiascoes and successes that are differentiated by the occurrence or non-occurrence of antecedent conditions, groupthink symptoms, and decision making defects.

In a subsequent volume, Janis further explicates the theory and adds an analysis of the Watergate transcripts and various published memoirs and accounts of principals involved, concluding that the Watergate cover-up decision also was a result of groupthink (Janis, 1983). Both volumes propose prescriptions for preventing the occurrence of groupthink, many of which have appeared in popular press, in books on executive decision making, and in management textbooks. Multiple advocacy decision-making procedures have been adopted at the executive levels in many organizations, including the executive branch of the government. One would think that by 1986, 13 years after the publication of a popular book, that its prescriptions might be well ingrained in our management and decision-making styles. Unfortunately, it has not happened.

On January 28, 1986, the space shuttle Challenger was launched from Kennedy Space Center. The temperature that morning was in the mid-20's, well below the previous low temperatures at which the shuttle engines had been tested. Seventy-three seconds after launch, the Challenger exploded, killing all seven astronauts aboard, and becoming the worst

Moorhead, G.; Ference, R.; & Neck, C.P., *Human Relations*, 44, 539–549. Copyright © 1991 by Sage Publications. Reprinted with permission of SAGE Publications.

disaster in space flight history. The catastrophe shocked the nation, crippled the American space program, and is destined to be remembered as the most tragic national event since the assassination of John F. Kennedy in 1963.

The Presidential Commission that investigated the accident pointed to a flawed decision-making process as a primary contributory cause. The decision was made the night before the launch in the Level I Flight Readiness Review meeting. Due to the work of the Presidential Commission, information concerning that meeting is available for analysis as a group decision possibly susceptible to groupthink.

In this paper, we report the results of our analysis of the Level I Flight Readiness Review meeting as a decision-making situation that displays evidence of groupthink. We review the antecedent conditions, the groupthink symptoms, and the possible decision-making defects, as suggested by Janis (1983). In addition, we take the next and more important step of going beyond the development of another example of groupthink to make recommendations for renewed inquiry into group decision-making processes.

THEORY AND EVIDENCE

The groupthink hypothesis has been presented in detail in numerous publications other than Janis' books (Flowers, 1977; Courtright, 1978; Leana, 1985; Moorhead, 1982; Moorhead & Montanari, 1986) and will not be repeated here. The major categories will be used as a framework for organizing the evidence from the meeting. Within each category the key elements will be presented along with meeting details that pertain to each.

The meeting(s) took place throughout the day and evening from 12:36 pm (EST), January 27, 1986 following the decision to not launch the Challenger due to high crosswinds at the launch site. Discussions continued through about 12:00 midnight (EST) via teleconferencing and Telefax systems connecting the Kennedy Space Center in Florida, Morton Thiokol (MTI) in Utah, Johnson Space Center in Houston, and the Marshall Space Flight Center. The Level I Flight Readiness Review is the highest level of review prior to launch. It comprises the highest level of management at the three space centers and at MTI, the private supplier of the solid rocket booster engines.

To briefly state the situation, the MTI engineers recommended not to launch if temperatures of the O-ring seals on the rocket were below 53 degrees Fahrenheit, which was the lowest temperature of any previous flight. Laurence B. Mulloy, manager of the Solid Rocket Booster Project at Marshall Space Flight Center, states:

> . . . *The bottom line of that, though, initially was that Thiokol engineering, Bob Lund, who is the Vice President*

> *and Director of Engineering, who is here today, recommended that 51-L [the Challenger] not be launched if the O-ring temperatures predicted at launch time would be lower than any previous launch, and that was 53 degrees* . . . (Report of the Presidential Commission on the Space Shuttle Accident, *1986, p. 91–92*).

This recommendation was made at 8:45 pm, January 27, 1986 (*Report of the Presidential Commission on the Space Shuttle Accident,* 1986). Through the ensuing discussions the decision to launch was made.

Antecedent Conditions

The three primary antecedent conditions for the development of groupthink are: a highly cohesive group, leader preference for a certain decision, and insulation of the group from qualified outside opinions. These conditions existed in this situation.

Cohesive Group   The people who made the decision to launch had worked together for many years. They were familiar with each other and had grown through the ranks of the space program. A high degree of *esprit de corps* existed between the members.

Leader Preference   Two top level managers actively promoted their pro-launch opinions in the face of opposition. The commission report states that several managers at space centers and MTI pushed for launch, regardless of the low temperatures.

Insulation from Experts   MTI engineers made their recommendations relatively early in the evening. The top level decision-making group knew of their objections but did not meet with them directly to review their data and concerns. As Roger Boisjoly, a Thiokol engineer, states in his remarks to the Presidential Commission:

> . . . *and the bottom line was that the engineering people would not recommend a launch below 53 degrees Fahrenheit* . . . *From this point on, management formulated the points to base their decision on. There was never one comment in favor, as I have said, of launching by any engineer or other nonmanagement person.* . . . *I was not even asked to participate in giving any input to the final decision charts* (Report of the Presidential Commission on the Space Shuttle Accident, *1986, p. 91–92*).

This testimonial indicates that the top decision-making team was insulated from the engineers who possessed the expertise regarding the functioning of the equipment.

Groupthink Symptoms

Janis identified eight symptoms of groupthink. They are presented here along with evidence from the *Report of the Presidential Commission on the Space Shuttle Accident* (1986).

Invulnerability   When groupthink occurs, most or all of the members of the decision-making group have an illusion of invulnerability that reassures them in the face of obvious dangers. This illusion leads the group to become overly optimistic and willing to take extraordinary risks. It may also cause them to ignore clear warnings of danger.

The solid rocket joint problem that destroyed Challenger was discussed often at flight readiness review meetings prior to flight. However, Commission member Richard Feynman concluded from the testimony that a mentality of overconfidence existed due to the extraordinary record of success of space flights. Every time we send one up it is successful. Involved members may seem to think that on the next one we can lower our standards or take more risks because it always works (*Time*, 1986).

The invulnerability illusion may have built up over time as a result of NASA's own spectacular history. NASA had not lost an astronaut since 1967 when a flash fire in the capsule of Apollo 1 killed three. Since that time NASA had a string of 55 successful missions. They had put a man on the moon, built and launched Skylab and the shuttle, and retrieved defective satellites from orbit. In the minds of most Americans and apparently their own, they could do no wrong.

Rationalization   Victims of groupthink collectively construct rationalizations that discount warnings and other forms of negative feedback. If these signals were taken seriously when presented, the group members would be forced to reconsider their assumptions each time they re-commit themselves to their past decisions.

In the Level I flight readiness meeting when the Challenger was given final launch approval, MTI engineers presented evidence that the joint would fail. Their argument was based on the fact that in the coldest previous launch (air temperature 30 degrees) the joint in question experienced serious erosion and that no data existed as to how the joint would perform at colder temperatures. Flight center officials put forth numerous technical rationalizations faulting MTI's analysis. One of these rationalizations was that the engineer's data were inconclusive. As Mr. Boisjoly emphasized to the Commission:

> . . . I was asked, yes, at that point in time I was asked to quantify my concerns, and I said I couldn't. I couldn't quantify it. I had no data to quantify it, but I did say I knew that it was away from goodness in the current data base. Someone on the net commented that we had soot blow-by on SRM-22 [Flight 61-A, October, 1985] which was launched at 75 degrees. I don't remember who made the comment but that is where the first comment came in about the disparity between my conclusion and the observed data because SRM-22 [Flight 61-A, October 1985] had blow-by at essentially a room temperature launch. I then said that SRM-15 [Flight 51-C, January, 1985] had much more blow-by indication and that it was indeed telling us that lower temperature was a factor. I was asked again for data to support my claim, and I said I have none other than what is being presented. (Report of the Presidential Commission on the Space Shuttle Accident, *1986, p. 89*).

Discussions became twisted (compared to previous meetings) and no one detected it. Under normal conditions, MTI would have to prove the shuttle boosters readiness for launch, instead they found themselves being forced to prove that the boosters were unsafe. Boisjoly's testimony supports this description of the discussion:

> . . . This was a meeting where the determination was to launch, and it was up to us to prove beyond a shadow of a doubt that it was not safe to do so. This is in total reverse to what the position usually is in a preflight conversation or a flight readiness review. It is usually exactly opposite of that . . . (Report of the Presidential Commission on the Space Shuttle Accident, *1986, p. 93*).

Morality   Group members often believe, without question, in the inherent morality of their position. They tend to ignore the ethical or moral consequences of their decision.

In the Challenger case, this point was raised by a very high level MTI manager, Allan J. McDonald, who tried to stop the launch and said that he would not want to have to defend the decision to launch. He stated to the Commission:

> . . . I made the statement that if we're wrong and something goes wrong on this flight, I wouldn't want to have to be the person to stand up in front of board in inquiry and say that I went ahead and told them to go ahead and fly this thing outside what the motor was qualified to . . . (Report of the Presidential Commission on the Space Shuttle Accident, *1986, p. 95*).

Some members did not hear this statement because it occurred during a break. Three top officials who did hear it ignored it.

Stereotyped Views of Others   Victims of groupthink often have a stereotyped view of the opposition of anyone with a competing opinion. They feel that the opposition is too stupid or too weak to understand or deal effectively with the problem.

Two of the top three NASA officials responsible for the launch displayed this attitude. They felt that they completely understood the nature of the joint problem and never seriously considered the objections raised by the MTI engineers. In fact they denigrated and badgered the opposition and their information and opinions.

Pressure on Dissent Group members often apply direct pressure to anyone who questions the validity of the arguments supporting a decision or position favored by the majority. These same two officials pressured MTI to change its position after MTI originally recommended that the launch not take place. These two officials pressured MTI personnel to prove that it was not safe to launch, rather than to prove the opposite. As mentioned earlier, this was a total reversal of normal preflight procedures. It was this pressure that top MTI management was responding to when they overruled their engineering staff and recommended launch. As the Commission report states:

> . . . At approximately 11 p.m. Eastern Standard Time, the Thiokol/NASA teleconference resumed, the Thiokol management stating that they had reassessed the problem, that the temperature effects were a concern, but that the data was admittedly inconclusive . . . (p. 96)

This seems to indicate that NASA's pressure on these Thiokol officials forced them to change their recommendation from delay to execution of the launch.

Self-Censorship Group members tend to censor themselves when they have opinions or ideas that deviate from the apparent group consensus. Janis feels that this reflects each member's inclination to minimize to himself or herself the importance of his or her own doubts and counter-arguments.

The most obvious evidence of self-censorship occurred when a vice president of MTI, who had previously presented information against launch, bowed to pressure from NASA and accepted their rationalizations for launch. He then wrote these up and presented them to NASA as the reasons that MTI had changed its recommendation to launch.

Illusion of Unanimity Group members falling victim to groupthink share an illusion of unanimity concerning judgments made by members speaking in favor of the majority view. This symptom is caused in part by the preceding one and is aided by the false assumption that any participant who remains silent is in agreement with the majority opinion. The group leader and other members support each other by playing up points of convergence in their thinking at the expense of fully exploring points of divergence that might reveal unsettling problems.

No participant from NASA ever openly agreed with or even took sides with MTI in the discussion. The silence from NASA was probably amplified by the fact that the meeting was a teleconference linking the participants at three different locations. Obviously, body language which might have been evidenced by dissenters was not visible to others who might also have held a dissenting opinion. Thus, silence meant agreement.

Mindguarding Certain group members assume the role of guarding the minds of others in the group. They attempt to shield the group from adverse information that might destroy the majority view of the facts regarding the appropriateness of the decision.

The top management at Marshall knew that the rocket casings had been ordered redesigned to correct a flaw 5 months previous to this launch. This information and other technical details concerning the history of the joint problem was withheld at the meeting.

Decision-Making Defects

The result of the antecedent conditions and the symptoms of groupthink is a defective decision-making process. Janis discusses several defects in decision making that can result.

Few Alternatives The group considers only a few alternatives, often only two. No initial survey of all possible alternatives occurs. The Flight Readiness Review team had a launch/no-launch decision to make. These were the only two alternatives considered. Other possible alternatives might have been to delay the launch for further testing, or to delay until the temperatures reached an appropriate level.

No Re-Examination of Alternatives The group fails to re-examine alternatives that may have been initially discarded based on early unfavorable information. Top NASA officials spent time and effort defending and strengthening their position, rather than examining the MTI position.

Rejecting Expert Opinions Members make little or no attempt to seek outside experts opinions. NASA did not seek out other experts who might have some expertise in this area. They assumed that they had all the information.

Rejecting Negative Information Members tend to focus on supportive information and ignore any data or information that might cast a negative light on their preferred alternative. MTI representatives repeatedly tried to point out errors in the rationale the NASA officials were using to justify the launch. Even after the decision was made, the argument continued until a NASA official told the MTI representative that it was no longer his concern.

No Continzgency Plans Members spend little time discussing the possible consequences of the decision and, therefore, fail to develop contingency plans. There is no documented evidence in the Rogers Commission Report of any discussion of the possible consequences of an incorrect decision.

Summary of the Evidence

The major categories and key elements of the group-think hypothesis have been presented (albeit somewhat briefly) along with evidence from the discussions prior to the launching of the Challenger, as reported in the President's Commission to investigate the accident. The antecedent conditions were present in the decision-making group, even though the group was in several physical locations. The leaders had a preferred solution and engaged in behaviors designed to promote it rather than critically appraise alternatives. These behaviors were evidence of most of the symptoms leading to a defective decision-making process.

DISCUSSION

This situation provides another example of decision making in which the group fell victim to the groupthink syndrome, as have so many previous groups. It illustrates the situation characteristics, the symptoms of groupthink, and decision-making defects as described by Janis. This situation, however, also illustrates several other aspects of situations that are critical to the development of groupthink that need to be included in a revised formulation of the groupthink model. First, the element of time in influencing the development of groupthink has not received adequate attention. In the decision to launch the space shuttle Challenger, time was a crucial part of the decision-making process. The launch had been delayed once, and the window for another launch was fast closing. The leaders of the decision team were concerned about public and congressional perceptions of the entire space shuttle program and its continued funding and may have felt that further delays of the launch could seriously impact future funding. With the space window fast closing, the decision team was faced with a launch now or seriously damage the program decision. One top level manager's response to Thiokol's initial recommendation to postpone the launch indicates the presence of time pressure:

> With this LCC (Launch Commit Criteria), i.e., do not launch with a temperature greater [sic] than 53 degrees, we may not be able to launch until next April. We need to consider this carefully before we jump to any conclusions . . . (Report of the Presidential Commission on the Space Shuttle Accident, *1986, p. 96*).

Time pressure could have played a role in the group choosing to agree and to self-censor their comments. Therefore, time is a critical variable that needs to be highlighted in a revised groupthink framework. We propose that time is an important

moderator between group characteristics and the development of the groupthink symptoms. That is, in certain situations when there is pressure to make a decision quickly, the elements may combine to foster the development of groupthink.

The second revision needs to be in the role of the leadership of the decision-making group. In the space shuttle Challenger incident, the leadership of the group varied from a shared type of leadership to a very clear leader in the situation. This may indicate that the leadership role needs to be clearly defined and a style that demands open disclosure of information, points of opposition, complaints, and dissension. Inclusion of leadership in a more powerful role in the groupthink framework needs to be more explicit than in the Janis formulation in which leadership is one of several group characteristics that can lead to the development of the groupthink symptoms. We propose the leadership style is a crucial variable that moderates the relationship between the group characteristics and the development of the symptoms. Janis (1983) is a primary form of evidence to support the inclusion of leadership style in the enhanced model. His account of why the same group succumbed to groupthink in one decision (Bay of Pigs) and not in another (Cuban Missile Crisis) supports the depiction of leadership style as a moderator variable. In these decisions, the only condition that changed was the leadership style of the President. In other words, the element that seemed to distinguish why groupthink occurred in the Bay of Pigs decision and not in the Cuban Missile Crisis situation is the president's change in his behavior.

These two variables, time and leadership style, are proposed as moderators of the impact of the group characteristics on groupthink symptoms. This relationship is portrayed graphically in Fig. 1. In effect, we propose that the groupthink symptoms result from the group characteristics, as proposed by Janis, but only in the presence of the moderator variables of time and certain leadership styles.

Time, as an important element in the model, is relatively straightforward. When a decision must be made within a very short time frame, pressure on members to agree, to avoid time-consuming arguments and reports from outside experts, and to self-censor themselves may increase. These pressures inevitably cause group members to seek agreement. In Janis's original model, time was included indirectly as a function of the antecedent condition, group cohesion. Janis (1983) argued that time pressures can adversely affect decision quality in two ways. First, it affects the decision makers' mental efficiency and judgment, interfering with their ability to concentrate on complicated discussions, to absorb new information, and to use imagination to anticipate the future consequences of alternative courses of action. Second, time pressure is a source of stress that will have the effect of inducing a policy-making group to become more cohesive and more likely to engage in groupthink.

FIGURE 1 / Revised Groupthink Framework

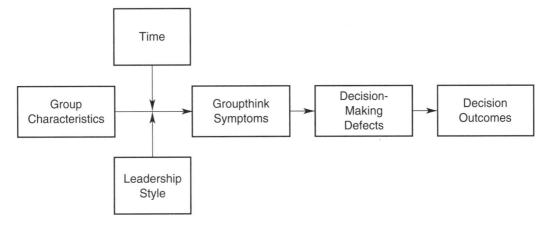

Leadership style is shown to be a moderator because of the importance it plays in either promoting or avoiding the development of the symptoms of the groupthink. The leader, even though she or he may not promote a preferred solution, may allow or even assist the group seeking agreement by not forcing the group to critically appraise all alternative courses of action. The focus of this leadership variable is on the degree to which the leader allows or promotes discussion and evaluation of alternatives. It is not a matter of simply not making known a preferred solution; the issue is one of stimulation of critical thinking among the group.

Impact on Prescriptions for Prevention

The revised model suggests that more specific prescriptions for prevention of groupthink can be made. First, group members need to be aware of the impact that a short decision time frame has on decision processes. When a decision must be made quickly, there will be more pressure to agree, i.e., discouragement of dissent, self-censorship, avoidance of expert opinion, and assumptions about unanimity. The type of leadership suggested here is not one that sits back and simply does not make known her or his preferred solution. This type of leader must be one that requires all members to speak up with concerns, questions, and new information. The leader must know what some of these concerns are and which members are likely to have serious doubts so that the people with concerns can be called upon to voice them. This type of group leadership does not simply assign the role of devil's advocate and step out of the way. This leader actually plays the role or makes sure that others do. A leader with the required style to avoid groupthink is not a laissez faire leader or non-involved participative leader. This leader is active in directing the activities of the group but does not make

known a preferred solution. The group still must develop and evaluate alternative courses of action, but under the direct influence of a strong, demanding leader who forces critical appraisal of all alternatives.

Finally, a combination of the two variables suggests that the leader needs to help members to avoid the problems created by the time element. For example, the leader may be able to alter an externally imposed time frame for the decision by negotiating an extension or even paying late fees, if necessary. If an extension is not possible, the leader may need to help the group eliminate the effects of time on the decision processes. This can be done by forcing attention to issues rather than time, encouraging dissension and confrontation, and scheduling special sessions to hear reports from outside experts that challenge prevailing views within the group.

Janis presents, in both editions of his book, several recommendations for preventing the occurrence of groupthink. These recommendations focus on the inclusion of outside experts in the decision-making process, all members taking the role of devil's advocate and critically appraising all alternative courses of action, and the leader not expressing a preferred solution. The revised groupthink framework suggests several new prescriptions that may be helpful in preventing further decision fiascoes similar to the decision to launch the space shuttle Challenger.

Much additional research is necessary to test the revised framework. First, laboratory research is needed to refine details of how time affects the development of groupthink. Second, the impact of various types of leadership style that may be appropriate for group decision-making situations needs to be investigated. Finally, research which tests the revised framework with real decision-making groups will be needed to refine new prescriptions for preventing groupthink.

CONCLUSION

This paper has reviewed the basic tenets of groupthink and examined the decision to launch the space shuttle Challenger in January 1986. The report of the Presidential Commission provided enough evidence of the antecedent conditions, the symptoms, and the decision-making defects to support a conclusion that the decision to launch can be classified as a groupthink situation. We have proposed, in addition, that other conditions may play important roles in the development of groupthink. These two variables, time and leadership style, are proposed as moderators of the relationship between group characteristics and groupthink symptoms. These two moderators lead to new prescriptions for the prevention of groupthink. Much additional research is needed to test the degree to which the revised framework can be used to guide prescriptions for prevention.

REFERENCES

Courtright, J. A. A laboratory investigation of groupthink. *Communications Monographs,* 1978, *45,* 229–246.

Flowers, M. L. A laboratory test of some implications of Janis's groupthink hypothesis. *Journal of Personality and Social Psychology,* 1977, *35,* 888–896.

Janis, I. L. *Victims of groupthink.* Boston: Houghton Mifflin, 1972.

Janis, I. L. *Groupthink* (2nd ed., revised). Boston: Houghton Mifflin, 1983.

Leana, C. R. A partial test of Janis's groupthink model: Effects of group cohesiveness and leader behavior on defective decision making. *Journal of Management,* 1985, *11,* 5–17.

Moorhead, G. Groupthink: Hypothesis in need of testing. *Group and Organization Studies,* 1982, *7,* 429–444.

Moorhead, G., & Montanari, J. R. Empirical analysis of the groupthink phenomenon. *Human Relations,* 1986, *39,* 399–410.

Report of the Presidential Commission on the Space Shuttle Accident. Washington, D.C.: July 1986.

Time. Fixing NASA. June 9, 1986.

CRITICAL THINKING QUESTIONS

1. Why do you think groupthink became a factor in the decision to launch the *Challenger?* In other words, why was no one involved in making the decision able to recognize what was going on and thus do something about it? How commonly understood is the concept of groupthink in the real world? Is it important that leaders in all walks of life know about groupthink? How could the message be spread to them?

2. The article states that one of the two moderating variables that influence whether groupthink symptoms develop is leadership style. To what extent can leadership style be taught to people? On the other hand, to what extent is leadership style a product of individual personality? Describe the personality characteristics of a leader who would not likely try to prevent the development of groupthink.

3. The second moderating variable discussed in the article is time. Design a laboratory study to investigate the impact of time on the development of groupthink.

4. Consult a social psychology textbook and read about different styles of leadership. Which styles might be most relevant to the development of groupthink? Design either a laboratory or a field study to examine the impact of leadership style on the emergence of groupthink.

ARTICLE 35 _____

Whenever two or more individuals act as a group, a central part of the interaction may involve trying to reach some agreement about an issue or activity. When the group consists of individuals or nations, reaching agreement is often a major concern.

Bargaining is one form that such negotiations take. The bargaining may be about something small and be informal in style, such as a couple deciding on which movie to see, or it may be major and formal, such as two nations trying to reach an agreement on nuclear arms control. In either case, central to the bargaining is the belief by both parties that reaching a mutually agreed-upon solution will possibly benefit both of them.

Two broad approaches to bargaining are cooperation and competition. In a *competitive* situation, individuals or groups view the situation in "win-lose" terms: I want to win, and it most likely will be at your expense. In a *cooperative* arrangement, the situation is more likely to be viewed as a "win-win" opportunity: We can both get something good out of this; neither one has to lose. Other things being equal, a cooperative strategy is more likely to ensure a good outcome for all concerned. But is that the strategy most likely to be used? Or do individuals and groups tend to use competitive strategies instead, even if it might not ultimately be in their best interest to do so?

The following classic contribution by Morton Deutsch and Robert M. Krauss examines the effect of threat on interpersonal bargaining. One major finding of the study is that the presence of threat, as well as whether only one or both parties are capable of threat, has a major impact on the outcome of the bargaining situation. Common sense might suggest that if my opponent has some threat that he or she can use against me, then I would be better off having the same level of threat to use against him or her, rather than having no threat to retaliate with. The findings of the study do not confirm this expectation, however, and may suggest a rethinking of the use of threat and power in real-world negotiations.

The Effect of Threat upon Interpersonal Bargaining

■ Morton Deutsch and Robert M. Krauss

A bargain is defined in *Webster's Unabridged Dictionary* as "an agreement between parties settling what each shall give and receive in a transaction between them"; it is further specified that a bargain is "an agreement or compact viewed as advantageous or the reverse." When the term "agreement" is broadened to include tacit, informal agreements as well as explicit agreements, it is evident that bargains and the processes involved in arriving at bargains ("bargaining") are pervasive characteristics of social life.

The definition of bargain fits under sociological definitions of the term "social norm." In this light, the experimental study of the bargaining process and of bargaining outcomes provides a means for the laboratory study of the development of certain types of social norms. But unlike many other types of social situations, bargaining situations have certain distinctive features that make it relevant to consider the conditions that determine whether or not a social norm will develop as well as those that determine the nature of the social norm if it develops.

Bargaining situations highlight the possibility that, even where cooperation would be mutually advantageous, shared purposes may not develop, agreement may not be reached, and interaction may be regulated antagonistically rather than normatively.

The essential features of a bargaining situation exist when:

1. Both parties perceive that there is the possibility of reaching an agreement in which each party would be better off, or no worse off, than if no agreement were reached.
2. Both parties perceive that there is more than one such agreement that could be reached.
3. Both parties perceive each other to have conflicting preferences or opposed interests with regard to the different agreements that might be reached.

Everyday examples of bargaining include such situations as: the buyer-seller relationship when the price is not fixed, the husband and wife who want to spend an evening out together but have conflicting preferences about where to go, union-management

Deutsch, M.; & Krause, R.M. (1960). The effect of threat upon interpersonal bargaining. *Journal of Personality and Social Psychology*, 61, 181–189.

negotiations, drivers who meet at an intersection when there is no clear right of way, disarmament negotiations.

In terms of our prior conceptualization of cooperation and competition (Deutsch, 1949) bargaining is thus a situation in which the participants have mixed motives toward one another: on the one hand, each has interest in cooperating so that they reach an agreement; on the other hand, they have competitive interests concerning the nature of the agreement they reach. In effect, to reach agreement the cooperative interest of the bargainers must be strong enough to overcome their competitive interests. However, agreement is not only contingent upon the *motivational* balances of cooperative to competitive interests but also upon the situational and *cognitive* factors which facilitate or hinder the recognition or invention of a bargaining agreement that reduces the opposition of interest and enhances the mutuality of interest.[1]

These considerations lead to the formulation of two general, closely related propositions about the likelihood that a bargaining agreement will be reached.

1. Bargainers are more likely to reach an agreement, the stronger are their cooperative interests in comparison with their competitive interests.
2. Bargainers are more likely to reach an agreement, the more resources they have available for recognizing or inventing potential bargaining agreements and for communicating to one another once a potential agreement has been recognized or invented.

From these two basic propositions and additional hypotheses concerning conditions that determine the strengths of the cooperative and competitive interests and the amount of available resources, we believe it is possible to explain the ease or difficulty of arriving at a bargaining agreement. We shall not present a full statement of these hypotheses here but turn instead to a description of an experiment that relates to Proposition 1.

The experiment was concerned with the effect of the availability of threat upon bargaining in a two-person experimental bargaining game.[2] Threat is defined as the expression of an intention to do something detrimental to the interests of another. Our experiment was guided by two assumptions about threat:

1. If there is a conflict of interest and one person is able to threaten the other, he will tend to use the threat in an attempt to force the other person to yield. This tendency should be stronger, the more irreconcilable the conflict is perceived to be.
2. If a person uses threat in an attempt to intimidate another, the threatened person (if he considers himself to be of equal or superior status) would feel hostility toward the threatener and tend to respond with counterthreat and/or increased resistance to yielding. We qualify this assumption by stating that the tendency to resist should be greater, the greater the

perceived probability and magnitude of detriment to the other and the less the perceived probability and magnitude of detriment to the potential resister from the anticipated resistance to yielding.

The second assumption is based upon the view that when resistance is not seen to be suicidal or useless, to allow oneself to be intimidated, particularly by someone who does not have the right to expect deferential behavior, is to suffer a loss of social face and, hence, of self-esteem: and that the culturally defined way of maintaining self-esteem in the face of attempted intimidation is to engage in a contest for supremacy vis-à-vis the power to intimidate or, minimally, to resist intimidation. Thus, in effect, the use of threat (and if it is available to be used, there will be a tendency to use it) should strengthen the competitive interests of the bargainers in relationship to one another by introducing or enhancing the competitive struggle for self-esteem. Hence, from Proposition 1, it follows that the availability of a means of threat should make it more difficult for the bargainers to reach agreement (providing that the threatened person has some means of resisting the threat). The preceding statement is relevant to the comparison of both of our experimental conditions of threat, bilateral and unilateral (described below), with our experimental condition of nonthreat. We hypothesize that a bargaining agreement is more likely to be achieved when neither party can threaten the other, than when one or both parties can threaten the other.

Consider now the situations of bilateral threat and unilateral threat. For several reasons, a situation of bilateral threat is probably less conducive to agreement than is a condition of unilateral threat. First, the sheer likelihood that a threat will be made is greater when two people rather than one have the means of making the threat. Secondly, once a threat is made in the bilateral case it is likely to evoke counterthreat. Withdrawal of threat in the face of counterthreat probably involves more loss of face (for reasons analogous to those discussed in relation to yielding to intimidation) than does withdrawal of threat in the face of resistance to threat. Finally, in the unilateral case, although the person without the threat potential can resist and not yield to the threat, his position vis-à-vis the other is not so strong as the position of the threatened person in the bilateral case. In the unilateral case, the threatened person may have a worse outcome than the other whether he resists or yields; while in the bilateral case, the threatened person is sure to have a worse outcome if he yields but he may insure that he does not have a worse outcome if he does not yield.

METHOD

Procedure

Subjects (*Ss*) were asked to imagine that they were in charge of a trucking company, carrying merchandise over a road to a

FIGURE 1 / Subject's Road Map

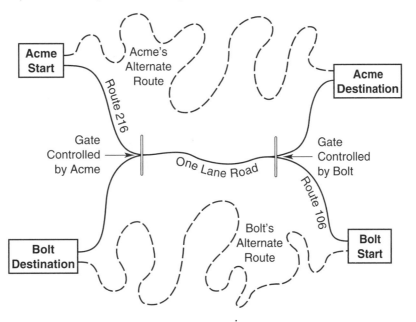

destination. For each trip completed they made $.60, minus their operating expenses. Operating expenses were calculated at the rate of one cent per second. So, for example, if it took 37 seconds to complete a particular trip, the player's profit would be $.60 − $.37 or a net profit of $.23 for that particular trip.

Each *S* was assigned a name, Acme or Bolt. As the "road map" (see Figure 1) indicates, both players start from separate points and go to separate destinations. At one point their paths cross. This is the section of road labeled "one lane road," which is only one lane wide, so that two trucks, heading in opposite directions, could not pass each other. If one backs up the other can go forward, or both can back up, or both can sit there head-on without moving.

There is another way for each *S* to reach the destination on the map, labeled the "alternate route." The two players' paths do not cross on this route, but the alternative is 56% longer than the main route. *S*s were told that they could expect to lose at least $.10 each time they used the alternate route.

At either end of the one-lane section there is a gate that is under the control of the player to whose starting point it is closest. By closing the gate, one player can prevent the other from traveling over that section of the main route. The use of the gate provides the threat potential in this game. In the bilateral threat potential condition (Two Gates) both players had gates under their control. In a second condition of unilateral threat (One Gate) Acme had control of a gate but Bolt did not. In a third condition (No Gates) neither player controlled a gate.

*S*s played the game seated in separate booths placed so that they could not see each other but could see the experimenter (*E*). Each *S* had a "control panel" mounted on a 12″ × 18″ × 12″ sloping-front cabinet (see Figure 2). The apparatus consisted essentially of a reversible impulse computer that was pulsed by a recycling timer. When the *S* wanted to move her truck forward she threw a key that closed a circuit pulsing the "add" coil of the impulse counter mounted on her control panel. As the counter cumulated, *S* was able to determine her "position" by relating the number on her counter to reference numbers that had been written in on her road map. Similarly, when she wished to reverse, she would throw a switch that activated the "subtract" coil of her counter, thus subtracting from the total on the counter each time the timer cycled.

S's counter was connected in parallel to counters on the other *S*'s panel and on *E*'s panel. Thus each player had two counters on her panel, one representing her own position and the other representing the other player's. Provision was made in construction of the apparatus to permit cutting the other player's counter out of the circuit, so that each *S* knew only the position of her own truck. This was done in the present experiment. Experiments now in progress are studying the effects of knowledge of the other person's position and other aspects of interpersonal communication upon the bargaining process.

The only time one player definitely knew the other player's position was when they had met head-on on the one-way section of road. This was indicated by a traffic light mounted on the panel. When this light was on, neither player could move forward unless the other moved back. The gates were controlled

FIGURE 2 / Subject's Control Panel

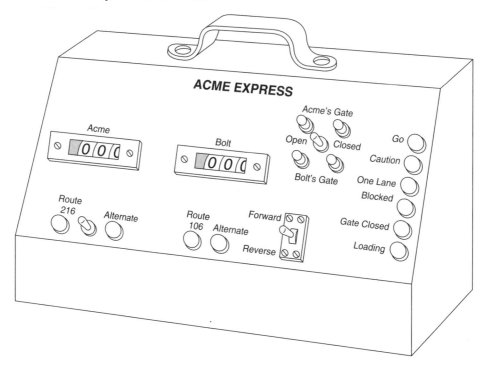

by toggle switches and panel-mounted indicator lights showed, for both *S*s, whether each gate was open or closed.

The following "rules of the game" were stated to the *S*s:

1. A player who started out on one route and wished to switch to the other route could only do so after first reversing and going back to the start position. Direct transfer from one route to the other was not permitted except at the start position.

2. In the conditions where *S*s had gates, they were permitted to close the gates no matter where they were on the main route, so long as they were on the main route (i.e., they were not permitted to close the gate while on the alternate route or after having reached their destinations). However, *S*s were permitted to open their gates at any point in the game.

*S*s were taken through a number of practice exercises to familiarize them with the game. In the first trial they were made to meet head-on on the one-lane path; Acme was then told to back up until she was just off the one-lane path and Bolt was told to go forward. After Bolt had gone through the one-lane path, Acme was told to go forward. Each continued going forward until each arrived at her destination. The second practice trial was the same as the first except that Bolt rather than Acme backed up after meeting head-on. In the next practice trial, one of the players was made to wait just before the

one-way path while the other traversed it and then was allowed to continue. In the next practice trial, one player was made to take the alternate route and the other was made to take the main route. Finally, in the bilateral and unilateral threat conditions the use of the gate was illustrated (by having the player get on the main route, close the gate, and then go back and take the alternate route). The *S*s were told explicitly, with emphasis, that they did *not* have to use the gate. Before each trial in the game the gate or gates were in the open position.

The instructions stressed an individualistic motivation orientation. *S*s were told to try to earn as much money for themselves as possible and to have no interest in whether the other player made money or lost money. They were given $4.00 in poker chips to represent their working capital and told that after each trial they would be given "money" if they made a profit or that "money" would be taken from them if they lost (i.e., took more than 60 seconds to complete their trip). The profit or loss of each *S* was announced so that both *S*s could hear the announcement after each trial. Each pair of *S*s played a total of 20 trials; on all trials, they started off together. In other words each trial presented a repetition of the same bargaining problem. In cases where *S*s lost their working capital before the 20 trials were completed, additional chips were given them. *S*s were aware that their monetary winnings and losses were to be imaginary and that no money would change hands as a result of the experiment.

Subjects

Sixteen pairs of *S*s were used in each of the three experimental conditions. The *S*s were female clerical and supervisory personnel of the New Jersey Bell Telephone Company who volunteered to participate during their working day.[3] Their ages ranged from 20 to 39, with a mean of 26.2. All were naive to the purpose of the experiment. By staggering the arrival times and choosing girls from different locations, we were able to insure that the *S*s did not know with whom they were playing.

Data Recorded

Several types of data were collected. We obtained a record of the profit or loss of each *S* on each trial. We also obtained a detailed recording of the actions taken by each *S* during the course of a trial. For this purpose, we used an Esterline-Angus model AW Operations Recorder which enabled us to obtain a "log" of each move each *S* made during the game (e.g., whether and when she took the main or alternate route; when she went forward, backward, or remained still; when she closed and opened the gate; when she arrived at her destination).

RESULTS[4]

The best single measure of the difficulty experienced by the bargainers in reaching an agreement is the sum of each pair's profits (or losses) on a given trial. The higher the sum of the payoffs to the two players on a given trial, the less time it took them to arrive at a procedure for sharing the one-lane path of the main route. (It was, of course, possible for one or both of the players to decide to take the alternate route so as to avoid a protracted stalemate during the process of bargaining. This, however, always results in at least a $.20 smaller joint payoff if only one player took the alternate route, than an optimally arrived at agreement concerning the use of the one-way path.)

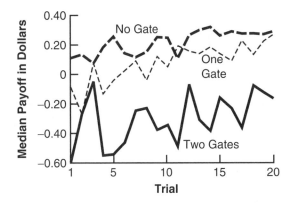

FIGURE 3 / Median Joint Payoff (Acme + Bolt) over Trials

Figure 3 presents the medians of the summed payoffs (i.e., Acme's plus Bolt's) for all pairs in each of the three experimental conditions over the 20 trials.[5] These striking results indicate that agreement was least difficult to arrive at in the no threat condition, was more difficult to arrive at in the unilateral threat condition, and exceedingly difficult or impossible to arrive at in the bilateral threat condition (see also Table 1).

Examination of Figure 3 suggests that learning occurred during the 20 trials: the summed payoffs for pairs of *S*s tend to improve as the number of trials increases. This suggestion is confirmed by an analysis of variance of the slopes for the summed payoffs[6] over the 20 trials for each of the 16 pairs in each of the 3 experimental treatments. The results of this analysis indicate that the slopes are significantly greater than zero for the unilateral threat ($p < .01$) and the no threat ($p < .02$) conditions; for the bilateral threat condition, the slope does not reach statistical significance ($.10 < p < .20$). The indicate that the pairs in the no threat condition started off at a fairly high level but, even so, showed some improvement

TABLE 1 / Mean Payoffs Summated over the Twenty Trials

	Means			Statistical Comparisons: *p* values[a]			
Variable	(1) No Threat	(2) Unilateral Threat	(3) Bilateral Threat	Overall	(1) vs. (2)	(1) vs. (3)	(2) vs. (3)
Summed Payoffs (Acme + Bolt)	203.31	−405.88	−875.12	.01	.01	.01	.05
Acme's Payoff	122.44	−118.56	−406.56	.01	.10	.01	.05
Bolt's Payoff	80.88	−287.31	−468.56	.01	.01	.01	.20
Absolute Differences in Payoff (A - B)	125.94	294.75	315.25	.05	.05	.01	*ns*

[a]Evaluation of the significance of overall variation between conditions is based on an *F* test with 2 and 45 *df*.

Comparisons between treatments are based on a two-tailed *t* test.

over the 20 trials; the pairs in the unilateral threat condition started off low and, having considerable opportunity for improvement, used their opportunity; the pairs in the bilateral threat condition, on the other hand, did not benefit markedly from repeated trials.

Figure 4 compares Acme's median profit in the three experimental conditions over the 20 trials; while Figure 5 compares Bolt's profit in the three conditions. (In the unilateral threat condition, it was Acme who controlled a gate and Bolt who did not.) Bolt's as well as Acme's outcome is somewhat better in the no threat condition than in the unilateral threat condition; Acme's, as well as Bolt's, outcome is clearly worst in the bilateral threat condition (see Table 1 also). However, Figure 6 reveals that Acme does somewhat better than Bolt in the unilateral condition. Thus, if threat-potential exists within a bargaining relationship it is better to possess it oneself than to have the other party possess it. However, it is even better for neither party to possess it. Moreover, Figure 5 shows that Bolt is better off not having than having a gate even when Acme has a gate: Bolt tends to do better in the unilateral threat condition than in the bilateral threat condition.

FIGURE 4 / Acme's Median Payoff

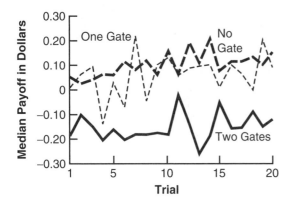

FIGURE 5 / Bolt's Median Payoff

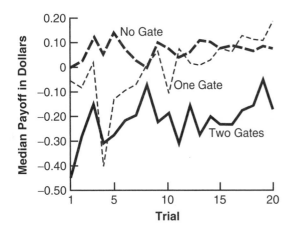

FIGURE 6 / Acme's and Bolt's Median Payoffs in Unilateral Threat Condition

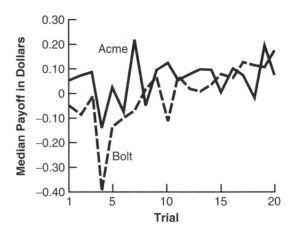

FIGURE 7 / Median Absolute Differences in Payoff

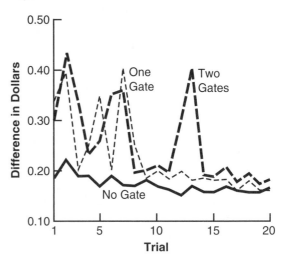

The size of the absolute discrepancy between the payoffs of the two players in each pair provides a measure of the confusion or difficulty in predicting what the other player was going to do. Thus, a large absolute discrepancy might indicate that after one player had gone through the one-way path and left it open, the other player continued to wait; or it might indicate that one player continued to wait at a closed gate hoping the other player would open it quickly but the other player did not; etc. Figure 7 indicates that the discrepancy between players in the no threat condition is initially small and remains small for the 20 trials. For the players in both the bilateral and unilateral threat conditions, the discrepancy is initially relatively larger; but it decreases more noticeably in the unilateral threat condition by the tenth trial and, therefore, is consistently smaller than in the bilateral condition.

By way of concrete illustration, we present a synopsis of the game for one pair in each of three experimental treatments.

No Threat Condition

Trial 1   The players met in the center of the one-way section. After some back-and-forth movement Bolt reversed to the end of the one-way section, allowing Acme to pass through, and then proceeded forward herself.

Trial 2   They again met at the center of the one-way path. This time, after moving back and forth deadlocked for some time, Bolt reversed to "start" and took the alternate route to her destination, thus leaving Acme free to go through on the main route.

Trial 3   The players again met at the center of the one-way path. This time, however, Acme reversed to the beginning of the path, allowing Bolt to go through to her destination. Then Acme was able to proceed forward on the main route.

Trial 5   Both players elected to take the alternate route to their destinations.

Trial 7   Both players took the main route and met in the center. They waited, deadlocked, for a considerable time. Then Acme reversed to the end of the one-way path allowing Bolt to go through, then proceeded through to her destination.

Trials 10–20   Acme and Bolt fall into a pattern of alternating who is to go first on the one-way section. There is no deviation from this pattern.

The only other pattern that emerges in this condition is one in which one player dominates the other. That is, one player consistently goes first on the one-way section and the other player consistently yields.

Unilateral Threat Condition

Trial 1   Both players took the main route and met in the center of it. Acme immediately closed the gate, reversed to "start," and took the alternate route to her destination. Bolt waited for a few seconds, at the closed gate, then reversed and took the alternate route.

Trial 2   Both players took the main route and met in the center. After moving back and forth deadlocked for about 15 seconds, Bolt reversed to the beginning of the one-way path, allowed Acme to pass, and then proceeded forward to her destination.

Trial 3   Both players started out on the main route, meeting in the center. After moving back and forth deadlocked for a while, Acme closed her gate, reversed to "start," and took the alternate route. Bolt, meanwhile, waited at the closed gate. When Acme arrived at her destination she opened the gate, and Bolt went through to complete her trip.

Trial 5   Both players took the main route, meeting at the center of the one-way section. Acme immediately closed her gate, reversed, and took the alternate route. Bolt waited at the gate for about 10 seconds, then reversed and took the alternate route to her destination.

Trial 10   Both players took the main route and met in the center. Acme closed her gate, reversed, and took the alternate route. Bolt remained waiting at the closed gate. After Acme arrived at her destination, she opened the gate and Bolt completed her trip.

Trial 15   Acme took the main route to her destination and Bolt took the alternate route.

Trials 17–20   Both players took the main route and met in the center. Bolt waited a few seconds, then reversed to the end of the one-way section allowing Acme to go through. Then Bolt proceeded forward to her destination.

Other typical patterns that developed in this experimental condition included an alternating pattern similar to that described in the no threat condition, a dominating pattern in which Bolt would select the alternate route leaving Acme free to use the main route unobstructed, and a pattern in which Acme would close her gate and then take the alternate route, also forcing Bolt to take the alternate route.

Bilateral Threat Condition

Trial 1   Acme took the main route and Bolt took the alternate route.

Trial 2   Both players took the main route and met head-on. Bolt closed her gate. Acme waited a few seconds, then closed her gate, reversed to "start," then went forward again to the closed gate. Acme reversed and took the alternate route. Bolt again reversed, then started on the alternate route. Acme opened her gate and Bolt reversed to "start" and went to her destination on the main route.

Trial 3   Acme took the alternate route to her destination. Bolt took the main route and closed her gate before entering the one-way section.

Trial 5   Both players took the main route and met head-on. After about 10 seconds spent backing up and going forward, Acme closed her gate, reversed, and took the alternate route. After waiting a few seconds, Bolt did the same.

Trials 8–10 Both players started out on the main route, immediately closed their gates, reversed to "start," and took the alternate route to their destinations.

Trial 15 Both players started out on the main route and met head-on. After some jockeying for position, Acme closed her gate, reversed, and took the alternate route to her destination. After waiting at the gate for a few seconds, Bolt reversed to "start" and took the alternate route to her destination.

Trials 19–20 Both players started out on the main route, immediately closed their gates, reversed to "start," and took the alternate routes to their destinations.

Other patterns that emerged in the bilateral threat condition included alternating first use of the one-way section, one player's dominating the other on first use of the one-way section, and another dominating pattern in which one player consistently took the main route while the other consistently took the alternate route.

DISCUSSION

From our view of bargaining as a situation in which both cooperative and competitive tendencies are present and acting upon the individual, it is relevant to inquire as to the conditions under which a stable agreement of any form develops. However, implicit in most economic models of bargaining (e.g., Stone, 1958; Zeuthen, 1930) is the assumption that the cooperative interests of the bargainers are sufficiently strong to insure that some form of mutually satisfactory agreement will be reached. For this reason, such models have focused upon the form of the agreement reached by the bargainers. Siegel and Fouraker (1960) report a series of bargaining experiments quite different in structure from ours in which only one of many pairs of *S*s were unable to reach agreement. Siegel and Fouraker explain this rather startling result as follows:

> *Apparently the disruptive forces which lead to the rupture of some negotiations were at least partially controlled in our sessions. . . .*
>
> *Some negotiations collapse when one party becomes incensed at the other, and henceforth strives to maximize his opponent's displeasure rather than his own satisfaction. . . . Since it is difficult to transmit insults by means of quantitative bids, such disequilibrating behavior was not induced in the present studies. If subjects were allowed more latitude in their communications and interactions, the possibility of an affront offense-punitive behavior sequence might be increased (p. 100).*

In our experimental bargaining situation, the availability of threat clearly made it more difficult for bargainers to reach a mutually profitable agreement. These results, we believe, reflect psychological tendencies that are not confined to our bargaining situation: the tendency to use threat (if the means for threatening is available) in an attempt to force the other person to yield, when the other is seen as obstructing one's path; the tendency to respond with counterthreat or increased resistance to attempts at intimidation. How general are these tendencies? What conditions are likely to elicit them? Answers to these questions are necessary before our results can be generalized to other situations.

Dollard, Doob, Miller, Mowrer, and Sears (1939) have cited a variety of evidence to support the view that aggression (i.e., the use of threat) is a common reaction to a person who is seen as the agent of frustration. There seems to be little reason to doubt that the use of threat is a frequent reaction to interpersonal impasses. However, everyday observation indicates that threat does not inevitably occur when there is an interpersonal impasse. We would speculate that it is most likely to occur: when the threatener has no positive interest in the other person's welfare (he is either egocentrically or competitively related to the other); when the threatener believes that the other has no positive interest in his welfare; and when the threatener anticipates either that his threat will be effective or, if ineffective, will not worsen his situation because he expects the worst to happen if he does not use his threat. We suggest that these conditions were operative in our experiment; *S*s were either egocentrically or competitively oriented to one another[7] and they felt that they would not be worse off by the use of threat.

Everyday observation suggests that the tendency to respond with counterthreat or increased resistance to attempts at intimidation is also a common occurrence. We believe that introducing threat into a bargaining situation affects the meaning of yielding. Although we have no data to support this interpretation directly, we will attempt to justify it on the basis of some additional assumptions.

Goffman (1955) has pointed out the pervasive significance of "face" in the maintenance of the social order. In this view, self-esteem is a socially validated system that grows out of the acceptance by others of the claim for deference, prestige, and recognition that a person presents in his behavior toward others. Since the rejection of such a claim would be perceived (by the recipient) as directed against his self-esteem, he must react against it rather than accept it in order to maintain the integrity of his self-esteem system.

One may view the behavior of our *S*s as an attempt to make claims upon the other, an attempt to develop a set of shared expectations as to what each was entitled to. Why then did the *S*s' reactions differ so markedly as a function of the availability of threat? The explanation lies, we believe, in the cultural interpretation of yielding (to a peer or subordinate) under duress, as compared to giving in without duress.

The former, we believe, is perceived as a negatively valued form of behavior, with negative implications for the self-image of the person who so behaves. At least partly, this is so because the locus of causality is perceived to be outside the person's voluntary control. No such evaluation, however, need be placed on the behavior of one who "gives in" in a situation where no threat or duress is a factor. Rather, we should expect the culturally defined evaluation of such a person's behavior to be one of "reasonableness" or "maturity," because the source of the individual's behavior is perceived to lie within his own control.

Our discussion so far has suggested that the psychological factors which operate in our experimental bargaining situation are to be found in many real-life bargaining situations. However, it is well to recognize some unique features of our experimental game. First, the bargainers had no opportunity to communicate verbally with one another. Prior research on the role of communication in trust (Deutsch, 1958, 1960; Loomis, 1959) suggests that the opportunity for communication would have made reaching an agreement easier for individualistically-oriented bargainers. This same research (Deutsch, 1960) indicates, however, that communication may not be effective between competitively oriented bargainers. This possibility was expressed spontaneously by a number of our Ss in a post-game interview.

Another characteristic of our bargaining game is that the passage of time, without coming to an agreement, is costly to the players. There are, of course, bargaining situations in which lack of agreement may simply preserve the *status quo* without any worsening of the bargainers' respective situations. This is the case in the typical bilateral monopoly case, where the buyer and seller are unable to agree upon a price (e.g., see Siegel & Fouraker, 1960). In other sorts of bargaining situations, however, (e.g., labor-management negotiations during a strike, international negotiations during an expensive cold war) the passage of time may play an important role. In our experiment, we received the impression that the meaning of time changed as time passed without the bargainers reaching an agreement. Initially, the passage of time seemed to place the players under pressure to come to an agreement before their costs mounted sufficiently to destroy their profit. With the continued passage of time, however, their mounting losses strengthened their resolution not to yield to the other player. They comment: "I've lost so much, I'll be damned if I give in now. At least I'll have the satisfaction of doing better than she does." The mounting losses and continued deadlock seemed to change the game from a mixed motive into a predominantly competitive situation.

It is, of course, hazardous to generalize from a laboratory experiment to the complex problems of the real world. But our experiment and the theoretical ideas underlying it can perhaps serve to emphasize some notions which, otherwise, have an intrinsic plausibility. In brief, these are that there is more safety in cooperative than in competitive coexistence, that it is dangerous for bargainers to have weapons, and that it is possibly even more dangerous for a bargainer to have the capacity to retaliate in kind than not to have this capacity when the other bargainer has a weapon. This last statement assumes that the one who yields has more of his values preserved by accepting the agreement preferred by the other than by extended conflict. Of course, in some bargaining situations in the real world, the loss incurred by yielding may exceed the losses due to extended conflict.

SUMMARY

The nature of bargaining situations was discussed. Two general propositions about the conditions affecting the likelihood of a bargaining agreement were presented. The effects of the availability of threat upon interpersonal bargaining were investigated experimentally in a two-person bargaining game. Three experimental conditions were employed: no threat (neither player could threaten the other), unilateral threat (only one of the players had a means of threat available to her), and bilateral threat (both players could threaten each other). The results indicated that the difficulty in reaching an agreement and the amount of (imaginary) money lost, individually as well as collectively, was greatest in the bilateral and next greatest in the unilateral threat condition. Only in the no threat condition did the players make an overall profit. In the unilateral threat condition, the player with the threat capability did better than the player without the threat capability. However, comparing the bilateral and unilateral threat conditions, the results also indicate that when facing a player who had threat capability one was better off *not* having than having the capacity to retaliate in kind.

REFERENCES

Deutsch, M. A theory of cooperation and competition. *Hum. Relat.,* 1949, *2,* 129–152.

Deutsch, M. Trust and suspicion. *J. Conflict Resolut.,* 1958, *2,* 265–279.

Deutsch, M. The effect of motivational orientation upon trust and suspicion. *Hum. Relat.,* 1960, *13,* 123–140.

Dollard, J., Doob, L. W., Miller, N. E., Mowrer, O. H., & Sears, R. H. *Frustration and aggression.* New Haven: Yale Univer. Press, 1939.

Goffman, E. On face-work. *Psychiatry,* 1955, *18,* 213–231.

Loomis, J. L. Communication, the development of trust and cooperative behavior. *Hum. Relat.,* 1959, *12,* 305–315.

Schelling, T. C. Bargaining, communication and limited war. *J. Conflict Resolut.,* 1957, *1,* 19–38.

Schelling, T. C. The strategy of conflict: Prospectus for the reorientation of game theory. *J. conflict Resolut.,* 1958, *2,* 203–264.

Siegel, S., & Fouraker, L. E. *Bargaining and group decision making.* New York: McGraw-Hill, 1960.

Stone, J. J. An experiment in bargaining games. *Econometrica,* 1958, *26,* 286–296.

Zeuthen, F. *Problems of monopoly and economic warfare.* London: Routledge, 1930.

ENDNOTES

1. Schelling in a series of stimulating papers on bargaining (1957, 1958) has also stressed the "mixed motive" character of bargaining situations and has analyzed some of the cognitive factors which determine agreements.

2. The game was conceived and originated by M. Deutsch; R. M. Krauss designed and constructed the apparatus employed in the experiment.

3. We are indebted to the New Jersey Bell Telephone Company for their cooperation in providing *S*s and facilities for the experiment.

4. We are indebted to M. J. R. Healy for suggestions concerning the statistical analysis of our data.

5. Medians are used in graphic presentation of our results because the wide variability of means makes inspection cumbersome.

6. A logarithmic transformation of the summed payoffs on each trial for each pair was made before computing the slopes for a given pair.

7. A post-experimental questionnaire indicated that, in all three experimental conditions, the *S*s were most strongly motivated to win money, next most strongly motivated to do better than the other player, next most motivated to "have fun," and were very little or not at all motivated to help the other player.

CRITICAL THINKING QUESTIONS

1. For many years, the mutually assured destruction (MAD) policy defined U.S. nuclear strategy. That is, nuclear war was to be prevented by the threat of assured destruction of the aggressor nation. What might be the implications of this study for the nuclear policies of nations?

2. The best performance in this study was obtained in the no-threat condition; the unilateral threat condition, in turn, produced better results than the bilateral threat condition, which did the worst. To what extent are these findings generalizable to other situations? In some situations, might it be best to have bilateral threat instead of unilateral threat? What variables might be important in determining when each would be preferred? Explain.

3. In an area such as international relations, how can the existence of threat be reduced? What role may communication play in the process?

ADDITIONAL RELATED READINGS

Pelc, A., & Pelc, K. J. (2009). Same game, new tricks: What makes a good strategy in the prisoner's dilemma? *Journal of Conflict Resolution, 53*(5), 774–793.

Poulsen, A., & Poulsen, O. (2010). Prisoner's dilemma payoffs and the evolution of co-operative preferences. *The Journal of Socio-Economics, 39*(2), 158–162.

ARTICLE 36 _____

Article 34 in this chapter presented the concept known as *groupthink*. Since Irving L. Janis proposed this hypothesis over 30 years ago, he and others have continued to refine understanding of the antecedent conditions, symptoms, and consequences of groupthink. Since its introduction, groupthink has been widely studied and broadly incorporated into the literature and knowledge base, not only in the field of social psychology but also in areas such as management and organizational behavior. For example, the ill-fated decision to launch the space shuttle *Challenger* (discussed in Article 34) and the Watergate fiasco are but two of the real-life decision-making processes that have been scrutinized according to the groupthink model.

As discussed in the explanation of groupthink found in Article 34, there are several factors that can contribute to the formation of groupthink, including group cohesiveness. *Group cohesiveness* refers to the qualities of the group that bind them together and promote a mutual liking for one another. One might think that being part of a highly cohesive group would be a good thing. Indeed, there are many studies that do show the positive benefits of high group cohesion. But according to Janis, high group cohesiveness may actually be negative, setting the stage for the occurrence of groupthink.

The following article by Esa Rovio, Jari Eskola, Stephen A. Kozub, Joan L. Duda, and Taru Lintuner examines the issue of whether high group cohesion was helpful or harmful to a group's functioning in a real-world setting. In doing so, the article also deals with some aspects of groupthink, and thus is a good example of a contemporary application of that theory. Additionally, this article involves a long-term field study, unlike many research studies you may have encountered thus far that tend to be short lived and done in a laboratory setting. Finally, the article also demonstrates the use of two different ways of gathering and analyzing data: qualitative and quantitative methodologies.

Can High Group Cohesion Be Harmful?
A Case Study of a Junior Ice-Hockey Team
■ Esa Rovio, Jari Eskola, Stephen A. Kozub, Joan L. Duda, and Taru Lintunen

High group cohesion is considered to be beneficial and lead to better performance. This qualitative case study describes a case in which high social cohesion led to a deterioration in a team's performance. The aim of the present study was to investigate the relationships between performance in a team sport and social psychological group phenomena such as cohesion, conformity, groupthink, and group polarization. The participants were members of a junior-league ice-hockey team, consisting of three adult coaches and 22 players aged 15 to 16 years. The data were derived from an interview with the main coach, continuous observation by the principal researcher, and a diary based on observations during one ice-hockey season. The Group Environment Questionnaire was used to assess group cohesion quantitatively. The qualitative data were analyzed by identifying themes that illuminated the research problem. In this study, the team did not perform as expected, and their performance deteriorated during the autumn. Social cohesion was high. In addition, the need to evaluate performance declined because of increased pressure to conform. Pressure to conform, groupthink, and group polarization increased owing to the high level of social cohesion which in turn was associated with the deterioration in the group's performance. Based on the findings it appears that high group cohesion may not always be beneficial to the team and does not necessarily lead to better performance in all situations.

According to the definition by Carron, Brawley, and Widmeyer (1998), group cohesion is "a dynamic process that is reflected in the tendency for a group to stick together and remain united in its pursuit of instrumental objectives and/or for the satisfaction of members' affective needs" (p. 213). The definition incorporates the concepts of task and social cohesion. As a group is usually founded to accomplish a purpose, task cohesion plays a fundamental role in the functioning of every group. Another cohesive force which often develops in time is that of social cohesion among the group's members.

Rovio, E.; Eskola, J.; Kozug, S.A.; Duda, J.L.; & Lintunen, T., *Small Group Research*, 40(4), 421–435. Copyright © 2009 by Sage Publications. Reprinted with permission of SAGE Publications.

Positive Outcomes of Cohesion

The relationship between cohesion and performance has been studied extensively (Carron, Colman, Wheeler, & Stevens, 2002; Mullen & Copper, 1994). According to a meta-analysis by Carron et al. (2002), the connection between cohesion and performance is reciprocal: High cohesion increases the group's performance and successful performance increases cohesion. Both task and social cohesion are related to group performance. Promoting both dimensions of cohesion through coaching thus seems warranted.

There are also other possible reasons for promoting cohesion. It has been found that adherence behavior (Prapavessis & Carron, 1997), adherence to training schedules (Carron, Widmeyer, & Brawley, 1988), conformity to group norms (e.g., Shields, Bredemeier, Gardner, & Boston, 1995), assuming responsibility for negative outcomes (e.g., Brawley, Carron, & Widmeyer, 1987), tolerance of the negative impact of disruptive events (e.g., Brawley, Carron, & Widmeyer, 1988), and collective efficacy (e.g., Paskevisch, Brawley, Dorsch, & Widmeyer, 1999) relate to greater cohesion. Weak cohesion has been found to be connected to weak training intensity (Prapavessis & Carron, 1997).

There are ways of improving cohesion. Cohesiveness is greater in smaller groups (Widmeyer, Brawley, & Carron, 1990). Cohesion is also boosted by altruism (Prapavessis & Carron, 1997), participation in team goal setting (Brawley, Carron, & Widmeyer, 1993), and democratic leader behavior (e.g., Kozub, 1993; Westre & Weiss, 1991). The relationship between cohesion and satisfaction (Williams & Hacker, 1982) would appear to be reciprocal.

Disadvantages of Cohesion

Cohesion may not always lead to more effective group performance. Paskevich, Estabrooks, Brawley, and Carron (2001) suggested that cohesion may be associated with pressure to conform, groupthink, and deindividuation. However, studies on the potential harmfulness of group cohesion in the area of sport psychology are few. According to Paskevich et al. (2001), one reason for the relative lack of research on the negative consequences of cohesion might be that researchers, coaches, and athletes take it as axiomatic that cohesion is always beneficial and thus should be encouraged whenever possible.

However, some evidence of the harmful aspects of cohesion in sport teams has been presented. Carron, Prapavessis, and Grove (1994) studied the connection between cohesion and self-handicapping behavior. They found that when the social dimension of group cohesion was high, athletes with strong self-handicapping traits made more excuses before an important competition. By excuses Carron et al. (1994) referred to cushioning and defensive comments in which the person would identify factors that can have the potential to hinder or impede performance (e.g., work, school, weather, family or personal problems, effects of alcohol, and influenza). When task cohesion was low, the athletes made fewer excuses. When discussing their results, Carron et al. (1994) considered cohesion to be both beneficial and harmful for a team. In a close group, athletes with a strong self-handicapping trait are salient. They may feel responsible for their performance, not wanting to let their teammates down, and consequently tend to make excuses for their failure.

In a highly unified team, teammates may feel the pressure of not to criticize social loafers (Carron & Hausenblas, 1998). Ignoring social loafing would help to preserve feelings of team unanimity. Athletes in more cohesive groups may therefore experience greater pressure to conform. The Carron et al. (1994) study also found signs of athletes experiencing pressure to act according to group members' wishes. Maintaining harmony is not always a good thing.

Different aspects of cohesion and performance-related norms are important in relation to perceptions of social loafing. In their study with 118 junior-league soccer players, Hoigaard, Säfvenbom, and Tonnessen (2006) found that when high social cohesion is combined with low task cohesion and the performance norm is low, the level of perceived social loafing is at its highest. However, when there is an increase in the performance norm, the level of perceived social loafing decreases appearing at its lowest level when combined with a high level of task cohesion and a high level of social cohesion. In addition, athletes seem to be aware of the possible disadvantages of task and social cohesion in a team. Similarly Hardy, Eys, and Carron (2005) also investigated a heterogeneous sample of 105 athletes. The results from the analyses revealed that 56% of athletes reported potential disadvantages in developing high social cohesion, whereas 31% reported disadvantages with respect to high task cohesion.

Multidimensional and Dynamic Cohesion

Previous cohesion studies have mainly used on a quantitative research methodology. Finding associations in cohesion research is difficult for two main reasons: multidimensionality and the dynamic nature of group phenomena (Paskevich et al., 2001). Many factors contribute to group cohesiveness and these factors vary depending on the nature of the group. A group that has been close in the past will not necessarily be a close group in the future. The factors influencing cohesion in a group that is in the stage of formation may differ from those in a more established group. In a newly formed group, the force maintaining group cohesion is the group's task. Normally, the developing of social relationships between group members begins only when the group is performing a task.

According to Brawley (1990), the question "Does cohesion affect performance?" might be more meaningfully rephrased as "How does cohesion come about and affect performance?" Widmeyer, Carron, and Brawley (1993) also saw studies that take account of the dynamic nature of cohesion as more important than one-off snapshot studies. There is a need for longitudinal and qualitative studies; the factors that contribute to cohesion should be studied more closely in authentic real life situations (Hoigaard et al., 2006; Widmeyer et al., 1993).

The present study is in the form of a qualitative case study. It describes a case in which high social cohesion led to a deterioration in the group's performance. The aim was to investigate the relationships between sport performance and social psychological group phenomena such as cohesion, conformity, groupthink, and group polarization.

METHOD

Participants

The participants were members of a junior-league ice-hockey team, consisting of three adult coaches and of 22 players 15 to 16 years of age. The main informant, the head coach, had 11 years experience in coaching at the junior and elite level. On average, the players had been playing ice hockey for 9 years. The club team played at the highest level in the national league. During the competition season the team practiced four or five times and had one or two games a week. The principal researcher had 25 years experience of team sports as a player and doctoral-level training in sport and exercise psychology.

Procedure and Design

The present study was based on part of a larger team-building intervention program, which aimed at creating a team that performed its tasks well and at the same time was highly cohesive. The methods used were group and individual goal setting, role clarifying, and team cohesion–enhancing strategies. Within the individual goal setting and role clarifying programs, the method of performance profiling (e.g., Butler & Hardy, 1992) was used. The program was implemented during one ice-hockey season.

The study was a mixed method case study. It can be regarded as an intrinsic qualitative case study, as it aimed to illustrate and understand particular issues and the detailed structures of specific events within a specific group of people in a natural situation (Dobson, 2001; Stake, 2005). In addition, this could also be considered an instrumental case study because it aimed at the refinement of theory.

Abductive content analytical procedures were used (Magnani, 2001). The approach can be considered abductive (Atkinson & Delamont, 2005), in that the analysis was guided by knowledge about cohesion derived from earlier research. In addition, theory development (the Conceptual Model of Group Performance Deterioration) was based on the findings concerning the target group and is thus the outcome of a dialogue between the data and theory.

The data were collected over the course of an entire ice hockey season starting at the end of April and ending in the April of the following year. The data were derived from continuous observation, a diary based on the observations, and an interview conducted in November with the main coach. The principal researcher kept a diary of all the team's events and all his contacts with the team. He was also present at the team training camp during the summer training season and observed most of the team's home matches. The 105-page (single spaced) diary produced by the principal researcher contained the following: descriptions of the actions of the team; summaries of discussions with the team members and other researchers with regards to their opinions, assumptions, suggestions, and preliminary interpretations; theoretical considerations; and feelings and emotions. The video-recorded interview (later transcribed verbatim, 15 single spaced pages) with the main coach was concerned with the team processes.

In addition, quantitative data were collected. To assess group cohesion, the 18-item Group Environment Questionnaire (GEQ; Carron, Widmeyer, & Brawley, 1985) was used. Measurements were taken four times during the season. Because the results of this study concern the beginning of the season, only the baseline measurement was used. The GEQ items were assessed on a 9-point scale, ranging from *strongly disagree* (1) to *strongly agree* (9). The questionnaire was based on a conceptual model in which cohesion is regarded as a multidimensional construct containing both individual and group aspects. Each aspect has a task and a social orientation. Thus, the GEQ assesses four manifestations of cohesion: (a) Individual Attraction to the Group-Task (ATG-T), (b) Individual Attraction to the Group-Social (ATG-S), (c) Group Integration-Task (GI-T), and (d) Group Integration-Social (GI-S). ATG-T (4 items) and ATG-S (5 items) were used to evaluate the individual team member's perception and personal involvement with the group's task and goals, and also their social involvement within the group. GI-T (5 items) and GI-S (4 items) were used to evaluate the magnitude of an individual member's perceptions concerning similarity and bonding around the group's task and the group as a social unit. Previous research has indicated that the GEQ possesses good factorial validity and moderate internal consistency with Finnish data (Salminen & Luhtanen, 1998).

Data Analysis

Central themes were identified from the research diary kept by the main researcher. Next, the interview with the coach was analyzed. In the first round, different themes and the times of their occurrence on the videotape were marked. In the second round accurate notes were made. In the third round, the observations surrounding the central themes were recorded. Three themes in the data caught the attention of the researchers: (a) a sudden and considerable rise in the team's level of performance after one feedback meeting, (b) poor team performance despite high group cohesion, especially social cohesion, and (c) the reluctance of the players to reveal their true personal opinions within the group. To understand these three unexpected findings, the researchers directed their attention to the changes in level of performance (winning, losing, practicing), group cohesion (social and task dimensions), group behavior, and individual players' behavior in the group (especially players' evaluation of the group's performance).

During the process of analyzing and writing the report, the researchers continuously referred to the theoretical literature and previous research. This enabled conclusions to be drawn about the influence of the changes in level of performance, team cohesion, and group phenomena on players' evaluation of the team's performance. The impact of the narrative analytical method (e.g., Polkinghorne, 1995) can be seen in the analysis and reporting of the present study. This type of analysis is common in case studies (Stake, 2005). It is especially suited to the study of an ongoing process at the group level. According to the practice of reporting qualitative research, the theory and earlier empirical research findings are presented in the results section, and not only in the discussion.

RESULTS

Performance

During the preseason, the team had not performed well for several weeks. In the last of the preliminary matches, the team lost to an opponent with a much lower ranking. After losing the game, the coach held a meeting with the team to review the progress made toward achieving their common goals. The aim of the meeting was to remind the players of their collectively set goals, such as "preparing for training and matches" and to strengthen the players' commitment to those goals. The statistics from the game showed that the players had performed their individual duties poorly. According to the coach, the discussion about the team's goals appeared to energize the team so that after the meeting performance in training was substantially improved. The researcher's (first author) diary entry for October 5 read: "'going all the way,' with respect to their common goals had really materialized for the players. For the first time in a long time the training session was imbued with the spirit of action." Later, the main coach (November 10) noted,

After the meeting, the problem seemed to have vanished. Group goals are tools that can be used if the team is underperforming.

Our willpower wasn't low—we just noticed that we could perform even better. If a player learns to act in a goal-oriented way, he will notice how much room for growth he has. There is no limit to what one can achieve in these things.

The improvement in the level of performance was clearly visible in the succeeding games as well. Such a significant increase in performance simply as the outcome of a single feedback meeting was interesting. Although the principal researcher has played soccer for 25 years, he had never in all that time witnessed such a sudden and notable rise in a team's level of performance. This was one of the three important themes that contributed to the researchers' interest in this phenomenon.

The poor performance of the team in the early part of the season was not temporary (i.e., the result of a bad day), but originated further back in time. In fact, the research diary from the preceding month (September 17) revealed that the main coach had regarded the team's training as not up to standard on several occasions. Also, the data from the first feedback meeting showed that perceptions of the team's achievement of its common goals were lower among the coaches than among the players. The mean score given by the 22 players for achievement of the team's 17 goals was 8.4 (scale 1 to 10) whereas that given by the three coaches was 6.5. "This difference between the coaches and the players was the greatest surprise. The players rated the team's achievement of its goals higher than did the coaches" (Research diary, August 19).

High Cohesion

Another interesting observation was that high group cohesion did not lead to better performance. This was the second important unexpected theme. The GEQ indicated that cohesion was clearly high during the early months of the season. The mean values and standard deviations (in parentheses) were: ATG-T, 7.82 (.85); ATG-S, 7.23 (.92); GI-T, 7.1 (1.02) and GI-S, 6.24 (1.19). All the means were above the mid-point of the 9-point scale. The measurements from the first month of the ice-hockey season indicated high personal involvement (ATG-T, ATG-S), especially with respect to task involvement (ATG-T, GI-T). Naturally, early on in the season, the group was not as integrated as a social unit (GI-S). In contrast to past studies, the performance of the group deteriorated, despite a high level of team cohesion.

The qualitative assessments were in line with the quantitative measurements. As the season progressed, the qualitative data pointed to an increase in social cohesion. During the summer and autumn the main coach reported high social cohesion in the team. This was also supported by players' comments on the internal relations in the team: "folks begun to chat with absolutely everyone" (July 20) and "it had a certain openness in it" (August 15). Communication relationships in the team appeared to be open and interconnected.

Conformity

What factors, then, contributed to the team's descent to a relatively poor level of performance? Higher social cohesion may have led to greater conformity (i.e., pressure to conform). Conformity is defined as submission to perceived group pressure where a direct request to conform has not been presented (Deaux, Dane, & Wrightsman, 1993). Conformity may have resulted from, in particular, normative influence, but informational influence may also have played a role (Deaux et al., 1993). Normative influence is defined as an individual's adaptation to the attitude of the majority in order to gain acceptance by the group. A situation in which an individual accepts the majority's attitudes as valid information is referred to as informational influence.

The principal researcher obtained crucial evidence of the pressure to conform and normative influence in the autumn when a high-status player (captain of the team) revealed that he had difficulties in giving critical feedback to his teammates (Research diary, September 14). He was afraid that this would negatively affect his position in the team. Also, extracts from the research diary (below, September 27) showed that the players hesitated to share their true personal opinions in the feedback meeting held in the autumn. Difficulties of the players to openly express their thoughts was the third theme that attracted the researchers' interest in the phenomenon.

> We had a round of talks where the players could assess the team's progress in the achievement of its goals. It appeared that many of the players didn't give their honest opinion. Nearly all of these players gave short answers and used the same words as many other players had used. It seemed that their only objective was to give the floor to the next player as soon as possible. The players who spoke at the beginning of the discussion were mainly those who spoke out during the season anyway.

As stated earlier, individuals in highly cohesive teams may feel pressure not to criticize their teammates for social loafing (Carron & Hausenblas, 1998). Ignoring social loafing can assist in preserving a feeling of unanimity within a team. In addition to cohesion, the large size of the group (see Deaux et al., 1993) and young age of the players (Costanzo, 1970) may have increased the pressure to conform in the present case.

Groupthink

High social cohesion and pressure to conform may have led to the phenomenon of groupthink. Groupthink is a group process that emphasizes the need for unanimity. Its manifestations are a lowered willingness to detect options, moral complacency, and self-censorship, and it leads to the deterioration of decision making in the group (Deaux et al., 1993). The research diary excerpts quoted above indicate that the players did not share their true opinions in the goal assessment meeting and that the coaches had a lower perception of the team's level of performance than did the players. These factors reflect over-estimation by the players of the team's performance and an unwillingness to openly identify and discuss problems. According to the groupthink model by Janis (1972; Deaux et al., 1993), high levels of cohesion and conformity are factors that lead to groupthink. Bernthal and Insko (1993) found that a group with high social cohesion was more susceptible to groupthink than a group with high task cohesion.

Group Polarization

The team showed symptoms of group polarization as well. Group polarization is defined as a shift towards the opinion of the majority in the group's decision-making process (Deaux et al., 1993). The development of group polarization was expected as it is assumed to be caused by normative and informational influence, as in the case of conformity (Jones & Roelofsma, 2000). Critical assessment of the teammates' performance decreased, whereas cohesion, especially social cohesion, and normative pressure to conform and maintain harmony increased. During the autumn, this was shown in the conformist comments made by the players when assessing the team's performance (short answers, use of same words of others). Finally, in the meeting held after their defeat, the players realized the true level of their training and playing. A significant change in the level of performance showed that the group's assessment of its performance had become too positive during the autumn.

Model of Group Performance Deterioration

It may be that high social cohesion led to a deterioration in group performance. A team with high social cohesion may be unaware of how it is performing. That was the case in this study. The team's performance deteriorated during the autumn and lasted several months. The field observations of this chain of events are combined in Figure 1, which illustrates the deterioration in the performance of the junior league ice-hockey team and the players' over-evaluation of the level of the team's performance in both training and games. Conformism, groupthink, and group polarization explain the illusion of unanimity—a collective misconception of reality—sustained by the players and why the deficient training and performance of their teammates was not criticized or the training tightened up. Pressure to conform, groupthink, and group polarization increased because of the high social cohesion in the team.

FIGURE 1 / Model of Group Performance Deterioration

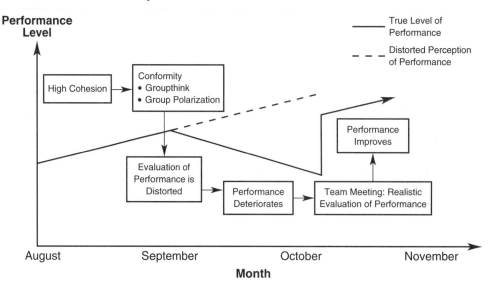

Finally, the players' unwillingness to evaluate the team's performance realistically led to further deterioration in performance.

DISCUSSION

The aim of the present study was to investigate the relationships between performance in a team sport and social psychological group phenomena such as cohesion, conformity, groupthink, and group polarization. Group cohesion has nearly always been considered a positive quality and there has been a tendency to seek to enhance it whenever possible. Numerous previous studies (see Carron et al., 2002; Paskevich et al., 2001) have shown that high cohesion is indeed associated with better performance. The performance of a group is better if its members are united and feel attraction towards one another and to the task they are performing. In the present case study, contrary to most previous research, high social cohesion was identified as a factor contributing to deterioration in group performance. The idea that of high cohesion can be harmful for effective group functioning has been supported in only a few earlier studies (e.g., Carron, 1994; Hardy et al., 2005; Hoigaard et al., 2006).

The present case study described how the performance of a team deteriorated during the autumn season, and the role played by group cohesion and other group factors in this process (Model of Group Performance Deterioration, Figure 1). As the season unfolded, three main observations or themes directed the investigation: (a) a sudden and considerable increase in the quality of the team's performance as an outcome of a single feedback meeting; (b) a deterioration in perform-

ance despite high levels of group cohesion, especially social cohesion; and (c) the reluctance of the players to reveal their true personal opinions within the team. The emergence of these events prompted the researchers to seek the underlying explanations for these occurrences on the basis of a number of data gathering methods, including field observations and research diaries, an interview with the head coach, and quantitative measurements.

A connection was identified between high social cohesion and deterioration in group performance. This finding conflicts with most of the previous research on the cohesion–performance relationship (Carron et al., 2002; Paskevich et al., 2001). In this case, high social cohesion was associated with a number of harmful group processes, including pressure to conform to norms revolving around the maintenance of unanimity, the reluctance of team members to express critical opinions regarding their teammates, and an unrealistically positive evaluation of the team's performance. In this respect, the team showed symptoms of groupthink and group polarization. These observations possibly explain the negative relationship observed between cohesion and performance.

Although high social cohesion in this case was found to have a negative impact on the team's performance, it can not be concluded that group leaders should reduce social cohesion or promote only task cohesion. In practice, the two aspects of cohesion are not separable. Coaching actions that aim to increase the attractiveness of a task also have implications for the social attractiveness of the group and vice versa. It continues to remain important to promote team cohesion. However, group leaders should be aware of the potential negative consequences associated with high social cohesion. Because of the combined pressure to conform to team norms and remain loyal to the group, team members may be unwilling to evaluate group performance critically. The main responsibility for assessing the team's performance lies with the group leader. When necessary, the group leader has to create space where the group members can safely and realistically evaluate the group's performance. Promoting a group environment in which communication is open and honest is an important aspect of the leader's role.

Collecting both qualitative and quantitative data in this study seemed to be an effective strategy. The qualitative data, such as the researcher's field observations, the video interview with the coach, and the collected notes of the discussions with the players enabled greater insights into the underlying processes into changes in cohesion and overall performance. Quantitative measures of cohesion supported the perceptions of the players and the interpretations of the researchers. The present study incorporated previous recommendations (e.g., Hoigaard et al., 2006; Widmeyer et al., 1993) that the observation of group phenomena should be long-term, preferably spanning a season or more, and involve both qualitative and quantitative methods. The strength of the present study was that the analysis focused on an ongoing process and on the activity of the group and the individuals. The study bears out the view of cohesion as dynamic and multidimensional in nature.

As the results were based mainly on the perceptions of the principal researcher and the main coach, the outcome of this study cannot be generalized to all team sports in all situations. To verify the relationships and processes identified here, we need more research on the influence of cohesion (both beneficial and harmful) on group functioning and performance. Further qualitative and quantitative research is necessary to identify the conditions under which cohesion has a positive or negative impact on performance and, most important, the group-related factors which contribute to this relationship.

As this study showed, high social cohesion may turn against itself. Cohesion may increase pressure to conform, groupthink, and group polarization, which in turn may impair the group's performance. Being cohesive may [become] such a strong norm, that group members lose their individuality (deindividuation), disappear into the crowd, and act in accordance with the hidden norms rather than in accordance with the task of the team. This way complex human-relationship networks may influence the decision-making process and behavior of individual group members. These findings possibly explain why a team may shift from a series of victories to a series of defeats. High group cohesion may not always be beneficial to the team and does not necessarily lead to better performance in all situations.

REFERENCES

Atkinson, P., & Delamont, S. (2005). Analytic perspectives. In N. K. Denzin & Y. S. Lincoln (Eds.) *The Sage handbook of qualitative research* (3rd ed., pp. 821–840). Thousand Oaks, CA: Sage.

Bernthal, P., & Insko, C. (1993). Cohesiveness without groupthink: The interactive effects of social and task cohesion. *Group and Organizational Management, 18,* 66–87.

Brawley, L. (1990). Group cohesion: Status, problems and future directions. *International Journal of Sport Psychology, 21,* 355–379.

Brawley, L. R., Carron, A. V., & Widmeyer, W. (1987). Assessing the cohesion of teams: Validity of the Group Environment Questionnaire. *Journal of Sport Psychology, 9,* 275–294.

Brawley, L., Carron, A., & Widmeyer, W. (1988). Exploring the relationship between cohesion and group resistance to disruption. *Journal of Sport & Exercise Psychology, 10,* 199–213.

Brawley, L., Carron, A., & Widmeyer, W. (1993). The influence of the group and its cohesiveness on perceptions of group-related variables. *Journal of Sport & Exercise Psychology, 15,* 245–260.

Butler, R. J., & Hardy, L. (1992). The performance profile: Theory and application. *The Sport Psychologist, 6,* 253–264.

Carron, A., Brawley, L., & Widmeyer, W. (1998). The measurements of cohesiveness in sport groups. In J. Duda (Ed.) *Advancements in sport and exercise psychology measurements* (pp. 213–226). Morgantown, WV: Fitness Information Technology.

Carron, A. V., Colman, M. M., Wheeler, J., & Stevens, D. (2002). Cohesion and performance in sport: A meta-analysis. *Journal of Sport & Exercise Psychology, 24,* 168–188.

Carron, A., & Hausenblas, H. (1998) *Group dynamics in sport* (2nd ed.). London, Ontario, Canada: Fitness Information Technology.

Carron, A. V., Prapavessis, H., & Grove, J. R. (1994). Group effects and self-handicapping. *Journal of Sport & Exercise Psychology, 16,* 246–258.

Carron, A. V., Widmeyer, W. N., & Brawley, L. R. (1988). Group cohesion and individual adherence to physical activity. *Journal of Sport & Exercise Psychology, 10,* 119–126.

Carron, A., Widmeyer, W., & Brawley, L. (1985). The development of an instrument to assess cohesion in sport teams: The group environment questionnaire. *Journal of Sport Psychology, 7,* 244–266.

Costanzo, P. R. (1970). Conformity development as a function of self-blame. *Journal of Personality and Social Psychology, 14,* 366–374.

Deaux, K., Dane, F., & Wrightsman, L. (1993). *Social psychology in the 90s* (6th ed.). Pacific Grove, CA: Brookes/Cole.

Dobson, P. J. (2001). Longitudinal case research: A critical realistic perspective. *Systemic Practice and Action Research, 14,* 283–296.

Hardy, J., Eys, M. A., & Carron, A. V. (2005). Exploring the potential disadvantages of high cohesion in sport teams. *Small Group Research, 36,* 166–187.

Hoigaard, R., Säfvenbom, R., & Tonnessen, F. E. (2006). The relationship between group cohesion, group norms, and perceived social loafing in soccer teams. *Small Group Research, 37,* 217–232.

Janis, I. L. (1972). *Victims of groupthink.* Boston: Houghton-Mifflin.

Jones, P. E., & Roelofsma, P. H. M. P. (2000). The potential for social contextual and group biases in team decision-making: Biases, conditions and psychological mechanism. *Ergonomics, 43,* 1129–1152.

Kozub, S. A. (1993). *Exploring the relationship among coaching behavior, team cohesion and player leadership.* Unpublished doctoral dissertation. University of Houston, TX.

Magnani, L. (2001). *Abduction, reason, and science: Processes of discovery and explanation.* New York: Kluwer/Plenum.

Mullen, B., & Copper, C. (1994). The relation between group cohesiveness and performance: An integration. *Psychological Bulletin, 115,* 210–227.

Paskevich, D. M., Brawley, L. R., Dorsch, K. D., & Widmeyer, W. N. (1999). Relationship between collective efficacy and team cohesion: Conceptual and measurement issues. *Group Dynamics: Theory, Research, and Practice, 3,* 210–222.

Paskevich, D., Estabrooks, P., Brawley, L., & Carron, A. (2001). Group cohesion in sport and exercise. In R. Singer, H. Hausenblas, & C. Janelle (Eds.) *Handbook of sport psychology* (2nd ed., pp. 472–494). New York: John Wiley.

Polkinghorne, D. (1995). Narrative cofiguration in qualitative analysis. In J. A. Hatch & R. Wisniewski (Eds.) *Life history and narrative* (pp. 5–23). London: Falmer.

Prapavessis, H., & Carron, A. (1997). Cohesion and work output. *Small Group Research, 28,* 294–301.

Salminen, S., & Luhtanen, P. (1998). Cohesion predicts success in junior ice hockey. *Perceptual and Motor Skills, 87,* 649–650.

Shields, D., Bredemeier, B., Gardner, D., & Boston, A. (1995). Leadership, cohesion, and team norms regarding cheating and aggression. *Sociology of Sport Journal, 12,* 324–336.

Stake, R. E. (2005). Qualitative case studies. In N. K. Denzin & Y. S. Lincoln (Eds.) *The Sage handbook of qualitative research* (3rd ed., pp. 443–466). Thousand Oaks, CA: Sage.

Westre, K., & Weiss, M. (1991). The relationship between perceived coaching and group cohesion in high school football teams. *The Sport Psychologist, 5,* 41–54.

Widmeyer, W. N., Brawley, L. R., & Carron, A. V. (1985). *The measurement of cohesion in sport teams: The Group Environment Questionnaire.* London, Ontario, Canada: Sport Dynamics.

Widmeyer, W., Brawley, L., & Carron, A. (1990). Group size in sport. *Journal of Sport & Exercise Psychology, 12,* 177–190.

Widmeyer, W., Carron, A., & Brawley, L. (1993). Group cohesion in sport and exercise. In R. N. Singer, M. Murhey, & L. K. Tennant (Eds.) *Handbook of research on sport psychology* (pp. 672–692). New York: Macmillan.

Williams, J. M., & Hacker, C. M. (1982). Causal relationship among cohesion, satisfaction and performance in women's intercollegiate field hockey teams. *Journal of Sport Psychology, 4,* 324–337.

CRITICAL THINKING QUESTIONS

1. As stated in the article, "Maintaining harmony is not always a good thing." Give an example of how you may have seen behavior in a group that would support this statement, including explaining why such behavior was not a good thing.

2. Examine the methodology used in this study. What are the advantages and disadvantages of the method that was employed? Explain your reasoning.

3. Based upon the information in this article, what ideas might you consider sharing with the coach of a sports team for improving the performance of the group?

4. Do you think the findings of this study could be generalized to other nonsports settings, such as business settings or classrooms? If so, explain what can be generalized and why. If not, explain why the findings cannot be generalized.

5. Have you ever observed or been part of a highly cohesive group? If so, did that high cohesiveness result in positive or negative (or both) behaviors for the group? Explain why you think those outcomes occurred using concepts found in this article.

CHAPTER INTEGRATION QUESTIONS

1. While the three articles in this chapter do not deal primarily with leadership per se, they all have implications for how leaders can affect the outcomes of group decisions. What are those implications?

2. Based on your own experience with working in groups, what factors other than those presented in the articles may influence the functioning and outcomes of groups? Explain why you think these factors are important.

3. Abraham Lincoln said, "Nearly all men can stand adversity, but if you want to test a man's character, give him power." Relate this quotation to a unifying theme or themes in the articles in this chapter.

Chapter Thirteen

BUSINESS PSYCHOLOGY

A MAJOR PART of your waking life will be spent at work. You may already be in a full-time position (or have been), or you may have had experience working at a part-time job. When you think about the work you are doing now or hope to do in the future, you may have many concerns. For instance, you may wonder how much money you will make. But you also may be concerned about whether you will enjoy what you do. If you become a manager and are responsible for other people's behavior, you may also be concerned with how best to utilize the human resources available for the benefit of the organization as well as that of the individual employee.

Social psychology has long been involved in the area of business, or *organizational,* psychology. Early work in the field looked at factors such as leadership style and how it may contribute to worker behavior. While work in that area has continued, the influence of social psychology has expanded into virtually all domains of work-related activities, including productivity, job satisfaction, and employee motivation, to name but a few. The articles in this chapter provide a sampling of the many ways in which social psychology contributes to our understanding of work behavior.

Article 37, "When Followers Become Toxic," examines the reciprocal relationship between leaders and followers. That is, while leaders have an influence over their followers, followers in turn have an influence on their leaders. Knowing how followers exert such influence, whether intentionally or not, provides valuable information for current leaders, future leaders, and followers, enabling all of them to more effectively perform their respective roles.

Article 38, "One More Time: How Do You Motivate Employees?" is a truly classic piece that examines the questions of what motivates people, what factors are involved in job satisfaction, and what conditions influence productivity. Your beliefs about what motivates you and others to work may change after you read this article.

Finally, Article 39, "Impact of Emotional Intelligence and Other Factors on Perception of Ethical Behavior of Peers," looks at the issue of ethical behavior in business as a function of various factors, including *emotional intelligence.* Emotional intelligence, a fairly recent concept, concerns the behaviors that seem to enhance successful social functioning. This article examines whether this factor is important in the realm of ethical behavior.

ARTICLE 37 _____

What makes an effective leader? Is it having a unique personality or the particular type of leadership needed in a particular situation? The study of what factors contribute to effective leadership has a long history and both theoretical and practical implications. After all, if we can identify the characteristics of effective leaders, then we can help move people to positions where their leadership abilities can be best utilized.

Broadly speaking, early work on leadership tended to focus on two types of factors: trait and situational. Interestingly, these two factors also parallel what has been found in much social psychological inquiry. *Situational factors* are those that can change depending on the specific context. By varying leadership styles in different situations, leaders often are able to elicit very different behaviors in their followers. *Trait factors*, on the other hand, pertain to those relatively enduring characteristics of the individual. Early research on leadership focused on such trait characteristics as intelligence. While being highly intelligent was shown to be important in an effective leader, ongoing research made it apparent that intelligence was not enough by itself.

While we may often think about how leaders influence their followers, it turns out that followers also may have an influence on their leaders. The following article by Lynn R. Offermann discusses some of the ways that followers can influence their leaders, often with negative consequences for the latter. Why this process occurs, and how a leader can effectively overcome these negative processes, is of practical value not only to current and future leaders but to those who follow as well.

When Followers Become Toxic
■ Lynn R. Offermann

ABSTRACT

Leaders are vulnerable, too. That is, they can be led astray just as their followers can—actually, by their followers. This happens in a variety of ways. Sometimes, good leaders end up making poor decisions because well-meaning followers are united and persuasive about a course of action. This is a particular problem for leaders who attract and empower strong followers. These executives need to become more skeptical of the majority view and push followers to examine their opinions more closely. At other times, leaders get into trouble because they are surrounded by followers who fool them with flattery and isolate them from uncomfortable realities. Charismatic leaders, who are most susceptible to this problem, need to make an extra effort to unearth disagreement and to find followers who are not afraid to pose hard questions. Organizational mechanisms like 360-degree feedback and executive coaching can help these leaders get at the truth within their companies. Finally, unscrupulous and ambitious followers may end up encroaching on the authority of the leader to such an extent that the leader becomes little more than a figurehead who has responsibility but no power. There's not much leaders can do to completely guard against a determined corporate Iago, but those who communicate and live by a positive set of values will find themselves better protected. And since followers tend to model themselves after their leaders, the straightforward

leader is less likely to have manipulative followers. In this article, George Washington University professor Lynn Offermann explores each of these dynamics in depth, arguing that leaders need to stir debate, look for friends who can deliver bad news, and communicate and act on a solid set of values.

Few leaders realize how susceptible they are to their followers' influence. A good set of values, some trusted friends, and a little paranoia can prevent them from being led astray

Douglas MacArthur once said, "A general is just as good or just as bad as the troops under his command make him." Almost as he made that remark, his country's president was proving the point. For in late 1961, John F. Kennedy, bowing to pressure from his advisers, agreed to the escalation of American intervention in Vietnam. Among the advisers pressuring him was the senior author of a report recommending military intervention. And that adviser's trusted friend—an American general—was chosen by the president to lead the new U. S. command in Saigon. Given his loyalties, the general wanted to make sure things looked good on the surface, so he stifled evidence from the field about potential setbacks and obstacles in Vietnam, making it tough for the president to discern the truth.

That, according to author and journalist David Halberstam, was how President Kennedy and his advisers led the United States into Vietnam. The story starkly illustrates just how easily, and with the best of intentions, loyal and able followers can get their leaders into trouble. If an accomplished politician like Kennedy could be misled in this way, it's no surprise that today's business leaders often fall into the same trap. No matter who we are, we are all influenced by those around us. Some of us are leaders, but we are all followers. Indeed, Ken Lay, the disgraced ex-chairman of Enron, may not be entirely wrong in blaming unscrupulous subordinates and advisers for his company's demise. As an executive coach to senior leaders in a variety of industries for more than 20 years, I've seen firsthand just how easily followers can derail executive careers.

How does it happen? In the following pages, I draw both on my experience as a consultant and executive coach and on decades of research in organizational psychology to describe when and why leaders become vulnerable to being led astray by their followers. In some cases, as the Kennedy story illustrates, effective leaders can end up making poor decisions because able and well-meaning followers are united and persuasive about a course of action. This is a particular problem for leaders who attract and empower strong followers; these leaders need to become more skeptical and set boundaries. At other times, leaders get into trouble because they are surrounded by followers who fool them with flattery and isolate them from uncomfortable realities. Charismatic leaders, who are most susceptible to this problem, need to make an extra effort to unearth disagreement and to find followers who are not afraid to pose hard questions. Charismatic or not, all leaders run the risk of delegating to unscrupulous followers. There's probably little they can do to completely guard against a determined corporate Iago, but leaders who communicate and live a positive set of values will find themselves better protected.

WHEN THE MAJORITY RULES

Although many leaders pride themselves on their willingness to take unpopular stands, research has consistently demonstrated that most people—including leaders—prefer conformity to controversy. And the pressure to conform rises with the degree of agreement among those around you. Even if widespread agreement doesn't actually exist, the very appearance of it can be hard to resist.

One of the most striking pieces of evidence for this was a series of experiments conducted in the 1950s by psychologist Solomon Asch. Asch showed participants a vertical line and then asked them to judge which of three other lines was most similar in length to the test line. Participants who made judgments on their own chose the correct answer 99% of the time. Yet when other participants answered as part of a group in which fake respondents had been coached to pick a particular incorrect line, almost three-quarters of the unknowing participants made at least one wrong choice and one-third of them conformed to the group choice half the time.

It's worth noting that the participants conformed without any pressure from the fake respondents. Indeed, the fake respondents were strangers whom the participants were unlikely to see ever again. In workplace situations where continued interactions are expected and where there may be concern about possible loss of face, one would reasonably expect conformity to be even more marked. What's more, most business decisions are urgent, complex, and ambiguous, which encourages people to depend on the views of others. We should hardly be surprised, therefore, to find that the ethical and capable individuals who served on the boards of companies like WorldCom and Enron turned "into credulous, compliant apparatchiks more focused on maintaining collegiality than maximizing long-term profitability," as the Washington Post put it.

What happens is that leaders faced with a united opposition can start to question their own judgment. And they should question themselves—the reason that unanimity is such a powerful influencing force is simply that the majority often is right. In general, research shows that using social proof—what others think or do—to determine our behavior leads us to make fewer mistakes than opposing the majority view does. But as even the smartest leaders have had to learn the hard way, the majority can be spectacularly wrong.

One reason that even well-informed experts so often follow the crowd is that people by nature tend to be what psychologists call "cognitive misers," preferring the shortcuts of automatic thinking over considered examination. These shortcuts can help us to process information more quickly but can also lead to monumental errors. For instance, product designers may assume that if they like a product, everyone will. Yet the flop of Dell's Olympic line of desktop and workstation computers taught managers there that products must appeal to more than the company's own technically savvy workforce. As Michael Dell put it, "We had gone ahead and created a product that was, for all intents and purposes, technology for technology's sake rather than technology for the customer's sake."

Cognitive miserliness can be reinforced by culture. In the United States, for instance, Americans have long tolerated—even encouraged—people who form and express quick opinions. It is not a reflective society. Americans like to brainstorm and move on. That shortcut mentality can be particularly dangerous if the opinions are presented publicly, because people will then advance their views tenaciously.

In such public forums, it falls to the leader to push followers to examine their opinions more closely. Alfred P. Sloan, the former chairman of GM, understood this very well. He once said at the close of an executive meeting: "Gentlemen, I take it we are all in complete agreement on the decision here. I propose we postpone further discussion until our next meeting to give ourselves time to develop disagreement and perhaps gain some understanding of what the decision is all about."

Another factor contributing to the power of the majority is that leaders worry about undermining their employees' commitment. This is a reasonable concern. Leaders do need to be careful about spending their political capital, and overruling employees one too many times can demotivate them. Indeed, there are times when going along with the majority to win commitment is more important than making the "right" decision. (For more on when it's wise to go along with the majority, see "Joining the Opposition") But other times, leaders need to listen instead to the single, shy voice in the background, or even to their own internal doubts. As Rosalynn Carter once said, "A leader takes people where they want to go. A great leader takes people where they don't necessarily want to go but ought to be." In going against the tide, the leader will sometimes boost rather than undermine his or her credibility.

FOOLED BY FLATTERY

Being swept along by their followers isn't the only form of influence that leaders need to be wary of. Sometimes, follower influence takes the subtler and gentler form of ingratiation. Most people learn very early in life that a good way to get people to like you is to show that you like them. Flattery, favors, and frequent compliments all tend to win people over. Leaders, naturally, like those who like them and are more apt to let those they are fond of influence them.

For their part, followers think that being on the boss's good side gives them some measure of job security. To an extent, they're probably right; even a recent Forbes guide to surviving office parties recommends: "Try to ingratiate yourself. In this market, people are hired and kept at their companies for their personal skills." Indeed, a recent study indicated that successful ingratiators gained a 5% edge over other employees in performance evaluations. This kind of margin by itself won't get someone ahead, but in a competitive market, it might well tip the scale toward one of two people up for a promotion.

Everyone loves a sincere compliment, but those who already think highly of themselves are most susceptible to flattery's charms. In particular, leaders predisposed toward narcissism may find their narcissistic tendencies pushed to unhealthy levels when they are given heavy doses of follower ingratiation. Gratuitous ingratiation can create a subtle shift in a leader's attitude toward power. Instead of viewing power as something to be used in the service of the organization, clients, and stakeholders, the leader treats it as a tool to further personal interests, sometimes at the expense of others in and outside the organization. This happens as a leader starts to truly believe his press and comes to feel more entitled to privileges than others. People often cite Jack Welch's retirement deal as an example of executive entitlement gone haywire. The resulting furor drew public scorn for a longstanding corporate icon.

But one of the most serious problems for leaders who invite flattery is that they insulate themselves from the bad news they need to know. In her memoir, Nancy Reagan relates how then-Vice President George Bush approached her with concerns about Chief of Staff Donald Regan. Mrs. Reagan said she wished he'd tell her husband, but Bush replied that it was not his role to do so. "That's exactly your role," she snapped. Yet followers who have witnessed the killing of previous messengers of unwelcome news will be unlikely to volunteer for the role. Samuel Goldwyn's words resonate strongly: "I want you to tell me exactly what's wrong with me and with MGM even if it means losing your job." As more staff ingratiate or hold back criticism, the perception of staff unanimity, often at the expense of the organization's health, increases as well.

The rare individual who won't join an ingratiating inner circle of followers is typically seen as a bad apple by both the leader and her peers. Even when this perception problem is acknowledged, it is tough to fix. Despite widespread publicity after the 1986 space shuttle Challenger disaster about the dangers of failing to attend to negative news, NASA is once again facing charges of having downplayed possible liftoff problems just before the Columbia disaster. In both cases, engineers allegedly did not inform senior NASA executives of safety concerns; they either withheld information or presented it in ways that diminished its importance or feasibility. Obviously, this tendency to withhold information is not limited to government agencies. Bill Ford, the new CEO of Ford Motor Company, believes that isolation at the top has been a big problem at Ford—a problem he has spent considerable time trying to rectify by a variety of means, including forcing debate and discussion among executives and having informal, impromptu discussions with employees at all levels.

In dealing with ingratiation, leaders need to begin by reflecting on how they respond to both flattery and criticism. In considering a follower's advice or opinion, ask yourself if you would respond differently if a staff member you disliked made the same comment, and why. Are followers really free to voice their honest assessments, or are they jumped on whenever they deviate from your opinions? Bill Ford makes a point of thanking people whom he has overruled because he wants them to know that their honesty is appreciated. One simple test of whether you're getting the feedback you need is to count how many employees challenge you at your next staff meeting. As Steven Kerr, chief learning officer of Goldman Sachs, says: "If you're not taking flak, you're not over the target."

Organizational mechanisms can also help. Greater exposure to external feedback from clients, well-run 360-degree feedback programs, and executive coaching may be more likely to reveal the full truth. It's hard to lead from a pedestal; open channels of communication can keep a leader far better grounded.

For honest feedback, some CEOs rely on longtime associates or family members, people who may even take pleasure at times in letting some of the air out of the executive's balloon. (Your teenage children might particularly enjoy this, though they might not have as much insight into your business). Bill Gates, for instance, has said that he talks to his wife, Melinda, every night about work-related issues. In particular, he credits her with helping him handle the transition period when he turned over the Microsoft CEO title to his old friend Steve Ballmer. Ballmer, too, has been one of Gates's closest advisers. Gates says of this peer relationship with Ballmer: "It's important to have someone whom you totally trust, who is totally committed, who shares your vision, and yet who has a little bit different set of skills and who also acts as something of a check on you." And Gates's well-known friendship with fellow billionaire and bridge buddy Warren Buffet serves as a sounding board for both men. Disney's Michael Eisner had a similar relationship with Frank Wells, until Wells's death in 1994, with Wells enjoying the role of devil's advocate, challenging Eisner to ensure that the best decisions got made.

In his book You're Too Kind, journalist Richard Stengel gives an account of flattery through the ages, noting that "the history of how ministers have used flattery to control leaders did not begin with Henry Kissinger's relentless and unctuous toadying to Richard Nixon. . . . Cardinal Richelieu was a famous user of flattery . . . and he was a famous sucker for it himself." Stengel argues that corporate VPs who suck up to their bosses are no different than the less powerful chimpanzees who subordinate themselves to more powerful ones in the animal world. Though it may feel great at the time, stroking a leader's ego too much, and protecting him or her from needed information, can have negative consequences for both the leader and the organization. It's worth remembering the words of cartoonist Hank Ketchum: "Flattery is like chewing gum. Enjoy it, but don't swallow it."

POWERS BEHIND THE THRONE

Caught between the Scylla of follower unanimity and the Charybdis of flattery, leaders might be tempted to keep their followers at a distance. But in today's world, this is simply not an option. CEOs of major firms cannot know everything about their own organizations. In coaching senior executives, I often hear them lamenting that they don't have full knowledge of what's happening in their companies. They report sleepless nights because they've been forced to make decisions based on incomplete information. They must rely on others for full, accurate, and unbiased input as well as for many operational decisions.

From the follower's point of view, this presents wonderful opportunities. He can learn and practice new skills as the leader relies on him more and more, and he may be presented with new opportunities for advancement and reward. At the same time, however, it opens the door for the occasional follower who uses his newfound power to serve his own interests more than the company's.

So how can leaders guard against that problem? They can begin by keeping ethical values and corporate vision front and center when delegating and monitoring work. Only then can they be certain that followers have a clear framework and boundaries for their actions. As Baxter CEO Harry Kraemer says, the key to ensuring that followers do the right thing is "open communication of values . . . over and over and over again."

Leaders can also protect themselves and their companies by setting good examples. Followers—especially ingratiators—tend to model themselves after their leaders. Thus, straightforward leaders are less likely to be manipulated than manipulative leaders are. And a leader who is seen to condone or encourage unethical behavior will almost certainly get unethical behavior in his ranks. Take the case of former WorldCom CEO Bernie Ebbers, who allegedly ridiculed attempts to institute a corporate code of conduct as a waste of time even as he pressed his followers to deliver double-digit growth. He shouldn't have been surprised to find that junior WorldCom executives cooked the books or at least turned a blind eye when others did.

Although competency is generally a good basis on which to grant followers greater influence, leaders need to avoid letting followers influence them based on competency alone. As W. Michael Blumenthal, former chairman and CEO of Unisys, once said, "When did I make my greatest hiring mistakes? When I put intelligence and energy ahead of morality." The danger here is that astute but unscrupulous followers can find ways of pushing their leaders in unethical directions and may even use the leader's stated values against him. Suggestions like "I know you like saving money, so you'll love the idea of . . . " followed by a shady proposal, force leaders into the position of having to choose between eating their words and accepting the proposal.

At the end of the day, leaders have to rely on their instincts about people. Fortunately, there is good news in this respect. Research by psychologist Robert Zajonc suggests that we process information both affectively and cognitively and that we experience our feeling toward something a split second before we intellectualize it. If leaders are attentive, therefore, they may be able to tune in to a fleeting feeling that something is not quite right or that they are being manipulated before they rationalize and accept what they would be better off rejecting. For example, one tactic favored by manipulative followers is to create a false sense of urgency to rush the leader into an uninformed decision. Recognizing that you're being pushed too fast and reserving judgment for a time may save you from an action you may regret.

It's not only the people you delegate to that you have to watch, it's also what you delegate. Clearly, leaders can never delegate their own responsibilities without peril. Smart leaders understand that even well-intentioned followers have their own ambitions and may try to usurp tasks that properly belong to their leaders. Harry Stonecipher, former president and COO of Boeing, likes to point to the great polar explorer Ernest Shackleton as an example of a leader who knew what responsibilities he could and couldn't afford to delegate. Stranded on an ice pack and crossing 800 miles of stormy seas in an open boat, Shackleton knew the deadly consequences of dissension and therefore focused his attention on preserving his team's unity. He was happy to delegate many essential tasks to subordinates, even putting one man in charge of 22 others at a camp while he sailed off with the remainder of the crew to get assistance. But the one task he reserved for himself was the management of malcontents, whom he kept close by at all times. Amazingly, the entire crew survived the more than 15-month ordeal in fairly good health, and eight members even joined Shackleton on a subsequent expedition.

By understanding how followers are capable of influencing them, top executives can improve their leadership skills. They can choose to lead by steadfastly refusing to fall prey to manipulative forces and try to guide the way toward more open and appropriate communications.

Followers, for their part, can better understand their power to inappropriately influence leaders. Once they recognize the danger they pose to their leaders—and ultimately to themselves ingratiators may come to realize that isolating leaders from reality can be as costly to themselves as to the company's shareholders. Realizing the value of dissent may force followers to take more care in forming and promoting their opinions.

Understanding that some tasks are best left to a leader may help followers to know where to stop and leaders to know what not to give away. In the final analysis, honest followers have just as great an investment in unmasking manipulative colleagues as their leaders do.

Joining the Opposition

The leader who automatically rejects his followers' opinions can be as unwise as one who unthinkingly goes along with them. In fact, there are times when it is advisable to go along with followers who are plainly wrong.

A senior executive in the health care field recently faced a united front of followers in an acquired facility. The followers wanted the executive to retain a popular manager despite an outside consultant's report that strongly recommended the manager's dismissal. Staff members felt that the manager had been wrongly blamed for the unit's problems and that the unit had been mishandled, under funded, and generally "done in" by previous management.

Although the senior executive was under pressure from her COO to dismiss the manager, she chose to keep and support him—and watch carefully. By choosing this course, the executive won the support and confidence of hundreds of employees who saw procedural justice in her willingness to give the manager a chance. With the full support of her staff, the executive then went on to lead a turnaround of the facility in short order, exceeding the COO's expectations. Indeed, the executive built so much credibility through her actions that she was eventually able to dismiss the manager, with the staff understanding that he had had a fair chance but had failed.

The executive recognized not only the unanimity of employees but also the importance of winning their buy in and commitment. She chose, intentionally, to defer to the staff's wishes in order to demonstrate her fairness and openness. After all, the employees could have been correct in their assessment. Even though that didn't turn out to be the case, the leader's considered decision to go along with her reports likely resulted in a better outcome than if she had summarily rejected their opinions.

Six Ways to Counter Wayward Influences

There's no guaranteed means of ensuring that you won't be misled by your followers. But adhering to these principles may help.

Keep vision and values front and center. It's much easier to get sidetracked when you're unclear about what the main track is.

Make sure people disagree. Remember that most of us form opinions too quickly and give them up too slowly.

Cultivate truth tellers. Make sure there are people in your world you can trust to tell you what you need to hear, no matter how unpopular or unpalatable it is.

Do as you would have done to you. Followers look to what you do rather than what you say. Set a good ethical climate for your team to be sure your followers have clear boundaries for their actions.

Honor your intuition. If you think you're being manipulated, you're probably right.

Delegate, don't desert. It's important to share control and empower your staff, but remember who's ultimately responsible for the outcome. As they say in politics, "Trust, but verify."

CRITICAL THINKING QUESTIONS

1. "Most people—including leaders—prefer conformity to controversy." Describe a situation that you have encountered that would support this quote from the article. Why might people prefer conformity?

2. What have you learned from this article that you can use to be a more effective leader? A more effective follower?

3. The article quotes a former chairperson and CEO as saying, "When did I make my greatest hiring mistakes? When I put intelligence and energy ahead of morality." Do you agree or disagree with this premise? Explain your reasoning.

4. The article maintains that leaders already predisposed toward narcissism are particularly susceptible to ingratiation. Give an example of when you might have seen "brown-nosing" negatively impacting a leader (teacher, coach, etc.).

ARTICLE 38 _____

Why do people work? Is it just to earn a living (or in some cases, to make a lot of money), or are there other reasons, too? If you look at the number of references in American culture to the "Monday morning blues" and "TGIF," you might get the impression that people would rather not work, if given a choice. Many people would consider it distinctly odd if someone expressed joy at the prospect of returning to work after a weekend off. Do most workers really feel that way? Is that the way it *should* be?

The question of what motivates people to work has been of major interest to industrial/ organizational psychologists for quite some time. Ultimately concerned with productivity and profits, business has an obvious interest in trying to discover ways to increase employee motivation, since increased motivation is often viewed as synonymous with increased output. Different theories of motivation have been drawn from areas in the behavioral sciences, ranging from learning theory to humanistic theories of motivation. All seek to identify the factors that motivate people and how to implement these factors to increase motivation levels.

One person who has made significant contributions to the understanding of motivation in the workplace is Frederick Herzberg. In the following classic article, he presents an analysis of commonly used methods of motivation and why they don't work, followed by his own theory and research. Whether you fully accept the tenets and suggestions found in the article, it will most likely get you to reexamine your own assumptions about what motivates people to work.

One More Time

How Do You Motivate Employees?

■ Frederick Herzberg

KITA—the externally imposed attempt by management to "install a generator" in the employee—has been demonstrated to be a total failure, the author says. The absence of such "hygiene" factors as good supervisor-employee relations and liberal fringe benefits can make a worker unhappy, but their presence will not make him want to work harder. Essentially meaningless changes in the tasks that workers are assigned to do have not accomplished the desired objective either. The only way to motivate the employee is to give him challenging work in which he can assume responsibility. Frederick Herzberg, who is Professor and Chairman of the Psychology Department at Case Western Reserve University, has devoted many years to the study of motivation in the United States and abroad. He is the author of Work and Nature of Man *(World Publishing Company, 1966).*

How many articles, books, speeches, and workshops have pleaded plaintively, "How do I get an employee to do what I want him to do?"

The psychology of motivation is tremendously complex, and what has been unraveled with any degree of assurance is small indeed. But the dismal ratio of knowledge to speculation has not dampened the enthusiasm for new forms of snake oil that are constantly coming on the market, many of them with academic testimonials. Doubtless this article will have no depressing impact on the market for snake oil, but since the ideas expressed in it have been tested in many corporations and other organizations, it will help—I hope—to redress the imbalance in the aforementioned ratio.

"MOTIVATING" WITH KITA

In lectures to industry on the problem, I have found that the audiences are anxious for quick and practical answers, so I will begin with a straightforward, practical formula for moving people.

What is the simplest, surest, and most direct way of getting someone to do something? Ask him? But if he responds that he does not want to do it, then that calls for a psychological consultation to determine the reason for his obstinacy. Tell him? His response shows that he does not understand you, and now an expert in communication methods has to be brought in to show you how to get through to him. Give him a monetary incentive? I do not need to remind the reader of the complexity and difficulty involved in setting up and administering an incentive system. Show him? This means a costly training program. We need a simple way.

Every audience contains the "direct action" manager who shouts, "Kick him!" And this type of manager is right. The surest and least circumlocuted way of getting someone to do something is to kick him in the pants—give him what might be called the KITA.

There are various forms of KITA, and here are some of them:

Negative Physical KITA   This is a literal application of the term and was frequently used in the past. It has, however, three major drawbacks: (1) it is inelegant; (2) it contradicts the precious image of benevolence that most organizations cherish; and (3) since it is a physical attack it directly stimulates the autonomic nervous system, and this often results in negative feedback—the employee may just kick you in return. These factors give rise to certain taboos against negative physical KITA.

The psychologist has come to the rescue of those who are no longer permitted to use negative physical KITA. He has uncovered infinite sources of psychological vulnerabilities and the appropriate methods to play tunes on them. "He took my rug away"; "I wonder what he meant by that"; "The boss is always going around me"—these symptomatic expressions of ego sores that have been rubbed raw are the result of application of:

Negative Psychological KITA   This has several advantages over negative physical KITA. First, the cruelty is not visible; the bleeding is internal and comes much later. Second, since it affects the higher cortical centers of the brain with its inhibitory powers, it reduces the possibility of physical backlash. Third, since the number of psychological pains that a person can feel is almost infinite, the direction and site possibilities of the KITA are increased many times. Fourth, the person administering the kick can manage to be above it all and let the system accomplish the dirty work. Fifth, those who practice it receive some ego satisfaction (one-upmanship), whereas they would find drawing blood abhorrent. Finally, if the employee does complain, he can always be accused of being paranoid since there is no tangible evidence of an actual attack.

Now, what does negative KITA accomplish? If I kick you in the rear (physically or psychologically), who is motivated? I am motivated; you move! Negative KITA does not lead to motivation, but to movement. So:

Positive KITA   Let us consider motivation. If I say to you, "Do this for me or the company, and in return I will give you a reward, an incentive, more status, a promotion all the quid pro quos that exist in the industrial organization," am I motivating you? The overwhelming opinion I receive from management people is, "Yes, this is motivation."

I have a year-old Schnauzer. When it was a small puppy and I wanted it to move, I kicked it in the rear and it moved. Now that I have finished its obedience training, I hold up a dog biscuit when I want the Schnauzer to move. In this instance, who is motivated—I or the dog? The dog wants the biscuit, but it is I who want it to move. Again, I am the one who is motivated, and the dog is the one who moves. In this instance all I did was apply KITA frontally; I exerted a pull instead of a push. When industry wishes to use such positive KITAs, it has available an incredible number and variety of dog biscuits (jelly beans for humans) to wave in front of the employee to get him to jump.

Why is it that managerial audiences are quick to see that negative KITA is *not* motivation, while they are almost unanimous in their judgment that positive KITA *is* motivation? It is because negative KITA is rape, and positive KITA is seduction. But it is infinitely worse to be seduced than to be raped; the latter is an unfortunate occurrence, while the former signifies that you were a party to your own downfall. This is why positive KITA is so popular: it is a tradition; it is in the American way. The organization does not have to kick you; you kick yourself.

Myths about Motivation

Why is KITA not motivation? If I kick my dog (from the front or the back), he will move. And when I want him to move again, what must I do? I must kick him again. Similarly, I can charge a man's battery, and then recharge it, and recharge it again. But it is only when he has his own generator that we can talk about motivation. He then needs no outside stimulation. He *wants to* do it.

With this in mind, we can review some positive KITA personnel practices that were developed as attempts to instill "motivation":

1. *Reducing time spent at work*—This represents a marvelous way of motivating people to work—getting them off the job! We have reduced (formally and informally) the time spent on the job over the last 50 or 60 years until we are finally on the way to the "6$\frac{1}{2}$-day weekend." An interesting variant of this approach is the development of off-hour recreation programs. The philosophy here seems to be that those who play together, work together. The fact is that motivated people seek more hours of work, not fewer.

2. *Spiraling wages*—Have these motivated people? Yes, to seek the next wage increase. Some medievalists still can be heard to say that a good depression will get employees moving. They feel that if rising wages don't or won't do the job, perhaps reducing them will.

3. *Fringe benefits*—Industry has outdone the most welfare-minded of welfare states in dispensing cradle-to-the-grave succor. One company I know of had an informal "fringe benefit of the month club" going for a while. The cost of fringe benefits

in this country has reached approximately 25% of the wage dollar, and we still cry for motivation.

People spend less time working for more money and more security than ever before, and the trend cannot be reversed. These benefits are no longer rewards; they are rights. A 6-day week is inhuman, a 10-hour day is exploitation, extended medical coverage is a basic decency, and stock options are the salvation of American initiative. Unless the ante is continuously raised, the psychological reaction of employees is that the company is turning back the clock.

When industry began to realize that both the economic nerve and the lazy nerve of their employees had insatiable appetites, it started to listen to the behavioral scientists who, more out of a humanist tradition than from scientific study, criticized management for not knowing how to deal with people. The next KITA easily followed.

4. *Human relations training*—Over 30 years of teaching and, in many instances, of practicing psychological approaches to handling people have resulted in costly human relations programs and, in the end, the same question: How do you motivate workers? Here, too, escalations have taken place. Thirty years ago it was necessary to request, "Please don't spit on the floor." Today the same admonition requires three "please"s before the employee feels that his superior has demonstrated the psychologically proper attitudes toward him.

The failure of human relations training to produce motivation led to the conclusion that the supervisor or manager himself was not psychologically true to himself in his practice of interpersonal decency. So an advanced form of human relations KITA, sensitivity training, was unfolded.

5. *Sensitivity training*—Do you really, really understand yourself? Do you really, really, really trust the other man? Do you really, really, really, really cooperate? The failure of sensitivity training is now being explained, by those who have become opportunistic exploiters of the technique, as a failure to really (five times) conduct proper sensitivity training courses.

With the realization that there are only temporary gains from comfort and economic and interpersonal KITA, personnel managers concluded that the fault lay not in what they were doing, but in the employee's failure to appreciate what they were doing. This opened up the field of communications, a whole new area of "scientifically" sanctioned KITA.

6. *Communications*—The professor of communications was invited to join the faculty of management training programs and help in making employees understand what management was doing for them. House organs, briefing sessions, supervisory instruction on the importance of communication, and all sorts of propaganda have proliferated until today there is even an International Council of Industrial Editors. But no motivation resulted, and the obvious thought occurred that perhaps management was not hearing what the employees were saying. That led to the next KITA.

7. *Two-way communication*—Management ordered morale surveys, suggestion plans, and group participation programs. Then both employees and management were communicating and listening to each other more than ever, but without much improvement in motivation.

The behavioral scientists began to take another look at their conceptions and their data, and they took human relations one step further. A glimmer of truth was beginning to show through in the writings of the so-called higher-order-need psychologists. People, so they said, want to actualize themselves. Unfortunately, the "actualizing" psychologists got mixed up with the human relations psychologists, and a new KITA emerged.

8. *Job participation*—Though it may not have been the theoretical intention, job participation often became a "give them the big picture" approach. For example, if a man is tightening 10,000 nuts a day on an assembly line with a torque wrench, tell him he is building a Chevrolet. Another approach had the goal of giving the employee a *feeling* that he is determining, in some measure, what he does on his job. The goal was to provide a *sense* of achievement rather than a substantive achievement in his task. Real achievement, of course, requires a task that makes it possible.

But still there was no motivation. This led to the inevitable conclusion that the employees must be sick, and therefore to the next KITA.

9. *Employee counseling*—The initial use of this form of KITA in a systematic fashion can be credited to the Hawthorne experiment of the Western Electric Company during the early 1930's. At that time, it was found that the employees harbored irrational feelings that were interfering with the rational operation of the factory. Counseling in this instance was a means of letting the employees unburden themselves by talking to someone about their problems. Although the counseling techniques were primitive, the program was large indeed.

The counseling approach suffered as a result of experiences during World War II, when the programs themselves were found to be interfering with the operation of the organizations; the counselors had forgotten their role of benevolent listeners and were attempting to do something about the problems that they heard about. Psychological counseling, however, has managed to survive the negative impact of World War II experiences and today is beginning to flourish with renewed sophistication. But, alas, many of these programs, like all the others, do not seem to have lessened the pressure of demands to find out how to motivate workers.

Since KITA results only in short-term movement it is safe to predict that the cost of these programs will increase steadily and new varieties will be developed as old positive KITAs reach their satiation points.

HYGIENE VS. MOTIVATORS

Let me rephrase the perennial question this way: How do you install a generator in an employee? A brief review of my motivation-hygiene theory of job attitudes is required before theoretical and practical suggestions can be offered. The theory was first drawn from an examination of events in the lives of engineers and accountants. At least 16 other investigations, using a wide variety of populations (including some in the Communist countries), have since been completed, making the original research one of the most replicated studies in the field of job attitudes.

The findings of these studies, along with corroboration from many other investigations using different procedures, suggest that the factors involved in producing job satisfaction (and motivation) are separate and distinct from the factors that lead to job dissatisfaction. Since separate factors need to be considered, depending on whether job satisfaction or job dissatisfaction is being examined, it follows that these two feelings are not opposites of each other. The opposite of job satisfaction is not job dissatisfaction but, rather, *no* job satisfaction; and, similarly, the opposite of job dissatisfaction is not job satisfaction, but *no* job dissatisfaction.

Stating the concept presents a problem in semantics, for we normally think of satisfaction and dissatisfaction as opposites— i.e., what is not satisfying must be dissatisfying, and vice versa. But when it comes to understanding the behavior of people in their jobs, more than a play on words is involved.

Two different needs of man are involved here. One set of needs can be thought of as stemming from his animal nature— the built-in drive to avoid pain from the environment, plus all the learned drives which become conditioned to the basic biological needs. For example, hunger, a basic biological drive, makes it necessary to earn money, and then money becomes a specific drive. The other set of needs relates to that unique human characteristic, the ability to achieve and, through achievement, to experience psychological growth. The stimuli for the growth needs are tasks that induce growth; in the industrial setting, they are the *job content*. Contrariwise, the stimuli inducing pain-avoidance behavior are found in the *job environment*.

The growth or *motivator* factors that are intrinsic to the job are: achievement, recognition for achievement, the work itself, responsibility, and growth or advancement. The dissatisfaction-avoidance of *hygiene* (KITA) factors that are extrinsic to the job include: company policy and administration, supervision, interpersonal relationships, working conditions, salary, status, and security.

A composite of the factors that are involved in causing job satisfaction and job dissatisfaction, drawn from samples of 1,685 employees, is shown in Exhibit I. The results indicate that motivators were the primary cause of satisfaction, and

hygiene factors the primary cause of unhappiness on the job. The employees, studied in 12 different investigations, included lower-level supervisors, professional women, agricultural administrators, men about to retire from management positions, hospital maintenance personnel, manufacturing supervisors, nurses, food handlers, military officers, engineers, scientists, housekeepers, teachers, technicians, female assemblers, accountants, Finnish foremen, and Hungarian engineers.

They were asked what job events had occurred in their work that had led to extreme satisfaction or extreme dissatisfaction on their part. Their responses are broken down in the exhibit into percentages of total "positive" job events and of total "negative" job events. (The figures total more than 100% on both the "hygiene" and "motivators" sides because often at least two factors can be attributed to a single event; advancement, for instance, often accompanies assumption of responsibility.)

To illustrate, a typical response involving achievement that had a negative effect for the employee was, "I was unhappy because I didn't do the job successfully." A typical response in the small number of positive job events in the Company Policy and Administration grouping was, "I was happy because the company reorganized the section so that I didn't report any longer to the guy I didn't get along with."

As the lower right-hand part of the exhibit shows, of all the factors contributing to job satisfaction, 81% were motivators. And of all the factors contributing to the employees' dissatisfaction over their work, 69% involved hygiene elements.

Eternal Triangle

There are three general philosophies of personnel management. The first is based on organizational theory, the second on industrial engineering, and the third on behavioral science.

The organizational theorist believes that human needs are either so irrational or so varied and adjustable to specific situations that the major function of personnel management is to be as pragmatic as the occasion demands. If jobs are organized in a proper manner, he reasons, the result will be the most efficient job structure, and the most favorable job attitudes will follow as a matter of course.

The industrial engineer holds that man is mechanistically oriented and economically motivated and his needs are best met by attuning the individual to the most efficient work process. The goal of personnel management therefore should be to concoct the most appropriate incentive system and to design the specific working conditions in a way that facilitates the most efficient use of the human machine. By structuring jobs in a manner that leads to the most efficient operation, the engineer believes that he can obtain the optimal organization of work and the proper work attitudes.

EXHIBIT I / Factors Affecting Job Attitudes, as Reported in 12 Investigations

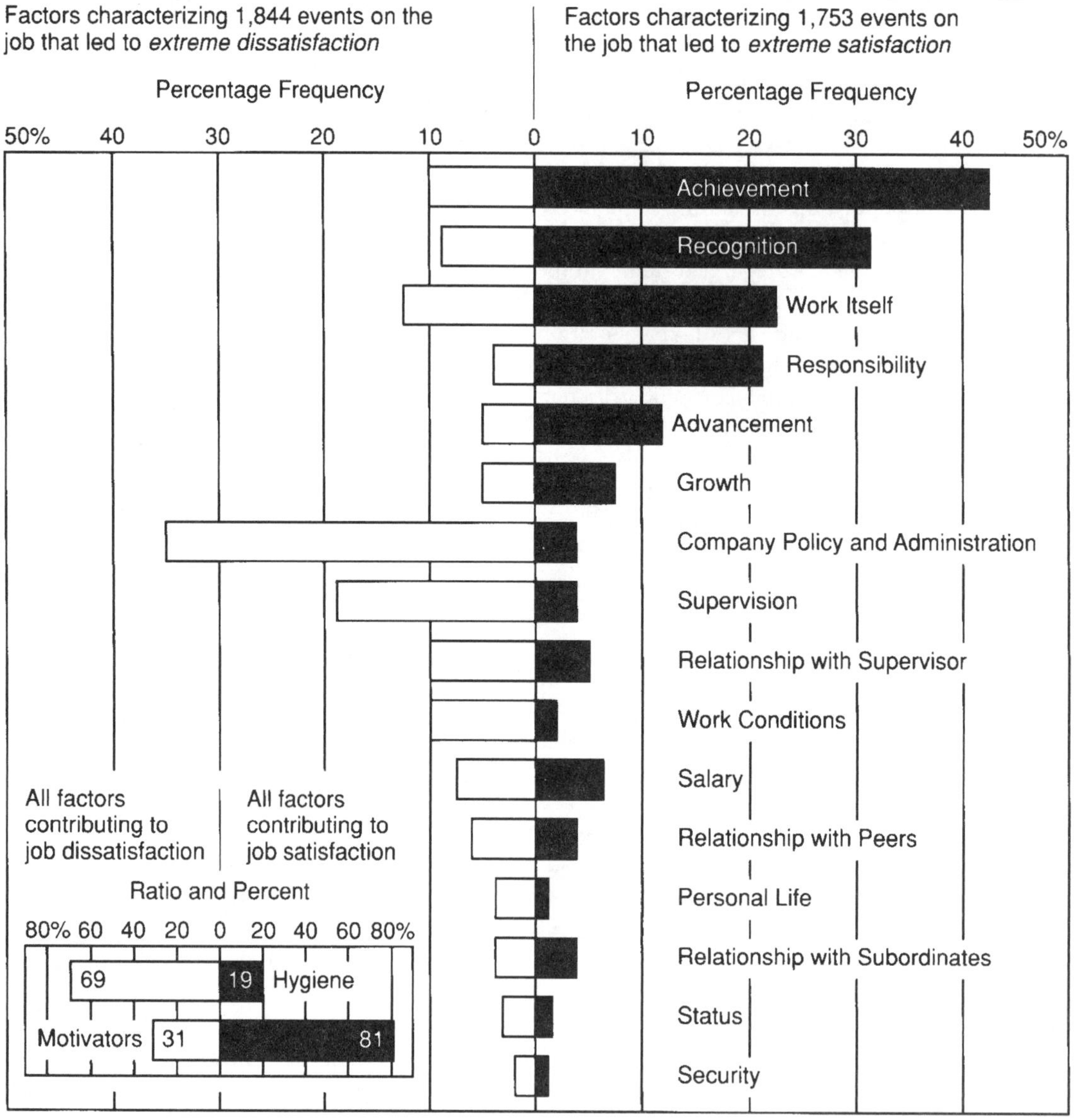

Factors characterizing 1,844 events on the job that led to *extreme dissatisfaction*

Factors characterizing 1,753 events on the job that led to *extreme satisfaction*

Percentage Frequency

Percentage Frequency

The behavioral scientist focuses on group sentiments, attitudes of individual employees, and the organization's social and psychological climate. According to his persuasion, he emphasizes one or more of the various hygiene and motivator needs. His approach to personnel management generally emphasizes some form of human relations education, in the hope of instilling healthy employee attitudes and an organizational climate which he considers to be felicitous to human values. He believes that the proper attitudes will lead to efficient job and organizational structure.

There is always a lively debate as to the overall effectiveness of the approaches of the organizational theorist and the industrial engineer. Manifestly they have achieved much. But the nagging question for the behavioral scientist has been: What is the cost in human problems that eventually cause more expense to the organization—for instance, turnover, absenteeism, errors, violation of safety rules, strikes, restriction of output, higher wages, and greater fringe benefits? On the other hand, the behavioral scientist is hard put to document much manifest improvement in personnel management, using his approach.

The three philosophies can be depicted as a triangle as is done in Exhibit II, with each persuasion claiming the apex angle. The motivation-hygiene theory claims the same angle as industrial engineering but for opposite goals. Rather than rationalizing the work to increase efficiency, the theory suggests that work be *enriched* to bring about effective utilization of

EXHIBIT II / "Triangle" of Philosophies of Personnel Management

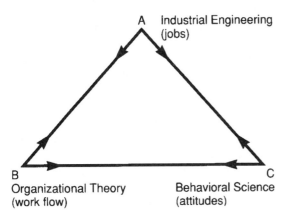

A Industrial Engineering (jobs)

B Organizational Theory (work flow)

C Behavioral Science (attitudes)

personnel. Such a systematic attempt to motivate employees by manipulating the motivator factors is just beginning.

The term *job enrichment* describes this embryonic movement. An older term, job enlargement, should be avoided because it is associated with past failures stemming from a misunderstanding of the problem. Job enrichment provides the opportunity for the employee's psychological growth, while job enlargement merely makes a job structurally bigger. Since scientific job enrichment is very new, this article only suggests the principles and practical steps that have recently emerged from several successful experiments in industry.

Job Loading

In attempting to enrich an employee's job, management often succeeds in reducing the man's personal contribution, rather than giving him an opportunity for growth in his accustomed job. Such an endeavor, which I shall call horizontal job loading (as opposed to vertical loading, or providing motivator factors), has been the problem of earlier job enlargement programs. This activity merely enlarges the meaninglessness of the job. Some examples of this approach, and their effect, are:

- Challenging the employee by increasing the amount of production expected of him. If he tightens 10,000 bolts a day, see if he can tighten 20,000 bolts a day. The arithmetic involved shows that multiplying zero by zero still equals zero.
- Adding another meaningless task to the existing one, usually some routine clerical activity. The arithmetic here is adding zero to zero.
- Rotating the assignments of a number of jobs that need to be enriched. This means washing dishes for a while, then washing silverware. The arithmetic is substituting one zero for another zero.
- Removing the most difficult parts of the assignment in order to free the worker to accomplish more of the less challenging assignments. This traditional industrial engineering approach amounts to subtraction in the hope of accomplishing addition.

These are common forms of horizontal loading that frequently come up in preliminary brainstorming sessions on job enrichment. The principles of vertical loading have not all been worked out as yet, and they remain rather general, but I have furnished seven useful starting points for consideration in Exhibit III.

A Successful Application

An example from a highly successful job enrichment experiment can illustrate the distinction between horizontal and vertical loading of a job. The subjects of this study were

EXHIBIT III / Principles of Vertical Job Loading

Principle	Motivators Involved
A. Removing some controls while retaining accountability	Responsibility and personal achievement
B. Increasing the accountability of individuals for own work	Responsibility and recognition
C. Giving a person a complete natural unit of work (module, division, area, and so on)	Responsibility, achievement, and recognition
D. Granting additional authority to an employee in his activity; job freedom	Responsibility, achievement, and recognition
E. Making periodic reports directly available to the worker himself rather than to the supervisor	Internal recognition
F. Introducing new and more difficult tasks not previously handled	Growth and learning
G. Assigning individuals specific or specialized tasks, enabling them to become experts	Responsibility, growth, and advancement

EXHIBIT IV / Shareholder Service Index in Company Experiment (Three-Month Cumulative Average)

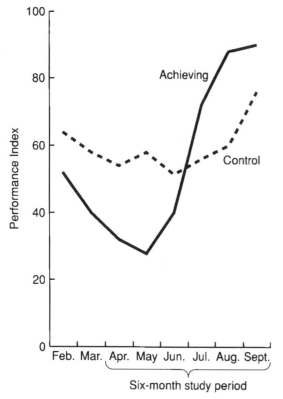

Six-month study period

achieving unit were found to be outperforming their counterparts in the control group, and in addition indicated a marked increase in their liking for their jobs. Other results showed that the achieving group had lower absenteeism and, subsequently, a much higher rate of promotion.

Exhibit IV illustrates the changes in performance, measured in February and March, before the study period began, and at the end of each month of the study period. The shareholder service index represents quality of letters, including accuracy of information, and speed of response to stockholders' letters of inquiry. The index of a current month was averaged into the average of the two prior months, which means that improvement was harder to obtain if the indexes of the previous months were low. The "achievers" were performing less well before the six-month period started, and their performance service index continued to decline after the introduction of the motivators, evidently because of uncertainty over their newly granted responsibilities. In the third month, however, performance improved, and soon the members of this group had reached a high level of accomplishment.

Exhibit V shows the two groups' attitudes toward their job, measured at the end of March, just before the first motivator was introduced, and again at the end of September. The correspondents were asked 16 questions, all involving motivation. A typical one was, "As you see it, how many opportunities do you feel that you have in your job for making worthwhile contributions?" The answers were scaled from 1 to 5, with 80 as the maximum possible score. The achievers became much more positive about

the stockholder correspondents employed by a very large corporation. Seemingly, the task required of these carefully selected and highly trained correspondents was quite complex and challenging. But almost all indexes of performance and job attitudes were low, and exit interviewing confirmed that the challenge of the job existed merely as words.

A job enrichment project was initiated in the form of an experiment with one group, designated as an achieving unit, having its job enriched by the principles described in Exhibit III. A control group continued to do its job in the traditional way. (There were also two "uncommitted" groups of correspondents formed to measure the so-called Hawthorne Effect—that is, to gauge whether productivity and attitudes toward the job changed artificially merely because employees sensed that the company was paying more attention to them in doing something different or novel. The results for these groups were substantially the same as for the control group, and for the sake of simplicity I do not deal with them in this summary.) No changes in hygiene were introduced for either group other than those that would have been made anyway, such as normal pay increases.

The changes for the achieving unit were introduced in the first two months, averaging one per week of the seven motivators listed in Exhibit III. At the end of six months the members of the

EXHIBIT V / Changes in Attitudes toward Tasks in Company Experiment (Changes in Mean Scores over Six-Month Period)

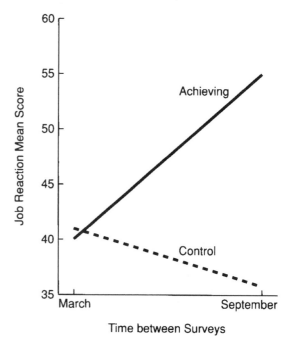

Time between Surveys

their job, while the attitude of the control unit remained about the same (the drop is not statistically significant).

How was the job of these correspondents restructured? Exhibit VI lists the suggestions made that were deemed to be horizontal loading, and the actual vertical loading changes that were incorporated in the job of the achieving unit. The capital letters under "Principle" after "Vertical loading" refer to the corresponding letters in Exhibit III. The reader will note that the rejected forms of horizontal loading correspond closely to the list of common manifestations of the phenomenon in Exhibit III, left column.

STEPS TO JOB ENRICHMENT

Now that the motivator idea has been described in practice, here are the steps that managers should take in instituting the principle with their employees:

1. Select those jobs in which (a) the investment in industrial engineering does not make changes too costly, (b) attitudes are poor, (c) hygiene is becoming very costly, and (d) motivation will make a difference in performance.

2. Approach these jobs with the conviction that they can be changed. Years of tradition have led managers to believe that the content of the jobs is sacrosanct and the only scope of action that they have is in ways of stimulating people.

3. Brainstorm a list of changes that may enrich the jobs, without concern for their practicality.

4. Screen the list to eliminate suggestions that involve hygiene, rather than actual motivation.

5. Screen the list for generalities, such as "give them more responsibility," that are rarely followed in practice. This might seem obvious, but the motivator words have never left industry; the substance has just been rationalized and organized out. Words like "responsibility," "growth," "achievement," and "challenge," for example, have been elevated to the lyrics of the patriotic anthem for all organizations. It is the old problem typified by the pledge of allegiance to the flag being more important than contributions to the country—of following the form, rather than the substance.

EXHIBIT VI / Enlargement vs. Enrichment of Correspondents' Tasks in Company Experiment

Horizontal loading suggestions (rejected)	Vertical loading suggestions (adopted)	Principle
Firm quotas could be set for letters to be answered each day, using a rate which would be hard to reach.	Subject matter experts were appointed within each unit for other members of the unit to consult with before seeking supervisory help. (The supervisor had been answering all specialized and difficult questions.)	G
The women could type the letters themselves, as well as compose them, or take on any other clerical functions.	Correspondents signed their own names on letters. (The supervisor had been signing all letters.)	B
All difficult or complex inquiries could be channeled to a few women so that the remainder could achieve high rates of output. These jobs could be exchanged from time to time.	The work of the more experienced correspondents was proofread less frequently by supervisors and was done at the correspondents' desks, dropping verification from 100% to 10%. (Previously, all correspondents' letters had been checked by the supervisor.)	A
The women could be rotated through units handling different customers, and then sent back to their own units.	Production was discussed, but only in terms such as "a full day's work is expected." As time went on, this was no longer mentioned. (Before, the group had been constantly reminded of the number of letters that needed to be answered.)	D
	Outgoing mail went directly to the mailroom without going over supervisors' desks. (The letters had always been routed through the supervisors.)	A
	Correspondents were encouraged to answer letters in a more personalized way. (Reliance on the form-letter approach had been standard practice.)	C
	Each correspondent was held personally responsible for the quality and accuracy of letters. (This responsibility had been the province of the supervisor and the verifier.)	B, E

6. Screen the list to eliminate any *horizontal* loading suggestions.

7. Avoid direct participation by the employees whose jobs are to be enriched. Ideas they have expressed previously certainly constitute a valuable source for recommended changes, but their direct involvement contaminates the process with human relations *hygiene* and, more specifically, gives them only a *sense* of making a contribution. The job is to be changed, and it is the content that will produce the motivation, not attitudes about being involved or the challenge inherent in setting up a job. That process will be over shortly, and it is what the employees will be doing from then on that will determine their motivation. A sense of participation will result only in short-term movement.

8. In the initial attempts at job enrichment, set up a controlled experiment. At least two equivalent groups should be chosen, one an experimental unit in which the motivators are systematically introduced over a period of time, and the other one a control group in which no changes are made. For both groups, hygiene should be allowed to follow its natural course for the duration of the experiment. Pre- and post-installation tests of performance and job attitudes are necessary to evaluate the effectiveness of the job enrichment program. The attitude test must be limited to motivator items in order to divorce the employee's view of the job he is given from all the surrounding hygiene feelings that he might have.

9. Be prepared for a drop in performance in the experimental group the first few weeks. The changeover to a new job may lead to a temporary reduction in efficiency.

10. Expect your first-line supervisors to experience some anxiety and hostility over the changes you are making. The anxiety comes from their fear that the changes will result in poorer performance for their unit. Hostility will arise when the employees start assuming what the supervisors regard as their own responsibility for performance. The supervisor without checking duties to perform may then be left with little to do.

After a successful experiment however, the supervisor usually discovers the supervisory and managerial functions he has neglected, or which were never his because all his time was given over to checking the work of his subordinates. For example, in the R&D division of one large chemical company I know of, the supervisors of the laboratory assistants were theoretically responsible for their training and evaluation. These functions, however, had come to be performed in a routine, unsubstantial fashion. After the job enrichment program, during which the supervisors were not merely passive observers of the assistants' performance,

the supervisors actually were devoting their time to reviewing performance and administering thorough training.

What has been called an employee-centered style of supervision will come about not through education of supervisors, but by changing the jobs that they do.

CONCLUDING NOTE

Job enrichment will not be a one-time proposition, but a continuous management function. The initial changes, however, should last for a very long period of time. There are a number of reasons for this:

- The changes should bring the job up to the level of challenge commensurate with the skill that was hired.
- Those who have still more ability eventually will be able to demonstrate it better and win promotion to higher-level jobs.
- The very nature of motivators, as opposed to hygiene factors, is that they have a much longer-term effect on employees' attitudes. Perhaps the job will have to be enriched again, but this will not occur as frequently as the need for hygiene.

Not all jobs can be enriched, nor do all jobs need to be enriched. If only a small percentage of the time and money that is now devoted to hygiene, however, were given to job enrichment efforts, the return in human satisfaction and economic gain would be one of the largest dividends that industry and society have ever reaped through their efforts at better personnel management.

The argument for job enrichment can be summed up quite simply: If you have someone on a job, use him. If you can't use him on the job, get rid of him, either via automation or by selecting someone with lesser ability. If you can't use him and you can't get rid of him, you will have a motivation problem.

NOTES

Readers of this article may be interested in "What Job Attitudes Tell About Motivation," by Lyman "W. Porter and Edward E. Lawler, III, *Harvard Business Review*, Vol. 46, January/February 1968, pp. 118–126.

Author's Note: I should like to acknowledge the contributions that Robert Ford of the American Telephone and Telegraph Company has made to the ideas expressed in this paper, and in particular to the successful application of these ideas in improving work performance and the job satisfaction of employees.

CRITICAL THINKING QUESTIONS

1. Suppose we change the topic of the article from how to motivate *employees* to how to motivate *students*. Can Herzberg's principles of employee motivation be used in the academic environment? How? As part of this question, conduct a survey of students to identify what school factors lead to extreme satisfaction and extreme dissatisfaction. Classify these as hygiene or motivation factors.

2. Would the principles of successful job enrichment outlined by Herzberg apply equally to all employees in all situations? What individual- or work-related factors might mediate whether the principles will work?

3. Conduct an informal survey of people you know who work full time, asking them the same questions about job satisfaction and dissatisfaction outlined in the article. How well do your observations correspond with the information presented by Herzberg?

4. After reading an article such as this, why might some managers still be reluctant to undertake recommended changes? Are any of these concerns legitimate? Why or why not?

ADDITIONAL RELATED READINGS

Boardman, C., & Sundquist, E. (2009). Toward understanding work motivation: Worker attitudes and the perception of effective public service. *The American Review of Public Administration, 39*(5), 519–535.

Lundberg, C., Gudmundson, A., & Andersson, T. D. (2009). Herzberg's Two-Factor Theory of work motivation tested empirically on seasonal workers in hospitality and tourism. *Tourism Management, 30*(6), 890–899.

ARTICLE 39 _____

At the heart of any organization—whether a small, family-run business or a large, multinational corporation—are its *people*. Perhaps nothing is more critical for the ultimate success or failure of an organization than the hiring of the best people for the appropriate jobs.

But what are the factors that might constitute *best* in terms of the person? Their intelligence? Willingness to work hard? The experiences and skills they bring with them? Certainly these and other factors can be important, depending on the specific position being looked at. But what about another factor, one that perhaps cuts across almost all work possibilities: *ethical* behavior. When we are dealing with a person who is working for an organization, whether it be a business, a school, or any such group, it's fairly safe to assume that most people would prefer that the other person was ethical rather than not. But what factors might be related to whether or not we behave ethically?

Recently, researchers Peter Salovey and John Meyer coined the term *emotional intelligence* to describe the qualities that seem to enhance successful social behavior. For example, factors such as empathy and delay of gratification often characterize people who are particularly socially successful. This concept became wildly popular with the publication of the best-selling book *Emotional Intelligence* by Daniel Goleman, who also introduced the shortened term *EQ* to refer to these qualities. The basic notion is that just as IQ (i.e., intelligence quotient) may give some indication of the overall level of a person's intellectual ability, EQ may give some insight into the level of social skills that an individual possesses.

Of course, having high social skills is no guarantee of acting ethically. In fact, having high social skills might make someone even better at "conning" someone. Yet our level of emotional intelligence may have an impact on our ethical behavior. The following article by Jacob Joseph, Kevin Berry, and Satish P. Deshpande examines how emotional intelligence and other factors may have an impact on the perception of ethical behavior in others. In turn, that perception of others' ethical behavior may be very related to one's own ethical conduct.

Impact of Emotional Intelligence and Other Factors on Perception of Ethical Behavior of Peers

■ Jacob Joseph, Kevin Berry, and Satish P. Deshpande

ABSTRACT

This study investigates factors impacting perceptions of ethical conduct of peers of 293 students in four US universities. Self-reported ethical behavior and recognition of emotions in others (a dimension of emotional intelligence) impacted perception of ethical behavior of peers. None of the other dimensions of emotional intelligence were significant. Age, Race, Sex, GPA, or type of major (business versus nonbusiness) did not impact perception of ethical behavior of peers. Implications of the results of the study for business schools and industry professionals are discussed.

INTRODUCTION

The popular media has paid considerable attention to the illegal and abusive lending practices of the financial-service industry and the subsequent collapse of the subprime-mortgage market in the United States (Sachdev, 2008). This mess has spiked foreclosure rates, damaged the US real estate market, and is expected to continue dampening the US economy late into 2008. Other major business scandals in the press last year include contaminated pet food that resulted in the deaths of several cats and dogs, recall of millions of toys that contained excessive amounts of lead, and evidence that a former manager at Siemens bribed government officials in Nigeria, Russia, and Libya. Unfortunately, ethical problems and scandals are not likely to fade away in the near future. In a recent national survey of human resource professionals by the Society for Human Resource Management (SHRM) and the Ethics Resource Center (ERC), only 33% of the respondents indicated that their firm had a comprehensive ethics and compliance program in place (Ethics Resource Center, 2008a).

But ethical abuses are not limited to for-profit organizations. Large non-profit organizations like the Smithsonian Institute,

With kind permission from Springer Science + Business Media. *Journal of Business Ethics*, "Impact of Emotional Intelligence and Other Factors on Perception of Ethical Behavior of Peers", 89(4), pp. 539–546. Joseph, J; Berry, K; & Deshpande, S.P. Copyright (c) 2009.

United Way, and Red Cross have been investigated for financial irregularities or violation of ethics rules (Harned, 2008; Wulfson, 2001). The Olympics, often associated with high ideals and true sportsmanship, have been tarred with issues like alleged drug use by high-profile athletes and alleged bribes paid to secure Olympic venues. Even government employees report a high incidence of ethical misconduct. More than half the respondents of a recent survey of government employees said that they had observed misconduct in the past year (Ethics Resource Center, 2008b). In addition, nearly one-third of the respondents said that the government is not socially responsible.

It is not surprising that business schools have been criticized for doing an inadequate job of teaching students how to apply ethical principles and to understand the social responsibility of firms (Verschoor, 2003). In 2003, the board of directors of The Association to Advance Collegiate Schools of Business (AACSB International), a not-for-profit organization devoted to the improvement and promotion of higher education in accounting and business administration, strengthened the focus on ethics in their new accreditation standards. In addition, they established the *Ethics Education Task Force* to examine how the crisis in business ethics can be used to strengthen business curricula. The task force in their 2004 report clearly identified a need for business educators to focus more on ethical responsibility of individuals and businesses.

While many business schools have responded to their critics by strengthening the ethics component in their curriculum, a big debate still exists among educators as to how business ethics should be taught (Lowry, 2003). AACSB International does not prescribe a set of courses but requires schools to justify how curriculum contents meet the mission of the school and learning goals of each program. Unfortunately, some business school faculty think teaching business ethics is a waste of time. Reasons cited by faculty include the belief that values are formed in childhood and cannot be changed during their short stay at universities and that employers do not really care about ethics (Mathieson and Tyler, 2008). Mathieson and Tyler (2008) examine these and other objections raised by business faculty, and present evidence to refute these negative perceptions and support the need for a strong commitment to ethics education.

LITERATURE REVIEW

In the last few years, a number of studies have examined factors impacting ethical behavior of students. Lawson (2004) reported that students felt that unethical behavior was the norm in the business world. This study also found a strong relationship between student's propensity to cheat in an academic setting and attitude toward unethical behavior in the business world. Deshpande and Joseph (2008) in a study of counterproductive behavior of 217 students of a large

northeastern public university found that business majors were no different than non-business majors when in came to unethical behavior. On the other hand, Bernardi et al. (2004) in a study of cheating behavior of 220 students from three universities reported that business students scored significantly lower on moral development and moral reasoning scales that other majors. In addition, they found that 66.4% of all students reported that they cheated in high school, college, or both high school and college. This is very disturbing because previous research suggests that these students are likely to continue their unethical behavior in a professional work setting (Nonis and Swift, 2001; Sims, 1993).

Previous reviews of studies done in business ethics have strongly recommended the need for additional investigation of "individual, situational, and issue-related influences" of the ethical decision-making process (O'Fallon and Butterfield, 2005, p. 399). Emotional intelligence is a relatively new concept and is being looked at by researchers across many disciplines (Ng et al., 2007). Emotional intelligence gained a lot of attention in the popular media after the publication of Daniel Goleman's book, *Emotional Intelligence*, in 1995. Mesmer-Magnus et al. (2008) in a study of 198 undergraduate students at a university found that overall emotional intelligence (EI) as measured by the 16 item Wong and Law EI scale was significantly correlated with both ethical behavior of peers and ethical behavior of self. They cogitate that employees with high EI may be less likely to interpret others' unethical actions as justification for their own unethical behavior. Past research has concluded that emotional intelligence positively impacts job performance, leadership effectiveness, and job satisfaction in a variety of jobs (Cherniss et al., 2006). Van Rooy and Viswesvaran (2004) in a meta-analysis found a correlation of 0.23 between EI and performance. The four-dimensional definition of emotional intelligence proposed by Davies et al. (1998) has been considered to be the most comprehensive (Law et al., 2004). The four dimensions are appraisal and expression of emotion in oneself (SEA), appraisal and recognition of emotion in others (OEA), regulation of emotions in oneself (UOE), and the use of emotions to facilitate performance (ROE). One of the objectives of this paper is to examine the impact of various dimensions/facets of EI on perception of ethical behavior of peers.

Reviews of the ethical decision-making literature have identified a number of studies over time that have suggested an ever present influence of significant others like coworkers or peers on ethical decision making by individuals (Loe et al., 2000; O'Fallon and Butterfield, 2005). Deshpande et al. (2006) in a study of 203 hospital employees in Midwestern and Northwestern United States found that ethical behavior of peers had the most significant impact on ethical behavior. These findings are in line with Bandura's Social Learning Theory (Bandura, 1977) which suggests that referent others have a significant impact on the behavior of individuals (O'Fallon and Butterfield, 2005). It is also consistent with Differential Association Theory which "assumes that ethical/unethical behavior is learned in the process of interacting with persons who are a part of intimate personal groups or role sets" (Ferrell and Gresham, 1985, p. 90). More recently, Kidwell and Valentine (2008) in a study of military reserve personnel found a negative relationship between perceptions of positive workgroup context and withholding efforts or neglecting job duties by employees.

While past research has used perception of ethical behavior of peers as an independent variable, current research suggests that a measure of ethical behavior of peers is a more valid measure of ethical misconduct than a self-reported measure of ethical behavior. According to Vardi (2001, p. 319), this measure "minimizes the potential perceived threat, as well as social desirability" associated with measures asking subjects their own misconduct. Studies done by the Ethics Resource Center in 2003 and 2005 have also used misconduct by others as the dependent variable. More recently, Andreoli and Lefkowitz (2008) also make a strong case for using ethical behavior of coworkers instead of measures self-reported misconduct. They suggest that self-report assessment of misconduct suffer from "fake good" bias. One of the arguments they make is that people often attribute their repressed thoughts and behavior to others or project their misconduct on others. This theory is based on the defensive mechanism of psychological projection or projection bias. We will use ethical behavior of peers as the dependent variable in our study. In addition, we will also examine if self-reported ethical behavior has an impact on perception of ethical behavior of peers. A review of ABI-INFORM and current literature reviews of the ethical decision-making literature did not identify any other study that has examined the impact of self-reported ethical behavior and various individual level variables on the perception of ethical behavior of peers. The variables we will examine in our study are self-reported ethical behavior of individual, level of emotional intelligence, GPA, color, sex, major in college. We will also test for overclaiming by subjects.

THE STUDY

The sample for this study came from four universities in the Midwestern and Northwestern United States. The survey used to collect data for this study was handed out in late 2007 and early 2008 in various classes on the participating campuses. There were no incentives given to the students to participate in the study. Two hundred and ninety-three surveys were deemed useable giving us a response rate of 85%. This was not unexpected given that the surveys were handed and collected during class to ensure a high response rate. Table I indicates that 62% of the respondents were females. The average age of a respondent was 22 years. The grade point average of an

TABLE I / Demographic Variables

Item	N	Mean	SD
Age	287	22.29	3.88
Male	293	0.33	0.51
White	293	0.82	0.38
Accounting	292	0.28	0.45
GPA	279	3.30	1.66

average respondent was 3.28. Of the respondents, 27.6% were accounting majors. Also 82.3% of the students were white.

The student survey covered measures of ethical behavior of peers, ethical behavior of self, emotional intelligence, and demographic measures. It also included a number of variables not included in this study. Ethical behavior of peers was measured using 12 items (e.g., students make personal calls at work). These items were based on previous business ethics research (Jackson, 2001; Viswesvaran et al., 2000). Ethical behavior of self was measured using 12 similar items (e.g., I make personal calls at work). These items, as presented in the Appendix, were rated on a four-point Likert scale (4 = very frequently, 1 = very infrequently). The Cronbach's alpha for ethical behavior of peers and self was 0.87 and 0.73, respectively.

The Wong and Law EI Scale (WLEIS) was used to measure four dimensions of emotional intelligence (Law et al., 2004). Self-emotions appraisal (SEA) was measured using the following items: I have a good sense of why I have certain feelings most of the time, I have good understanding of my own emotions, I really understand what I feel, and I always know whether or not I am happy. Others-emotions appraisal (OEA) was measured using the following items: I always know my friends' emotions from their behavior, I am a good observer of others' emotions, I am sensitive to the feelings and emotions of others, and I have good understanding of the emotions of people around me. Use of emotions (UOE) was measured using the following items: I always set goals for myself and then try my best to achieve them, I always tell myself I am a competent person, I am a self-motivating person, and I would always encourage myself to try my best. Regulation of emotions (ROE) was measured using the following items: I am able to control my temper so that I can handle difficulties rationally, I am quite capable of controlling my own emotions, I can always calm down quickly when I am very angry, and I have good control of my own emotions. This scale was recently used by Deshpande and Joseph (2008) to examine tendency of nurses to engage in unethical behavior. Cronbach's alpha for SEA, OEA, UOE, and ROE was 0.80, 0.80, 0.80, and 0.85, respectively.

Overclaiming scales were used to control for social desirability bias in our survey. The procedure to detect overclaimers in this study was initially proposed by Randall and

Fernandes (1991). Respondents were asked to rate their degree of familiarity with different categories like movies, products, TV shows, and designer labels on a three-point Likert scale (3 = very familiar, 1 = not at all familiar). All these items were nonexistent. These fake items are presented in the Appendix. Overclaiming score were arrived at by adding up score of fake items and dividing by the number of items. High scoring respondents claimed that they were aware of nonexistent items. Cronbach's alpha for this scale was 0.78. Respondents were also asked to provide their age, race, sex, GPA, and college major.

RESULTS

Table II indicates that self-reported ethical behavior, OEA, age, and Business major were significantly correlated with ethical behavior of peers (EBP). While overclaiming was not significantly correlated with EBP, it was significantly correlated with ethical behavior of self. We also observed a number of significant correlations between other predictors of EBP. Thus, it would be hasty and premature to draw conclusions on the impact of various independent variables as the intercorrelations can impact significance of the relationships of interest. Correlations also have another limitation. They give us an estimate of the association among the variables, but they do not tell us if a variable is dependent upon the others.

Regression analysis allows us to examine the dependence of a variable on various explanatory variables. Therefore, regression analysis will allow us to draw more valid conclusions. The most widely used method of estimation for the regression model, ordinary least squares (OLS), was used in our study. Regression analysis presented in Table III provides a stronger test of the variables investigated in our study. Regression analysis indicated that among the independent variables only ethical behavior of self and OEA significantly influenced EBP.

IMPLICATIONS AND CONCLUSIONS

Both business schools and industry professionals can benefit from the results of this study. Previous research has indicated that on an average, students have weaker ethical values than working professionals (Cole and Smith, 1996). While there could be a number of reasons for this conclusion (e.g., more liberal viewpoints of what is unethical or less experience in dealing with unethical behaviors), it is important that students learn about repercussions of their unethical actions and change their behavior before entering the workplace. Among various disciplines, business schools have specially come under a lot of criticism for creating an environment that has produced graduates that are unethical. Business school faculty have also

TABLE III / Regression Analysis for Ethical Behavior of Peers

Independent variables	β
Ethical behavior of self	0.29*
Self Emotions Appraisal (SEA)	0.04
Others Emotions Appraisal (OEA)–	−0.25*
Use of Emotions (UOE)	−0.05
Regulation of Emotions (ROE)	0.06
Age	0.02
White	0.00
Male	0.04
GPA	−0.04
Business	0.05
Overclaiming	0.02
N	276
R-square	0.19
F	5.57*

*$p < 0.01$,   **$p < 0.05$.

TABLE II / Correlations Among the Variables

	1	2	3	4	5	6	7	8	9	10	11	12
1 Ethical beh of peers	1.00											
2 Ethical beh of self	0.29**	1.00										
3 SEA	−0.04	0.02	1.00									
4 OEA	−0.31**	−0.13*	0.36**	1.00								
5 UOE	−0.11	0.04	0.29**	0.27**	1.00							
6 ROE	0.05	0.13*	0.35**	0.06	0.30**	1.00						
7 Age	0.13*	0.20**	−0.06	−0.20**	−0.03	−0.16**	1.00					
8 White	−0.01	−0.03	0.04	−0.01	0.01	−0.07	0.03	1.00				
9 Male	0.09	−0.16**	−0.01	−0.25**	−0.11	−0.01	0.08	0.07	1.00			
10 GPA	−0.05	0.01	−0.02	0.02	0.05	0.03	−0.03	−0.12	−0.06	1.00		
11 Business major	0.12*	0.03	−0.04	−0.23**	−0.07	−0.08	0.23**	−0.06	0.20**	0.05	1.00	
12 Overclaiming	−0.05	−0.21**	0.05	0.06	0.03	0.00	−0.06	−0.01	0.01	−0.03	0.04	1.00

*$p < 0.05$ (two-tailed),   **$p < 0.01$ (2-tailed).

Listwise *n* = 276.

been accused of making unreasonable assumptions like student's values are rigid and fixed by the time they reach business school and faculty have an insignificant role in teaching values (Mitroff, 2004). In our study, business school students perceived ethical behavior of their peers no differently than nonbusiness students. Klein et al. (2007) in their study on cheating found no significant difference among cheating by business and professional students. But they also report that business students tend to be more lax in their definition of cheating compared to other students. Borkowski and Ugras (1998) in a meta-analysis of 47 studies also did not find a significant effect of academic major on ethical attitudes/behavior. Our results support the view that unethical student behavior is a global phenomenon and not a domain of business students alone.

Previous reviews of studies done in business ethics have strongly recommended the need for additional investigation of "individual, situational, and issue-related influences" of the ethical decision-making process (O'Fallon and Butterfield, 2005, p. 399). The concept of emotional intelligence is relatively new and is being looked at by researchers in a wide range of disciplines (Ng et al., 2007). This investigation opens up a new line of research by looking at the impact of dimensions of emotional intelligence on perception of ethical behavior of peers. Students with greater ability to perceive and understand emotions of others (OEA) or empathy were significantly more likely to be aware of unethical behavior of peers. But other dimensions of emotional intelligence—a student's ability to be aware of their own mood and thought (SEA), regulate their emotions (UOE), or facilitate performance (ROE)—had no significant impact on perception of ethical behavior of peers. This could be due to high intercorrelations among the various dimensions of emotional intelligence as seen in Table II. Daniel Goleman (2006) in his latest book *Social Intelligence* makes a strong case on the importance of social awareness for success in life and examines ways in which these skills can be nurtured and developed. Research needs to be done on the best way to enhance empathy and social awareness skills among students and employees.

Those who reported higher levels of ethical behavior of self were significantly more likely to report higher levels of ethical behavior of peers too. This suggests that perceptions of ethical behavior of peer is a reflection of individual's ethical behavior. Previous research using regression analysis has found that ethical behavior of peers significantly impacts ethical behavior of self (Deshpande and Joseph, 2008). This raises an interesting topic of investigation for future researchers. What is the directional relationship between the two variables? Andreoli and Lefkowitz (2008) examine this issue and conclude that there exists no appropriate basis to anticipate directionality. In their study they combined the two variables into one variable since the correlation between the two variables in their study was

high (0.43) and the reliability of their measure of observed misconduct of others was low (0.43). But the correlation between the two variables in our study was not as high as in theirs (0.29) and both the variables had high reliabilities in our study (peers = 0.87, self = 0.73). Future researchers can further examine if it makes sense to combining these two variables into a single measure of ethical behavior.

But it should be noted that unlike ethical behavior of peers, ethical behavior of self is significantly correlated with overclaiming. This suggests that in spite of the facts that there was no way of tracking down responses of specific respondents, subjects still inflated their responses on their own ethical behavior. This raises questions about validity of studies that have used self-reported ethical behavior and not controlled for overclaiming. Future business ethics research must control for social desirability bias.

This study was limited to four universities in the US. In an analysis not shown in the paper, the type of university (private versus public) or location did not impact the significance of the results of this study. Future research can examine if the nature of the university (religious versus secular) or the type of business major (HR versus Finance) impacts the results. Future research can use a longitudinal design to examine if values of the students change once they leave the university and enter the workforce.

APPENDIX

Items used to measure various constructs

Ethical behavior of peers

   a. Students make personal calls at work.
   b. Students surf the web at work.
   c. Students take office supplies home.
   d. Students share music on the internet.
   e. Students download term papers off the internet.
   f. Students give friends an extra discount at a store or free food at a café/restaurant.
   g. Students sometimes help themselves to food if working at a fast food joint.
   h. Students do homework for friends.
   i. Students have used fake ID to purchase alcohol.
   j. Students have used fake ID to get into a bar.
   k. Students have cheated on an exam.
   l. In order to get ahead in life, students believe that one has to compromise on ethical standards.

Ethical behavior of self

   a. I'd make personal calls at work.
   b. I'd surf the web at work.
   c. I'd take office supplies home.
   d. I'd share music on the internet.
   e. I download term papers off the internet.

f. I'd give a friend an extra discount at a store or free food at a café/restaurant.

g. I'd sometimes help myself to food if I worked at a fast food joint.

h. I'd do homework for my close friends.

i. I've used fake ID to purchase alcohol.

j. I've used fake ID to get into a bar.

k. I've cheated on an exam.

l. In order to get ahead in your future career you will have to compromise your ethical standards.

Overclaiming scales

a. How familiar are you with each of the following movies?
Turned to Gold
Katherine's Mistake

b. How familiar are you with each of the following products?
Microsoft Statistical Assistant
New Life Spices

c. How familiar are you with the following albums?
Cosmic Being
Offender After Dark

d. How familiar are you with each of the following TV programs?
The Adventure of Johnnie
Chicago Heat

e. How familiar are you with each of the following designer labels?
Ocean City
Jones, L.A.

REFERENCES

Andreoli, N. and J. Lefkowitz: 2008, 'Individual and Organizational Antecedents of Misconduct in Organizations', *Journal of Business Ethics,* Retrieved on June 23rd, 2008 through http://www.springerlink.com/content/e1u286241t084402/.

Bandura, A.: 1977, *Social Learning Theory* (Holt, Rinehart and Winston, Englewood Cliffs, NJ).

Bernardi, R. A., R. L. Metzger, R. G. Scofield Bruno, M. A. Wade Hoogkamp, L. E. Reyes and G. H. Barnaby: 2004, 'Examining the Decision Process of Students' Cheating Behavior: An Empirical Study', *Journal of Business Ethics* **50**(4), 397–414. doi:10.1023/B:BUSI.0000025039.47788.c2.

Borkowski, S. C. and Y. J. Ugras: 1998, 'Business Students and Ethics: A Meta-Analysis', *Journal of Business Ethics* **17**(11), 1117–1127. doi:10.1023/A:1005748725174.

Cherniss, C., M. Extein, D. Goleman and R. Weissberg: 2006, 'Emotional Intelligence: What Does the Research Really Indicate?', *Educational Psychologist* **41**(4), 239–245. doi:10.1207/s15326985ep4104_4.

Cole, B. and D. Smith: 1996, 'Perception of Business Ethics: Students Versus Business People', *Journal of Business Ethics* **15**, 889–896. doi:10.1007/BF00381856.

Davies, M., L. Stankov and R. D. Roberts: 1998, 'Emotional Intelligence: In Search of an Exclusive Construct', *Journal of Personality and Social Psychology* **75**, 989–1015. doi:10.1037/0022-3514.75.4.989.

Deshpande, S. P. and J. Joseph: 2008, 'The Impact of Ethical Values and Perceptions of Ethical Conduct on Counterproductive Behavior of Future Managers', *Advances in Competitiveness Research* (in press).

Deshpande, S. P., J. Joseph and R. Prasad: 2006, 'Factors Impacting Ethical Behavior in Hospitals', *Journal of Business Ethics* **69**, 207–216. doi:10.1007/s10551-006-9086-5.

Ethics Resource Center: 2008a, 'Performance Reviews Often Skip Ethics, HR Professionals Say', Retrieved on June 23rd, 2008 through http://ethics.org/about-erc/press-releases.asp.

Ethics Resource Center: 2008b, 'Governments at All Levels Show High Rates of Misconduct; "Next Enron" Could Be in Public Sector', Retrieved June 23rd, 2008 through http://www.ethics.org/about-erc/press-releases.asp.

Ferrell, O. C. and L. G. Gresham: 1985, 'A Contingency Framework for Understanding Ethical Decision Making in Marketing', *Journal of Marketing* **49**(Summer), 87–96. doi:10.2307/1251618.

Goleman, D.: 2006, *Social Intelligence* (Bantam Books, New York).

Harned, P. J.: 2008, 'Your Online Resource for a Broad Range of Organizational Ethics and Character Development Issues', Retrieved June 23rd, 2008 through http://www.ethics.org/ethics-today/0408/pat-column.asp.

Jackson, T.: 2001, 'Cultural Values and Management Ethics: A 10-Nation Study', *Human Relations* **54**, 1267–1302.

Kidwell, R. E. and S. R. Valentine: 2008, 'Positive Group Context, Work Attitudes, and Organizational Misbehavior: The Case of Withholding Job Effort', *Journal of Business Ethics*. Published Online 4 June, 2008.

Klein, H. A., N. M. Levengurg, M. McKendall and W. Mothersell: 2007, 'Cheating During the College Years: How Do Business School Students Compare?', *Journal of Business Ethics* **72**, 197–206. doi:10.1007/s10551-006-9165-7.

Law, K., C. Wong and L. Song: 2004, 'The Construct and Criterion Validity of Emotional Intelligence and Its Potential Utility for Management Studies', *The Journal of Applied Psychology* **89**(3), 483–496. doi:10.1037/0021-9010.89.3.483.

Lawson, R. A.: 2004, 'Is Classroom Cheating Related to Business Students' Propensity to Cheat in the "Real World"?', *Journal of Business Ethics* **49**, 189–199. doi:10.1023/B:BUSI.0000015784.34148.cb.

Loe, T., L. Ferrell and P. Mansfield: 2000, 'A Review of Empirical Studies Assessing Ethical Decision Making in Business', *Journal of Business Ethics* **25**, 185–204. doi:10.1023/A:1006083612239.

Lowry, D.: 2003, 'An Investigation of Student Moral Awareness and Associated Factors in Two Cohorts of an Undergraduate Business Degree in a British University: Implications for Business Ethics Curriculum Design', *Journal of Business Ethics* **48**, 7–19. doi:10.1023/B:BUSI.0000004383.81450.96.

Mathieson, K. and C. Tyler: 2008, '"We Don't Need No Stinking Ethics": The Struggle Continues', *Journal of College & Character* **9**(4), 1–12.

Mesmer-Magnus, J., C. Viswesvaran, J. Joseph and S. S. Deshpande: 2008, 'The Role of Emotional Intelligence in Integrity and Ethics

Perceptions', in W. Zerbe, N. Ashkansky and C. Hartel (eds.), *Research on Emotions in Organizations: Emotions, Ethics, and Decision-Making*, Vol. 4 (Quorum Books/Greenwood Publishing Group, Westport, CT).

Mitroff, I. I.: 2004, 'An Open Letter to the Deans and Faculties of American Business Schools', *Journal of Business Ethics* **54**(7), 185–189.

Ng, K., C. Wang, C. Zalaquett and N. Bodenhorn: 2007, 'A confirmatory Factor Analysis of the Wong and Law Emotional Intelligence Scale in a Sample of International College Students', *International Journal for the Advancement of Counseling*, 173–185. doi:10.1007/s10447-007-9037-6.

Nonis, S. and C. O. Swift: 2001, 'An Examination of the Relationship Between Academic Dishonesty and Workplace Dishonesty: A Multicampus Investigation', *Journal of Education for Business*, 69–76.

O'Fallon, M. J. and K. D. Butterfield: 2005, 'A Review of the Empirical Ethical Decision-Making Literature: 1996–2003', *Journal of Business Ethics* **59**, 375–413. doi:10.1007/s10551-005-2929-7.

Randall, D. M. and M. F. Fernandes: 1991, 'The Social Desirability Response Bias in Ethics Research', *Journal of Business Ethics* **10**, 805–817. doi:10.1007/BF0038 3696.

Sachdev, A.: 2008, 'Mortgage Mess Becomes Prime Territory for Law Firms', Retrieved on May 28, 2008 through www.chicagotribune.com/business/chi-tue-law-notebookmar11,1,968395.story.

Sims, R. L.: 1993, 'The Relationship Between Academic Dishonesty and Unethical Business Practices', *Journal of Education for Business* **68**(4), 207–212.

Van Rooy, D. and C. Viswesvaran: 2004, 'Emotional Intelligence: A Meta-Analytic Investigation of Predictive Validity and Nomological Net', *Journal of Vocational Behavior* **65**, 71–95. doi:10.1016/S0001-8791(03)00076-9.

Vardi, Y.: 2001, 'The Effects of Organizational and Ethical Climates on Misconduct at Work', *Journal of Business Ethics* **29**, 325–337. doi:10.1023/A:1010710 022834.

Verschoor, C. C.: 2003, 'Is Ethics Education of Future Business Leaders Adequate?', *Strategic Finance* **85**, 20–21.

Viswesvaran, C., S. P. Deshpande and J. Joseph: 2000, 'Are Ethical Perceptions of Various Practices Affected by Workplace Dependencies?', *Journal of Applied Social Psychology* **30**, 2050–2057. doi:10.1111/j.1559–1816. 2000.tb02423.x.

Wulfson, M.: 2001, 'The Ethics of Corporate Social Responsibility and Philanthropic Ventures', *Journal of Business Ethics* **29**, 135–145. doi:10.1023/A:1006459 329221.</

CRITICAL THINKING QUESTIONS

1. Think of a person you know whom you consider to be socially very successful. Does he or she seem to possess the qualities associated with emotional intelligence, as discussed in this article? Elaborate on how these (or other) qualities may contribute to this person's social success.

2. According to the article, some business professors have "the belief that values (of students) are formed in childhood and cannot be changed during their short stay at universities . . . ". Do you agree or disagree with this statement? Explain your reasoning.

3. "Students felt that unethical behavior was the norm in the business world." React to this statement from the article. Do the beliefs of you, your family, and/or your friends support or contradict this statement? Explain.

4. Design a study to test whether student's ethical values change during their four years at a college or university. What variables would you include in your study? Why?

5. Should emotional intelligence be taught to children? Why or why not? What issues would need to be considered? For example, what emotional responses are deemed proper, and by whom would that be determined? Defend your position.

6. Would it be possible to teach a sort of remedial emotional intelligence to adults? Why or why not? Describe a study that would attempt to answer this question empirically.

CHAPTER INTEGRATION QUESTIONS

1. The first article on leadership dealt with followers, the second with employee motivation, and the third with ethical behavior and emotional intelligence. What do these three articles have in common? Explain what you see as a common thread or threads running through all of the articles in this chapter.

2. What other factors besides those discussed in these articles may be important in understanding business psychology? For example, what topics of previous chapters may have particular relevance for the study of business psychology? Discuss why you think these topics/chapters may be relevant.

3. An old proverb tells us, "It is not whether you win or lose but how you play the game." Yet according to Vince Lombardi, a former professional football coach, "Winning isn't everything, it's the only thing." These quotes typically are associated with sports, but can they be applied to how people approach business, as well? How so? What are both the potential short-term and long-term implications for someone who follows either of these quotes in his or her approach to business? Explain.

Chapter Fourteen

FORENSIC PSYCHOLOGY

You PROBABLY HAVE had some contact with the legal system, in one form or another. Perhaps you (or someone you know) have been arrested and even tried for some offense. Maybe you have been asked to be a juror. More likely, you have watched televised trials or read about real or fictional trials in the media. Given your experience, does the legal system, as it presently operates, guarantee an objective, unbiased outcome?

Forensic psychology has emerged in recent years as a major discipline that tries to understand the entire judicial process and make it as fair as possible. Originally an outgrowth of social psychology and other psychological disciplines, forensic psychology has become an area of study in its own right. Nonetheless, it remains strongly rooted in the principles and findings of social psychological research.

Social psychologists working in the field of forensic psychology have examined a number of factors that may influence the outcomes in legal settings. Many of the findings summarized in previous articles in this book can be applied to forensic settings, as well. For example, the findings pertaining to prejudice, discrimination, social influence, and attitude change, to name but a few, can easily be extended to the courtroom. Some of the biases that enter into the judicial process may be by-products of how we think and process information (i.e., social cognition). Some of these biases may stem from how we naturally deal with the complex world around us, and as such, they may have been present from the first time that someone's guilt or innocence was put in question. However, there may also be some new biases entering the modern courtroom based on technological changes.

Article 40, "The Psychology and Power of False Confessions," examines why someone might do the unthinkable: namely, confess to a crime he or she did not commit. The article addresses some of the social psychological factors that may play a role in getting someone to admit guilt when he or she is actually innocent.

The classic study found in Article 41, "Beautiful but Dangerous: Effects of Offender Attractiveness and Nature of the Crime on Juridic Judgment," looks at the relationship between the attractiveness of the offender and the nature of the crime and how it may influence a jury's judgment. Often (but not always), having good looks is an asset when someone is on trial.

Finally, Article 42, "Attractive but Guilty: Deliberation and the Physical Attractiveness Bias," is a good contemporary article that looks at the variables introduced in the classic study mentioned earlier (Article 38). This more recent study found that having a juror reach his or her decision alone or via jury deliberations in a group had an impact on the likelihood of convicting someone based on his or her physical attractiveness. It further demonstrates the constant need to expand and refine a topic over time in order to come up with a fuller understanding of how it operates.

ARTICLE 40 _____

Since the advent of DNA testing, many individuals who have committed crimes have been convicted and sentenced based on genetic evidence. As any viewer of the myriad police shows on television will attest, the use of DNA evidence seems to be a cornerstone of modern forensic police work.

While the use of DNA testing has provided evidence to convict criminals who would not confess to their acts and for whom other evidence was lacking, the use of such testing has also produced another result. Namely, DNA testing has provided evidence that someone already convicted for a crime could not have committed it.

There are many reasons an innocent person may be convicted of a crime. The person's physical similarity to the actual offender, the existence of eyewitnesses who maintain he or she was the criminal, and the lack of competent legal representation are but a few of the reasons a person professing innocence may be convicted of a crime he or she did not commit. However, sometimes people are convicted of crimes they did not commit because they confess to committing them.

To many people, the last sentence seems implausible. Why in the world would an innocent person confess to a crime he or she did not commit? Common sense would lead most people to believe that if you voluntarily confess to something, you must be telling the truth. We expect people to lie to get out of being charged or convicted of a crime, not to get charged or convicted.

So why would someone confess to a crime of which he or she was innocent? Topics from many of the previous chapters pertain to this issue. Using just a few examples, *social influence* deals with how people respond by conforming to social pressure, *social cognition* addresses how people think and make sense of the world, and *attitudes* reflect how people sometimes use a process known as *cognitive dissonance* to justify their initial beliefs or statements. But other processes are at work, as well.

The following article by Ian Herbert explores some of the reasons people may confess to crimes they did not commit. It also discusses some of the ways the legal system might be improved to minimize the possibility of people being wrongfully convicted due to a false confession.

The Psychology and Power of False Confessions

■ Ian Herbert

On July 8, 1997, Bill Bosko returned to his home in Norfolk, Virginia, after a week at sea to find his wife murdered in their bedroom. A few hours later, Bosko's neighbor, Danial Williams was asked to answer questions at the police station. And after eight hours there, Williams confessed to the rape and murder of Michelle Moore-Bosko.

Five months later, because of inconsistent physical evidence, the Norfolk police became convinced that Williams did not act alone and turned their attention to Joseph Dick, Williams' roommate. Dick confessed as well. He later pled guilty, testified against two other co-defendants, named five more accomplices who were never tried, and publicly apologized to the victim's family. "I know I shouldn't have done it," Dick said just before the judge gave him a double life sentence. "I have got no idea what went through my mind that night—and my soul."

Dick now says that all of that is untrue, and he has a team of lawyers who believe him. In 2005, the Innocence Project filed a petition on behalf of Williams, Dick, and the other two members of the group called the "Norfolk Four." They petitioned Virginia Governor Tim Kaine for clemency on the basis of new physical evidence, and in August 2009, the outgoing governor issued conditional pardons, which set the men free but forced them to be on parole for the next 20 years. It was a decision that Kaine struggled with, and he granted conditional pardons because he said the men failed to fully prove their innocence. "They're asking for a whole series of confessions . . . to all be discarded," Kaine said on a radio show in the fall of 2008. "That is a huge request."

We know that false confessions do happen on a fairly regular basis. Because of advances in DNA evidence, the Innocence

Project has been able to exonerate more than 200 people who had been wrongly convicted, 49 of whom had confessed to the crime we now know they didn't commit. In a survey of 1,000 college students, four percent of those who had been interrogated by police said they gave a false confession.

BUT WHY?

False confessions seem so illogical, especially for someone like Joseph Dick of the Norfolk Four, who got a double life sentence after confessing. Why do people confess to crimes they didn't commit? Some do it for the chance at fame (more than 200 people confessed to kidnapping Charles Lindbergh's baby), but many more do it for reasons that are far more puzzling to the average person. In the November 2004 issue of *Psychological Science in the Public Interest,* APS Fellow Saul Kassin looked at the body of research and described how the police are able to interrogate suspects until they confess to a crime they didn't commit.

Generally, it starts because people give up their Miranda rights. In fact, Richard A. Leo found that a majority of people give up the right to remain silent and the right to an attorney. In fact, according to self-report data, innocent suspects gave up their rights more often than guilty suspects (most told Leo either that this was because they felt that they didn't have anything to hide because they were innocent or that they thought it would make them look guilty).

Once a suspect starts talking, the police can use a variety of techniques to make the accused feel as though they are better off confessing than continuing to deny (these include promises of leniency and threats of harsher interrogation or sentences). If a suspect feels like a conviction is inevitable no matter what he or she says, confessing may seem like a good idea.

But, in some cases, the accused comes to believe that he or she actually did commit the crime. It's been shown repeatedly that memory is quite malleable and unreliable. Elizabeth Loftus has repeatedly shown that the human brain can create memories out of thin air with some prompting. In a famous series of experiments, Loftus, APS Past President, was able to help people create memories for events that never happened in their lives simply through prompting. She helped them "remember" being lost in a shopping mall when they were children, and the longer the experiment went on, the more details they "remembered." The longer police interrogate a suspect, emphatic about his guilt and peppering their interrogation with details of the crime, the more likely a suspect is to become convinced himself.

Joseph Dick claims that this is what happened to him. His confession, testimony, and apology to the family were not lies, he maintains, but rather the product of a false memory. "It didn't cross my mind that I was lying," he said. "I believed what I was saying was true."

CORRUPTING THE OTHER EVIDENCE

Despite the evidence that false confessions are a regular occurrence, most jurors struggle with the concept just like Kaine did with the Norfolk Four. Confessions are difficult to discount, even if they appear to be coerced. Years ago, Kassin noticed that cases with confessions have an unusually high conviction rate, and since then he has dedicated his life to studying why that happens and what can be done about it.

In a 1997 study, Kassin and colleague Katherine Neumann gave subjects case files with weak circumstantial evidence plus either a confession, an eyewitness account, a character witness, or no other evidence. Across the board, prospective jurors were more likely to vote guilty if a confession was included in the trial, even when they were told that the defendant was incoherent at the time of the confession and immediately recanted what he said.

Kassin and Neumann also did two simultaneous studies to further explore the power of confessions. In one, they had people watch a trial and turn a dial to rate the extent to which evidence convinced them the defendant was guilty or innocent. The other asked potential jurors after the trial which evidence was most powerful. In both the mid-trial and post-trial ratings, jurors saw the confession as the most incriminating. Other studies have shown that conviction rates rise even when jurors see confessions as coerced and even when they say that the confession played no role in their judgment. "I don't honestly think juries stand a chance in cases involving confessions," Kassin says. "They're bound to convict."

Kassin says he doesn't blame jurors. He travels around the country lecturing on the psychology of false confessions and he says "the most common reaction I get from a lay audience is, 'Well, I would never do that. I would never confess to something I didn't do.' And people apply that logic in the jury room. It's just that basic belief that false confessions don't occur." What's more, the evidence juries are given in conjunction with the false confessions is very damning, Kassin says. False confessions of guilt often include vivid details of how a crime was committed—and why. Confessions sometimes even come with an apology to the family. It's no wonder jurors have trouble discounting them.

What confessions rarely include is an explanation of why the person confessed. In most states, police are not required to videotape the interrogations, just the confessions. So juries don't get to see any potential police coercion and they don't get to see the police planting those vivid details in the minds of the suspects.

And that may be just the tip of the iceberg. Kassin believes that confessions can have a dramatic impact on trials even if they never make it into a courtroom. They can influence potential eyewitnesses, for example, and taint other kinds of evidence.

Kassin recently teamed up with psychologist Lisa Hasel to test the effect of confessions on eyewitnesses. They brought subjects in for what was supposed to be a study about persuasion techniques. The experimenter briefly left the room and, during that time, someone came in and stole a laptop off the desk. The subjects were then shown a lineup of six suspects, none of whom was the actual criminal, and they were asked to pick out which member of the lineup, if any, committed the crime. Two days later, the witnesses were brought back for more questioning. Those who had identified a suspect were told that the person they identified had confessed, another person had confessed, all suspects continued to deny their involvement, or that the identified suspect had continued to deny his involvement. Those who had (correctly) said none of the people in the lineup committed the crime were told either that all suspects denied the crime, that an unspecified suspect had confessed, or that a specific suspect had confessed.

The results show that confessions can have a powerful effect on other evidence. Of the people who had identified a subject from the original lineup, 60 percent changed their identification when told that someone else had confessed. Plus, 44 percent of the people who originally determined that none of the suspects in the lineup committed the crime changed their mind when told that someone had confessed (and 50 percent changed when told that a specific person had confessed). When asked about their decision, "about half of the people seemed to say, 'Well, the investigator told me there was a confession, so that must be true.' So they were just believing the investigator," Hasel said. "But the other half really seemed to be changing their memory. So that memory can never really be regained once it's been tainted." What's more, people who were told that the person they wrongly pinpointed as the culprit had confessed saw their confidence levels soar. After that confirmation, they remembered the crime better and were more sure about details. The implications for inside the courtroom are obvious if eyewitnesses who incorrectly picked someone out of a lineup can become so sure of their choice after learning that the person confessed. "It is noteworthy that whereas physical evidence is immutable (once collected and preserved, it can always be retested), an eyewitness's identification decision cannot later be revisited without contamination," Kassin and Hasel write.

Kassin and Hasel suspect that false confessions may also affect the memories of people who are potential alibis for defendants. Kassin worked on the actual case of John Kogut, who was accused of raping and murdering a 16-year-old girl. Kogut was at a party for his girlfriend at the time the crime was committed, and he had multiple alibi witnesses. But after 18 hours of interrogation, Kogut confessed to the grisly crime. "After he confessed to the crime, [the witnesses] started dropping off one-by-one," Hasel said. " 'You know, maybe I saw him earlier in the night but not later; maybe I saw him later in the night but not earlier; it must have been a different night,

I must be wrong.' " Kassin and Hasel are currently working on an experiment similar to their eyewitness study to test this theory on a broad basis.

This phenomenon may be explained by the same Loftus research about creating false memories that may have led to the false confession in the first place. So it is plausible that eyewitnesses or alibi witnesses might begin to remember things differently when told about something as powerful as a confession. But what about scientific evidence? At least confessions can't change something as concrete as DNA evidence or fingerprints, right? Even that belief may be untrue.

In 2006, University College London psychologist Itiel Dror took a group of six fingerprint experts and showed them samples that they themselves had, years before, determined either to be matches or non-matches (though they weren't told they had already seen these fingerprints). The experts were now given some context: either that the fingerprints came from a suspect who confessed or that they came from a suspect who was known to be in police custody at the time the crime was committed. In 17 percent of the non-control tests, experimenters changed assessments that they had previously made correctly. Four of the six experts who participated changed at least one judgment based on the new context. "And that's fingerprint judgments," Kassin said. "That's not considered malleable. And yet there was some degree of malleability and one of the ways to influence it was to provide information about the confession."

The practical importance of this research extends well beyond the laboratory. In a white paper set to be published in *Law and Human Behavior* in 2010, Kassin and four other prominent confession experts make recommendations, including, most notably, mandatory taping of all interrogations in capital cases. Kassin has begun to research this idea. His preliminary data illustrates that, shown two versions of known false confessions (one that just included the confession or another that included the entire interrogation), subjects were significantly less likely to vote guilty when shown the entire interrogation. "The information that the jury doesn't have and needs is how did this guy come to confess and then, when he did confess, how did he know all this information about the crime if he in fact wasn't there," Kassin says. "So yes, I think videotaping is probably the single best protection to be afforded to a defendant."

That would help defendants who were coerced into confessing by police, but would do nothing to help those who lost alibi witnesses or were convicted with the help of eyewitness testimony because of knowledge of a confession. To combat that problem, Hasel and much of the scientific community argues for double-blind testing when handling evidence, meaning that the police officer handling the lineup doesn't know which of the member of the lineup is the suspect. "So they can't consciously or unconsciously direct [witnesses] to a particular person," she says.

And she wants to investigate whether judges and jurors can understand this topic of evidence dependence—the idea that a confession contaminates other evidence. If jurors are told that a false confession may have tainted other evidence, are they able to look at it objectively and make their own judgment? Can judges grasp its ramifications on appeals? Kassin believes that, because of the persuasive potency of confessions and evidentiary dependence, it's not good enough for judges to look at the other evidence and determine that a jury would have convicted even without the coerced confession.

"If it turns out that the confession corrupted the other evidence, then there is no such thing as harmless error," Kassin said. "I don't think you can look at that other evidence once there is a confession out of the box because once the confession is out there, it corrupts all that other evidence."

CRITICAL THINKING QUESTIONS

1. The article states that jurors seeing the videotape of a false confession are less likely to convict if they see the videotape of the entire interrogation and not just the confession piece. Do you think courts should require juries to see the entire interrogation recording and not just the confession part? Why or why not? Defend your position.

2. Working within the legal system, would better educating lawyers, judges, and juries about the psychology of false confessions help lessen the possibility of wrongful convictions? If so, how would you go about educating these individuals, especially jury members?

3. For what possible reasons might police use coercive techniques during interrogations that result in false confessions? In addition to better educating police about the psychology of false confessions, what other safeguards could be implemented to help reduce the likelihood of an innocent person being convicted of a crime he or she did not commit?

4. Based on the information in Chapters 2 and 3 (on social perception and social cognition, respectively), what other sources of bias may affect courtroom proceedings? Explain your answer.

ARTICLE 41 _____

What factors may have an impact on determining the defendant's guilt or innocence? Jurors are asked to weigh the evidence presented during the trial. Hopefully, they will not permit irrelevant characteristics of the defendant—such as his or her physical appearance, race, or sex—to affect their judgment. But is it really possible to be totally objective in such situations? Or do irrelevant factors play a role in our beliefs about guilt or innocence?

The following article by Harold Sigall and Nancy Ostrove is a classic piece of research that investigated the impact of the defendant's physical attractiveness on the severity of sentences given to her. Earlier studies had indicated that physically attractive individuals often have great advantages over less attractive people in a variety of situations. This study not only examined the role of physical attractiveness in a trial-like setting but also how the nature of the crime and attractiveness interact to influence judgments about the defendant. The article also tests two different models that may explain why this particular effect occurs.

Beautiful but Dangerous
Effects of Offender Attractiveness and Nature of the Crime on Juridic Judgment
■ Harold Sigall and Nancy Ostrove

The physical attractiveness of a criminal defendant (attractive, unattractive, no information) and the nature of the crime (attractiveness-related, attractiveness-unrelated) were varied in a factorial design. After reading one of the case accounts, subjects sentenced the defendant to a term of imprisonment. An interaction was predicted: When the crime was unrelated to attractiveness (burglary), subjects would assign more lenient sentences to the attractive defendant than to the unattractive defendant; when the offense was attractiveness-related (swindle), the attractive defendant would receive harsher treatment. The results confirmed the predictions, thereby supporting a cognitive explanation for the relationship between the physical attractiveness of defendants and the nature of the judgments made against them.

Research investigating the interpersonal consequences of physical attractiveness has demonstrated clearly that good-looking people have tremendous advantages over their unattractive counterparts in many ways. For example, a recent study by Miller (1970) provided evidence for the existence of a physical attractiveness stereotype with a rather favorable content. Dion, Berscheid, and Walster (1972) reported similar findings: Compared to unattractive people, better-looking people were viewed as more likely to possess a variety of socially desirable attributes. In addition, Dion et al.'s subjects predicted rosier futures for the beautiful stimulus persons—attractive people were expected to have happier and more successful lives in store for them. Thus, at least in the eyes of others, good looks imply greater potential.

Since physical attractiveness hardly seems to provide a basis for an *equitable* distribution of rewards, one might hope that the powerful effects of this variable would occur primarily when it is the only source of information available. Unfair or irrational consequences of differences in beauty observed in some situations would cause less uneasiness if, in other situations given other important data, respondents would tend to discount such "superficial" information. Unfortunately, for the vast majority of us who have not been blessed with a stunning appearance, the evidence does not permit such consolation. Consider, for example, a recent study by Dion (1972) in which adult subjects were presented with accounts of transgressions supposedly committed by children of varying physical attractiveness. When the transgression was severe the act was viewed less negatively when committed by a good-looking child, than when the offender was unattractive. Moreover, when the child was unattractive the offense was more likely to be seen as reflecting some enduring dispositional quality: Subjects believed that unattractive children were more likely to be involved in future transgressions. Dion's findings, which indicate that unattractive individuals are penalized when there is no apparent logical relationship between the transgression and the way they look, underscore the importance of appearance because one could reasonably suppose that information describing a severe transgression would "overwhelm the field," and that the physical attractiveness variable would not have any effect.

Can beautiful people get away with murder? Although Dion (1972) found no differences in the punishment recommended for offenders as a function of attractiveness, Monahan (1941) has suggested that beautiful women are convicted less often of crimes they are accused of, and Efran (1974) has recently demonstrated that subjects are much more generous when assigning punishment to good-looking as opposed to unattractive transgressors.

The previous findings which indicate a tendency toward leniency for an attractive offender can be accounted for in a number of ways. For example, one might explain such results with the help of a reinforcement-affect model of attraction (e.g., Byrne & Clore, 1970). Essentially, the argument here would be that beauty, having positive reinforcement value, would lead to relatively more positive affective responses toward a person who has it. Thus we like an attractive person more, and since other investigators have shown that liking for a defendant increases leniency (e.g., Landy & Aronson, 1969), we would expect good-looking (better liked) defendants to be punished less than unattractive defendants. Implicit in this reasoning is that the nature of the affective response, which influences whether kind or harsh treatment is recommended, is determined by the stimulus features associated with the target person. Therefore, when other things are equal, benefit accrues to the physically attractive. A more cognitive approach might attempt to explain the relationship between physical appearance and reactions to transgressions by assuming that the subject has a "rational" basis for his responses. It is reasonable to deal harshly with a criminal if we think he is likely to commit further violations, and as Dion's (1972) study suggests, unattractive individuals are viewed as more likely to transgress again. In addition, inasmuch as attractive individuals are viewed as possessing desirable qualities and as having relatively great potential, it makes sense to treat them leniently. Presumably they can be successful in socially acceptable ways, and rehabilitation may result in relatively high payoffs for society.

There is at least one implication that follows from the cognitive orientation which would not flow readily from the reinforcement model. Suppose that situations do exist in which, because of his high attractiveness, a defendant is viewed as more likely to transgress in the future. The cognitive approach suggests that in such instances greater punishment would be assigned to the attractive offender. We might add that in addition to being more dangerous, when the crime is attractiveness related, a beautiful criminal may be viewed as taking advantage of a God-given gift. Such misappropriation of a blessing may incur animosity, which might contribute to severe judgments in attractiveness-related situations.

In the present investigation, the attractiveness of a defendant was varied along with the nature of the crime committed. It was reasoned that most offenses do not encourage the notion that a criminal's attractiveness increases the likelihood of similar transgressions in the future. Since attractive offenders are viewed as less prone to recidivism and as having greater potential worth, it was expected that under such circumstances an attractive defendant would receive less punishment than an unattractive defendant involved in an identical offense. When, however, the crime committed may be viewed as attractiveness-related, as in a confidence game, despite being seen as possessing more potential, the attractive defendant may be regarded as relatively more dangerous, and the effects of beauty could be expected to be cancelled out or reversed. The major hypothesis, then, called for an interaction: An attractive defendant would receive more lenient treatment than an unattractive defendant when the offense was unrelated to attractiveness; when the crime was related to attractiveness, the attractive defendant would receive relatively harsh treatment.

METHOD

Subjects and Overview

Subjects were 60 male and 60 female undergraduates. After being presented with an account of a criminal case, each subject sentenced the defendant to a term of imprisonment. One-third of the subjects were led to believe that the defendant was physically attractive, another third that she was unattractive, and the remainder received no information concerning appearance. Cross-cutting the attractiveness variable, half of the subjects were presented with a written account of an attractiveness-unrelated crime, a burglary, and the rest with an attractiveness-related crime, a swindle. Subjects were randomly assigned to condition, with the restriction that an equal number of males and females appeared in each of the six cells formed by the manipulated variables.

Procedure

Upon arrival, each subject was shown to an individual room and given a booklet which contained the stimulus materials. The top sheet informed subjects that they would read a criminal case account, that they would receive biographical information about the defendant, and that after considering the materials they would be asked to answer some questions.

The case account began on the second page. Clipped to this page was a 5× 8 inch card which contained routine demographic information and was identical in all conditions.[1] In the attractive conditions, a photograph of a rather attractive woman was affixed to the upper right-hand corner of the card; while in the unattractive conditions, a relatively unattractive photograph was affixed. No photograph was presented in the control conditions.

Subjects then read either the account of a burglary or a swindle. The burglary account described how the defendant,

Barbara Helm, had moved into a high-rise building, obtained a pass key under false pretenses, and then illegally entered the apartment of one of her neighbors. After stealing $2,200 in cash and merchandise she left town. She was apprehended when she attempted to sell some of the stolen property and subsequently was charged with breaking and entering and grand larceny. The swindle account described how Barbara Helm had ingratiated herself to a middle-aged bachelor and induced him to invest $2,200 in a nonexistent corporation. She was charged with obtaining money under false pretenses and grand larceny. In both cases, the setting for the offense and the victim were described identically. The information presented left little doubt concerning the defendant's guilt.

The main dependent measure was collected on the last page of the booklet. Subjects were asked to complete the following statement by circling a number between 1 and 15: "I sentence the defendant, Barbara Helm, to _____ years of imprisonment." Subjects were asked to sentence the defendant, rather than to judge guilt versus innocence in order to provide a more sensitive dependent measure.

After sentencing had been completed, the experimenter provided a second form, which asked subjects to recall who the defendant was and to rate the seriousness of the crime. In addition, the defendant was rated on a series of 9-point bipolar adjective scales, including physically unattractive (1) to physically attractive (9), which constituted the check on the attractiveness manipulation. A post-experimental interview followed, during which subjects were debriefed.

RESULTS AND DISCUSSION

The physical attractiveness manipulation was successful: The attractive defendant received a mean rating of 7.53, while the mean for the unattractive defendant was 3.20, $F(1, 108) = 184.29$, $p < .001$. These ratings were not affected by the nature of the crime, nor was there an interaction.

The criminal cases were designed so as to meet two requirements. First, the swindle was assumed to be attractiveness-related, while the burglary was intended to be attractiveness-unrelated. No direct check on this assumption was made. However, indirect evidence is available: Since all subjects filled out the same forms, we obtained physical attractiveness ratings from control condition subjects who were not presented with a photograph. These subjects attributed greater beauty to the defendant in the swindle condition ($X = 6.65$) than in the burglary condition ($X = 5.65$), $F(1, 108) = 4.93$, $p < .05$. This finding offers some support for our contention that the swindle was viewed as attractiveness-related. Second, it was important that the two crimes be viewed as roughly comparable in seriousness. This was necessary to preclude alternative explanations in terms of differential seriousness. Subjects rated the seriousness of the crime on a 9-point scale extending from not at all serious (1) to extremely serious (9). The resulting responses indicated that the second requirement was met: In the swindle condition the mean seriousness rating was 5.02; in the burglary condition it was 5.07 ($F < 1$).

Table 1 presents the mean punishment assigned to the defendant, by condition. Since a preliminary analysis demonstrated there were no differences in responses between males and females, subject sex was ignored as a variable. It can be seen that our hypothesis was supported: When the offense was attractiveness-unrelated (burglary), the unattractive defendant was more severely punished than the attractive defendant; however, when the offense was attractiveness-related (swindle), the attractive defendant was treated more harshly. The overall Attractiveness × Offense interaction was statistically significant, $F(2, 108) = 4.55$, $p < .025$, end this interaction was significant, as well, when the control condition was excluded, $F(1, 108) = 7.02$, $p < .01$. Simple comparisons revealed that the unattractive burglar received significantly more punishment than the attractive burglar, $F(1, 108) = 6.60$, $p < .025$, while the difference in sentences assigned to the attractive and unattractive swindler was not statistically significant, $F(1, 108) = 1.39$. The attractive-swindle condition was compared with the unattractive-swindle and control-swindle conditions also, $F(1, 108) = 2.00$, *ns*. Thus, strictly speaking, we cannot say that for the swindle attractiveness was a great liability; there was a tendency in this direction but the conservative conclusion is that when the crime is attractiveness-related, the advantages otherwise held by good-looking defendants are lost.

Another feature of the data worth considering is that the sentences administered in the control condition are almost identical to those assigned in the unattractive condition. It appears that being unattractive did not produce discriminatory responses, per se. Rather, it seems that appearance had its effect through the attractive conditions: The beautiful burglar got off lightly, while the beautiful swindler paid somewhat, though not significantly, more. It can be recalled that in the unattractive conditions the stimulus person was seen as relatively unattractive and not merely average looking. Therefore, the absence of unattractive-control condition differences does not seem to be the result of a weak manipulation in the unattractive conditions.

Perhaps it is possible to derive a small bit of consolation from this outcome, if we speculate that only the very attractive receive special (favorable or unfavorable) treatment, and that others are treated similarly. That is a less frightening conclusion than one which would indicate that unattractiveness brings about active discrimination.

TABLE 1 / Mean Sentence Assigned, in Years ($n = 20$ per cell)

Offense	Defendant Condition		
	Attractive	Unattractive	Control
Swindle	5.45	4.35	4.35
Burglary	2.80	5.20	5.10

As indicated earlier, previous findings (Efran, 1974) that attractive offenders are treated leniently can be interpreted in a number of ways. The results of the present experiment support the cognitive explanation we offered. The notion that good-looking people usually tend to be treated generously because they are seen as less dangerous and more virtuous remains tenable. The argument that physical attractiveness is a positive trait and therefore has a unidirectionally favorable effect on judgments of those who have it, would have led to accurate predictions in the burglary conditions. However, this position could not account for the observed interaction. The cognitive view makes precisely that prediction.

Finally, we feel compelled to note that our laboratory situation is quite different from actual courtroom situations. Most important, perhaps, our subjects made decisions which had no consequences for the defendant, and they made those decisions by themselves, rather than arriving at judgments after discussions with others exposed to the same information. Since the courtroom is not an appropriate laboratory, it is unlikely that actual experimental tests in the real situation would ever be conducted. However, simulations constitute legitimate avenues for investigating person perception and interpersonal judgment, and there is no obvious reason to believe that these processes would not have the effects in trial proceedings that they do elsewhere.

Whether a discussion with other jurors would affect judgment is an empirical, and researchable, question. Perhaps if even 1 of 12 jurors notes that some irrelevant factor may be affecting the jury's judgment, the others would see the light.

Especially now when the prospect of reducing the size of juries is being entertained, it would be important to find out whether extralegal considerations are more likely to have greater influence as the number of jurors decreases.

REFERENCES

Byrne, D., & Clore, G. L. A reinforcement model of evaluative responses. *Personality: An International Journal,* 1970, *1,* 103–128.

Dion, K. Physical attractiveness and evaluation of children's transgressions. *Journal of Personality and Social Psychology,* 1972, *24,* 207–213.

Dion, K., Berscheid, E., & Walster, E. What is beautiful is good. *Journal of Personality and Social Psychology,* 1972, *24,* 285–290.

Efran, M. G. The effect of physical appearance on the judgment of guilt, interpersonal attraction, and severity of recommended punishment in a simulated jury task. *Journal of Research in Personality,* 1974, *8,* 45–54.

Landy, D., & Aronson, E. The influence of the character of the criminal and victim on the decisions of simulated jurors. *Journal of Experimental Social Psychology,* 1969, *5,* 141–152.

Miller, A. G. Role of physical attractiveness in impression formation. *Psychonomic Science,* 1970, *19,* 241–243.

Monahan, F. *Women in crime.* New York: Washburn, 1941.

ENDNOTE

1. This information, as well as copies of the case accounts referred to below, can be obtained from the first author.

This study was supported by a grant from the University of Maryland General Research Board.

CRITICAL THINKING QUESTIONS

1. This article used pictures only of females to show defendants of varying attractiveness. Would the same results be obtained if male defendants were used? In other words, do you think that attractiveness stereotypes operate in the same way for males as for females? Defend your answer.

2. As the authors of the article noted, the methodology of the study differed from real-life jury trials in several ways. For example, subjects made their decisions alone and were presented with a paper description of the person and deed, not a real-life person and crime. Design a study that would investigate the same variables studied in the article in a more natural environment.

3. Would the results of this study be generalizable to situations other than jury trials? Think of a situation in which the attractiveness of a person making a request or performing a certain action may result in his or her being treated differentially as a result of his or her attractiveness. Explain your answer.

4. What implications do these findings have for the U.S. legal system? How could the effects of irrelevant factors such as attractiveness somehow be minimized in the real-world courtroom? For example, would telling the jurors beforehand about the tendency to let attractiveness influence their judgments make any difference? Why or why not?

ADDITIONAL RELATED READINGS

Ahola, A. S., Christianson, S. Å., & Hellström, Å. (2009). Justice needs a blindfold: Effects of gender and attractiveness on prison sentences and attributions of personal characteristics in a judicial process. *Psychiatry, Psychology and Law,* *16*(Suppl 1), S90–S100.

Beckham, C. M., Spray, B. J., & Pietz, C. A. (2007). Jurors' locus of control and defendants' attractiveness in death penalty sentencing. *The Journal of Social Psychology,* *147*(3), 285–298.

ARTICLE 42 _____

In the legal systems of the United States, Canada, and many other countries, the conviction and sentencing of a defendant is supposed to be based on the admissible evidence presented in the courtroom. What is considered *admissible* is usually based on precedent and other rules concerning the appropriateness of certain types of evidence. However, there are certain factors pertaining to the defendant that, while not admissible as evidence, are impossible to conceal from the jury. For example, Article 41 demonstrated how the physical attractiveness of the defendant may play an important role in the likelihood of his or her being convicted and the severity of his or her recommended punishment.

Besides physical attractiveness, many other personal characteristics of the defendant are obvious to the jury yet should not necessarily affect the decision it makes. Race, ethnic background, and perceived intelligence are but a few of the defendant characteristics that cannot be concealed from the jury. While such factors presumably should not enter into the decision making of the jury, they certainly may.

Most research studies examining the impact of various personal characteristics on the likelihood of being found guilty by a jury typically involve the use of mock juries, that is, not real-life juries. Furthermore, the methodology often involves having a subject read over trial information with a photograph of the attendant attached, with the subject then making a decision about guilt or innocence. However, these decisions are often made alone by the subjects whereas in the real world juries deliberate as a group. Can these jury deliberations influence the potential impact of factors such as physical attractiveness? The following article by Mark W. Patry examines the effect of deliberating on the physical attractiveness bias found by others. It may be that how a decision is reached mitigates the impact of physical attractiveness. This article, along with the information presented in Article 40 and 41, further demonstrates the many potential sources of bias and error that may influence the workings of the criminal justice system.

Attractive but Guilty: Deliberation and the Physical Attractiveness Bias[1,2]

■ Marc W. Patry

SUMMARY

The current study examined the effect of jury deliberation on the tendency for mock jurors to find attractive defendants guilty less often. It was expected that there would be an interaction between group deliberation (yes or no) and defendant's appearance (plain-looking or attractive). It was hypothesized that mock jurors who did not deliberate would be more likely to find a plain-looking defendant guilty and that deliberation would mitigate this effect. The study was a 2 × 2 between-subjects factorial design. Participants were assigned randomly to one of four conditions: attractive defendant/deliberation, attractive defendant/no deliberation, plain-looking defendant/deliberation, and plain-looking defendant/no deliberation. A total of 172 undergraduates from a small, rural college in Vermont contributed to this study: mock jurors were 70 men and 52 women, ages ranged from 18 to 52 years (M = 20.5, SD = 4.9). The hypothesis was supported. Mock jurors who did not deliberate were more likely to find the plain-looking defendant guilty, whereas mock jurors who deliberated were more likely to find the attractive defendant guilty.

Dion, Berscheid, and Walster (1972) were the first to examine a well-documented phenomenon in an article entitled "What is beautiful is good." They found that physically attractive individuals were thought to be more occupationally successful, have happier marriages, and generally have happier lives. Meta-analyses regarding this physical attractiveness bias have indicated that attractive people are perceived to be more intelligent, socially competent, better adjusted, i.e., having better mental health and higher self-esteem, and are generally evaluated more positively than unattractive individuals across a wide range of research paradigms (Eagly, Ashmore, Makhijani, & Longo, 1991; Feingold, 1992; Jackson, Hunter, & Hodge, 1995).

Researchers have also demonstrated a physical attractiveness bias in legal contexts. Mock jurors perceived attractive defendants as more trustworthy, likeable, sociable and intelligent than plain-looking defendants (Darby & Jeffers, 1988; Castellow, Wuensch, & Moore, 1990; Wuensch, Chia, Castellow, Chuang, & Cheng, 1993). Physical appearance has also affected legal decisions by mock jurors. Plain-looking defendants are more likely to be found guilty than attractive defendants (Efran, 1974; Izzett & Leginski, 1974; Deitz & Byrnes, 1981; Darby & Jeffers, 1988; MacCoun, 1990), and plain-looking defendants receive significantly longer prison sentences than attractive defendants (Sigall & Ostrove, 1975; Smith & Hed, 1979; Wuensch, *et al.*, 1993; DeSantis & Kayson, 1997). Meta-analysis of research on mock jurors confirms that physically attractive defendants are perceived as being less guilty and receive less severe punishments than plain-looking defendants (Mazzella & Feingold, 1994). There is also some evidence that attractiveness may aid both plaintiffs and defendants in civil trials (Stephan & Tully, 1977; Castellow, *et al.*, 1990). The few research studies conducted in actual courtroom settings to examine the real life occurrence of this bias have yielded strong relationships between physical attractiveness and lenient sentences (Stewart, 1980, 1985) as well as bail and fines (Downs & Lyons, 1991). However, physical attractiveness appears to be an advantage only for certain defendants and may even be a disadvantage when the facts suggest that they used their attractiveness in the execution of a crime (Sigall & Ostrove, 1975; Smith & Hed, 1979; Wuensch, *et al.*, 1993).

Research on physical attractiveness bias often relates directly to the judgment of a single mock juror instead of the opinion of a mock jury, a more realistic representation of actual courtroom proceedings (Mazzella & Feingold, 1994). The few studies conducted with jury deliberation and the physical attractiveness bias have yielded conflicting results. MacCoun (1990) reported that mock juries were more likely to acquit attractive defendants than plain-looking defendants. In his study, attractiveness was only an advantage for a defendant when the jury needed to reach a unanimous decision; predeliberation, jurors' ratings of guilt and innocence did not differ between the attractive and plain-looking defendants. Other research has shown that the physical attractiveness bias may actually be reduced through the use of small mock juries (Izzett & Leginski, 1974; Kaplan & Miller, 1978). Izzett and Leginski (1974) reported that prior to deliberation subjects gave plain-looking defendants significantly more severe punishments than attractive defendants. Following deliberation there were no differences between sentences issued by these two groups.

If juries are a successful means of reducing bias in jurors, what accounts for this effect? Kaplan and Miller (1978) proposed biases in jurors can be minimized through jury deliberation. They argued that an increase in informational content derived from jury deliberation is the mechanism through which juror bias can be reduced. According to their model, a juror's verdict is the weighted average of an individual's opinions prior to the trial, or preexisting bias, and the probative value of each piece of information presented in the trial. Deliberation has the effect of increasing the probative value of

the evidence presented in a trial, which reduces the effects of pre-existing bias.

The present study was based on dichotomous decisions of guilt from two groups of participants: mock jurors who deliberated before reaching a verdict and mock jurors who did not deliberate. The hypotheses for the present study were based on prior research and theory suggesting (a) bias in favor of physically attractive defendants and (b) the bias-reduction effect of jury deliberation. An interaction was expected between group deliberation prior to individual judgments (yes or no) and defendant appearance (plain-looking or attractive). More specifically, it was hypothesized that mock jurors who did not deliberate would be more likely to find a plain-looking defendant guilty, and that deliberation would mitigate this effect.

METHOD

Experimental Design

This study was a 2 × 2 between-subjects factorial design. Participants were assigned randomly to one of four conditions: attractive defendant/deliberation, attractive defendant/nondeliberation, plain-looking defendant/deliberation, and plain-looking defendant/nondeliberation.

Participants

A total of 172 undergraduates from a small, rural college in Vermont contributed to this study. Fifty pilot participants helped with selection of stimulus photographs, and 122 participants (70 men and 52 women; ages 18 to 52 years, $M = 20.5$, $SD = 4.9$) acted as mock jurors. Participants were recruited by word-of-mouth and flier advertisements. Most participants were volunteers, and in some cases received extra course credit in exchange for their participation.

Materials

Participants received a copy of a case summary describing an armed robbery. The stimulus case used in the study was based on an actual armed robbery which had been described in the media several months previously. Names and other case facts were changed to reduce participants' familiarity with the case. The 3-page summary detailed the case of a young woman accused of robbing a retail business at gun point. The victim of the robbery had identified the defendant from a mug shot book and a lineup. During her testimony, the victim also described a tattoo on the assailant's hand that matched a tattoo on the defendant's hand. The defendant testified that she could not have committed the acts because she was 75 miles away from the crime, staying at a motel. The case summary ended with closing remarks from both the prosecutor and the defense attorney.

The last page of the stimulus packet includes a 1-in. × 3-in. black and white photograph of the defendant (head and shoulders). The photograph appeared after the case summary to minimize the saliency of the attractiveness manipulation.

To operationalize attractiveness, 20 photographs were chosen from a high school senior yearbook unfamiliar to 20 pilot participants. These participants, 10 men and 10 women, were asked to rate each of the 20 pictures as either "plain-looking" or "attractive." The three photographs most often rated "attractive" and the three most rated "plain-looking" were used in a paired-comparison activity completed by an additional 30 pilot participants. These participants were asked to select the more attractive photograph in each pair. Each of the photographs was compared to the other five, resulting in 15 separate forced-choice comparison trials. The photograph most often chosen as more attractive was selected to be the "attractive" defendant, while the photograph least often chosen became the "plain-looking" defendant in this study.

Procedure

Mock jurors were randomly assigned to one of four conditions: non-deliberating/attractive, nondeliberating/plain-looking, deliberating/attractive, deliberating/plain-looking. Those in nondeliberating conditions reviewed a stimulus packet and immediately issued a written verdict of not guilty or guilty beyond a reasonable doubt. Deliberating participants were placed into mock juries numbering six. Though mock juries were not matched for sex, all mock juries contained at least one member of each sex. All participants in a given mock jury received the same set of stimulus materials. Brief oral instructions were provided to the mock juries asking them to discuss the case with a predisposition to changing their opinion based on the arguments of others. Participants were also encouraged to persuade others to see the case as they did. The mock juries were specifically admonished not to reach a formal group decision. Deliberation was limited to 20 min. All mock juries exhausted their discussion within the allotted time. Deliberating participants then provided written juror-level verdicts.

RESULTS

Logistic regression was used to analyze the effects of attractiveness and deliberation on the dichotomous guilt decisions. The overall model was significant [χ_3^2 ($N = 122$) = 46.55, $p < .001$]. There was a weakly significant main effect for deliberation. In comparison to participants who deliberated, participants who did not deliberate were more likely to find a defendant guilty beyond a reasonable doubt (odds ratio = .39, Wald = 3.70, $p = .054$). There was also a main effect of defendant's attractiveness: the plain-looking defendant was more

likely than the attractive defendant to be found guilty beyond a reasonable doubt (odds ratio = 3.13, Wald = 4.20, $p = .04$). However, these main effects were qualified by an interaction between deliberation and defendant physical attractiveness (odds ratio = .03, Wald = 8.08, $p = .004$).

Follow-up analyses showed that this interaction was in the expected pattern. Mock jurors who did not deliberate were more likely to issue guilty verdicts for the plain-looking defendant than for the attractive defendant [χ_1^2($N = 62$) = 4.35, $r = .27$, $p = .04$]. Conversely, mock jurors who deliberated were more likely to find guilty the attractive defendant [χ_1^2 ($N = 60$) = 6.41, $r = -.33$, $p = .01$; see Table 1].

DISCUSSION

The hypothesis was supported: mock jurors who did not deliberate were less likely to find an attractive defendant guilty than a plain-looking defendant. Deliberation seemed to eliminate a predeliberation bias in favor of the attractive defendant.

Deliberation had the expected effect in the sense that the bias against plain-looking defendants was not present: deliberating mock jurors were not more likely to issue guilty verdicts for the plain-looking defendant than for the attractive defendant. In fact, attractiveness had an opposite effect on jurors who deliberated; they were more likely to find an attractive defendant guilty. This finding is somewhat counterintuitive. Although previous research has suggested that deliberation can either mitigate the physical attractiveness bias (Izzett & Leginski, 1974) or exacerbate this bias (MacCoun, 1990), something new was observed in the present data: a reversal of the effect. Participants in the current study who deliberated in mock juries exhibited a bias against the attractive defendant.

TABLE 1 / Distribution of Participants' Verdict Decisions by Experimental Condition

| Group | Attractiveness Condition | | | |
| | Attractive | | Plain-looking | |
	n	%	*n*	%
Did not deliberate				
Not Guilty	13	48.1	8	22.9
Guilty	14	51.9	27	77.1
Total	27	100.0	35	100.0
Deliberated				
Not Guilty	22	73.3	29	96.7
Guilty	8	26.7	1	3.3
Total	30	100.0	30	100.0

Mazzella and Feingold (1994) suggested that attractive defendants are held to a higher standard than plain-looking defendants and may be more harshly reprimanded when they do not live up to those standards. More recent research has also shown that mock jurors are more likely to find an attractive defendant guilty when that attractive defendant is also perceived to be more responsible for the accused crime (Abwender & Hough, 2001). It is possible that, through the process of deliberation, participants in the current study came to feel the attractive defendant did not live up to this "higher standard."

This research has some limitations. Jurors who deliberated prior to making their judgment were instructed to deliberate with a predisposition to changing their minds. It is possible that this instruction, and not the deliberation process, reduced the physical attractiveness bias observed in the post-deliberation judgments or that the instruction at least contributed to that effect. There is also the possibility that placement of the photograph of the defendant at the end of the materials had the unintended effect of making it more salient to participants, in line with the well-established recency effects from cognitive psychology. Another limitation to the current study was that deliberation and time were confounded. Because mock jurors who did not deliberate made immediate judgments and because deliberating mock jurors had a delayed judgment (i.e., the amount of time that the mock jury deliberated), the effects of deliberation from the current study must be replicated, perhaps with a filler task for nondeliberating participants to eliminate the problem of time and deliberation. As such, further research is required to clarify the effects of deliberation on physical attractiveness bias, and more generally as well.

Research, including the present study, is somewhat limited with regard to external validity. Mock juror participants are not jurors in actual cases, and paper-and-pencil stimuli are not very similar to actual trials. By minimizing the artificiality of experimental conditions, researchers could improve upon these limitations. Researchers should attempt to use participants who are representative of the types of individuals likely to serve on actual juries. Experimental stimuli and other conditions should be as realistic as possible. Jury size is another consideration for these types of studies: it has been well-documented that juries numbering 12 differ in their decision-making processes from juries comprising fewer jurors (see Saks & Marti, 1997). It may also be worthwhile to examine the effects of deliberation on reducing predeliberation biases when the juries are required to reach unanimous decisions. Jurors' sex is another potentially important issue which was not addressed in the current study. Researchers should examine the effects of deliberation in terms of jurors' biases with regard to defendants' attractiveness.

The present study adds to the literature by contributing an experimental manipulation of jury deliberation to an already well-established bias in favor of attractive criminal defendants. Analyses suggested that group deliberation can have a bias-reduction function with respect to the physical attractiveness bias. Researchers should replicate and extend these findings in more externally valid settings to specify the exact nature and parameters of the effects of deliberation on juror bias.

REFERENCES

ABWENDER, D. A., & HOUGH, K. (2001) Interactive effects of characteristics of defendant and mock juror on U.S. participants' judgment and sentencing recommendations. *The Journal of Social Psychology*, 141, 603–615. [electronic version]

CASTELLOW, W. A., WUENSCH, K. L., & MOORE, C. H. (1990) Effects of physical attractiveness of the plaintiff and defendant in sexual harassment judgments. *Journal of Social Behavior & Personality*, 5, 547–562.

DARBY, B. W., & JEFFERS, D. (1988) The effects of defendant and juror attractiveness on simulated courtroom trial decisions. *Social Behavior and Personality*, 16, 39–50.

DEITZ, S. R., & BYRNES, L. E. (1981) Attribution of responsibility for sexual assault: the influence of observer empathy and defendant occupation and attractiveness. *Journal of Psychology*, 108, 17–29.

DESANTIS, A., & KAYSON, W. (1997) Defendants' characteristics of attractiveness, race, and sex and sentencing decisions. *Psychological Reports*, 81, 679–683.

DION, K., BERSCHEID, E., & WALSTER, E. (1972) What is beautiful is good. *Journal of Personality and Social Psychology*, 24, 285–290.

DOWNS, A. C., & LYONS, P. M. (1991) Natural observations of the links between attractiveness and initial legal judgments. *Personality and Social Psychology Bulletin*, 17, 541–547.

EAGLY, A. H., ASHMORE, R. D., MAKHIJANI, M. G., & LONGO, L. C. (1991) What is beautiful is good, but . . . : a meta-analytic review of research on the physical attractiveness stereotype. *Psychological Bulletin*, 110, 109–128.

EFRAN, M. G. (1974) The effect of physical appearance on the judgment of guilt, interpersonal attraction, and severity of recommended punishment in a simulated jury task. *Journal of Research in Personality*, 8, 45–54.

FEINGOLD, A. (1992) Good looking people are not what we think. *Psychological Bulletin*, 11, 304–341.

IZZETT, R., & LEGINSKI, W. (1974) Group discussion and the influence of defendant characteristics in a simulated jury setting. *Journal of Social Psychology*, 93, 271–279.

JACKSON, L. A., HUNTER, J. E., & HODGE, C. N. (1995) Physical attractiveness and intellectual competence: a meta-analytic review. *Social Psychology Quarterly*, 58, 108–122.

KAPLAN, M. F., & MILLER, L. E. (1978) Reducing the effects of juror bias. *Journal of Personality and Social Psychology*, 36, 1443–1455.

MACCOUN, J. M. (1990) The emergence of extralegal bias. *Criminal Justice and Behavior*, 17, 303–314.

MAZZELLA, R., & FEINGOLD, A. (1994) The effects of physical attractiveness, race, socioeconomic status, and gender of defendants and victims on judgments of mock jurors: a meta-analysis. *Journal of Applied Social Psychology*, 24, 1315–1344.

SAKS, M. J., & MARTI, M. W. (1997) A meta-analysis of the effects of jury size. *Law & Human Behavior,* 21, 451–467.

SIGALL, H., & OSTROVE, N. (1975) Beautiful but dangerous: effects of offender attractiveness and nature of crime on juridic judgment. *Journal of Personality and Social Psychology,* 31, 410–414.

SMITH, E. D., & HED, A. (1979) Effects of offenders' age and attractiveness on sentencing by mock juries. *Psychological Reports,* 44, 691–694.

STEPHAN, C., & TULLY, J. C. (1977) The influence of physical attractiveness of a plaintiff on the decisions of simulated jurors. *Journal of Social Psychology,* 101, 149–150.

STEWART, J. E. II (1980) Defendant's attractiveness as a factor in the outcome of criminal trials: an observational study. *Journal of Applied Social Psychology,* 10, 348–361.

STEWART, J. E. II (1985) Appearance and punishment: the attraction-leniency effect in the courtroom. *Journal of Social Psychology,* 125, 373–378.

WUENSCH, K. L., CHIA, R. C., CASTELLOW, W. A., CHUANG, C., & CHENG, B. (1993) Effects of physical attractiveness, sex, and type of crime on mock juror decisions. *Journal of Cross-cultural Psychology,* 24, 414–427.

CRITICAL THINKING QUESTIONS

1. Are the findings of studies such as this one, which employed simulated jury trials, relevant to the real world of jury trials? Why or why not? How might the results of such studies be of use in making real-world jury trials more impartial and fair? Explain your answers.

2. What other issues from social psychology might be used to explain the findings of this study? For example, what concepts from topics such as prejudice, interpersonal attraction, social perception, social cognition, and attitudes may be of use in understanding these findings?

3. The previous article (Article 41) found that attractive defendants were generally less likely to be convicted of crimes than less attractive individuals. The present study, which added jury deliberation to what was examined, reversed that finding, with attractive defendants being more likely to be convicted when the decision was reached by jury deliberation. How would *you* explain these differential results, going beyond what was presented in the article, in discussing your answer?

4. The author of the article suggests that limitations of laboratory studies such as this one as well as most others could be improved "by minimizing the artificiality of experimental conditions." What are those artificial conditions, and how could they possibly be controlled? Are there any external limitations constraining how such research can be done? Explain your reasoning.

*CHAPTER INTEGRATION QUESTIONS*_____

1. By this time, you have undoubtedly read many of the previous chapters in this book. What other chapters and topics have particular relevance to the field of forensic psychology? Be specific in discussing how these chapters/topics may be of importance to forensic psychology.

2. What theme or themes are common to all three of the articles in this chapter? Explain.

3. "Justice is truth in action," according to Benjamin Disraeli, former British Prime Minister. What does this quotation mean to you? Based on the research presented in this chapter, how true is this quote? Explain your answer.

Chapter Fifteen

HEALTH PSYCHOLOGY

THIS FINAL CHAPTER addresses the contributions of social psychology to health issues. When we think of health, often the first thing that comes to mind is the medical or biological component of illness. But what about the behaviors that are linked to illness? Obviously, we can do many things to increase or decrease the likelihood of becoming ill. *Health psychology,* which has a long and strong connection with social psychology, is concerned with the psychosocial factors affecting the prevention, development, and treatment of physical illness.

Think of the various chapters and topics that you have read about in this book thus far. In one way or another, virtually every one of them has some implications for health psychology. For example, how we think about the social world around us (social cognition), our views of ourselves (social identity), how we form and change attitudes and the connection between attitudes and behaviors (attitudes), the impact of being subject to prejudice (prejudice), the role of supportive relationships (helping behavior), and the role of conformity in starting (or stopping) unhealthy behaviors (social influence) are all topics in social psychology that have direct implications for health.

Article 43 discusses the current thinking regarding the causes of stress and how in turn stress negatively impacts our psychological and physical well-being. "Understanding the Have-Knots" reports that even small negative events can affect us in major ways over the long run. However, we also have the power to change many of these factors that ultimately might cause us harm.

We all know that stress can cause illness, but can even positive events make us sick? Perhaps it is not just negative events but anything that makes us adapt and change that causes stress. From this view, getting married may be almost as stressful as getting fired from work. Article 44, "The Social Readjustment Rating Scale," is a classic article about pioneering work on how life changes in general may affect health.

Finally, Article 45 examines how the terrorist attacks of September 11, 2001, may have affected people. Unlike many studies on people's reactions to traumatic events, "Psychosocial Predictors of Resilience After the September 11, 2001 Terrorist Attacks" looked at the underlying reasons why quite a number of people who were exposed to the trauma did not exhibit lasting, negative reactions to it. The heartening message from this study is that people may be a lot more resilient to trauma than is commonly believed. By identifying the factors that help promote such resilience, we may be able to help people in their adjustment to other traumatic events.

ARTICLE 43 _____

Over the years, numerous connections have been made between personality/lifestyle factors and health. Perhaps the best-known link is that between stress and health. But what is *stress?* To a large extent, it is subjective. What is a source of stress for one person may be a neutral or even positive experience for another. Effectively, then, *stress* may be defined as physical, mental, or emotional strain or tension. It has evolved as a shortened version of the word *distress.*

Many studies have linked the amount of stress people experience with negative health consequences. Sometimes, these negative consequences are the direct result of stress—for instance, developing cardiovascular disease as a result of having elevated blood pressure. In other cases, the health problems may stem from behaviors developed in response to stress, such as smoking out of nervousness and contracting lung cancer. Thus, an important factor in determining the impact of stress on health is one's ability to cope. Someone who has developed effective coping mechanisms in response to stress is less likely to develop stress-related health problems than someone with less effective coping mechanisms.

While the sources and manifestations of stress may be unique to each individual, certain factors seem to predispose most people to health risks. For example, anger and hostility have been linked to cardiovascular disease in numerous studies. Likewise, factors such as social isolation may not only predispose individuals to disease but also impair their recovery from illness. The following article by Eric Wargo examines contemporary thinking on the nature of stress. The bad news is that the experience of stressors may have lasting physical and psychological impacts on people. The good news is that we can learn to experience a less stressful life.

Understanding the Have-Knots

■ Eric Wargo

"I can't express anger. I grow a tumor instead."
—Woody Allen

You live in a majorly stressed out world. You're never very far from a ringing cell phone or a guilt-inducing laptop. Traffic makes you flip out. And as if stressing out over lines, health, your job, your grades, or global terrorism wasn't enough, along comes the APS *Observer* with one more thing in your life to stress out over: *Stress.*

Stress, to put it bluntly, is bad for you. It can kill you, in fact. Medicine used to be skeptical that the mind could have a direct effect on the body, but any doubt of that has, alas, gone the way of the dinosaur or the relaxing weekend. Study after study now reveals that stress causes deterioration in everything from your gums to your heart and can make you more susceptible to everything from the common cold to cancer. The mind-body connection is real, and it is powerful, and thanks to new research crossing the disciplines of psychology, medicine, neuroscience, and genetics, the mechanisms underlying the connection are rapidly becoming understood.

AXIS POWERS

The first clues to the link between stress and health were provided in the 1930s by Hans Selye, the first scientist to apply the word "stress"—then simply an engineering term—to the strains experienced by living organisms in their struggles to adapt and cope with changing environments.

One of Selye's major discoveries was that the stress hormone cortisol had a long-term effect on the health of rats. Cortisol has been considered one of the main culprits in the stress-illness connection, although it plays a necessary role in helping us cope with threats.

When an animal perceives danger, a system called the hypothalamic-pituitary-adrenal (or HPA) axis kicks into gear: A chain reaction of endocrine signals beginning in the hypothalamus results in the release of various hormones—most notably epinephrine ("adrenaline"), norepinephrine, and cortisol—from the adrenal glands above each kidney. These hormones boost heart rate, increase respiration, and increase the availability of glucose (cellular fuel) in the blood, thereby enabling the famous "fight or flight" reaction. Because these responses take a lot of energy, cortisol simultaneously tells other costly physical processes—including digestion, reproduction, physical growth, and some aspects of the immune system—to shut or slow down.

The HPA axis is a self-regulating (homeostatic) mechanism, a lot like a thermostat. Stress hormones act back upon the hypothalamus to inhibit production of more signaling chemicals, thus causing less stress hormones to be released down the line. When occasions to fight or flee are infrequent and threats pass quickly, the body's stress thermostat adjusts accordingly: Cortisol levels return to baseline (it takes 40-60 minutes), the intestines resume digesting food, the sex organs kick back into gear, and the immune system resumes fighting infections. But problems occur when stresses don't let up—or when, for various reasons, the brain continually perceives stress even if it isn't really there.

DANGER! DANGER!

Stress begins with the perception of danger by the brain, and it appears that continued stress can actually bias the brain to perceive more danger by altering brain structures such as the medial prefrontal cortex (mPFC) and amygdala, which govern the perception of and response to threat. Prolonged exposure to cortisol inhibits the growth of new neurons in the mPFC, an area that ordinarily acts to inhibit the HPA axis, and can cause increased growth of the amygdala, the portion of the brain that controls fear and other emotional responses. The end result is heightened expectation of and attention to threats in the environment (see Fox et al., 2007).

Stress hormones also inhibit neuron growth in parts of the hippocampus, a brain area essential in forming new memories. In this way, stress results in memory impairments and impairs the brain's ability to put emotional memories in context (Sapolsky, 1994). Think of it this way: Too much stress and you forget not to be stressed out. These brain changes are thought by some researchers to be at the heart of the link between stress and depression—one of stress's most devastating health consequences—as well as posttraumatic stress disorder (PTSD).

The best known of stress's health impacts are on the heart.

The idea that stress directly causes coronary heart disease has been around since the 1950s; although once controversial (or thought to be mediated solely by behavioral responses like smoking or overeating), the direct stress-cardiac link is now well-documented by many studies. For instance, men who faced chronic stresses at work or at home ran a 30 percent higher likelihood of dying over the course of a nine-year study; in another study, individuals reporting neglect, abuse, or other stressors in childhood were over three times as likely as nonstressed individuals to develop heart disease in adulthood (Miller & Blackwell, 2006).

Stress appears to be cumulative. Although when we think of stressors we might think of big things like abuse, illness, divorce, grieving, or getting fired, it is now known that the little things—traffic, workplace politics, noisy neighbors, a long line at the bank—can add up and have a similar impact on our well-being and our health. People who report more minor irritants in their lives also have more mental and physical health problems than those who encounter fewer hassles (Almeida, 2005). And recent research shows that PTSD may be the result of stressors adding up like building blocks, remodeling the plastic brain in a cumulative rather than a once-and-for-all fashion (Kolassa and Elbert, 2007).

To designate the cumulative wear and tear on physical systems due to long-term overactivation of the stress response, Rockefeller University neuroendocrinologist Bruce McEwen (1998) developed the concept of "allostatic load." Studies showing serious health consequences of allostatic load on the rest of the body's systems are numerous and growing. Besides heart disease, PTSD, and depression, chronic stress has been linked to ailments as diverse as intestinal problems, gum disease, erectile dysfunction, adult-onset diabetes, growth problems, and even cancer. Chronic rises in stress hormones have been shown to accelerate the growth of precancerous cells and tumors; they also lower the body's resistance to HIV and cancer-causing viruses like human papilloma virus (the precursor to cervical cancer in women; see Antoni & Lutgendorf, 2007).

Adding insult to injury, stress may even have a self-perpetuating effect. Depression and heart disease, for example, are not only the results of stress, but also causes of (more) stress. Consequently, the chronically stressed body can appear less like a thermostat than like a wailing speaker placed too close to a microphone—a feedback loop in which the stress response goes out of control, hastening physical decline with age.

TUNING THE STRESS RESPONSE

Growing evidence shows that our sensitivity to stress as adults is already "tuned," so to speak, in infancy. Specifically, the amount of stress encountered in early life sensitizes an organism to a certain level of adversity; high levels of early life stress may result in hypersensitivity to stress later, as well as to adult depression. A history of various stressors such as abuse and neglect in early life are a common feature of those with chronic depression in adulthood, for example (see Gillespie & Nemeroff, 2007).

At McGill University in Montreal, Michael J. Meaney and his colleagues have studied mother and infant rats, using rat maternal behavior as a model of early life stress and its later ramifications in humans. The key variable in the world of rat nurturance is licking and grooming. Offspring of rat mothers who naturally lick and groom their pups a lot are less easily startled as adults and show less fear of novel or threatening situations—in other words, less sensitivity to stress—than offspring of less nurturant mothers. The same thing is true of offspring of naturally less nurturant mothers who are raised (or "cross-fostered") by more nurturant ones. By the same token, low-licking-and-grooming rat mothers are themselves more fearful than the more nurturant rat moms; but again, female offspring of those non-nurturant mothers foster-parented by nurturant mothers show less fear and are themselves more nurturant when they have pups of their own. This indicates that the connection between maternal nurturance and stress responsiveness is not simply genetic, but that fearfulness and nurturance are transmitted from generation to generation through maternal behavior (Parent et al., 2005).

A mechanism responsible for this tuning of the stress response is found at the "top" part of the HPA axis. One of the signaling chemicals released by the hypothalamus in response to stress is called CRF (for corticotropin-releasing factor—so-named because its function is to tell the pituitary gland to release another hormone, corticotropin, or ACTH, which in turn signals the adrenal glands to kick into action). Adult rats who had been well licked and groomed as pups show inhibition of CRF receptors in the amygdala (Parent et al., 2005).

In its extreme form, the human equivalent of low licking and grooming is child abuse and neglect. Research on abuse and neglect in humans and its connection to anxiety disorders, depression, and PTSD in later life shows the same CRF-mediated mechanism. Elevated levels of CRF are found in the cerebrospinal fluid of individuals with depression, and people who have committed suicide have been found to have changes in the frontal cortex consistent with chronic elevation of CRF (Gillespie & Nemeroff, 2007). More subtly, the degree of maternal care predicts trait anxiety and the responsiveness of an individual's HPA axis to stress. In one study, adult children of Holocaust survivors showed altered HPA response and higher PTSD incidence, indicating that responsiveness to stress can be transmitted behaviorally from generation to generation in humans, as in other animals (Yehuda et al., 2000).

A GOOD RESPONSE GONE BAD

The vicious cycle of stress hormones biasing us to perceive more threat and react with an increased stress response might seem like some kind perverse joke played by nature—or at least a serious design flaw in the brain. But it makes better sense if we take the brain out of its modern, urban, "civilized" context.

The stress response is a necessary response to danger. For animals, including most likely our hominid ancestors, behavioral transmission of individual differences in stress reactivity from parents to offspring makes sense as an adaptation to fluctuating levels of danger in the environment. Animals raised in chronically adverse conditions (e.g., high conflict, material deprivation) may

expect more of the same in the near future; so in effect the maternal treatment of offspring attunes them to the level of stress they may expect to encounter in their lives (Parent et al., 2005). As such, a response that seems baffling and counterproductive in a modern, civilized context may make more sense in the context of our distant evolutionary past.

Even depression has been theorized as playing an adaptive role in certain contexts. The inactivity, lack of motivation, loss of interest in pleasurable activities like sex, and withdrawal from social relationships experienced by depressed people closely resemble "sickness behavior"—the energy-saving lethargy activated by the immune system in response to infection (see Miller & Blackwell, 2006). In a natural setting, the hopeless attitude of depression may be the most adaptive for an organism infected with a pathogen: The best strategy for survival is not to expend energy fruitlessly and become exposed to predators, but to hunker down, hide from threats, and direct energy to immune processes where it's needed.

According to Stanford neuroendocrinologist Robert Sapolsky, who has studied stress in baboon troops, it is the relative safety from predators and high amounts of leisure time enjoyed by some primates—including humans—that has transformed these useful biological coping mechanisms into a source of pointless suffering and illness (Sapolsky, 1994). (Yes, it turns out that baboons suffer from depression and other stress-related disorders, just like people do.)

MIND-BODY MECHANISMS

The great challenge in stress psychology—and the necessary precursor to developing interventions against stress's harmful effects—has been understanding the mechanisms by which thoughts and feelings and other "mental" stuff can affect bodily health. For many years, it was believed that the main causal link between stress and disease was the immune suppression that occurs when the body redirects its energy toward the fight-or-flight response. But recent research has revealed a far more nuanced picture. Stress is known to actually enhance one important immune response, inflammation, and increasingly this is being seen as the go-between in various stress-related diseases.

Ordinarily, inflammation is how the healthy body deals with damaged tissue: Cells at the site of infections or injuries produce signaling chemicals called proinflammatory cytokines. These cytokines in turn attract other immune cells to the site, to help repair it. Cytokines also travel to the brain and activate the HPA axis, and they are responsible for initiating sickness behavior. Overactive cytokine production has been found to put individuals at greater risk for a variety of aging-related illnesses (Robles, Glaser, & Kiecolt-Glaser, 2005).

Cytokines may be an important mediator in the relationship between stress and heart disease. When the arteries feeding the heart are damaged, cytokines induce more blood flow, and thus more white blood cells, to the site. White blood cells accumulate in vessel walls and, over time, become engorged with cholesterol, becoming plaques; these may later become destabilized and rupture, causing heart attacks (Miller & Blackwell, 2006). Cytokine action also has been implicated in the link between stress and depression. People suffering from clinical depression have shown 40–50 percent higher concentrations of certain inflammatory cytokines. And about 50 percent of cancer patients whose immune responses are artificially boosted through the administration of cytokines show depressive symptoms.

The close connection between inflammation and both depression and heart disease has led some researchers to theorize that inflammation may be what mediates the two-way street between these two conditions: Depression can lead to heart disease, but heart disease also often leads to depression (Miller & Blackwell, 2006). Sleep may be part of this puzzle too, as disturbed sleep, which often goes with anxiety and depression, increases levels of proinflammatory cytokines in the body (Motivala & Irwin, 2007).

STRESSED-OUT PERSONALITIES

Not everyone responds the same way to stress. Personality traits like negativity, pessimism, and neuroticism are known to be risk factors for stress-related disease, as are anger and hostility.

In the late 1950s, Friedman and Rosenman (1959) identified a major link between stress and health with their research on the "Type A" personality: a person who is highly competitive, aggressive, and impatient. This personality was found to be a strong predictor of heart disease, and later research clarified the picture: The salient factors in the relationship between the Type A personality and health are mainly anger, hostility, and a socially dominant personality style (for example, tending to interrupt other people when they are talking; see Smith, 2006). When negative emotions like anger are chronic, it is as if the body is in a constant state of fight or flight (with the allostatic load this state entails).

There is now evidence that another trait associated with success-striving in the modern world—persistence—may also lead to health problems in some circumstances. When goals are not readily attainable, the inability to detach from them may produce frustration, exhaustion, rumination on failures, and lack of sleep. These in turn activate harmful inflammatory responses that can lead to illness and lowered immunity (Miller & Wrosch, 2007).

The bottom line: Woody Allen's neurotic character who grows a tumor instead of releasing his anger isn't far from the truth.

By the same token, studies have shown that optimistic people have lower incidence of heart disease, better prognosis after heart surgery, and longer life. The effects of a positive attitude on immunity were shown in a study by APS Fellow

---

The Social Side of Stress

Any kind of frustration or challenge can cause stress, but by far the most powerful stressors, as measured by physiological stress responses, are those caused by disrupted or absent social relationships (Koolhaas, de Boer, & Buwalda, 2006). Loss of friends and loved ones, inadequate nurturance, and social isolation all have major impact on health and well-being.

At the University of Chicago, APS President John Cacioppo and Louise Hawkley have studied the health effects of social isolation, an increasingly common malady in the modern world. Among their findings are that lonely older adults show more arterial stiffening and higher blood pressure than their nonlonely counterparts and that the association between loneliness and blood pressure increases with age (see Hawkley & Cacioppo, 2007, for a review).

Cacioppo and Hawkley also found that loneliness directly impacts the HPA axis. In middle-aged and older adults (but not young adults), loneliness is associated with higher levels of epinephrine in the blood, and lonely people of all ages show elevated levels of cortisol. By

desensitizing the mechanism whereby cortisol turns off more cortisol production, the social isolation frequently experienced by older adults may hasten physical decline (Hawkley & Cacioppo, 2007). Lonely individuals of all ages also have poorer sleep than nonlonely people and therefore get less of sleep's essential restorative benefits.

Humans and other social animals particularly seek the company of others when facing threats—both for safety and for social support. The general affiliative response—what APS Fellow and Charter Member Shelley Taylor, UCLA, has called "tending and befriending" (Taylor, 2006)—is mediated by the hormone oxytocin. Oxytocin rises during times of separation or disrupted social relations. Just as the familiar "adrenaline rush" of epinephrine induces the familiar fight-or-flight reaction, it is oxytocin that causes us to desire company and social togetherness. It may be especially important in females, reflecting their different reproductive and survival priorities from those of males—i.e., caregiving (tending offspring) and lessening social tensions through friendly overtures (befriending).

and Charter Member Sheldon Cohen, Carnegie Mellon University, and his colleagues, in which individuals were exposed to a cold virus in a laboratory setting and watched over six days. Those with a positive emotional style were less likely to develop colds than were individuals with low levels of positive affect (Cohen & Pressman, 2006). (Note that researchers like Cohen distinguish low levels of positive affect from negative affect—a low level of positive affect does not necessarily mean a high level of negative affect, and vice versa.) Positive affect was also found to be correlated with reduced symptom severity and reduced pain. Conscientiousness also has been found to predict longevity (see Smith, 2006). Cohen's research earned him APS's top honor, the James McKeen Cattell Award, in recognition of his contributions toward understanding the effects of social and environmental stress on human behavior and health and the impact of his research across a range of fields.

THE FUTURE: BEHAVIORAL GENETICS

Personality and environmental factors are not the whole story when it comes to stress. The next frontier of stress research is the rapidly growing field of behavioral genetics. Modeling the interaction of genetic and environmental influences is no longer a matter of weighing the relative input of nature and nurture. The two intertwine in subtle and complicated ways, with environments affecting gene expression, and vice versa, throughout life. Thus, the current watchword is "stress-diathesis" models, in which environmental stressors have varying impact on individuals due to preexisting inherited vulnerabilities.

One major advance in this area was the discovery by APS Fellow and Charter Member Avshalom Caspi, University of Wisconsin, and his colleagues of a link between stress sensitivity and a particular gene called *5HTTLPR*. This gene controls a protein that regulates the amount of the neurotransmitter serotonin (5HTT) available in the synaptic cleft (space between neurons). Individuals possessing two "short" variants (or alleles) of this gene and who also had experienced five or more stressful life events were more likely to have a depressive episode than similarly stressed individuals who had two "long" alleles of the gene (Caspi et al., 2003). In other words, a certain genetic makeup seems to increase risk for a serious illness through the mechanism of increased sensitivity to stressful occurrences.

Nathan Fox, University of Maryland, and his colleagues subsequently reported that children with two short alleles of the *5HTTLPR* gene whose mothers also reported receiving low social support were more likely to show behavioral inhibition (fearfulness and a tendency to withdraw) at age 7. Those receiving high support did not show the tendency, and those with the long alleles but receiving low support also appeared "protected" by

their genetic makeup. Behavioral inhibition may put a child at risk for mental illness in later life (Fox et al., 2007).

Genetic predisposition to stress sensitivity may in some cases become a self-fulfilling cycle. Fox and colleagues found that some very behaviorally inhibited children were regarded by their mothers as hard to soothe and received less care and sensitivity as a result; this in turn tuned up the child's sensitivity to stress through the alterations in the mPFC and amygdala mentioned earlier. In the model Fox and colleagues propose, genetically influenced temperament in early childhood influences the quality of caregiving children receive, which in turn shapes a child's attention bias to threat.

A CUP HALF FULL

So Nietzsche's strenuous view of life, "whatever doesn't kill me makes me stronger," just plain isn't true. Stressors that don't kill you in the short run may yet shorten your life or drastically lessen its quality.

But quit your moping and look on the bright side: The newly refined science of stress could lead to new drug therapies that can control stress or inhibit its effects on health. Also, depression and anxiety are not only results of stress, but also causes, and existing therapeutic and medical treatments for these conditions can help change how people perceive threats, put their life challenges in context, and cut stressors down to manageable size. The cycle doesn't have to be vicious, in other words.

What's more, the confirmation that the mind directly affects the body can work as much in our favor as it does to our detriment, as the personality-and-stress research above indicates. As APS Fellow Carol Dweck, Stanford University, has argued, personality is mutable (see Herbert, 2007); if our outlooks and beliefs about ourselves can be changed, so (theoretically) can our vulnerability to life's slings and arrows.

The bottom line: Stress is not inevitable. Even with more than one's fair share of vulnerability genes, there's plenty of room to take one's life and one's mind in a less stressful direction. Relaxation techniques such as meditation and yoga, for example, have been confirmed to quell stress demons. Even if you are a determined workaholic glued to your cell phone or a fearful and angry urban neurotic like Woody Allen, stress-reduction methods are readily available to cope with stress in the short term and even alter perceptions of stressors in the long term.

Meyer Friedman, co-discoverer of the link between "Type A" behavior and heart disease, is a case in point. A self-described Type-A personality, Friedman wound up suffering a heart-attack at age 55. He made the conscious choice to change his ways in accordance with his own discoveries—including following his own prescription by reading the classics. To get more in touch with his slow, patient, and creative side, he read Proust's languid seven-volume opus *Remembrance of Things Past* three times. In short, he trained himself to relax and enjoy life, and he had the last laugh at stress by living to the ripe old age of 90.

REFERENCES

Almeida, D.M. (2005). Resilience and vulnerability to daily stressors assessed via diary methods. *Current Directions in Psychological Science, 14*, 64–68.

Antoni, M.H., & Lutgendorf, S. (2007). Psychosocial factors and disease progression in cancer. *Current Directions in Psychological Science, 16*, 42–46.

Caspi, A., Snugden, K., Moffitt, T.E., Taylor, A., Craig, I.W., Harrington, H., *et al.* (2003). Influence of life stress on depression: Moderation by a polymorphism in the 5-HTT gene. *Science, 301*, 386–389.

Cohen, S., & Pressman, S.D. (2006). Positive affect and health. *Current Directions in Psychological Science, 15*, 122–125.

Cutrona, C.E., Wallace, G., & Wesner, K.A. (2006). Neighborhood characteristics and depression: An examination of stress processes. *Current Directions in Psychological Science, 15*, 188–192.

Fox, N.A., Hane, A.A., & Pine, D.S. (2007). Plasticity for affective neurocircuitry: How the environment affects gene expression. *Current Directions in Psychological Science, 16*, 1–5.

Friedman, M., & Rosenman, R.H. (1959). Association of specific overt behavior patterns with blood and cardiovascular findings: Blood cholesterol level, blood clotting time, incidence of arcus senilis and clinical coronary artery disease. *Journal of the American Medical Association, 169*, 1286–1296.

Gillespie, C.F., & Nemeroff, C.B. (2007). Corticotropin-releasing factor and the psychobiology of early-life stress. *Current Directions in Psychological Science, 16*, 85–89.

Hawkley, L.C., & Cacioppo, J.T. (2007). Aging and loneliness: Downhill quickly? *Current Directions in Psychological Science, 16*, 187–191.

Herbert, W. (2007, August). How beliefs about the self shape personality and behavior. *APS Observer, 20*(7), 9–11.

Kolassa, I.-T., & Elbert, T. (2007). Structural and functional neuroplasticity in relation to traumatic stress. *Current Directions in Psychological Science, 16*, 321–325.

Koolhaas, J.M., de Boer, S.F., & Buwalda, B. (2006). Stress and adaptation: Toward ecologically relevant animal models. *Current Directions in Psychological Science, 15*, 109–112.

McEwen, B.S. (1998). Protective and damaging effects of stress mediators. *New England Journal of Medicine, 338*, 171–179.

Miller, G.E., & Blackwell, E. (2006). Turning up the heat: Inflammation as a mechanism linking chronic stress, depression, and heart disease. *Current Directions in Psychological Science, 15*, 269–272.

Miller, G.E., & Wrosch, C. (2007). You've gotta know when to fold 'em: Goal disengagement and systemic inflammation in adolescence. *Psychological Science, 18*, 773–777.

Motivala, S.J., & Irwin, M.R. (2007). Sleep and immunity: Cytokine pathways linking sleep and health outcomes. *Current Directions in Psychological Science, 16*, 21–25.

Parent, C., Zhang, T.-Y., Caldji, C., Bagot, R., Champagne, F.A., Pruessner, J., & Meaney, M.J. (2005). Maternal care and individual differences in defensive responses. *Current Directions in Psychological Science, 14*, 229–233.

Robles, T.F., Glaser, R., & Kiecolt-Glaser, J.K. (2005). Out of balance. A new look at chronic stress, depression, and immunity. *Current Directions in Psychological Science, 14*, 111–115.

Sapolsky, R. (1994). *Why zebras don't get ulcers: A guide to stress, stress-related disease and coping.* New York Scientific American/Freeman Press.

Smith, T.W. (2006). Personality as risk and resilience in physical health. *Current Directions in Psychological Science, 15*, 227–231.

Taylor, S.E. (2006). Tend and befriend: Biobehavioral bases of affiliation under stress. *Current Directions in Psychological Science, 15*, 273–277.

Yehuda, R., Bierer, L.M., Schmeidler, J., Aferiat, D.H., Breslau, I., & Dolan, S. (2000). Low cortisol and risk for PTSD in adult offspring of Holocaust survivors. *American Journal of Psychiatry, 157*, 1252–1259.

CRITICAL THINKING QUESTIONS

1. Examine a social psychology textbook to learn more about the psychosocial factors associated with disease. Based on this evidence, what factors may predispose *you* to disease later in life? What interventions can you make now to lower your risk from these factors?

2. The article indicates that how we think about the world may impact what we experience as stress. Chapter 3 of this book dealt with the concept of social cognition. What cognitive tendencies from that section might make us more or less likely to experience stress? Explain your reasoning.

3. As a culture, do Americans endorse certain values and/or behaviors that might make them more susceptible to stress? If so, what are they and how might they negatively affect them? Are there other cultures that have a value system that might be less stress-prone? Give an example of such a group and what values they may have that might make them less susceptible to stress.

4. The article gives some examples of how our responses to stress may be learned from our environment and those around us. What other experiences might have an impact on us, making us more or less likely to experience stress?

5. Have you known someone who has successfully reduced stress in their lives? If so, how did they do it? If you know someone who has not made such changes already, what information from this article could you share with them as possible things they could change? Explain your answer.

ARTICLE 44 _____

Just about everyone these days accepts the idea that stress can cause illness. However, this concept was not always deemed to be true. In the past, it was commonly believed that illness was due to germs and organ pathology. There was not much focus on what was going on in a person's life that actually might be causing the illness.

A new view of the relationship between stress and illness was pioneered by the work of Hans Selye a half century ago. Selye defined *stress* as the body's physiological response to threatening events, whether physiological or psychological in nature. Thus, Selye was the first to clearly demonstrate that a purely psychological state, such as worrying too much about something, could produce a negative physiological state.

While Selye began to expand our understanding of how psychological states could produce physiological consequences, other researchers began to examine specifically what types of events might produce stress and consequently physical changes. The following classic article by Thomas H. Holmes and Richard H. Rahe represents the beginning of a line of research that tried to relate life events and health. Holmes and Rahe suggest that *stress* is the extent to which people have to readjust or change their lives in response to an outside event. Thus, a great deal of stress would be associated with a major life change, such as getting divorced, while considerably less stress would be associated with a lesser life change, such as getting a parking ticket. Furthermore, any life change, positive or negative, could produce such stress. Getting married, which involves many changes in a person's life, is a good example of how an event typically thought of as positive may nonetheless produce stress.

This article by Holmes and Rahe discusses the methodology that they used in developing their scale, which has been widely reproduced and used in many research studies. For example, several subsequent studies have found that the higher a person scores on this scale, the more likely his or her physical health will suffer.

Our understanding of the relationship between stress and health has become much more complex over the years. For example, the original Holmes and Rahe scale assumed that anyone experiencing a divorce would find that event to be extremely stressful. But isn't it possible that someone in a terribly abusive relationship might actually find that getting divorced lessens his or her stress? A critical factor may be our subjective interpretation of the events that we experience. That is, it may not be the event itself that causes stress but how we subjectively react to it. Certainly, a given event is not viewed the same by everyone who experiences it. While the Holmes and Rahe scale does not take this subjective reaction into account, it is nonetheless a good example of how the research on stress and health began.

The Social Readjustment Rating Scale[1]

■ Thomas H. Holmes and Richard H. Rahe

In previous studies [1] it has been established that a cluster of social events requiring change in ongoing life adjustment is significantly associated with the time of illness onset. Similarly, the relationship of what has been called 'life stress,' 'emotional stress,' 'object loss,' etc. and illness onset has been demonstrated by other investigations [2–13]. It has been adduced from these studies that this clustering of social or life events achieves etiologic significance as a necessary but not sufficient cause of illness and accounts in part for the time of onset of disease.

Methodologically, the interview or questionnaire technique used in these studies has yielded only the number and types of events making up the cluster. Some estimate of the magnitude of these events is now required to bring greater precision to this area of research and to provide a quantitative basis for new epidemiological studies of diseases. This report defines a method which achieves this requisite.

METHOD

A sample of convenience composed of 394 subjects completed the paper and pencil test (Table 1). (See Table 2 for characteristics of the sample.) The items were the 43 life events empirically

Holmes, T.H.; & Rahe, R. H. "The social readjustment rating scale." *Journal of Psychosomatic Research*, 11, 213–218. Copyright © 1967 Elsevier. Reprinted with permission.

TABLE 1 / Social Readjustment Rating Questionnaire

Events	Values
1. Marriage	500
2. Troubles with the boss	—
3. Detention in jail or other institution	—
4. Death of spouse	—
5. Major change in sleeping habits (a lot more or a lot less sleep, or change in part of day when asleep)	—
6. Death of a close family member	—
7. Major change in eating habits (a lot more or a lot less food intake, or very different meal hours or surroundings)	—
8. Foreclosure on a mortgage or loan	—
9. Revision of personal habits (dress, manners, associations, etc.)	—
10. Death of a close friend	—
11. Minor violations of the law (e.g. traffic tickets, jay walking, disturbing the peace, etc.)	—
12. Outstanding personal achievement	—
13. Pregnancy	—
14. Major change in the health or behavior of a family member	—
15. Sexual difficulties	—
16. In-law troubles	—
17. Major change in number of family get-togethers (e.g. a lot more or a lot less than usual)	—
18. Major change in financial state (e.g. a lot worse off or a lot better off than usual)	—
19. Gaining a new family member (e.g. through birth, adoption, oldster moving in, etc.)	—
20. Change in residence	—
21. Son or daughter leaving home (e.g. marriage, attending college, etc.)	—
22. Marital separation from mate	—
23. Major change in church activities (e.g. a lot more or a lot less than usual)	—
24. Marital reconciliation with mate	—
25. Being fired from work	—
26. Divorce	—
27. Changing to a different line of work	—
28. Major change in the number of arguments with spouse (e.g. either a lot more or a lot less than usual, regarding childrearing, personal habits, etc.)	—
29. Major change in responsibilities at work (e.g. promotion, demotion, lateral transfer)	—
30. Wife beginning or ceasing work outside the home	—
31. Major change in working hours or conditions	—
32. Major change in usual type and/or amount of recreation	—
33. Taking on a mortgage greater than $10,000 (e.g. purchasing a home, business, etc.)	—
34. Taking on a mortgage or loan less than $10,000 (e.g. purchasing a car, TV, freezer, etc.)	—
35. Major personal injury or illness	—
36. Major business readjustment (e.g. merger, reorganization, bankruptcy, etc.)	—
37. Major change in social activities (e.g. clubs, dancing, movies, visiting, etc.)	—
38. Major change in living conditions (e.g. building a new home, remodeling, deterioration of home or neighborhood)	—
39. Retirement from work	—
40. Vacation	—
41. Christmas	—
42. Changing to a new school	—
43. Beginning or ceasing formal schooling	—

TABLE 2 / Pearson's Coefficient of Correlation between Discrete Groups in the Sample

Group	No. in Group		Group	No. in Group	Coefficient of Correlation
Male	179	vs.	Female	215	0-965
Single	171	vs.	Married	223	0-960
Age < 30	206	vs.	Age 30–60	137	0-958
Age < 30	206	vs.	Age > 60	51	0-923
Age 30–60	137	vs.	Age > 60	51	0-965
1st Generation	19	vs.	2nd Generation	69	0-908
1st Generation	19	vs.	3rd Generation	306	0-929
2nd Generation	69	vs.	3rd Generation	306	0-975
< College	182	vs.	4 Years of College	212	0-967
Lower class	71	vs	Middle class	323	0-928
White	363	vs.	Negro	19	0-820
White	363	vs.	Oriental	12	0-940
Protestant	241	vs.	Catholic	42	0-913
Protestant	241	vs.	Jewish	19	0-971
Protestant	241	vs.	Other religion	45	0-948
Protestant	241	vs.	No religious preference	47	0-926

derived from clinical experience. The following written instructions were given to each subject who completed the Social Rating Questionnaire (SRRQ).

(A) Social readjustment includes the amount and duration of change in one's accustomed pattern of life resulting from various life events. As defined, social readjustment measures the intensity and length of time necessary to accommodate to a life event, *regardless of the desirability of this event.*

(B) You are asked to rate a series of life events as to their relative degrees of necessary readjustment. In scoring, *use all of your experience* in arriving at your answer. This means personal experience where it applies as well as what you have learned to be the case for others. Some persons accommodate to change more readily than others; some persons adjust with particular ease or difficulty to only certain events. Therefore, strive to give your opinion of the average degree of readjustment necessary for each event rather than the extreme.

(C) The mechanics of rating are these: Event 1, Marriage, has been given an arbitrary value of 500. As you complete each of the remaining events think to yourself, "Is this event indicative of more or less readjustment than marriage?" "Would the readjustment take longer or shorter to accomplish?" If you decide the readjustment is more intense and protracted, then choose a *proportionately larger* number and place it in the blank directly opposite the event in the column marked "VALUES." If you decide the event represents less and shorter readjustment than

marriage then indicate how much less by placing a *proportionately smaller* number in the opposite blank. (If an event requires intense readjustment over a short time span, it may approximate in value an event requiring less intense readjustment over a long period of time.) If the event is equal in social readjustment to marriage, record the number 500 opposite the event.

The order in which the items were presented is shown in Table 1.

RESULTS

The Social Readjustment Rating Scale (SRRS) is shown in Table 3. This table contains the magnitude of the life events which is derived when the mean score, divided by 10, of each item for the entire sample is calculated and arranged in rank order. That consensus is high concerning the relative order and magnitude of the means of items is demonstrated by the high coefficients of correlation (Pearson's r) between the discrete groups contained in the sample. Table 2 reveals that all the coefficients of correlation are above 0-90 with the exception of that between white and Negro which was 0-82. Kendall's coefficient of concordance (W) for the 394 individuals was 0-477, significant at $p = < 0-0005$.

DISCUSSION

Placed in historical perspective, this research evolved from the chrysalis of Psychobiology generated by Adolph Meyer [14]. His invention of the 'life chart,' a device for organizing the

TABLE 3 / Social Readjustment Rating Scale

Rank	Life Event	Mean Value
1	Death of spouse	100
2	Divorce	73
3	Marital separation	65
4	Jail term	63
5	Death of close family member	63
6	Personal injury or illness	53
7	Marriage	50
8	Fired at work	47
9	Marital reconciliation	45
10	Retirement	45
11	Change in health of family member	44
12	Pregnancy	40
13	Sex difficulties	39
14	Gain of new family member	39
15	Business readjustment	39
16	Change in financial state	38
17	Death of close friend	37
18	Change to different line of work	36
19	Change in number of arguments with spouse	35
20	Mortgage over $10,000	31
21	Foreclosure of mortgage or loan	30
22	Change in responsibilities at work	29
23	Son or daughter leaving home	29
24	Trouble with in-laws	29
25	Outstanding personal achievement	28
26	Wife begin or stop work	26
27	Begin or end school	26
28	Change in living conditions	25
29	Revision of personal habits	24
30	Trouble with boss	23
31	Change in work hours or conditions	20
32	Change in residence	20
33	Change in schools	20
34	Change in recreation	19
35	Change in church activities	19
36	Change in social activities	18
37	Mortgage or loan less than $10,000	17
38	Change in sleeping habits	16
39	Change in number of family get-togethers	15
40	Change in eating habits	15
41	Vacation	13
42	Christmas	12
43	Minor violations of the law	11

medical data as a dynamic biography, provided a unique method for demonstrating his schema of the relationship of biological, psychological, and sociological phenomena to the processes of health and disease in man. The importance of many of the life events used in this research was emphasized by Meyer: ". . . changes of habitat, of school entrance, graduations or changes or failures; the various jobs, the dates of possibly important births and deaths in the family, and other fundamentally important environmental influences" [14].

More recently, in Harold G. Wolff's laboratory,[2] the concepts of Pavlov, Freud, Cannon and Skinner were incorporated in the Meyerian schema. The research resulting from this synthesis adduced powerful evidence that 'stressful' life events, by evoking psychophysiologic reactions, played an important causative role in the natural history of many diseases [15–19]. Again, many of the life events denoted 'stressful' were those enumerated by Meyers and in Table 1 of this report.

Beginning in this laboratory in 1949, the life chart device has been used systematically in over 5000 patients to study the quality and quantity of life events empirically observed to cluster at the time of disease onset. Inspection of Table 1 reveals that each item derived from this experience is unique. There are 2 categories of items: those indicative of the life style of the individual, and those indicative of occurrences involving the individual. Evolving mostly from ordinary, but some from extraordinary, social and interpersonal transactions, these events pertain to major areas of dynamic significance in the social structure of the American way of life. These include family constellation, marriage, occupation, economics, residence, group and peer relationships, education, religion, recreation and health.

During the developmental phase of this research the interview technique was used to assess the meaning of the events for the individual. As expected, the psychological significance and emotions varied widely with the patient. Also it will be noted that only some of the events are negative or 'stressful' in the conventional sense, i.e. are socially undesirable. Many are socially desirable and consonant with the American values of achievement, success, materialism, practicality, efficiency, future orientation, conformism and self-reliance.

There was identified, however, one theme common to all these life events. The occurrence of each usually evoked or was associated with some adaptive or coping behavior on the part of the involved individual. Thus, each item has been constructed to contain life events whose advent is either indicative of or requires a significant change in the ongoing life pattern of the individual. The emphasis is on change from the existing steady state and not on psychological meaning, emotion, or social desirability.

The method for assigning a magnitude to the items was developed for use in Psychophysics—the study of the psychological perception of the quality, quantity, magnitude, intensity of physical phenomena. This subjective assessment of the observer plotted against the physical dimension being perceived (length of objects, intensity of sound, brightness of light, number of objects, etc.) provides a reliable delineation of man's ability to quantify certain of his experiences [20]. In this research, the assumption was made that participants in the contemporary American way of life could utilize this innate psychological capacity for making quantitative judgments about psychosocial phenomena as well as psychophysical phenomena [21, 22]. The data generated by this investigation appear to justify the assumption. Although some of the discrete subgroups do assign a different order and magnitude to the items, it is the degree of similarity between the populations within the sample that is impressive. The high degree of consensus also suggests a universal agreement between groups and among individuals about the significance of the life events under study that transcends differences in age, sex, marital status, education, social class, generation American, religion and race.

The method used in this research, when applied to psychophysical phenomena, generates a ratio scale. A discussion of whether or not the magnitudes assigned to the items in Table 3 actually constitute a ratio scale is beyond the intent of this report [21, 22]. However, this issue will be dealt with in a subsequent report [23].

REFERENCES

1. Rahe R. H., Meyer M., Smith M., Kjaer G. and Holmes T. H. Social stress and illness onset. *J. Psychosom. Res. 8,* 35 (1964).

2. Graham D. T. and Stevenson I. Disease as response to life stress. In *The Psychological Basis of Medical Practice* (H. I. Lief, V. F. Lief, and N. R. Lief, Eds.) Harper & Row, New York (1963).

3. Greene W. A., Jr. Psychological factors and reticulo-endothelial disease—I. Preliminary observations on a group of males with lymphomas and leukemias. *Psychosom. Med. 16,* 220 (1954).

4. Greene W. A. Jr., Young L. E. and Swisher S. N. Psychological factors and reticulo-endothelial disease—II. Observations on a group of women with lymphomas and leukemias. *Psychosom. Med. 18,* 284 (1956).

5. Greene W. A., Jr. and Miller G. Psychological factors and reticulo-endothelial disease—IV. Observations on a group of children and adolescents with leukemia: an interpretation of disease development in terms of the mother-child unit. *Psychosom. Med. 20,* 124 (1958).

6. Weiss E., Dlin B., Rollin H. R., Fischer H. K. and Bepler C. R. Emotional factors in coronary occlusion. *A.M.A. Archs. Internal Med. 99,* 628 (1957).

7. Fischer H. K., Dlin B., Winters W., Hagner S. and Weiss E. Time patterns and emotional factors related to the onset of coronary occlusion. [Abstract] *Psychosom. Med. 24,* 516 (1962).

8. Kissen D. M. Specific psychological factors in pulmonary tuberculosis. *Hlth Bull. Edinburgh 14,* 44 (1956).

9. Kissen D. M. Some psychosocial aspects of pulmonary tuberculosis. *Int. J. Soc. Psychiat. 3,* 252 (1958).

10. Hawkins N. G., Davies R. and Holmes T. H. Evidence of psychosocial factors in the development of pulmonary tuberculosis. *Am. Rev. Tuberc. Pulmon. Dis. 75,* 5 (1957).

11. Smith M. Psychogenic factors in skin disease, Medical Thesis, University of Washington, Seattle (1962).

12. Rare R. H. and Holmes T. H. Social, psychologic and psychophysiologic aspects of inguinal hernia. *J. Psychosom. Res. 8,* 487 (1965).

13. Kjaer G. Some psychosomatic aspects of pregnancy with particular reference to nausea and vomiting, Medical Thesis, University of Washington, Seattle (1959).

14. Lief A. (Ed.) *The Commonsense Psychiatry of Dr. Adolf Meyer,* McGraw-Hill, New York (1948).

15. Wolff H. G., Wolf S. and Hare C. C. (Eds.) *Life Stress and Bodily Disease,* Res. Publs. Ass. Res. Nerv. Ment. Dis. Vol. 29. Williams & Wilkins, Baltimore (1950).

16. Holmes T. H., Goodell H., Wolf S. and Wolff H. G. *The Nose. An Experimental Study of Reactions Within the Nose in Human Subjects During Varying Life Experiences,* Charles C. Thomas, Springfield, Illinois (1950).

17. Wolf S. *The Stomach,* Oxford University Press, New York (1965).

18. Wolf S., Cardon P. V., Shepard E. M., and Wolff H. G. *Life Stress and Essential Hypertension,* Williams & Wilkins, Baltimore (1955).

19. Grace W. J., Wolf S. and Wolff H. G. *The Human Colon,* Paul B. Hoeber, New York (1951).

20. Stevens S. S. and Galanter E. H. Ratio scales and category scales for a dozen perceptual continua. *J. Exp. Psychol. 54,* 377 (1957).

21. Sellin T. and Wolfgang M. E. *The Measurement of Delinquency,* John Wiley, New York (1964).

22. Stevens S. S. A metric for the social consensus. *Science 151,* 530 (1966).

23. Masuda M. and Holmes T. H. This issue, p. 219.

ENDNOTES

1. This investigation was supported in part by Public Health Service Undergraduate Training in Psychiatry Grant No. 5-T2-MH-5939-13 and Undergraduate Training in Human Behavior Grant No. 5-T2-MH-7871-03 from the National Institute of Mental Health; O'Donnell Psychiatric Research Fund; and The Scottish Rite Committee for Research in Schizophrenia.

2. Harold G. Wolff, M.D. (1898-1962) was Anne Parrish Titzell, Professor of Medicine (Neurology), Cornell University Medical College and the New York Hospital.

CRITICAL THINKING QUESTIONS

1. Examine the methodology that Holmes and Rahe used. For example, subjects were asked not only how stressful they found the events to be but also how stressful they thought other people typically found the events to be. Is this a problem? If so, why? If not, why not? What other issues in how Holmes and Rahe collected their data might limit the conclusions that they have drawn? Be specific in your answers.

2. Examine the items on the Social Readjustment Rating Scale (Table 3). Are any "life events" missing from the scale that you think are important stressors? If so, what are they, and why are they important? Why do you think these items were not included in the original scale?

3. The introduction to the article mentioned how the subjective perception of events may be more critical in determining stress reactions than the objective events themselves. In other words, not everyone reacts to the same situation in the same manner. Select an item from the scale, and give a concrete example of how you have seen two people react to it in very different ways.

4. According to this scale, getting married is more stressful than getting fired and hence more likely to cause physical illness. Do you accept the premise that *positive* life events, such as getting married, are just as stressful as *negative* life events, such as getting fired? Why or why not? If positive life events cause stress and hence illness, why do people seek them out in the first place? Explain your reasoning.

ADDITIONAL RELATED READINGS

Guoping, H., Yalin, Z., Yuping, C., Momartin, S., & Ming, W. (2010). Relationship between recent life events, social supports, and attitudes to domestic violence: Predictive roles in behaviors. *Journal of Interpersonal Violence, 25*(5), 863–876.

van den Berg, A. E., Maas, J., Verheij, R. A., & Groenewegen, P. P. (2010). Green space as a buffer between stressful life events and health. *Social Science & Medicine, 70*(8), 1203–1210.

ARTICLE 45 _____

Do you remember exactly where you were and what you were doing when you first heard of the terrorist attacks on September 11, 2001? For most people in the United States, and indeed the world, the destruction of the World Trade Center in New York City and the attack on the Pentagon in Arlington, Virginia, are events they will always remember. Whether we were 10 or 10,000 miles away from the horrific events of that day, few of us can say that we were not profoundly affected by them.

Given the impact of the events of 9–11, it only stands to reason that they represented a stressor in the lives of many people. Obviously, the more directly affected someone was by the attacks—such as knowing a person who was killed or injured—the more stressful the events were. But even people far removed from the events were profoundly affected. And so, the events of 9–11 were believed to be a major stressor and, as such, to have many negative effects on people's psychological well-being and physical health.

At least, that was what common sense and much media reporting reasoned. In the weeks, months, and years following the events of 9–11 (and other terrorist acts as well, such as the Madrid train bombings), commentators and experts alike took to the press and the airwaves to discuss how these events were going to affect us all. In particular, they claimed, children's sense of safety and security would be greatly diminished in the aftermath.

But do you think that all of the people who witnessed the events of 9–11 were affected in the same way? Current thinking on the impact of stress is that the subjective interpretation we make of the events is what causes stress, rather than the events per se. Thus, two people experiencing the same event could react quite differently to it, depending on their individual subjective interpretations of it.

The following article by Lisa D. Butler, Cheryl Koopman, Jay Azarow, Christine M. Blasey, Juliette C. Magadalene, Sue DiMiceli, David A. Seagraves, T. Anderew Hastings, Xin-HuaChen, Robert W. Garlan, Helena C. Kraemer, and David Spiegel examines the resilience of the population indirectly exposed to the September 11 terrorist attack. Indirectly exposed means those individuals who were not present at the sites of the attacks nor knew someone who was, but instead experienced it indirectly via television, radio, and/or newspaper reporting. Most studies on reaction to trauma have focused on the symptoms or problems people experience after being exposed to trauma. This study, in a sense, focuses on the opposite questions: Namely, how many people were resilient to the traumatic event and did not experience any negative effects, and perhaps most importantly, why were they not negatively affected?

Psychosocial Predictors of Resilience After the September 11, 2001 Terrorist Attacks

■ Lisa D. Butler, Cheryl Koopman, Jay Azarow, Christine M. Blasey, Juliette C. Magdalene, Sue DiMiceli, David A. Seagraves, T. Andrew Hastings, Xin-Hua Chen, Robert W. Garlan, Helena C. Kraemer, and David Spiegel

ABSTRACT

The terrorist attacks of September 11, 2001 inflicted distress beyond those directly exposed, thereby providing an opportunity to examine the contributions of a range of factors (cognitive, emotional, social support, coping) to psychological resilience for those indirectly exposed. In an Internet convenience sample of 1281, indices of resilience (higher well-being, lower distress) at baseline (2.5–12 weeks post-attack) were each associated with less

emotional suppression, denial and self-blame, and fewer negative worldview changes. After controlling for initial outcomes, baseline negative worldview changes and aspects of social support and coping all remained significant predictors of 6-month outcomes, with worldview changes bearing the strongest relationship to each. These findings highlight the role of emotional, coping, social support, and particularly, cognitive variables in adjustment after terrorism.

Butler, L.D.; Koopman, C.; Azarow, J.; Blasey, C.B.; Magadalene, J.C.; DiMiceli, S.; Seagraves, D.A.; Hastings, T.A.; Chen, X.; Garlan, R.W.; Kraemer, H.C.; & Spiegel, D. "Psychosocial predictors of resilience after the September 11, 2001 terrorist attacks". *The Journal of Nervous and Mental Disease, 197*(4), 266–273. Copyright (c) 2009 Wolters Kluwer Health. Reprinted with permission.

The events of September 11, 2001 were a collective trauma without parallel in modern American experience. The scale of death and destruction, the sinister nature of the attacks as deliberate acts of terrorism, and the repeated presentation of disturbing images in the mass media made for a potentially traumatic experience not only for those directly exposed, but also for millions of others around the country and world. Not surprisingly, several epidemiological surveys documented negative effects both in the New York and Washington DC areas and in the United States as a whole, including acute stress, posttraumatic stress disorder (PTSD) symptoms, and depression (DeLisi et al., 2003; Galea et al., 2002; Knudsen et al., 2005; Schlenger et al., 2002; Schuster et al., 2001; Silver et al., 2002), with much higher rates among those directly exposed to the attacks or residing near the World Trade Center (Galea et al., 2002) and among relief workers at Ground Zero (Zimering et al., 2006).

Findings from these national probability samples also indicate considerable impact on those who were neither personally affected nor living near an attack site. Schuster et al. (2001) found that, 3 to 5 days after the attacks, two-thirds of a representative sample of 560 Americans acknowledged being troubled by one or more stress symptoms of at least moderate intensity. Silver et al. (2002) documented that 17% of the US population outside of the New York area reported September 11, 2001-related PTSD symptoms 2 months after the attacks, even though less than 2% of that sample had firsthand experience of the attacks or knew someone injured or killed during them. It is worth noting that indirect exposure, particularly through mass media, is the type of exposure that the greatest number of people will likely experience in the event of future terrorism, and consequently reactions in this context warrant study.

However, most individuals exposed—even directly—to terrorism or other large-scale collective trauma experiences are not severely traumatized, but instead, exhibit remarkable resilience (Norris et al., 2002; North, 2001). Yet the factors that account for positive outcomes in the face of such events are not well understood.

Psychological resilience refers to "the process of, capacity for, or outcome of successful adaptation despite challenging or threatening circumstances" (Masten et al., 1990, pp. 426; Butler et al., 2003, 2007; O'Leary and Ickovics, 1995). When the term resilience is applied to the process of adaptation it may refer to positive characteristics of the recovery trajectory, such as suffering less initial disturbance before full recovery from the event or faster recovery from the setback (Butler et al., 2007). However, resilience is most widely used to refer to event-relevant outcomes. For example, in developmental studies of resilience among at-risk children, resilience is typically defined in terms of specific age-salient outcomes, such as the achievement of specific social competencies or developmental tasks (Luthar and Cicchetti, 2000; Masten et al., 1999).

In the present study, individual-level resilience is examined with respect to two relevant psychological outcomes in the aftermath of September 11, 2001. Specifically, resilience is operationalized as the maintenance or achievement of a relatively low level of distress and/or a high level of psychological well-being. With respect to distress, Luthar and Cicchetti (2000) have noted that "optimal outcome indicators are those that are conceptually most relevant to the risk encountered, so that when there are serious life adversities such as exposure to war, the absence of psychiatric distress can be a more logical outcome than excellence in functioning" (pp. 858). Psychological well-being offers another psychological dimension of import after trauma because it represents more than the absence of distress or dysphoria; instead, it encompasses overall satisfaction with life and global happiness, and also existential concerns such as meaning and self-realization (Diener et al., 1999; Ryan et al., 2000; Ryff and Keyes, 1995).

Resilient outcomes appear to be the product of a range of psychosocial and other factors (Butler et al., 2007; Garlan et al., 2005; Norris et al., 2002; O'Leary and Ickovics, 1995), including beliefs and attitudes, such as worldview/existential outlook, emotional expression, the availability and quality of social resources, specific coping strategies, and demographic features, in addition to characteristics of the traumatic event. Several studies have examined one or more of these psychosocial variables after the September 11, 2001 attacks. Silver et al. (2002) assessed coping styles in a national sample and found that behavioral disengagement, denial, self-distraction, self-blame, or the seeking of social support were associated with distress and trauma symptoms, while active coping and acceptance appeared to be protective. Galea et al. (2002) found that those who reported higher levels of social support in the 6 months before the attacks had lower levels of attack-related depression and PTSD, while Wayment (2004) found that the presence of a social environment that inhibited discussion of feelings after the terrorist attacks was associated with higher levels of distress. Furthermore, research on disasters has shown that trauma-related changes in existential worldview correlate with both positive and negative psychological outcomes (Joseph et al., 1993), and this holds true for the events of September 11, 2001 (Butler et al., 2005; Linley et al., 2003). Similarly, after the first World Trade Center attack in 1993, Difede et al (1997) noted that patients reported that the most distressing aspect of their experience—more distressing even than their PTSD symptoms—was that fundamental beliefs about themselves, others, and the world had been damaged (Janoff-Bulman, 1985; Janoff-Bulman, 1989). Thus, understanding resilient outcomes requires attention to cognitive as well as affective, social, and coping variables. Additionally, because the majority of people are exposed to terrorism through the media, and because the degree of such exposure has been found to be associated with outcomes (Ahern et al., 2004; Pfefferbaum et al., 1999; Schlenger et al., 2002), assessing media exposure appears to be necessary to understanding the determinants of psychological adjustment in the context of terrorism.

However, despite the clinical and empirical research attesting to the importance of cognitive, emotional, social support, and coping factors to adjustment during and after traumatic experience, few studies have compared the contributions of these factors when examined together in the prediction of psychological outcomes. The present study, which used a large Internet convenience sample, was designed in the immediate wake of the September 11, 2001 terrorist attacks to assess variables from these 4 psychosocial domains as potential correlates and predictors of negative and positive psychological responses to the event. Because previous research indicates that adjustment (Norris et al., 2002), coping (Blanchard et al., 2004), and processing of the event (Fivush et al., 2003) may vary with the level of traumatic event exposure, in the present analyses we restricted our sample to those indirectly exposed to the events to examine the relative contributions of cognitive, emotional, coping, social support, and media variables in the immediate aftermath of the attacks to short and longer-term indices of resilience. Indirect exposure, in this case, refers to those without firsthand experience of the attacks or loss or injury of someone close due to the attacks.

METHODS

Data Collection

To acquire data as quickly as possible, we developed a brief initial questionnaire package, obtained Institutional Review Board approval, and posted a research website on a secure University server on September 28, 2001 (described in Butler et al., 2002). Over 7000 individuals accessed the website and consented to participate (and to be recontacted for the 6-month follow-up), provided information on at least 4 demographic variables (sex, age, ethnicity, and education), and were 18 years of age or older. This group included 6659 American citizens (from all 50 states and Washington, DC) and 579 individuals who had foreign citizenship (representing 39 countries) or who failed to provide citizenship data. Baseline part 1 assessments were collected between September 28, 2001 and December 4, 2001 (mean = 41 days post-attack, SD = 12.07, range = 17–84). Baseline part 2 assessments were collected between November 3, 2001 and December 4, 2001 (mean = 61 days post-attack, SD = 8.68, range = 53–84), with about one third

of the initial sample (n = 2566) completing some or all of this second part of the baseline survey. On March 11, 2002 we initiated the 6-month follow-up survey by attempting to contact all participants who had provided email or mailing addresses at the initial session. These 6-month follow-up assessments were collected between March 12, 2002 and May 19, 2002 (mean = 194 days or 6.5 months post-attack, SD = 13.26, range = 182–251), and about one half of the sample who initially consented and provided demographic data (n = 3744) completed some or all of this follow-up survey. Overall, only about one quarter (n = 1762) of these initial participants completed some or all of each of the 3 assessments.

Participant Recruitment

Participants were recruited through a variety of sources, including forwarded links to the site, a press release that resulted in local and national media stories, links and advertising placed on Internet search engines and resource referral sites, contacts with ethnic minority-oriented organizations, professional associations, and agencies, and promotion by organizations with related interests such as the National Mental Health Association, who put an endorsed link to our survey on their website and issued a press release (for more information on recruitment, see Butler et al., 2002).

Participants

The present analyses were restricted to examining data from those who had completed all necessary baseline and follow-up measures and were American citizens, a sample of 1444 individuals (70.4% of those who provided complete data on these measures at baseline). To limit the analyses to those indirectly exposed, participants were excluded if their experience of the attacks included having a relative, friend, or colleague die or be injured in the attacks and/or they had experienced firsthand (in person) event exposure, resulting in the exclusion of 163 directly-exposed participants and thereby leaving a sample of 1281 (analyses examining persons directly exposed will be reported elsewhere).

See Table 1 for baseline demographic characteristics of the sample used in the present analyses. Compared with the initially consenting baseline sample (BS), the present longitudinal sample (LS) was significantly older (LS mean age = 45.19, BS mean age = 40.20; t [6267] = 12.18, p < 0.001), more female (LS = 77.2% female, BS = 71.5% female, χ^2 [1] = 16.75, p < 0.001), better educated (median LS = some graduate school, median BS = bachelor degree, t [6267] = 9.09, p < 0.001), and more European/white in ethnicity (LS = 92.1% white, BS = 86.5% white, χ^2 [1] = 29.80, p < 0.001).

TABLE 1 / Demographic Composition of Eligible Participants at Baseline (*N* = 1281)

Variable	Level	No. (%)
Gender	Male	292 (22.8)
	Female	989 (77.2)
Age range	18–24	51 (4.0)
	25–34	257 (20.1)
	35–44	266 (20.8)
	45–54	402 (31.4)
	55–64	237 (18.5)
	65 or older	68 (5.3)
Racial/Ethnic background	African-American	16 (1.2)
	Asian-American	30 (2.3)
	European/White	1183 (92.3)
	Hawaiian Native/Pacific Islander	2 (0.2)
	Hispanic/Latino	23 (1.8)
	Native American/Alaska Native	9 (0.7)
	Other	18 (1.4)
Education	Less than high school	1 (0.1)
	Graduated from high School	30 (2.3)
	Completed trade school	20 (1.6)
	Some college	274 (21.4)
	Bachelor's degree	302 (23.6)
	Some graduate school	135 (10.5)
	Master's degree	364 (28.4)
	PhD, MD, and/or JD	155 (12.1)
Household income* (*n* = 1237)	Less than $20,000	66 (5.3)
	$20,000–$39,000	167 (13.5)
	$40,000–$59,000	218 (17.6)
	$60,000–$79,000	221 (17.9)
	$80,000–$99,000	157 (12.7)
	$100,000 or more	408 (33.0)

*These data were collected at baseline part 2.

Measures

Cronbachs α for all scaled measures are listed in Table 2.

Outcome Variables

Psychological Well-Being

The short-form version of the Scales of Psychological Well-being (Ryff, 1989; Ryff and Keyes, 1995) was used. This measure assesses how respondents feel about themselves and their lives across 6 dimensions of well-being (autonomy, environmental mastery, personal growth, positive relations with others, purpose in life, and self-acceptance) using a Likert-type scale (1 = strongly disagree to 6 = strongly agree). The short version has satisfactory internal consistency (Ryff

and Keyes, 1995). Based on the results of a principal components analysis using the present sample, a summary well-being score was created by averaging scores on the 6 subscales. Baseline and follow-up scores were strongly correlated ($r = 0.73$).

Global Distress

General symptomatic distress was assessed with the widely used 53-item Brief Symptom Inventory (Derogatis and Melisaratos, 1983). The Brief Symptom Inventory asks respondents to rate how distressed or bothered they were by a variety of symptoms over the past 7 days (0 = not at all to 4 = extremely). Test-retest reliability and internal consistency for this measure have been demonstrated (Derogatis and

TABLE 2 / Descriptive Statistics and Cronbach's α for Longitudinal Sample on Predictor and Outcome Variables ($N = 1281$)

	Mean (SD)	Range	Cronbach's α
Baseline			
Age	45.19 (12.43)	18–84	—
Education	5.72 (1.52)	1–8	—
Media exposure	5.14 (1.30)	1–7	—
Emotional suppression	46.72 (11.93)	21–84	0.94
Cognitive changes (positive)	43.27 (9.43)	11–64	0.85
Cognitive changes (negative)	34.12 (12.99)	15–83	0.90
Social constraints	1.92 (0.64)	1–4	0.76
Social support network size	3.30 (0.91)	1–5	—
Coping—self-distraction	4.95 (1.65)	2–8	0.59
Coping—active coping	4.98 (1.74)	2–8	0.73
Coping—denial	2.52 (0.98)	2–8	0.54
Coping—substance use	2.60 (1.27)	2–8	0.96
Coping—emotional support	5.15 (1.75)	2–8	0.83
Coping—instrumental support	4.13 (1.65)	2–8	0.79
Coping—beh. disengagement	2.57 (1.00)	2–8	0.63
Coping—emotional venting	4.85 (1.50)	2–8	0.67
Coping—positive reframing	4.22 (1.77)	2–8	0.75
Coping—planning	4.94 (1.79)	2–8	0.77
Coping—humor	2.99 (1.30)	2–8	0.81
Coping—acceptance	6.59 (1.31)	2–8	0.58
Coping—religion	4.46 (2.11)	2–8	0.88
Coping—self-blame	2.78 (1.16)	2–8	0.52
Baseline			
Well-being total score	14.11 (2.06)	5.83–18.00	0.83
Distress total score	0.55 (0.53)	0.00–3.06	0.97
6-mo Follow-up			
Well-being total score	14.12 (2.11)	6.67–18.00	0.84
Distress total score	0.44 (0.50)	0.00–3.30	0.97

Melisaratos, 1983). For the present analyses we calculated the Global Severity Index score as the indicator of current distress levels. Baseline and follow-up scores were strongly correlated ($r = 0.81$).

Predictor Variables

Demographics

A variety of demographic and personal characteristics were assessed at baseline (Table 1); age, gender, education, and ethnicity were used in the present analyses.

Media Exposure

Respondents indicated the amount of time per day they had spent attending to September 11, 2001-related media in the first few days after the attacks, which was scored as follows: 1 = none;

2 = up to 1 hour; 3 = 1 to 2 hours; 4 = 2 to 4 hours; 5 = 4 to 8 hours; 6 = 8 to 12 hours; 7 = more than 12 hours.

Emotional Suppression

The Courtauld Emotional Control Scale (Watson and Greer, 1983) is a 21-item questionnaire that measures the extent to which individuals generally suppress their emotional responses to stress by "smothering" or "bottling-up" negative affect, including anger, sadness, and anxiety (1 = almost never to 4 = almost always). The Courtald Emotional Control Scale has good internal consistency and relatively good test-retest reliability (Watson and Greer, 1983).

Cognitive Outlook

Positive and negative changes in existential outlook or worldview after the attacks were assessed with the 26-item Changes in Outlook Scale (Joseph et al., 2005; Joseph et al., 1993). The instructions for this measure, used previously in disaster (Joseph et al., 1993) and September 11 (Linley et al., 2003) research, were adapted for the present study to read, "each of the following statements have been made at some time by survivors of disaster, like the terrorist attacks" and ask respondents to indicate their agreement with each statement (1 = strongly disagree to 6 = strongly agree), such as "I value my relationships much more now" (positive change) and "My life has no meaning anymore" (negative change). Psychometric analyses indicate that positive and negative changes are orthogonal components, each with satisfactory internal reliability (Joseph et al., 2005). In the current sample, the subscales were slightly negatively correlated ($r = -0.13$).

Social Support

The Single-Item Measure of Social Support (Blake and McKay, 1986) was used to examine the size of the social support network available to each participant. The item reads, "How many people do you have near you that you can readily count on for help in times of difficulty, such as to watch over children or pets, give rides to the hospital or store, or help when you are sick?"

To assess the quality of emotional support, specifically whether respondents experienced a social environment that inhibited discussion of, or emotional expression about, the terrorist attacks, respondents completed a 5-item version of the 10-item Social Constraints Scale (Lepore et al., 1996) adapted for this study (1 = never, 2 = rarely, 3 = sometimes, and 4 = often). Items were keyed to the past week and, where appropriate, referred to the terrorist attacks. The measure has demonstrated good internal consistency (Lepore et al., 1996).

Coping

Coping strategies were assessed with the widely used 28-item Brief COPE (Carver, 1997), which includes subscales that assess self-distraction, active coping, denial, substance use, use of emotional support, use of instrumental support, behavioral disengagement, emotional venting, positive reframing, planning, humor, acceptance, religion, and self-blame. Respondents were instructed that the items "deal with way you've been coping with the stress in your life, including stress related to the terrorist attacks" and asked how often they had engaged in specific coping strategies in the past week (1 = I haven't been doing this at all to 4 = I've been doing this a lot).

Overview of Analyses

Statistical analyses were conducted with SPSS for Windows, version 11.5.0 (SPSS, Inc.). Model-building analyses included stepwise regressions to maximize the R^2 with the fewest number of variables in the prediction of the 4 resilience outcomes of interest, namely psychological well-being and distress, each

measured at baseline and 6-month follow-up. Zero-order correlations were examined to identify the independent variables that accounted for at least 1% of the variance (i.e., $r > 0.10$) in each outcome, and these were included in their respective regressions. A criterion of $p < 0.05$ was used as the threshold for entry of any given variable into the final stepwise regression equation. Additionally, eigenvalues and bivariate correlations were examined for collinearity, and all correlation coefficients among the independent variables were less than 0.50. All independent variables were centered at their mean (Aiken and West, 1991), and all reported p values are 2-tailed.

RESULTS

Table 2 presents the descriptive statistics for the baseline and follow-up variables. Table 3 presents the zero order correlations of the independent variables with the dependent variables.

Stepwise Regression Results

Baseline

The final stepwise model predicting well-being at baseline accounted for 36% of the variance (Adjusted $R^2 = 0.35$), $F(8, 1272) = 88.36$, $p < 0.001$ (Table 4). Significant baseline factors associated with greater well-being were more education, less emotional suppression, fewer negative worldview changes, larger social network size, less denial and self-blame, and more active coping and seeking of emotional support.

The final stepwise model predicting distress at baseline accounted for 49% of the variance (Adjusted $R^2 = 0.49$), $F(9, 1271) = 136.034$, $p < 0.001$ (Table 5). Significant factors at baseline associated with lower distress were more education, less media exposure, less emotional suppression, fewer negative worldview changes, lower social constraints, and less denial, self-blame, substance use, and seeking of instrumental support.

Six-Month Follow-Up

The final stepwise model predicting well-being at the 6-month follow-up accounted for 66% of the variance (Adjusted $R^2 = 0.66$), $F(4, 1276) = 632.62$, $p < 0.001$ (Table 4). As expected, baseline well-being was a significant predictor of well-being at 6 months ($B = 0.74$, $\beta = 0.726$, $p < 0.001$); however, other baseline variables also predicted higher follow-up well-being, including more education, fewer negative worldview changes, and more seeking of emotional support.

The final stepwise model predicting distress at 6 months accounted for 56% of the variance (Adjusted $R^2 = 0.56$), $F(6, 1274) = 270.052$, $p < 0.001$ (Table 5). As expected, baseline distress was a significant predictor of distress at 6 months ($B = 0.56$, $\beta = 0.582$, $p < 0.001$); however, other baseline

TABLE 3 / Zero-Order Correlations of Independent With Dependent Variables (N = 1281)

	Baseline Well-Being	Follow-Up Well-Being	Baseline Distress	Follow-Up Distress
Sex	−0.09	−0.09	−0.09	−0.05
Age	0.06	0.05	−0.15	−0.10
Education	0.21	0.21	0.15	−0.15
Ethnicity	0.01	0.01	−0.05	−0.06
Media	−0.11	−0.14	0.24	0.22
CECS	−0.26	−0.25	0.18	0.15
CIO (negative)	−0.50	−0.50	0.64	0.56
CIO (positive)	0.15	0.16	−0.01	0.01
SIMSS	0.30	0.29	−0.18	−0.20
Social constraints	−0.32	−0.30	0.44	0.42
COPE—self-distraction	−0.08	−0.08	0.22	0.18
COPE—denial	−0.25	−0.23	0.30	0.28
COPE—substance use	−0.20	−0.20	0.28	0.23
COPE—behavioral disengagement	−0.31	−0.29	0.35	0.29
COPE—venting	0.09	0.08	0.10	0.09
COPE—positive reframing	0.13	0.14	−.01	0.01
COPE—humor	−0.02	−0.03	0.00	0.02
COPE—acceptance	0.19	0.20	−0.21	−0.17
COPE—religion	0.06	0.09	0.06	0.06
COPE—self-blame	−0.32	−0.31	0.44	0.41
COPE—active coping	0.17	0.17	0.00	0.02
COPE—planning	0.05	0.05	0.16	0.15
COPE—seeking instrumental support	0.04	0.06	0.20	0.15
COPE—seeking emotional support	0.18	0.20	0.07	0.00

TABLE 4 / Stepwise Regression Results for Psychosocial Correlates and Predictors of Psychological Well-Being

Baseline Variable	Baseline PWB			Follow-Up PWB		
	B	t	p	β	t	p
Education	0.122	5.31	0.001	0.042	2.52	0.012
CECS	−0.104	−4.32	0.001	—	—	—
CIO (negative)	−0.335	−12.39	0.001	−0.123	−6.56	0.001
SIMSS	0.141	5.91	0.001	—	—	—
COPE—self-blame	−0.158	−6.20	0.001	—	—	—
COPE—active coping	0.076	3.08	0.002	—	—	—
COPE—seeking emotional support	0.074	2.88	0.004	0.048	2.89	0.004
COPE—denial	−0.064	−2.65	0.008	—	—	—
Baseline PWB*	—	—	—	0.726	37.57	0.001

*Only included in follow-up regression. All continuous IVs were centered at their mean. Categorical variables were coded 1/m and 1-1/m. PWB = psychological well-being; CIO = changes in outlook; SIMSS = single-item measure of social support; CECS = Courtald Emotional Control Scale.

TABLE 5 / Stepwise Regression Results for Psychosocial Correlates and Predictors of Distress

Baseline Variable	Baseline BSI			Follow-Up BSI		
	B	t	P	β	t	P
Education	−0.075	−3.69	0.001	−0.044	−2.34	0.019
Media	0.049	2.36	0.019	—	—	—
CECS	0.051	2.39	0.017	—	—	—
CIO (negative)	0.424	15.86	0.001	0.094	3.59	0.001
SIMSS	—	—	—	−0.045	−2.33	0.020
Social constraints scale	0.119	5.04	0.001	0.077	3.47	0.001
COPE—self-blame	0.167	7.36	0.001	0.087	4.10	0.001
COPE—denial	0.066	3.09	0.002	—	—	—
COPE—seeking instrumental support	0.124	5.83	0.001	—	—	—
COPE—substance use	0.063	2.98	0.003	—	—	—
Baseline BSI[*]	—	—	—	0.582	22.92	0.001

[*]Only included in follow-up regression. All continuous IVs were centered at their mean. Categorical variables were coded 1/m and 1-1/m. BSI = Brief Symptom Inventory; CECS = Courtald Emotional Control Scale; CIO = Changes in Outlook; SIMSS = Single Item Measure of Social Support.

variables also predicted lower follow-up distress, including more education, fewer negative worldview changes, lower social constraints, less self-blame, and a larger social network.

DISCUSSION

This study complements the findings of previous research on the psychological effects of the terrorist attacks of September 11, 2001 by focusing on a range of psychosocial characteristics in the immediate aftermath and their associations with resilience outcomes initially and in the longer term. In each analysis, demographic, media exposure, cognitive, emotional, social support, and coping variables were examined. Although media exposure and education had predictive value—less media exposure was associated with less initial distress, and educational attainment was associated with higher well-being and lower distress at both time points—most of the variability in outcomes was associated with psychosocial variables. Greater psychological well-being and lower distress at baseline were each associated with fewer negative worldview changes, less emotional suppression, and less denial and self-blame. Greater psychological well-being in the short-term was also associated with having a larger social network and with coping actively and seeking emotional support, and lower distress in the short-term was also associated with lower constraints on social communication, less substance use, and less seeking out of instrumental support.

After controlling for baseline levels of respective outcomes, the degree of negative changes in worldview remained a significant predictor of outcomes at 6-month follow-up. Greater well-being over the longer term was also predicted by seeking emotional support at baseline, while lower long-term distress was also predicted by engaging in less self-blame, having a larger social network, and experiencing lower social constraints at baseline. Despite differences in sampling methodology and timing, these results are congruent with previous studies on the psychological aftermath of September 11, 2001, including in the degree of global distress reported (Silver et al., 2002), and the contributions of coping styles (Silver et al., 2002), social support (Galea et al., 2002), social constraints (Wayment, 2004), and media coverage (Ahern et al., 2004; Schlenger et al., 2002) to levels of distress. However, the important contributions of negative changes in worldview and emotional suppression to psychological adjustment after the attacks are relatively unique findings, and it is noteworthy that negative world-view changes accounted for the most variance in both indices at both time points. These results suggest that positive adjustment may depend in large part on both avoiding lapsing into overgeneralized negative views of the world in the aftermath of societal traumatic events (see also Janoff-Bulman, 1985; Janoff-Bulman, 1989) and seeking out emotionally supportive environments that do not inhibit thoughtful discussion of, or emotional expression about, the experience (Lepore et al., 1996). Although some researchers (e.g., Knudsen et al., 2005) have noted that there is little evidence for a lasting impact of the terrorist attacks on Americans' well-being generally; nonetheless, for those who did continue to experience impairment, early negative changes in worldview appears to be the most important contributor among the variables we examined.

Taken together, the findings of this study suggest that the person most likely to be resilient after indirect exposure to the attacks of September 11, 2001 was someone who was open to his/her emotional reactions, who inhabited a social environment that did not constrain expression and discussion of those reactions, and who did not suffer a damaged worldview. In this case, resilience involved making use of cognitive, emotional, and social resources to face rather than avoid tragedy, although it appears from the present findings that the way the individual thinks about the event is most critical.

One difference between our findings and previous studies on terrorism (DeLisi et al., 2003; Galea et al., 2002; North et al., 1999; Schlenger et al., 2002; Schuster et al., 2001; Silver et al., 2002) and other disasters (Norris et al., 2002) is that in previous research men have tended to experience less distress than women. In the present study, however, gender was found to account for less than 1% of the variance in the resilience indices. Another difference is that coping through behavioral disengagement or self-distraction—previously found to be a significant predictor of September 11, 2001 distress (Silver et al., 2002) and moderately correlated with distress in the present sample—did not significantly improve prediction in the context of the present models, presumably because they included a greater breadth of psychosocial variables that accounted for that variance.

The sampling design and data collection methods of this study have a number of methodological strengths and limitations. Specific strengths include timeliness of data collection, focus on positive as well as distress outcomes, breadth of the predictor variables allowing for a head-to-head comparison of the strength of their associations with outcomes, use of widely employed, well-validated measures, wide geographic distribution of the sample, large sample size, and prospective design.

Nevertheless, an Internet-based survey is inherently limited with respect to generalizability. Because we did not use probabilistic sampling, we do not claim that this sample is representative of a specific population. We were not seeking to assess the prevalence of specific characteristics within a particular population, but rather to examine the relationships among key variables within the sample as is traditionally done with convenience samples. Nonetheless, the present sample was similar to other large Internet samples (Best et al., 2001; Witte et al., 2001) in levels of educational attainment and minority representation; it differed, however, in its high proportion of female participants. Additionally, we did not have pre-911 measures of distress or wellbeing, and so the potential contribution of pre-event levels of adaptation to postevent psychosocial resources or outcomes could not be examined (Thoits, 2006). The present analyses were also restricted to those who experienced the attacks indirectly, and so the relationships found here may not be applicable to those who experienced the attacks firsthand, or to those who experience individual (vs. community-wide) traumas.

Additional limitations may include low rates of participation by individuals with little access to the Internet or insufficient interest in the events of September 11, 2001. In particular, individuals who were uninterested in examining their own reactions, or who felt so overwhelmed that they avoided further exposure, are probably underrepresented. In addition, longitudinal Internet surveys that do not provide compensation for participation rely on the goodwill of participants to complete follow-ups. Our longitudinal sample comprised only about 20% of those who initially indicated interest in the study because some participants failed to complete all measures in one or more assessments and perhaps also because some individuals may have consented and provided initial demographic information so they could proceed through the web pages to examine the survey without actually intending to participate. There were some difficulties as well in contacting participants for additional assessments (if they did not provide contact information or it had changed in those intervening months) and there was significant attrition in participation in the second part of the baseline and in the 6-month follow-up among those who were contacted. This study also used self-report measures that depend on recall and may be biased by social desirability of responses, although several authorities on Internet surveys (Tourangeau et al., 2003) argue that social desirability effects in web-based surveys are less pronounced than in paper-and-pencil or interviewer-administered surveys.

Future research could build upon our finding that negative changes in worldview were the strongest predictor of well-being and distress in both the short and longer-term. Previous research (Janoff-Bulman, 1985; Janoff-Bulman, 1989; Joseph et al., 1993) has found that traumatic events can profoundly affect people's assumptions about the world and themselves, and the present study demonstrates the association of such changes with long-term adjustment. The next steps would be to identify those at risk for such changes after trauma, the characteristics of worldviews vulnerable to negative changes, and the psychosocial and environmental factors that may precipitate and/or mediate such changes. Additionally, clinical studies could seek to determine whether interventions designed to address such negative worldview changes could remediate terrorism-related distress.

Our findings also suggest several other directions for future inquiry, including whether encouraging specific kinds of coping can bolster successful adaptation in the aftermath of terrorism, and elucidating the negative roles of emotional suppression and social constraints in long-term adjustment. In the present study, constriction of emotional expression, whether self-imposed or imposed by one's social environment, was predictive of poorer emotional adjustment over time. Research is needed to clarify whether and how emotional expression can facilitate cognitive and interpersonal processing of stressful events. Additionally, as Thoits (2006) has noted, little empirical attention has been paid to the role of personal agency in determining the psychological and other resources that may be brought to bear on trajectories of adaptation to such events, even though such examinations could "help unpack and explain phenomena that are currently labeled as 'resilience' . . . or 'vulnerability' . . . to stress" (p. 318).

Given the increased frequency of terrorism in the industrialized world in recent years, research is also needed to identify ways in which governments and the mass media can perform their primary roles in the dissemination of information and opinion without fomenting widespread maladaptive changes in the public's worldviews, but instead prophylactically promoting adaptive ones.

CONCLUSIONS

Although much clinical and empirical research attests to the importance of cognitive, emotional, social support, and coping factors to adjustment during and after traumatic experience, few studies have compared the contributions of these factors when examined together in the prediction of psychological outcomes. In the present study, which used a large Internet convenience sample in the immediate wake of the September 11, 2001 terrorist attacks, we assessed variables from these 4 psychosocial domains as potential correlates and predictors of negative (distress) and positive (well-being) psychological responses to the event. We found that education, media viewing, negative changes in worldview, social constraints on discussing traumatic experience, suppression of negative affect, social network size, and coping behaviors were each associated with distress and/or well-being in the short-term, and negative changes in worldview at baseline remained the strongest and most consistent predictor of 6-month adjustment (after controlling for baseline outcome levels), underlining the apparent importance of cognitive assessment and attribution to psychological resilience, and highlighting a possible avenue for postevent intervention. Cognitive and affective variables—largely unexamined in the previous literature on psychological effects of terrorism—deserve further attention from clinical researchers and policy makers as they design and implement educational programs and preventive and therapeutic interventions to foster resilient outcomes at both the individual and population-level in an era of increased terrorism.

ACKNOWLEDGMENTS

The authors thank all those who took the time to participate in this study and the individuals, organizations, and businesses that contributed to the implementation of this study or supported its objectives, in particular the National Mental Health Association; Heather Abercrombie, Catherine Classen, Nancy Daniels, Janine Giese-Davis, Mareile Grumann, Carolina Gutierrez, David Hardisty, Shelly Henderson, Stephen Joseph, Andrea Kwan, Shannon McCaslin, Daphne Nayar, Eric Neri, Bita Nouriani, Lori Peterson, Randy Rodriguez, Tukey Seagraves, Liz Seibert, Andy Winzelberg, and Krista Thorne Yocam for contributing to study planning and implementation; and Laura Lazzeroni for additional statistical consultation.

REFERENCES

Ahern J, Galea S, Resnick H, Vlahov D (2004) Television images and probable posttraumatic stress disorder after September 11—The role of background characteristics, event exposures, and preievent panic. *J Nerv Ment Dis.* 192:217–226.

Aiken L, West S (1991) *Multiple Regression: Testing and Interpreting Interactions.* Thousand Oaks, CA: Sage Publications, Inc.

Best SJ, Krueger B, Hubbard C, Smith A (2001) An assessment of the generalizability of Internet Surveys. *Soc Sci Comput Rev.* 19:131–145.

Blake RL Jr, McKay DA (1986) A single-item measure of social supports as a predictor of morbidity. *J Fam Pract.* 22:82–84.

Blanchard EB, Kuhn E, Rowell DL, Hickling EJ, Wittrock D, Rogers RL, Johnson MR, Steckler DC (2004) Studies of vicarious traumatization of college students by the September 11th attacks: Effects of proximity, exposure, and connectedness. *Behav Res Ther.* 42:191–205.

Butler LD, Blasey CM, McCaslin S, Garlan RW, Azarow J, Chen XH, Desjardins JC, DiMiceli S, Seagraves DA, Hastings TA, Kraemer HC, Spiegel D (2005) Posttraumatic growth following the terrorist attacks of September 11, 2001: Cognitive, coping and trauma symptom predictors of posttraumatic growth in an Internet convenience sample. *Traumatology.* 11:247–267.

Butler LD, Hobfoll SE, Keane TM (2003) *Fostering Resilience In Nonclinical Adults—American Psychological Association Board of Directors Task Force on Resilience in Response to Terrorism.* Washington, DC: American Psychological Association.

Butler LD, Morland LA, Leskin GA (2007) Psychological resilience in the face of terrorism. In B Bongar, LM Brown, L Beutler, et al. (Eds), *Psychology of Terrorism* (pp 400–417). New York (NY): Oxford University Press.

Butler LD, Seagraves DA, Desjardins JC, Azarow JA, Hastings TA, Garlan RW, DiMiceli S, Winzelberg A, Spiegel D (2002) How to launch a national Internet-based panel study quickly: Lessons learned from studying how Americans are coping with the tragedy of September 11, 2001. *CNS Spectr.* 7:597–603.

Carver CS (1997) You want to measure coping but your protocol's too long: Consider the Brief COPE. *Int J Behav Med.* 4:92–100.

DeLisi LE, Maurizio A, Yost M, Papparozzi CF, Fulchino C, Katz CL, Altesman J, Biel M, Lee J, Stevens P (2003) A survey of New Yorkers after the Sept 11, 2001, terrorist attacks. *Am J Psychiatry.* 160:780–783.

Derogatis LR, Melisaratos N (1983) The Brief Symptom Inventory: An introductory report. *Psychol Med.* 13:595–605.

Diener E, Suh EM, Lucas RE, Smith HL (1999) Subjective well-being: Three decades of progress. *Psychol Bull.* 125:276–302.

Difede J, Apfeldorf WJ, Cloitre M, Spielman LA, Perry SW (1997) Acute psychiatric responses to the explosion at he World Trade Center: A case series. *J Nerv Ment Dis.* 185:519–522.

Fivush R, Edwards VJ, Mennuti-Washburn J (2003) Narratives of 9/11: Relations among personal involvement, narrative content, and memory of the emotional impact over time. *Appl Cogn Psychol.* 17:1099–1111.

Galea S, Ahern J, Resnick H, Kilpatrick D, Bucuvalas M, Gold J, Vlahov D (2002) Psychological sequelae of the September 11 terrorist attacks in New York City. *N Engl J Med.* 346:982–987.

Garlan RW, Butler LD, Spiegel D (2005) Psychosocial resilience and terrorism. *Dir Psychiatry.* 25:151–163.

Janoff-Bulman R (1985) The aftermath of victimization: Rebuilding shattered assumptions. In CR Figley (Eds). *Trauma and its Wake.* New York (NY): Brunner/Mazel.

Janoff-Bulman R (1989) Assumptive worlds and the stress of traumatic events: Applications of the schema construct. *Soc Cogn.* 7:113–136.

Joseph S, Linley PA, Andrews L, Harris G, Howle B, Woodward C, Shevlin M (2005) Assessing positive and negative changes in the aftermath of adversity: Psychometric evaluation of the Changes in Outlook Questionnaire. *Psychol Assess.* 17:70–80.

Joseph S, Williams R, Yule W (1993) Changes in outlook following disaster: The preliminary development of a measure to assess positive and negative responses. *J Trauma Stress.* 6:271–279.

Knudsen HK, Roman PM, Johnson JA, Ducharme LJ (2005) A changed America? The effects of September 11th on depressive symptoms and alcohol consumption. *J Health Soc Behav.* 46:260–273.

Lepore SJ, Silver RC, Wortman CB, Wayment HA (1996) Social constraints, intrusive thoughts and depressive symptoms among bereaved mothers. *J Pers Soc Psychol.* 70:271–282.

Linley PA, Joseph S, Cooper R, Harris S, Meyer C (2003) Positive and negative changes following vicarious exposure to the September 11 terrorist attacks. *J Trauma Stress.* 16:481–485.

Luthar SS, Cicchetti D (2000) The construct of resilience: Implications for interventions and social processes. *Dev Psychopathol.* 12:857–885.

Masten AS, Best KM, Garmezy N (1990) Resilience and development: Contributions from the study of children who overcome adversity. *Dev Psychopathol.* 2:425–444.

Masten AS, Hubbard JJ, Gest SD, Tellegen A, Garmezy N, Ramirez M (1999) Competence in the context of adversity: Pathways to resilience and maladaptation from childhood to late adolescence. *Dev Psychopathol.* 11:143–169.

Norris FH, Friedman MJ, Watson PJ, Byrne CM, Diaz E, Kaniasty K (2002) 60,000 disaster victims speak: Part I. An empirical review of the empirical literature, 1981–2001. *Psychiatry.* 65:207–239.

North CS (2001) The course of post-traumatic stress disorder after the Oklahoma City bombing. *Mil Med.* 166:51–52.

North CS, Nixon SJ, Shariat S, Mallonee S, McMillen JC, Spitznagel EL, Smith EM (1999) Psychiatric disorders among survivors of the Oklahoma City bombing. *JAMA.* 282:755–762.

O'Leary VE, Ickovics JR (1995) Resilience and thriving in response to challenge: An opportunity for a paradigm shift in women's health. *Womens Health.* 1:121–142.

Pfefferbaum B, Nixon SJ, Krug RS, Tivis RD, Moore VL, Brown JM, Pynoos RS, Foy D, Gurwitch RH (1999) Clinical needs assessment of middle and high school students following the 1995 Oklahoma City bombing. *Am J Psychiatry.* 156:1069–1074.

Ryan RM, Deci EL (2000) On happiness and human potentials: A review of research on hedonic and eudaimonic well-being. *Ann Rev Psychol.* 52:141–166.

Ryff CD (1989) Happiness is everything, or is it? Explorations on the meaning of psychological well-being. *J Pers Soc Psychol.* 57:1069–1081.

Ryff CD, Keyes CL (1995) The structure of psychological well-being revisited. *J Pers Soc Psychol.* 69:719–727.

Schlenger WE, Caddell JM, Ebert L, Jordan BK, Rourke KM, Wilson D, Thalji L, Dennis JM, Fairbank JA, Kulka RA (2002) Psychological reactions to terrorist attacks: Findings from the National Study of Americans' Reactions to September 11. *JAMA.* 288:581–588.

Schuster MA, Stein BD, Jaycox L, Collins RL, Marshall GN, Elliott MN, Zhou AJ, Kanouse DE, Morrison JL, Berry SH (2001) A national survey of stress reactions after the September 11, 2001, terrorist attacks. *N Engl J Med.* 345:1507–1512.

Silver RC, Holman EA, McIntosh DN, Poulin M, Gil-Rivas V (2002) Nationwide longitudinal study of psychological responses to September 11. *JAMA.* 288:1235–1244.

Thoits PA (2006) Personal agency in the stress process. *J Health Soc Behav.* 47:309–323.

Tourangeau R, Couper MP, Steiger DM (2003) Humanizing self-administered surveys: Experiments on social presence in Web and IVR surveys. *Comput Human Behav.* 19:1–24.

Watson M, Greer S (1983) Development of a questionnaire measure of emotional control. *J Psychosom Res.* 27:299–305.

Wayment HA (2004) It could have been me: Vicarious victims and disaster-focused distress. *Pers Soc Psychol Bull.* 30:515–528.

Witte JC, Amorso AM, Howard PEN (2000) Method and representation in Internet-based survey tools: Mobility, community, and cultural identity in Survey 2000. *Soc Sci Comput Rev.* 18:179–195.

Zimering R, Gulliver SB, Knight J, Munroe J, Keane TM (2006) Posttraumatic stress disorder in disaster relief workers following direct and indirect trauma exposure to ground zero. *J Trauma Stress.* 19:553–557.

CRITICAL THINKING QUESTIONS

1. This article found that certain variables were predictive of being positively adjusted following the event. Although this study focused exclusively on people's reactions to the 9-11 terrorist attacks, might similar findings be expected for those exposed to other traumatic events, such as Hurricane Katrina? Why or why not? Explain your reasoning.

2. A psychology database search will indicate that a lot more studies have been done on PTSD (post-traumatic stress disorder) than on resilience. In some ways, this parallels much of the research in psychology in

general, in which there is a stronger tendency to study pathology rather than the lack of pathology. Why do you think this may be the case? What, if any, potential problems might be associated with the studying of pathology as the main subject matter? Explain.

3. How might the media contribute to the common perception that people are more traumatized than they really are by certain events (e.g., hurricanes, floods, tornadoes, oil spills)? In other words, how might the way an event is reported influence how widespread the trauma is perceived to be? Use examples to support your answer.

4. The findings of this article highlight the importance of certain variables in adjustment to this traumatic event. What are those variables, and how might they be applied to possibly assist people in being better able to deal effectively with traumatic events?

CHAPTER INTEGRATION QUESTIONS

1. "That which does not kill me, makes me stronger," wrote Friedrich Nietzsche, German philosopher. Discuss this quotation in the context of the three articles in this chapter.

2. The three articles in this chapter all dealt with stress in one form or another. Integrate the findings of the articles into one or more conclusions on how stress affects people. Explain your conclusions.

3. Again, all three articles in this chapter looked at stress. What social psychological factors other than stress might have an impact on health? Explain your answers.

Author Index

Subject Index